The German War of 1866

The Bohemian and Moravian Campaign

Theodor Fontane

Illustrations by Ludwig Burger

Translated by Frederick Steinhardt
Edited by Gerard W. Henry

Helion & Company

Dedicated to Victoria Cundiff Steinhardt without whom this book would never have happened.

Helion & Company Limited
Unit 8 Amherst Business Centre
Budbrooke Road
Warwick
CV34 5WE
England
Tel. 01926 499 619
Email: info@helion.co.uk
Website: www.helion.co.uk
Twitter: @helionbooks
Visit our blog at blog.helion.co.uk

Published by Helion & Company 2021
Designed and typeset by Mary Woolley (www.battlefield-design.co.uk)
Cover designed by Paul Hewitt, Battlefield Design (www.battlefield-design.co.uk)

English translation © Gerard W. Henry 2021
Images © as individually credited 2021

ISBN 978-1-914059-29-2

British Library Cataloguing-in-Publication Data.
A catalogue record for this book is available from the British Library.

For details of other military history titles published by Helion & Company Limited contact the above address or visit our website: http://www.helion.co.uk.

We always welcome receiving book proposals from prospective authors.

Contents

Editor's Foreword to the English Edition

Theodor Fontane was born on the 30 December 1819 in the small town of Neuruppin in the Mark Brandenburg. An apothecary by trade, he practiced first in Dresden and then at his father's shop in Letschin, before quitting the profession in 1849 to become a full time writer. Although politically liberal (he had briefly flirted with revolution in 1848), the need to secure a regular income forced him to accept a position in Berlin with the pro-government *Adler-Zeitung*. A committed Anglophile, Fontane spent many years in London as their British correspondent, before returning to edit another right wing newspaper, the *Neue Preussische Zeitung,* and then another, the *Kreuzzeitung.* These moves, which were occasioned by financial considerations alone, caused him considerable anguish: *I sold myself to the reaction for thirty pieces of silver* he wrote on joining the *Adler, 'these days one cannot survive as an honest man.*

Throughout his long and productive life, Fontane would embrace many literary disciplines. He is probably best known today for his novel *Effi Briest*, and for his travel writing, but he was also a poet and a noted chronicler of what later became known as the German wars of unification, the Schleswig Holstein War of 1864, the Austro–Prussian War of 1866, and the Franco–Prussian War of 1870-71.

This book is the first, unabridged, translation of Fontane's history of the second of these wars, the Austro–Prussian War (which he refers to as *Der deutsche Krieg von 1866* or The German War of 1866), and as such represents a significant contribution to the Anglophone literature of the period. In his introduction to *Literature and History in the Bismarck Reich,* the late Professor Gordon Craig acknowledged Fontane's contribution to his own hugely influential work, Königgrätz (Weidenfeld & Nicholson, London, 1965);

> [The] war books ... I read with enthusiasm and gratitude, rightly so, for what would my own book have become had I not read Fontane's 'The German War of 1866?

Given that *The German War* first appeared in 1870, it is still remarkably fresh. Fontane's background as a journalist and novelist is evident throughout, the amount of detail is unsurpassed, while the narrative has a pace and colour rarely if ever found in works of this kind. Professor Craig again;

> Anyone [who obtains this volume]... with the expectation that it will conform to conventional nineteenth century military ... literature will be happily surprised ... by the clarity and essentially literary quality of the style, which makes technical detail and complicated manouevres comprehensible to the general reader, by the masterful description of the historical and political context, and of the terrain in which the

hostilities take place, by Fontane's eye for the critical turning points in battle, and his dramatic re-creation of individual passages of arms.

The German War of 1866 is the second of Ted Steinhardt's translations that I have had the pleasure to commission and edit (the first being *Oberst* Ernst Heidrich's *The Battle for the Swiepwald 3rd July 1866* (1902). As with Heidrich, Ted's exceptional knowledge of the period and his painstaking attention to detail is evident throughout. A distinctive feature of his work is the inclusion of extensive footnotes, which provide the reader with an abundance of background material, indispensable to a fuller understanding of the text, and indeed of the war. My job as editor has been to render this meticulous translation of a 19th century classic into modern form, it is not, and was never intended to be, a word for word transliteration. Certain phrases, sayings, or figures of speech are unique to the German language and here appropriate parallels have been used. Fontane's tendency to repetition when making or emphasizing a point can on occasions become tautologic, here I have taken the liberty of winnowing the original to clarify the intended meaning. Unsurprisingly, some of Fontane's literary mannerisms now sound slightly anachronistic, these have been refined or discarded without (I hope), losing the essential character of the original.

For anyone comparing the original text with this edition, two chapter sub-headings are absent (though not the contents). In the original section headed *Bohemia and the Iser Region*, there is a sub-heading entitled *The War Plans*. However, Fontane makes no mention of any war plans, instead expatiating on his theme, *Bohemia, its land and its people*. Similarly, the Iser Army's order of battle does not appear separately but is included by the author in the chapter *Austria Prepares*. To avoid reader confusion, these sub-heading have been omitted.

Fontane was a patriotic Prussian, and this history, while professing impartiality, is certainly not unbiased. His tendency to overlook or exonerate Prussian failings should be seen in this light. Similarly, his consistently favourable opinion of the Saxons and their High Command is partly based on historical evidence (they generally performed well), and partly on the politics of the new Germany (Saxony was now a key Prussian ally). Despite this, I did not consider the redress of perceived bias as being within my remit as editor. For that reason, no observation, nor opinion, nor judgement, no matter how tendentious, has anywhere been contradicted or altered. Where the author is wrong in point of fact, an aside to this effect might appear either as a footnote or as a supplementary comment in square brackets.

This volume, six years in the making, has been a huge undertaking. Despite our infinite pains, it will almost certainly contain errors. For these I bear the sole responsibility, and for which, I beg the reader's indulgence.

Translator's Preface to the English Edition

I have observed certain conventions throughout this translation. Prussian Corps are in Roman Numerals, Prussian Armies, Divisions, Brigades, Regiments, Battalions and Companies are in Arabic. Austrian Corps are in Arabic, Austrian Cavalry Divisions are in Arabic, Austrian Brigades are designated using the name of the Brigade Commander, e.g. Brigade Piret (Infantry), Brigade Wallis (Cavalry). Austrian infantry regiments are usually prefixed by IR and may also carry the name of the honorary colonel (Inhaber) as a suffix. Unit designations are generally given as the English equivalent. Upon the first appearance, where needed, the German spelling is given in square brackets e.g. Hess Kassel Hussars [*Hessen - Cassel Hussaren*]. Titles such as Archduke (*Erzherzog*) and Prince (*Prinz*) are generally translated unless there is no suitable English equivalent or as with *Freiherr* and *Baron*, the distinction between the two would be lost in translation. The abbreviation KK where it appears stands for *Kaiserlich Königlich*, Imperial Royal (Austria).

Military ranks are italicized and left in German; *Feldzeugmeister, General, General der Kavallerie, General der Infanterie, Generalmajor, Oberst, Oberstlieutenant, Major, Hauptmann, Premiere Lieutenant, Lieutenant.* In the Austrian army the term Ad Latus is also used to designate the Corps Second in Command. The reader may note that military ranks still reflect French influence to some degree, *Lieutenant* and *Premiere* or *Secondelieutenant* rather than the more recent German *Leutnant* and the like. In the Imperial Austrian Army, the rank of *Feldmarschalleutnant* corresponds to that of *Generalleutnant* in the Prussian Army, that of *Feldzeugmeister* to *General der Infanterie* and that of *Feldmarschall* to that of *Generalfeldmarschall*.

Text in square brackets [ ] have been added by me or the editor for edification. Text in curved brackets ( ) has usually been added by the author. Occasionally, for the purpose of clarity, the editor has placed curved brackets around dependent or subordinate clauses.

The spelling of place names is a problem. The original place names are Czech or German, and each author seems to use a different rendition or modification thereof. I have generally used the spelling employed in the work at hand, since that is the spelling used on that source's maps. Major place names, such as Bohemia, Moravia, Saxony etc. are given as their English equivalents.

Times are as written by the author, occasionally with the editor's addition of am or pm.

Except for the German Schritt, or pace (a German Schritt measures approximately 30 inches or 75cms), distances have been converted from the contemporary Prussian to (British) Imperial measures; thus Fuss, a Prussian foot measures 12.5 inches or 31.6 cm; Meile, a Prussian mile measures 4.53 Imperial miles or 7.3kms; Klafter, an Austrian fathom, measures 6 feet 3¼ inches or 1.9 meters. Similarly, Pfund, a Prussian pound weighs 1 pound 1½ ounces or 546gms.

Finally, a word about maps. Military history without maps is incomprehensible. Fontane includes a wealth of sketch maps in the text, but they are limited. For the reader wishing to better follow the course of the campaign, I have included a list of recommended map renderings in the bibliography.

Frederick Steinhardt, Colorado, 2021

Der

deutsche Krieg

von

1866.

Book I

Origins of the War

The Elbe Army and 1st Army to Gitschin

Contents

Gastein.

Introduction

To 14th August 1865 (Gastein)

The War of 1866 was conceived in the Peace of 1864,[1] it's very first paragraph bore the seed of the impending discord. Austria and Prussia had jointly agreed that Schleswig - Holstein was the common property of both victors, and this joint possession was at the heart of a virtually inevitable conflict. The joint administration would, in the long term, be impossible to sustain the moment a disagreement arose. The only question was, in what spirit would the *Condomini*[2] embark on this attempt.

The nature of the relationship was such that the northern power [Prussia], as a close neighbour, would have to make very different demands to those of the southern joint occupying force [distant Austria]. Everything would depend on the degree to which both Austria and Prussia would recognize each other's position and attempt to accommodate each other. However, as could be anticipated, this did not happen. It is possible that Prussia fell somewhat short of amicable cooperation. It is certain that Austria was arrogant, in any event it was clear that Prussia had no choice, that it was facing a *nunc aut numquam* [now or never] situation. Its demands were not whimsical, it was a question of its very existence. Austria did not fully recognize this; it could not rise above its old feelings of jealousy and this resulted in war.

Our initial task will be to follow the developing course of events step by step, and analyse the details of the preceding sentences.

Paragraph I of the Vienna Peace Treaty, unconditionally placed the duchies under the rule of Prussia and Austria. The concluding section of this paragraph stated:

> That the King of Denmark is obligated to recognize the measures that their Majesties of Austria and Prussia institute regarding this duchy.

Neither the hereditary rights of either pretender, nor the federal law, was mentioned in the conditions of the peace treaty. It was a surrender in accordance with the laws of war. The peace treaty made no mention of the various claims to hereditary rights, even though they did exist. Even Prussia did not dispute these, at least initially. There were certain original hereditary claims of the Prince of Augustenburg that were not in question.

---

1   Tr. Note: The Preliminary Peace Treaty concluded on 1st August 1864, finally separated the duchies from Denmark, placing them in the hands of the two allies that had conquered Denmark in the 1864 Schleswig - Holstein War, Austria and Prussia. The final Vienna Peace Treaty was signed on 30 October 1864. With that, the German Federal Execution in Holstein was superfluous and the removal of the Hannoverian and Saxon troops was demanded by Prussia.

2   Tr. Note-*Condominus* (pl. *condomini*), Latin, one who shares domain.

However, the treaty refrained from a decision as to whether these original hereditary claims were extinguished by the Document of Cession of June 1852,[3] and emphasized that however the decision on these points might turn out, [Prussia] would only be willing to surrender its own rights under certain conditions. The German Confederation took a different stance from that of Prussia. This too, was well founded. Prussia based its stance on the Vienna Peace Accord. The German Confederation based its position on Federal law. Prussia said Schleswig - Holstein is a possession of Austria and Prussia, therefore only Austria and Prussia have the right to dispose of it. The Confederation stated the King of Denmark could not surrender what did not belong to him; the conditions of the Vienna Peace Accord are null and void; Schleswig - Holstein belongs to the German Prince whose hereditary rights give him a claim to this land, and the German Confederation is the guardian of these rights.

It was obvious that there was a question of legality here, there was also a question of power. Everything depended on the positions that Austria and Prussia, the *beati possessores* took towards each other. If they were in agreement, then they would stand on a legal basis that would be recognized by all of the great powers (signatories of the Vienna Peace Accord), in which case, the Confederation would be too weak to challenge their legal claim. In this case peace would remain and the outcome would be some kind of compromise. If however, Austria and Prussia disagreed, if Austria shifted its legal foundation from the Vienna Agreement to that of the hereditary rights, it would lead to war. This alternative lay ahead. The course of politics turned on the question, would Austria stand with Prussia or with the Confederation? In the event, the position of the Vienna cabinet during the next year and a half was nothing but a constant

3   Tr. Note: In 1849 there was a revolution against Denmark in the duchies of Schleswig and Holstein. Austria and Prussia joined in suppressing the revolution and restoring the duchies to Denmark. On 8th May 1852, the Treaty of London (known in Germany as the London Protocol) was signed by Russia, Austria, Prussia and Great Britain. It stated that the preservation of the entire Danish kingdom was a matter of significance to all of Europe, and that the successor to the throne of Frederick VII, who had no heir, would be Prince Christian of Holstein - Glücksburg. Duke Christian August von Schleswig - Holstein Sonderburg - Augustenburg († 1869), who had taken a leading part in the revolt and had hereditary claims for rule in Schleswig – Holstein, ceded his estates to the Danish government in exchange for a payment of 2½ million Danish *Thaler*, and promised to live outside of the Danish Monarchy. He promised 'not to undertake anything whereby the tranquility of His Majesty's dominions and lands might be disturbed, nor in any way to counteract the resolution which His Majesty might have taken, or in future may take, in reference to the succession to all the lands now united under His Majesty's sceptre or to the eventual reorganization of His monarchy.' He further promised 'for ourselves and our heirs and descendants, that we will faithfully fulfil on our side all that has been stipulated ... and will not allow any of ours to do or to undertake anything against it.' (Steefel, p. 80) His sons, who were already of legal age, however, did not join him in this. Sybel (vol. III of English translation) discusses this and its implications at length. Immediately upon hearing of the death of Danish King Frederick VII, Christian August renounced his claims in favour of his eldest son, Prince Frederick. Nor did the German Confederation agree to the above renunciation. The 1852 Treaty of London (known in Germany as the London Protocol) confirmed Danish possession of the duchies and affirmed their inseparability. Denmark accepted the obligation to respect the independence of the duchies under international law and to avoid infringing on the national rights of the Germans there. It made no change in the relationship of Holstein and Lauenburg to the German Confederation.

Immediately after affirming the Treaty of London however, Denmark began ignoring the protocol and incorporating Schleswig fully into Denmark, which in 1864, led Austria and Prussia to declare the war against Denmark that preceded the above mentioned London Peace Treaty that is the start of this volume's history.

wavering between these alternatives. When at last it made its decision, and finally shifted from Prussia's side to that of the Confederation, its decision resulted in war.

However, this outcome (and here we shift to a chronological presentation of events) still lay far in the future. In the late autumn of 1864, the details of the Vienna Peace Treaty became known, and Austria and Prussia were declared sole possessors of the conquered duchy, but the first clouds were not long appearing on the horizon. Austria confidentially asked Prussia whether it would agree to surrender its claim to Schleswig - Holstein in favour of a third party. Prussia did not directly refuse but evaded the question. Entering into such discussions (against which it raised no objections in principal) so soon after the conclusion of peace seemed premature. The ensuing negotiations over this complicated point, where differences in interpretation would be nearly inevitable, should for the time being, be postponed. [Prussia] asked Austria to join it in a common appeal to the Confederation, which, in its decisive reference to Paragraph I of the Vienna Peace Accord, made it unmistakably clear that Prussia was determined to place itself on the side of the new agreement. The joint Austrian Prussian appeal to the Confederation read as follows:

> The Federal Diet will consider the Federal Execution approved on 7th December of this year in the duchies of Holstein and Lauenburg as completed and the governments of the Kingdoms of Saxony and Hannover that were tasked with its consummation will withdraw their troops from the above duchies and recall the civil commissioners they appointed there.

This motion was adopted by a majority of nine to six (Bavaria, Saxony, Würtemberg, Hesse - Darmstadt, Braunschweig - Nassau and the Thuringian states). Hannover and Saxony withdrew their troops in mid-December. Friend and foe believed that the two great German powers would now cooperate in the light of this motion. The south German press recognized the danger lying therein, however in Vienna itself, where at that time sentiment still favoured Prussia, this development in German affairs was widely seen as the only legitimate one (because it was natural). The *Österreichische Zeitung* wrote, with notable perspicacity:

> Whoever examines the nature and underlying concept of the German Confederation from a free, unselfconscious, political viewpoint, whose awareness of the significant position of the German Confederation in the European community of nations has not been obfuscated by the press and by schoolboy wisdom, that person must unconditionally recognize that the top and bottom, indeed, the indispensable prerequisite for any possible effectiveness and longevity of the Confederation, is *the true and firm cooperation of Austria and Prussia*. If this exists, then the German Confederation remains powerful, assuring peace in the heart of Europe, and its people rejoice together, strong and secure. Its integrity is inviolable, its welfare secure. If however, the prerequisite upon which the entire structure rests (the firm cooperation of Austria and Prussia) is lacking, then that is the end, not only of internal peace, but also of the security and integrity of all the German lands. Even though the leadership of the Confederation was erroneous in principle from its founding to the year 1848, the historical fact remains that up to that point, so long as Austria and Prussia remained hand in hand, the power of this

relationship kept war far from central Europe. *This will certainly remain true just as long as Austria and Prussia remain joined in close friendship.*

That was generally how people viewed the situation in Austria. The war in Denmark, where [no foreign power] dared to intervene, had proved the truth of these statements. This was how the ruling circles in Vienna still thought in mid-December, but a change loomed in the days ahead, *the ancient jealousy reared its head.*

In Schleswig - Holstein itself, seventeen members of the nobility gathered to prepare an address, one passage of which (even though not intended as a trigger) rekindled the smouldering embers. This passage read:

> If this attempt (regarding the succession) results in a change in the basis of the succession that results in a division of the Duchies, we place our trust in the wise solicitude of your Majesty. *Demands of one part can have no legitimate basis regarding the inseparable whole.* Such demands must be judged in light of the wellbeing of the entire land. This calls for possible protection … which Your Majesty cannot deny to the Arch Duchies. We are convinced that there can be no better assurance than by the most urgent appeal to one of the German great powers, and indeed to the *Prussian* monarchy, as the closest one.

This address, along with the deputation that brought it, was warmly received in Prussia and almost immediately the King directed that the Prussian royal jurists report on the claims of the Prince of Augustenburg to the succession. That was no more than Vienna should expect to take place, if from the very start, she was determined to take a sympathetic view of Prussia and her natural demands. As events would prove, that was not the case. The Emperor refused to receive the address. Displeasure was expressed in the recall of *Freiherr* von Lederer from Kiel and his replacement by *Baron* von Halbhuber, a less affable man. *Baron* von Halbhuber arrived in Altona in the final days of the year and his arrival inaugurated an era of friction and discord.

The purpose of *Herr* von Halbhuber's special mission did not emerge in the first few weeks, on the contrary, January passed with friendly relations. Austria again took up its inquiry from mid-November as to, 'whether it is not time for a possible imminent settlement of the Schleswig - Holstein question and the establishment of an independent government for the duchies.' In and of itself, there was nothing in this inquiry that was inappropriate, let alone offensive. At that time Prussia was still far from thinking of annexing the duchies, and just as far from any intention of continuing to share *ad infinitum*, joint custody and administration of the duchies with Austria. Transfer to a third party with the most legitimate claim appeared as the most natural solution, only two conditions had to be met: the third party's legitimacy must first be conclusively proven, and after such proof, it must agree on specific concessions to Prussia, as the guardian of Northern Germany. All parties were actually in agreement on this. Austria, the German Confederation, even the Prince von Augustenburg, were not opposed *in principle* to these Prussian views. Therefore, everything depended on what concessions were required, and what demands Prussia would make. Initially Prussia sought to postpone specifying these demands, but as Austria became ever more pressing, [Prussia] proceeded to formulate the essential elements, which were transmitted to Vienna in a dispatch of 22nd February. These later became famous as the *February Demands*.

The importance of this document seems to merit an inspection of its contents. In its introduction, the point was raised that the duchies, by their geographical location and in consideration of the existing political situation, constituted a weak spot for the attack of all of northern Germany. Since they would be unable to defend themselves, Prussia must undertake their protection, and if Prussia was to assume such an extensive responsibility, she must be given the means to fulfill this obligation effectively. That meant that the combat forces and military installations in Schleswig must closely cooperate with those of Prussia, and that the duchy must, militarily, be a part of [the Prussian] system so that it could immediately and effectively withstand an attack. Such was the rationale to which the demands themselves were appended. These were essentially as follows:

1. That the newly formed state of Schleswig - Holstein conclude an eternal and indissoluble Alliance for Protection and Defense with Prussia, empowering and obligating the latter to protect and defend the duchies against any enemy attack. Schleswig - Holstein for its part, is to place *the entire combat forces of both duchies* at the disposal of the King of Prussia so that they may serve within the Prussian army and fleet, in the defense of both lands and their interests.

2. The conscription and strength of the manpower to be provided to the Prussian army and fleet from Schleswig – Holstein, will be determined according to standards current in Prussia. The same basis will apply for the navy, as for the land army.

3. The Prussian fleet is be granted freedom of movement and stationing of warships in all Schleswig - Holstein waters. To enable effective coastal defense, the Prussian government will be granted control over the piloting, buoys and coastal lighting facilities on the Baltic and North Seas.

4. The Prussian government reserves to itself, in cooperation with the Austrian government, the right to propose to the German Confederation that Rendsburg be made a Federal Fortress and that the putative regime of the new state gives its advance approval to this proposal. Until the establishment and completion of this arrangement, Rendsburg will continue to be garrisoned by Prussia.

5. The obligation to protect the duchies and the situation in which Schleswig is exposed to foreign attack, make it necessary for Prussia, with respect to the effective construction of fortifications, to have *direct possession of ground and earth*, which is to be transferred to Prussia with full sovereignty rights. These transfers will, as a minimum, include:
   a) For the protection of North Schleswig: The city of Sonderburg with a corresponding region on both sides of the Alsen Sound and sufficient territory on Alsen for construction and fortification of a military harbour in the Hörup Haff.
   b) Regarding construction of a Prussian military harbour in the Bay of Kiel: the Friedrichsort Fortress.
   c) The mouths of the North Sea – Baltic Canal, for the purpose of constructing military harbours and fortifications.

6. Control of the adjacent North Sea – Baltic Sea Canal.

7. Entry into the Customs Union [*Zollverein*].

8.   Unification of the postal and telegraph service with those of Prussia.

These were the February Demands. To these were appended, *All of the above conditions must be assured before the duchies will be transferred to their future ruler.*

In Vienna it seemed that people did not want to acknowledge the full seriousness of the Prussian demands (even though these were explicitly designated as a *minimum*). The answer arrived in Berlin in the first half of March, wherein the demands were described as 'too far reaching.' That is how the matter rested. The exchange of dispatches, at least in so far as it concerned this matter, ended. The feud between the cabinets was at a standstill.

The larger feud slumbered, but not the little ones. The duchies themselves were the natural theater of bickering, which must inevitably result in the revival of the main feud. It was possible to maintain a certain level of courtesy between Vienna and Berlin despite ever more frequent disagreements, this was not the case in Kiel where the respective governments had to function in close proximity with each other.

Between Vienna and Berlin, the conflict was considered a 'major question', whose solution involved serious considerations, but could be postponed until wide ranging negotiations could take place. In the meantime, every day, the matter was a burning issue between our Civil Commissioner, *Herr* von Zedlitz and the Austrian *Herr* von Halbhuber. Here there was no possibility of politely pretending problems did not exist, no convenient postponement. What each day brought, had to be dealt with that day. Here, the demands and denials that were initially of a purely factual nature, very soon transformed into personal friction and inaugurated an unhappy six months of strife. Not a day passed without a fresh pinprick. It would be too much to follow these little clashes step by step, but a few moments can be spent characterizing the style of this petty warfare. *Freiherr* von Zedlitz requested a ban against the *F. VIII.* (Frederick VIII [Duke of Augustenburg]) on the Schleswig - Holstein banners and flags, *Freiherr* von Halbhuber refused. *Freiherr* von Zedlitz proposed that, after the unification of the customs services of the two duchies, [the service] should no longer spoken of as *herzoglich holsteinschen* [Ducal Holstein] but (deleting the *herzoglich*) it should now be referred to as the Schleswig - Holstein Customs Bureau, *Freiherr* von Halbhuber refused. Prussia celebrated the 18th April (anniversary of Düppel)[4], *Herr* von Halbhuber refused to take part. There were days and weeks where the activity of the Austrian Civil Commissioner was limited to refusals and protests. *Freiherr* von Halbhuber believed he could bring about (indeed, it is said that he dreamed of) a 'second Olmütz'.[5]

These incessant protests, which only too clearly produced an impression of outright harassment and frivolous governmental interference, caused bad feeling in Berlin. *Herr* von Zedlitz complained bitterly about his colleague's lack of professionalism. Nevertheless, one has

---

4   Tr. Note: The Battle of Düppel, 7th-18th April 1864, in which Prussian forces stormed and took the major Danish fortifications at Düppel. It resulted in a Prussian-Austrian victory over Denmark.

5   Tr. Note: After the former German Confederation was dissolved in the revolutions of 1848, Prussia took the lead in forming a new confederation but excluded Austria from the new arrangement. Complex political events, including the question of Schleswig – Holstein, resulted in Prussian mobilization. In response Austria moved troops to the Prussian border. Confronted by the threat of war Prussia backed down and on 29th November 1850, Prussia and Austria signed the 'Olmütz Declaration,' agreeing to the demobilization of Prussia's troops and an effective return to the *status quo ante*. In Prussia this was viewed as a serious, shameful humiliation.

to admit that there was some provocation in the Prussian behaviour too. Although it did not infringe upon the rights of [the Austrian co-administration], it made far reaching use of its own rights, even where these impinged upon the unclear line of demarcation. It dealt with the Düsternbrook bathing establishment[6] in relation to construction of a naval facility. It involved purchase of land for the construction of fortifications. It involved excavation and surveying, measuring and buoying. It fortified Düppel. It supported the establishment of a '*Norddeutschen Schiffbau – Gesellschaft*' [North German Ship building Company]. Put simply, it made itself at home. The only answer to the various questions and protests from the Austrian co-administration was that [Austria] was free to do the same.

The Austrian administration, however, did not do the same. It simply persisted in its negative stance and its only activity was to encourage Augustenburg agitation. *Herr* von Halbhuber supported all endeavours that would undermine Prussia's chartered rights in Schleswig - Holstein. He made common cause with the Hereditary Prince's shadow regime,[7] and as opportunity presented itself, gave the legal Schleswig - Holstein local government (which consisted of friends of the Augustenburgers) an anti-Prussian character, so that the local government, when possible, did what the shadow regime desired. If the Prussian administration, by rapidly initiating construction projects, disturbed Vienna, Halbhuber's making joint cause with the Augustenburg faction caused even more disturbance in Berlin.

And for good reason. This agitation mocked the existing legal status and ignored the Vienna peace treaty, it was nothing more than high treason (and in the later stages of the dispute, Prussia had the courage to simply call it by that name). [As Austria saw it] the treaty rights accompanying the Vienna Peace Treaty were nothing, whereas the hereditary claims of the Augustenburgers were everything.

The reality was this, Prussia was in the land but wrongfully. It was taking possession of what did not belong to it, but it considered itself legally entitled to do so (and did so because Austria permitted it) and said so daily. If 1848 was generally spoken of as a time of cosy anarchy, here was a situation of cosy high treason. Thereby one gloried in extensive gratitude. 'First our Duke', it was said, 'the rest will take care of itself. We will ask the people of the land what they want to do about Prussia, but first our Duke.' Prussia was an admonisher, an uninvited guest, and not the master. *Freiherr* von Zedlitz demanded that *Freiherr* von Halbhuber put an end to his agitation or at least limit its growth. *Herr* von Halbhuber refused to act or simply ignored it.

The agitation continued. The agitation was particularly stoked by the 'memorial days.' Whenever there was something to remember or commemorate, use was made thereof. Obviously, the family celebrations of the House of Augustenburg were especially welcome. 6th July was the birthday of the 'Duke' and therefore a celebration was proclaimed. 'Six thousand valiant men,' were to assemble in Nienstädten[8] and show the prince 'how many he could count on.' When

---

6   Tr. Note: The Düsternbrook bathing facility is a bathing beach in Kiel harbour.
7   Tr. Note: The Austrian Civil Commissioner von Halbhuber, allowed the development of an extra legal 'Ducal co-regime' under the pretender, Prince von Augustenburg. According to Sybel (vol. IV, p. 103), nearly all of the local officials it appointed were Augustenburg supporters and decisions regarding all measures that were of importance to the Augustenburg party were covertly presented to the 'pretender', the Prince of Augustenburg for 'sovereign approval'.
8   Tr. Note: Nienstädten is a quarter in the city of Hamburg, Germany. It is in the borough of Altona on the right bank of the Elbe river.

the day actually arrived, there was no demonstration. There was supposed to have been a parade as part of the celebration, which as one can well imagine, could not have taken place without confrontation, thus accomplishing the main objective, intensifying the conflict between *Herr* von Zedlitz and *Herr* von Halbhuber. That is what it was all about. While the newspapers argued about whether *Herr* von Halbhuber had granted his permission for an intervention or had denied it, *Herr* von Zedlitz finally declared 'that neither the one nor the other would have been possible, since *Herr* von Halbhuber's permission had not been requested. The matter was the affair of the Military High Command, which would best know whether intervention was required in the interests of law and order.' This declaration immediately added fuel to the fire, as might 'the great parade at Nienstädten' have done.

So, one had to be satisfied with limited success, the fact that the demonstration of the '6,000 valiant men' did not take place. This 6,000 were members of the *'Kampfgenossen'*, the 'combat comrades' and *Schleswig – Holstein Verein*, the 'Schleswig - Holstein Societies', which numbered 171 or more. They were like a net stretched over the entire land and terrorized the broad mass of the people that actually stayed far from politics and simply followed whoever was stronger. They agreed on common measures, they armed themselves directly, they sent speakers throughout the land that harangued the people and they controlled the press. Their organs were the *Kieler Zeitung*, the *Schleswig - Holstein Zeitung* and the *Itzehoer Nachrichten* which was important because of its wide readership.

Conflict was inevitable, the Prussian troops and the *Schleswig – Holstein Verein* were like separate garrisons in the same cities, and as always happens in such cases, friction arose. The public speakers and the newspapers of the Schleswig - Holstein side were eager to provoke the 'Prussian battalions' and the moment could not be far off that would show which was the stronger. Had the *Vereine* shown more moderation things might have been different but the increasingly provocative attitude they took hastened the confrontation. Prussian troops were mocked, sentinels insulted and the children of our officers (in the schools they attended) were exposed to foul language and violence. Public speakers spoke of the 'Prussian pack,' the 'hungry wolf that no one had called for.' Here and there, the slogan was heard, 'Better Danish than Prussian.' This kind of talk stirred things up in Berlin! In the meantime, the *Kronsyndikat's*[9] opinion was made known, it denied every claim of the Hereditary Prince (the pretender). Naturally, this did not increase the inclination of the Augustenburg supporters to moderate their behaviour. The inevitable confrontation came about at the end of July, this is how it happened.

Prominent men led the Augustenburg organization, but as their straw man, they chose an industrious, otherwise insignificant personality, the newspaper editor May. His publication, (the *Schleswig - Holsteinische*) was the dumping ground for everything anti – Prussian, and of late had taken an increasingly provocative tone. In recent weeks he had made the *Bremer Schützenfest* [Bremen rifle match][10] an occasion for offensively personal remarks about Prussia, the Prussian army and even the King. The first blow fell on him. May's arrest was decided on

9   Tr. Note: Until 1918, the *Kronsyndikat* were the legal advisors of the Prussian Crown. Permanently in office to give impartial legal opinions they included two pensioned ministers of justice, six presidents and councillors of the Supreme Court, two presidents of courts of appeal and four professors of the Universities of Berlin and Bonn (Sybel, vol IV p. 158).

10 Tr. Note: The *Bremer Schützenfest*, a major rifle match and festival, was inaugurated in 1846 in Bremen by the *Bremer Schützenverein*, or Bremen Shooting Club.

at a conference of ministers that was held regarding the events in Schleswig - Holstein on 21st July, during King Wilhelm's trip from Karlsbad to Gastein. This was carried out on 25th July. A military detachment surrounded May's house in Altona where he was still sleeping, and took him from Altona to Rendsburg, where he was detained at the local police station. The next day the Prussian delegate, Frese, who was a friend of May's and had spent the recent weeks in the duchies, was advised to leave the country within twenty four hours.

This bold action demonstrated that Prussia was tired of, and would no longer tolerate, such inappropriate behaviour. There was, naturally, no shortage of protests, *Freiherr* von Halbhuber also protested, and we present his protest here:

> According to an oral communication I received from the Prussian Civil Commissioner, *Freiherr* von Zedlitz, I discovered that the editor of the *Schleswig - Holsteinsche Zeitung*, May, has been arrested in Altona because he is a Prussian subject and has acted contrary to Prussian laws. I protest against this act that was taken without my consent as a violent violation of the Austrian rights as co - ruler, of my sphere of activity and of the laws of the land. I urgently request that the Prussian Civil Commissioner revoke this action that he has unilaterally taken.
>
> Schleswig, 25 July 1865.
> *Freiherr* von Halbhuber.

So long as only *Herr* von Halbhuber himself stood behind this protest, it was trivial, everything would depend on how the Prussian action was seen in Vienna. If it was seen as an infringement, and taken formally as such, then conflict was unavoidable.

The clouds were gathering, but once again a breach was avoided. Austria did not want to strike, nor was she able. Negotiations were started, *Graf* Blome came to Gastein, the two rulers met in Salzburg, everything seemed to be smoothed over. In the event, agreement was reached, and the result of this agreement was the Gastein Convention.

To 13th March 1866 (initial armament)

In the Gastein Convention we had an attempt to maintain peace. Peace was endangered less by the mood of the cabinet than by the difficulty of conducting a joint administration for Schleswig-Holstein. *Herr* von Halbhuber and *Herr* von Zedlitz were in the front line of those carrying on the feud, not the prince, nor *Graf* Mensdorff, nor *Herr* von Bismarck. The joint administrations in *Schloss* Gottorp caused friction. The goal of the Convention, whose basic concept was 'divide the administrations', was intended to eliminate this [daily friction]. Two administrations replaced one. The Gastein Convention created one administration for Holstein and a second for Schleswig. The individual stipulations of the convention were as follows:

> Exercise of rights over the duchies will henceforth be geographically separated so that those regarding the Duchy of Schleswig will be exercised by the King of Prussia and those regarding the Duchy of Holstein will be exercised by the Emperor of Austria.
>
> The two sovereigns will cause the formation of the German fleet for the Confederation and the Harbour of Kiel is specified as the Federal harbour. Until then command and policing of the same will be exercised by Prussia, which is empowered in

itself to construct the necessary fortifications and facilities and to garrison these with Prussian troops and guard them.

Application will be made to the Federal Diet to elevate Rendsburg to the status of a Federal fortress. Until then this fortress will receive a garrison of Prussian and Austrian troops. Command of these will alternate annually on 1st July.

The Prussian regime is to receive two military roads through Holstein, one from Lübeck to Kiel, the other from Hamburg to Rendsburg. It will be given control over a telegraph wire to link Kiel and Rendsburg, as well as the right to let Prussian postal wagons with their own officials to pass on both lines through the Duchy of Holstein.

The duchies will join the Customs Union [*Zollverein*].

Prussia is empowered to extend the yet to be constructed North Sea – Baltic Canal through the territory of Holstein as well as to exercise control over the same and its maintenance. In exchange for payment of compensation to the Austrian government, the Emperor of Austria turns over his claims to the Duchy of Lauenburg to the King of Prussia, so that the entire rule over this Duchy will finally be transferred to the King of Prussia. Lauenburg pays no costs of the war.

The Duchy of Holstein will be evacuated by Prussian troops, Schleswig evacuated by Austrian troops.

Measures to be taken as a result of this agreement, also including the dissolution of the previous joint administration for the two duchies, will presumably be completed by 15th September of this year.

They were completed by 15th September, and were carried out on both sides, in a spirit of reconciliation. The Emperor's birthday (18th August) was celebrated with special ceremonies by the Prussian troops, salutes were fired in Kiel, the national hymn was sung, and the flag flown on all warships. There was a joint parade in Rendsburg and even in the Lockstädter *Lager* [camp], where (between Itzehoe and Neumünster) about 10,000 Prussian troops were stationed. Austria, for its part, did not fall short in gestures of friendship either. *Herr* von Halbhuber, the source of so many annoyances and complaints, was recalled, and *Feldmarschalllieutenant* von Gablenz was appointed Governor of the administration of Holstein. This was an outstanding choice. Without prejudices against Prussia, charming, with all those virtues that make interaction with soldiers so pleasant, there was every expectation of an epoch of friendly cooperation, even as the 'Halbhuber era' had been one of conflict and discord. Prussia, for its part, appointed *Generallieutenant* von Manteuffel as Governor of Schleswig. Von Manteuffel resided in *Schloss* Gottorp, *Feldmarschalllieutenant* von Gablenz in *Schloss* Kiel. Under both of them the actual administration of the land was, as before, placed in the hands of civil commissioners. *Freiherr* von Zedlitz remained in office in Schleswig. *Geh. Hofrath* von Hoffmann took over the administration in Holstein. Everything went well. In Prussia at least, there were hopes of a final settlement. The transfer of Lauenburg, as stipulated in the Gastein Convention, was only a prelude. Nobody doubted that a measure would also be found for Schleswig - Holstein that was equivalent to what had served for Lauenburg. At most people disagreed on what the equivalent measures would consist of.

One can assume that such questions did indeed concern the two regimes, and that at least for the time being, such intentions were seriously raised on the Austrian side. Only later could this be viewed with certainty. Without doubt a spirit of reconciliation existed at that time, at least for a matter of weeks. To give only one example, Austria joined with Prussia in approaching Frankfurt, whose senate was requested, in very uncompromising language, to forbid the meetings and provocations of democratic (at the same time Augustenburg) societies within its walls. Austria was half - hearted in the matter but went along with it. In any case, an atmosphere of cooperation and soldierly comradeship developed between Kiel and Schleswig. This spirit of comradeship withstood the various trials which could not fail to take place. Nothing could be less to the liking of the Augustenburg party than this spirit of cooperation. Its only chances depended on discord between the *condomini*. This discord must be restored exactly as it had been between *Baron* von Halbhuber and *Freiherr* von Zedlitz and every endeavour was made to find new ways of bringing it about.

They were inventive enough, or perhaps it was the very nature of the thing. There may be some doubt about the first incident when Duke Friedrich decided to visit *Schloss* Karlsburg in Southern Schleswig (the Schwanken district) from Kiel. Various motives for this visit were offered. Early on 14th October the Duke departed and (whether intended or not) found himself in a suburb of Eckernförde, in the midst of an Augustenburg demonstration, with banners and welcoming speeches proclaiming him as Friedrich VIII, the rightful Duke of Schleswig - Holstein. That was too much. The Prussians were determined that on Schleswig soil at least, these claims to dukedom had to be ended once and for all. The Vienna Treaty clearly stated that only Austria and Prussia could rule here. The rejection of the February Demands had reduced the likelihood of a voluntary cession to a very low level, and after the *Kronsyndikat* had delivered its expert verdict three months earlier, the Augustenburg house and its claim, had been to all intents and purposes, stricken from the alternatives under consideration. Once more, settlement of the question was only between Austria and Prussia and there was no longer any inclination to confuse the issue by appealing to a third party. It was from this viewpoint that *Freiherr* von Manteuffel wrote the following letter to Prince Friedrich as the result of the Eckernförd incident:

Schloss Gottorp, 18 October 1865.

On the 14th of this month in Borbye, during a change of horses, Your Serene Highness got out and took the opportunity to be addressed by various people in which you were greeted as the Sovereign and to which you replied. During the preparations for this trip various agitators found time to gather 6 or 7 horsemen, that rode ahead of your carriage and assembled a part of the populace in Eckernförde.

Your Serene Highness' drive through Eckernförde and stay in Borbye thus took on the character of a political demonstration. Such [demonstrations] disturb the peace of the land, endangering the existence of individuals and are an offense against the law and order of the duchy, for whose maintenance I am responsible. I have therefore issued appropriate orders that, in the event of a similar repetition, all appropriate legal means, including, if necessary, arrest, will be employed to preserve public order and avoid further disturbances.

His majesty the King, my most gracious master, has had so much mercy toward your Serene Highness, your noble father and his entire house, that it would be painful to me if your Serene person became involved with the police of the Duchy of Schleswig, and I therefore feel impelled to inform your Serene Highness of the measures instituted, and therefore most humbly request that you inform me in timely fashion if your Serene Highness intends to visit the Duchy of Schleswig, so that I can make the arrangements necessary to protect your Serene Highness from any personal unpleasantness.

I have informed the Governor of the Duchy of Holstein, *Feldmarschallieutenant* von Gablenz, of the events in Eckernförde and Borbye where your Serene Highness did not maintain the private position that you, at present, hold in the Duchy of Holstein.

Freiherr von Manteuffel.

This was uncompromising language, but it was unavoidable. To eliminate the slightest doubt regarding the position of the Prussian regime, a few days later the *'Staatsanzeiger'* published a communiqué that stated, 'the action taken by the Governor in this respect had the full endorsement of His Majesty the King,' and another official organ found it appropriate to give the following expression, 'The prince must finally realize that his former position in the duchies did not exist as the result of his rights, but out of pure patience [of the authorities] and that the only legal basis for further developments in the duchies is the right of possession of Prussia and Austria.'

In conjunction with this, *Freiherr* von Manteuffel brought up another old grievance, requesting that *Freiherr* von Gablenz ban use of the designation, *'Graf* Friedrich VIII' or 'our Duke', as daily employed in the Holstein newspapers. At nearly the same time as this, all Holstein newspapers, so far as they supported Augustenburg (and that was the great majority of them) were banned in the Duchy of Schleswig.

Politically, all of these requests and bans, contained between the lines at least, the gentle reproach, 'Government of Holstein, you are not doing what you should,' and also contained a dig at the Imperial *condominus* in Vienna, especially against its representative, the Governor of Holstein (*Freiherr* von Gablenz). Whether his temperament and spirit of comradeship allowed him to overlook a great deal, or whether he basically recognized the Prussian demands (harsh though they might appear) as correct, he did not take offense and remained on good terms with *Schloss* Gottorp. He deserves credit (where his feelings as a soldier, may have played a major role) for avoiding, to the very last, instituting another 'Halbhuber era'. However, personal amiability could not prevent the final confrontation, circumstances were more powerful than individuals. The imperatives of the situation prevailed, pleasantries could only modify it, not change its fundamental nature.

Again, it was 'memorial days' and ducal demonstrations that prepared the way for the break. In the meantime, the new year (1866) arrived, and it happened like this.

The Augustenburgers had called for a general assembly of all Schleswig - Holstein societies [*Schleswig - Holsteinsche Vereine*] and brothers in arms for 23rd January at Altona. A mass meeting was to choose revolution and to call for the assembly of the Estates[11]. Already on 16th

---

11   Author's Note: It was certain that the majority of the *Holsteinschen Stände* [or Estates], were on the side of the hereditary Prince von Augustenburg. All, therefore, who were anti - Prussian wanted to have the Estates assembled as soon as possible so as to occasion a pro - Augustenburg demonstration, and with this demonstration, as with a factionalized popular vote, to influence the German Federal Diet as well as the European courts. Prussia could not possibly have anything to gain from such a vote. It recognized the right of the Estates to be assembled and heard, but it reserved to itself, as *Condominus*,

November, on the second anniversary of the Dolzig Proclamation[12], there had been similar demonstrations in a wide variety of locations, with feasts and reunions, to force the Estates to assemble and install the duke. The call, which had at that time been isolated, was now to be *en mass*. This was expected to have an effect.

In Berlin, which was fully informed of all these plans, little significance was attributed to this 'General Assembly' and the resolutions it was to take. However, it considered it far more important that the Holstein regime, as the *Condominus*, had permitted a demonstration that was in such flagrant violation of the Vienna Peace Treaty and the Gastein Convention.

In Vienna, [the Austrian government] seemed aware of the tension [in Berlin]. They realized our irritation and hesitated to make the final, irremediable breach. On the other hand, from week to week, the inclination to settle the prevailing question in a manner pleasing to Prussia diminished. The mood shifted back and forth, finally settling on a half measure. This half measure was that a ban would be announced of the planned assembly, but only on the day when it was scheduled to take place, and that the ban would be rescinded on the simple promise of the party leader, that he did not want to start a revolution.

Revolutions were of course, not now intended, but in their choice of language, the assemblies seemed to be trying to avert blame for such. 'With God's help', so said one of the leaders, 'the despised public opinion will swell to a river that will sweep away *Junkerthum* and despotism'. Bergmann remarked from Altona, ' With a million eyes the world is watching Schleswig - Holstein. It must remain true, otherwise it will be despised by the women and cursed by its own children.' Eckstorff (also from Altona) proclaimed in low German that, 'the Holsteiners must support Schleswig, lying in Prussian chains, and protect the rights of the land from the Berlin *Putzenmacher.*' This was the type of language employed. Many proposed a 'refusal to pay taxes,' all pushed for an assembly of the Estates and were convinced, 'that the Prussians had already gone too far.'

Thus dawned 23rd January. There were wild speeches whose clear-cut violation of the law was indisputable. Berlin came to a quick decision; this was enough and too much. On 26th January *Graf* Bismarck sent a dispatch to Vienna that could be seen as the starting point of the final rupture. This dispatch, after expressing indignation over the fact that the Austrian regime in Holstein had permitted such subversive activities, then continued:

> It seems nearly incomprehensible that things could get to this point when we look back on the days of Gastein. . . The current behaviour of the Imperial Regime in Holstein is of an entirely different character. We must view this as emphatically directed against us, and the Imperial Regime does not hesitate to employ exactly the same means to inspire sedition against us in the field that they were willing to join with us in disputing in Frankfurt. . . .[13] Through the Gastein Convention, each of the two duchies is entrusted

the right to share in the decision regarding the timing. All of the Augustenburgers on the other hand, urged Austria, without consideration of Prussia, to take unilateral action on this question.

12   Tr. Note: On 16th November 1863, from his residence on *Gut* Dolzig, in Prussian Niederlausitz, Friedrich proclaimed himself Friedrich VIII, Duke of Schleswig - Holstein.

13   Tr. Note: Prussia and Vienna had agreed, in Gastein and Salzburg, that they would conduct the affairs of Germany as a whole, in concert, with a firm and conservative policy. When the 'Committee of Thirty Six', in angry response to the Gastein Treaty, called together a new assembly of deputies

equally as surety for the loyalty and conscientiousness of each of the co - owners. We had hoped on that basis to achieve a broader understanding, and we have the right to demand that until the attainment of that understanding, each surety will be kept intact. Damage of the sort that you have caused through these disorders we cannot and will not allow. We require no concessions, no surrender of any of Austria's rights in the duchies, only the maintenance of the rights we hold in common, nothing more than Austria is responsible for, for its own interests as much as ours. Nothing more than the Imperial regime is in a position to carry out without sacrifice of or injury to its own interests. If the rights we hold in common are of little value to Austria, for Prussia the determination and execution of these is a vital question that is inseparable from the overall politics of the present government of His Majesty the King. A negative or evasive reply to our request will convince us the Imperial government does not intend, in the long run, to follow a common path with us, but that in Austria, the tendencies that are negative toward Prussia, and the traditional antagonism toward Prussia, is more powerful than the feeling of solidarity and the common interest! This would be a painful disappointment for His Majesty the King, from which we hope to be spared. However, it is an imperative necessity for us to bring clarity to our relationship. We must, if the inner solidarity of the overall policy of both powers that we have sincerely striven for cannot be achieved, *gain complete freedom for our entire policy* and make use of the same in accordance with what we consider to be Prussia's interests.

The Austrian reply (7th February), simply refuted the allegations contained in the above dispatch. It emphasized that the Imperial Administration based its refutation on the conditions of the Gastein Convention, that it was in no way subordinate to Prussian controls in its administration of Holstein, and remarked in conclusion, citing the words of *Graf* Bismarck, 'if a solidarity of the overall policy of both powers cannot be achieved, the reasons for this must be found somewhere other than in the attitudes and activities of the Imperial court.'

With these dispatches, the peaceful exchange of opinions over the Schleswig - Holstein question came to an end. The respective intentions were now clear, and these intentions were opposed to each other. Enough had been said. Prussia wanted Schleswig – Holstein, Austria was clear about that, and Austria would permit no rival [to attain] this increase in power, Prussia was clear about that too. Adjoining regimes were impossible in the long run. In the most favourable conditions the question could only be postponed. The moment when force must be invoked as the ultimate solution was drawing ever nearer.

None of the many dispatches[14] that were still exchanged until the outbreak of war, took up the controversy of the Schleswig - Holstein question again, new elements entered the discussions

to meet at Frankfort on the 1st of October, resulting in an outpouring of vituperation against the Gastein agreement, Bismarck suggested to Vienna, taking some common measure against the free city [Frankfurt], which had allowed such an attack upon the German Great Powers within its borders. Prussia and Austria then each sent a severe note to the Frankfurt senate demanding the prohibition of any future repetition of such an occurrence. Otherwise, the Prussian note added, [Austria and Prussia] would, themselves, be forced to interfere [Sybel, volume IV, p. 222 ff and 273ff].

14   Author's Note: The only exception was the Austrian dispatch of 6th March. In this the Vienna cabinet referred to the Prussian February Demands of 1865 without otherwise fully and plainly approving them. Prussia would only, and with difficulty, have been content with an unreserved acceptance [of the

and the snowball became an avalanche. In the next chapter we shall see what questions gained the upper hand before the actual fighting began.

Prussia remained silent throughout February and remained silent during the first weeks of March. That was significant, even more significant than if the heated controversy had continued, that was also the opinion in Austria. In mid-March, news arrived in Berlin that on 10th March, a military conference had taken place in Vienna and that on 13th March, the decision to mobilise had been taken. Against whom? There could be no doubt about the answer.

To 5th June (The Holstein Estates are called to session)

Until mid-March, there could still be doubts as to whether it was known in Berlin that Austria was arming, henceforth there could be none. News arrived simultaneously from Vienna, Bohemia, Galicia and Hungary, of regiments being brought up to full strength and of troop movements toward the north. In Saxony too, forces were being brought up to strength. Every day confirmed the reports. The Vienna press, to the extent that it was independent, made no secret of this armament. The official organs at least, did not deny it.

For the time being, Prussia held back, satisfying itself with carefully watching what was happening on the far side of the border. Opinions varied as to whether Austria was in earnest or whether all this troop movement and the accompanying commotion in the press, was only an attempt at intimidation. But this uncertainty did not last long. In the final week of March all signs (including the sudden silence of the press) indicated that Austria wanted war, or at least believed it was going to happen, and that Prussia was obliged to react if it wished to avoid a situation similar to that which had taken place in 1850, when an Austrian army stood ready to attack on our border, without ourselves being in a position to offer any resistance. The result was Olmütz.

Despite *Herr* von Halbhuber's prophecies, there was to be no second Olmütz. Prussia initiated a counter mobilization, partial to begin with as we did not want to appear provocative, but neither were we ready to strike our colours. On 28th March the order was issued to arm the [Prussian] fortresses of Glatz, Kosel, Neisse, Torgau, Wittenberg, Spandau and Magdeburg. Several field artillery regiments were augmented, and the infantry regiments of the 5th, 7th, and 9th Divisions, as well as the entire VI (Silesian) Army Corps, received orders to call up the reserves. This was an important step. Though Austria might appear to be on the defensive, or at least give that impression, it was clear that she would respond with increased mobilisation, and so she did. Now the pace quickened. The main Austrian force moved in echelon to Moravia, while smaller units were dispatched to Bohemia. On 6th April *Oberstlieutenant Graf* Waldersee was arrested in Prague (despite having a proper pass in his name) and was brought before a military commission of investigation. Upon receipt of orders from Vienna he was released, but forcibly ejected from Austria. This was already an act of war, a hostile act before the opening of hostilities. It confirmed Austrian mobilization, and it proved that there was something in Bohemia to hide and that they wanted to hide it. Now Prussia knew what it was facing. Without fuss, but also without concealment, the work was set in motion on our side. At the beginning

February Demands]. Since February 1865 the situation had changed (for example as the result of the opinions of the *Kronsyndikat*) and what might have been satisfactory at that time, was no longer so.

of May, the III, IV, V and VI Corps were mobilised as well as the Guards. On 8th May the entire army was mobilised, and by the middle of the month, eight weeks after the start of the first mobilisations, two great armies stood facing each other, greater and more prepared for immediate action, than either opponent had ever put in the field before.

However, as all this was taking place, while the railroads transported hundreds of thousands of men to the Silesian and Saxon borders in a continuous relay, the pens did not rest, and dispatches were exchanged in ever increasing numbers. New questions (we mentioned these already at the close of our preceding chapter) pushed the old ones aside, and as always in a conflict between two parties, all the bystanders, all those closely or distantly involved, sought to help and to advise, to soothe and to reconcile, or at least get credit for so doing.

Reading through the documents that were exchanged in these months is initially somewhat confusing. If however, one eliminates the trivial and examines what remains, the bigger picture emerges. The first exchange of dispatches dealt with the hot question of, 'Who initiated the mobilisation?' Prussia stated that it did not respond to Austria's mobilisation of 13th March until 28th March, [when it did so] with a partial, strictly defensive call up of its reserves. Austria, however, claimed that it had not, for its part, provoked Prussia's mobilisation. It declared most resolutely, 'that no significant assemblies of troops, let alone a concentration of such on the border has been ordered … no unusual purchase of horses, no recall of men on leave to any *significant* degree has taken place.' Such declarations understandably, led nowhere. Each side shoved the blame onto the other. Finally, the exchange of dispatches entered a second stage. The question of, 'Who started it?' was dropped. Austria, 'As proof of its love of peace,' declared, in a dispatch of 18th April, that it was ready to engage in the demobilisation proposed by Prussia, if Prussia for its part, was ready on the proposed day (25th April) to return its army to its peacetime state, as it had been prior to 28th March. Prussia accepted and the mutual demobilisation was agreed in principle. The possibility of a reconciliation returned but vanished as quickly as it had come. 25th April came with no visible signs of an Austrian demobilisation, indeed in Venetia, the [Austrian] mobilisation (from 22nd April on), took on ever increasing proportions.[15]

---

15   Tr. Note: Just as the possibility of mutual demobilisation began to gain credibility in Austria and Prussia, Italy upset the applecart. Usual Italian practice was for half of the annual levy of 80,000 men to serve for five years in the standing army, the other half to be trained for six to eight weeks and then sent home. As a result of a serious budget crisis, and with no immediate expectation of war, in December Italy decided to forego the annual January [1866] conscription for the army. To avoid leaving the land defenseless, the already trained soldiers would be retained in service for an extra year rather than be sent home, as was usual. When Prussia approached Italy in March with the prospect of a mutual military alliance as part of Prussia's preparation for impending war with Austria, conditions changed. Now anticipating the long awaited opportunity to attack Austria and regain Venetia for Italy while Austria was at war with Prussia, Italy needed to strengthen its army. On 11th March it ordered that the second category of the 1865 levy, instead of being sent home on leave or released as was usual after training, would be retained for active service. This was followed on 25th March by a decree that the normal levy, which had been deferred in January as an economy measure, would take place to its normal extent, beginning on 25th April What was most significant was that, in spite of the new, not unusual recruiting, the men conscripted earlier would not be released, thereby increasing the normal complement of the army. On 18th April the strict order was issued that there would be no leaves and no releases. Thus, after normal recruiting, the Italian army would have an entire annual class more than its normal complement, as well as the second levy from 1865. The Austrian General Staff calculated that Italy would thereby increase its army by 100,000 men. At the same time there were substantial transfers

Prussia declared that such a partial demobilisation[16] (if such had even been seriously attempted) did not provide it with the necessary guarantees, that [the demobilisation] must be uniform, meaning in Venetia *and* in Bohemia, if [Prussia] for her part, was to restore the conditions as they were before 28th March. Austria refused with the excuse that she was also threatened by Italy. With this, the second stage of the exchange of dispatches regarding mobilisation came to an end. Mobilisation continued, more energetically and more openly that ever. On 13th May, *Feldzugmeister* Benedek went to the North Army, to Olmütz. These two groups of dispatches relating to mobilisation, the first dealing with the controversial point, 'Who started in all', the other dealing with the even hotter question, 'Who is demobilising?' was now over.

But already a new group of dispatches opened a third question, the question of the reform of the German Confederation. This question, which had been controversial since the *Fürstentag von Frankfurt* (1863),[17] was now raised again in a circular letter to the Prussian representatives at all the German courts (except Austria). The insertion of this new and vexing question into an already complex situation, might appear surprising at first glance, the more so since it seriously diminished the prospects of peace. In actual fact the reverse proved true, and the situation was more clarified than complicated. Let us look more closely. In Vienna and Berlin, while still writing about peace, people believed only in war, and from 13th March onwards, when it was known in Prussia that 'Austria is arming', the talk in Berlin was not only of counter mobilisation, but also, who are our allies?

The alliance with Italy found its basis in these days, but even before Berlin formally concluded this alliance, it wanted to know what position the small and medium sized German states would take if a conflict broke out. It wanted to know who would irrevocably stand for the old, and who for the new, who would be for Austria and who for Prussia.

Thus, Prussia prepared a proposal for the reformation of the German Confederation. In its Circular Dispatch of 24th March, [Prussia] urged reform of the Confederation, essentially calling for Prussian hegemony, exclusion of Austria, and subordination of the other Confederation states. The position that the other German states would take toward this Prussian proposal, would in truth, do more to simplify the situation than to complicate it. The prospect for war

of Italian troops from the south toward the Venetian border. Austria saw Italian forces massing for a possible attack and therefore felt forced to mobilize and concentrate sufficient forces in its south to counter this threat. (Friedjung, vol. I, pp. 218 ff.)

16 Tr. Note: The Austrian Foreign Minister, *Graf* Mensdorff, informed Prussia, on 26th April, that Austria remained true to its former intention of demobilising in the north, but that it was necessary to mobilise in the south to defend against Italy. Prussia, however, could hardly be expected to distinguish whether a mobilized Austrian corps or regiment was going to head north or south or remain there. On 27th April Austria issued the first order for mobilization of the North Army. The die had been cast.

17 Tr. Note: In the summer of 1861, Julius Fröbel sent a memorandum to Anton von Schmerling, Minister of State, proposing that a German *Fürstentag* [Congress of Princes, analogous to the *Bundestag*] be called at Frankfurt under the chairmanship of the Austrian Emperor, a standing committee of monarchs to rule the hitherto disunited Germany with the aid of a chamber selected from the *Landtag*. The matter rested a long time until, in May 1863 the Hereditary Prince von Thurn und Taxis interested Emperor Franz Joseph in the plan. The emperor enthusiastically made the plan his own, seeing himself in the position proper for the Holy Roman Emperor directing the future of a new Germany. After much intrigue, to make a long story short, the assembly was summoned. However, with great difficulty, Bismarck persuaded Prussia's King William I not to attend, with the result that the whole enterprise foundered. (Friedjung, vol I, pp. 56 ff.)

(even though it was considered a certainty) could hardly be heightened. The reform proposal would crystalise matters and force the other German states to decide who's side they were on; Prussia would rather have clear cut enemies than dubious friends.

However, even though war seemed unavoidable, [Prussia] did not want to miss the opportunity to put a final and permanent end to a situation she regarded as unnatural and unendurable. The question of the duchies should not dominate the situation. The battle between Austria and Prussia, if inevitable, should be for a greater reason than Schleswig - Holstein. *Born out of the Schleswig- Holstein question, it should, at the same time, solve the German question.* The first step toward that, which as we know, preceded the motion placed before the Federal Diet, was the Circular Dispatch of 24th March. This document, sent to the German representatives at all German courts (except Austria), initially sought to present the necessity for Prussian defensive measures and then emphasized that, due to the unreliability of Austrian support, [Prussia] was forced to seek security against impending future dangers in a *closer connection with the German states* and in a *stronger organization of the German Confederation.* The vital sentences of Bismarck's circular letter read as follows:

In the [conditions of the] present moment, I have not been able to refrain from giving the preceding elucidation (regarding the undeclared and therefore threatening mobilisation of Austria) and I urgently and most sincerely request that you speak out against the regime that you believed to be honourable, so that the preparations that we too are now forced to make will be seen in the proper light.

However, measures for our present security are not all that the situation demands from us. The experience that we have gained regarding the reliability of an Austrian alliance, requires of us that we also turn our attention to the *future* and look for guarantees that can assure us of the security that we have not only vainly sought in the Confederation with the other major German powers, but indeed see threatened by these very powers. Prussia, by reason of its position, its German character and, above all, the German patriotism of its princes, initially turns in search of these guarantees within Germany itself.

However, whenever we contemplate these thoughts, we are again forced to recognize that the Confederation, in its present form, is not adequate for that purpose. It was set up with the expectation that the two major German powers would always be in accord. It has been able to survive so long as this condition was maintained by continuous Prussian flexibility toward Austria, it could not survive a serious conflict between the two powers. Indeed, we have experienced that even when the two powers were in accord, the Confederal arrangements were insufficient to allow Germany to take an effective national and political role.

We have repeatedly spoken out to our comrades in the Confederation that the Confederation's military arrangements are insufficient to provide adequate security for Germany. In the present state of things, we cannot trust in effective help from the Confederation in the event that we are attacked. In any attack, whether by Austria or by another power we would have to depend on our own forces if the especial goodwill of individual German regimes did not set in motion means to support us, which would happen far too late through the usual Federal channels to be of any help to us. We are, at present, in light of the threatening mobilisation of Austria, in a situation where we must ask our comrades in the Confederation when and to what degree can we count on this goodwill?

But even the goodwill that may, perhaps, exist toward us in some of our federal comrades, gives us no assurance for the impending dangers, because *in the existing state of the Confederation* and the *condition of Federal military relationships* the legitimate or practical possibility of manifesting it will, in many cases, be lacking. These considerations and the entirely extraordinary situation in which Prussia finds itself due to the hostile attitude of the other major power in the Confederation, forces upon us the necessity of moving for *reform of the Confederation* that will reflect existing circumstances. We reserve to ourselves the right to present further announcements in this regard soon. For now however, we have to request an answer to the question stated above, whether and to what degree can we count on support in the event that we are attacked by Austria or are forced to war by unambiguous threats.

This circular letter was followed almost immediately by a corresponding motion by Prussia in the Confederation. In the 9th April session Prussia made the following motion:

That the Federal Diet will resolve: To summon an assembly for a yet to be appointed day that will be chosen by direct vote and universal suffrage, to consider and discuss proposals of the German governments regarding a reform of the Federal system. In the meantime, however, until the assembly takes place, [that the Federal Diet will] through communication between the individual governments [move] to give form to these proposals.

The preamble was comprehensive and was based on the above circular letter of 24th March. Neither this motion nor the accompanying preamble stated what the Federal reform would comprise. It was already known that it would deal with the major points we had already presented, exclusion of Austria, supremacy of Prussia and subordination of the small and medium states. It would, 'recognize the realities of the existing situation.' Prussia was well aware that it would not win the support of the Confederation with the prospect of 'reform' that signified to any significant degree, subordination to Prussia. However, it was felt that in the given situation, things had already reached a point where what was correct politically, was also politically shrewd. Even Austria was clear beyond any doubt that this would put an end to the equality of rights in the Confederation, and that naturally, relationships would be established based on power. 'It is against the order of the world,' a Vienna daily newspaper had written on an earlier occasion, 'that great bodies should be reined in by smaller. Politics are violating the laws of nature ... all attempts to eliminate this rule of the powerful by assemblies of the people, *Paulskirchen*[18] or parliamentary majorities, must always fail.'

---

18 Tr. Note: The Constitution of the German Empire (*Verfassung des Deutschen Reiches*), adopted and proclaimed by the Frankfurt Parliament after the Revolutions of 1848, was an unsuccessful attempt to create a unified German state from the successor states of the Holy Roman Empire. The Frankfurt Constitution (*Frankfurter Reichsverfassung*), contained a charter of fundamental rights and a democratic government in the form of a constitutional monarchy, it was also known as the Constitution of St. Paul's Church *(Paulskirchenverfassung)*.

Prussia's plan for the reform of the German Confederation, everywhere heightened the antipathies that were already felt against us in the German lands (we have already indicated this), antipathies that were openly expressed. Desirous of war, or seeing it as unavoidable, the Vienna cabinet searched for Federal allies in Germany, but employed opposite means [to Prussia] to win them over. Being friendly towards them, no longer distant, even at the danger of a *pater peccavi* [Latin: Father, I have sinned, a reference to the parable of the 'Prodigal son' in the New Testament. Here the author is suggesting that Austria's rapprochement with the confederal German states, might have involved a degree of humble pie], in order to make peace with the Confederation. Its guilt, primarily, lay in the Schleswig - Holstein question, where making common cause with Prussia had distanced it from the Confederation. Now it turned back to the Confederation. The Confederation (suddenly) was again in the right, the Confederation was now to determine who Schleswig - Holstein belonged to, and an Austrian dispatch of 26th April expressed this altered viewpoint. [Austria] gave up [its alliance with] Prussia and now placed itself on the side of the Confederation. The essential points of this extremely important dispatch that was sent to *Graf* Karoly[19] [to be forwarded to the Prussian court] were as follows:

> Honourable *Graf.* The Imperial Government places extreme importance on the reciprocal declaration through which, in recent days, the imminent danger of a conflict between the German great powers is so happily overcome. Accordingly, the Emperor, our most gracious Sovereign, keenly wishes, that the return of this danger, the recognition of which must be painful for Your Majesty [William I], must be prevented forever. For that, however, it is requisite that the agreement of the cabinets from Vienna and Berlin regarding mutual disarmament be achieved along with and tied to, an agreement regarding the *fundamental elimination of the causes of the existing tension.*

The dispatch referred the 'causes of the existing tension,' in other words, to the Schleswig - Holstein question. It then stated that Austria had always viewed the transfer of the duchies, as stated in Article III of the Vienna Peace Treaty, as 'an interim measure' upon which further arrangements (meaning the installation of the Duke of Augustenburg) would be based. Austria conceded that, in the meantime, certain concessions (Kiel, Rendsburg, Sonderburg) had been granted to Prussia. After specifying these concessions, which were designated as 'the disparaged February Demands,' it concluded as follows:

> If Prussia wantonly rejects our legal and honourable proposals, we will be left with no other alternative than to place the entire matter before the German Confederation and to trust the joint deliberation of our Confederation colleagues, employing this means to achieve a resolution of the Schleswig - Holstein situation through determination by the German Confederation in default of agreement between Austria and Prussia. Also, the voice of the land of Holstein, which, doubtless, should be heard, indeed, cannot any longer remain unheard, as in any case, the Holstein Estates, as validly constituted, must be called into session in the course of this year.

---

19   Tr. Note: Austrian ambassador to Berlin.

So much for the 26th April dispatch. The Schleswig - Holstein question, as it had inspired the strife, now brought it to life. Prussia, of course, denied 'the legal and honourable proposals,' as this dispatch had presented them, and to use the words of Mensdorff's dispatch, 'the Austrian Government was left with no other alternative than to place the entire matter before the German Confederation.' This ensued during the Confederation session on 1st June. Just as the Prussian petition to the Confederation on 9th April merely expressed what had already been stated in the circular dispatch of 24th March, the Austrian petition of 1st June merely expressed the opinions and changes that had already first been stated in the Austrian dispatch of 26th April. The relevant declaration stated, essentially, 'that a recrudescence of the danger of war can only be avoided if Prussia is willing to recognize the decisions of the German Confederation and if (in the present special case) the Schleswig - Holstein question is resolved according to Confederation and international law rather than by unilateral action.'

At this point the Austrian representative added the concluding paragraph:

> That Austria's endeavours to achieve a resolution of the question of the duchies ... has proven fruitless, and therefore, the Imperial Government turns the entire matter over to the determinations of the German Confederation, which Austria will follow. The Imperial Governor in Holstein is authorized to call the Holstein Estates into session so that the wishes and legal viewpoints of [the people of Holstein] can be made valid as a legal factor in the decision.

With this, the matter was concluded and the rupture complete. The Prussian government (in a dispatch of 3rd June) declared in immediate response to these proceedings, that it considered the declaration by the Austrian representative to the Confederation to be an explicit repudiation of the Gastein Convention and thereby the original Vienna Treaty, and further declared that the unilateral calling to session of the Holstein Estates, was a violation against which the Prussian Government reserved to itself further measures. Vienna however, had already gone beyond consideration of what was legally admissible, and only asked what appeared politically achievable.

At this point, however, nothing seemed more politically desirable than to gain the backing of the Confederation and the medium sized German states against the hated rival. The Vienna press gave animated expression to this feeling. 'Finally, at last!', said the *Ostdeutsche Post*, 'What we have so long recognized and encouraged as an indispensable step in Austrian policy, has become fact. Austria has returned the matter of the duchies to the hands of the German Confederation and will call into session the Holstein people's assembly. . . At this point there is no longer a treaty in effect between Prussia and Austria. It is the German Confederation that fought at Königsberg and Oeversee.[20] It is the German Confederation that helped take the

---

20   Tr. Note: Two battles in the Schleswig-Holstein War of 1864. *Feldmarschalllieutenant* Gablenz, leading the Austrian forces, was ordered to capture the hills in front of the first major Danish defense, the Dannewerk. On 3rd February the Austrian Brigade Gondrecourt captured the villages of Jagel and Overselk, which covered the outworks of the fortification. Although their mission for the day was accomplished, the victorious troops charged onwards after the retreating Danes, storming the steep Königsberg hill that commanded the Danish fortifications. The impetus of their assault carried them to the very base of the Danish fortifications, so shaking the confidence of the Danes that they evacuated

duchies from Denmark. It is the German Confederation that jointly signed the Vienna Peace Treaty. Austria was simply its deputy, the benefits accruing therefrom that Austria gained, were gained for the Confederation.' Nearly all the Vienna papers echoed this tone. The *Presse*, in fairly measured prose, wrote, 'The peace of central Europe requires the political reorganization of Germany in an anti-Prussian sense; a reorganization that will make it impossible for Prussia to diminish the significance of the other German lands and thereby increase its own importance by annexing territory in Germany, or by agreements with other German states. It is impossible to accomplish this by peaceful means. Therefore, it seems to us that peace itself is impossible, and certainly not desirable. A successful war against Prussia would obviously result in an acceptable solution to the greater German problem. It would help expand the larger German states and achieve a much better balance of power between them than presently exists. If, for example, Saxony and Hannover were doubled in size, much would be gained.' Other newspapers far surpassed this moderate language, and presuming victory of the new alliance, pompously proclaimed, 'Not Olmütz, but Jena. Prussia must be rendered harmless. The *intermezzo* of Frederick the Great must come to an end.' That was the mood in Vienna, the words were provocative enough, but the deed was still lacking. This (the convocation of the Holstein Estates) was imminent, and everything depended on whether it would be convoked or not. That would not be in doubt for long, on 5th June, the following patent (convocation order) appeared in the *Kieler Zeitung*:

> By order of His Majesty the Emperor, my Supreme Lord, I, the Imperial Royal Governor of the Duchy of Holstein, hereby announce that I call the Estates for the Duchy of Holstein to assemble on 11th June. The delegates, or their lawful deputies, are to assemble on the specified day in the city of Itzehoe and attend to the business that will be presented for their consideration by the commissioner that I shall name. The assembly is to conduct its business so that these matters will be concluded within three months.

> Gablenz, Feldmarschalllieutenant.
> Imperial Governor of the Duchy of Holstein.
> Kiel, 5th June 1866.

To 14th June (The Federal Diet's resolution against Prussia)

The elections would wait. The patent of 5th June had thrown down the gauntlet and Prussia picked it up, instituting the 'further steps' that it had referred to in its 3rd June dispatch. [Prussian troops] crossed the Eider, entering Holstein (on 7th June). Every possibility was anticipated, but for the present moment, the main question was whether *Feldmarschalllieutenant* von Gablenz was resolved to permit, or to prevent, [Prussian] entry into Holstein. The Governor made his decision, perhaps for political reasons, but more likely from purely military considerations (the

the position. During the subsequent Danish retreat from the Dannewerk, the village of Oeversee was the site of a battle between Austrian and Danish forces on February 6th 1864. These two battles were viewed as triumphs for the massed bayonet assault tactics of the Austrian troops.

Prussian force was twice the size of his own and [Prussian] gunboats were on the Elbe River). All the odds were against him, as the Prussians advanced into Holstein, the Austrians withdrew to the south and at noon on the 7th, the Governor himself left Kiel. At this point there was still a desire to express the comradely sentiments that had characterized the preceding months. All of the Prussian officers and men paraded at Kiel railway station and the band of the Prussian Marines played the Austrian National Hymn, but the Hereditary Prince of Augustenburg, to give him that title,[21] had already fled Kiel that very morning. Governor von Gablenz departed Kiel under protest stating that, 'subject to further decisions by [the Austrian] cabinet,' he felt compelled, for the time being, to remove the seat of government to Altona. Thereupon he departed, followed by the Austrian Brigade (Kalik), which had for so long been the occupying force in Holstein. Now the Governor waited to see whether Prussia would prevent the assembly of the Estates, it did, Prussian troops entered Itzehoe on Sunday the 10th, along with *Freiherr* von Manteuffel. The Prussians made themselves master of the situation without opposition. During the night of 11/12th the Austrians evacuated Altona and crossed the Elbe to Harburg. The [Austrian] brigade then proceeding to the Bohemian theater of war via Hannover and Kassel. We shall meet them again there, in courageous but unsuccessful combat.

Throughout Germany, the impression made by these events made was overwhelming. To the very last, perhaps even in Vienna, people had resisted believing in the seriousness of Prussia's intentions. The sudden display of energy had a somewhat paralysing effect, the more so since it was unexpected after the earlier events at Olmütz. One could almost say that the weaknesses of 1850 bore golden fruit for us in 1866.

Motion upon motion was now proposed at the German Federal Diet. The Austrian representative called for an extraordinary session on the 11th [June], and declared, with respect to Prussia's advance into Holstein, 'that this is a breach of the Vienna Treaty and of the Gastein Convention, regarding which Austria is prepared to await the decision of the Confederation … The Emperor will remain true to the laws of the Confederation, which forbid members of the German Confederation from engaging in armed conflict with each other. Prussia has undertaken to act unilaterally, which must be stopped at all costs. The Confederation Parliament is therefore requested and obligated to take action through Article 19 of the Vienna Final Act.[22] Austria

---

21 Author's Note: Seldom had a pretender more ignominiously departed the stage with less applause. It was not granted to him, hardly even among those who had stood by him, to awaken a lively interest, let alone that poetical charm which, even if nothing else remains, is usually the ineluctable heritage of a pretender. No deeply felt sympathy followed him, and it was not due to caprice, not by chance, not due to disloyalty, nor the result of 'Prussian conspiracy'. It was only the natural result of cause and effect. *Graf* Bismarck described him as 'ignorant of statesmanship,' and 'a diplomat in turn-down boots,' who thought he could outwit [Bismarck], striving for the highest demands while employing the slightest of means, never [showing] personal devotion, never exhibiting that passion that arises from belief in oneself. And thus, he concluded the course of his life, silent and cautious. Among all the traits of personality that a pretender can best dispense with, caution is perhaps highest on the list.

22 Tr. Note: This *Artikel 19 der wiener Schlussakte* refers to the Final Act of the Viennese Ministerial Conference of 1820, not to the Final Act of the Congress of Vienna of 1815. In the 1820 Viennese Ministerial Conference, at which all the governments of the German Confederation were represented, the principles of the original Act of Confederation that was part of the 1815 Final Act of the Conference of Vienna were to be more clearly and exactly defined so that they could be better put into practice, thus producing the second fundamental set of laws of the Confederation. Unfortunately for future students of history, this was also called the Vienna Final Act. Article 19 of the 1820 Final Act reads: 'When acts

therefore moves for: The *rapid mobilisation of the entire Confederation Army within fourteen days*, with the exception of the corps belonging to the Prussian army.'

Three days later, on the 14th, the Federal Parliament resolved to vote on the Austrian motion. In the meantime, (on the12th) the Austrian ambassador in Berlin, *Graf* Karolyi, requested his passport and departed. On that same day (the 12th) Prussia released a circular letter in which it stated its position regarding the Austrian motion of the previous day. 'The motion is devoid of any basis in Confederation law', it stated. 'In voting on this, *the members dissolve the Confederation* and initiate the unfederated condition with an act of hostility against Prussia. In the war that is starting, Prussia will only look to its own interests and those of the states allied to it.'

Thus, the 14th of June arrived, and with it the vote. Austria's motion of the 11th (mobilisation of the Confederation army against Prussia) was approved by nine votes to six. Voting with Austria were Bavaria, Saxony, Würtemberg, Hannover, Grand Duchy of Hesse, Kurhessen, Nassau and the sixteenth *Kurie* [curia] (Liechtenstein, Reuss *et.al.*).[23]

Voting against Austria were Saxon - Weimar and the Thüringian [duchies] (except Meiningen), Oldenburg - Anhalt - Schwarzburg, Mecklenburg, the free cities (except Frankfurt), Luxemburg and Baden. Prussia did not, actually vote, since it had, at the very start of the session, declared the entire proceeding to be in violation of Confederation law.

Immediately after the vote, which signified war between Austria and the medium German states against Prussia, the Prussian representative to the Confederation Parliament (*Herr* von Savigny) rose to deliver a final declaration, stating that the old Confederation was dead. Prussia demands the formation of a new one.

The concluding sentences of this declaration read:

> As a result of the Austrian motion and the vote declaring war against a member of the Confederation, the Prussian government considers the destruction of the Confederation to be accomplished. In the name of and by the supreme order of His Majesty the King, his Most Gracious Lord, the ambassador hereby declares that Prussia considers the previous Confederation Treaty to have been broken and therefore no longer considers it binding, considering it dissolved and will act accordingly. Nevertheless, His Majesty the King does not view the national foundation upon which the Confederation was built to be destroyed with the dissolution of the previous Confederation. Far more,

of violence between members of the Confederation are feared or have actually occurred, the Federal Assembly is to be summoned to take provisional measures to obviate the necessity for self-defense and to put an end to measures that have already been taken. To this end, above all, it shall take care to uphold vested rights.' Sybel (vol. 1, p.66) and Huber, *Dokumente zur Deutschen Verfassungsgeschichte. Band 1: Deutsche Verfassungsdokumente 1803 – 1850.*

23 Tr. Note: According to Friedjung (vol. 1, pp 341-2), the actual motion that was voted on 14th June was not the Austrian motion, which was technically in violation of the Confederation law in being directed against Prussia, but that of Bavaria, which was legal and called for putting the four Confederation corps of the medium states on a war footing, without being specifically directed against Prussia. Voting for this motion were: Austria, Bavaria, Hannover, Württemberg, Saxony, Kurhessen, Hessen - Darmstadt, Nassau, Meiningen, Frankfurt. Against the motion: Prussia, Luxemburg, both Mecklenburgs, Weimar, Koburg, Altenburg, Braunschweig, Oldenburg, Schwarzburg, Anhalt, Hamburg, Lübeck, Bremen. The mood of the 6th *Kurie* (Liechtenstein, both Reuss, Lippe, Waldeck and Schaumburg) was not clear. Baden abstained from voting.

Prussia holds firm to this basis and to the unity of the German nation and sees it as an imperative duty of the German states to find a suitable expression for that. The royal government, for its part, hereby proposes the basic principles for a new unification more in tune with the conditions of the times (this proposal follows) and declares itself ready to form a new Confederation on a foundation transformed by such reforms with those German governments that will join hands with it. The ambassador [thus] carries out the orders of his Supreme Ruler in declaring herewith that his former activity is ended.

Immediately following these events (of 14th June) Prussia notified all the European powers, 'that the former Confederation according to international law of the German states no longer exists.'

Who is at fault?

So now it was war! Who was to blame? It seems almost improper to raise this question, when at least in our opinion, the blessings of the outcome mitigate the guilt of its beginning (no matter which side may have been at fault). Yet we do consider the question, because we are firmly of the opinion that Prussia has no need to avoid it. *Prussia did not desire this war.* Her enemy (granted, with some provocation) pushed for it and with it, [Prussia's] victory. Prussia was within its rights regarding Austria and the Confederation. Clearly and above board in regard to Austria, for the most part, in regard to the Confederation. Politics and national needs justified Prussia, but it must be recognized that technically, at the start of the conflict, law was on the side of the Confederation.

It will be rewarding to examine the difference in Prussia's position in respect of Austria, and of the Confederation. From the start, Prussia was fully justified in her actions towards Austria but only partially justified in her actions towards the confederation. That partial justification became entire following the resolution of the 14th June, putting the Confederation entirely in the wrong and Prussia entirely in the right in respect of both its opponents.

First a word about Prussia's position regarding the Confederation. For this we must briefly return to November 1863 and the death of Friedrich VII of Denmark.

Prussia's actions immediately following the death of the above prince, were technically contrary to the law of the Confederation. The Confederation had never recognized the London Protocol [Treaty of London, 8th May 1852] (that dealt with the claims of the house of Augustenburg). As seen by the Confederation, the hereditary Prince of Augustenburg was the legitimate heir to the thrones of Schleswig - Holstein and it was the Confederation's duty to establish him in his hereditary position. At this point Friedrich VII of Denmark died. The Confederation considered that from the day of his death (15th November 1863), the hereditary prince was his legal successor, and it was only necessary to make the Duke *de jure*, into the Duke *de facto*. The necessary steps to achieve this end were instituted and Prussia, if it recognized the formal laws of the Confederation as higher than its national mission, had the duty, as the agent of the Confederation, to occupy Holstein, and as the agent of the Confederation, to conquer Schleswig, and still as the agent of the Confederation, to hand over the conquered Schleswig - Holstein to the legitimate hereditary Prince von Augustenburg. Prussia took another path, and at this point we add, fortunately. Nevertheless, [Prussia's] actions, however we may rejoice in them, technically violated the law of the Confederation.

The Confederation skillfully maintained its formal rights, with consequences. It did not let itself be blinded by the brilliance of the victory that had been attained, nor was it diverted from its legal position. 'We were not able to conquer Schleswig - Holstein because we were prevented from doing so. We thank the victor for nothing. Prussia did for its own purposes, what it had to do for the Confederation. [Prussia] has gone above and beyond our resolution. It has ignored the Confederation. The only thing that we can do is to forget the insult, but we must not forget our laws. Our law is to watch over the rights of a German prince and to secure his inheritance. There is only one way that the breach can be healed, if Prussia gives up its demands as a victor, retrospectively submits to our resolution, and gives to the Duke what is rightfully his.'

Technically, from the standpoint of law, this statement was correct. It is also correct, so long as the stipulations of the Vienna Peace Treaty, the Confederation and its protégé, the hereditary Prince von Augustenburg, are disregarded. The Confederation reasoned that, 'The King of Denmark has turned Schleswig - Holstein over to the victors, but he cannot do that. It is not possible to surrender something that one does not possess. The new King of Denmark was never the Duke of Schleswig - Holstein. With the death of Friedrich VII, the ancient Danish realm split into two parts. The inheritor of the one part had no control over the other, and any control that he attempted over the other part, was null and void.'

Prussia, as is known, disagreed with the Confederation on the basis of the Vienna peace treaty, and defended the rights that [the treaty] promised to it. However, these were rights that had only come to it [through the treaty] and that it had, from the very beginning, unjustly maintained against the Confederation. This injustice to anyone who is not blinded and inhibited by their own selfish interests, has long been recognized a political necessity and a national duty, a blessing and a salvation, but however politically justified, it was from the very start, a technical violation of the law, and if the Confederation had possessed the strength to punish this violation, to overcome Prussia in war by way of the Execution,[24] then we would, though with reservations and excuses, have to answer the question that is the point of this chapter 'Who is to blame?' by stating, Prussia is to blame. However, it is recognized that the war which broke out against us, was not conducted as a Confederation war against Prussia, but that Austria, the ally of Prussia, its co-victor and co-ruler [of the captured duchies], initiated this war in which it was then joined by certain of the medium and smaller [German] states, not to punish Prussia for violating the [laws of the] German Confederation, but to punish Prussia for challenging Austria. But Prussia was entirely within its rights in its dispute with Austria, as we intend to demonstrate.

Prussia's relationship with Austria was completely different from its relationship with the Confederation. If we confirm that Prussia was technically in the wrong in its action toward the Confederation, then Austria was equally guilty. All steps taken by Prussia that followed upon the death of Friedrich VII were taken jointly with Austria. Jointly they ignored the Confederation, jointly they vanquished the enemy, jointly they made peace and jointly they took possession of the conquered land, after they had already agreed at the start of their alliance (January 1864), to *exclude the Confederation* from their subsequent deliberations. If there was an injustice in this (and we have indicated the extent of that injustice above), then that injustice was equally shared. Austria and Prussia were equally guilty, but they were guilty with respect to a third party, not

24   Tr. Note: when the German Confederation wished to engage in military action it voted on what was termed 'an Execution' against the malefactor.

toward each other. This third party might legitimately indite them, saying 'You are guilty', but a mutual accusation of guilt was inadmissible.

Their attitude toward the Confederation, in which both were equally blameworthy, did not however result in war. The war arose from the fact that the victors could not agree over the fruits of their conquest of 1864. The conflict developed from the articles that Austria and Prussia had agreed to as *Condomini*, as joint possessors of Schleswig - Holstein. What was in the past remained in the past. To find the party responsible for the outbreak of war between the two *Condomini* we must simply determine who, on the basis of the Vienna Treaty, exceeded his authority and injured the joint possessor. Who was it then, that did this?

The facts that we recounted in the first chapter of this section, provide the answer to this question. Let us recapitulate and take another look at the situation as it then was. Austria and Prussia had taken joint possession of Schleswig - Holstein. There were only two possibilities, either both parties agreed to turn [the duchies] over to a third party or [Austria and Prussia] ruled them jointly, with certain guarantees as to their respective rights. Both solutions were attempted. Initially, despite doubts raised over the much discussed rights of inheritance, there was easy agreement regarding the 'third party'. However, it was impossible to reach agreement about what this third party would have to agree *to*, in order to recompense Prussia for all that it had done, and especially, for all that was *yet* to be done. The February Demands were not accepted but Prussia did not make this the justification for war. It accepted the rejection and then, after one alternative had failed, proceeded with a second. That meant establishing joint government without impairing the respective interests [of Austria and Prussia]. That was the mission.

One can search in vain from autumn 1864 to the spring of 1866, for actions or ordinances through which Prussia damaged the interests of its co - ruler. It is true that Prussia was constantly active, that it built and surveyed, that its troops came and went, that it organized and administered, and through this activity, might well have given the impression that it was taking permanent possession. But in all that it did, it was well within its rights and never infringed the right of Austria (which remained quietly in the background) to change its own garrisons, to build barracks, and moor warships in the harbour of Kiel. Austria's rights were never in doubt, and no matter how much Prussia might wish that sooner or later, Austria might be willing to drop its claims in exchange for a sum of money (as it had already done with Lauenburg), and turn over its half to Prussia, Prussia had no intention of gaining Schleswig - Holstein by means of a great war, thereby (for who could guarantee the outcome), placing its own existence at stake. Prussia made itself at home, but never, by word or deed, attempted to secure the other half of the house.

Not so Austria. Knowing full well that postponement of the question could only work to the advantage of its co-ruling rival, and that in the long run, Schleswig - Holstein would fall into Prussia's lap like ripe fruit, Austria unilaterally, without securing Prussia's agreement, went back to the plan of solving the Schleswig - Holstein question by promoting the interests of the 'third party'.

We say unilaterally, and therein lay the provocation. Prussia itself, as we have seen, did at one point want to negotiate with this third party, but the negotiations had failed. That was in the past and only by joint agreement could it be resurrected. Austria however, proceeded unilaterally, and aligned itself with the policy of the Confederation, decisively taking the side of the Hereditary Prince. With diminishing restraint, it canvassed in favour of [Augustenburg]

Leaving Schleswig.

and thereby prejudiced the interests of its joint ruler. It could not agitate for Augustenburg to rule only its own half, any agitation in favour of Augustenburg affected the whole, and stirred up the Prussian half along with its own.

The refusal to accede to [Prussia's] demands, supporting a third party and allying itself with this third party against its ally, must inevitably lead to a breach. The refusal to ban the Altona assembly on 23rd January, the unilateral convocation of the Holstein Estates, the corresponding petition to the Confederation, constituted neither more nor less than the end of the alliance with Prussia, the departure from the stipulations of the Vienna Peace Treaty, turning the matter over to the decisions of the Confederation, which hitherto been disputed *jointly* by Austria and Prussia, all of this meant, as we have already indicated elsewhere, that this breach was decided upon in Vienna. The complete change in its legal position was an insult. Austria was allied with Prussia and had no right to make this change. However, it did so, leaving Prussia no choice if

Halbhuber's, 'second Olmütz,' was not finally to become reality. Technically, the Confederation had every right, for its own part, to call for the convocation of the Holstein Estates, to bring the resolution of the question of the hereditary succession before its forum, and the right to push for the installation of the 'Duke'. The Confederation had this right. *Austria did not.* The Austrian provocations, as we have listed them above (calling the Holstein Estates *et alia*), were what forced the start of the war. Without these provocations, Prussia would not have been drawn into war, and trusting in its natural chances, for which the existing situation was undoubtedly favourable, would have bided its time. As proof of this we cite the words of the King, spoken again and again both before and after the conflict, 'I did not want this war.'[25]

And thus, we should finally take an unbiased look at the events themselves. The Confederation vote on 14th June did not start the war. It only gave closure to an existing situation. It simply showed who was for us and who was against. It decided the alliances of the medium and small states and it stripped the Confederation of its formal rights against us when it too, finally fell into error. The decision to go to war was taken when *Feldmarschalllieutenant* von Gablenz published the order calling the Holstein Estates into session. That was the gauntlet, Austria threw it down, Prussia only picked it up. For us, the question Who is to blame? has been answered.

Austria and Prussia Prepare for War

Even as the notes and dispatches we have quoted above fanned the flames, or at times dampened them, the mobilisation on both sides proceeded, seemingly unaffected by the tone of the negotiations. We will first turn our attention to the arming of our opponent.

In mid-March, perhaps even earlier, Vienna began to make military preparations for war. Initially it was kept secret. Troops were relocated as Italian and Hungarian regiments, provisionally still on a peacetime footing, were shifted to Bohemia, others to Italy. Vienna, as the centre of communications, was significantly reinforced, all other troops were ordered to the railways. The uniform manufacturers worked day and night and accomplished so much, as perhaps to make this army the best dressed ever. The number of battalions in the *Grenz Regimenter*[26] were doubled. The fourth battalions [of all regiments] (which in peacetime only served as depot cadres) were brought up to strength and the activation of a fifth battalion was

---

25   Author's Note: As Prince Friedrich Karl departed for the army and took leave of the King, the latter said, with deep emotion, 'I am an old man, nearly 70 years old. Why should I now think of war? I want nothing more than to leave my people in peace when I die. I also know that I must answer to God and to my conscience. I can bear witness before God that I have done all that I can. I have implored the Emperor, *implored*, as intensely as one can. Also, I do not want one square foot of land. I will concede anything that is consistent with the honour of Prussia. I have offered much, but they want war. They want to have things again the way they were before the Seven Years War, and that cannot be, for then Prussia would no longer be Prussia!' An eyewitness to this meeting noted down these words.

26   Tr. Note: Archduke Ferdinand I, younger brother of Emperor Charles V of Spain, and after Charles V, Holy Roman Emperor, solved the problem of defense of his southeastern frontiers through a system of fortifications and military colonies. Small groups of mercenaries garrisoned a crude but effective chain of fortifications along the Hungarian border. He settled Christian Balkan refugees in a network of fortified villages, watchtowers and blockhouses protecting the Croatian uplands. In return for military service he granted these colonists substantial privileges. These colonies, in time, became a significant military force. The *Militärgrenze* thus became a permanent part of the Habsburg military system. In 1851 the Transylvanian *Grenz* regiments were dissolved as unreliable, leaving the regiments of Croatia,

ordered for every infantry regiment. *All of these measures were already instituted in March* and were of a semi warlike nature. If it came to war (so Vienna reasoned), she would not enter it entirely unprepared, the machine would at least be ready, so that if necessary, it could be quickly set in motion. If on the other hand, the enemy was not entirely serious, perhaps the mere *demonstration* of [Austrian] mobilisation, might induce Prussia to give in. Accordingly, preparations were made [for war] such that if they raised enemy fears, they would be sufficient to shake him, and at the same time were sufficiently covert, so that if circumstances required, their existence could be denied.

These half measures continued right through April, only on 4th May, when Prussia ordered the mobilisation of five army corps (the other four army corps being brought up to wartime strength), did Austria openly arm with all its strength. The time of mere display, 'to cause fear and trembling,' was past, there was no longer any point in secrecy and games of concealment. The enemy (Austria), by openly arming, rendered any further deception superfluous.

Austria prepares!

Austria now mobilised at full speed. The mood in the land assisted the process and helped overcome existing difficulties. The press and the clergy succeeded in enthusing the masses and the war was made popular. Not only was it, if one listened to the Austrian sources, a war of right against wrong, in more than one place (we will come back to this), it was successfully given the mantle of a holy crusade. The Vienna press surpassed itself. Long kept in bondage, it was suddenly able to rejoice in freedom. Granted the freedom it was permitted was nothing other than to be able to say anything and everything unpleasant about the 'allies' and their governments, the Prussian people and their army, but that too, was still a freedom. And they made full use of it. The phrases, 'second Olmütz' and 'second Jena' (we already met these), were constantly repeated and hundreds of times we were invited 'to Canossa'[27] Indeed, they went further, 'The yoke of humiliation is not enough. It is not enough to drive these Prussians through the Caudinian Pass[28]. The troublemaker that has disturbed the peace in Germany for a century and a half must be rendered harmless. Prussia must be broken up into fragments. The epoch of Frederick the Great must come to an end.' Such was daily fare. The Silesian War, the great uprising in 1813, the victorious battles of Düppel and Alsen[29] that the Austrians had recently witnessed, all these were forgotten. Instead, in fevered fantasies they envisioned 30,000 horsemen under *Baron* Edelsheim[30] swarming over Silesia anew, as in the time of the Tartars

---

Slavonia and the Banat of Temesvár. These remaining *Grenzer* regiments were mobilized for the Austro Prussian war in February 1866. (Rothenberg, 'The Army of Francis Josef', pp. 2, 43 , 61 and 67.)

27   Tr. Note: The Holy Roman Emperor Henry IV was forced to walk to Canossa Castle, in Emilia Romagna, in 1077 to obtain revocation of the excommunication imposed on him by Pope Gregory VII. He was forced to humiliate himself, kneeling for three days and three nights in a raging blizzard before the castle gate.

28   Tr. Note: Referring to the final humiliation of the defeated Roman Army by the Samnites in the Second Samnite War, (321 – 327 BC).

29   Tr. Note: Two crucial Prussian victories in the Schleswig - Holstein War.

30   Tr. Note: *Baron* Edelsheim, commander of the Austrian 1st light cavalry Division in 1866, was already famous for his brilliant and dashing cavalry exploits at the Battle of Solferino, in the war of 1859 in Italy.

and Mongols, where they imagined the decisive battle would take place, naming it beforehand as the 'Grave of the Prussians.' Derisory songs about Prussia and its army were the order of the day. The following appeared in the Vienna '*Presse*,' the most widely read newspaper in the capitol.

> Commendable editorial! Since *Graf* Bismarck thinks of meeting us in the field as a *Landwehrmajor*, and I wish to make the *Graf* something other than a guest of our Emperor, I promise one hundred *gulden* to whatever warrior captures the said *Graf* Bismarck, whether alone or with the help of others, whether with whole or riddled hide, dead or alive.
>
> Dr. Joseph Hundegger, Advocate in Murau.

Such was the attitude of the press. The attitude of the clergy was, perhaps, of even greater effect. More than one pulpit preached against, 'the Turks', and the horrors of a religious war (through Gods merciful grace, finally rejected by us), were at least, ominously invoked. The high prelates led the pack. The Bishop of Brixen opened his pastoral letter with, 'Otherwise may my office be that of a messenger of peace, but today I preach war to you.'

An ecclesiastical manifesto of the *Cardinal – Fürstbischof* Rauscher stated:

> The second German state places itself under the leadership of a man whom Mazzini[31] and his associates chose as a role model [Bismarck]. He cannot claim that Prussia has any more claim to Schleswig - Holstein than has Austria. However, Prussia needs the duchies and therefore has a right to possess them, and the man who is throwing the fatherland into a frivolous civil war has learned more from Young Italy, than the mockery of the law by fresh deeds of violence. The base intrigues, the malicious artifices, the shameless lies whereby he has sought for months to delude foreign countries, to incite Prussia's people and to exhaust Austria's patience *have nothing German about them*.

Such language was not employed in vain and the people listened willingly. Never was a war more popular, from every part of the land, with the sole exception of Italy, people joyfully flocked to the flag. The strict Catholics came from confessional antagonism, the German Austrians as rivals, the Hungarians and Slavs from racial hatred. The great majority, among the people as in the army, promised themselves an easy victory.

'With peculiar logic,' a south German officer later wrote, 'the Viennese concluded from the unfortunate battles of Magenta and Solferino, that the French Army might be the first army in the world, but that the Austrian army was immediately behind them as the second army in the world. . . . Nobody had even a suspicion that in the event, the forces would prove their relative values to be like an Austrian paper *gulden* to a Prussian [silver] *Thaler*.'

The mobilisation was completed by the beginning of May, men on leave were recalled and the battalions brought up to full strength. Already, on the 11th of May (six days earlier than Prussia), the concentration of the brigades closest to the front could begin. On 20th May the mass transport of the most distant corps to Moravia commenced.

---

31 Tr. Note: Giuseppe Mazzini (1805-72), founded the secret revolutionary society Young Italy (1832). He was a Genoese propagandist and revolutionary and a champion of the movement for Italian unification known as the Risorgimento.

Austria arms.

This was the situation on 10th June:

1st Army Corps (Clam-Gallas), headquarters Prague.
2nd Army Corps (*Graf* Thun), headquarters Zwittau, Moravia.
3rd Army Corps (Archduke Ernst), headquarters Brünn, Moravia.
4th Army Corps (*Graf* Festetics), headquarters Littau, Moravia.
6th Army Corps (Ramming), headquarters Prerau, Moravia.
8th Army Corps (Archduke Leopold), headquarters Auspitz, Moravia.
10th Army Corps (*Graf* Huhn, later Gablenz), headquarters Hlansko, Moravia.

Thus, six army corps, as the sketch shows, were arrayed along the railway lines that traverse Moravia.

Initial Austrian deployment.

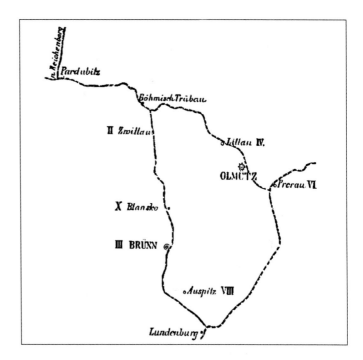

It was a good central position from which, if necessary, operations could easily be conducted in front or on the flanks. The organization of the individual corps[32] (and this seems to us to be the best place to give it) was as follows:

1st Army Corps (Clam-Gallas)

Brigade Poschacher.
    18th Jäger Battalion (Bohemia)
    Infantry Regiment King of Prussia Nr. 34 (Hungary)
    Infantry Regiment Martini Nr. 30 (Galicia).
Brigade Leiningen.
    32nd Jäger Battalion (Bohemia).
    Infantry Regiment *Graf* Chulai Nr. 33 (Hungary)
    Infantry Regiment *Graf* Haugwitz Nr. 38 (Italy).
Brigade Piret.
    29th Jäger Battalion (Hungary).
    Infantry Regiment *Grossfürst* Constantin Nr. 18 (Bohemia).
    Infantry Regiment Archduke Sigismund Nr. 45 (Italian).

---

32 Author's Note: Here we give exclusively the composition of the infantry brigades, four of which always form an army corps. (Only the 1st Army Corps had five brigades, after the arrival of Brigade Kalik from Holstein). Each individual brigade had one 4pdr battery attached (Austrian batteries had 8 guns), and attached to each individual corps, was always a regiment of Hussars or Uhlans [or Dragoons] and a corps artillery reserve, usually consisting of six batteries.

Brigade Ringelsheim.
>26th Jäger Battalion (Carinthia).
>Infantry Regiment King of Hannover Nr. 42 (Bohemia).
>Infantry Regiment Würtemberg Nr. 73 (Bohemia).

Brigade Abele (Formerly Kalik, arrived from Holstein 16th June)
>22nd Jäger Battalion
>Infantry Regiment Graf Khevenhüller-Metsch Nr. 35 (Bohemia).
>Infantry Regiment Ramming Nr. 72 (Hungary).

2nd Army Corps (*Graf* Thun)

Brigade Thom.
>2nd Jäger Battalion (Bohemia).
>Infantry Regiment Rossbach Nr. 40 (Galicia).
>Infantry Regiment Jellacic Nr. 69 (Hungary).

Brigade Henriquez.
>9th Jäger Battalion (Styria).
>Infantry Regiment Hessen Nr. 14 (Upper Austria).
>Infantry Regiment King of the Belgians Nr. 27 (Styria).

Brigade Saffran.
>11th Jäger Battalion (Styria).
>Infantry Regiment Sachsen - Weimar Nr. 64 (Hungary).
>Infantry Regiment Holstein Nr. 80 (Italy).

Brigade Würtemberg.
>20th Jäger Battalion (Styria).
>Infantry Regiment Hartung Nr. 47 (Styria).
>Infantry Regiment Mecklenburg Nr. 57 (Galicia).

3rd Army Corps (Archduke Ernst)

Brigade Appiano.
>4th Jäger Battalion (Moravia).
>Infantry Regiment Sachsen - Meiningen Nr. 46 (Hungary).
>Infantry Regiment Archduke Heinrich Nr. 62 (Siebenbürgen [Transylvania]).

Brigade Benedek.
>1st Jäger Battalion (Bohemia).
>Infantry Regiment Archduke Franz Karl Nr. 52 (Hungary).
>Infantry Regiment Sokcsevics Nr. 78 (Croatia/Slavonia).

Brigade Kirschberg.
>3rd Jäger Battalion (Upper Austria).
>Infantry Regiment Archduke Albrecht Nr. 44 (Hungary).
>Infantry Regiment *Baron* Hess Nr. 49 (Lower Austria).

Brigade Prohaska.

    Combined Jäger Battalion Nr. 33.

    Combined Jäger Battalion Nr. 34.

    Grenzer Regiment Nr. 13 (Romanian Banat).

    4th Battalion from Regiment Gondrecourt Nr. 55 (Galicia).

    4th Battalion from Regiment Gorizutti Nr. 56 (Galicia).

4th Army Corps (*Graf* Festetics)

Brigade Brandenstein.

    27th Jäger Battalion (Styria)

    Infantry Regiment Archduke Wilhelm Nr. 12 (Hungary).

    Infantry Regiment *Grossfürst* Michael Nr. 26 (Italy).

Brigade Fleischhacker.

    13th Jäger Battalion (Bohemia).

    Infantry Regiment *Graf* Coronini Nr. 6 (Hungary).

    Infantry Regiment *Grossfürst* Thronfolger Nr. 61 (Hungary).

Brigade Poeckh.

    8th Jäger Battalion (Carinthia).

    Infantry Regiment Archduke Joseph Nr. 37 (Hungary).

    Infantry Regiment Archduke Karl Ferdinand Nr. 51 (Siebenbürgen [Transylvania]).

Brigade Archduke Joseph.

    30th Jäger Battalion (Galicia).

    Infantry Regiment *Ritter* von Schmerling Nr. 67 (Hungary).

    Infantry Regiment *Freiherr* von Steininger Nr. 68 (Hungary).

6th Army Corps (Ramming)

Brigade Waldstätten.

    6th Jäger Battalion (Bohemia).

    Infantry Regiment *Graf* Hartmann Nr. 9 (Galicia).

    Infantry Regiment *Ritter* von Frank Nr. 79 (Italy).

Brigade Hertwek.

    25th Jäger Battalion (Moravia).

    Infantry Regiment *Baron* Kellner Nr. 41 (Bukowina).

    Infantry Regiment Gorizutti Nr. 56 (Galicia).

Brigade Jonak.

    14th Jäger Battalion (Bohemia).

    Infantry Regiment Prince of Prussia Nr. 20 (Hungary).

    Infantry Regiment Wasa Nr. 60 (Hungary).

Brigade Rosenzweig.

    17th Jäger Battalion (Moravia).

    Infantry Regiment *Deutschmeister* Nr. 4 (Vienna).

    Infantry Regiment Gondrecourt Nr. 55 (Galicia).

8th Army Corps (Archduke Leopold)

Brigade Fragnern.
    5th Jäger Battalion (Moravia).
    Infantry Regiment Nassau Nr. 15 (Galicia).
    Infantry Regiment Karl Salvator Nr. 77 (Hungary)
Brigade Kreyssern.
    24th Jäger Battalion (Galicia).
    Infantry Regiment *Baron* Reischach Nr. 21 (Bohemia).
    Infantry Regiment Este Nr. 32 (Hungary).
Brigade Schulz.
    31st Jäger Battalion (Slovakia).
    Infantry Regiment *Baron* Gerstner Nr. 8 (Moravia).
    Infantry Regiment Nobili Nr. 74 (Bohemia).
Brigade Rothkirch.
    Infantry Regiment *Baron* Mamula Nr. 25 (Hungary).
    Infantry Regiment Toscana Nr. 71 (Hungary).

10th Army Corps (*Graf* Huhn, later Gablenz)

Brigade Mondl [Mondel].
    12th Jäger Battalion (Galicia).
    Infantry Regiment Mazzuchelli Nr. 10 (Galicia).
    Infantry Regiment Parma Nr. 24 (Galicia).
Brigade Grivicics.
    16th Jäger Battalion (Moravia).
    Infantry Regiment *Kaiser* Alexander Nr. 2 (Hungary).
    Infantry Regiment Airoldi Nr. 23 (Banat).
Brigade Knebel.
    28th Jäger Battalion (Siebenbürgen [Transylvania]).
    Infantry Regiment *Kaiser* Franz Joseph Nr. 1 (Silesia).
    Infantry Regiment Archduke Karl Nr. 3 (Moravia).
Brigade Wimpffen.
    Infantry Regiment *Freiherr* von Bamberg Nr. 13 (Italy).
    Infantry Regiment Archduke Stephan Nr. 58 (Galicia).

In addition to seven army corps, there were also five cavalry divisions (also deployed to Moravia) [two light cavalry divisions comprising Hussars and Dragoons, and three reserve cavalry divisions comprising Uhlans and cuirassiers] and the great army artillery reserve. Later Brigade Kalik would arrive from Holstein. All in all, this amounted to 58 Infantry Regiments [57?],[33] 28 Jäger Battalions, 158 [cavalry] squadrons, 744 guns and 6 rocket batteries. The Saxon

---

33 Author's Note: If we group these 58 infantry regiments according to nationality, which is not unimportant, then we find that Upper and Lower Austria, Vienna, Silesia, Siebenbürgen, Banat, Croatia, Bukowina and the Szekler Land each provided one regiment, Moravia and Styria each two.

Army Corps that joined with the Imperial Army in the latter part of June is not included in these numbers. The totality of the seven Austrian corps (including artillery and cavalry, about 240,000 men strong) was named the 'North Army'. It was commanded by *Feldzeugmeister* von Benedek with *Feldmarschalllieutenant Baron* Henickstein as chief of staff. Before we examine the Prussian mobilisation, a word regarding the *Feldzeugmeister*, who was called to lead the army in a rare display of solidarity between army and people.

Ludwig von Benedek, the son of a protestant physician, was born in 1804 at Oedenburg in Hungary. From his youth he was inclined toward a military career. He started in the *Militair Bildungsanstalt* [Military Training Facility] at Neustadt, then at age 18 (1822) he entered the army as a cadet. In 1829 he became an *Unterlieutenant*. He was promoted to the next grade in 1831 and was transferred to the general staff in Italy. In 1835 he was promoted to *Hauptmann*, then in 1840 he went to Galicia as *Major* and adjutant of the *Generalkommando* [corps headquarters]. There he was promoted in 1843 to *Oberstlieutenant* and in 1846, to *Oberst*. That was the year when the Polish population of Galicia, especially the peasants, revolted against the nobility. The number of Austrian troops was limited, and they would have been unable to suppress the revolt nor contain the rage of the peasants, if capable and energetic officers had not made victory possible. Benedek was one of these who, by defeating the Poles at Gdow, made *General* Collin's victory at Krakau possible. Archduke Ferdinand Esta, at that time Governor of Galicia, gave the 42 year old *Oberst* the highest praise. The true story of this uprising, which was extremely murderous on all sides, has not yet been told. Benedek was awarded the Leopold Cross for restoring order in the eastern part of the Polish province, and one year later, was ordered to the army in Italy with his Infantry Regiment Chulai that had been recruited in Hungary.

His sangfroid and presence of mind became famous during the Italian revolt of 1848. He particularly shone in the attack on the double gun studded line at Curtatone, which its defenders considered impregnable. Such devotion to the cause of Austria did not pass unnoticed. Radetzky praised him in the next order of the day in the warmest terms and recommended him for the Order of Maria Theresa. When the following year (1849), the Piedmontese renewed the desperate battle, Benedek entered Mortara (21st March) at the head of his regiment, forced the Italians out and captured a brigade. He also made an essential contribution to victory at Novara by holding out until the arrival of the 3rd Army Corps.

On 3rd April 1849, Benedek was promoted to *Generalmajor* and transferred to the army in Hungary (under Haynau). There he initially commanded a brigade in the corps of *Felmarschalllieutenant* Vogel, then a brigade in the fourth, or Reserve Army Corps. He fought

---

In addition, six were recruited in Italy (Haugwitz, Sigismund, Holstein, *Grossfürst* Michael, *Ritter* Frank, *Freiherr* von Bamberg), seven in Poland (Galicia), ten in Bohemia and twenty one in Hungary. Among the Jäger battalions, which formed a *corps d'elite*, none were [exclusively] Italian. The six infantry regiments recruited in Venetia, however, constituted a particularly weak point in the Austrian army and may have contributed to the failures of some of their formations. 'The Italians are generally unsuitable, but when they are good, they are outstanding,' was a frequent and often repeated judgement amongst Austrian officers. Here again, the judgement may have proven itself both in general and in particular. Individual battalions (for example from Regiment Bamberg at Trautenau, from Regiment Frank at Nachod) displayed great bravery despite enormous losses. In general, the conduct of the Italian regiments was lacking in energy and reliability, and it is striking that this fact is not mentioned in any of the many Austrian reports that we have read. Is this a deliberate omission or chivalry, or just indifference?

with distinction in a variety of engagements and battles, at Raab, at Komorn and Szegedin. His courage was a byword in the army. He was lightly wounded at Szegedin, but in the battles of Szöreg and Ozs - Ivany, he was so severely wounded (by a shell fragment in the foot) that he could take no further part in the war in Hungary. Following his recovery, he was named Chief of the *General Quartiermeister* Staff of the Second Army under Radetzky, an appointment that brought him back from Hungary to Italy. At the same time, he was named *Inhaber*[34] of Regiment Latour and promoted to *Feldmarschialllieutenant* in 1853. In the following year (1854), in expectation of the Austrian Army fighting in the Crimean War, he was given command of the 4th Army Corps in Lemberg (as is well known, in the event, the Austrian Army did not take part in the Crimea).

In the war of 1859 [in Italy, where Austria was challenged in Lombardy by the Piedmontese, backed by the French under Napoleon III], that brought so little general fame, but in which the name of Benedek achieved renown, he commanded the 8th Army Corps. Initially he found little opportunity to shine. The Po crossing at Cornale produced only insignificant skirmishes. At the Battle of Magenta only one regiment of his Corps took part, late in the evening. During the retreat however, he took part in the bloody battle at Melegnano (8th June) with one of his divisions. In the position behind the Mincio River, Benedek took the extreme right wing, east of Peschiera. In the new advance (23rd June) he crossed the Mincio at Salionza, marched to Pozzolengo and pushed his advanced guard even further forward. The next day, the day of Solferino, was his day of fame. As all of the other corps were attacked by the enemy, he stood on the extreme [right] wing with the 27,000 men of 8th Corps, facing the entire Piedmontese army which numbered at least 40,000 men. He repulsed all their attacks at San Martino, until a heavy thunderstorm interrupted the fighting between four and five o'clock. Shortly thereafter he was ordered to retreat. He obeyed under protest. It was said that he shed tears and expressed himself in bitter words regarding the army command. Already it is said that he was going to resign when he was named *Feldzeugmeister ad honoures* (meaning without the salary of the rank) and then named to replace Hess as *Generalquartiermeister der Armee*. In April 1860, he replaced Archduke Albrecht as Governor General of Hungary and leader of the political administration of this land. However, he left this position in November of that same year to take command of the Italian Army as *Obercommandant*. He remained there until immediately before the start of the war against Prussia.

This was the man whom Emperor Franz Joseph called to command the Great North Army. The people and the army were one in their belief that this was the only possible choice. His undisputed courage, his soldier's luck which had remained true to him, even on the unfortunate day of Solferino, his middle class origins', his forthright language against *Erzherzöge* [archdukes], magnates and others, made him the most popular man in the land in the weeks before or immediately following his appointment. Everywhere, on the streets and in the theater, he was the occasion of the loudest ovations, and the women of Vienna pushed their way through to his carriage to throw floral bouquets to him. This enthusiasm was well founded, Austria had no

---

34   Tr. Note: The *Inhaber* was the proprietor, or honourary colonel of the regiment. In earlier times he raised the regiment, funded its needs and shared in its plunder. In the Austrian army the position was regarded as a great honour. When the *Inhaber* was a famous or royal person, as with the *Kaiser* Franz Josef, a second colonel might be chosen from among the nobility to perform his duties. Until the system was finally abolished in 1868 the proprietor held considerable influence over promotions

general who had achieved more success. Nevertheless, it seems that some individuals who were better informed, already had misgivings about his suitability as a *Feldherr* [field commander]. The Emperor himself, if one is to lend credence to rumours, considered that he was brave, favoured by luck and the feelings of the people, but limited in his abilities.[35] Even at the outbreak of the war a former general who had served under Benedek in 1859 wrote, 'Benedek can be compared with a heavy hammer, which, wherever it falls, strikes a mighty blow. *If he is directed by a skillful hand*, then wherever his blows fall, they will certainly be felt. But if he is directed by an unskilled hand, then he will mostly miss his target and be in danger of being broken himself. Benedek will bring quick victory or the army will not long survive his command.' This judgement implies that the 'hammer' must, in all circumstances, be directed by a dominant hand. Now however, the direction was left with the hammer itself.

It almost seems as if Benedek himself considered the mission assigned to him beyond his capabilities. On every side there are indications that from the very start, he was mistrustful of success, the only remaining doubt is whether this mistrust was in himself, or in the army. Some of his statements suggest that he believed that he must loyally obey [his sovereign's] call, and that perhaps he was the only one who did not underestimate his opponent.

A south German officer, who was near him at the start of the campaign, later wrote, 'Despite all of his popularity, Benedek felt isolated within the army. His instincts that had been sharpened by experience and shrewdness, allowed him to clearly see the deep faults in the military machine. All of his efforts to eliminate the most serious evils, for example the *Inhaber* system, had failed. The *Feldzeugmeister* dreaded the outcome of the war, he trusted neither himself nor the army. His attempts to maintain a superficial veneer of confidence created a false

Benedek.

---

35 Author's Note: At the court he was opposed by the aristocratic and clerical parties, in the army, despite his general popularity, by the 'young intelligentsia,' those know it alls in which the Austrian Army, as its military literature shows, is richer than any other. *Not* to its advantage.

atmosphere which was quickly detected by the more perceptive in his headquarters.' Other statements confirm this. He was lacking neither in pride nor vanity, yet vanity does not always blind one, and while it may use soaring rhetoric, it is terrified by the impending responsibility and yields to self-knowledge. Benedek's first order to the army (12th May) emphasized his old 'soldier's luck'. Perhaps he was well aware that he would need this luck in the battles that were approaching.

Prussia prepares!

Not until the 27th [March], only fourteen days after the example set by Austria, did orders go out to the troops of the five divisions garrisoning the Austrian and Saxon borders, to go to a heightened state of readiness. This order, which increased the army by 20,000 men, was a mere 'warning' to Vienna. Everything was done to avoid giving the wrong impression [of aggression], our response did no more than match the Austrian actions and indicated that [Prussia] intended to keep in step with its opponent, or more correctly, to follow in its footsteps. Prussia's task was to refer to Austria's progress and match it with its own military preparations, thereby securing a political advantage without putting itself at a military disadvantage.

Right up until the last week of April, Prussia clung to the possibility of peace. For an uncomfortable four weeks it went no further than the steps it had already taken on 27th March. Finally, faced with the increasingly ominous situation (which was also evident in the mobilisation of the medium German states), Prussia was forced into full mobilisation if it was not to suddenly find itself defenseless with enemies on all its borders. The military arrangements then followed one another in quick succession. On 24th April, orders were issued to bring five army corps up to wartime strength, on 4th May these five corps were declared ready for service, as was the entire army on 7th May.

The mood that accompanied these steps was exactly the opposite of that which prevailed in Austria. People were serious, there was no conceit, no talk of fame, no derision, no mockery. People felt the significance of the moment, and in the seriousness of the situation, the people themselves became serious. There was no arrogance, no exuberance. That is what we said, and the fact that it was so, for whatever reason, was a blessing. But we must not delude ourselves with the belief that our moderate attitude was in the least due to genuine humility. The people were not fired with arrogance because, by and large, the people did not want war. This lack of desire for war pervaded all levels of society, it was general, only the motives differed.

One group, a dominant part of the conservative party, not in numbers, but in reputation and influence, were against the war because they considered that to break with Austria was a serious political mistake. They remembered the testament of Friedrich Wilhelm III, who had established cooperation with Austria as a political necessity for Prussia. In agreement with the late king, they saw Austria as the bulwark of conservative interests and they viewed the break with Austria, particularly in alliance with Italy, as an alliance with the revolution. Right up until the last moment, with our troops already on the border, they warned against a war that they saw as stupid and wrong, and that could have no other result than to make the 'man on the Seine' [Emperor Napoleon III], the arbiter of Germany.

The second group were against the war because they mistrusted our strength, especially the combat readiness of the army. It was not that they thought it absolutely bad, they simply considered Austria's army to be better. The entire 'Prussian system,' even though it was fifty years old and had trained two generations, had not actually undergone a serious test. Düppel - Alsen could not be considered such a test, so their concern that the 'old soldiers of the Emperor' (only the war would show that we too, had old soldiers), would prove themselves superior to our short service people, was not unreasonable. The needle gun, despite its trial combat at Lundby, had yet to prove its superiority against a worthy enemy. In any case, the Austrian army with its complement of veteran officers and non commissioned officers, understood war. They were brave (they had proven that even on the unfortunate days of Magenta and Solferino), and above all, they had proven commanders, Ramming, Gablenz, Benedek, of whom the last named, 'undefeated, on the day of disaster,' had good reason to point to his soldier's luck.

The third group (and they were the most numerous) were against the war because they sullenly and indignantly opposed the people who, despite the dangers that increased hourly, would venture a war for the honour of the land. This third group saw the danger not in Austria, but solely and entirely at home, in the fragmentation of our own strength, in the unsolved budget strife, in the unpopularity of those who, knowing their unpopularity, still planned to go to war. This third group wanted the war, which they considered right and necessary, but they wanted to wage it themselves. Only the politically acceptable, only the [politically] liberal Prussians, were fit to undertake this mission. Under the given circumstances war was impossible, one could not allow a Bismarckian Prussian to lead this battle for survival.

In Austria, people were very well informed about this anti-war mood in Prussia. 'Prussia cannot wage war, for the Prussian people will not have it,' was the feeling in Vienna, and it was the basis of their policy of intimidation. They considered a 'second Olmütz' inevitable. But they made their reckoning without consulting the innkeeper. They failed to consider that instinctive Prussian discipline, which, while permitting 'internal debate' (which was given complete freedom), will respond with dutiful willingness as soon as the King has called. This is something specifically Prussian, and can only occur in a land where, for a century and a half, the monarchy has led the people in devotion to duty and where, despite occasional grumbling and complaining, the common man feels in his very being that, 'My king calls me only when he needs me.'

Vienna failed to include in its reckoning the proud, 'I serve' [Ich diene], which is inscribed on the heart of every Prussian. It should have, for its effect surprised even those who well knew this trait in our character and had counted on it, it was, and we dare to use this word, *magnificent*. Willing or not, every [Prussian] rests his honour on being in the right place at the right time. Nobody hung back. It was as if an entire people had given their word that, no matter what the cost, they would do their duty. Sometimes this took place under the most difficult circumstances. We shall give a few examples from our own experience. In the same house as us, lived a simple old worthy, a railroad official. His three sons, all *Landwehr Unteroffiziere* [non commissioned officers] were called up. The oldest (a master plumber) worked in Birmingham. The second (a cabinet maker) was in Lüttich [Liege]. The third (a postman) had already set the date for his wedding. Before ten days had passed each one of them was standing in the ranks, the youngest now limps, at Nachod a bullet smashed his hip joint.

Gottlieb Kruschel was called up in Posenschen, he had formerly been in the Guards. He was married with five children and lived on his father's farm. When the call up order came there was quite a commotion in the house. An unmarried man came up to Kruschel and said, 'I will go in your place,' everyone thought this was a good idea. Kruschel thought for a bit, then he said, 'The King has never waged war without me,' and as if that was not enough, he ended the discussion

Prussian arms.

with, 'The King has called me and not you, what would happen if everyone wanted to send a replacement, I will go.' And he went. He died in an epidemic and is buried in the Pohrlitz[36] churchyard near Brünn.

Perhaps the most beautiful example is in a letter that a reservist from the Mark, if we remember correctly, from Tilsit or Gumbinnen, who wrote to his old mother in Lunow (Uckermark). This reservist had been working in Russia along with many others, when he heard of the King's summons (we will present this summons later). He left Russia and now wrote from the Prussian border, which he had just crossed on his return:

> My dear, beloved mother! . . . I was working in Orly (near Pskow), forty five miles from Petersburg. I had no more news of Germany than any other of my countrymen, of which there were a good three hundred in the city. One hundred twenty of them were Prussians, the others mostly Saxons and Bavarians.

36   Tr. Note: Pohrlitz is a town in southern Moravia, approximately 25 km south of Brünn.

One day we learned that the Czar was coming to the city. Everyone was preparing to welcome him. However, before that day arrived, we received other news through the Prussian embassy in Petersburg, namely that the country is in danger and that the King had summoned all brave Prussians back to the fatherland. The word was passed from one to another, but all of us had only one thought, back to Prussia and take up the sword! That was the cry with which we all gave notice at work that day. Dear Mother, there is not one Prussian left there. The day of our departure was the very day that the Czar came. The military were there at the railroad station to receive him very early in the day. We gathered to leave Russia, perhaps forever. Many curious bystanders crowded around us awaiting our departure with admiration. Each of us had received a black and white sash, and now with a band leading us we marched to the strains of the song, 'Ich bin ein Preusse' [I am a Prussian] to the railroad station. There the windows opened, and we received many good wishes and many farewells from the Russians, with whom we were dear guests.

All of a sudden military music rang out in front of us. The Czar was there and was entering the city at the head of his Guards. We wanted to turn off into another street, but that was no longer possible, and the Czar suddenly stopped in front of us. Halt! Rang out and everything was deathly still. The Russians were chalk white from anxiety, we were calm and relaxed, awaiting whatever would come. Then the Czar rode forward, and after he had inspected us for a long time asked, 'Who are you?' I answered 'Prussians, your Majesty.' 'What is this about?' 'We are returning to our fatherland.' 'Are you no longer happy in my land, or is someone driving you out?' Dear Mother! Then I stepped forward a pace and said, 'No, Majesty! But our King summons us to help save our fatherland, which the enemy threatens, and we must not be lacking!' Then his eyes lit up. He gazed long at us and then spoke: 'I think it is beyond salvation!' Mother! A fiery pain pierced my chest. We had not thought the danger that great. 'Then we will let ourselves be buried with it!' That was how we answered him. Then, my dear Mother, I saw how the man before whom millions trembled, held back the tears that filled his eyes with difficulty. 'Go in peace, do your duty and rely on Prussia's friends. It will never be defeated no matter what may come. Go with God.' Then he spoke a few words to his adjutant, waved his hand, and the band of the Ingermanland Guards Regiment was at our head. Then 'Present Arms!' and the shout, 'Long live the Czar, long live the Prussian,' and we went on, to the thundering cries of the Guards. That, my Mother, was a glorious moment in my life that I shall never forget. Now I am in Prussia again to await what comes, and I wanted to write to you immediately.'

This spirit, as he so beautifully expresses it in this letter, animated all those who had ever served under Prussia's flag.[37] Everyone flocked to the depots, and as military music rang out again

37 Author's Note: We cannot restrain ourselves from recounting yet another story, even though it originates a few weeks after the war, which yet throws a retrospective light on how seriously it was taken at that time in Prussia. This is the story. King William, on his journey to Dresden (February 1867) passed through the little town of Hertzberg. The station platform was crowded with people, also with reservists who wore on their chests their military decorations from Düppel - Alsen and Sadowa [Königgrätz]. The King waved the closest one to him, spoke kindly and asked him in a cheerful mood,

on the streets, and as departure drew near, then the Prussian hearts began to beat and all the griping and complaining vanished like a bank of fog, and the long awaited sunlight shone again over the land.

Silesia was in the lead. Here first (in the most exposed location) a pure flame swept away the murk and smoke that had long darkened the mood. Breslau, a name that had already been inscribed on the most luminous pages of our history, put the discontent behind it, and with a, 'here we are again,' sent a letter filled with patriotic devotion to the throne. This example will never be forgotten. The words that the capital city of Silesia addressed to the King were:

> Most Gracious King and Lord! In this serious time in which Prussia and Germany are threatened with grave dangers of war, it is the city government of Breslau, as the capital city of the very province, which first and initially is exposed to the war with its events, that should approach the throne of Your Majesty with a respectful affirmation.
>
> Your Majesty has ordered mobilisation of the entire army. We know that Your Majesty has resolved upon this with a heavy heart. Your Majesty knows the suffering that the Prussian people have already endured in the long years of profitable peaceful employment and which, in the event of outbreak of war, will be a far greater burden. There must, therefore, be weighty reasons that have brought Your Majesty to this serious decision. We believe at the very highest levels that we can assure you that, just as in 1813, Breslau will not fall behind any other city in Prussia in its willingness to make sacrifices.
>
> Along with Your Majesty we feel the affliction of the war, we no not underestimate the burden that the Prussian people will have to bear. We know the sacrifices that war demands. Regardless of all that we state and believe that we well know the mood of our fellow citizens, who, if it is a matter of the might and honour of Prussia, its position in Germany and what goes with this position in connection with the unity of our common fatherland, will face the dangers and needs of the war with the same spirit of self-sacrifice and devotion that the men of Silesia demonstrated under the leadership of Your Majesty's noble father. If Prussia and Germany can attain their highest well-being in peace, then we celebrate this with joyful hearts. Should, however, as happened in 1850, the enemy of Prussia and Germany again seek a diminution of Prussia's position of power, again attempt to humiliate Prussia, then Silesia would rather take upon itself all the burdens and suffering of war than allow the historic mission of Prussia, the unification of Germany again be postponed for decades.

Thus wrote Breslau (15th May).

The King replied:

> I have happily received the words that the magistrates and municipal council addressed to me in their statement of the 15th of this month. I recognize in them the outpouring of the same spirit that, in 1813, inspired the fathers of today's citizens of Breslau. It

---

'whether he was well and strong of heart?' The man addressed did not hesitate, looked the King square in the eye and then said, modestly, 'I fought for my King and fatherland.' King Wilhelm patted his cheek, fell silent and got back in his railway compartment.

has done my heart good that the representatives of the city expressed this spirit in earnest and with warmth. No one can feel more painfully than I do the weight of the sacrifice which the war will require from the fatherland, no one feel the burdens more heavily that the ruler and people will bear in unalloyed harmony. May my words serve as a guarantee to the city of Breslau, *that no arrogant endeavour, certainly not that which can be considered justified in the interest of the great common fatherland, rather it is only the obligation to defend Prussia and its most holy goods that causes me to summon my people to arms.*

The royal answer placed the seal on the change of mood, on the transformation that took place in the feelings of the people when it first became clear that the prospect of war was inevitable. The basic mood remained serious, people were on guard against overconfidence and arrogance, but there was a certain joy (a joy like that which arises from hope) that grew out of it.

On the 19th the King's reply arrived in the city of Breslau. Already, on the 15th, the troop concentrations began from the east and west. At the start of June, the deployment (a preliminary one, that was changed fourteen days later) was completed. Four corps under the Crown Prince (the II, or Silesian, Army) covered Silesia. Four and a half corps, under Prince Friedrich Karl and *General* Herwarth von Bittenfeld (1st and Elbe Army) covered the Lausitz and the Mark. The positions, at this point, were primarily of a defensive nature. 'The diplomat must go closely, hand in hand, with the military'. The particular difficulty was that, while the political situation called for defensive measures, the chance to take the offensive, if the opportunity presented itself, could not be allowed to slip. The plan (a relatively good one) remained in place, not in detail, but in broad outline, entirely in agreement with the Napoleonic dictum, 'One must calculate two thirds and leave one third to chance.' One who calculates too little will be confused as events unfold, one who calculates too much will confused by events taking an unforeseen course. The people began to hope, as we said. One however, had entire confidence in victory, *Graf* Bismarck. He knew the forces on both sides. 'The [Austrian] Cabinet and the people underestimate us. The world will watch in amazement what power the despised Prussia is capable of deploying.'

The Occupation of Saxony – The Manifestos

In mid-July Prussia was in a defensive position on the Saxon Silesian border. Political considerations dictated this, but it offered certain military advantages too, such as an immediate occupation of Saxony and an advance from north to south, depending on the actions of the Confederation. Confederation neutrality in the forthcoming battle was still a possibility, and therefore it was necessary to avoid any action that might prejudice this. When the vote of the Confederation on 14th June went against Prussia, any remaining doubts were removed, thereby relieving Prussia of the need to take [the Confederation's] position into consideration. The moment had arrived to take the offensive, which consisted of the immediate occupation of Hannover, Kassel and Dresden. At this point we shall consider this advance.

On the 15th, Prussia presented its ultimatum. During the night of 15/16th June, after King Johann [of Saxony] had turned down the ultimatum, the Prussians advanced to the border, and on the following morning, crossed it at a number of places along the line between Leipzig and Görlitz.

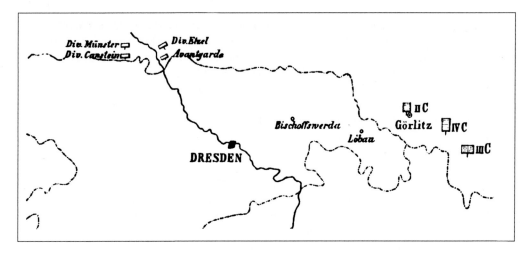

Initial deployment of the Prussian 1st and Elbe armies.

Elbe Army (Herwarth von Bittenfeld), proceeded via Riesa and Meissen towards Dresden. The 1st Army (Prince Friedrich Karl), advanced via Bautzen and Löbau to Zittau. Both armies sought to maintain contact via their flanking corps at Bischofswerda, halfway between Dresden and Bautzen, however this contact could not be maintained as the advance continued. It was not until the fighting at Münchengrätz, eleven days later, that contact between the two armies was re-established.

After crossing the border, the Saxons merely attempted to hinder the Prussian advance by tearing up railway lines, removing locomotives and Elbe steamers, and finally by destroying bridges as they withdrew, evacuating Dresden in the process, and retreating up the Elbe through the valley of the *Sächsischen Schweiz* [Saxon Switzerland]. Belief was widespread among the withdrawing troops that they were only leaving their Saxon homeland for a short time, and that only 'a short distance,' separated them from the main allied army under Benedek. It was assumed that only the rash Prussian initiative, and perhaps the Austrian [habit of being] 'always slow to advance,' had prevented [Benedek's army] from being in what was believed to be the decisive spot at the right time.

Keeping on the left, or more accurately, on the left bank of the Elbe, they crossed the Bohemian border. Nowhere had there been a clash of arms. The attempts to delay the Prussian advance, proved to be a failure. From the beginning, the Prussians had made good use of the railways (which only had to be cut) from near the border to Dresden. Even more pointless had been the destruction of the beautiful bridges at Riesa and Meissen. The Saxons themselves, shook their heads over this. Setting fire to the bridge piers, the towering flames seemed to serve no purpose other than that of a beacon, a landmark. The soaring flames proclaiming far into the land, 'The war is here!' On our side the pontoon detachments immediately set to work. While they were busy restoring communications between the banks [of the Elbe], the divisions that had crossed the border were already advancing toward Dresden in forced marches on both sides of the river. On 16th June the little localities on the Lepzig Dresden railroad line, Wurzen, Dahlen, Oschatz and, on the 17th, Meissen, was occupied.

The next day the advance – guard would enter the Saxon capital. Already, on the 16th, immediately after crossing the border, *General* Herwarth von Bittenfeld issued the following proclamation:

> Saxons! I am advancing into your land, [but] not as your enemy, for I know that your sympathies do not coincide with the actions of your government. What has happened would not have taken place if the alliance between Austria and Prussia had not given rise to hostilities. That alone is the reason that your beautiful land has, initially, become the theater of war. However, my troops will treat you as friends, just as they would treat the citizens of our own country, to the same degree that you welcome us and are ready to willingly bear the inevitable burdens of war. It is therefore in your hands to ameliorate the sufferings of the war, and to thwart efforts that might give rise to hostility between the related peoples.

Everywhere there were troops, people looked upon them with amazement. Their carriage, their cheerfulness, their smart uniforms, all caused general surprise. A letter from Meissen written at the time, best expresses this. '. . . Early on Sunday blue Hussars rode through our city. At midday and in the afternoon the influx increased and lasted into the night. All headed toward Dresden. Early on Monday more followed, infantry, Uhlans and about a hundred cannon. We were stunned. We had never seen such a show. We had been told that Prussia was destitute in everything, that it lacked the means to put a great army in the field, and now the weapons and harness glinted, and the procession seemed endless.'

On the 18th, at about noon, the first Prussians entered Dresden, the Royal Hussars Regiment [*Königs Husaren Regiment*]. They moved in from three sides, from the *Albertsbahnhof* [Albert Railroad Station], through the *Gehege*[38] and from Neustadt, linking up at the bridge before the Catholic church. They were immediately followed by infantry, the commanders leading, the Hohenzollern Fusilier Regiment Nr. 40, the East Prussian Fusilier Regiment Nr. 33, Uhlans, Jäger and artillery. The main government buildings were immediately occupied, the postal and telegraph service, the *Leipziger, Böhmische, Schlesische* and *Albertsbahnhof* [Leipzig, Bohemian, Silesian and Alberts Railroad Stations], and the royal palace. Individual officers hastened to other buildings. The old bridge over the Elbe was only blocked for a short time, then it was reopened to traffic. The occupation continued until late in the afternoon. *General* Herwarth, who set up headquarters in the Hotel Bellevue, reviewed the arriving regiments as they filed past him. The troops, those that were not passing through, were housed, partly in the barracks, partly in private homes. The next day high mass was held in the Catholic church (the men who had come into the city were Rhinelanders and Westphalians) [predominantly Catholic]. Nowhere had there been any resistance. The people accepted peacefully what they could not change. Their attitude was polite but reserved. Only the many Prussians living in Dresden gave lively expression to their patriotic joy. They waved with sheets and saluted the arriving men with hails and hurrahs.

---

38   Tr. Note: The *grosse Gehege* is a meadow area within a bend of the Elbe northwest of the city boundary on the south bank of the Elbe. The area is beautifully depicted in an 1832 painting, *Das Grosse Gehege*, or *Ostra-Gehege*, by Caspar David Friedrich.

The 19th was a day of rest for the Elbe Army. While *General* Herwarth's troops rested however, Leipzig was occupied by advance elements of a Reserve Corps that was still in the process of mobilisation. This occupation of the second major city of the land was only a defensive measure and served no other purpose than to cover the right flank of the Elbe Army. An advance on this line (Leipzig – Hof) was not intended, nor at that time, possible. Due to the limited forces available this [corps] would have to prevent any Bavarian advance from that direction.

Already on 18th June, patrols of Hussars arrived at Reudnitz, a village suburb just outside Leipzig, to see if Bavarian forces were in the vicinity. It was not until early on the 19th that the city was occupied. At 4 o'clock in the morning, about thirty farm wagons with 150 infantry arrived outside the Dresden Gate. They disembarked at the *Johanniskirche* and proceeded through the city to the *Bayerschen Bahnhof* [Bavarian Railway Station]. Guards were posted while the remainder of the men climbed back into the wagons and continued on to Altenburg.

We shall let an eyewitness provide a description of the advances of this day:

> At 9:30 in the morning a 40 man patrol of Brandenburg Dragoons rode through the *Grimmaische Strasse*, the leading man with drawn pistol, as is usual in times of war. They were surrounded and subject to many friendly greetings from a large group of curious people that had assembled. The commander proceeded to the *Rathhaus* [city hall] and demanded that the proclamation of the Prussian commanding general in Saxony, Herwarth von Bittenfeld, be publicly posted by the city council (which was refused, whereupon the military authority itself employed force and posted it). At 11:00 in the morning infantry columns finally arrived in the outskirts of Dresden. It was a battalion of the fourth Guards Regiment, a thousand strong, under the command of *Oberstlieutenant* von Conta. They had come on Monday from Torgau, whence they had arrived from Berlin eleven days earlier on poor roads and had marched here yesterday in five hours. They arrived covered in dust and sweat, but not exhausted. The battalion marched without drums across the *Augustusplatz* on the *Schillerstrasse* into the castle, the old *Pleissenburg*. The rifles were stacked in the courtyard of the castle and the men made themselves comfortable. At midday such a large number of curious people pressed into the *Pleissenburg* that the gates had to be closed. In a short time all of the men were refreshed. They had a warlike appearance. They were tall, strong men, bearded, sunburned, and for the most part, decorated with the *Düppelkreuz* [a cross indicating service at the battle of *Düppel* in the Danish War 1864]. They were proper and friendly in their dealing with the public, and this was reciprocated. People fraternized.

The welcome in Leipzig was warmer than in any other city [in Saxony], to such a degree that it was ours by the 19th. Prussian sympathies were unmistakable, however it was only in the eastern part of Saxony, between Stolpen, Neustadt, Hohenstein and that narrow spit of land where Saxony, Silesia and Bohemia meet, that an unsolicited inclination toward Prussia manifested itself. Here, as a result of long interaction across the border in both directions, people had long learned the difference between Prussian and Austrian ways, and the comparison was not to our disadvantage.

Initially however, we must accompany the Elbe Army in its advance (which as you know, had a day of rest on the 19th). On the morning of the 20th, the entire Elbe Army crossed the Dresden bridges with bands playing, passed the Neustadt, and marched singing, past the

Waldschlösschen on the beautiful mountainside, and on to Bischofswerda and Stolpen. The latter were occupied on the evening of that same day. Neustadt, that little spot that is so close to the border, was not occupied until the 21st. That otherwise peaceful plateau now became a single, great armed camp. The view was beautiful, especially as night fell. From the heights of Schloss [castle] Stolpen one could see bivouac fires burning all the way to the border, in between, like dark shadows, were the villages. Great plumes of smoke rose into the sky and here and there, when a gust of wind came, they sank down and covered the field and its lights.

So we have brought the Elbe Army to the Bohemian border. On 22nd June it was announced, 'Early in the morning we move on.' This was received with loud jubilation. The advanced guard marched that same day (22nd) to Schluckenau.

As the Elbe Army advanced through Dresden, the 1st Army (Prince Friedrich Karl) advanced via Bautzen and Löbau to the border. The scenes and events here were the same. The railroads, where they had been destroyed, were quickly restored to service, the telegraph put back in action, the officials, so far as the service required, recalled to duty. The Prince issued a proclamation which stated, just as in *General* Herwarth's announcement, 'that the war would not be waged against the land and its citizens, but only against the government, a government whose hostile attitude toward Prussia had provoked this action.' It was announced that requisitions would be made and receipts issued for them. On the 22nd the 1st Army was in the Zittau, Ostritz, Seidenburg triangle. Early on the 23rd, it would cross into Bohemia.

The common field of action of the 1st and the Elbe Army was the Iser region. In the mid - course of this river, between Turnau and Münchengrätz, the two armies, one marching southeast, the other southwest, must presumably meet. And so it happened, we shall see how.

The manifestos

Early on 16th June the telegraphic report of the invasion of Saxony arrived in Vienna. On the 17th Emperor Franz Joseph issued the following manifesto:

To My Peoples!

In the midst of the work of peace that I have undertaken in order to lay the foundations for a form of constitution which will confirm the unity and position of the entire empire, its individual lands and peoples, yet at the same time, secure their free inner development, my sovereign duty has required that I summon my entire army to arms. On the borders of the empire, in the south and in the north, stand the armies of two allied enemies who intend to shake Austria from its position as a European great power. I have, for my part, given neither of them an excuse for war.

As God the Omniscient is my Judge, I have always considered my first and most sacred sovereign duty, to secure the blessings of peace for my people. Alone, one of the two hostile powers needs no excuse. In its lust to steal parts of my empire, a favourable moment is sufficient reason for war.

Two years ago, allied with the Prussian troops that now face us as enemies, a part of my loyal and courageous army reached the shores of the North Sea. I entered this armed alliance with Prussia to protect the rights of the treaty, to protect an endangered German people, to limit an unavoidable war in this smallest of countries. In addition, as one of the two, major, central powers which had in part, been given the task of maintaining European peace, to win such a lasting guarantee of peace for the good of my Empire, Germany and Europe. I have not sought conquest. In selflessly concluding the alliance with Prussia I did not seek any advantages for myself in the Vienna Peace Treaty. Austria bears no guilt in the tarnished series of unfortunate developments that would never have come to pass, if Prussia had maintained the same sort of selfless intentions and shown the same sense of loyalty to the alliance.

These were brought about to accomplish selfish ends, and therefore, there was no peaceful way for my government to find a peaceful solution.

Thus the seriousness of the situation constantly increased as warlike preparations were instituted in the two hostile states, and daily it became more apparent that there was an agreement between them that could only be based on the intention of a common, hostile attack on my Empire. I resolved, in the deepest peace, in awareness of my royal duties, to be ready for anything consistent with the honour and well - being of my people.

However, as I realized that further delay endangered the effective defense against enemy attacks and thereby the safety of the monarchy, I had to choose the heavy sacrifices that are inseparably linked with preparations for war.

Prussia responded to the assurances given by my government of my love of peace, and the repeated declarations of my readiness for simultaneous reciprocal demobilization, with counter demands whose acceptance would have meant the surrender of the honour and security of my Empire.

Prussia demanded demobilisation not only against itself, but also against the enemy forces on the border of my Empire in Italy, for whose love of peace no guarantee was offered, and for which none could be given.

All negotiations with Prussia regarding the question of the duchies, have merely added more evidence that a solution in accordance with the dignity of Austria, the rights and the interests of Germany, and of the duchies, cannot be attained by agreement with Prussia with its clear and open policy of power and conquest.

The negotiations were broken off, the entire matter referred to the German Confederation, and at the same time, the legal representatives of Holstein have been called into session.

The threat of war has caused the three powers, France, England and Russia to invite my government to take part in joint discussions whose objective should be keeping the peace. My government, in accordance with my intention, whenever possible to maintain peace for my peoples, has not declined taking part, but has [stipulated] that European laws and the existing treaties have to form the starting point for this attempt at mediation, and that the powers taking part have no special interests in upsetting the European balance of power and the rights of Austria.

If the attempted peace talks foundered on these natural prerequisites, therein lies proof that talks in themselves could never result in keeping and assuring peace.

Most recent events prove incontrovertibly that Prussia now replaces law with naked power. Prussia no longer considers the rights and honour of Austria, nor the rights and honour of the entire German people, to constitute any limit on its own fatally inflated pride. Prussian troops invaded Holstein, forcibly dispersed the Estates that had been called into session by the Imperial Governor, and assumed sole rulership of Holstein, which the Vienna Peace Treaty had jointly turned over to Austria and Prussia. The Austrian garrison was compelled to fall back in the face of tenfold superiority.

When the German Confederation, at Austria's request, resolved to mobilise the Confederation troops, Prussia, which so liked to present itself as the champion of German interests, went its own disastrous way. Tearing apart the national union of Germans, it declared its withdrawal from the Confederation, demanding that the German governments adopt a so called reform plan which would achieve the separation of Germany, and advance with military power against the sovereigns loyal to the Confederation. And thus the most disastrous thing, a war of German against German, has become unavoidable. I summon those that have brought this about, before the judgement seat of history, before the eternal, almighty God, to answer for the misfortunes that they would bring upon the individuals, families, communities and lands. I march to battle with the confidence in victory that a righteous cause gives, with the feeling of power that lies in a great Empire, where prince and people are imbued with only one thought, the rights of Austria, encouraged by the sight of my brave, battle ready army, that forms a bulwark against the strength of the enemies of Austria.

The pure flame of patriotic inspiration blazes everywhere in the expanses of my Empire. Joyfully the warriors who have been summoned, hasten to the ranks of the army. Volunteers press forward for military service. All who are capable of bearing arms in the most exposed lands, arm themselves for battle, the noble willingness for self - sacrifice, lessens their misfortunes, and thereby support the needs of the army.

A single feeling animates the peoples of my land, the feeling of togetherness, of the power of unity, of disgust at such an unheard of violation of law. I am doubly pained that the work of agreeing upon an internal constitution has not gone far enough, so that in this serious, moment, the representatives of all my peoples would be able to gather at my throne. Deprived of this support for now, my sovereign duty is all the clearer, my resolve all the stronger, to secure my Empire for all of the future.

We shall not stand alone in this battle. Germany's princes and people know the danger that threatens their freedom and independence, from a country whose methods of operation are guided solely by selfishness and a ruthless lust for power. They know what sort of bulwark they find in Austria, what support for the power and integrity of the entire German fatherland. Our German Confederation brothers stand in arms as do we, in defense of highest good.

The weapons have been forced into our hands. So be it! Now, when we have taken them up, we shall not and must not lay them down until my realm, as well as the allied German states, are assured that their free internal development, and their position in Europe, is again confirmed. Our trust and hopes rest not only on our unity and strength.

I place them before a higher authority, the almighty, just God, whom my house has served from its very beginning, and who never abandons those who in righteousness trust in him.

To him I shall pray that he be with us, and grant us victory, and I call upon my people to join with me in so doing.

Given in my residence and Imperial capital, Vienna, on the Seventeenth of June, One Thousand Eight Hundred Sixty Six.

Franz Joseph *m.p.*

Such was the Emperor's manifesto.

One day later (June 18th), on the anniversary of Fehrbellin and Belle - Alliance, the Prussian manifesto also appeared:[39]

To My People!

At the moment when Prussia's army anticipates a decisive battle, I am compelled to speak to my people, to the sons and grandsons of the brave fathers, to whom half a century ago, my father who now rests with God, spoke these memorable words|:

'The Fatherland is in Danger' Austria and a large part of Germany is in now in arms against this same Fatherland!

It is only a few years since, of my own accord and thinking of no prior wrong, I stretched out the hand of alliance when it was a matter of freeing a German land from foreign rule. I hoped that a brotherhood in arms would blossom from the blood that was jointly shed, that this would lead to a firm alliance based on mutual respect and recognition, the fruit of which would be internal German well - being and external importance. However, my hopes have foundered.

Austria will not forget that its princes once ruled Germany. In the young Prussia, that is however, becoming powerful, it will not recognize a natural ally, but only a hostile rival. Prussia, so Austria thinks, must be thwarted in all its endeavours, for what is good for Prussia, injures Austria. The old fatal jealousy has flared up again, and blazes brightly. Prussia must be weakened, destroyed, dishonoured. Treaties no longer apply to Prussia. The princes of the German Confederation are not just incited against Prussia, but are encouraged to break the Confederation. Wherever we look in Germany, we are surrounded by enemies whose battle cry is 'Humiliate Prussia!'

However, the spirit of 1813 is alive in my people. Who can take from us a single foot of Prussian soil when we are firmly resolved to preserve what our fathers conquered, when King and people are united, stronger than ever, by the danger threatening the Fatherland, when they consider it their highest and holiest duty to expend wealth and blood for its honour?

---

39   Tr. Note: The Battle of Fehrbellin, which has been considered Prussia's 'baptism of fire', was fought on June 18th 1675. Brandenburg - Prussian troops of Frederick William, the Great Elector, defeated Swedish forces that had invaded and occupied parts of Brandenburg.

On 18th June 1815, La Belle Alliance, an inn situated a few miles south of Brussels in Belgium, became Napoleon Bonaparte's headquarters for the Battle of Waterloo. After the battle Blücher and Wellington met near the inn to mark the end of the battle. Blücher, the Prussian commander, suggested la Belle Alliance as the name for the battle to commemorate the great alliance that had joined to defeat Bonaparte. Wellington, who had chosen the field of battle and commanded the allied army that had fought throughout the day before Blücher's fortunate arrival, preferred that the battle be named Waterloo.

In concerned anticipation of what now begins, for years I have considered that I must recognize as the first duty of my royal office, the preparation of Prussia's valiant people for a strong display of power. Confident and content, every Prussian will join me and the armed forces that protect our borders. With its King at its head, Prussia's people will feel like an entire people in arms. Our enemies delude themselves if they think that Prussia is crippled by internal conflict. In the face of the enemy it is united and strong. In the face of the enemy it smooths out the differences that divided it and then stands united for good or ill. I have done everything to spare Prussia from the burdens and sacrifices of a war. My people know that. God, who examines the heart, knows that. Right up to the last moment I have, in common with France, England and Russia, sought and held open the way for a worthy reconciliation. Austria has not wanted this, and other German states have openly placed themselves at its side. So be it, then. The guilt is not mine if my people must fight difficult battles and perhaps, endure hard affliction. We are, however, left with no other choice! We must fight for our existence, we must enter a battle for life and death against those who would hurl the Prussia of the Great Elector,[40] of the Great Frederick, from the level to which it arose from the War of Independence.

We implore the Almighty, the director of the fates of peoples, the director of battles, that he bless our weapons! May God grand us victory. Then we will also be strong enough to renew the loose bond that unites the German lands more in name than in fact, and which is now torn apart by those who fear the right and the might of the national spirit, in another form that will be stronger and healthier.

May God be with us!

Berlin, 18th June 1866.
(Signed) Wilhelm.

On that same day (as we already know) Dresden was occupied. This step was morally and militarily of the highest importance. Until then, though highly unlikely, a settlement of the conflict was always possible. With the invasion of Saxony this possibility ended. When the Riesa bridge went up in flames, that truly marked the beginning of the war. Everyone in Prussia recognized the significance of the four days that had brought us to the Bohemian border and the possession of Saxony. A battle had been won even before the first shot was fired. A joyful confidence filled every heart, everyone felt a strong will, a skilled hand. The mere demonstrations were over, 'It is happening,' and the warlike spirit of our fathers that rested deep within, in which one had almost lost faith, was there again.

This first step accomplished all this. If there was any further need for proof of its significance, we can find it in the behaviour of our enemy. A south German officer exclaimed, 'Now we are lost.' The news even affected Vienna and the people instinctively recognized the significance of the occupation. Confidence was shaken and doubts began to be voiced about Benedek's

---

40   Tr. Note: Friedrich Wilhelm (1620-88), known for his prowess and accomplishments as The Great Elector, or in German, *Der Große Kurfürst,* was Elector of Brandenburg and Duke of Prussia from 1640 until his death in 1688.

infallibility. There was already talk of 'omissions.' The leading circles felt the need to calm the excited mood. Various newspapers were told to provide proof that nothing had been lost, that all that had happened or not happened, was part of a well thought out plan, and that the calm, the waiting, the *stability* of the Austrian army command, was grounded in the confidence of having superior forces.

'The occupation of Dresden by the Prussians,' said a military technical journal, 'has been given a significance that it absolutely lacks. Reinforcement of the Saxons with an Austrian corps in order to hold Dresden would have resulted in the loss of all the advantages that our North Army has in its concentrated position ... Whoever will defend everything, defends nothing. That is a strategic and tactical principal that has constantly proven itself and has been illustrated in the defeats of those who ignore it. It could be anticipated that the Prussians would occupy Dresden. Everyone should be convinced that the [failure] to occupy Dresden by our side ... was fully reasoned and is in full compliance with Benedek's plan for the campaign.'

This discussion, as we know, was in accordance with the truth to the extent that a belated completion of the mobilisation of the Austrian forces, *had* prevented the *Feldzeugmeister* from considering any offensive operations. Instead, he had either to await the enemy in a good position or advance to meet him between the Iser and the Elbe. On 22nd and 23rd June, our columns entered the Bohemian basin. Before we follow their advance, we will take a look at the ground on which the battle would be decided with unforeseen rapidity.

Bohemia and the Iser Region

The land and its people

Bohemia, the old battle ground between Prussia and Austria, is the bastion - like part of the Empire that juts northwards. From the mountain ranges that border it to the north and northwest, foothills extend southwards over rolling terrain, for the most part, far into the land. Deeply incised river valleys alternate with steeply rising, wooded, sugarloaf hills [a sugarloaf hill is pointed or conical in appearance]. The landscape is similar nearly everywhere.

The greatest part of the country is in the drainage basin of the Elbe whose most significant tributary is the Moldau. Both the Elbe from Melnik, and the Moldau downstream from Königsaal, were navigated by small steamers which primarily served as towboats.

Bohemia has long been known for the fertility of its soil. Bohemian fruit and Bohemian hops (the latter unsurpassed for goodness), are to this very day the object of cultivation and demand. All the conditions for economic prosperity are there. However, great though the natural fertility of the land may be, the fruits of the soil are almost nowhere harvested to their full potential. The way that the land is distributed, the damaging effects of political and religious influences, and finally, a certain *indolence* in the character of the people that is accompanied by an excitability easily aroused to fanaticism, make conditions such that the land is not fully utilized. The agricultural economy suffers at the two economic extremes. On the one hand it is concentrated into overly large agricultural estates, and on the other, excessive breakup of agricultural holdings resulting in frequent changes of ownership. With regard to the 'overly large agricultural estates,' it should be noted here, that of the 146 great *Fideikommiss* [entailed] estates that were in the hands of only 52 families of the high landed nobility, some were as large as a small German *Länder*. For example, the *Krumau* estate of Prince [*Fürst*] Schwarzenberg, not counting its other areas, included over 205 square miles of forest. Despite these, and other similarly extensive holdings, the high landed nobility, with few exceptions, is deeply in debt. The best that can be said for the ordinary people is that they are not moving ahead. The high taxes that they are subject to, make general agricultural prosperity impossible.

The people of Bohemia, according to the 1857 census, numbered about five million, including three million Czechs and two million Germans. The Czech statistics, on the other hand, indicate that the Czechs greatly outnumber the Germans, who make up barely a quarter of the population. Such contradictory figures are common in all lands of mixed nationality, though not always to the extent that they are in Bohemia, where there is great internal agitation regarding the nationality question. A major point of controversy concerns the relationship of the nationalities in the capital city. Of the 140,000 residing there, the Germans claim that there are only 60,000 Czechs, so that they consider Prague to be a German city, and claim it as such, unsuccessfully however, as the Czechs rule it.

Recently attempts have been made, with great energy and care, though clearly not without an element of party politics, to draw boundaries within the broad territory of the kingdom according to language and nationality. The only unquestionable result of this attempt is that the northern border district (the strip of land along the *Fichtel* and *Erzgebirge)*, as well as individual districts near the Lausitz and Silesian *Riesengebirge*) [the old Sudetenland], are almost exclusively inhabited by Germans, while in the center, as well as in the east and the south, the Czech nationality predominates. Since throughout the entire land, both nationalities live intermingled, the members of one community are also frequently and entirely at home in the language of the other, and many Czech family names are found among the Germans, and German family names among the Czechs. This makes it extremely difficult to assign nationalities in some cases.[41] It seems safe to say that the Czech nationality provides the mass of the lower classes of people in the cities and on the land, the majority of the peasant holdings, the small artisans, and a few noble families, while the Germans include the greater land holdings [most of the high nobility] and the larger trade and industrial enterprises. This is also the case in Prague, though here (as we stated earlier) the predominantly Czech municipal representatives have succeeded, with a few exceptions, in *Czechifying* the public schools.

41   Author's Note: We take the following from a report on this interesting question. There is no actual language boundary in Bohemia. German and Czech are thoroughly mixed. There are German localities between entirely Bohemian localities, and on the other hand, there are entirely Bohemian localities between German ones. Bohemian or Czech are spoken, not only in Bohemia, but also in Moravia, as well as in substantial parts of Hungary and Slavonia, and with a variation, also in Austrian Silesia. The Czech language is pliable and rich. The Bohemian language includes many examples of onomatopoeia such as Kruta, the turkey cock, Kachna, the duck. The sound of Bohemian is pleasant and melodious, for they can in their language, express the alphabets of all languages. Granted, Bohemian has a shortage of sonorous vowels, and the consonants are emphasized. This however, is only seen in the writings of talentless scribblers, for in the mouth of the people the language seems strong and expressive. Bohemia had an extremely rich literature. In 1620, after the Battle at the White Mountain, all of the Bohemian books condemned as heretical, were burned, the German language introduced, and the Bohemian suppressed. So it came about that in the years 1729 to 1749, the Bohemians nearly ceased to speak Bohemian (Tr. Note: The Battle of The White Mountain, 8th Nov 1620, was one of the early battles of the Thirty Years War. Fought near Prague in Bohemia, it was a major victory of the Roman Catholic Habsburgs over the Protestant Union and gave the house of Habsburg dominion over Bohemia and its neighbours).

The nationality question, the resurgence of the Czech population seeking political control, is a recent phenomenon, a product of the year 1848. Until then, the Metternich regime had been equally repressive of Germans and Czechs alike, and a Czech national rebellion against the German government, seemed even more remote than a liberal revolt against the absolute power of the Imperial government. For those who traveled at that time in Bohemia, nowhere was conflict evident in daily life. Harmless, equally mishandled by the bureaucracy, equally in awe of [the bureaucracy], the people lived in city and land, undifferentiated with respect to nationality. Here and there the German had a strange and sharp accent. That was all, nothing gave any premonition of what would suddenly and explosively appear in the spring of 1848. Hardly had the youth of Vienna cast aside an outmoded system that had fallen behind the times, when suddenly, a uniquely Bohemian element pushed itself forward among the intoxicated actors of the capital city. Arising from literary inspired hotheads, stalking along in fantastic Slav costume, speaking in an idiom that the world had come to look upon as already vanishing, they suddenly began to incite wild agitation among the Czechs, initially seeking unlimited autonomy for Bohemia, an objective that demanded unconditional dominance of the Czech over the German element. It was characteristic that, in the guise of the general liberal uprising, the Germans initially favoured this endeavour, indeed numbering themselves among its supporters. The sobering up after the great intoxication in which they too had participated, was not long in coming, and soon the nationalities were bitterly opposed. The Czech nationals, gradually purging themselves of the revolutionary elements, drew on the forces of Czech culture, including the clerical element, and skillfully and effectively pursued its goal in all intellectual fields, in the church, in the schools, in art and in literature, thereby succeeding in displacing German culture from its dominant position. During the past eighteen years the German element had lost much ground.

Czech nationalism entertained far reaching hopes. For our part, we see in this passionate attempt at resurrection, merely a last flaring of the fire before it finally goes out. We see these efforts as hopeless, more futile than those of the Poles who comprise the great front of the Slavic world, while Bohemia (separated [from Poland] by Silesia) is a semi Germanized Slavic island which, because it is surrounded by German culture, must remain under modified, but necessarily German, political rule. A [Czech] rearguard is resisting this, drawing inspiration from the distant past and introducing the stuff of ballads into politics, but it is merely the last gasp. We see the failure of the same [hopeless romanticism] in 'the Green Harps of Ireland' and in Denmark. In the same way, this evocation of *Czech-ism* will founder on the reality of power politics.

For us, during the war that we just waged, this *Czech-ism* (despite all of the Germanophobia that characterized it) was more of an ally than an enemy. An imperially united and Austria - minded people, would have had an easy time organizing a people's war behind our back, which, though it would not have altered the outcome, could easily have increased our losses. This did not happen because the German and Czech elements of the population could not unite in a common cause. With regard to the Czechs, an eyewitness in the theatre of the war could write, 'I must finally and openly state, that I never believed I would find such a total lack of loyalty to the Empire as here in Bohemia. There may well be blind, fanatical hatred of the enemy and heresy, but here I find only loyalty and piety for *Bohemian kings and Bohemian deeds*.'

The entire kingdom of Bohemia (which we have tried to sketch previously) was not the theatre of the war, only its eastern half, and the decisive blow fell on only half of this half, in the northeast. The southeastern half was only traversed.

Bordered to the south by other lands of the Habsburg crown, bounded on the west by Bavaria and never seriously exposed on that side to Prussia, the north and northeastern part of Bohemia was always the most strategically significant, because it was the only part that was seriously exposed. It is here that we find most of the battlefields and fortresses of Bohemia.[42] However, as elsewhere (for example we think of the great Saxon plain), the most important locations for war, and therefore the most frequently visited by war, are also the most developed. It is here that commerce and industry, more than anywhere else, have their place. Despite the friction of the nationalities that is the land's worst enemy, the intellectual vitality, energy and fertility of the land, has turned large areas of the upper Elbe, for example around Königgrätz, into some of the most intensely populated in all of Germany.

And just as it is noted for its fertility, this stretch of land is also characterized by scenic beauty. This beauty is concentrated along the rivers that flow from the mountains to the Elbe, especially along the Iser. Constrained in its upper course by baroque rock formations, the river soon broadens into the plain. Here with little islands in its midst, there flowing below ruined castles, the banks of this river provide constantly changing and always attractive pictures. Especially beautiful is the stretch of railway between Eisenbrod and Turnau. We can best depict the beauties of this landscape and its uniqueness with excerpts from a letter that was written almost immediately after the great events and expatiates over 'the land and its people':

> I have now driven through this region between the Elbe and the Iser for eight days, that has been the subject of so much negative talk of late, and if you ask me how I found it to be, I must say that I have formed the most pleasing impression.
>
> Nowhere have I come across a lack of hospitality, brutishness, degenerate behaviour or depravity. Allow me to describe the landscape, the villages and cities, and also the people as I have found them. Despite all that may be lacking (and I shall point out what is lacking), this is a blessed land, a land the senses may feast themselves upon, an alluring piece of the earth, and over it all there is something heavenly in the atmosphere that proclaims, 'This is historic a land!' Thus, did I find it in Brandeis and Münchengrätz, in Sobotka and Gitschin. Jung Buntzlau is most beautifully situated, with its row of houses and its *Castell* [fortified Barracks] looking down in to the Iser valley.
>
> The fertility of the land also gives it a unique agricultural character. As a result of its highly productive soil, broad grasslands are largely absent. The numerous villages on the roadside or in the fields are more reminiscent of lower Saxony, and the rich Bohemian landscape, especially near the Elbe, presents a picture similar to that of the Oder hills in the *Oderbruch*,[43] a carpet of fields and villages.
>
> So much for the outward appearance of the Bohemian villages. The question remains what are they like when you walk into one, how do they function? Well, they are at least better than their reputation. There are no large houses with stately porches and walled verandas, there are no bay windowed towers and balconies. Indeed, in nine

---

42 Author's Note: Here, in this northeast quarter of the land lie Josephstadt, Königgrätz and Theresienstadt. On both sides of the Elbe, the battlefields of Soor and Czaslau, of Lowositz, Prague and Kolin. Even at Chlum there were earlier encounters.

43 Tr. Note: The *Oderbruch* is a low lying, originally marshy area bordering the River Oder extending from Oderberg and Bad Freienwalde in the north, to Lebus in the south, in Mark Brandenburg.

cases out of ten, there is no tile roof and the old fashioned moss covered thatch sits on a low, small windowed blockhouse built of horizontal timbers. However, although one seldom sees a conspicuous new building rising above its neighbours (as is so characteristic of our own villages), indicative of increasing prosperity, neither does one meet the opposite. The picture of wealth may be lacking, but so is that of poverty, and even the begging that could indicate poverty, and undoubtedly is a plague on the land, appears to me in many cases, more of a bad custom, more like an indolent avoidance of work rather than actual need and deprivation. Perhaps the picturesqueness that seems inherent in everything in this beautiful land like an inalienable dowry, has concealed the magnitude of this need, and the vine covered houses and huts that one glimpses through the innumerable green fruit trees, and the gracious, half dressed women and children, have blinded me to it. Even the picturesque has the power to corrupt.

Just as picturesque as the Bohemian villages are the Bohemian towns, to the extent that I have come to know them in the northeastern part of the land. They are in no way impaired by the fact that they are not large. They are small, but they are not insignificant. On the contrary, all are striking, and the Ring [the town square] gives even the smallest little town an air of greatness. Here are the churches and the town hall. In the center a *Mariensäule* [a tall column with a statue of the Virgin Mary on its top], with arcades or arbors surrounding the square and adding to the imposing impression of the whole. One senses something of an old culture here, ancient connections are evident with the south, with Italy.

A Bohemian village.

In the Ring one also finds the *hostinec*, the inn. Just as everything here is typical, so too is the inn. It is large and roomy; a broad hall separates the guest rooms on the left from the kitchen on the right, whose hearth fire burns constantly and whose steaming fatty vapours pervade the house. The *hostinec* keeps no culinary secrets. If the fragrance is insufficient to reveal what is cooking, then the eye sees it, for everything, the baking and roasting, even the distasteful process of stuffing the sausages, takes place before the eyes of the guests, indeed with a certain ostentation that says, 'Here I am, I have nothing to hide from the light of day.' Just as interesting as the kitchen is the public room. Generally extending for the entire depth of the house, the front is sunny, the back, dark and shaded. People choose their place in the light or in the dark as they please. Broad, leather covered benches extend along the walls with sturdy, massive tables before them. Everything exhibits that smoke darkened tone, that unsought for patina that so well clothes a public room and makes it so homely. And this feeling of homeliness is what matters. Our big city hotels lack what provides this feeling of contentment, of being 'at home'. They give us glitter instead. The guest may consider himself lucky if he finds courtesy, but he will certainly not find homeliness. There is no elegance in this place, no gilded moldings, no expensive pictures. Whatever art hangs on the walls is only passable, but it is entirely right and goes perfectly with the long, dimly lit table from whose lower end the bottles will be cleared away to make room for a steaming bowl of mulled Melniker and upper Hungarian wine.

A Bohemian Inn.

The common complaint one encounters is that of uncleanliness, but now a word about this too. To me there is some truth in this, but it depends on who makes it. Many of those whom I have heard complain, would do well to first sweep before their own door. Certainly, nobody has a right to describe a Bohemian *hostinec* as uncivilised, on the contrary. The food is, all in all, superb. Coffee, white bread and butter are good, the beer, as in neighbouring Bavaria, is sheer bliss, the pastries a delicacy. The wild game is excellent and the meat dishes wholesome. The mode of serving gives rise to some concerns, there is no argument about that. The table linen more often comes from the press than from the cupboard [everyday quality, not the best]. The luxury of water and a hand towel is still unknown, and the one washbasin principle is still rigorously maintained. But how many small towns, even in the praiseworthy north [Germany], have not successfully broken free from this practice? So much for villages and towns, for the Ring and the *hostinec*. How about a word regarding the people? I have not found them that bad. Friend or foe, the truth does them credit. Whatever their antipathies may be, the Czechs are companionable and friendly. Whenever we asked for information, we were generally provided with it courteously. Where, out of justified patriotism, this obligingness was not shown, there was a certain reserved attitude, but this reserved attitude never took the form of a direct refusal. Now and then something like hatred burned in their eyes. They looked sharply at us, looked us up and down and seemed to want to say, 'We shall meet again,' but all the resentment that may have been simmering inside did not prevent them from giving a quiet answer to the calmly stated question. There was no trace of trickery, of intentional misleading and such like games. Even the poorest folk were always ready to provide a drink of water. The outstanding trait in the character of the people seems to me to be a shy, softly spoken, gently expressed, civility. Everyone gives the impression of moving round on stocking feet, while the Prussian walk has entirely too much of boots and spurs. The Czechs, judging by their appearance, are refined people. They have, 'proprieties' and these proprieties incline the more or less propriety free northern Germans to speak of falseness and deceit.

Generally, in the northeastern corner of Bohemia that formed the actual theatre of war and that is the exclusive basis for my description, it is doubly incorrect to attribute any unseemliness that may have occurred, to the Czech nature, to its moral inferiority or to racial hatred. This northeastern corner of Bohemia, as I have already said, is the very part of the land where Bohemian and German live most completely together. Indeed, near Saxony and Silesia it is like Germany, and Trautenau and Reichenberg are German cities.

We have nothing to add to this description. Perhaps in the attempt to present the truth, it has, here and there, been 'truer' than the truth itself. Through what sort of rose tinted glasses the writer of the letter (from which we have extracted this description), may have looked, and however many indefensible things may have escaped his eye, it is not, as some have erroneously tried to depict, an uncultured land of need and of misery, into which our battalions descended from the Lausitzer and Silesian mountains. It was a smiling garden, a parkland, on which the dice of fate had fallen.

The Prussian plan, General von Moltke

We return to the army.

The occupation of Saxony (like the simultaneous occupation of Hannover and Hesse) ended the prelude to war, whose first, quickly concluded act, had been the crossing of the Eider [in Schleswig - Hostein] by *General* von Manteuffel.

Now, at the conclusion of the prelude, we stand along an obtuse angle at the bastion of northern Bohemia, with the *Riesen Gebirge* on the left, the *Lausitzer Gebirge* on the right, ready to descend in long columns through the mountain passes from Silesia and Saxony into the Bohemian basin.

The entirety of the army, part of it organized in corps, part organized in divisions (as we will explain later) formed three main groups, three separate armies:

> **2nd Army** (Crown Prince Friedrich Wilhelm) on the Silesian border, formed the left wing.
> **1st Army** (Prince Friedrich Karl) in the Saxon *Oberlausitz*, formed the center.
> **Elbe Army** (*General* Herwarth von Bittenfeld) to the right of the latter, formed the right wing.

Separately (that was the plan), these three armies were to march through the various passes along the border, advance concentrically and link up for the decisive battle, presumably on the plateau between Gitschin and Königgrätz. It is known with what precision and what success this plan (to which we will return) was carried out. It was the work, the idea of *General* von Moltke.

Helmuth Karl Bernhard *Freiherr* von Moltke was born on 26th October 1800, in Parchim, Mecklenburg. Von Moltke received his early education in the house of his father, who had served in the Möllendorf Regiment and died as a Royal Danish *Generallieutenant*. His father had bought an estate in Holstein and [von Moltke] remained there until his twelfth year. In 1811 he was taken to Copenhagen with his elder brother, where he spent six years at the *Landcadetten Institut* [Danish military cadet school]. There the youngster lived under strict discipline and became accustomed early on to all sorts of deprivation. Seldom was there any youthful lightheartedness. On 22nd January 1818, von Moltke was named a page of the King of Denmark with the rank of an officer and remained such until 1st January 1819. On that day he entered the Danish Infantry Regiment Oldenburg. On 5th January 1822, von Moltke left the Danish service to transfer to the Prussian army that was to form his enduring home. Here, on a broader field, the talents of the young officer could more richly develop than had hitherto been possible.

On 12th March von Moltke became the youngest *Secondelieutenant* in the 8th *Infanterie (Leib) Regiment* and was posted to the garrison in Frankfurt *am Oder*. He graduated from the *Kriegschule* [war college] in Berlin just at the time his parents lost their estate through a series of misfortunes. After his return to the regiment he was entrusted with command of the Divisional School, and thence to the topographical survey department of the General Staff. In this position he took part in mapping the provinces of Silesia and Poland. On 30th March 1833, he was promoted to *Premierlieutenant* and was transferred to the General Staff, and on 30th March 1835, promoted *Hauptmann* [captain]. In that same year (on 23rd September) he traveled to

Constantinople where he was tasked with the instruction and organization of Turkish troops, and later, assisted by four Prussian officers, succeeded in accomplishing this extremely difficult mission. After four years absence von Moltke returned from Turkey in August 1838. During this period, he gathered a wealth of experience and was decorated by the Sultan (*Nischan Orden* with diamonds and sword of honour) and also by King Friedrich Wilhelm III with the *Orden pour le mérite*, for his outstanding contribution to the 1838 Campaign in Asia Minor.

After this period von Moltke anonymously published an account of his experiences in Turkey and a military historical work, *Der russisch- türkische Feldzug von 1828-1829* [Russian-Turkish Campaign of 1818-1829]. This last appeared under his name. His writing is remarkable for the clarity of its description and the acuteness of its military judgement, thus proving it to be the product of a military thinker as well as of an experienced soldier. Von Moltke's stay in Turkey was also useful for cartographic purposes. After the battle of Nisib in Asia Minor, von Moltke studied this area in order to improve the extremely incomplete maps, covering approximately

7,500 English miles in his journeys of exploration. He traversed the Mesopotamian deserts, studied the passage of the Euphrates through the Kurdish mountains and floated down the Euphrates on inflated camel skins, just like Xenophon. The passage of time had left no trace in this area. The tribes that inhabit the mountains of Kurdistan isolate themselves from the influence of civilization and kill every European they encounter. Before von Moltke, it can be proven that only Xenophon had observed the passage of the Euphrates [through these mountains]. Hitherto all travelers had fallen victim to the barbarism of the local inhabitants.

Moltke.

After von Moltke was promoted to *Major* on 12th April 1842, he married *Fraulein* von Burt, from Holstein. He lived in Rome from 1845 to 1846 and served as personal adjutant to the ailing Prince Heinrich of Prussia. His '*Contorni die Roma,*' which remains incomplete, is a product of this sojourn. After the death of the prince, to whom *Major* von Moltke had been a loyal companion, he was transferred to Magdeburg where he remained for seven years. On 22nd August 1848, he became Chief of Staff of IV Army Corps. On 26th September 1850, he was promoted to *Oberstlieutenant*, on 2nd December 1851, to *Oberst.*

On 1st September 1855, he was named first personal adjutant of Prince Friedrich Wilhelm of Prussia, during which time he attended the marriage of the prince with the Royal Princess[44] in Balmoral. He spent the next year with the prince in Breslau and accompanied him on several more occasions to England. On 9th August 1856, he was promoted to *Generalmajor* and on 29th October 1857, he exchanged his former position for command of the General Staff of the Army. On 18th September 1858, he was named Chief of the General Staff. He remained in this position and the gradual increase and reorganization of the General Staff is essentially recognized as his work.

General von Moltke played a major role in the Schleswig - Holstein war. After the storming of Düppel, various personnel changes were made to the army in Schleswig and Jutland. Von Moltke worked with *Feldmarschall* Wrangel on a plan for landing on Fünen, which might well have been achieved, but could only be accomplished with the help of the Austrians since the Prussian forces were in Sundewitt and in Jutland, while the Austrians were on the Schleswig Jutland border, at Kolding. Command over a mixed corps was offered to *Feldmarschalllieutenant* von Gablenz, but however much the daring nature of the expedition appealed to his intrepid nature, the landing was too remote from the special interests of the Vienna cabinet for it to be carried out. Therefore, the only remaining option was the attack on Alsen and the complete occupation of Jutland. In 1859 von Moltke was promoted to *Generallieutenant*. On 8th June 1866, shortly before the outbreak of hostilities, he was named *General der Infanterie*.

That year, 1866, would provide him with the opportunity to fully develop his outstanding abilities. As we will demonstrate, his was the strategic thinking that initiated and concluded this glorious war. And yet despite a series of successes such as military history can hardly match, this thinking has not escaped sharp criticism. Abroad he has been repeatedly condemned, while at home, his correctness has at least been doubted. Rivalry and the blind adherence to doctrine, which are nowhere so endemic as in the realm of strategy, have not withheld their criticism. Particularly the 'young and old Napoleons' of the Austrian army, have endeavoured to prove that, 'the strategic calculations of the Prussian military command were hardly more than mediocre.' This relative judgement concerns itself, in every case, with Moltke's basic concept of, 'separating the overall body and approach of the army into three, then uniting these three axes of advance at one focal point.' For our part, we are deeply convinced of the wisdom of this plan, in contrast with the fashionable axiom that speaks of, 'unconditional concentration,' and an, 'advance with the entire strength.' It seems questionable to us, whether such a maxim can be elevated forevermore to the status of strategic, 'First Principle.' It is only correct for as long as it works, and we might venture the opinion that this, 'First Principle,' at least in its exclusivity, was shattered during the war of 1866. We do not set out to *correct* this difficult question, but

---

44   Tr. Note: Princess Victoria, daughter of Queen Victoria and Prince Albert.

two points strike the layman. First of all, in accordance with the time served rule that, 'getting jammed up is even worse than being split up,' the *terrain* might raise the separation of forces to the highest priority. However, entirely aside from this point, whose significance should not be underrated, it also appears to us that a right angled formation, or a semi-circular formation, obviously not too large in its extent, provides the possibility of envelopment, of encircling the enemy and thereby achieving a rapid overall result such as can never be attained by a concentrated frontal attack, that strikes the enemy head on, but does not prevent him from escaping to the right of left. Nobody can deny that Moltke's plan might have failed! A plan never produces victory by itself, no matter how clear the thinking, no matter how correct the calculations may be. However, a lucid plan, even though it is not victory in itself, is a promise of victory. Like an electric spark it pervades the body, stimulates it and thereby fills the whole with energetic life. Only the truly inspired concept has this capacity.

Our opinion, which we recorded in the first months after the war, has subsequently been confirmed by a judgement from an authoritative source:

The Austrians,' it states, 'have described our Prussian army leadership as mediocre. That it may have been. One seldom attains the *ideal* in the complicating element of war, but even the mediocre can (as success has shown) still attain the objective. The junction of the Prussian armies at the right moment was never, at least by the Prussian General Staff, viewed as an especially brilliant or erudite concept. It was the rationally conceived and energetically conducted solution to an unfavourable but unavoidable situation. Our strategy has been criticized because, before the start of the campaign, two or three armies were positioned separately instead of concentrating all the forces in the Lausitz. We can only respond to this criticism by pointing out that no time could be lost in the concentration of the Prussian army (that was only ordered at such a late date). More railroads led to two (or three) assembly areas than to a single one, and however much one might like the theory of, 'concentrating all the forces,' in the event, a rich province like Silesia could never be left entirely defenseless on the border of a concentrating enemy.

The indisputable advantage of interior lines of operation (which accrued to the Austrian army as a result of its concentration), is only valid so long as there is sufficient space to engage one enemy force, while the other is still several marches distant, so that there is time to smash one, and then turn against the other, which in the meantime, has merely been observed. If however, this space (as was true almost from the start of operations) is such that one can no longer attack the first enemy without running the danger of simultaneously having to deal with the second, who may fall on your flank or rear, then the strategic advantage of interior lines of operation is transformed into the tactical disadvantage of envelopment.

If we had concentrated our entire armed forces in the Lausitz, then on a front extending from Torgau to Görlitz, our depth would have extended all the way back to Berlin and Frankfurt *am Oder*. All of the passable roads that lead from this region into Bohemia, crowd together in a narrow space 23 miles wide when they cross the mountains between Rumburg and Friedland. The sheer valley walls of the *Schandauer* and the *Sandsteingebirges* on either side prevent any greater breadth. Accordingly, in an advance through this pass, the leading division could come against the enemy without the possibility of any support from those echeloned two or three days behind. Such a narrow concentration of great masses is itself a calamity. It can only be justified and recommended if it leads immediately to the battle. It is dangerous to deploy from [such a concentration] in the face of the enemy and impossible, in the long run, to persist in it.

It is the difficult task of a good army commander, to maintain the separate condition of his forces *while assuring the possibility of their concentration at the correct time.* Therefore, there can be no general rule. Every time it will be different.

Once more, we can see no advantage that would have accrued to us if a Prussian army of over 200,000 men had been concentrated in the forests and swamps of the Lausitz, on the contrary. Furthermore, we believe that it would have greatly simplified the supply, quartering and approach march of the *Austrian* army, if at the start of the campaign, instead of being concentrated in a single main group [at Olmutz], it had been concentrated in two groups, at Olmütz and Prague, entirely aside from the strategic advantages that would have arisen from the presence of a significant army massed in northern Bohemia.

It would be difficult to deny the truth of this statement.

The Austrian plan

Offensive or defensive? This question was weighed on both sides. Neither of the two commands could say for sure which role [offense or defense] would be theirs. Only the Confederation resolution of the 14th and the resulting invasion of Saxony (on the 16th) clarified the situation.

From that day on the Prussians took the offensive, the Austrians the defensive. The latter, if they did not want to break out from Moravia into Silesia, and march on Berlin on the left of our army while we advanced on Vienna, were left with no other choice than the defensive. For a moment it appears that there was indecision as to whether the defensive battle would be fought in Moravia, between Olmütz and Brünn, or in Bohemia between the Iser and the Elbe. On approximately the 19th, Benedek opted for the latter. On the 20th, the six corps that were concentrated on the Moravian railways moved out in a march that, until the arrival of the main body of the army, had only the Saxons and the 1st Corps (Clam-Gallas) for its protection.

Benedek's plan, as it now stood, was as follows. During the advance, the main army was divided into two parts, a smaller part (two corps), and a larger part (four corps). With the smaller part detached to the right, the larger part would proceed with its advance toward the north [west]. Clam-Gallas and the Saxons would then link up with it, and now increased to six corps, it would deliver a decisive blow against our 1st and Elbe Armies. After this battle the army would swing to the east. The two corps that had been thrown out to the right would disengage, and in a second battle, defeat, or as the case might be, destroy the army of the Crown Prince.

Operations conformed to this plan, but it miscarried. It would be incorrect however, to attribute this failure to the plan, as one flawed from the very start by confused thinking. Benedek's plan, as we have briefly outlined, was in no way to be condemned outright. It was clearly based more on the actual situation, more on personal evaluations than on theory, and that is more usually a matter for praise than for blame. It is possible that a concentration of the army in Bohemia instead of Moravia (which as we shall see, was more the result of circumstance than choice), might have provided significant advantages. Furthermore, it is highly probable that it would have been better to roll up the individual corps of the 2nd Army as they emerged from the mountain passes, than to march past the enemy on the flank (the Crown Prince [2nd Army]) in order to reach the enemy in front (Prince Friedrich Karl [1st Army and Elbe Army]). Granted, all that. Nevertheless, however open we may be to these considerations, even though the plan tempted danger, it was still more bold than bad, indeed it was so good a plan that had it succeeded, it would certainly have been greatly admired. It was denied that success. The plan failed for two reasons. Firstly, our great tactical superiority, in which the needle gun played a not insignificant roll. Secondly, a multitude of limitations that in short, one is accustomed to describing as, 'the Austrian system.'

It was by no means for lack of intellectual capacity that the Austrian command failed, but rather it was a matter of morale, and the lack of clear, decisive, well thought out execution. Primarily it foundered, not due to an offense against so called fundamental principles, but on the 'system,' on excessive secrecy and know it all behaviour, on rivalry and foolish recklessness, on mistrust and egotism. Other factors also contributed.

It is true that, in the course of events, especially from the 28th onwards, the situation more resembled a chaos of plans than one 'plan.' However, this confusion was already the product of accumulating failures and does not in itself cast doubt upon the correctness of the original strategic thinking. We shall, in later sections, find opportunity to return to this question.

The Campaign in the Iser Region

The Elbe and the 1st Army to Gitschin.

On 20th June, as we said, Benedek marched the main body of his army from Moravia. The objective was the Iser line, or the plateau of Gitschin extending south of it. Here the *Feldzeugmeister* hoped to find Prince Friedrich Karl (1st and Elbe Armies), to pin [his forces] and to destroy [them].

Given the significant distance from Olmütz, it might well be impossible for the main army to reach Gitschin, or even the Iser, before the 27th or 28th, in which case a single Austrian army corps (Clam-Gallas) and the attached Cavalry Division Edelsheim[45] might be faced with the

---

45   Author's Note: Cavalry Division Edelsheim consisted of:
    Brigade *Oberst* Appel:
        Windischgrätz Dragoons (Bohemia),
        Liechtenstein Hussars,
        4 pdr Horse Artillery Battery.
    Brigade *Oberst Graf* Wallis:
        Savoy Dragoons (Bohemia),
        King of Prussia Hussars
        4 pdr Horse Artillery Battery.
    Brigade *Oberst* Fratricievic:
        Radetzky Hussars,
        Hesse - Kassel Hussars
        4pdr Horse Artillery Battery.

difficult task of having to repulse or delay the advance of an enemy that was already, on the 21st, at the Bohemian border with 120,000 men.

It should be noted here that 1st corps (Clam-Gallas), had been brought up to a strength of five brigades since the appearance on 16th June of Brigade Abele [formerly Brigade Kalik, from Holstein] (22nd Jäger Battalion and Regiments IR 72 Ramming and IR 35 Graf Khevenhüller*).* The composition of this corps makes it clear that the intention, so far as possible, was to leave the defense of Bohemia to its own native sons. Among the thirty five battalions of the corps, thirteen were Bohemian. Similarly, Cavalry Division Edelsheim included two Bohemian regiments, the Savoy and Windischgrätz Dragoons. Similar considerations may have placed *Graf* Clam-Gallas in command of the corps. With rich estates in northern Bohemia, he not only had to defend his country, but also his own holdings. His competence was admittedly much mistrusted, and the old saying was again making the rounds, 'Gallas, the army drum! You only hear of him when he is beaten.' Anecdotes, less than complimentary, passed from mouth to mouth. Errors at Solferino were revived. However, it seems certain that rancour and political antagonism played a large part in this judgement. Much as we are inclined, wherever possible, to be on the side of the *Feldzeugmeister*, here we must, in the feud between Benedek and Clam-Gallas, to a considerable degree place ourselves on the side of the latter. We shall return to this point after the Battle of Gitschin.

To carry out the mission that had been assigned to Clam-Gallas' corps, calmly, firmly and prudently, was not a small thing. However, after the arrival of the Saxons[46] (on the 22nd and 23rd), the Iser Army was increased to about 60,000 men, of which the Crown Prince of Saxony assumed command. Nevertheless, the situation of this army remained extremely difficult if the enemy advanced rapidly, and circumstances delayed the approach of the main body, as indeed happened. A definite order to fall back on the main army with light fighting and specifying the point to fall back to, would have simplified the situation and made it less difficult. However, specific orders were not Benedek's style, and thus a series of engagements ensued, first on the Iser line and then to hold the position at Gitschin. These decimated and deeply shook Clam-Gallas' corps and could probably have been avoided if precise orders been issued for a well-considered, firmly executed plan.

As we describe these engagements, we shall consider those fought by the 1st and Elbe Armies separately, or (as at Münchengrätz) by both together, and in which, initially, they faced only individual regiments of Cavalry Division Edelsheim, then (at Hühnerwasser and Podol), Brigades Leiningen and Poschacher, and finally (at Gitschin), nearly the entire Austro-Saxon Iser Army.

---

46   The Saxon Corps consisted of four Brigades, each with five battalions:
  1st Infantry Brigade (Crown Prince); *Oberst* **von Vorberg [red facings]:**
      Infantry Battalions 1,2,3,4 and 1st Jäger Battalion.
  2nd Infantry Brigade; *Generalmajor* **von Carlowitz [yellow facings]:**
      Infantry Battalions 5,6,7,8 and 2nd Jäger Battalion.
  3rd Infantry Brigade; *Oberst* **von Hake [black facings]:**
      Infantry Battalions 9,10,11,12 and 3rd Jäger Battalion.
  4th (*Leib*) Infantry Brigade; *Oberst* **von Hausen [white facings]:**
      Infantry Battalions 13,14,15,16 and 4th Jäger Battalion.
  In addition, four cavalry regiments and ten batteries.
      The 1st and 4th Brigades formed Division Stieglitz, the 2nd and 3rd Division Schimpff.

The Elbe Army, General Herwarth von Bittenfeld

The Elbe Army consisted of Westphalian and Rhineland troops of the 14th, 15th and 16th Divisions.

The individual divisions consisted of:

14th Division (*Generallieutenant Graf* Münster - Meinhövel)

Brigade Schwarzkoppen.
Infantry Regiment Nr. 16, *Oberst* Schwarz.
Infantry Regiment Nr. 56, *Oberst* von Dorpowski.
Brigade Hiller.
Infantry Regiment Nr. 17, *Oberstlieutenant* von Kottwitz.
Infantry Regiment Nr. 57, *Oberst* von der Osten.
Westphalian Jäger Battalion Nr. 7.
Divisional Cavalry.
Westphalian Dragoon Regiment Nr. 7, *Oberst* von Ribbeck.

15th Division (*Generallieutenant* von Canstein)

Brigade Stückradt.
Hohenzollern Fusilier Regiment Nr. 40, *Oberstlieutenant* von Zimmermann.
Infantry Regiment Nr. 65, *Oberst* du Troffel.
Brigade Glasenapp.
Infantry Regiment Nr. 28, *Oberst* von Gerstein - Hohenstein.
Infantry Regiment Nr. 68, *Oberst* von Gayl.
Divisional cavalry
King's Hussar Regiment Nr. 7, *Oberst* von Lindern.

16th Division (*Generallieutenant* von Etzel)

Brigade Schöler.
Infantry Regiment Nr. 29, *Oberst* Schuler von Senden.
Infantry Regiment Nr. 69, *Oberst* von Beyer.
Fusilier Brigade.
East Prussian Fusilier Regiment Nr. 33, *Oberst* von Wegerer.
Pomeranian Fusilier Regiment Nr. 34, *Oberst* von Schmeling.
Rheinisches Jäger Battalion Nr. 8.

[VIII Corps consisted of the 15th and 16th Infantry Divisions, 14th Infantry Division was one half of VII Corps]. The Elbe Army's cavalry consisted of the 8th Cuirassiers, the 5th and 7th Uhlans, and the 11th Hussars. Its artillery had 120 guns. At its head of all three divisions was *General* Herwarth von Bittenfeld, Commander in Chief of the entire Elbe Army.

Karl Eberhard Herwarth von Bittenfeld was born on 4th September 1796 at Grosswerther in the former *Grafschaft* Hohenstein (*Provinz Sachsen*).[47] Raised in the family home and at the *Gymnasium* in Brandenburg *a. H.*, he followed the family tradition and on 15th October 1811, the young Eberhard joined the Prussian Army. All of his forefathers had worn the soldier's jacket. His father had been wounded at Auerstädt. His grandfather fell at the head of his regiment at Kolin.

Eberhard von Herwarth entered the *Normal Infanterie Bataillon*. In 1812 he became *Portepee Fähnrich* [officer candidate entitled to wear the sword knot] and on 21 February 1813, he was commissioned. He was denied the opportunity to take part in the first battles of the war that soon broke out, because he was assigned to the *Ersatz* [replacement] battalion. Following the armistice however, he was transferred to the 2nd Foot Guards, which had been activated in the meantime, and he took part in the campaigns of 1813 and 1814, serving in the Fusilier Battalion of this regiment. Present at a number of engagements, on 30th March he participated in the assault on the Montmartre (Belleville), and was personally decorated in this action in which the 2nd Guards Regiment shone.

Returning to the Berlin garrison, he remained with the 2nd Guards Regiment from 1815 to 1835. In 1835, having been promoted on 30th March 1821 to *Hauptmann,* and named as company commander, he received command, now as *Major,* of the 2nd Battalion of the Guard Reserve Regiment (now the Guard Fusilier Regiment) that was garrisoned at Spandau, with which, in that same year, he took part in the Prussian – Russian review in Kalisch.

In 1839 he was entrusted with the command of the 1st Battalion of the 1st Foot Guards Regiment. In 1846 (as *Oberstlieutenant*) he commanded the *Kaiser* Franz Grenadier Regiment. Then on 30th March 1847, he was appointed commander of the 1st Guards Regiment, which a year later he led onto the streets of Berlin.

As *Oberst* since 10th May, von Herwarth remained in command of his regiment until the spring of 1850. In June of that year he assumed command of the combined brigade in Division Bonin, which as a result of the impending conflict with Austria, was concentrated at Kreuznach. In October he proceeded with his brigade to Hesse. Soon afterwards, he was placed in command of the Prussian occupation force in Frankfurt *am Main*. On 23rd March he was promoted to *Generalmajor*, in 1854 to Commander of the Confederation fortress of Mainz. In 1856 (in June) he was named commander of the 7th Division (Magdeburg). On 17th March 1863, he was promoted to *General der Infanterie*.

He participated in the 1864 war against Denmark, in which the 13th Infantry Division Wintzingerode (from the VII Army Corps), took part under the command of Prince Friedrich Karl of Prussia. In May of that year, after the Prince assumed supreme command of the Prussian army following the recall of *Feldmarschall Graf* von Wrangel, von Bittenfeld assumed command of the Prussian Combined I Army Corps (6th and 13th Infantry Divisions).

Since the London peace talks had produced no results, shortly before the expiry of the armistice with Denmark (26th June), the Combined Corps that had up to that point been in cantonments in Schleswig, was concentrated in Sundewitt to deliver the decisive blow by capturing the last territory in Schleswig that was still held by the Danes, the island of Alsen.

---

47   Tr. Note: More properly *Grafschaft* Hohnstein, in the Prussian *Provinz Sachsen*

The capture of the island of Alsen, to which there is practically nothing comparable in military history, resulted in the Peace Treaty that was concluded in Vienna between Denmark and the German Great Powers on 1st September 1864. On that most memorable day, His Majesty the King awarded the *pour le mérite* to the commander of the Combined Corps, and shortly thereafter, he was appointed *a la suite* of the 6th Westphalian Infantry Regiment Nr. 55, which had been given abundant opportunities to distinguish itself in that campaign. As a result of the Vienna Peace Treaty, a joint government of duchies was instituted between Prussia and Austria. *General* von Herwarth was given command over the Austro Prussian Corps that remained in occupation with headquarters in Kiel.

When, after the Gastein Convention, Prussia took over the administration of Schleswig and Austria that of Holstein, the previous joint military command was dissolved. *Generallieutenant* von Manteuffel was named Governor of Schleswig, *General* von Herwarth was called to Coblenz, on 29th June 1865, to become the Commanding Officer of VIII Army Corps. He now led this corps, as well as the 14th Division, against the enemy.

Austrian Hussar.

The Elbe Army from 22 to 26 June

The double fight at Hühnerwasser[48]

Five battalions strong, the advanced guard of the Elbe Army entered Bohemia. The composition of this force was as follows:

King's Hussar Regiment Nr. 7.
Rheinisches Jäger Battalion Nr. 8.
Fusilier Battalion from the 28th, 2nd Battalion from the 33rd, 2nd Battalion from the 40th, Fusilier Battalion from the 69th and two batteries.

Oberst von Gerstein - Hohenstein commanded the infantry, *Generalmajor* von Schöler the entire advance - guard. The border was crossed with a hurrah, the main body followed on directly.

The first march reached Schluckenau on the 22nd, Rumburg on the 23rd, Gross Mergenthal on the 24th and on the 25th, the village of Dorstrum. Nowhere was there any sign of the enemy. The formidable Gabel Pass, so frequently mentioned in the wars of the previous century, was left unoccupied. Only on the 26th did we meet them. We take the following passage from the letter of an *Unteroffizier* in the Hohenzollern Fusilier Regiment Nr. 40, describing the first peaceful day of the march:

'. . . On 22nd June at 6:00 in the morning we crossed the border. We proceeded via Hainspach, Schönay and Kaiserswalde. By 12:00 we were already in Schluckenau. We set up outposts and bivouacked in the marketplace. Food was brought. We could purchase beer and other small needs. To our great amazement our silver coins, small or big, were exchanged for paper money and every one of us curiously examined the little notes that represented ten *Kreuzer*. Now we were in Austria! From now on we had to get used to keeping an entire price list in our heads. The difference between paper and silver was immediately evident. I paid for my glass of beer with a silver *Thaler* and received one paper *thaler* and ten *Kreuzer* back . . . . On the 23rd, in Rumburg, we 'requisitioned' tobacco, filled our pouches, sat at the table and lit the first pipe full of Austrian tobacco . . . . On the 24th we reached the pass. We had reason to believe that the enemy would contest our passage as we crossed the crest, accordingly we marched in column of attack. Since there was no sign of the enemy however, we continued our march, and at about 10:00 we passed the '*hohe Lausch*', whose peak was entirely hidden by clouds. We bivouacked in Gross Mergenthal . . . . The 25th was very hot. In the course of the day an intense thunderstorm broke, and we were soaked by the time we reached Dorstrum. We bivouacked on a potato field, whose thoroughly soaked ground soon became a pond. We were close to some woods that provided us with wood and

---

48   Author's Note: This is the correct spelling, not 'Hünerwasser' or 'Hünnerwasser'. It is a literal translation of the Bohemian *kuri* (*Hühner* [chicken]) and *voda* (*Wasser* [water]). Granted, the road signs and the name board bear the designation '*Hünerwasser*' without the '*h*', but anyone who has traveled in Bohemia has experienced what the Bohemians do with correct German spelling!

brush to build shelters. The hastily constructed shelters provided us with some degree of protection from the rain that came down again in streams toward evening. On the 26th we had our first battle.'

We will now describe this battle (actually a double battle, one in the morning and another in the evening of the same day). Early on the 26th the advanced guard moved out from Dorstrum. The 3rd Squadron (*Rittmeister* von der Goltz) of the King's Hussars took the lead. The other troops followed with the 2nd Battalion of the 33rd Infantry Regiment, *Oberstlieutenant* von Marschall, in the lead. At 9:00 the 3rd Squadron reached the little town of Niemes. *Rittmeister* von der Goltz trotted on towards Hühnerwasser.

Hühnerwasser is approximately 4½ miles beyond Niemes. At first the road is open, then there are woods on both sides, and then it is open again. Then comes Hühnerwasser, at whose far side (thus toward Münchengrätz and the Iser River) the woods commence again. These woods on the near and far side of Hühnerwasser are the points that were contested, the near side of Hühnerwasser in the morning, the far side in the evening.

After passing through Niemes, when he again came into the open, *Rittmeister* von der Goltz ran into a squadron of Nicolaus Hussars between the town and the woods. He immediately attacked, sent them flying and took a number of prisoners, including two officers. Pursuing

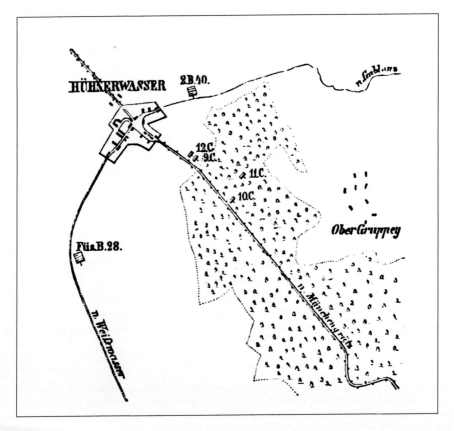

Sketch map of Hühnerwasser.

his advantage too enthusiastically, he came under volley fire from some enemy infantry that had lined the edge of the woods. He could go no further and the prisoners escaped. *Lieutenant Graf* Moltke fell from his horse, severely wounded, and was captured. The squadron fell back on Niemes, the infantry had to advance.

Generalmajor von Schöler issued the appropriate orders. The 2nd Battalion of the 33rd Regiment advanced at the double, the 8th Jäger Battalion followed. That sufficed and the enemy was driven from the outlying woods back to Hühnerwasser with practically no resistance, then on through the little village to the woods on the far side. There was no halting there either. Three of our battalions, in hot pursuit, immediately took up an outpost position on the far side of the village, two towards Weisswasser and Gablonz, the third (Fusilier Battalion Nr. 69) toward Münchengrätz. The remainder of the advance - guard, which had been reinforced at noon by the 1st and 3rd Battalions, 40th Regiment, took up alarm quarters [ready for an instant response] in Hühnerwasser.

Only now, after bringing in about 80 prisoners that had surrendered without resistance in the woods between Niemes and Hühnerwasser, and then in Hühnerwasser itself, was the identity of the enemy unit established. They were Italians from IR 38 Haugwitz, therefore it was evident that we were facing Brigade Leiningen, IR 38 Haugwitz, IR 33 Chulai [Hungarian] and the 32nd Feldjäger Battalion. Brigade Leiningen formed the left wing of the Austro - Saxon Iser Army[49] *Graf* Gondrecourt (the *Adlatus*[50] of Clam-Gallas) commanded operations at this location.

The midday and afternoon passed quietly. Fifty, even up to a hundred men were billeted in each house. All of the residents had fled, taking foodstuffs, livestock and everything movable with them. However, at least the men were under a roof for the first time since Dresden. Nevertheless, the evening peace was only the preliminary to a second, more serious encounter. It was almost expected. The woods before Hühnerwasser had been the scene of the morning's fighting. Now the woods on the far side of Hühnerwasser would be the scene of the evening fighting.

'Within these woods,' wrote a man of the 1st Battalion of the 40th Infantry Regiment, 'were our outposts. We ourselves belonged to the support battalions that had remained in the village. Rations were just being distributed when the alarm sounded and an orderly rushed in with a report that our outposts were under heavy attack. We all jumped up and everyone hastened to the site of the alarm. Already heavy skirmisher fire was audible from the woods that were a quarter of an hour distant, in six minutes our battalion was already advancing to support the outposts. The 33rd Fusiliers and the 8th Jägers (which had already joined the dance in the morning) advanced with us. We maintained contact between them. Two of our companies were

---

49   Author's Note: On the evening of the 25th, the entire Iser Army, with the exception of Brigade Ringelsheim, and several cavalry detachments that were skirmishing with our 1st Army, was concentrated in positions at Jung Bunzlau and Münchengrätz. (Brigade Ringelsheim, which had been detached to Teplitz to cover the approach of the Saxons, did not get back to Münchengrätz until the 26th.) Several attacks were launched from this Jung Bunzlau – Münchengrätz position against our two advancing armies (Elbe Army and 1st Army): Brigade Leiningen in the morning and again in the evening of the 26th at Hühnerwasser, and in the evening of the 26th, Brigade Poschacher against Podol. Then calm until the 28th.

50   Tr. Note: In the Austrian Army the *Adlatus* was more than just an assistant to the commanding officer. He was the pre-selected, on the spot replacement in the event the commander was killed or disabled.

sent forward in skirmish order, the other two companies followed behind, closed up in reserve, I was with the latter. The sporadic fire of the skirmishers was broken by the volleys of entire columns. Twigs rained down on us but we had no wounded. The men of the 33rd and the Jäger, who advanced at a faster pace, had the luck and the honour to get in on the last moments of the fighting, perhaps to be able to decide the outcome. We only followed on. Enemy dead and wounded lay on the road and in the hedges. The onset of darkness and the heavily overgrown terrain prevented further pursuit. On all sides signals recalled our riflemen and at about 9:00 we returned to our quarters to carry on with preparations for our meal.' So much for the letter. Let us now look at the fighting itself, whose din only reached the ears of our man of the 40th while it raged in the woods.

Jaegers in the wood.

Our three outpost battalions had taken positions such that the 2nd Battalion of the 40th Regiment, *Major* von Henning, was on the left, the Fusilier Battalion of the 69th Regiment, *Major* von Gulicki, was in the center, and the Fusilier Battalion of the 28th Regiment, *Major* Mettler was on the right. Sentries and pickets were posted, it was now 6:00pm.

It was at this hour that *Graf* Gondrecourt chose to attempt the recapture of Hühnerwasser. He placed himself at the head of the 32nd Feldjäger Battalion and one battalion of IR 33 Chulai, advanced down the Münchengrätz road into the woods (thus into the center of our position) and attacked the 10th and 11th Companies of the 69th Fusilier Battalion, who were furthest forward. The assault was powerfully delivered and those elements that were initially attacked fell back. But before they were forced out of the woods, two other companies (9th and 12th) came up in support, giving them a breather and taking up the fight. The enemy, in good positions and energetically led, fired volley after volley. The Fusilier battalion of the 69th Regiment had to hold its own in this fight, the losses began to mount.

The battalion adjutant (*Lieutenant* Albrecht) was wounded, yet there was still no firing from our side. An eyewitness wrote:

> One may well ask why we delayed, but the waiting was correct. The calm requisite for an effective volley had not yet arrived. A misdirected volley would have filled our own people with self - doubt. Moreover, the volleys of the enemy that passed over us in the trees, convinced us that their fire was more noisy than accurate. With every new volley the initial frightening impression diminished, and to the same degree, our own confidence increased. This was exactly why we refused to yield to the impatience of our own men, who were urging us to let them fire. We required them to follow our orders under enemy fire, thereby establishing the desired discipline. The success would soon be evident. Already, after the enemy Jäger's third volley, our men could be heard making mocking remarks, like, 'What can those fellows over there be aiming at?' Now, however, came the command, 'Four hundred paces, *kleine Klappe*,[51] aim, fire! And our bullets whistled through the woods. Within a few seconds the powder smoke cleared, and we could see a number of our enemies lying on the ground, their officers trying to rally the men who were shaken by these losses. But they were not given much time for that. A second volley tore into the packed ranks of the Austrians, further devastating them, and it sufficed to send all those who had not yet been hit fleeing, terrified, to both sides in the woods.
>
> It seemed that new [Austrian] companies were brought up and briefly resumed the fight, but now the time had come when, from the right and left, we were joined by the men of the 28th and 40th, and only a few moments later, by the supports hastening from Hühnerwasser, the 40th (1st and 3rd Battalions), the 33rd and 8th Jäger, who in their initial charge, hurled the enemy back over the Teperberg and all the way to Ober Gruppay. On our side, *Hauptmann* Moldenhauer of the 40th Regiment was killed. Three officers were wounded. Our total losses were 4 officers, 46 men.

The enemy's losses (relatively) must have been extremely heavy. When a day and a half later, in the early morning coolness, our men resumed their advance, the terrain that we passed through presented a sad sight:

> The grainfield beyond Hühnerwasser showed clear signs of the fighting. The stems at the edge of the spruce woods, through which our road led, were downtrodden.

---

51   The infantry models of the Dreyse *Zündnadelgewehr*, or needle gun, had rear sights with range adjustments by flipping up rear sight *Klappen*, or leaves. The rear sight on the *Füsiliergewehr M/60*, for the 1855 cartridge with *Langblei*, or ovoid bullet, had a *Standvisier* (fixed sight) for 300 *Schritt* (about 250 yards), a *kleine Klappe* (little leaf) for 450 *Schritt* (about 375 yards) and a *grosse Klappe* (large leaf) with a *Kreissegment* (lower opening) for 600 *Schritt* (about 500 yards) and an *obere Kimm* (upper notch in the top) for 800 *Schritt* (about 655 yards). Thus, the command, *kleine Klappe*, or 'small leaf' meant flip up the shorter rear sight for 450 *Schritt*, or 375 yards. (Wirtgen, Rolf, 'Das *Zündnadelgewehr*,' p. 150. See also von Witzleben, vol. I, p. 412.)

Everywhere lay Austrian *Jäger* hats (the bunches of feathers already torn off). Scattered among them were mess tins, knapsacks, gaiters and broken rifle stocks. We strode through the grainfield hoping to find dead or wounded. However, the field had already been searched and all the living removed. Farther on the woods bordered the highway. On both sides lay the corpses of Austrian *Jäger*, the pale, bloodless faces covered by sympathetic hands with bits of uniform or spruce boughs. Right at the road lay a *Jägerlieutenant*, a youngster, his sword still in his right hand. Farther into the woods others lay in the underbrush, there where they had crawled and died. In the early light of dawn, we passed them by.'

Such was the field, early on the 28th.

The 1st Army of Prince Friedrich Karl

On that day [the 28th], the Elbe Army proceeded toward Münchengrätz. Even before it was noon this important point was taken in cooperation with the 1st Army. Before we describe this day of battle, let us join the 1st Army (Prince Friederich Karl) on its advance to the Iser. The 1st Army stood on the border, immediately to the left of the Elbe Army (which we have accompanied in the previous chapter as far as the action at Hühnerwasser), and on the same day (the 23rd), advanced into Bohemia. Before we follow it in its advance, we shall first give its composition. It consisted of three army corps, the II, III and IV, and a cavalry corps specially activated for this war under the command of Prince Albrecht (father).

II Army Corps (Pomerania)

Commanding General: *Generallieutenant* **von Schmidt.**
Chief of Staff: *Generalmajor* **von Kameke.**
Commander of Artillery: *Generalmajor* **Hurrelbrinck.**
Commander of Pioneers: *Oberst* **Leuthaus.**

3rd Division (*Generallieutenant* **von Werder**)

Brigade Januschowsky.
 Grenadier Regiment King Friedrich Wilhelm IV, *Oberst* von Reichenbach.
 5th Pomeranian Infantry Regiment Nr. 42, *Oberst* von Borcke.
Brigade Winterfeld.
 3rd Pomeranian Infantry Regiment Nr. 14, *Oberst* von Stahr.
 7th Pomeranian Infantry Regiment Nr. 54, *Oberstlieutenant* von Kurowski.
 Pomeranian Jäger Battalion Nr. 2.
Divisional Cavalry.
 Blücher Hussars Nr. 5, *Oberst* von Flemming.

4th Division (*Generallieutenant* Herwarth von Bittenfeld)

Brigade Schlabrendorff.
2nd Pomeranian Grenadier Regiment (Colberg) Nr. 9, *Oberst* von Sandrart.
6th Pomeranian Infantry Regiment Nr. 49, *Oberst* von Wietersheim.
Brigade Hanneken.
4th Pomeranian Infantry Regiment Nr. 21, *Oberst* von Krane.
8th Pomeranian Infantry Regiment Nr. 61, *Oberst* von Michaelis.
Divisional Cavalry.
1st Pomeranian Uhlans Regiment Nr. 4, *Oberst* von Kleist.
Corps Reserve Artillery under *Oberst* von Puttkamer.
4 rifled batteries. In addition, 4 batteries with each division, a total of 72 guns.

III Army Corps (Brandenburg)

5th Division (*Generallieutnent* von Tümpling)

Brigade Schimmelmann.
1st Brandenburg Infantry Regiment (*Lieb*) Nr. 8, *Oberst* von Berger.
5th Brandenburg Infantry Regiment Nr. 48, *Oberst*, von Diringshofen.
Brigade Kamiensky.
2nd Brandenburg Grenadier Regiment Nr. 12, *Oberst* von Debschutz.
1st Posen Infantry Regiment Nr. 18, *Oberst* von Kettler.
Divisional Cavalry.
1st Brandenburg Uhlans Regiment Nr. 3, *Oberstlieutenant* von Tresckow.
Divisional Artillery.
4 rifled batteries under *Major* Rüstow.

6th Division (*Generallieutenant* von Manstein)

Brigade Gersdorff.
Brandenburg Fusilier Regiment Nr. 35, *Oberst* von Rothmaler.
7th Brandenburg Infantry Regiment Nr. 60, *Oberst* von Hartmann.
Brigade Kotze.
4th Brandenburg Infantry Regiment Nr. 24, *Oberst Graf* von Hacke.
8th Brandenburg Infantry Regiment Nr. 64, *Oberst* von Götz.
Brandenburg Jäger Battalion Nr. 3, *Major* von Witzleben.
Divisional Cavalry.
Brandenburg Dragoon Regiment Nr. 2, *Oberstlieutenant* Heinichen.
Divisional Artillery.
4 batteries under *Major* Roeckner.

IV Army Corps (Magdeburg – Thüringen)

7th Division *(Generallieutenant* von Fransecky)

Brigade Schwartzhoff.
1st Magdeburg Infantry Regiment Nr. 26, *Oberst Freiherr* von Medem.
3rd Magdeburg Infantry Regiment Nr. 66, *Oberst* von Blanckensee.
Brigade Gordon.
2nd Magdeburg Infantry Regiment Nr. 27, *Oberst* von Zychlinski.
4th Magdeburg Infantry Regiment Nr. 67, *Oberst* von Bothmer.
Divisional Cavalry.
Magdeburg Hussar Regiment Nr. 10, *Oberst* von Besser.
Divisional Artillery.
4 batteries under *Major* Weigelt.

8th Division *(Generallieutenant* von Horn)

Brigade Bose.
1st Thuringen Infantry Regiment Nr. 31, *Oberst* von Freyhold.
3rd Thuringen Infantry Regiment Nr. 71, *Oberst* von Avemann.
Brigade Stückradt.
4th Thuringen Infantry Regiment Nr. 72, *Oberst Graf* Gneisenau.
Magdeburg Jäger Battalion Nr. 4, *Oberstlieutenant* von Colomb.
Divisional Cavalry.
Thuringen Uhlans Regiment Nr. 6, *Oberstlieutenant Freiherr* von Langermann und Erlenkamp.
Divisional Artillery.
4 batteries under *Major* Heinrich.

Cavalry Corps *(General der Cavallerie* Prince Albrecht of Prussia)

1st Heavy Cavalry Brigade, *Generalmajor* **Prince Albrecht (son).**
Garde du Corps, Oberst Graf Brandenburg.
Guards *Cuirassier* Regiment, *Oberstlieutenant* von Lüderitz.
2nd Heavy Cavalry Brigade, *Generalmajor* **von Pfuel.**
Brandenburg *Cuirassier* Regiment (*Kaiser* Nicolaus) Nr. 6, *Oberst* von Rauch.
Magdeburg *Cuirassier* Regiment Nr. 7, *Oberst* von Hontheim. 3rd Heavy Cavalry Brigade, *Generalmajor* von der Goltz.
Pomeranian *Cuirassier* Regiment (*Königin*) Nr. 2, *Oberst* von Schaevenbach.
2nd Pomeranian Uhlans Regiment Nr. 9, *Oberst Freiherr* von Diepenbroick - Grüter.
1st Light Cavalry Brigade, *Generalmajor Baron* **von Rheinhaben.**
1st Guards Uhlans Regiment, *Oberst* von Colomb.
2nd Guards Uhlans Regiment, *Oberst Graf* Brandenburg.
1st Guards Dragoon Regiment, *Oberstlieutenant* von Barner.

2nd Light Cavalry Brigade, *Generalmajor* **Duke Wilhelm von Mecklenburg - Schwerin.**

   2nd Guards Dragoon Regiment, *Oberst* von Redern.

   Brandenburg Hussar Regiment (Zieten) Nr. 3,[52] *Oberstlieutenant* von Kalkreuth.

   2nd Brandenburg Uhlans Regiment Nr. 11, *Oberstlieutenant* Prince Hohenlohe - Ingelfingen.

3rd Light Cavalry Brigade, *Generalmajor Graf* **von der Gröben.**

   Neumärkisches Dragoon Regiment Nr. 3, *Oberstlieutenant* von Willisen.

   Thuringen Hussar Regiment Nr. 12, *Oberst Freiherr* von Barnekow.

Two brigades were detached from these six brigades, probably because it was realized in advance how difficult it would be to operate with such a mass of cavalry:

   The 1st Heavy Cavalry Brigade to the 2nd (Crown Prince) Army.
   The 3rd Heavy Cavalry Brigade to the II (*Pommern*) Army Corps.

Two divisions were formed from the remaining four brigades: Division Alvensleben and Division Hann. In addition, the Cavalry Corps had five horse artillery batteries, totaling 30 guns. As can be seen from this brief overview, the III and IV Army Corps had no special corps headquarters,[53] being directly under the command of the 1st Army. This High Command consisted of:

   Commander in Chief: Prince Friedrich Karl of Prussia.
   Chief of Staff: *Generallieutenant* von Voigts - Rhetz.
   General Quartiermeister: *Generalmajor* von Stülpnagel.
   Commander of Artillery: *Generalmajor* von Lengsfeld.
   Commander of Pioneers: *Generalmajor* Keiser.

Prince Friedrich Karl, son of Prince Carl of Prussia (brother of King Friedrich Wilhelm IV) was born in Berlin on 20th March 1828. Raised, as were all the princes of the royal household, for military service, he displayed his burning love of the army at an early age, and eagerly studied the life and the battles of the 'Great King' [Frederick the great]. When the First Danish War broke out in 1848, he was a *Hauptmann* on the staff of *General* Wrangel. He was present at the Battle of Schleswig where, right at the start, [*General* Wrangel] had to specifically order him to stop exposing himself to danger and to remain at his side. In the further course of the battle, by order of the Commander in Chief, the prince led the 2nd Kings [*Königs*] Regiment into the right flank of the enemy, a movement that was decisive for the day's outcome. In the campaign of 1849 in Baden, Prince Friedrich Karl served as a *Major* on the staff of his uncle, then the

---

52   Tr. Note: The Brandenburg Hussar Regiment (Zieten) of the Prussian, and later the Imperial German Army, was founded in 1730 and named after its first Colonel, Hans Joachim von Zieten.

53   Author's Note: The reason for this may have been that Prince Friedrich Karl, formerly commanding the III Army Corps, now commanded the 1st Army, while *General* von Schack, Commander of IV Corps, remained behind in Dresden as Governor of Saxony (Province and Kingdom).

Prince of Prussia, today King Wilhelm I, where he personally led a squadron of the 9th Hussars that was only 87 men strong, against 400 Baden infantry. He was severely wounded in the arm and shoulder.

His adjutant, *Premierlieutenant* von Busche-Münch, fell at his side, mortally wounded by five bullets. In the ensuing years the prince rose through the military ranks to *Generallieutenant*. In 1858 he was briefly in Paris. On 18th October 1861, he was promoted to *General der Cavallerie* and named Commander of III Army Corps, which he led in the great autumn maneuvers of 1863 against the Guards Corps (Prince August von Würtemberg). A few months later war began against Denmark. *Feldmarschall* Wrangel was Commander in Chief of the allied army, consisting of three corps.

I Corps (comprising a Brandenburg and Westphalian division) was commanded by Prince Friedrich Karl. This was the corps that saw the most action, attacking at Missunde, conducting the flanking march over the Schlei, entered Flensburg and Sundewitt, and after a two months siege, (after being reinforced by the Guards and the 5th Division) stormed the Düppel fortifications on the glorious 18th of April. At this point, replacing the retiring *Feldmarschall*, the Prince assumed command of all three corps and carried out the final shining act of the war, the crossing of the Limfjord, the conquest of Alsen and the occupation of the Friesian *Westsee* Islands. Even before peace was concluded, he returned to Berlin, where he resumed command of the III (Brandenburg) Army Corps.

He was not granted much time to rest. When in the spring of 1866, war with

Fritz Karl

Austria seemed inevitable, attention focused on him as a proven leader. The King placed the prince in command of the 1st Army. 'Karl, you have accomplished your first task well, now you have a far more difficult one.' These were roughly the words of King Wilhelm with which he said farewell to the prince upon his departure to the army. [The prince] soon arrived in Görlitz, where he was warmly welcomed by the soldiers of his old command, namely the men of the III Corps. During the night of 15/16th June, as already recounted, he led the 1st Army over the Saxon border, and on the 23rd, over the Bohemian border.

Prussian Hussars crossing the border.

Advance of 1st Army

The initial encounters

Prussian songs again rang out in the mountains, as four divisions of the 1st Army, two Magdeburg-Thuringen (7th and 8th) and two Brandenburg (5th and 6th) entered Bohemia early on the 23rd along three main routes, via Zittau, Seidenberg and Marklissa. We will initially describe the crossing of the border, and then the minor encounters of the first day which were exclusively cavalry skirmishes.

At all three points the invasion took place nearly simultaneously (between 7:00 and 8:00 in the morning) with bands playing and cries of hurrah. The troops of the 7th and 8th Divisions, advancing via Zittau, formed the right wing. It was here that Prince Friedrich Karl halted and allowed the regiments to march past him. An eyewitness who was beside the prince described the scene as follows:

> A toll house with a black and yellow barrier marked the border between Saxony and Bohemia. Here the prince stopped. Uhlans, who formed the advance guard, crossed the border first, then the infantry. As soon as the leading ranks of the battalions reached the turnpike and saw the Austrian colors, they raised a cry of joy that was immediately taken up by the ranks to the rear, and was constantly renewed, until the men reached the toll house and saw their 'Soldier Prince' standing by the border marker. Upon seeing him the hurrahs turned into a roar of jubilation, whose loud demonstrations only ceased to be replaced by a war song that was taken up by each battalion in turn and repeated as it crossed onto Bohemian soil.
>
> The commander himself, waited silently at the side of the road. With quiet pride he looked upon the passing regiments, and well might he feel this pride, for never had an army crossed the border of an enemy, better equipped, better supplied[54] or inspired with greater spirit than the one that marched today from Saxony into Bohemia. Now and then the prince greeted an officer or a soldier who had already served under him, and won the heart of that man with a friendly question, for soldiers feel love for the superior officer who shows a personal interest in them.

Of the four divisions that crossed the border early on the 23rd, the 7th, 5th and 6th advanced toward Reichenberg while the 8th Division bore off to the right to establish contact with the Elbe Army. We shall temporarily lose sight of this last division to meet it again on the 26th at Liebenau and Podol. Until then we shall follow the other three divisions on their concentric advance toward Reichenberg, which was occupied early on the following day (the 24th). The column marching in the center (5th Division) had no contact with the enemy aside from fleeting encounters.

---

54   Tr. Note: The eyewitness was unaware that almost immediately, serious deficiencies in arrangements for supply, especially rations and fodder, would plague the 1st Army. These reached critical dimensions at Münchngrätz.

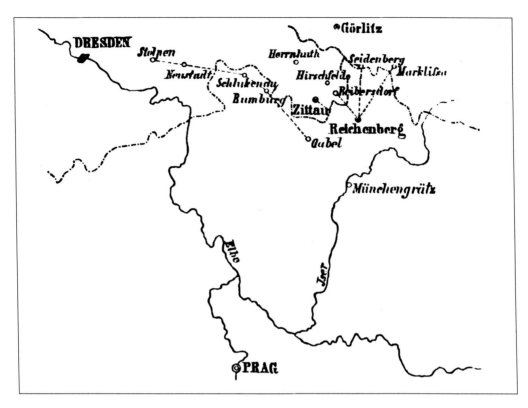

March route of Prussian 1st and Elbe armies.

The two columns on the wings however, had minor encounters with enemy Hussars. In light of the special respect with which the celebrated, and also feared, enemy cavalry was viewed, it might be well to more closely examine these minor encounters on the day of invasion.

The 10th Hussars led the right wing column (7th Division). The 3rd Squadron, under *Major* von Hymmen, was ordered to advance via Wetzwalde and Ober Wittig on the road toward Einsiedel in hopes of bringing in a prisoner. As the van of the advanced guard reached a group of hills just before Einsiedel from which one could see the road from Einsiedel toward Friedland, *Major* von Hymmen, who was in the lead, spotted an enemy patrol of eight to ten Hussars. He immediately charged, calling *Lieutenant* von Maltzahn to follow him with the advance guard. The enemy, recognizing the danger they were in, turned and sought to evade the attack with our men in hot pursuit. One of the enemy horsemen fell, and another, despite the lead they had, was overtaken by *Lieutenant* von Maltzahn and captured. They were Radetzky Hussars. We learned from them that the enemy was in Reichenberg. The objective of the reconnaissance had been achieved.

In the meantime, the 23rd brought another encounter for the 10th Hussars that was less fortunate. The division had advanced to Kratzau and had established outposts on the road to Reichenberg. These consisted of parts of the 27th Regiment and a squadron of the 10th Hussars. The troops had not yet cooked their meals when a report arrived that a squadron of enemy Hussars was approaching at a fast trot. *Premierlieutenant Graf* von der Schulenburg went at them with his two troops [a 'troop' in this case being a sub-division of a squadron]. However, before he drew near the enemy, he realized that two or three new troops of enemy cavalry were charging out from behind a farmstead and heading for his flank. Now he turned, but too late. The leading rank was already fighting hand to hand and our men had to fall back. We had several wounded. One, Hussar Ahlefeld, who had fought a heroic fight with four of the enemy, had fallen into their hands.

So much for the right wing. The left, too, as we indicated above, had its skirmishes. At the head of the left wing column marched the Brandenburg Dragoon Regiment Nr. 2, '*die Schwarzklappigen*', [the Black Hats]. The newly activated 5th Squadron in the lead. Similarly, near Einsiedel (as with the 10th Hussars) they came upon the enemy. Two platoons under *Lieutenants* von Haugwitz and von der Heydt immediately attacked and quickly sent the enemy flying, capturing horses and prisoners. *Lieutenant* von Haugwitz was lightly wounded. The enemy left several dead on the field. Our '*Schwarzklappigen*' soon sang a fine song in honour of their 'Fifth Squadron'. It ran:

> *We rode into battle, an old regiment,*
> *That Prussia's history named with joy,*
> *The old squadrons, the first four,*
> *And we had a new one, the Fifth.*

> *The First, it is the staff squadron,*
> *The Second already fought at Dennewitz,*
> *The Third bravely carried the standard,*
> *The Fourth rode flank before our front, the Fifth?*

> *The Fifth, it must first win new renown*
> *For its very own,*
> *So that it, which is still so new,*
> *Can be equal to the others, the Fifth.*

> *Heydt nobly attacked,*
> *Pigur hacked down six,*
> *Haugwitz bravely dashed forth,*
> *Hungarian Hussars fled, before the Fifth.*

> *So now the Fifth is equal to the others,*
> *Rich in fame and honours of war,*
> *And now, in the entire regiment,*
> *Every man now names with pride, the Fifth*

(slightly abridged).

Such were the minor clashes on the 23rd. They had their significance. On the right and left wings, our forces had fought with the Radetzky and Liechtenstein Hussars, had exchanged blows and gained the confidence that we were able to engage them equally in horsemanship and in fighting with the *arme blanche* [in this case, the sword]. Now we could look forward with confidence to further engagements, the next day would bring them.

It also brought the occupation of the important town of Reichenberg. The advance - guards of the 5th and 7th Divisions had advanced toward Reichenberg on the 23rd, and early in the morning, at 6:00 on the 24th, the black and white banner of the Brandenburg Uhlans waved on the high hills that enclose Reichenberg. Two hours later the first battalions entered the town.

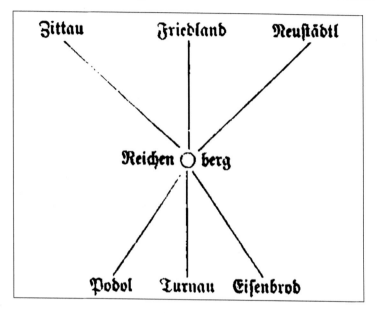

Roads to and from Reichenberg.

The *Leib* Regiment had the lead, so wrote an eyewitness:

> All the battalions marched nobly. After a long day's hike under pouring rain, they came in dressed ranks and in perfect step as if they were on parade. There was not a sign of weariness. The 64th Regiment, whose '*Chef*' [honourary colonel] is the prince, followed on. Many bore the Düppel Medal, they were old soldiers. Their faces showed that they knew their prince. They marched past him without a cry, but with a carriage that said more to one who understands soldiers than jubilation and hurrahs.

Nowhere, as noted above, had there been any resistance. Since the town was commanded by the surrounding hills, it would have been futile to defend it. The enemy forces fell back over the Iser. Our leading elements followed and bivouacked at Gablonz (halfway between Reichenberg and Turnau). An attack by the Liechtenstein Hussars, attempting to disrupt the bivouac, was repulsed.

The 7th Division to the Iser

Turnau

The movement of the 1st Army to Reichenberg had initially been concentric. The columns that had crossed the mountains through Zittau, Friedland and Neustädtl came together in and around Reichenberg, only then to split and continue south on three separate roads.

The sketch above shows the march to and beyond Reichenberg. Three divisions led off, three divisions followed. Their mission was to arrive at the three eastern crossings of the Iser (Turnau, Podol and Eisenbrod) at approximately the same time that the Elbe Army would reach the more westward crossing of the Iser at Münchengrätz. This mission was accomplished. On the evening of the 26th the Elbe Army was between Hühnerwasser and Münchengrätz. On that same day the three eastward crossings of the Iser were occupied by the three leading divisions of the 1st Army, Turnau and Eisenbrod without a fight, Podol after an intense fight. We will accompany all three divisions on their advance from Reichenberg to the Iser. First the Seventh.

The 7th Division (*Generallieutenant* von Fransecky) advanced to Turnau which was occupied by the leading battalions of the advanced guard on the 26th. The Achserlebner Hussars had already pushed forward to the Iser bridges, the main body of the advanced guard arriving on the 27th. The advance, as well as the occupation of the town (on the 26th), took place without the enemy's rearguard putting up any serious resistance. A pleasant description of this march (which follows), gives us the opportunity to accompany the division on its advance to the Iser that was, for them, only a series of peaceful interludes. And all the better for that, since in the course of our account, there is much of battle and horror and little of the light - hearted side of military life.

An *Unteroffizier* of 67th Regiment, whose battalion did not arrive in Turnau until the 27th, tells us:

> The 26th passed peacefully. We had reached Massersdorf, halfway between Reichenberg and Gablonz, the previous evening. Since we did not receive our marching orders until 10:00 in the morning, we could count with certainty on a day of rest. We dug our cooking pits and impatiently waited for our rations to be issued. However, the desired rest was not for us, even before out rations were completely issued, we heard alarm signals simultaneously on all sides, and the news ran through our ranks like wildfire that our outposts had been attacked.
>
> We immediately moved out. Fortunately, the news turned out to be false, but once we were on the march, we continued and reached the little town of Gablonz without incident. Here we had a short rest. The inhabitants, with great submissiveness, brought us water and beer (refusing any payment). Then we resumed our march, often cross country so as to avoid losing time on the extensive windings of the road. In so doing I discovered that, almost without exception, all of our men had a great appreciation for the beauties of nature. The same people who were so concerned with shortening our route, passed up no opportunity to climb a jutting rock from which they could gain a view of the picturesque valley lying to the side. I seriously believe that no nation other than the Germans could have such an appreciation for the beauties of nature, in such a solemn moment as we were in, and as we were approaching.

The views were of incomparable beauty. Pointed sugar loaf hills here and there crowned with ruined castles, jutted out into the valley below, in which lay towns and villages, their churches evident from afar, with streams and fields between them, and away in the distance, the blue Silesian mountains, framing the view from the east. Only one thing was lacking, life. Not a man could be seen on the roads or in the fields, not a single animal was in the meadows, no wagon moved along the roads. Everything was hidden or had fled.

Occupation of Turnau.

Several companies were detached to the various exits of the town to secure us against surprise attacks. They made the streets impassible, turning over wagons, rolling barrels and bringing up heavy timbers to construct barricades. Furthermore, in the corner houses the windows were removed so that they could be used as loopholes in the event of an attack. Reconnaissance, however, suggested that the enemy was disinclined to contest our possession of Turnau. So the rifles were stacked, packs removed, and half of the men were allowed to find places to cook in the surrounding houses. The life of a soldier (and herein lies part of its charm), is just such a constant alternation of bodily exhaustion and recuperation. Every moment of rest is used to recover from the strenuous endeavours one has made, and to gain strength for the deprivations that lie ahead. Turnau was such a moment. What a miracle that we had nothing more pressing, than to take the best possible care of ourselves. I called the officers to have tables and benches set up in front of the bakery near to which our company was positioned, and in less than a quarter of an hour, the table was set and white bread, fresh butter and steaming coffee was served. Only sugar was missing. However, a shop keeper on the other side of the street, who had hitherto kept his shop locked for fear of 'requisitions.' soon helped us out of our predicament. When we guaranteed his safety and he made acquaintance with our silver money, he brought us cigars and presented them with the remark that they were, 'good smuggled cigars.'

Our friend the shopkeeper had a good day's business, but what was most in demand, and therefore what was soon exhausted, was writing materials, paper, ink, pens and the like. Everywhere, in the houses and in the squares, you could see soldiers busy writing letters. Here was one of the bandsmen using his drum as a table. There, stretched out on the ground lay another, knapsack and writing pad before him, and so often, because of the soft surface, the hard pencil poked through the paper, but this did not prevent him from completing his letter. Those were pleasant hours in Turnau. However, for the residents they were difficult and exhausting. While we rested and took care of ourselves, they had to work for us. The departing Austrians had required them to break up the fixed bridges over the Iser, and we now forced them to rebuild them, since the pontoon bridges on which we had crossed the river on our entry, now had to be lifted for our further advance.

The *Bürgermeister* and the town council declared that it was impossible to fulfill this task. First there was no wood, no timbers, no boards, no nails and axes, and, finally, no able bodied workers. All of these excuses, however, were to no avail, and the available military support soon solved the problem. Every house was searched and all those who were not absolutely incapable due to age or illness were put to work. In less than an hour, 100 workers were assembled, a colourful mixture of all levels of society. Here a stooped old man, stepped forward as the foreman. Right behind him a young man, obviously a member of the richer classes, clenching his fists and muttering curses and imprecations. Then working folk in shabby clothes, one of them staggering under the influence of brandy, the others calling upon God and all the Saints to free them from our hands. In stark contrast to this despair, one saw the half grown youths playing and shouting and curiously crowding around the strange guests. We had brought them an unrestrained freedom which they seemed to want to celebrate.

From our positions we could follow the gradual progress of the work on the bridges. Finally (it was now late in the afternoon) we heard music, and our Fusilier battalion, in spite of an exhausting day's march under the scorching sun, marched in step into the town, some accompanying the music with song, others joking and changing the words. The Fusiliers relieved us. An hour later we returned to the same bivouac that we had left in the early hours of this same day. On the next day (the 28th) we had the fighting at Münchengrätz.

We have presented this description of the march to Turnau and the occupation of the town, initially for its own sake, but also for another reason. The occupation of the town was in itself, every bit as important as the apparent unimportance of the events that accompanied our advance. The troops that carried this out had at least a suspicion of its importance. Only with our later knowledge of the orders of the Austrian high command, did it become evident just how important the occupation of Turnau was. If this had not been accomplished before the arrival of an order from the [Austrian] High Command on the afternoon of the 26th, the operations of *General* Clam-Gallas would very probably have taken a different form. Instead of attempting resistance at Münchengrätz, he would have attempted to hold the more easterly crossings of the Iser with all his available forces, and thereby at least *attempt* to halt the advance of the Prussians to Gitschin, the [planned] rendezvous for 1st and 2nd Armies. This plan, which was significant, was given up, indeed *had* to be given up, because Turnau was already in our hands when the order - *The Iser line must be held* - arrived.

The 8th Division on the Iser

As mentioned above, General Horn with 8th Division, was directed towards the right from Grottau on the first day of the march into Bohemia, and thenceforth advanced on the right flank of the 7th Division toward the Iser. The advance proceeded such that the 7th Division that was marching toward Turnau, maintained contact between the III Army Corps (5th and 6th Divisions) on its left, and the 8th Division on its right, while the 8th Division, in its turn, maintained contact between the 7th Division on its left and the Elbe Army on its right.

The advance of the 8th Division was initially accompanied by the same scenes we outlined in the previous chapter. The difference was it was granted an opportunity to engage in a serious action before the other elements of the 1st Army.

On the 23rd the division marched via Spittlegrund and Pass, reaching Pankraz, where it bivouacked without contacting the enemy. On the 24th it reached Eichicht via Schönbach and Ehriesdorf. This had been a hard day, the steep, nearly 3,000 foot high Jeschenberg caused the division much difficulty, particularly the artillery and the transport. On this day there was also a skirmish. Between Eichicht and Langenbrück the 6th (Thuringen) Uhlans ran into some Hungarian Hussars, exchanged blows and sent them flying. One Uhlans was killed, *Major* von Guretzki was wounded. The Hussars lost three dead.

The 25th was a day of rest (and the division needed it after the exertions of the last two weeks), remaining in close cantonments between Eichicht and Lanbenbrück. The four dead of the previous day (friend and foe alike), were interred in the Langenbrück cemetery. The 72nd's regimental band played the chorale, the Catholic priest gave the blessing. The next day brought the first proper combat.

On the 26th, the division was ordered by Army Command to carry out a forward reconnaissance towards the Iser. Accordingly, *General* von Horn ordered Brigade Schmidt towards Liebenau. The brigade consisted of Infantry Regiment Nr. 72, the Magdeburg Jäger Battalion, one 4pdr [rifled] battery, and a squadron of the Thuringen Uhlans, they were to rendezvous at Gerzmanitz. Liebenau, which had been evacuated by the Austrians, was soon reached, and on the far side of the town, the brigade made contact with the enemy. It developed into a cannonade of several hours duration, variously known as the Artillery Fight at Liebenau, at Gillowey or at Schloss

Sichrow, all three points were in the immediate vicinity of the encounter. As for the fight itself, we present the description of an eyewitness (from the 72nd Regiment):

The action at Liebenau

The sides of the valley on the far side of Liebenau were bounded by substantial heights with precipitous sides. These heights were held by dismounted Austrian cavalry (no infantry had yet been brought forward). The 1st Battalion of the 72nd Regiment and the 4th Jäger Battalion formed the advance - guard. Both battalions marched in column on the valley floor, the main body followed on behind. The first bullets began to whistle over our heads, at 8:30 one drilled through the chest of a man of the 72nd, the first of our regiment to be killed. Two companies of Jäger were sent forward from the village of Gillowey to the hills on the left. The 1st Company of the 72nd followed on the highway, the 3rd along the railroad, the 2nd and 4th Companies followed on. When the infantry reached the foot of the heights and began to climb them, the Austrian Hussars withdrew at the trot.

An abatis had been constructed across the road as it crested the rise. It only delayed the 2nd and 4th Companies for a few minutes, their combined pioneer sections quickly removed it.[55] When they reached the plateau, the companies came under shell fire, so they left the road and proceeded into the woods on the right, toward Sichrow and *Golden Stern*. On a second hill, separated from the first by a deep, narrow valley, an Austrian half battery (consisting of four rifled guns) was situated in a superb position, and its fire began to cause us real problems. If we succeeded in rapidly crossing the valley and reaching the far side, then we could get underneath its fire and would then be able to scale the steep slope, surprise the battery and capture it. That was the objective of the 4th Company under *Premierlieutenant* Freytag. The Battalion Commander, *Major* Hensel, marched at the head of the company and showed it the way, with the 2nd Company following closely behind. Enemy fire was most intense on the valley floor, about fifty shells were fired but fortunately most of them went too high. Only one exploded twenty feet in front of the company, tearing off one man's leg and part of

---

55   Author's Note: It is hard to get a clear picture of the 'Action at Liebenau', in part because the reports have gaps in them, in part (for lack of good maps) because they cannot be followed in detail. If we use the letter of the man of the 72nd Regiment that is printed above, and the report in the Austrian General Staff Work (the two descriptions supplement each other well), we come up with a battlefield bounded by two ridges, one on the north, the other on the south, with the highway cutting across at right angles. The advancing Prussians stood on the northern ridge, the Austrians on the southern ridge, the so-called 'Semmelberg.' The center of the enemy positions was where the highway reaches the height of the Semmelberg. Behind an abatis, were dismounted troops of the Prussian Hussars [the Austrian *Preussen Husaren*], with the Liechtenstein Hussars on their left, the Radetzky Hussars on their right, the Savoy Dragoons and a battery of horse artillery on the extreme left flank in a position at right angles to their line. Our 72nd advanced against this line of defense. The Preussen Hussars [Austrian] fired their volleys and then fell back, the Hussars to their right and left following them, as did the guns. The entire Division Edelsheim, three brigades and three batteries strong, now took up a [new] position farther to the rear (at Dauby). The artillery on both sides fired away, however as our infantry threatened to flank their position, the enemy broke off the fight. This is how it went. Essentially, the reports are correct.

another's shoulder, while lightly wounding a third. Most of the shells fell in the field dressing station. The first had just exploded there, when the doctor's three horses, wanting no more to do with the business, escaped from the hands of the soldiers of the train and galloped off with all their gear toward the Austrian lines. Despite heavy fire, the 4th Company advanced splendidly with the 2nd behind it, only breaking the regulation formation for a moment. The skirmishers [*Schützenzüge*][56] were thrown out 150 paces ahead under *Lieutenant* von Bömcken. Finally, we reached the foot of the valley floor. Enemy fire constantly showered us with twigs and branches from the trees over our heads, but at least we could catch our breath for a moment in relative cover. Marching over hill and dale through man high fields of grain, combined with our heavy packs and gear, had nearly taken all of our breath away, and this was urgently needed to scale the hill! We could only advance slowly due to the extreme steepness and had to pause briefly several times to rest. Finally, the rifle platoon reached the crest. It found itself 200 paces from the battery and opened a lively, effective fire against the horses and crews to prevent them from escaping. Unfortunately the main body of the company was too far back to help. The Austrians however, decided it would be advisable to limber up, and in such haste that they left sponges, schnapps flasks, caps and even cartridges lying behind, which our people jubilantly carried off as trophies. If we had not had to carry our knapsacks, we would have taken that battery. The company was next assigned to hold the edge of the woods toward Sichrow. A squadron of Austrian Hussars did not dare to attack us there.

Meantime, after passing the abatis and the shell fire, the 1st Company advanced on Zbiarek and remained there while the 3rd Company followed the railway and advanced toward *Wilde Gans* [Husa]. It was constantly harassed by a squadron of Hungarian Hussars that did not leave it alone for a minute. A General Staff officer brought the 4th Company orders to occupy *Golden Stern* [a small hamlet astride the road], which was to serve as the base for a reconnaissance to be carried out by the Zieten Hussars. The 1st Battalion gradually concentrated at *Golden Stern*, with the exception of the 3rd Company, and advanced toward Schloss Sichrow and *Wilde Gans*. East of that it took position with the other battalions of the brigade to cover a line of 18 guns that engaged, first two and then three Austrian batteries. The latter fired very bravely, but at first they

56   Tr. Note: The standard formation of a Prussian infantry company was two platoons, side by side, with the men in three ranks, the best shots and most skilled men in the third rank. When the company formed the normal fighting formation, the company column, the front two ranks of the two platoons now formed two platoons, each with two ranks, one behind the other, while the skilled riflemen in the third ranks of the two platoons now formed a third, *Schützenzug*, or rifle platoon, also of two ranks, behind the other two. When preparing for combat, the rifle platoon advanced 100 paces in front of the column. Upon the command, '*Schwärmen,*' one or two sections (12-15 men) of the *Schützenzug* advanced another 150 paces and deployed as skirmishers, the remainder of the *Schützenzug* remaining behind as *Soutien*, or supports. The skirmishers fought under the direction of their *Unteroffizier* [NCO] who observed fire and gave sight settings for the range to target. Since the breech loading rifle could be loaded in any position, the men were trained to take full advantage of available cover and fire from prone, kneeling, sitting or standing position as needed. When the tactical situation so demanded, a greater part of the company might be employed as skirmishers. The Prussian regulations emphasized the need for flexibility to take advantage of cover and terrain.

Sichrow.

were a hundred paces short, then several hundred paces over. Only one round hit our battery without doing any damage, a significant number of the enemy shells failed to explode. Our battery fired its first (ranging) round too short, but then corrected round by round, and finally fired so well that the Austrian batteries had to cease firing and withdraw. The artillery battle lasted three quarters of an hour. In the meantime, the entire 8th Division had concentrated, and the Austrians broke off the action at 12:30.

Our regiment, and especially the 1st Battalion, had received its baptism of fire, our losses were minimal. After the fighting ended, an outpost was set up at *Wilde Gans* to cover our disengagement. Toward evening the division advanced to the Iser, to bivouac on the near side of the river. This advance led to the night action at Podol.

Before we describe this action, we shall examine the overall situation as it was (in the Iser region) on the afternoon of the 26th. First the Prussians, who had everywhere reached the Iser or its immediate vicinity, their left wing (7th Division) held Turnau, their center (8th Division) was south of Schloss Sichrow towards Podol, their right wing (Elbe Army) was in and around Hühnerwasser, about seven miles from Münchengrätz.

Where were the Austrians? They held the same line, essentially unaltered, that they had held since the 18th, from Jung Bunzlau to Münchengrätz. All their detachments (Brigade Ringelsheim, the Radetzky and Lichtenstein Hussars), had been pulled in, and were even now about to fall back through Sobotka to Gitschin, from whence they hoped to link up with the main army. Then at noon on the 26th, new orders arrived from Army Headquarters (Benedek), to hold the Iser line (meaning the stretch between Turnau and Münchengrätz), *at all costs*. So far as was possible, this order had to be carried out. Turnau, if it proved possible to recapture, was not a place that could be held by a merely passive defense. Moreover, it would be dangerous to divide the forces between Turnau and Münchengrätz. Therefore, it was decided to advance to the attack early on the 27th, to cross the Iser and take up a position near Gillowey, on approximately the same ground where the cannonade described above had taken place. Preparatory movements were to be carried out on the evening of the 26th, Turnau was to be recaptured in a surprise [night] attack, and north of Podol the hill by Schloss Swigan was to be occupied and held by Brigade Poschacher (18th Jäger Battalion, IR 30 Martini, and IR 34 King of Prussia).

Thus, the overall situation foreshadowed an encounter within a matter of hours. The 8th Division had orders to advance south to the Iser (Podol) on the evening of the 26th. Brigade Poschacher had orders, at the same time, to advance north to Podol and beyond. A clash at this Iser crossing, halfway between Turnau and Münchengrätz was inevitable, and in the event, it took place.

The action at Podol

Podol is a small hamlet on the north bank of the Iser consisting of a single street that meets the river almost at right angles. The houses, aside from an angular but extensive farmstead at the entrance, are small blockhouses built of tree trunks. It is a picturesque place. Between the blockhouses and the road embankment are front gardens with yellow Parnassus flowers and dark hollyhocks, while gourds and false jasmine entwine every window. At the back, fruit trees hide every house and rise above the old thatched roofs. These, in places sunken in, have moss and common houseleek growing on them, with far spreading eaves, and little wooden benches under the windows. The village's only significance is strategic, because here, highway and railway cross the Iser.

The wide riverbed, half dried up in summer, but with a number of channels, has steep banks and is crossed by two embankments side by side, road and rail. The road embankment is broken by three bridges,[57] the railway embankment by a single, long, lattice bridge [made of iron]. The highway embankment is an extension of the village street and is flanked on the right by the railway embankment. The first bridge past the village is a plank bridge. Past the third and last bridge, on the way to Münchengrätz, a massive house [it was an inn] rises to the left, beyond and behind this house, the terrain sinks again and forms a good covered position.

---

57   Tr. Note: According to Regensberg (*Von Dresden bis Münchengrätz*, p. 48), the highway crosses over four bridges in a row, the first over a mill race or pond, the second over the river itself, and the other two over dry arms of the Iser. This is correct and they can still be seen today though now built of modern materials. The 'river bed' described above could be more accurately rendered as the 'flood plain.' The mill race is now dry, the mill stream having been diverted up river, but the low, stone-arched bridge, remains.

So much for the locality. As for the fighting, we shall start with the Austrian report, which is notable for its brevity and clarity, and which will serve to help us with the uncertainties and contradictions of the contemporary reports.

Clam-Gallas' report observed:

> As Brigade Poschacher, which had occupied Podol earlier in the course of the afternoon with one, and later with a second company of IR 30 Martini, reached the above village on the evening of the 26th on its way towards the heights above Schloss Swigan, it found the village [Podol] already held by the enemy. These had forced the two advanced companies that were already there, back over the bridges as far as the massive house. The 18th Jäger Battalion and the subsequently arriving battalions of IR 30 Martini and IR 34 King of Prussia, under *Oberst* Bergou, forced the enemy out of Podol and reoccupied the village. The enemy for his part, did not intend to leave us in possession of this important position, and a stubborn and bloody night action ensued that caused great loss to the above named units. The enemy losses must have been even greater.
>
> The Corps Commander (Clam-Gallas), who was constantly in the front rank directing the lead battalions (a task complicated by darkness and fog), also committed Brigades Abele (Kalik) and Piret in support. The fighting continued with varying success until 2:00 in the morning when it was broken off and Regiment Martini, along with the 18th Jäger Battalion, was pulled back behind the 2nd Battalion of IR 72 Ramming (which had initially recaptured the enemy held bridges).
>
> The enemy, himself, extremely exhausted and battered, did not follow. The [planned] surprise attack on Turnau was abandoned due to the altered situation.

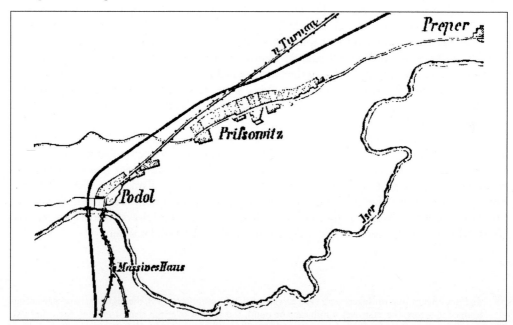

Sketch map of Podol.

So much for the Austrian report which divides the fighting into two parts. The first part, in which after initial success on our side, Brigade Poschacher forced us out of the village, and a second part, in which after being reinforced, we forced [Brigade Poschacher] back out of the village, and that is how it happened.

This division of the fighting into two parts is not always recognized in descriptions of the combat, nor in the criticism that troops who were engaged in the action, subsequently made of each other. It must be acknowledged that the first half of the fighting, even though it ended in failure, initially produced brilliant results, while the victorious second half, which did indeed transform failure into success, was unable to match the results achieved in the first, most favourable part of the battle (before the arrival of Austrian reinforcements).

Only in the first half of the battle did our men advance over all three [four] bridges, and most probably over the parallel railway embankment too, as far as the 'massive house.' In the second half [our forces] had to settle for the recapture of the village. In the first half, the Fusiliers of the 72nd Regiment and the 4th Jäger Battalion were engaged. In the second half, four battalions of the 31st and 71st Regiments. We shall initially turn to a description (of the first half) in a letter by a soldier of the 72nd:

> About 5:00 in the afternoon while our battalion was covering the outpost positions, Uhlans brought the news that Podol was already held [by the enemy]. Now fighting started which could hardly have taken a more gallant form. The village was prepared for defense with abatis. Enough said. With no knowledge of the ground, and no idea who or how many were in the village, we charged with a hurrah down the road that leads between the village on the left and the railroad embankment on the right. On the far side of the bridge it bends to the left around the village, and on a level with [the village], crosses over an arm of the Iser.[58] As we reached the village we detached two companies to the left for flank cover, two companies (the 10th and 11th) advanced to the second bridge and there detached a half company to the railway embankment that was on the right, which at most, is about 200 feet from the Iser. We stood in this narrow area after we had crossed the second Iser bridge and came to a massive enemy held house, one and a half companies alone against the Austrians, for the two companies that had been detached within the village as flank cover, were now separated from us by the Iser (This is correct). The massive house was soon cleared out and here, 200 feet from the Austrians, our people, barely 400 strong, stood under fire for 33 minutes. The bullets flew over and around us like bees. The moon was shining brightly. We saw the Austrians charge toward us and we opened fire on their columns with a fire such as we would never have believed possible.[59] As the report showed the next day, our 11th Company fired 5700 rounds in 33 minutes, an average of 22 rounds per man. The highway on which we were standing had a hollow 125 feet in front of us in which the

58   Author's Note: As is usual in reports written immediately after the action, the description of the terrain includes substantial errors. These however, are unimportant to the action described (the battle for the massive house). We refer you to the above sketch for the obvious corrections of the description.

59   Tr. Note: The Prussian General Staff Study describes this 'file fire' (p. 110): 'The battalion halted [and] had the two front ranks kneel down to receive the closed up charging enemy with a volley from four ranks.'

Austrian battalion had been concealed. The Austrians have a signal for their attack. As soon as it sounded they rose up before us, brightly lit by the moonlight that shone on their faces, and charged at us with a hurrah. The front ranks collapsed, the men behind them stepped into their places, they got to within less than forty paces, then turned back. Four times they charged, three times we repulsed them. On the fourth we slowly fell back to the first bridge, and then back over that. Our people could no longer hold their rifles, the barrels burned like fire. Then a hurrah rang out behind us. Two battalions of the 31st and 71st advanced to our assistance. We greeted them with loud shouts. We had held the village for two hours. Our people sank from exhaustion.

This report, written with great animation, is one sided as are all such descriptions. For example, it overlooks the outstanding, and what another version described as, the *preceding* part, played in the first half of this action by two companies of the 4th Jäger Battalion. A Jäger wrote:

We were (it must have been 9:00 [in the evening]) within 200 paces of the village when we were met with a battalion volley. We scattered to right and left, seeking cover from the enemy fire. Only our beloved *Hauptmann* (von Michalowski) sat firm in the saddle, and shot down one of the Austrians who had charged toward us with his revolver. Our *Feldwebel* now leaped forward. 'Jäger, are you going to leave your *Hauptmann* in the lurch?' he shouted at us, and the entire company charged after him. The Austrians stopped short, then turned back to the village, in whose houses and barnyards they tried to hold out. However, we left them little time for that and pursued them, first through the village and then over the embankment and the bridges. Thus we came (in the meantime it had become completely dark) as far as a massive house, which the Austrians, whom it appeared had found fresh battalions, had turned into a real fortress. We were met with a hail of fire that poured from the attic, the cellar and the windows. Fortunately, they fired too high and the bullets whistled past over our heads. However not for long, it got more and more intense and we had to retreat.

Our *Hauptmann's* horse collapsed. Right afterward he took a bullet in the left side of his chest. He died the beautiful death for the fatherland, our first. We buried him on the other side of the village, right beside the road that leads to Turnau, under some young pear trees.

This letter not only expands on the account of the man of the 72nd, it also confirms some essential points. We shall come back to it.

The fighting (by now it must have been 10:30), moved into its second phase. The men of the 72nd and the Jäger could not hold Podol. *Generalmajor* von Bose, who now brought up fresh troops for our side (the two 2nd Battalions of Regiments Nr. 31 and Nr. 71), met the retreating troops at the exit to the village. He immediately resolved to recapture Podol (which he succeeded in doing after three hours of fighting), after *Oberst* von Avemann arrived with the two Fusilier battalions of the above regiments as further support.

We take this description of the second part of the fighting, which developed with increased ferocity, from the following letter of an officer of the 2nd Battalion of 31st Regiment:

We had bivouacked in Preper, about 2¼ miles north of Podol. It must have been about 9:00 or a bit later, when we heard lively rifle fire in the direction of the river. 'To your rifles!'[60] We advanced at the double. Our second battalion was the first on the scene. The 2¼ mile distance was covered in half an hour. Shortly before the village the 4th Jäger Battalion came towards us (perhaps only single companies). They had initially taken the village, but after a brave defense had been forced out by superior Austrian forces. The Jäger called out to us, 'Fire low, the Austrians all fire too high!' Five more minutes advancing, in a hail of bullets from the houses and the gardens and farmyards between them, as well as from the abatis, all of which went over us. They really did aim too high. The battalion (under *Major* von Hagen) advanced, the 6th Company on the right on the railway embankment, so as to be able to fire from there on the village. The 5th and 7th Companies remained on the road, to force entry. The 8th advanced on the left to attack the farmsteads that were about 125 feet from the road on the left flank. We immediately came under heavy fire from all points. Granted, in the existing darkness that reduced visibility to barely fifty feet, the aim was a bit uncertain.[61] The flashes of the rifles, as well as the dark masses that appeared and disappeared here and there, were the only visible targets. Nevertheless, the heaps of dead and wounded Austrians that we saw the next morning showed how well our men had fired.

Gradually the enemy on our right flank was driven back to the Iser by the well-aimed volleys of the two battalions of the 71st Infantry Regiment that were advancing to our support. At the same time, our two companies (the 5th and 7th), forced their way into the village and over the abatis with great difficulty. It was here that *Hauptmann* von Prittwitz was mortally wounded by two bullets. Here too, the battalion commander and *Generalmajor* von Bose, who stood at the front with a rifle in his hand, provided the soldiers with an inspiring example of coolness and courage.

Meantime, on the left flank, the 8th Company had also been active, and despite the heavy fire had driven the enemy out of the farmsteads on the left. Unfortunately, the above company did not dare to push on further, the ground beyond was completely unknown, and the meadows, which were covered in fog, had the appearance of water. As daylight later revealed the [true nature] of the ground, [it seemed that] pursuit might have been possible, and by enveloping the left side of the village, then wading through the river (which was fordable in many places), the company might have cut the enemy off at the Iser bridges, or at the very least, given him a hard time.

During this battle the incessant sound of the enemy signal horns was unnerving, their dull moan encouraging the enemy riflemen in their resistance. Two musketeers of the 8th Company were assigned to silence one of these troublesome buglers. This was no easy task, for [the bugler] was in good cover behind one of the buildings and bravely sounded his frightful instrument. [The men assigned] however, resolutely crept on their stomachs along the wall of the house, and covered by the darkness, safely

---

60   Tr. Note: When the troops have stacked their rifles in neat little pyramids, (each *Rotte*, or three- man file, stack their rifles together), '*An die Gewehre*' is the command that sends them back to their arms, to pick them up again and prepare to march.

61   Tr. Note: The first action was conducted in complete darkness as the moon had not yet risen. The full moon then rose at about 11:30 and shone brightly until it disappeared again behind clouds.

made it to the front corner. Now he was done for. When the bugler was silenced, the fire gradually died down. The 2nd battalion gained possession of the village as far as the area of the Iser bridges, dragging out dozens of Austrians who had hidden in the houses.

The battle however, was not yet over. Our brave *General* von Bose did not settle for a half victory. Advancing down the road toward the bridge with the first section of the 8th company beside him, the audible result of several trial rounds fired toward the bridge, convinced him that it was still in enemy hands.

At this moment *Oberstlieutenant* von Drigalski appeared with Fusilier Battalion Nr. 31, and received permission to attack. The Fusiliers charged impetuously and threw the enemy back from the bridge in their first onslaught. The fight was short but intense. Among the fallen on our side was the heroic commander of the Fusilier Battalion (who was at that time also the regimental commander), *Oberstlieutenant* von Drigalski, who sank to the ground while leading his men, felled by two bullets through the head.[62] The desire to avenge their brave leader was a fresh spur to the Fusiliers. Irresistibly they forced their way forward, also capturing the second bridge. This broke the enemy's spirit and they quickly retreated. The Iser crossing was ours but there could be no thought of pursuit in the darkness. The Fusilier Battalion supplied outposts and by order of the general, the 2nd battalion returned to its previous bivouac, where it arrived at about 2:00 in the morning. Our losses were amazingly small in comparison to those of the enemy (we alone had taken about 600 prisoners). The enemy's bullets mostly went too high. Our opponent was the Brigade Poschacher, the so-called 'Iron Brigade.'[63] Securing the Iser crossings was a magnificent result in itself, but so too was the self confidence that our young troops gained from it. Our enemy was just as depressed [as we were elated]. According to prisoner statements, the Austrian commander had intended to mount a further attack, but had to give up the idea because, *the men could no longer be persuaded to advance.*

---

62   Author's Note: *Oberstlieutenant* von Drigalski was buried in the same spot as *Hauptmann* von Michalowski. The grave of the first bears a headstone with the inscription, 'In the assault on the village of Podol the Royal Prussian *Oberstlieutenant* Eugen von Drigalski, Commander of the Fusilier Battalion of the 1st Thuringen Infantry Regiment Nr. 31, died a hero's death for King and Fatherland at the head of his Fusiliers during the night of 26th June 1866 [erected by] The Comrades of His Regiment.' By the way, during a visit to Podol, it was interesting to see how soon after an event it becomes a legend and is often molded anew in the first few weeks. Thus it was, on that very spot, we were told of Drigalski's death in the following way. 'The *Oberstlieutenant*, as he advanced to attack, came upon an Austrian Jäger corporal in the middle of the bridge who had caught his mortally wounded officer in both arms. He still held his rifle firmly in his left hand. 'Drop the rifle', called the *Oberstlieutenant* to him. 'Drop the rifle,' a second time. At that moment the [corporal] quickly glanced upon the countenance of his officer and, realizing that he only held a corpse in his arms, quickly let the one he had so carefully held, fall to the ground, and grabbing his rifle with his right hand, felled the *Oberstlieutenant* with the broad bladed bayonet.' Such was the tale. It was entirely fictitious. Von Drigalski fell as we described it above.

63   Author's Note: A *Hauptmann* of Regiment Martini, who was wounded and captured three days later at Gitschin, said to a Prussian Officer, 'What did you expect?! If the Iron Brigade couldn't do it, the others certainly couldn't.'

We have only a few remarks to add to these first - hand accounts. It is clear that the first part of the combat, as we already stated, led momentarily to a farther reaching success than that which the later arriving men of the 31st and 71st Regiments were able to achieve. Only the 4th Jäger Battalion and the 72nd Fusiliers forced their way, at the start of the action, past the third bridge (the report incorrectly says the second) [in fact it was the *fourth* bridge] as far as the 'massive house.' In the second half of the action, in the face of ever increasing enemy reinforcements, our 31st and 71st Regiments had to settle for recapturing the village and forcing the enemy back over the first bridge [Fontane probably means the second bridge, i.e. the one that actually spanned the river, not the one that crossed the mill race].

Fighting at Podol.

Afterwards, our forces bivouacked on the near side of the Iser (in the village itself), and to protect ourselves against surprise attacks, part of the bridge was removed and set on fire. The Austrians had already attempted this earlier to prevent *Oberstlieutenant* von Drigalski from capturing it, however the [Austrian] officer (*Oberlieutenant* von Zimmermann), illuminated by the flames of his torch, was immediately a target for our Fusiliers, and was wounded and captured before he could carry out his mission.

Losses on our side amounted to 101, 2 officers and 21 men were killed, 7 officers and 69 men were wounded with 2 men missing. Austrian losses were incomparably higher. 33 officers and 1,015 men, according to their reports. 9 Officers were killed, 21 were wounded, 3 were captured, unwounded. Hardest hit was the Regiment Martini (they lost 20 officers and 600 men) and the 18th Jäger Battalion (6 officers and 189 men).

Here too, just as with the Elbe Army, the first serious fighting showed the superiority of our weapons and the futility of the tactics the Austrians employed against them.

The 1st Army Links Up with the Elbe Army

Münchengrätz

The 1st Army now stood on the Iser and had taken both of the eastern bridges at Turnau and Podol. The advance to link up with the 2nd (Crown Prince's) Army, which as we will show later, was entering the enemy's territory through the 'Three Gates of Bohemia,' would proceed southeast toward Gitschin. This advance to the southeast however, as we have already indicated in earlier chapters, was dependent upon the arrival of the Elbe Army that was marching on [1st Army's] right wing. But it would not do to simply hold the Turnau - Podol position while awaiting the Elbe Army (which was advancing from Hühnerwasser). The entire Austro - Saxon army stood in a strong position between our right wing [Elbe Army] and our center [1st Army]. The Elbe Army was too weak to force this position unaided, therefore Prince Friedrich Karl decided to divert from his eastward march while the Elbe Army continued to advance, and by means of this maneuver, to catch the enemy between two fires. This led to the double action at Münchengrätz.

Münchengrätz, on the left bank of the Iser, is a small Czech town of nearly 4,000 inhabitants. Its architecture is similar to that of most Bohemian cities, a large market place surrounded with arcades where streets meet from all points of the compass, with columns bearing statues of either the Virgin Mary or of Nepomuk.[64] In and of itself, it is rather ordinary, but it has a certain historic significance. After resting for 150 years in the *Karthaus* [Carthusian monastery], Wallenstein's remains were reinterred in the chapel of his great castle to the north of the town. The tomb is now empty.[65] In the castle itself, which is greatly elevated and surrounded by a

64   Tr. Note: John of Nepomuk (Jan Nepomucký) is a Bohemian saint. Confessor to the Queen of Bohemia, he was drowned (March 1393) in the Vltava (Moldau) river at the behest of King Wenceslaus, reputedly for refusing to divulge the secrets of the confessional.

65   Author's Note: On 12th July, *Graf* Leonhard von Schwerin, *Etappenkommandant* [rear army area commandant] of Münchengrätz, in the company of the administrator of the castle, the *Bürgermeister,* and a number of officers of the Düsseldorf *Garde Landwehr* Battalion, entered the chapel at Schloss Münchengrätz (the Annen *Kapelle*) to answer the question, 'Where are Wallenstein's remains?' At that time there appeared to be no doubts regarding this. The Annen *Kapelle* is east of the Schloss, on a hill surrounded by trees. Inside it are paintings and wood carvings of no artistic significance. As one enters, to the right, elevated above the floor is a white painted wooden double door, like that of a cupboard. Here, according to the residents of Münchengrätz, were Wallenstein's remains. Since the key could not be found, a locksmith, who had been brought along as a precaution, had to open the vault. He did it with visible unwillingness. Finally, the iron bar that was before the door fell off and the doors were opened, but the room was empty. The *Bürgermeister* when questioned, said he had earlier seen Wallenstein's casket there. This statement was confirmed by a large sheet of paper that was attached to the inside of the right hand door, and which had to all appearances, been glued there for a long time, for it was yellowed, partially torn and its writing had faded. In part in *Fraktur* and in part, in ordinary Latin script, was the following (the two opening lines are probably not entirely correct):

magnificent old park, an historic meeting took place in 1833 between the Emperors of Russia and Austria, and the King of Prussia. So much for Münchengrätz.

Perhaps it has greater strategic significance as a superb defensive position against an enemy approaching from Saxony. Regardless of which road the enemy uses for his approach, whether directly via Mohelnic on the Iser, or from the right via Hühnerwasser, or from the left via Turnau or Podol, he must pass through a difficult defile of sunken roads and bridges [Hühnerwasser], or a road commanded by rugged hills [Turnau / Podol].

The deeply scarred terrain and sunken roads (especially around the village of Kloster, one mile from Münchengrätz), lies primarily to the west, from which direction the Elbe Army was approaching. The dominating hills discussed above rise primarily to the east, in the direction from which the 1st Army, under Prince Friederich Karl was to be expected. The three highest of these peaks are the Kaczow, the Horka and the Musky Berg,[66] which form a semi - circle

Supra cooperculum tumbae stanneae Waldecensium religiosa pietas et grata posteritas extrui jussit in scuto ex parte. Quaeris Viator, quis hic jacet? Albertus Eusebius Waldstein, Dux Fridlandiae, qui 1634 die 25. Februarii aegre fatis cessit Egrae, fulgebat olim Splendore Martis, dum pro Deo, pro Ecclesia, pro Caesare, pro Patria fortiter pugnavit et triiumphavit heros Inclytus. Eum, quoniam legitime certavit, Deus ad se vocavit coelestique corona praemiavit.

Cujus jam bello fossa
Hic in pace quiescant ossa.

Freely translated as:

The piety of the Walditzer monks and the gratitude of posterity have placed this notice above the cover of this tin casket. Wanderer, do you ask who rests here? Albert Eusebius Waldstein, Duke of Friedland, whose fate it was to die at Eger on the 25th day of February 1634, renowned for military valour, he had triumphed as a hero for God, Church and Emperor. After he had fought a good fight, God called him to himself and honoured him with a heavenly crown.

His bones, broken in war,
Shall sleep here, here shall they find peace.

These words (clearly a copy of the original inscription in the Walditzer *Karthaus*), were accompanied by further lines in Latin to the effect that his corpse had been moved from Gitschin to the chapel of Schloss Münchengrätz. These lines that have been added are more difficult to decipher, but the following at least can be made out:

Under the rule of Joseph II, Emperor of Austria and King of Bohemia, Vincent *Grafe* von Waldstein und Wartenbergy, had the sarcophagus that was hitherto in the *Karthaus* at Gitschin, transferred to the Capuchins in the Saint Anna *Kapelle* and ceremonially reinterred on the 3rd day of March 1785.

There can be no doubt therefore, that Wallenstein's casket (presumably for at least eighty years) had rested in the Saint Anne *Kapelle* at Münchengrätz. But where is it now? *Graf* Leonhard von Schwerin expressed the suspicion that the casket had not been removed from the Schloss chapel, but had only been moved to a different place inside it. Probably, to make it more difficult to find, it had been moved from its own special vault to [another] family tomb. This may be. However, we must state that in response to our inquiry, we were told in Gitschin at the end of August, that the corpse of Wallenstein had already been moved from Münchengrätz, *a long time ago*, and taken farther west, to a Waldstein estate near Eger. Unfortunately, we do not recollect the name of the estate. Our inquiries directed to Bohemia had received no answer.

66   Tr. Note: Hozier describes the Musky Berg as rising to a height of about 500 feet, the Kaczow Berg being considerably lower.

around Münchengrätz. Each of these had its significance for the defense of the town or the Iser line respectively, but the last named Musky Berg was first in importance.

Such were the points that dealt with the double approach marches, the village of Kloster to the west, the Musky Berg to the east, and in the event, it was here where the battle was decided. The dispositions for the day were essentially:

Elbe Army

The 15th and 16th Divisions proceeding (eastwards) via Nieder Gruppay and Weissleim.
The 14th Division proceeding (southward) via Mohelnic.

1st Army

The 8th Division (westward) via Brezina.
The 7th Division (also westward) via the Musky Berg to Münchengrätz.
The 6th Division followed the 8th.

If one follows these movements on the map, they result in an envelopment of the enemy on three sides. The only escape route left open is to the south, but this too would be exposed if (as nearly happened) the outflanking columns on the left and right succeeded in cutting the roads leading to Sobotka and to Jung Bunzlau.

The overall dispositions, as we have broadly outlined above, were good enough if the Prussians expected to meet serious opposition, and that had to be expected. However, if the enemy only chose to defend the Iser line lightly, or even to give it up without a fight, then the concentration of a 60,000 man army at Münchengrätz made no sense. It was desirable therefore [for the Austro - Saxons], to fall back on the [Austrian] main army that was approaching from the east, but not to make a stand against the [Prussian] army that was approaching from the north [and west]. And in the event, that is what happened.

[Seen from the Prussian perspective] the [Austrian] position on the Iser could have only one purpose, and that was to *hold the Iser*. If that was to be done with the entire [Austro - Saxon] force, that is with 60,000 men in a superb defensive position, then it would be appropriate [for the Prussians] to attack them with five divisions, and thus with about equal forces. In the event, that is not what happened, and the battle that ensued could be compared to using a bludgeon where a rapier would have sufficed. Those however, who would cast blame, should not forget that all of what we now know, was not known at the time, and for reasons that we shall give, could not even have been suspected at the time. Resistance was indeed offered at Münchengrätz, but not with the enemy's entire strength, only with half, he simply covered his withdrawal.

First, we shall describe the enemy's dispositions and numbers. On the 27th the entire Austro - Saxon Army was concentrated at Münchengrätz, 37,000 Austrians and 23,000 Saxons. Their intention was to hold the Iser line. The order that had arrived at noon on the 26th was still in force and left no alternative. However, on the evening of the 27th the situation changed. A new order arrived from headquarters directing them to fall back on Gitschin, where they would be met by the Commander in Chief [and the main Austrian Force] coming from the south. In carrying out this order the Iser Army (in brigade echelons) began to move out during the night of 27/28th June. The Saxons proceeded via Jung Bunzlau, Brigade Ringelsheim via Sobotka, Brigade Poschacher, passing Brigade Ringelsheim, proceeded directly to Gitschin.

Only three brigades remained in Münchengrätz as our attack began, they were located as follows:

Brigade Leiningen (on the left) held Münchengrätz itself, along with all of the advance positions to its west, Kloster, Haber and Weissleim.
Brigade Piret (on the right) had taken up position on the Musky Berg.
Brigade Abele was positioned at right angles to Brigade Piret at the foot of the Musky Berg, between the hill and the town.

Most critical, as was later proved, was the position of the artillery.

This was the complex position against which our columns advanced from three sides. The column advancing from the north (14th Division) had no actual combat, that fell to the columns that advanced from the west and east. Both actions took place entirely independently of each other. For ease of differentiation, we shall name one, 'The Action at Kloster,' and the other, 'The Action at the Musky Berg.'

The action at Kloster

The 15th and 16th Divisions, as we said above, proceeded via Nieder Gruppay and Weissleim directly toward Münchengrätz. This was held by Brigade Leiningen with:

The 32nd Jäger Battalion at the Wildstein Castle.
IR 38 Haugwitz (Italian) on the plateau north of Kloster and in the village itself.
IR 33 Chulai (Hungarian) had the south facing position.

The brigade battery was positioned alongside Regiment Haugwitz, north of Kloster. A second battery went into position at the Jewish cemetery, immediately west [actually southwest] of the town [Münchengrätz].

On our side, only the advance - guard, under *Generalmajor* von Schöler took part in the fighting. This consisted of the same battalions that had already taken part in the evening fighting at Hühnerwasser:

The Hohenzollern Fusilier Regiment Nr. 40 (*Oberst* Zimmermann), all three battalions.
The 2nd Battalion Fusilier Regiment Nr. 33.
The Fusilier Battalion Infantry Regiment Nr. 28.
The Fusilier Battalion of Infantry Regiment Nr. 69.
The 8th Jäger Battalion.

They moved out of Hühnerwasser at 4:30 in the morning, marching over the battlefield of the previous evening that we have already described. At 6:30 the lead battalion reached the villages of Nieder Gruppay and Unter Rosita, and from there towards the village of Weissleim (the main body of the advance guard was already there), which is only about 2¼ miles from Münchengrätz. Before the battalion reached Weissleim, the enemy battery positioned north of Kloster opened fire. *General* von Schöler rapidly disposed his battalions so that:

The Fusilier Battalion Infantry Regiment Nr. 28 and two companies of the 8th Jäger Battalion continued their march toward Weissleim.

The 2nd Battalion Fusilier Regiment Nr. 33, along with the Fusilier Battalion Infantry Regiment Nr. 69 formed a left wing column.

The 1st Battalion Fusilier Regiment Nr. 40 along with two Jäger companies formed a right wing column.

The 2nd and 3rd Battalions Fusilier Regiment Nr. 40 were to follow on the main road in support.

At the same time, Batteries Wolf and Fuchsias went into position to the right and left, to return the fire of the enemy's artillery. Events now moved extremely rapidly. The center column, the 2nd and 3rd Battalions of Regiment Nr. 40, took Weissleim, then Haber and finally, with a sharp turn to the left, the position at Kloster. With that, the action on the western battlefield was decided. The enemy, falling back over the Iser, destroyed the only available bridge and thereby made it necessary for our forces (those that did not wade across the river), to build a pontoon bridge. The time that this required was insignificant, and at 11:30, the advance guard entered Münchengrätz.

On arrival they found that it was already held by Fusilier Battalion Nr. 56, which advancing at the head of the 14th Division via Mohelnic, had entered the town with hardly any fighting and had captured nearly 200 men of the [Austrian] 32nd Jäger Battalion.

In general, our opponents displayed little energy, this can be ascribed to a variety of reasons. First, their orders were to conduct a fighting *retreat*. Second, the Italians of Regiment Haugwitz had little desire to fight. Third and most important, the thunder of cannon from the east that drew ever closer, signaled that their line of retreat was about to be cut. There was yet a fourth reason that would have a decisive effect on the possession of Kloster and thereby on the outcome of the battle. It was the envelopment of the enemy position that was carried out by the left wing column which, by skillfully exploiting the Sabrtitzer Gorge [shown on some maps as the *Kleine Iser Br.*], allowed us to enter the village of Kloster from the north, while the enemy was facing the center column along the main road from the south [southwest].

We have an interesting account of this skillful advance by an officer of Fusilier Battalion Nr. 69, from which we take the following:

> When we got to the village of Nieder Gruppay, the 2nd Battalion of the 33rd Regiment and the Fusilier Battalion of the 69th Regiment (the former farther forward) were detached to cover the left flank of the advance guard. The detour that we had to make was substantial, however the heat and the terrain were worse than the detour. After a short march we stood before a precipitous gorge. The battalion had to make its way down a narrow path, sometimes stumbling, sometimes slipping, supporting ourselves with our rifle butts so as not to fall. Slowly we climbed back up the other side, now using our rifles for support, our upper bodies bent far forward, our left hands clutching at the bushes to pull us up.
>
> When we reached the top, we closed ranks and breathing heavily proceeded onwards. Before long (barely 400 paces) yet another gorge yawned before us, even deeper, and if possible, even steeper than the last. Again we had to make it down and

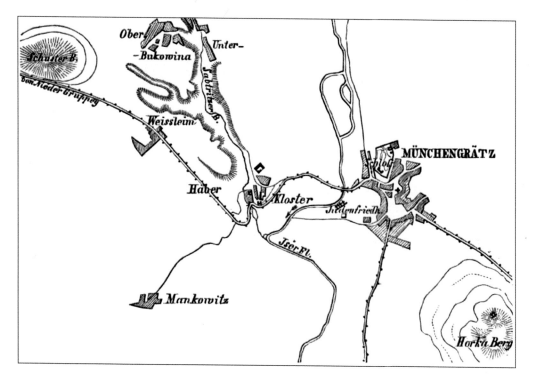

Sketch map of Kloster.

up the other side, our knees were already failing us. Some could go no farther and were left behind, the battalion continued its march until we stood at a third gorge.

Gasping for breath, utterly exhausted, we needed fully 20 minutes to climb up the third slope. I cannot but express my amazement and admiration that our soldiers, who for the most part were not as strong as myself (I am blessed with a strong constitution), and moreover, carried twenty two pounds more gear, had managed this far. I must state that the willpower that made it possible for them to do this deserves the highest praise.

On the last ascending hill, our path led us through a great farmstead. At the same time, we heard the chatter of skirmishing fire and the crack of volleys to right and left. Behind the farm we saw the lie of the land. 1500 paces ahead of us was a village (Ober Buckowina). Beyond it to the right was a hill, and beyond this hill (the Schusterberg), the battle seemed keenest, it was at Weissleim, where the center column was engaged.

We advanced at the double, the excitement, the thirst for battle, giving us new strength. 'Forward,' the men shouted to each other, 'Forward,' urged the officers, now we were on the field of battle. Along the way lay scattered dead. The battalion halted on the road from Weissleim to Ober Buckowina.'

We break the narrative here so that we can briefly outline what took place in the ensuing half hour, then to take up the story again at the decisive point. The 9th and 12th companies were placed in the lead while the 10th and 11th companies followed closed up, in support. Thus, the advance continued over the plateau until (already level with Kloster) a 70 foot deep gorge, with a stream running through it, cut through the terrain from north to south. [These companies] were already coming under rifle fire from the enemy, who [were shooting] from the plateau on the far side, especially from a field of hops. Inexplicably however, they were not at the edge of the ravine, but positioned several hundred yards beyond. We now return to the narrative:

The floor of the gorge was covered with lush meadow and a small meandering stream approximately 15 feet wide (the Sabrtitzer), which now impeded the advance of our riflemen. It was impossible to leap over it with our heavy gear. My men looked questioningly at me, so thrusting my revolver and pipe into my jacket, I stepped forward. However, when one goes down a flight of stairs and there are two steps when one believed there was only one, one falls, and so it was that I fell forward into the unexpected depths and lay up to my neck in the water. Faster than I can say, I pulled myself up and out of there, but my revolver and pipe were in the stream. The Fusiliers, who threw their rifles across the stream, also waded across. Then everyone threw themselves down, unslung their cooking kettles and began eagerly to quench their thirst. Here on the banks of the stream we were safe, at least for the time being, and heard with a certain discomfiture the whistle and hiss of bullets passing far above our heads. If the Austrians had positioned even one section on the slope whose foot we were now at, not one of us would have come out alive.

We rested for a few minutes and then it was forward again and up the opposite face. We could tell what was going on above us from the whistle of the bullets. Dead tired, hungry, and with heavy knapsacks, we clambered up yet again under the scorching sun. Most ran out of steam halfway up, unable to move, hanging onto a tree for support to avoid rolling back down the slope. There is a degree of exhaustion which overcomes even the strongest will.

Finally, I reached the upper rim of the gorge with perhaps eight men still by my side. Our helmets were barely visible when we were greeted with heavy rifle fire. We hastily threw ourselves down in a field of barley thereby making ourselves invisible, while the enemy, standing nearby in a hop field, was almost without of cover. We opened fire,[67] then I called a sergeant who had now joined us with a number of riflemen from the 9th Company, to flank the enemy from the left while I pushed forward to the hop field. The enemy peppered us with fire as we approached when (at about 150 paces distant), I stumbled and fell. The wing man of my platoon, *Gefreiter* Aufdermauer, bent over me and asked, 'Are you dead, *Herr Lieutenant?*' Unable at this moment to enjoy the naivety of his question I simply said, 'No.

'Then we must go on,' said Aufdermauer. 'We can't stay here. The *Zwockels*[68] have us right in their sights.' I pulled myself up and went forward again.

The Austrians thought, 'The cleverest ones retreat,' and when we were about 80 paces from them, they turned and ran. We followed with hurrahs. The more they ran,

67   Tr. Note: One of the advantages of the breech loading needle gun was that the Prussian rifleman could reload and fire from any position, even prone, without exposing himself, while the Austrian, with his muzzle loading Lorenz rifle had to stand to reload.

68   Author's Note: In Mainz and in Frankfurt am Main, *Zwockel* is a derisive term for Austrian soldiers, originating as a corruption of the *Tschako* headgear that the Austrian infantryman wore.

The Sabritzer Gorge at Kloster.

the louder we yelled, and the more we yelled, the faster they ran. Action and reaction! As soon as we were out of the hop field, from whose fire our advancing company columns had suffered substantial casualties, we swung to the right and pursued the enemy toward Kloster. I had only four men with me by now, *Gefreitern* Aufdermauer and Weber, *Füsilier* Herpel of the 12th company and *Füsilier* Gross of the 9th. That was the first wave. Following 100 paces behind were eight to ten riflemen of the 9th and 12th Companies. All the others had been left behind.

We may have followed the Austrians for about 200 paces when they suddenly vanished. Advancing over a road that ran parallel with the Sabrtitzer gorge to Kloster, bullets suddenly began to whistle around our ears. I ducked, Herpel likewise. In the same instant I heard a crunch and crack, then a muffled cough. Herpel, hit in the mouth by a bullet, fell dead on the ground. As he fell, he stretched out his hands and convulsively grasped my right arm. This contact cut me to the quick, and at the sight of this horrible transition from life to death I was completely shaken.[69] However, my own danger pulled me out of it. When I looked ahead of me, I saw a large group of Austrians in a hollow by the roadway, who were now charging us with fixed bayonets, an officer swinging his sword in the lead. The only hope was for us to counter - charge the enemy, 4 against 22. Running in a single rank (Aufdermauer, Weber, Gross and I) and yelling like men possessed, we rushed forward. Now we were within ten paces and started closing our accounts with God, when, overcome with panic, the enemy turned and fled as fast as his legs could carry him. The Austrian officer stood for a moment, transfixed. I could see in his face an expression of fury and disappointment, but what else could he do? He had to retreat but he did not get far. Twenty paces further on he turned and flourished his sword, at that moment a bullet from Aufdermauer hit him right in the head. Two more shots from my companions dropped an enemy *Unteroffizier* and a private soldier.

The fallen lay side by side, right by the road that led from Givina to Kloster. Scarcely ten paces farther on was a substantially built little monastery behind which the Austrians had fled. We four Prussians dived into a little ditch twenty paces in front of it, but hardly were we down, when rifles with white handkerchiefs were waving back and forth from behind the wall of the monastery. It was the sign of surrender, we took 18 men prisoner. During this little fight in the hop field the battle was decided at Kloster. The 10th and 11th companies, which were following on as supports, had also clambered down into the Sabrtitzer Gorge, and following the course of the stream, had taken the village of Kloster from the north, even as the center column launched an assault on the front.

The first into the village (from the north) was *Feldwebel* Schmidt of the 11th company, *Lieutenant* Keller entered the village with his rifle platoon [*Schützenzug*] shortly after. The capture of Kloster was decisive for the possession of Münchengrätz.

The fighting at Musky Berg[70]

At the same time that the Elbe Army was advancing on the enemy, those parts of 1st Army that were farthest west advanced towards Münchengrätz. These were the 8th and 7th Divisions. The 8th Division was ordered to move out from Podol via Brezina, the 7th Division to advance from Mokry and Wschen as left flank cover. The tasks were equally difficult for both divisions, though the difficulties were of different sorts. The 8th Division had to traverse a valley floor that was commanded throughout by artillery positioned on the massive heights to its left. The

---

69   Author's Note: 'Half an hour later I looked for and found my brave Herpel among the dead. A tear stole to my eye. Then I covered the mutilated head of the brave man with a cloth. 'May God grant you eternal rest.' Whenever I hear the song of the good comrades:
  '*A bullet came flying, Is it for me, or is it for you?*
  It took him away, He lies at my feet, as if he was a part of me'
  I think of that field of hops near Kloster, and of my brave Herpel. He was a *Landwehr* man and left his wife and two children in need.

70   Tr. Note: According to von Seebach's history of the 72nd Infantry Regiment of the 8th Division (p. 33), the temperature during the advance to Münchengrätz was 28° Reaumur (95° Fahrenheit/35° Celsius).

7th Division however, had to cross over these heights, the Musky Berg, whether along the slope or over the top (which was supposed to be impassible). The entire enterprise, at least initially, seemed insuperable. However, it was clear that if the 8th Division was not to be exposed to extremely heavy losses, it was dependent on the 7th Division, which could at least avoid most of the fire. And it was accomplished. Let us see how.

Generallieutenant von Fransecky placed Regiments Nr. 27 and Nr. 66 in the lead and formed three columns from them, each consisting of two battalions. The first column, the 2nd Battalion and the

Fusilier Battalion of Infantry Regiment Nr. 27, was led by *Oberst* von Zychlinski. The second column, the 2nd Battalion and the Fusilier Battalion of Infantry Regiment Nr. 66, was led by *Oberst* von Blanckensee. The third column, the 1st Battalions from Infantry Regiments Nr. 27 and Nr. 66, was led by *Generallieutenant* von Fransecky himself. Only the first column, *Oberst* von Zychlinski, was an actual outflanking column. It was ordered to climb the Musky Berg from the east and take the enemy artillery position that was located on the northern slope from the rear, while the two other columns were ordered to advance by taking advantage of the dead ground at the foot of the mountain. All three columns accomplished their missions, and while *Oberst* von Zychlinski led the first column over the steep Musky Berg, *Oberst* von Blanckensee and *Generallieutenant* von Fransecky led their columns round its base. Thus, the village of Musky on the heights, and the village of Dneboch on the slope, were captured. On the west side of the mountain [southwest], after all three columns were reunited, the ruins of Bossin (the best defended enemy position) were stormed. This was between 12:00 and 1:00, at the same time as the decisive events at Kloster and Münchengrätz. The enemy fell back to Fürstenbrück, his withdrawal was not interfered with.

It cannot be disputed that the skillful outflanking of the enemy artillery position was the crucial factor. The battle would have been won in any event, but without this there would have been far greater casualties. *Oberst* von Zychlinski himself, gave an outstanding account of his 'Passage over the Musky Berg,' from it we extract the following:

So, over the Musky Berg! Those were our orders. The rocks of this isolated little mountain appeared to us like an interwoven wreath [of stone and vegetation], in whose center the pointed hill, the 'Musky *Kegel*,' served as a *point d'appui*. Guides that we had brought with us repeated the assertion that there was no way to march over this mountain (the Musky Berg).

Finally, I found a German whose home was in the village of Zdiar, and who was in the process of packing all of his belongings onto a wheelbarrow to flee somewhere (he himself had no idea where). His young wife carried a child at her breast, two others lay wrapped in bedding in the wheelbarrow which the father was attempting to push through a stream. I explained to the man the foolishness of his actions and reassured him, whereupon he finally declared, 'there is a way to Przihraz that goes between ponds and over swampy meadows, but … only a footpath goes over the Musky Berg.' Good, that's how we'll go!

Nevertheless, I still believed that a green stretch between two strips of woods that was in front of me would prove easier and allow us to march on a broader front. I sent two Hussars ahead to reconnoiter but they soon came back saying that they had nearly been swallowed up by the swampy ground. I now realized that the treacherous slope

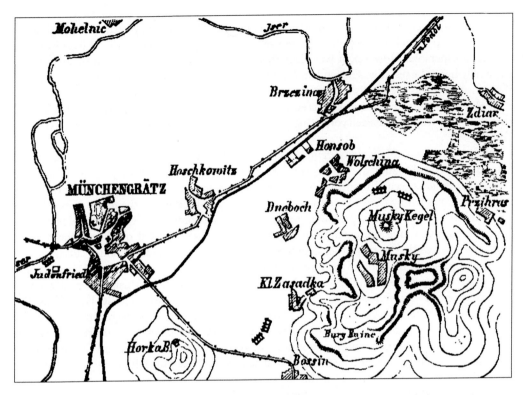

Sketch map of the Muskyberg.

rising before me (it was composed of scree) was similar to some I had encountered during a Staff Ride in the Falkenberg area near Neisse. Alerted to the danger I decided to follow my guide up the footpath. At first, we proceeded passably, but soon we were surrounded by woods and thick underbrush, then by narrow rocky gorges that resembled the *Anna tal* [valley] at Eisenach, more often however, like the paths around the Heuscheuer[71] which are hard going, even for the solitary walker. The mounted men had to leave their horses with the Hussars. Only my adjutant and the adjutant of the 2nd Battalion brought theirs. Later all of the horses followed the same path, I never believed that the beasts could climb like that.

In every clearing of the woods, every widening of the ravine, we expected to be met with a hail of lead, but no. Only the highest and narrowest point of the pass had been blocked with an abatis. This had been anticipated and the pioneers quickly cleared it away. We moved on, neither hearing nor seeing the enemy until we reached the thinner woods on the plateau when we heard heavy shell fire. The direction was rather

---

71   Tr. Note: probably referring to the Heuscheuer mountains in the Glatz area, where erosion has shaped the sandstone into fanciful and grotesque forms.

uncertain since the echoes in the woods were deceptive. Small arms fire sizzled around us so that twigs splintered and fell, but [strangely] it sounded like the hiss of our *own* bullets. A road led downwards to the right, probably to Dneboch, and several followed this path where they were met by *Prussian* rifle fire. We had correctly identified the unique hiss [of our own bullets]. The 14th Brigade, soon the 13th as well, were in the valley on the northern side of the Musky Berg and were already engaged with the enemy infantry, but held in check and harassed by an [Austrian] battery [situated on the heights]. At that very moment we heard a small hurrah on the left side in the woods. One section had captured an Austrian patrol of six men.

We now kept to the left where the going was easier, and just as we reached the edge of the woods, the pointed peak of the Musky Berg appeared before us. At the same moment however, we were peppered with well-aimed fire from some Austrian Jäger, probably from the 29th Jäger Battalion.[72] The 11th and 8th Companies, exhausted from climbing (although we carried out our expedition without packs) assembled inside the woods and the rifle platoons [*Schützenzüge*], were advanced to the wood's edge. Initially I wanted to wait for both battalions to come up, however I relinquished that idea and organized an enveloping attack instead, to be carried out by the Fusilier battalions that had already assembled. It was an immediate success, though not without losses. The Fusilier companies fanned out in all directions, down the deep ravines and over the dissected plateau. The 10th Company proceeded directly to the village of Musky, the 11th headed off to the right to take an enemy battery that was positioned there in the rear (however it moved out before we could capture it). The 9th and 12th Companies went around the village [of Musky] on the left.

In the meantime, the 2nd Battalion had concentrated and followed on behind, to right and left, in two half battalions. The general objective [*point d'appui*], was some castle ruins on a rocky peak near the village of Bossin.

Our advance was so rapid that the enemy (although he was present in significantly superior numbers), was unable to take up the numerous defensive positions available to him in the various scattered villages and farmsteads separated by ravines and strips of forest. The Italians from Regiment Sigismund [IR 45 recruited in Venetia] surrendered to us in droves, happy to escape our needle guns which, in spite of the constant advance and minimal expenditure of cartridges, were terrifyingly effective. Further on we ran into stronger resistance, but even that was only momentary, from the Hungarians of IR 72 Ramming, who had previously been stationed in Holstein. Later, in the capture of Bossin we had to deal with the Bohemians of IR 35 Khevenhüller, and here the fighting was most serious. All in all, 400 prisoners were captured. The enemy then fell back to Fürstenbrück.

72 Author's Note: Here we repeat what has already been said about the enemy position, adding somewhat. The enemy had two brigades in action here which had taken positions nearly at right angles to each other. Brigade Piret, initially facing north, held the plateau of the Musky Berg and the village of Musky. Brigade Abele (Kalik) stood at the western slope of the mountain, with Regiment Ramming in and around Dneboch, Regiment Khevenhüller in Sasadka and Bossin. The first clash was with Brigade Piret, the second, more serious clash, with Brigade Abele. The artillery, probably eight guns [a battery], was positioned halfway up the slope, east of Dneboch.

Our success this day was achieved with relatively small losses. They were nearly the same in both actions. The Elbe Army (von Schöler's advance guard), lost 167 men at Weissleim and Kloster, the 1st Army lost 164 men on the Musky Berg. *Major* Junk, of Hohenzollern Fusilier Regiment Nr. 40 was killed as he led his 3rd Battalion against Haber. Austrian losses were substantial, particularly in the number captured (1400 men).

Fighting at Boissin.

In Münchengrätz

Von Schöler's advanced guard had in the meantime established itself in Münchengrätz and Kloster, while the main body of the Elbe Army bivouacked on the meadow ground that lies between the two (and through which the Iser flows).

Barely fifty residents remained behind in Münchengrätz, even fewer in Kloster, and all exhibited hostility and bitterness. The wells had been blocked in the most disgusting fashion, and the water rendered undrinkable. All provender had been carried off or buried and hidden.

All of this put our extremely exhausted[73] men in a bad humour, and then came an event, or at least the rumour thereof, that raised this discontent to the most extreme rage. In Kloster, so it was said, about 60 men had been lured into the back of a vaulted cellar under the pretext of 'wanting to give them a good drink.' [At some point] a cask of spirits towards the front [of the cellar], was set on fire, and its [blazing] contents soon spread, blocking all escape, there was talk of thirteen men burned.

The news of this ran like wildfire from battalion to battalion and gave rise to immense rage. Two of the workers at the distillery were considered guilty. One was cut down, the other, bleeding from a deep neck wound and with his hands tied behind him was dragged away to be questioned and condemned. He was later released, 'despite his sullen looks, which, at the end, was no proof,' (as a report put it). Upon interrogation it was determined that his own wife and children were in the burning house. Enough said. We are firmly convinced that our own faults, boisterousness, immoderation and carelessness caused the accident. In tapping the distilled spirits someone forgot, or didn't think it worth the trouble, to close the tap. The liquid flowed through the dark rooms and someone carelessly set it on fire. Such things are hard to believe until they are proven. Not virtue, but fear [of punishment], prevents men in moments like these from becoming vengeful savages.

Fortunately, the spirit cellar in the cloister was not opened up, but the adjoining beer cellar put all of us back in a good mood. When, after ten hours of marching, our need was at its greatest, and everyone was happy to scoop up muddy water from puddles with their mess tins, a treasure was discovered, an unfathomably deep, broad, rock hewn cellar. The *Braumeister* was summoned as people began to suspect the contents, and immediately full barrels of the most magnificent, ice cold beer, were brought out with block and tackle. Thirstily everyone thronged towards the dark cavern in which the treasure lay. 'The supply is inexhaustible', the official reassured us. 'The Austrians and Saxons hauled casks out for three days, but even if you stayed here for eight days, you could not exhaust the supply.' How wonderful that sounded after the torments of thirst our men had endured! This Waldstein brewery with its bottomless cellars was the most beautiful find our Elbe Army made during the whole campaign. Throughout the entire afternoon, officers of all arms of the service pushed their way to this source. More and more the news of it spread to every campsite, and requisition details came and dragged the casks to the most distant bivouacs. 'What priceless nectar! An ocean was consumed!' So said one who had shared in the drinking.

However, not a bite of bread was to be had. The lords of the corps headquarters who had quartered themselves in Waldstein's castle had nothing for supper but champagne and potatoes. A few were fortunate in their find. They were 'Sunday's children.' 'I had just lain down,' said

---

73 Author's Note: The following [officer] description sheds light on the extremity of their exhaustion. 'The heat at midday was unbearable. Finally, our route carried us past a marsh, and we drank greedily. However, immediately after the delight of the repulsive and lukewarm water, I began to stagger and to fall down like a drunkard. I fell upon our drum major, who good - naturedly took my rifle on his shoulder and gave me his arm. However, I was ashamed of my weakness and tore myself away. For a moment my will was victorious, and then I collapsed. There I lay and saw, as in a dream, the men march on past me. I did not have the strength to stand. Fortunately, my batman saw me and gave me some liquid to drink, whether schnaps or water I cannot say, and helped me. At that moment, I made a quick decision and threw away my knapsack, thereby making it possible to move more freely. Finally, we received the order to 'Halt!' and in the same moment, the entire squad lay down on the ground. All of our strength was gone.'

an officer of the 69th, 'when my servant burst breathlessly into the room and shouted, '*Herr Lieutenant*', there is a piglet down below in the courtyard!' A piglet! What news! I dashed down without cap, tunic or neck cloth, grabbing a *Hauptmann's* servant as reinforcements along the way, and now began the hunt for the divine piglet, which finally expired under the blows of the two servants. My servant, versatile and able for anything, brought a burning wisp of straw and singed the hide and scraped it with a sword, now to the kitchen. There were pots and pans in abundance, finally under a cupboard, we found a basin with a dubious substance that we thought might be a mixture of butter and syrup. Whatever it was it served our purpose, and the suckling pig was done. Then potatoes from the cellar and we had a feast for the Gods. Drawn by the aroma, our *Major* was the first to appear, and smiling, received his portion. Younger officers who could no longer make their way into the jam packed room, lined up outside, gazing ravenously through the door and windows, suffering the torments of hell until it was their turn.'

However, suckling pigs were not to be found everywhere. Until the middle of the night, when the supply columns arrived, most of the men had nothing but the beer from the Waldstein cellar. 'Never,' wrote one, 'did I so greatly appreciate the truth that beer is liquid bread.' And so came the night. From the castle on the hill our men had a magnificent view of the Iser valley. Flickering campfires stretched as far as the eye could see. Here and there a swirling cloud of smoke, and overhead, the dark, still, starry heavens.

The 3rd Division to Gitschin

In the Podkost Woods

On the afternoon of the 28th, immediately after the actions at Münchengrätz [and Kloster] that led to the union of the 7th and 8th divisions [of 1st Army], and the three divisions of the Elbe Army, the remaining elements of the 1st Army were located as follows:

> The 6th Division at Brzina facing the Musky Berg.
> The 5th Division (to its left) at Rowensko.
> The 4th Division between Daubrow and Zidar.
> The 3rd Division between Zidar and Zehrow.

Until the 28th, Horn and Fransecky (8th and 7th divisions), had the taken the lead. Now the 5th and 3rd divisions were placed in front and received orders to advance on Gitschin, the 5th Division via Rowensko and the 3rd Division via Podkost and Sobotka.

Both divisions made contact with the enemy, the 3rd first. Therefore, we will initially follow the 3rd Division on its advance, starting with a bit of background.

The 3rd Division followed behind the 8th Division, marching from Zittau (on the Bohemian border) to Grottau on the 23rd, Kratzau on the 24th, cantonments in and around Kratzau on the 25th and 26th, and on the 27th, first to Reichenberg and then [bearing right], to Liebenau. On the 28th (after witnessing the fighting at Münchengrätz from the Sichrow plateau), to Zehrow and Zidar, where the main body bivouacked.

However, on the assumption that the advance the following day [the 29th], would proceed through the pass at Podkost, it seemed advisable to carry out a reconnaissance in advance. Accordingly, *Oberst* von Stahr, commander of the 14th Infantry Regiment, was ordered to reconnoiter the route on the evening of the 28th, and this resulted in the ensuing night action.

Before describing this action, we shall give a short account of the situation and the terrain. On the evening of the 28th, after the fighting at Münchengrätz [and Kloster], the Austro - Saxon Army was between Münchengrätz and Gitschin in Brigade echelons as follows:

Brigade Poschacher (farthest forward) at Gitschin.
Brigade Piret at Sobotka.
Brigade Leiningen (behind Brigade Piret) at Wosek.
Brigade Abele (behind Brigade Leiningen) at Ober Bautzen.[74]

These positions entailed significant danger [for the Austrians]. If the Prussian 3rd Division (which had orders to advance to Gitschin via Podkost and Sobotka) was lucky enough to reach Sobotka during the night of 28/29th, while Brigades Leiningen and Abele were still to the [west], then Brigades Leiningen and Abele would be cut off.[75] In order to avert this danger, Brigade Ringelsheim had already been detached on the evening of the 27th to close the easily defended pass at Podkost, and thereby block the only road leading from the north to Sobotka.

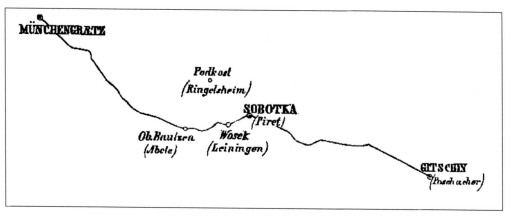

The road to Podkost, winds through woods and between strange rock formations of great picturesque charm. From east of the Musky Berg, the road initially passes through a fir forest whose flatness and uniformity give no hint of what is to come. Suddenly, isolated cones of rock

---

74 Author's Note: The Saxons took a more southerly route, via Unter Bautzen, Brezno and Liban.
75 Tr. Note: A map of the larger area shows Sobotka at the intersection of two roads. The northern (minor) one, comes from Podol via Podkost, the southern (major) one, comes from Münchengrätz via Bossin, Fürstenbrück and Ober Bautzen, to Sobotka. The northern route, upon which the Prussian 3rd Division was advancing, was shorter, the southern route, along which the Austrian brigades were proceeding from Münchengrätz, was longer. Therefore, the pinch point at Schloss Podkost had to be held if Brigades Leiningen and Abele were to make good their escape to Gitschin.

like sugar loaves, thrust upwards from between the trees, gradually increasing in number until the rock has displaced the forest and forms a high wall on either side of the ever narrowing road. After about ten minutes the rocky defile widens, the fir trees and rocks recede, and linden trees and old nut trees begin to fill the broad, empty space. Behind the trees however, towering over them by more than a hundred feet, loomed the forbidding presence of Schloss Kost. Anyone who wished to continue [to Sobotka] would first have to pass through its courtyard and gate. On the other side of the gate a stream (the Bili Rybnik), had filled the basin that lay between the castle gate and the rocks behind [forming a small lake]. This was the pass which Brigade Ringelsheim had held for the past 24 hours and towards which the 3rd Division was now advancing, Detachment Stahr in the lead.

Detachment Stahr was about ten companies strong and consisted of two battalions of the 14th Regiment, two companies (1st and 3rd) of the Greifswalder Jäger, plus one hundred Pioneers and a troop of Blücher Hussars, Jägers leading. At 10:00 the detachment moved out of its Bivouac at Zehrow, and one hour later arrived at the pass. Soon our Jäger came up against the enemy outposts, some in the woods, others behind an abatis. The narrowness of the road and the height of the trees made everything dark despite the bright moon overhead. Our men exchanged a few shots with the enemy who, without attempting any serious resistance, fell back to a second position (another abatis), where a lengthier firefight developed.

Fighting at Podkost.

The darkness prevented any further advance so at about 1.00, *Oberst* Stahr chose to break off the engagement. Not for long however, as soon as there was sufficient light to take aim, our Jäger (reinforced by two companies of the 14th Regiment) renewed the attack, and despite a stubborn defense, forced [the enemy] back to Schloss Kost itself. During this advance *Lieutenant* L'homme de Courbière, of the 1st Jäger Company, fell with a bullet in his heart. Facing the ancient rock castle, whose highest windows were already lit with the first light of dawn, the detachment now halted. Should it launch an attack? That seemed rash. All points of access were barricaded, the enemy was in a good position and shortly thereafter opened fire. In addition to the [Austrian] 26th Jäger Battalion, which up to this point had opposed our Pomeranian Jäger, several infantry regiments were also present, the castle itself being held by two companies of IR 73 Würtemberg. At 6.00 [in the morning] *Oberst* Staher sent a situation report and requested further orders, however before these could arrive the Austrians withdrew, and at 7:45 the 14th Fusiliers entered Schloss Kost without meeting any resistance, sending a few rounds after the [Austrian] detachments that were already disappearing on the far side of the waters of the Bili Rybnik.

The enemy's withdrawal was voluntary. By 6:30 in the morning *Generalmajor* Ringelsheim had been informed that Brigades Leiningen and Abele were past Sobotka. Accordingly, there was no longer any reason to hold the position and he issued the appropriate orders. Once the main body of the [Prussian 3rd] division had arrived, our force followed in pursuit. The night action at Podkost had cost us three dead (including *Lieutenant* Courbière) and 17 wounded. Enemy losses consisted of five officers and 72 other ranks, almost entirely from the 26th Jäger Battalion.

The fight for Unter Lochow

We left the main body of the 3rd Division in its bivouac at the Musky Berg between the villages of Zidar and Zehrow.

On the morning of the 29th orders arrived from the headquarters of Prince Friedrich Karl, 'Capture Schloss Kost, pursue the enemy on the Sobotka Gitschin road and take [Gitschin]' (at the time the order was issued, the capture of Schloss Kost was not yet known).

And so, on to Gitschin! The pass between Podkost and Sobotka was open and the enemy was in retreat. If there was to be a battle this day it would be in the afternoon somewhere on the road between Sobotka and Gitschin, and in the event, that is what happened.

The [3rd] Division, *Generallieutenant* von Werder, moved out of its bivouacs at 12:00 noon in scorching sunlight. At 1:00 it reached Schloss Kost, Detachment Stahr rejoining their battalions, or as the case might be, their regiments. After the formation of a new advanced guard (one squadron of Blücher Hussars, two companies of Greifswalder Jäger, two companies from the 14th Regiment, Fusilier Battalion (Malotki) from the 42nd Regiment, and the 4pdr Battery Gallus, the march to Sobotka was resumed. The 5th Brigade followed a short distance behind, the 6th brought up the rear. The composition of both was as follows:

5th Brigade (*Generalmajor* von Januschowski):
Grenadier regiment Nr. 2 (*Oberst* von Reichenbach).
1st and 2nd Battalions Infantry regiment Nr. 42.
4pdr Battery Ekensteen.
6pdr Battery Dewitz.
12pdr Battery Grüger 2nd Field Artillery Regiment.

6th Brigade (*Generalmajor* von Winterfeld):
1st and Fusilier Battalions from the 14th Regiment.
1st and 2nd Battalions from 54th Regiment.
1st and 3rd Companies from 2nd Jäger Battalion.
2nd Pioneer Battalion.

Three squadrons of the Blücher Hussars made up the vanguard, the reserve artillery of II Army Corps brought up the rear. Only the advanced guard and 5th Brigade took a direct and active part in battle that developed in the afternoon.

At 2:30 the little town of Sobotka was reached. The march had only lasted for an hour and a half, but already a large number of men had fallen out along the way due to the burning sun and oppressive humidity. The march was halted at the market square where everyone hastened to quench their burning thirst and threw themselves down in the shade of the surrounding stone arcades. After a short rest it was, 'pick up your rifles,' and the heavily laden, dust covered columns, wound out of the narrow streets with the sun reflecting off helmets and rifle barrels, bearing off to the left on the broad, fortunately tree lined, highway, that led from Jung Buntzlau and Münchengrätz to Gitschin.

Rolling along this road in a light carriage on a bright autumn day is a joy for the eye and the heart. The Bohemian landscape is always beautiful but here it achieves its full charm. The rolling landscape stretches before you, wooded plantations alternate with farm fields and broad expanses of grain extend to the blue horizon. In the distance one can see ridges and ruined castles, none more beautiful than the famous *Burg* Trosky,' destroyed by Ziska,[76] its ruins still commanding the view for miles around. Such is the route between Sobotka and Gitschin, but the dusty battalions marching that day under a scorching sun, had no eyes for *Burg* Trosky. Their tongues stuck to the roofs of their parched mouths.[77] The song that one or another started, soon died away - but what's that! (all heads turned toward it) the thunder of guns could be heard from Rowensko, from the Turnau Gitschin road, that's where our 5th Division was advancing! All were electrified, exhaustion forgotten, are we in contact with the enemy, this was the question that ran through the columns.

The distant firing kept up but perceptibly shifted towards Gitschin, and soon was so far ahead that the men gave up their hopes of an encounter, but they were wrong. As the advanced guard (by now it was 6:00) emerged from Woharitz into the open, it came under short range fire. Before them, on either side of the road, were the villages of Ober and Unter Lochow. Passing between them was unavoidable, and this led to the bloody battle of Unter Lochow. First we shall look at the terrain and the enemy positions.

---

76   Tr. Note: Jan Ziska, c. 1370 -1424, was a leader of the Bohemian Hussites.

77   Author's Note: On this march, in the village of Samsin, a group of soldiers crowded around the well, and several wanted to put the bucket to their lips, when a [soldier's] voice called, 'Don't drink, the well is poisoned.' Stunned, the thirsty men dropped the bucket and let it lie on the ground, suffering the torments of Tantalus. Then a young German -Bohemian girl, came from a house they had thought abandoned and stepped, half sympathetic, half indignant, through the close packed group of enemy soldiers to the well. Silently she took the mess tin from a soldier's hand, dipped it in the bucket and drank. The scornful way that she gazed with burning cheeks at those around her was more eloquent than a thousand words. The men now drank like those dying of thirst in the desert.

The terrain, the enemy positions

The [main] road that passes through Woharitz between Ober and Unter Lochow, leads over a wooded plateau that gradually falls off to the right. On the left it rises and ends in a rock formation (The Prachow Heights, *Prachower Felsen*) that runs parallel with the road. Directly in front of Ober and Unter Lochow (the first to the north, the other to the south of the road), rise several ridges that command the ground before them, the woods and the road that runs through their midst.

The ground is such that two northern ridges, a short distance apart, extend in front of [west of] Ober Lochow, while in front of Unter Lochow there is only a single ridge which rises towards St. Anne peak [Anna Berg]. Behind [Unter Lochow] is a plateau that drops rather steeply to the west (toward the village). Therefore, Unter Lochow is in a sort of hollow and can only be occupied by an enemy advancing from the west after the capture of the preceding ridge. It cannot be held until the commanding edge of the plateau behind it has also been captured. In the event, it was the capture of the edge of this plateau that decided the battle for Unter Lochow. The advance to the left (in front of Ober Lochow), was of only secondary importance.

The twin spires of Wohawec church with the Annaberg in the background.

Before we describe the events that led to the capture of the plateau's edge, and thereby to the opening the road to Gitschin, we shall describe the Austrian positions.

Ober and Unter Lochow were held by Brigade Ringelsheim (that had fought in the night action at Podkost) and by several battalions of Brigade Abele. A Saxon cavalry regiment was positioned in reserve, somewhat to the left and rear. The individual units were positioned as follows:

First echelon:

> Unter Lochow (center) 1st and 2nd Battalions IR 42 Hannover.
> Ober Lochow (right wing) 3rd Battalion IR 42 Hannover.
> Anna Berg (left wing) Saxon cavalry.
> In front of Ober Lochow, two (according to other statements, three) batteries.

Second Echelon:

> On the plateau between Unter Lochow and Wohavec (Center) 26th Jäger Battalion, all three
> Battalions IR 73 Würtemberg.
> Prachow Heights, behind Ober Lochow (right wing) 22nd Jäger Battalion, 1st Battalion IR 72 Ramming, both from Brigade Abele.
> Behind the Anna Berg, as far as Wostruzno (left wing) Nicolaus Hussars.

The advanced guard captures Unter Lochow, the artillery battle, failure on the Left Wing

We shall leave our advanced guard in Woharitz at the point where they deployed from the main road. The first task was to reconnoiter the woods. The 4pdr Battery Gallus went into position (on the left), soon joined by batteries Ekensteen and Dewitz (on the right), and under the protection of their combined fire (Battery Gallus had already forced the enemy to fall back), our advanced guard moved forward on both sides of the road. The Greifswalder Jäger, who were on the right flank, took possession of the Anna Berg. The 42nd Fusiliers, *Major* von Malotki, forced the enemy out of Unter Lochow. The two companies of Infantry Regiment Nr. 14 that were advancing on the left side of the highway, advanced to Ober Lochow.

Up to this point everything seemed to be going well and it looked as if we would have an easy victory like Podkost. However, the situation soon changed. So far we had only been dealing with the enemy's outposts, now he attacked with his full strength. The [Austrian] 22nd Jäger Battalion and the 1st Battalion IR 72 Ramming, which had hitherto been by the Prachow Heights, attacked our left flank (the two companies of Infantry Regiment Nr. 14) and drove them easily back through the woods. Battery Gallus, which had now lost its infantry cover, had to follow suit and pulled back to its original position, on the [Prussian] left in front of Woharitz. The situation seemed to be taking an equally unfavourable turn in Unter Lochow (the actual key to the position), where four companies of the 42nd Fusiliers faced a numerically superior enemy. Things weren't going well for the Fusiliers, *Major* von Malotki had been wounded and *Hauptmann* von Puttkamer was dead. At this moment of extreme danger, one of the Jäger companies at the foot of the Anna Berg (the 4th Company under *Hauptmann* von Reibnitz), was ordered to move back to the village to support the Fusiliers, it was a move that nearly ended in disaster. We shall give it a moment.

In order to reach Unter Lochow, the company first had to leave the hollow in which it was located and proceed along a sunken road that cut across it. The Greifswalders (marching four abreast) had hardly made their way along this trough (6 feet deep and barely 30 paces wide), when their left flank was suddenly attacked with musket butts and sword bayonets, while 12 yards ahead of them, the grey coats and dark feather hats of Austrian Jäger came into view. It was the [Austrian] 26th Jäger battalion which had been on our left flank unnoticed, and now charged with loud *hochs* to the Emperor. Only a few of our men could climb to the top of the bank to fire, the others were blocked in, defenseless. But this dangerous situation did not last long. Following an impulse, the company ran 50 yards to the side and hastily scrambled up [the opposite] bank from which they delivered a well - directed, rapid fire. For no more than half a minute the powder smoke obscured the scene, then, as the smoke cleared, the enemy was gone.

Our Jäger now approached Unter Lochow unhindered, where at nearly the same time, the first units of 5th Brigade were arriving (2nd Battalion of Grenadier Regiment Nr. 2, King Friedrich Wilhelm IV), here too the fight resumed as the enemy fell back.

Envelopment of the enemy Left Wing, breaking through the Center

The battle had begun at 6:00. It may have been 7:30 (the frequent halts and rests had separated the advance guard from the main body), when the 5th Brigade, and soon thereafter, the 6th Brigade, arrived in the immediate vicinity of the battlefield at Woharitz. The 6th Brigade bore off to the left where it contented itself with preventing a second breakthrough at this position.

In the meantime, Grenadier Regiment Nr. 2 formed two assault columns, outflanking the enemy's left with their right hand column, while breaking through the enemy's center with the left.

We shall follow both columns in their advance:

> The outflanking column, two battalions strong, was personally led by *Oberst* von Reichenbach, the Regimental Commanding Officer. Consisting of the 1st and Fusilier Battalions, it kept to the south, passed the woods and swung right around the Anna Berg, then climbed up (from the south) onto the plateau between Unter Lochow and Wohawec, and advanced in line as if it was on exercise, to that last named village. The enemy reserves that were there, who were also being attacked from the front, did not feel strong enough to resist the advance of both of our battalions (now supported by Battery Dewitz on their right), and fell back, thus exposing their line of retreat.

Apparently the situation in the center was decided at the same time. Here the 2nd Battalion, *Major* von der Osten, advanced parallel to the highway and forced its way into Unter Lochow. Up to this point, the fighting, as conducted by the advance guard, had been primarily in the nature of an intense infantry action. Ground had been gained only to be lost again. Only a few farmsteads, maybe only one, were still in our hands. However, this was not where the danger lay. On the plateau, to the rear of the village [Wohawec], were two Battalions of IR 42 Hannover that had previously been fighting in the center, and two Battalions of IR 73 Würtemberg. If they all advanced together before our main body arrived, they could have smashed our already decimated advance - guard. Fortunately, we forestalled this. *Major* von der Osten [2nd Battalion 2nd Grenadiers], had the men drop their knapsacks and advance onto the densely held slope of the plateau in assault column.[78] The battalion had scarcely advanced 40 yards when it was halted by an intense flanking fire from the far side of the highway to its left, and also to its front. The battalion started to falter, those that were toward the rear showed an inclination to fall back to the village [Unter Lochow], *Major* von der Osten was wounded. Only with extreme effort was *Hauptmann* von Keyserlink, who assumed command, able to keep the battalion in its position.

Our rapid fire finally cleared the slope in front [of enemy] while the main body of the battalion, seeking cover everywhere, was at least able to establish itself in the ground between the village and the slope. To the left, the road embankment provided excellent cover. One Battalion of Regiment Hannover that dared to ascend it from the far side suffered heavy losses. An immediate danger had been averted, indeed a certain measure of success was achieved. However, it was more apparent than real, and in any case, it was only secondary. We had regained the village [Unter Lochow], and had even cleared the slope of the plateau, but the plateau itself remained in enemy hands. There they stood with three intact battalions, firmly resolved not to give up the position without making a last, decisive effort. The enemy was still superior to us in numbers and position, all the odds were with him if he tried.

With hurrahs and beating drums, the three columns advanced downhill towards the edge of the plateau and our exhausted Grenadiers. *Hauptmann* von Keyserlink quickly realized there was only one thing to do. Throwing skirmishers onto the highway, he formed up the battalion, moved two companies of the advanced guard (which had been pulled back into the second line upon the arrival of the Grenadiers) forward on the right flank, and met the charging enemy with a counter charge by the remaining [Prussian] forces. The thick powder smoke that hung between the combatants made it impossible to recognize the weak state of the [Prussian] battalion (it had already been reduced to 400 men). There was a brief clash and then the enemy scattered, the edge of the plateau was attained and the [Austrians], pursued by our fire (in which Batteries Gallus and Ekensteen joined), now flooded back.

The enemy suffered extremely heavy losses in this flight (the plateau afforded no cover), some from the rapid fire that we sent after him, yet more from the shells of the two batteries, whose bursts were still evident the next day. The dead of friend and foe lay in equal numbers at the edge of the plateau where the clash had taken place. 500 paces eastwards however, nearly halfway to

78   Tr. Note: One of the conclusions that the Prussian army drew from its study of the Second Italian War, was to emphasize the use of small units trained to work independently. It was then that the company column became the basic formation for manoeuvre and combat. The Prussian company column rearranged the company line of two platoons side by side (each of three ranks, with the best shots and most experienced soldiers in the third rank), with the company column of *three* platoons, one platoon wide and three deep. In the company column, each of the three platoons now had two ranks. The rearmost platoon, the *Schützenzug*, consisted of what had been the rearmost rank of the original two platoons, now forming a third, two ranked platoon, consisting of the best shots and most experienced soldiers. In action these *Schützenzüge*, or rifle platoons might be thrown out as skirmishers in advance of the remainder of the column. Regensberger quotes Moltke on this unique instance, where the formerly standard, but now outmoded and discouraged Battalion Column (*Kolonne nach der Mitte*), was employed. 'The most extensive use, with the greatest success, is made of the company column. Only one single case can be found in the records where a battalion column was led into enemy infantry fire. It was the 2nd Battalion, 2nd Grenadier Regiment King Friedrich Wilhelm IV, at Gitchin, and the losses that it suffered warn against future use of this formation.' (Regensberg, *1866, Gitschin*, p. 66. Footnote).

Fighting at Gitschin.

Wohawec, there were only Austrians, more than a hundred (including three officers), whom our pursuing fire had felled. The slope and its edge, and also the plateau itself, was ours. A cavalry attack that was delivered without much commitment was repulsed. The enemy, his center broken and with darkness falling (it was now 9:00), fell back to Gitschin.

At the same time, the other two battalions of the 2nd Grenadier Regiment were bypassing the plateau. [At the other end of the battlefield] the 5th Division was storming the Brada position. Things developed so favourably for us this day that the advance of the 3rd Division supported the advance of the 5th, and conversely the advance of the 5th Division supported the advance of the 3rd. Whether the courageous action that we have described above was decisive to the outcome of the battle or not, it will always remain as one of the most brilliant and most poetic episodes of this war. Thus, it is hardly surprising that more than one song of the 2nd Battalion [of the 2nd Grenadier Regiment] has been written to celebrate it.

It already looked the enemy in the eye,
Far greater their numbers,
Five against one, it is almost too much.
It pauses and looks around for help,

Only enemies everywhere.
Down they kneel, 'God, Lord God,
Help us Father, Help us in our need,
Even through death, to victory.'

And now, in God's name, onward,
And the cry could be heard, far and near, as they charged,
'Help us, God, through death to victory.'[79]

The losses

Among the fallen was a Massow, a Borcke and a Dewitz, bearers of three of the oldest Pomeranian names. They rest in a single grave. Von Dewitz was shot by an Austrian officer to whom he was offering mercy. As he requested his sword, the Austrian officer shot him with his revolver. Even in his death throws von Dewitz managed to thrust his own sword through the breast of his perfidious foe. We do not know whether another event that we shall describe is related to the above. A young officer, it is said, who fought and fell at Unter Lochow had a dream on the day of the invasion of Bohemia, that we would be hit by a bullet in the evening of June 29th. There was no lack of the usual jokes. Then came the 29th, the fighting was over, the troops went to their bivouacs and his comrades asked with as much merriment as the moment allowed, how things stood now with fulfilment of his dream. He answered that it was not yet evening. Soon afterward came the order to advance. The young officer led the first platoon of skirmishers. 30 Austrians had taken cover under a bridge on the road to Gitschin. They had already surrendered their rifles and stood behind the leader of the skirmishers (who was helping a wounded enemy comrade out of the ditch), when one of the captured soldiers grabbed a rifle from the ground and shot him through the heart from behind.

---

79   Author's Note; This report, written with great vividness, was the basis of the lines above: 'We were met by fearsome rifle fire as we moved out of the village. The commander, *Major* von der Osten, collapsed. The officers took post at the front and again the battalion advanced with beating drums. We could only feel the enemy, since we could see nothing in the thick powder smoke. We could not fire since we believed that our own skirmishers were ahead of us … soon the smoke cleared. New skirmishers were thrown out and the battalion advanced, however the enemy fire seemed to increase. Every moment one heard a cry, or saw a comrade fall without a sound. Two thirds of the officers were already dead or wounded. We were in danger of losing our strength. The enemy outnumbered us greatly (four battalions, so it seemed, faced us) and our battalion began to pray out loud: 'Father help us, No shame, Victory or death!' *Hauptmann* von Keyserlingk, who assumed command of the battalion after von der Osten was wounded, grasped the colours, the drums beat, everyone summoned up their last strength and we charged with hurrahs toward the enemy, who surrendered or fled. The plateau was ours and we held it fast.'

The action at Unter Lochow cost the Division 28 officers and 466 men. The heaviest losses were suffered by the Fusilier Battalion of the 42nd Regiment and the 2nd Battalion of Grenadier Regiment Nr. 2 Friedrich Wilhelm IV, which in the advance - guard, defeated superior enemy forces at Unter Lochow and finally repulsed them after repeated assaults. The Grenadiers lost 11 officers and 131 men dead or wounded. The Fusilier Battalion of the 42nd lost 7 officers and 126 men. The first named battalion [Fusiliers of the 42nd Regiment] returned from the fight with only five unwounded officers.

Enemy losses, despite the advantage provided by his position, were far heavier. Brigade Ringelsheim lost close to 1,000 men, including 55 officers. The losses suffered by the individual battalions of Brigade Abele in Ober Lochow were limited.

The Saxon cavalry regiment (the 3rd Reiter) that was attached to Brigade Ringelsheim, was deployed on the extreme left wing of the Austrian position where it was unable to take part in the battle and suffered relatively heavy losses from the fire of Batteries Dewitz and Gallus (the better known cavalry attacks appear to have been made by Austrian Hussars). Three officers, including *Oberst* von Ludwiger, the Regimental Commanding Officer, were wounded. *Rittmeister* von Fabrice[80] was killed.

---

80 Author's Note: *Rittmeister* von Fabrice was (as it later turned out) was buried with many others in a common grave. About three weeks later, a retired Saxon general, *General* von Heygendorf, arrived to search for the fallen *Rittmeister*, and bring his body back to Saxony. This happened many times, and on the Saxon side, with as much discretion as courage and persistence. In this case *General* von Heygendorf was successful in locating the body of the fallen officer. He first obtained permission to have the graves opened. He then proceeded to Unter Lochow, near which the *Rittmeister* was supposed to have been killed (all sources agreed on this). He found several large graves in which Austrians, Saxons and Prussians, 50 to 100 in a grave, had been buried by train soldiers [soldiers who accompanied the wagons and attended to matters of supply, logistics etc.] after the battle. Who however, among the Bohemian speaking locals, would be able to provide information as to where the Saxon *Rittmeister* was buried? And yet he succeeded. *General* von Heygendorf went to a priest, explained his intentions to him, and had him (as interpreter) offer the residents of Unter Lochow a *gulden* for each Saxon military artefact they produced. First an old woman brought an epaulet of a Saxon *Rittmeister*. She received her *gulden* and that encouraged the suspicious Bohemians, who next brought an Order of the Iron Crown, then a wedding ring, and then, after receiving their rewards, repeated everything that they knew. The *Rittmeister* had appeared behind a farm late in the afternoon of the 29th, apparently severely wounded. The people called out to him that he should come in, there were no Prussians there. He then dismounted and fell dead in the garden. The next morning he was buried in a great grave at the roadside with about 50 other dead. Since the Order and the wedding ring (with his wife's initials), undoubtedly belonged to *Rittmeister* von Fabrice, it seemed certain to *General* von Heygendorf that he would find the body of his friend in the designated grave. It was opened, but, after the three weeks that had passed, features were no longer recognizable. The first row had already been searched through in vain when the light blue tunic of a Saxon Guards cavalryman was spotted. It was evident that he was an officer, and the markings in his socks, *v. F.*, with the numbers *3* and *4* (socks with the corresponding other two numbers were found in the *Rittmeister's* luggage, which remained with the regiment) left no doubt that the sought - for body was there. *General* von Heygendorf had a coffin brought from Gitschin and carriage to Dresden followed. (This mission, as we noted above, was carried out with great sensitivity. Whether in general it is advisable to carry out such missions, must be left an open question. It is a matter of feelings. For our part, we might prefer that the resting place of the dead be left undisturbed.)

The march to Gitschin

The fighting ended at about 9:00 [pm]. After nine hours of marching, to say nothing of the stress of battle, the troops were extremely exhausted. Nevertheless, a last effort had to be made. The orders were most specific: Gitschin was to be occupied in the course of the 29th.

So, forward! There was no water to speak of on the plateau, nor even in the villages. Gitschin however, must at the very least have a few wells. Thus, the prospect of being able to quench their thirst helped the columns to overcome their weariness, to soundlessly move along the dusty highway and over the already downtrodden grainfields to its right and left, to the town, only distinguishable in the dark by its towers. The Fusilier Battalion of the Grenadier Regiment was in the lead, the 2nd Battalion of the 54th following after. Prisoners were brought in. Where the enemy held out in individual farmsteads along the way, his resistance was quickly broken.

Just before Gitschin there was water, poor and muddy, but still nectar for those already half dead from thirst. Advanced patrols soon brought in reports that the town was not occupied and *Major* von Stölting was ordered to enter it with his Fusiliers. This took place and an easily won success seemed likely to close the day, but it turned out otherwise. A momentary check at least was still in store for us, we shall come back to it in a subsequent chapter.

The 5th Division to Gitschin

Reconnaissance by *Oberstlieutenant* Heinichen

After crossing the border at Seidenberg, the 5th Division proceeded to Reichenberg. (Its first bivouac was at Dittersbach, the advance guard at Einsiedel).There were no signs of the enemy, not even minor skirmishes such as the 7th and 8th Divisions had experienced with their cavalry patrols (the Ascherslebner Hussars and Thuringen Uhlans).

The 25th was a day of rest in Reichenberg. On the 26th the division reached Gablonz and on the 27th, Eisenbrod. Early on the 28th (camp was broken at 3:00) it reached Rowensko with the advance guard on the Gitschin road past Ktowa.

The next day the division was to proceed to Gitschin, and so it seemed prudent to determine whether Gitschin was occupied by the enemy, and whether he intended to hold it. A reconnaissance was decided on and a combined cavalry detachment was formed under the command of *Oberstlieutenant* Heinichen, commander of the 2nd (Brandenburg) Dragoons. The detachment consisted of six squadrons of cavalry and one mounted battery (the Fürstenwald Uhlans, the Aschersleben Hussars and the Schwedt Dragoons each contributing two squadrons). Shortly after 9:00 they rode out, the 1st Squadron of the Fürstenwald Uhlans in the lead. We take the following from an account obtained from the last named regiment:

> After we had gone nearly nine miles at a steady trot on dusty highways and in great heat, two troops of our 1st Squadron encountered the enemy at the village of Kbelnitz, a bit over half a mile from Gitschin. (The position on the Brada hill that was to be so stubbornly defended the next day had not yet been occupied). Three Jäger, presumably from the 18th Feldjäger Battalion, whom we captured in a field of grain near Kbelnitz, and soon afterwards, the bullets whistling around us, made it evident that the town was in enemy hands. In order to encourage the enemy to reveal his forces, the remainder of

the two squadrons joined up with the vanguard and trotted forward, while the enemy lying in the grain kept up a steady fire without actually hitting any of us. Suddenly thick clouds of dust appeared on our right flank to the south of Gitschin (thus coming from Münchengrätz), presumably caused by approaching cavalry. We were deploying for an attack when that well known whistle unique to shells, made clear our error. Since the ground seemed to offer no passable cover anywhere, and the purpose of the reconnaissance (to determine whether Gitschin was held or not), had been completed, *Oberstlieutenant* Heinichen ordered a retreat. The first ordeal of fire had been passed. 30 to 40 shells burst in the immediate vicinity of the squadron. Our *Lieutenant* von Busse had his horse torn apart from beneath him by a shell, three others landed in *Rittmeister Graf* Häfeler's squadron (of the Schwedt Dragoons) without causing notable damage. The Uhlans lost two men killed, four wounded. The losses of the other squadrons were even less. After a ride (there and back) of 18, 27 or 36 miles, depending on the point from which the unit had started, the detachment was back between Rowensko and Ktowa just after mid - day, riders and horses completely exhausted. Thirty hours later (on the 29th), our Uhlans would again stand on the same ground, under shell fire for a second time, with greater losses but without getting to attack.

The outcome of the reconnaissance thus read, 'Gitschin is held,' and the attack was put off to the next day. In the event, Gitschin *was* held, but not as we imagined. The enemy was far weaker than he appeared and consisted, in so far as infantry goes, of a single detached company of the 18th Jäger Battalion, that had only just arrived on the morning of the 28th (or shortly before) from Eisenbrod. In fact, there was nothing facing us apart from the 1st Light Cavalry Division under *Generalmajor* von Edelsheim, and three attached batteries of horse artillery.

Oberstlieutenant Heinichen was justified in not attacking this body of cavalry with his own inadequate force (six squadrons against six regiments), but it appears that he was deceived by the weak Jäger detachment and the heavy fire of the horse artillery and returned to the camp at Rowensko with a picture that did not correspond to the actual situation.

Austrian skirmishers at Gitchin.

Gitschin

Orders arrived at noon on the 29th for the 5th Division to proceed immediately to Gitschin, to capture the town and to occupy it. Carrying out these orders led in the course of the afternoon, to a series of bloody engagements. Before we describe these, we shall first give a short description of the town and its surroundings.

Gitschin (in Bohemian *Jicin*) is the [county town] of the *Kreis* of the same name, and one of the most fertile in the kingdom. The inhabitants, about 6,000, are predominately Czech. The locality, larger and more extensive than the number of its population would suggest, has an historical character entirely in accord with its history. Until the time of the outbreak of the Bohemian revolution (1618), it was an impoverished place consisting of about 200 clay and weatherboard houses, which if it was possible, became even less significant during the years of the insurrection. In 1623 Albrecht *Graf* von Waldstein (Wallenstein), purchased the town and its surroundings, and united them with his dominion of Friedland, raising it (by Imperial rescript) to the status of Duchy two years later. Gitschin was his residence. In the same year, Wallenstein started the construction of a large palace[81] in the Florentine style. He took a lively interest in the building and kept track of its progress, even in his absence. A garden adjoined the palace, which was in turn adjoined by a pheasantry, and that by a large and richly endowed zoo. The stud farm that he established was renowned, he bought the costliest Palfreys from

---

81   Author's Note: This palace was built on the site of the old Smirsitzki manor house that was destroyed in 1620 by a gunpowder explosion. At the same time, the old, above mentioned family line, came to an end. The events have a very characteristic old Bohemian stamp, which is why we shall briefly recite them here. In 1618 the last male heir of the Smirsitzki family died. He left two sisters. The elder was imprisoned at Schloss Kumburg as the result of a forbidden love affair. The younger was married to a Slawata. The brother had declared this younger sister to be his sole heiress. However, she was not to be happy with this inheritance. The older sister was freed from her imprisonment by Heinrich Otto von Wartenberg, who married her immediately upon her release. Both now raised claim to the inheritance that had been denied them, armed 1,000 peasants and took possession of Gitschin, town and castle. The Slawatas, however, had Friedrich von der Pfalz, the so called 'Winter King,' on their side, who now named a commission that was to evict Wartenberg and his wife, 'with force from possession of Gitschin.' A *Kursachsisch* [Electorate of Saxony] attaché's report describes what now happened. 'When the appointed commission, which also included Slawata, arrived on Saturday the 4th of February 1620, [at the house of] von Wartenberg and his wife in Gitschin, a most imposing building which had been constructed by the deceased *Herr* Smirsitzki, it was blown up by gunpowder that had been placed under the house. Not only *Herr* von Slawata and his brother, but all the other commissioners that were present, including *Frau* von Wartenberg, who was at that time, great with child, along with a great many other people (over 60 were counted), were miserably killed.' Another report says, 'The Lady of the Castle, *Frau* von Wartenberg, who was considered responsible for the explosion, had to pay most horribly for her fanaticism. She was found, alive, half buried, her face and hands terribly burned. She begged for a drink, but the administrator of the castle (who was in service to the opposing party) not only refused her this drink, but forcibly tore the valuable earrings from her ears so that blood flowed from them, and then tore the chains and clothes from her neck and body, and also the rings from her fingers. He then left her, thus naked, to die miserably of thirst. In such condition the corpse was carried to a respectable citizen who, out of pity, provided her with a shroud and a black coffin and buried her in a little church before the town.' So ended this feud. The younger sister, *Frau* von Slawata, now a widow, had to flee to the White Mountain [site of the Battle of the White Mountain, in the 30 Years War] and the estate, which had now been appropriated by the emperor, was purchased three years later by Wallenstein.

Italy, Arabian stallions from Turkey, and the noblest and strongest breed from Mecklenburg. The actual construction of the palace was completed in 1630. The Duke particularly enjoyed spending the months here between his dismissal (1630), and the resumption of his command. Here he developed that much described magnificence; here he made his plans. Gitschin always remained dear to him and he expressed this in his wishes to be buried in the 'Charterhouse at Gitschin.' This wish was not fulfilled until 1636 after his corpse had lain in the Franciscan Cloister at Mier. His final rest at Gitschin was frequently disturbed. In 1639, *Felmarschall* Bauer had his head and right arm removed from the tomb and sent both to Sweden. In 1785 *Graf* Vincenz von Waldstein finally received permission to have the remains of his great ancestor moved from the Gitschin Charterhouse to what was now the Waldstein family tomb in the St. Anne Chapel at Münchengrätz (see earlier).

After Wallenstein's death, Gitschin initially went to his former companion in arms, *General* von Tiefenbach, and from him to *Reichsgraf* von Sternberg, and from the Sternbergs, finally to the *Graf* (now Prince) von Trauttmannsdorff, who currently owns it.

In 1813 Gitschin again enjoyed brief prominence. The Emperor Franz spent five weeks here, in the old Wallenstein palace, during the months of the armistice, while the alliance between Russia, Prussia and Austria was agreed. The signing of the treaty took place at the Palace of Gitschin, and the room in which the signing took place (with Metternich, Nesselrode and Wilhelm von Humboldt), would be preserved as it then was, for all times.

Gitschin is surrounded by three suburbs [*Vorstädte*], the Prague, Holin and Walditz suburbs. Gitschin itself consists of the Ring [town square] and several immediately adjoining streets. Taking up the greatest part of one side of the ring, is the above described Waldstein Palace, which now serves as a government building, and also as the location of various bureaus, the Superior Court, the Forestry Bureau and the like. Between the Ring and the Walditz suburb, which only communicate through a gated tower, stands the beautiful Jesuit church, which was built in the style of the pilgrimage church of Santiago de Compostella. Attached to the church is the Jesuit College, whose construction, also by Wallenstein, was undertaken at the same time as the construction of the palace.

Near the town, whose surroundings provide an abundance of the most delightful landscapes, are a number of small, picturesque localities, Wockschütz, the Charterhouse, Libun, Lomnitz and Eisenstadtl, all much mentioned on the 29th. The Charterhouse [*Karthaus*], linked to the town by a magnificent avenue with two double rows of trees, is closest to the town. After the battle we shall go there.

The Encounter at Gitschin

On the afternoon of the 29th, two Prussian columns advanced towards Gitschin on two separate roads. One column (3rd Division), came from the west, we accompanied it along the Gitschin highway as it passed between Ober and Unter Lochow in the preceding chapter. The other column (5th Division), came from the north. We shall accompany it now after a preliminary description of the terrain.

About four and a half miles north of Gitschin, the road from Turnau runs [through] the village of Libun, then [turning half right] across a plateau for a little over three miles, [through] Kniznitz, past Ginolitz, Poduls and Kbelnitz. It then descends in a straight line to the south where it continues along the valley floor to Gitschin. This route over the plateau is the shortest.

It is however, flanked to the east by three isolated peaks, and to the west, by a rugged [massif], the forested Priwysin.[82] Passing between the peaks and the Priwysin would prove difficult, and given an adequate defense, anyone who attempted it would have to overcome fire from three directions, from the front and from both sides.

Nearly parallel with the Turnau highway, a secondary road runs from north to south. At the foot of the plateau [in the dead ground], it follows the course of the Cidlina stream, running through the villages of Cidlina, Bresca and Zames, before bending east towards Eisenstadtl, [south] past the Walditz Charterhouse, and finally [southwest] behind the Zebin Berg and Spitzberg, to Gitschin.

These two roads offer a choice. The first one (over the plateau), has no cover at all and is open to enemy observation, but is reliable with firm ground underfoot. The second (at the foot of the plateau), is less commanded by enemy fire but the going is uncertain and for the most part it runs over swamp and meadow, thus it is a byway.

General von Tümpling, less concerned about the danger of the enemy than the danger of the ground, and thereby making the best choice, chose the most direct route of advance down the main road, supporting it with diversions to the right and left. He therefore divided the 12 battalions of his division into three attacking forces, two flanking columns and one in the center.

Accordingly, orders were issued that:

The left flanking column advance along the Cidlina.
The right flanking column advance over the nearly pathless Priwysin.
The center column advance on the Turnau highway. On this last road lay the key to the enemy position, the villages of Poduls and Brada.

Before we follow the individual columns on their advance, we shall examine the enemy position.

The enemy positions

The enemy's dispositions made natural use of the terrain and corresponded to *our* dispositions as we have just given them.

One brigade, Brigade Piret, was positioned at Eisenstadtl. It formed the extreme [Austrian] right wing and had the task of blocking the Cidlina valley. Presumably the Prussian left flanking column must run into this brigade.

---

82   Authors Note: The three isolated peaks to the east are the *Tesin* or *Eisenberg* near Eisenstadtl, the *Zebin Berg* by the Walditz Charterhouse, and the *Soudna* or *Spitzberg*, before Gitschin. Only the latter two were held by troops [most credible sources say there was also artillery on the third peak, the Eisenberg]. The 'Priwysin,' on the opposite side of the plateau, is a forested, flattened cone of rock about a mile square. Towards the west it merges into the Prachow Rocks [*Prachower Felsen*], which from their southern slopes, command the Sobotka to Gitschin highway. To the north [of the Priwysin], is a broad strip of swamp with the villages of Ginolitz and Klein Ginolitz. Our map is not entirely accurate in this respect. The Priwysin has its actual front facing east. Falling more or less steeply, its slopes here approach the Turnau highway, which it commands completely. At the foot of the slope [divided into two widely separate parts by the highway], is the village of Poduls. Behind it, halfway up the slope, is the village of Brada. Behind Brada is a truncated cone, the Brada Berg. These are the points that will be decisive.

Sketch map of Gitschin east.

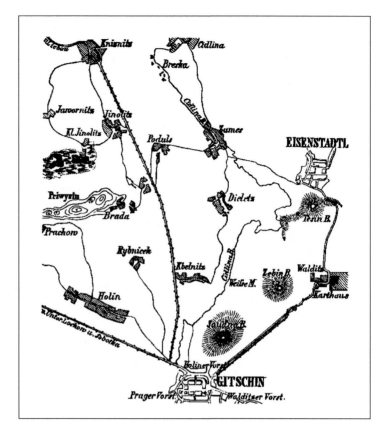

A second brigade, Brigade Poschacher (the so called 'Iron Brigade' that had already been under fire at Podol), held the [Austrian] center and left, with IR 34 King of Prussia defending the eastern slope of the Priwysin, and IR 30 Martini defending the northern slope (the *Waldberg*).

The [Prussian] center column that was advancing on the Turnau road, must therefore come under the flanking fire of the Regiment King of Prussia, while the battalions advancing as our right flanking column, would come under frontal fire from Regiment Martini.

These two brigades (Piret and Poschacher), comprised the first echelon and were principally tasked with barring the road to Gitschin. Two other brigades were tasked with supporting them, Brigade Leiningen was positioned to the rear of IR 34 King of Prussia, while Brigade Abele was positioned to the flank and rear of IR 30 Martini, extending the [Austrian] left wing[83] [westwards] and thus increasing the difficulty of envelopment.

Even more important was the bringing up of a third reserve brigade, the Saxon Brigade *Crown Prince*. This was moved forward at the start of the battle from the second echelon to the first and occupied the southern slope of the plateau that extended between the Cidlina stream

---

83   Author's Note: Only half of Brigade Abele, IR 35 Khevenhüller, was positioned to the flank and rear of regiment Martini facing north. The other half, IR 72 Ramming, was positioned with front facing south at Ober Lochow at the foot of the Prachower Felsen, and was engaged there, as we know, in the action against our 3rd Division.

and the hamlet of Diletz (located east of the Turnau road). The overall position had great natural strength. 96 guns made it rather unapproachable, seven batteries of the Corps Artillery Reserve extended at right angles across the plateau between the villages of Poduls and Zames.

Behind them was the Cavalry Division Edelsheim. In addition, additional batteries were positioned on the Priwysin on the left [including a rocket battery], and the two isolated peaks (the Tesin and Zebin Berg) on the right [according to most other sources, artillery was also positioned on the *Eisenberg*]. The Prussians advanced against these positions at 3:30.

The Center Column takes Poduls, thwarted at Brada

At about 3:30 Division Tümpling stood astride the highway between Libun and Unter Kniznitz, from where there was a good overview of the ground and the enemy position. *General* von Tümpling had the divisional artillery go into action on a ridge between Kniznitz and Cidlina, and open fire on the enemy gun line between Poduls and Zames. At 5:30 our forces went over to the attack in accordance with the dispositions given above.

The center column (comprising [two] musketeer battalions from the 48th and [two] Grenadier battalions from the *Leib* Regiment), passed Unter Kniznitz, proceeded toward Cidlina (avoiding the main highway), and then advanced diagonally across the plateau towards [the Brada - Poduls] position. The other two columns, which were advancing at the same time, covered both flanks. Ginolitz and Daubrowitz, located to the right and left of the line of march, had already been captured by the vanguard.

Initially the advance was directed toward Poduls. We must here explain that Poduls consists of two halves, the built up half is on the near [northern] side of the great Turnau highway, while on the other [southern] side (of the highway), it continues as separate farmsteads that transition almost immediately into the village of Brada. Both halves were strongly held by the enemy (IR 34 King of Prussia and the 18th Jäger Battalion).

The first attack was directed against the built up half of the village as it was the most advanced point. *General* von Tümpling placed the 1st Battalion of Regiment Nr. 48, *Major* Spieler, in the lead, with two battalions of the *Leib* Regiment following. The 2nd Battalion of the 48th, on a level with the 1st Battalion, accompanied its advance such that its 5th Company was on its right [i.e. closest to the 1st battalion]. The 1st battalion now advanced, skirmishers of the 3rd Company (*Hauptmann* von Steinbach) in the lead, and these now opened up with rapid fire while *Hauptmann* von Steinbach himself led the rest of the company, drums beating, against Poduls. The village was captured in the first rush, the enemy falling back to the extended farmsteads on the far side of the road with not insubstantial losses, exacted for the most part thanks to the skillful involvement of the 5th Company [of the 2nd battalion, which had apparently joined the attack], that rapidly climbed up from the Cidlina bottom and enveloped the eastern and southern edges of the village. A *Hauptmann* and 60 men fell into our hands as prisoners.

One strong point had been captured, but this was no more than an outwork. The actual Brada Poduls position remained in enemy hands and it was now a matter of capturing it. Three of the [1st] battalion's companies (1st, 2nd and 4th) were still intact. *Major* Spieler decided to have the 2nd Company turn toward the Priwysyn and the 1st and 4th Companies (brought forward on the right and left), advance against the farmsteads of Poduls on the far side of the highway. With hurrahs the companies advanced, but despite the greatest bravado on the part of the officers and the other ranks, this attack was repulsed by enemy fire. Fresh companies of IR 34 King of

Prussia and the 18th Jäger Battalion, reinforced by those who had fallen back from the built up half of the village, had set up the houses for a sort of tiered fire. The best shots stood in the front line and were handed loaded rifles from behind so that they achieved a rate of fire equal to the rapid fire of our needle guns. *Premierlieutenant* von Massenbach, who led the 2nd Company, *Lieutenant* von Ledebur of the 1st, and *Premierlieutenant* Von Borkowski of the 4th Company were all killed. Many other officers and other ranks were wounded. *Major* Spieler brought the 3rd and 5th Companies, which had remained in the village after the capture of Poduls, up to the highway and had them open up with rapid fire against the extended farmsteads, but they too were unable to renew the attack without reinforcements. A success was achieved here, but only a half success, Poduls remained in enemy hands. The 2nd Battalion of the 48th, or at least the majority of its companies [less the 5th], continued the advance along the Cidlina bottom. The two Grenadier battalions of the *Leib* Regiment remained in reserve.

It was now 6:00 and *General* von Tümpling felt satisfied for the time being with what had been achieved. Any further advance in the center would be dependent on the success of the flanking columns. We shall first look at the right flank column.

Advance on the Right Flank, the woodland fighting of the 18th and 12th regiments

At the same time (5:00) as the center column advanced over the plateau toward Poduls and Brada, the right flank column moved off. This column (almost the entire 10th Infantry Brigade) consisted of five battalions under *Brigadier Generalmajor* von Kamiensky, three from the 18th regiment and two Grenadier battalions from Regiment Nr. 12. Directly after passing Libun, the 1st Battalion of the 18th Regiment was ordered south against Jawornitz, and after capturing this village, to continue its advance against the northern wooded slopes of the Priwysin. The 2nd Battalion followed the 1st battalion which was followed in turn by the Fusilier battalion. The two Grenadier Battalions of the 12th were held in reserve.

The 1st Battalion of the 18th occupied Jawornitz and immediately thereafter, a hill behind it [to the south]. When it attempted to take a second line of hills running parallel to the first, it found its progress blocked by a broad stretch of swampy meadow that lay between the two. Nowhere could a bridge, a causeway or a dry crossing be found, nor was it possible to wade across as our troops immediately came under heavy fire from enemy riflemen echeloned on the opposite slope. Under the circumstances, *General* von Kamiensky decided to extend our right wing, in the hope of outflanking the enemy with a wider movement that avoided the impassable terrain that had blocked [the first attempted envelopment].

The two battalions of the 18th Regiment (the 2nd and Fusilier battalions) that were closest, were brought up. The 2nd Battalion took up position to the right of the 1st, the Fusilier Battalion to the right of the 2nd, thereby prolonging the line [to the right] about 1,600 yards southwest of Jawornitz, until we came upon a passable site. Here the two battalions moved forwards (to the south) as quickly as the ground allowed, however they did not reach the northern slope of the Priwysin as intended, but instead came up against the Prachow Rocks that were farther to the west and rear of the Brada - Poduls position. As if more was needed, these were also strongly held by IR 35 Khevenhüller (Brigade Abele), which was positioned here with front facing north in an extension of the enemy's left wing.

Fighting on the Prachow.

A firefight now developed in the pathless wooded terrain in which enemy riflemen had concealed themselves. Casualties were high on both sides, but the losses weren't the main concern. The [Prussian] 18th were locked in combat with an opponent whose flank they wished to get around, without becoming [drawn into a frontal assault], at the cost of time and blood. For the Austrians, their concern was that if our Pomeranians [3rd Division] pressed forward at Unter Lochow, they would come under two fires and be cut off.

Both sides thus took precautionary measures. *Oberst* Kettler of the 18th had [his force] turn half left to restore the correct direction of the advance, while *Oberst* von Abele ordered a strong push to gain the space to accomplish his retreat. The Austrians attacked with closed up columns,[84] the fighting among the rocks was renewed, fiercer than before, degenerating

---

84   Tr. Note: If the column formation retained the same distance between ranks as in line formation it was an extended column. If the distance between ranks was shortened it was a closed up column.

into a brawl with rifle butts and bayonets. When this resulted in a momentary retreat by our 18th, *Oberst* von Abele used the time to carry out his retreat. On our side the 5th, 7th and 8th companies were primarily involved in the combat. *Hauptmann* Schorr (7th) was killed, *Lieutenant* von Unruh (5th) also. *Premierlieutenant* Offermann and *Lieutenant* von Divszehy were both severely wounded. The 5th company suffered the most casualties.

The 12th Grenadier Regiment at Klein Jinolitz

The flanking movement by the18th [Infantry Regiment] that led to the Prachow Rocks rather than the Priwysin, was in the event a failure. A failure because it came up against an unexpected enemy in the rocks, and a failure because the attack was delivered [too far to the west], thereby putting no pressure on the Priwysin, where the pressure would actually have been useful.

Generalmajor Kamiensky therefore resolved to carry out a less sweeping envelopment with the two battalions of the 12th [Grenadier Regiment] that he still had on the left flank of the 18th Regiment. This envelopment must necessarily lead to the Priwysin, assuming that it was fortunate enough to find a way to cross the swampy strip (the 1st Battalion of the 18th Regiment had not been so lucky).

The two battalions of the 12th set out at 6:00, *Oberst* von Debschitz leading them in person. After a short fight, Klein Jinolitz was taken by the leading company (the 1st), but more importantly, a corduroy road [a road made of tree trunks laid parallel with each other] that led across the swampy ground to the Priwysin, was spotted behind it. Here was the passable way, however the enemy, well knowing this was the only place from which our attack could come, had echeloned the riflemen from Regiment Martini in the wooded hills opposite. There was a lot of firing back and forth, resulting in many casualties. An enemy attack to regain Klein - Jinolitz failed, as did an attack on our part to force the enemy from his position in the woods. He held the key to his position firmly, the Priwysin and the village of Brada. Here, as in the center, the fighting was at a standstill.

Advance on the Left Flank, the Fusilier Battalions of the 12th and 48th take Zames and Diletz (6:00 and 7:30)

The left wing column (Fusilier Battalions of the 12th and 48th) turned left at the northern entrance to Ober Kniznitz and proceeded through Unter Kniznitz to Cidlina. As our flanking movement became evident, Cidlina and Breska were set ablaze by enemy shellfire, which did not however, halt our advance. This continued along the Cidlina bottom, though the Fusilier Battalion of the 48th had to be diverted [to the right] back onto the plateau for a short time, to protect the 1st 6pdr. Battery that had gone into position there, from enemy cavalry (that appeared by Poduls).

The Fusilier Battalion from the 12th [Grenadier Regiment] advanced until it was level with, and to the left of, Zames. Here *Major* des Barres, who was leading the battalion, observed cavalry and infantry (rapidly advancing elements of Brigade Piret) coming from the left [from Markt Eisenstadtl] that wanted to reach the village before him. The Fusilier Battalion now advanced at the run and occupied Zames (which was under shell fire from the Priwysin on one side, and from the batteries that were positioned at the foot of the Eisen - and Zehin - *Berge* on the other) and was in flames in a few minutes. However, *Major* des Barres held the village both against the fire from left and right, and also against the above mentioned enemy cavalry and infantry, who did not give up in their attempts. They were companies of Regiment Sigismund (Italian). Several volleys were sufficient to repulse the attack, which was delivered with no particular determination. Zames remained in the hands of our Fusiliers. In the meantime, the Fusilier Battalion of the 48th was brought up (6:00).

Zames was already in the flank of the enemy position. Its possession, however, in light of the enemy's superior forces, was not sufficiently effective to make him abandon his position, at least his position on the Priwysin.

Perhaps a broader and bolder advance would accomplish what the simple gain on the flank had not. Therefore, the two Fusilier battalions were ordered to advance from Zames against Diletz, which was located on the southern slope of the plateau. If this succeeded, much would be gained, a wedge would be driven between Brigade Poschacher and Brigade Piret, and the position of the Privysin would be taken half in the rear. The advance was therefore directed toward this important village where the events at Zames would be repeated, but (at least initially) with less favourable results. Diletz too, was unoccupied. At 6:00 the Saxons were still at Gitschin, at 6:30 they passed Kbelnitz and now advanced toward Diletz in order to occupy it with the Brigade Crown Prince. Once again there was a race to see who would get there first.

Generalmajor von Schimmelmann, commander of the 9th Infantry Brigade, when he observed the rapid advance of the Saxon battalions, galloped to Diletz and ordered the two leading rifle platoons to double through the village and occupy its farther edge. Before the general was able to get more troops into the village however, the Saxon battalions got there first and forced our rifle platoons out. At 6:45, Diletz was in Saxon hands. The position that they occupied will best be clarified by the Saxon report (see later).

This important point could not be allowed to remain in enemy hands, it had to be recaptured if there was to be any thought of success in the center. *Generallieutenant* von Tümpling therefore attempted to concentrate all the forces that he could at this point, without weakening the others. First, *Major* Rüstow of the 3rd Artillery Regiment, was ordered to advance with three batteries and occupy a position north of the road between Zames and Poduls, which would allow him to fire on both the enemy forces advancing against Diletz, and also on the enemy batteries on the Eisen - and Zehin - *Berge*.

At the same time, he detached the 2nd Battalion of the *Leib* Regiment from its position at Poduls, to support the Fusilier battalions that were advancing against Diletz. On the other side, three companies, (the 11th Company of the *Leib* Regiment, and the 6th and 7th Companies of Regiment Nr. 48) had joined the attack of the advancing Fusilier battalions.

Accordingly, three battalions and three companies were committed there:

> The Fusilier battalion of the 12th [Grenadier Regiment].
> The Fusilier battalion of the 48th [Infantry Regiment].
> The 2nd Battalion of the *Leib* Regiment.
> One company (11th) of the *Leib* Regiment.
> Two companies (6th and 7th) of the 48th [Infantry Regiment].

The attack now ensued against the village from three sides. The two Fusilier battalions and the 11th Company of the *Leib* Regiment attacked the village from the north and northwest, the 2nd Battalion of the *Leib* Regiment from the southwest, the 6th and 7th Companies of the 48th attacked more from the northeast. The Saxon reserve, the *Leib* Brigade, was at Kbelnitz, 2.000 paces behind Diletz.

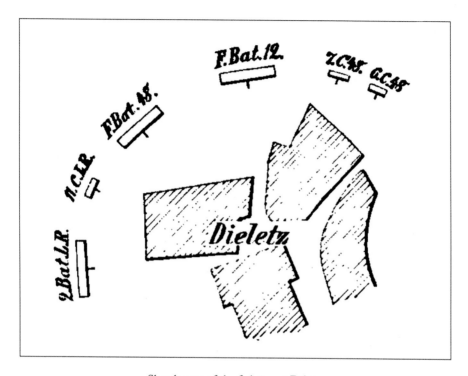

Sketch map of the fighting at Diletz.

The concentric attack by our 15 companies took place with great elan. The enemy battalions had little time to establish themselves in the village or in the immediate vicinity (the *Jäger* were in a fruit orchard) and were driven from their positions and forced back into the lanes and farmsteads. Our men followed them with loud hurrahs and heavy fighting developed in the village, where the determination of our officers and soldiers, combined with the superiority of the needle gun, resulted in victory. A rapid series of small volleys stretched rows of the enemy on the ground. Several squadrons of the Liechtenstein and Nicolaus Hussars got caught up in the fighting and were driven off. Several volleys were accidentally fired at the Saxon *Jägers* [who were in the orchard at the western end of the village] from the far side of the Cidlina stream (where a battalion of Regiment Sigismund was located), adding to the confusion and losses of our enemy. At 7:30 Diletz was entirely in our hands.

The [Saxon] Brigade Crown Prince attempted to rally and reform outside the village, but heavy fire from the southern edge caused great destruction in their ranks and forced them to retreat across the Cidlina stream. Our men followed as far as the center mill.

The Saxon report differs greatly from this account. We extract the following from it:

At about 6:30 the Saxon 1st Infantry Brigade (Crown Prince) appeared before Diletz, which had shortly before been occupied by enemy infantry coming from Zames. Both columns appeared nearly simultaneously at the southern edge, attacked with the bayonet and took the village in their first charge. The perimeter was now occupied by three battalions (the 2nd, 4th and 1st) holding the northern and western edges of the village, the 1st *Jäger* Battalion took post in a fruit orchard [adjoining the village to the east] while the 3rd Infantry Battalion was positioned (as immediate reserve) south of the village. The *Leib* Brigade, our main reserve, also was positioned to the south under cover of the Diletz hill.

The enemy immediately attacked with reinforced numbers. A lively firefight developed at the edges of the village, which in conjunction with the enemy shrapnel, exacted heavy losses from the brigade. The extended and scattered layout of the village, as well as the lack of a continuous enclosure, greatly complicated command and control. Nevertheless, the battalion (which very soon lost the majority of its company commanders, *Hauptleute* [Captains] Fickelscherer, von Rex, and Klette were all killed, five others wounded) , stoutly held its position. Also, thanks to an unfortunate misunderstanding, the Austrian forces on the right wing at Eisenstadtl, mistook the Saxons for Prussians, and fired on the rear of the 1st *Jäger* Battalion, causing it additional losses.[85] The fighting came to a standstill and it was obvious that the enemy attempt to break through the center would not succeed either at Brada (where Brigade Poschacher stood unshaken), nor at Diletz.

This was the situation at 7:30, when an order from *Feldzeugmeister* Benedek arrived at [Corps Headquarters] and changed everything. This order stated that the *Feldzeugmeister* had suspended his movement toward the Iser, that control of Gitschin would be pointless, and that the Austro - Saxon Army was to link up with the main body of the army and should avoid major fighting.

When this order arrived, the situation was such that the Saxon troops could undoubtedly hold the village of Diletz for the remainder of the day, but notwithstanding, they had to obey [Benedek's] order. At 7:30 the command was given to break off the action.

Due to the nature of the fighting in the village, and given the exhausted condition of the troops, the evacuation of Diletz by the 1st Infantry Brigade (Crown Prince) could not be conducted in good order. The companies were extremely intermixed (some were without officers), and had to retreat over entirely open terrain, criss-crossed with ditches and sunken roads. Accordingly, the enemy forces that were rapidly pushing into the village caused our troops heavy losses from infantry fire, during which the

---

85   Author's Note: As if this incident was not sufficiently grievous, it led to a greater misfortune. Saxon *Jäger*, when they realized they were under fire [from friendly forces], leaped forward and waved white handkerchiefs to give the Austrians a sign. However, this handkerchief waving was also seen by the advancing Prussians who drew the erroneous conclusion that [the Saxons] were surrendering. [The Prussians] came nearer and were met with lively fire. Now the cry was, 'Treachery!' It was not possible to correct this misunderstanding during the battle, however Battalion Commander von Nostitz, has [subsequently] declared, 'We had no intention of deceiving the Prussians. Such a deception would have been so despicable that no one would believe that brave troops and honourable officers such as the Saxons have proven themselves to be, would be capable of such a thing.'

Brigadier, *Oberst* von Boxberg and *Major* von Sandersleben, were wounded. The 1st *Jäger* Battalion, on the right flank, retreated to St. Magdalena in good order. The divisional cavalry, which up to this point had maintained contact with the Brada hills, turned toward Gitschin. The 1st Brigade (Crown Prince) also proceeded to the north side of the town. Darkness fell. Nowhere did the enemy pursue.

Thus, is the excerpt from the Saxon report. As we pointed out earlier, its divergences from the Prussian account are significant. According to the Prussians, the Saxons were forced out of Diletz. According to the Saxons, they fell back from Diletz in accordance with higher orders. It is difficult and at the same time painful to sort out such differences of opinion, to place the conflicting claims of both sides in perspective. In the above case however, we must state that we are not convinced by the Saxon statement that Brigade Crown Prince evacuated Diltez voluntarily and entirely due to higher orders. Withdrawal from a securely held position takes place in a different [less disorderly] fashion and presents another kind of picture. On the other hand, we readily concede that if the *Leib* Brigade (which had been held in reserve), had been committed in a renewed attack, the Saxons would most probably have succeeded in regaining Diletz. We shall return to this.

The assault of Brigade Piret (7:45 to 8:00)

At 7:30 Diletz was in Prussian hands, a wedge had been driven between the Priwysin and the position at Eisenstadtl. When *General* Piret de Bihain (whose brigade held Eisenstadtl and the adjoining points), saw the Saxons set out from Diletz on their retreat, he considered the battle lost. Whether they were retreating because they could not withstand the Prussian assault, or merely as the result of higher orders,[86] did nothing to alter the situation for him. Our left flanking column had severed his contact with the center. He was in an exposed position and even though his line of retreat was not immediately threatened (his right flank was still open), he must at least fear that the Austrian batteries in position near Diletz and at the foot of the Zehin and Eisen *Berge,* might be lost to a bold Prussian *coup*. He therefore decided to launch an attack in order to save these exposed batteries.

His brigade debouched from Eisenstadtl in three columns. The first column, two Battalions from IR 18 Constantin in the first wave and a Battalion from IR 45 Sigismund in the second, crossed the Cidlina and proceeded to Diletz. With music playing the battalions advanced to the northeast corner of the village, to the same fruit orchard that the Saxon 1st *Jäger* Battalion had so courageously defended against our forces an hour earlier.

By now two companies (the 6th and 7th) of the [Prussian] 48th [Infantry Regiment] had established themselves there and awaited the attack. At 350 paces [the order was given] … Fire! The Austrians wavered, but only for a moment. With a loud shout from the officers they

---

86   Author's Note: Given their scattered (sometimes isolated) positions, it was extremely difficult to inform the Austrian Brigadiers of Benedek's order, and it was often delayed in its arrival. The order reached the Saxon Crown Prince (commanding the Austro - Saxon Iser Army) at 7:30. It was a full half hour later before it was possible to get the same order to *General* Clam-Gallas (who was on the Priwysin), so that some units did not receive the order to break off the fighting until 9:00 or even 10:00.

continued their advance. A second volley and the ranks thinned. Throwing away their rifles they sought to make it over the hill at a run.

The second column (one Battalion and one Squadron) crossed the Cidlina at the same location, then headed northwards to the edge of the plateau and proceeded toward Zames. *General* von Tümpling, who observed this advance from [his position at] Poduls, threw the only intact battalion he had available (the 1st Battalion of the *Leib* Regiment under *Major* von Rheinbaben), against the approaching column. Bearing to the left, the battalion proceeded over the plateau and took shellfire, *Major* von Rheinbaben himself was killed by a shell fragment. *Hauptmann* von Wussow assumed command. All pressed forward in order to get off the plateau and reach the Cidlina bottom, where the Austrian battalion was approaching. [The Austrians] for their part, were climbing the slope from the Cidlina bottom to the plateau, the two forces met at the rim. Our men forced the Austrians back down into the Cidlina bottom where [they] attempted to establish themselves. The cavalry squadron (from the Liechtenstein Hussars) pressed forward, but received with rapid fire, they hastily fell back. There were no further attempts. On our side the fight was essentially waged by the 1st and 3rd companies of the *Leib* Regiment.

The third column (two battalions strong) likewise proceeded toward Zames, but this time on the far bank of the Cidlina stream. Only when it arrived opposite Zames (which was on this side of the Cidlina), did it cross the stream and advance to the strains of 'God Save Franz the Emperor' [*Gott erhalte Franz den Kaiser*] to the eastern edge of the village.

The 2nd and 4th companies of the *Leib* Regiment now turned against this third column, receiving it at 250 paces with rapid fire. The music died, the battalions turned to flight, some to the north, some back over the stream. Those that tried to remain on the near side of the Cidlina in the brush, were driven back over the stream by rifle platoons led by *Lieutenants* von Rohr, von Studnitz and Petersen.

Overall a quick and brilliant outcome. With six companies we had repulsed six battalions of Brigade Piret.

To recapitulate:

> The 6th and 7th Companies of the 48th Regiment repulsed the attack of three battalions on Diletz.
> The 1st and 3rd Companies of the *Leib* Regiment, south of Zames, drove an enemy battalion from the plateau into the Cidlina bottom.
> The 2nd and 4th Companies of the *Leib* Regiment, east of Zames, beat back the two battalions that had crossed the Cidlina across from [Zames].

General Piret for his part, could still take pride in having achieved some success, the batteries on the Eisen and Zehin *Berge* were able to withdraw during the above action (which as we know, was the primary objective of the attack).

Storming the position on the Priwysin at 8:30 in the evening

The assault by Brigade Piret was really just a digression, all of its attacks were repulsed. The situation at 8:00 was essentially the same that it had been at 7:30. Let us take a look at the overall situation as it appeared at 8:00 before we turn to the decisive advance in the center.

Our center column (only five companies strong) held that part of Poduls that lay on the near side of the highway. The attack on the farmsteads on the far side had failed.

The right flanking column, after lengthy attempts back and forth, had finally found a passage over the swampy strip that extended along the front of the Priwysin position. However, even after the passage [across the swamp] had been discovered, the position, defended by troops firing from echeloned positions on the opposite slope, could not be taken by the Grenadier battalions of the 12th Regiment. The men of the 18th [Regiment] had gone too far to the right.

The left flanking column had taken Cidlina, Bresca, Zames and finally Diletz. In so doing the Priwysin position was outflanked and nearly taken in the rear, Brigade Piret was cut off. Such was the situation at 8:00. In the center and on the right, there were small successes. On the left, the capture of Diletz achieved a greater one. Nevertheless, even after the repulse of the assault by Brigade Piret, our situation was most precarious. We faced a greatly superior enemy force and the enemy *only needed to become aware of his superiority* to throw our battalions, exhausted by the fighting and by the heat, from the positions they had gained. Our enemy still had (to say nothing of his cavalry), two entirely intact brigades, Brigade Leiningen and the Saxon *Leib* Brigade. On our side, *we had nothing more in reserve*. Had Clam-Gallas recognized this before he passed on the order to retreat, and had he gone over to the offensive instead, then so far as can be humanly foreseen, we would have been vanquished. Despite our successes the situation was critical, if only the enemy had been aware of the actual situation.

General von Tümpling was fully aware of this. The retreat of the Saxons to Gitschin, and the repulse of Brigade Piret, had indeed improved the situation, but had not in any way eliminated its ominous character. The enemy center still stood firm. What if the enemy now, for his part, *went over to the offensive* and broke through our weak center and outflanked *our* flanking columns? Such an assault, which would have been decisive, must be met with force. *General* von Tümpling therefore decided to bring the two Grenadier battalions of Regiment Nr. 12, back from the right wing to his center, thereby protecting his position on the Turnau highway against a sudden enemy advance. If such an attack did not take place, the enemy would thereby reveal that he was too shaken or too threatened from the west by the [3rd] Pomeranian Division, to be able to still think of an attack. Accordingly, *General* von Tümpling (now reinforced with two fresh battalions), now resolved to go over to the offensive himself, and at 8:30, to make a second attempt against the Brada position. The first assault at 6:00 had foundered, as we related earlier.

At 8:30 the two Grenadier battalions arrived in the center from the right wing. Since the enemy still showed no indication of attacking, *General* von Tümpling formed his assault columns. The 1st Battalion of Regiment Nr. 48, to which isolated companies (the 5th of the 48th and the 9th of the *Leib* Regiment) had attached themselves, took the lead. The Grenadier battalions of the 12th followed on. They crossed the highway in *Sturmschritt* [storm pace, a fast run] and took the extended farmsteads of Poduls in the first assault. The 2nd and 4th companies (closed up) swung to the right, and with hurrahs and beating drums, captured the village of Brada. The position on the Priwysin was ours.

The 5th Division had come through victorious against four brigades, Poschacher, Piret, half of Abele and Brigade Crown Prince. The enemy, outflanked by parts of the 18th Regiment now also in his rear, fell back in disorder to Gitschin. Exhaustion and the onset of darkness prevented a rapid pursuit.

The Night Fighting in Gitschin

The bloody day still had an epilogue, the night fighting in the streets of Gitschin. Description of this extremely complex action is only possible if it is separated into its various parts:

Capture of two Chulai battalions and one Khevenhüller battalion in the approaches to Gitschin (11:00).
The first street fighting (11:30). The Pomeranians are repulsed.
The later street fighting (12:30). The leading elements of 5th Division take possession of the town.

Before we embark on a description of these separate phases, we shall try to shed some light on the course of the Austrian retreat. A Saxon report is very much to the point:

Any attempt to break off an action is fraught with difficulties. These difficulties increase however (as in the present case), when [the retreat] it is complicated by a flanking movement, when it leads over terrain crossed by sunken roads and ditches, and when darkness falls. Because of the enemy advance from Sobotka to Unter Lochow (where Brigade Ringelsheim had vainly sought to stem his advance), it was necessary that all troops still outside Gitschin, pass rapidly back through the town. The order to this effect was issued soon after 9:00 (at roughly the same time that the battle at Unter Lochow was decided in favour of the Prussians, and that the battle at the Priwysin was decided by the storming of the Brada hill).

The retreat proceeded to Horsitz and Miletin, in the direction of Königgrätz. The greatest difficulty arose from the fact (correctly pointed out in the above report), that all of the forces that were north and west of Gitschin, had to pass through the town itself. This resulted in bewilderment and confusion.

Nevertheless, and with great good fortune, this retreat was accomplished without significant losses. Only three battalions were lost, more through their own fault than due to our actions. They ran into our hands.

Capture of the two Chulai Battalions and one Khevenhüller battalion in the approaches to Gitschin

Exhaustion and darkness prevented a rapid pursuit of the enemy forces falling back on Gitschin, but not a general following on. *General* von Tümpling (wounded while bringing the two Grenadier battalions forward) had relinquished his command with the specific order, 'That the advance on Gitschin was to begin, and that this important point was to be captured and held at all costs.' *Generalmajor* von Kamiensky assumed command of the division, and immediately took steps to comply with this order. The advance commenced in two columns, one on the highway and one on the left parallel to the highway, past the village of Kbelnitz.

The main column marching on the highway comprised:

The 1st Battalion of the 18th [Infantry Regiment].
The two Grenadier battalions of the 12th [Grenadier Regiment].
The 1st Battalion of the 48th [Infantry Regiment].
The 9th and 10th Companies of the *Leib* Regiment.

Marching along the left side of the highway:

The Fusilier battalion of the 12th [Grenadier Regiment].
The Fusilier battalion of the 48th [Infantry Regiment].
Two battalions of the *Leib* Regiment (as reserve).

The rest of the division remained on the field of battle. While *en route,* many scattered [Austrian] units were captured, but it was only just before Gitschin (to which the Pomeranian division had already advanced), that it was possible to capture a more significant number of the enemy.

Each of the two division operated independently in achieving this. Two battalions of IR 33 Chulai (Hungarian) were captured by the Pomeranians [3rd Division], while the Brandenburgers [5th Division], captured a Battalion of IR 35 Khevenhüller (Bohemian).

The circumstances of the capture of the two Chulai Infantry battalions by the Pomeranians is nowhere specifically explained, not even in the Pomeranian accounts, but [it is possible to arrive at a credible version of events] by a process of comparison and deduction. The Austrian report states that the two Chulai battalions and one Khevenhüller battalion were particularly unfortunate, in that they did not join the retreat in time, and then stumbled into a swampy pond and lost very many captured.

The Pomeranian report states that a short distance before Gitschin, at about 11:00, the Fusilier Battalion of Grenadier Regiment Nr. 2, King Friedrich Wilhelm IV, under *Major* von Stölting, took the lead. The 2nd Battalion, *Major* von Voss, followed. The lead battalion then came under fire from a farmstead and forced its way into it. Immediately thereafter, a large body of Austrians that were approaching from the direction of the village of Holin (and thus from the northwest) were captured by the (Pomeranian) battalions that were following on.

The Brandenburg report states that soon after 11.00, the left wing column advanced towards Gitschin. The Fusilier Battalion of the 48th Regiment crossed the Cidlina near the white mill, and it was here that the Battalion Khevenhüller, under attack from various sides, had been forced into a swamp, and for the most part surrendered. One *Oberstlieutenant*, five other officers, one cadet and 478 other ranks were captured.

When we compare these three reports, it is not difficult to fill in the gaps. The Austrian report confirms the capture of three battalions. The Brandenburg report specifically claims one of these, leaving the two Chulai Battalions for the Pomeranian division.

The capture of the three battalions did not take place at the same time, nor in the same place, as can be deduced from the brief Austrian report. The two Chulai battalions were captured west of Gitschin near the Sobotka road at 11:00. The Khevenhüller battalion was captured to the north of Gitschin near the Turnau road at 12:00. (Since the Pomeranians had their street fight in Gitschin at 11:30, and the Brandenburgers had theirs at 12:30, the times given above for the captures are approximately correct).

First street fighting (11:30), the Pomeranians are repulsed

The Saxon *Leib* Brigade was selected to cover the retreat from the town, which until 11:00 had proceeded without interference. It received orders to occupy Gitschin and to halt the pursuing enemy, which it did with as much courage as skill.

[The brigade] repulsed the first attack, which was made by the Pomeranians. We shall give such details as are available.

At 11:00 the advanced guard of the 3rd Division had reached the northwest corner of Gitschin, the *Holiner Vostadt* [Holin suburb], Fusilier Battalion Grenadier Regiment Nr. 2, King Friedrich Wilhelm IV, in the lead. *Major* von Stölting sent patrols into the town that reported, 'Gitschin is not occupied.' It was solely on the basis of this report that the decision to occupy the town was made. The commanding general, *General* von Werder, wanted to avoid street fighting and night fighting. That was not to be.

At 11:00, when *Major* von Stölting had sent his first patrols into the town, it *was* unoccupied. The Austrian brigades had left, and the Saxon *Leib* Brigade had not yet arrived. Half an hour later the situation had changed, the Saxon brigade had entered the town from the north and had taken possession of the Ring as well as all the approaches to it.

Thus it was, that the Pomeranians of Battalion Stölting and Battalion von Voss, who were advancing from the suburb toward the town centre at the same time (11:30), quite unexpectedly ran into the enemy. As the leading platoons entered the Ring, they came under fire from the front and flank. The men in front stopped and fell back which caused disorder and confusion. In the dark it was impossible to see what was facing them. Our advanced detachments were pulled back into the *Vorstadt*.

Having arrived at the bridge and regrouped, Battalion Stölting was led forward for the second time, however the outcome was the same. A closely packed mass of the enemy, which so far as could be ascertained greatly outnumbered our detachments, were firing on them at short range in the dark from adjoining houses. *General* von Werder ordered total evacuation of the town. Battalion Voss posted outposts. The Saxons had repulsed our first attack.

Street fighting 12:30, the advanced guard of the 5th Division occupies Gitschin

The Saxon *Leib* Brigade entered Gitschin at 11:30, at which time it had the encounter with the Pomeranians described above. At 12:30, after another round of fighting, it fell back before the advance guard of the Brandenburg Division. It had held the town for one hour.

There are extensive accounts of this second round of street fighting by both the Brandenburgers and the Saxons. At 12:00, according to our reports, the Fusilier Battalions of the 12th and 48th Regiments were at the northern edge of the town, and (as already described) had captured a battalion of IR 35 Khevenhüller. *Oberstlieutenant* Birodz von Gaudy, who led our column, now placed the Fusilier Battalion of the 12th Regiment, *Major* des Barres, in the lead and entered the spacious courtyard of the former Jesuit cloister. As he started to advance from this courtyard towards the Ring, the leading platoons came under heavy fire. This fire came from the Saxon *Jäger*, whose 4th Battalion formed the [Saxon] rear guard, while the four infantry battalions of the brigade (the 13th, 14th, 15th and 16th) had mostly withdrawn. *Major* des Barres now assembled his Fusiliers again in the Jesuit courtyard, left one company (the 9th) behind as reserve, and advanced with the other three, drums beating and without stopping, through the maze of alleys to the market square. He took it and the Saxons fell back. In the meantime, to the left of the 12th, the Fusiliers of the 48th, under *Major* von Zglinitzki, had entered the town from the east at another location, first occupying the great square in the Walditzer *Vostadt* [suburb] and then the actual Ring itself. Everywhere the Saxons fell back, Gitschin was ours. Lights had to be placed in the windows. The houses were searched, 300 were found hiding and another 400 to 500 wounded in the Gitschin hospital.

The Saxon report is particularly vivid, especially with respect to the locality and the last moments of the fighting.

All battalions (including the 4th *Jägers*), had already left the town, and only a small detachment (a half company from the 14th Battalion) was kept back with instructions, 'to remain in the marketplace for the time being, to await and repulse the [first] enemy attack, then to fall back to the Tower Gate located about 100 paces east of the market place, and only after an attempt to defend this also, to follow the other battalions.' This rear guard, only 90 men strong, continued the fight against the pursuing Prussians. We now quote from the Saxon report:

> The marketplace or Ring of Gitschin, formed a square whose sides corresponded to the four points of the compass. Extending at right angles from the center of the north side, an alleyway ran straight for 50 to 60 paces and then split into several arms. The next attack could be expected from there. In the southeastern corner, a long, somewhat broader alleyway ran east from the marketplace, in which was the afore mentioned rather high Tower Gate, which separated the town from the *Vorstadt* [suburb]. The road to Arnau was the direct extension of this alleyway, the road to Neu Biczow and Königgrätz branched off it at right angles, about 100 paces beyond the Tower Gate. The Saxon troops marched off on the Neu Biczow road. The platoon that had been left behind stood in the marketplace in section columns.[87] The full moon hid behind gray clouds and only appeared for brief moments. Deep stillness ruled in the town. Nowhere was anyone to be seen on the streets, at most, a lighted window. The assertion that inhabitants of the town took part in the fighting and fired from the windows is just as nonsensical as the fairy tale of Saxon buglers imitating Prussian signals.
>
> The *Hauptmann* delivered a brief, inspiring speech to his men and warned them not to fire too high. Better to shoot into the pavement a few yards in front of them than over their heads. His soldiers gazed back at him, trusting and inspired. The little group was well aware of the gravity of the situation and of the importance of their mission, but they went bravely into the unequal combat.

87   Tr. Note: The Saxons were similar to the Prussians, in that a company (100 to 150 men in peacetime, up to 250 men in wartime) was divided into two equal *Züge*, or platoons. If the number of *Rotte*, or files (of three men) was uneven, the platoon on the right got the extra *Rotte*. If the platoon had sixteen or more *Rotte*, it was divided into *Halbzüge* or half platoons, and these in turn, subdivided into *Sektionen*, or sections. Platoons of fifteen or less *Rotte* were not divided into half platoons, merely into sections. The sections were to contain no more than six and no less than four *Rotte* each, i.e. 12 - 18 men. So, in the section column (*Sectionscolonne*), the platoon was in a column, 12 to 18 men wide, and apparently, two sections deep.

Fighting at the Tower Gate.

Soon the commanding voices and measured tread of [the enemy] could be heard, then a shrill bugle call. A dark mass now filled the alleyway. It rolled forward and reached the marketplace. Then the fire of the foremost section cracked out. This made way and a new Saxon volley followed. The enemy turned back with loud groans from the wounded. Within a few seconds stillness reigned again.

The first part of the mission was accomplished. Now it was a matter of occupying the Tower Gate before the enemy renewed the attack. Furniture was quickly brought from the adjoining houses and the gateway blocked with a makeshift barricade. It was still incomplete when the bugle call that customarily preceded the Prussian attacks, sounded again. The recently abandoned marketplace was again the location of this attack, which began like the first, with drums and hurrahs. A minute of unbroken fire and the crash of shattered windowpanes gave notice that the enemy was in undisputed possession of the marketplace [but we had flown]. He must have soon realized where he had to look for his vanished opponent, and the silence that followed the tumult associated with taking possession of the *Ring Platz,* made it evident that he would now proceed to attack the Tower Gate without delay. The *Hauptmann* and the *Oberlieutenant* were busy organizing their men behind the weak barricade, when the sudden shout, 'We are surrounded!', rang out. And in truth, barely 100 paces behind them, a dark line appeared in the street, unmistakably an enemy detachment in superior strength (it was the Fusiliers of the 48th).

They had probably come through the gardens of the eastern suburbs and then along the street (with front facing south), but it would only take a 'right about face' and the Saxon's only line of retreat would be cut. The platoon now hastened in open order to the narrow exit that still offered salvation. However, it was necessary to run the length of a daunting firing line (no farther off than a width of an ordinary street), in order to escape capture. A deafening volley met the fleeing men, yet despite (or perhaps because of), the unusually close range, only a few fell to the enemy fire. Most of the bullets struck above the windows of the ground floors of the houses. Unfortunately, the leader of the 2nd *Section* (half platoon), *Sergeant* Schütze, was among the wounded left behind. It was only several weeks later, after the courageous *Unteroffizier* had been awarded the silver 'Military Service Medal '[*silberne Militairverdienstmedaille*],that [his men] received news that Schütze had died the following day (30th June) as a result of his wounds. The *Hauptmann* also was hit in the hip by a ricochet and fell to the ground. On standing up he had to endure yet another volley, but fortunately he escaped. The Neu Biczow road that led off to the right (a few yards from the fateful location) was not occupied, and this allowed the little group to escape (an escape only made possible in the confusion engendered by street fighting at night).

The platoon's assignment, to cover the Saxon withdrawal and to delay the enemy for as long as possible, had for the most part been completed. Although times cited under such conditions may be subject to error … we believe that we are not far from the truth when we estimate that the time during which the platoon stood alone against the enemy in Gitschin … to have been around 25 to 30 minutes. According to his own statements, the enemy had sent several regiments into the fight for the town.

The battle for Gitschin, which after nine hours of fighting (from 3:30 to 12:30) and had ended with this street fighting, was a great strategic success.

Just as the day of Münchengrätz (the 28th) had resulted in the linking of 1st Army with the Elbe Army, the day of Gitschin established contact, or at least, nearly established contact, between these two armies on the one hand, and the 2nd (Crown Prince's) Army on the other. The actual link up took place four days later on the battlefield of Königgrätz, but the victory of the 29th (Gitschin) resulted in the first contact between the two great army groups. They could now freely communicate. No longer did any enemy stand between them.

We repeat that the action at Gitschin was a great strategic success, an opinion with which the Austrians finally agreed, but without placing any great emphasis on the battle itself. They acknowledged the significance of the result, without fully appreciating what led to it. In other words, they underestimated (indeed almost contest) the outstanding bravery with which our men fought and placed all the emphasis on the night march that led to the occupation of the town. Granted, this night march certainly crowned the work, but it could never have been carried out if the enemy had not first been shattered first. The actual glory of the day arises from the fact that this shattering, given the enemy's formidable position and superiority in numbers, took place before Benedek's retreat order had arrived or was known of. The Austrian military critics ignore this. Thus, for example, the following:

> In the Prussian accounts of the war, it sounds quite remarkable that the Austro-Saxon position that was naturally so strong and studded with an immense number of guns, was taken by only two [Prussian] divisions in such a short time. On the Austrian side … there were only two entire brigades [as well as], two battalions … and the Corps Artillery Reserve, thus 16 battalions, four squadrons [of cavalry] and six batteries (48 guns[88]) in the battle, which was nearly exclusively limited to a cannonade. If one looks more closely at the matter and only speaks the truth, the picture is far less surprising, and the deeds of heroic invincibility [of which we hear], become reduced to the level of entirely ordinary undertakings.

88   Author's footnote– The Austrian officer who made this statement claimed, 'only to speak the truth,' but he failed to do so, which leaves us wondering whether he could not or would not. Even if the Brigade Leiningen, from which we finally took two battalions prisoner, and the Saxon *Leib* Brigade, with which we twice fought in the streets of Gitschin, and finally, if we entirely leave out of the reckoning the six regiments of Edelsheim's Light Cavalry Division, as well as all of the Saxon cavalry and artillery, we are still left with the following strengths:

Austro-Saxons:

Brigade Ringelsheim	7 battalions.
Brigade Poschacher	7 battalions.
Brigade Piret	7 battalions.
Brigade Abele	7 battalions.
Brigade Crown Prince	5 battalions.
Artillery	96 guns.

Thus, 33 infantry battalions and 96 guns (namely, five brigade batteries including the battery of Brigade Leiningen plus seven batteries of the corps artillery reserve).

Prussian:

Division Werder	12 battalions.
Division Tümpling	12 battalions.
Pomeranian artillery	18 guns.
Brandenburg artillery	18 guns.

Thus, 24 infantry battalions and 36 guns.

These numbers are reliable. In addition, there was the formidable position. And what losses! Everyone can then come to their own conclusions as to whether Gitschin was a hard fight or not. And to finally quote the Austrian officer once more, 'the deeds of heroic invincibility [of which we hear], become reduced to the level of entirely ordinary undertakings,' could be said about everything, even Morgarten and Sempach. [The Battle of Morgarten occurred on 15th November 1315, when a 1,500 strong force from the Swiss Confederacy defeated a body of Austrians on the shores of Lake Ägeri near the Morgarten Pass in Switzerland. The Battle of Sempach was fought on 9th July 1386, between Leopold III, Duke of Austria and the Old Swiss Confederacy. The battle was a decisive Swiss victory in which Duke Leopold and many of the Austrian nobles died.

The above Austrian report exhibits their underestimation of the significance of the Battle of Gitschin. The next short report, of a more official character, demonstrates the overestimation of the significance assigned to the entry into the town:

> It was not the battle but the subsequent conditions of the retreat that disrupted the organization of some of our units . . . The regrettable fact of the Prussian entry into Gitschin had several deleterious effects on the outcome of the day. The corps headquarters was still in the town when the Prussians entered. It was disturbed by the appearance of the enemy while in the process of preparing the necessary orders and was in danger of being captured.

In this short statement, we see that the corps headquarters only placed special significance on what was *personally disturbing* and *inconvenient* for them. The actual occupation of Gitschin had only this special significance, of being disturbing and uncomfortable, perhaps there was also a moral effect, though more for us than for the enemy. Otherwise, if our battalions had halted at the edge of the town (since there was no thought of further pursuit and his line of retreat was nowhere threatened), the tactical and strategic success of the day would have remained essentially the same. However, the [Austrian] Corps Headquarters seems to want to avoid any mention of that. If it had asked Regiment Würtemberg that was in Unter Lochow, Regiment Constantin that was at the Cidlina stream, or Brigade Crown Prince that was decimated in Diletz, before preparing this report (instead of merely glancing over the casualty lists with bureaucratic indifference), the [badly mauled] battalions would have said where the main actions of the day had and had not been.

The losses

The great success of the day was also achieved by the 5th Division, but with substantial sacrifices. Gitschin cost the Brandenburgers 43 officers (11 dead) and 1016 men. Regiments Nr. 12 and 48 suffered the heaviest casualties, the 12th losing 13 officers and 278 men, the 48th losing 12 officers and 353 men.

Our enemy's losses were five times higher. The Saxons (at Diletz) lost 27 officers and 566 men. The Austrians (not counting Brigade Ringelsheim, whose losses we gave in our account of the fighting at Unter Lochow) lost 111 officers and 3,600 men. The 18th *Jägers* and Regiments Constantin, Sigismund and King of Prussia were the hardest hit. The first two of these losing up to a quarter of their complement. Regiment Chulai lost the most prisoners, and it must therefore be surprising that, while the official Austrian account simply states the loss of two battalions of Chulai infantry, the official list of losses only speaks of 217 wounded and unwounded prisoners. One or other of these statements is in need of correction.

Gitschin on 30th June

Not until the next morning was it possible to see how fierce the fighting had been on the previous day. Early in the morning, details of stretcher bearers began to search the battlefield, and by noon more than a thousand wounded had already been placed in private houses and public buildings. Most were in the palace, government buildings, barracks and schools. However, hundreds more

Prince Albert of Saxony.

were brought in, and soon the unfortunates, for want of space, were placed under the arcades of the marketplace, some on hay or straw or on a blanket that had been thrown down, most on the bare stone. All of Gitschin was a hospital. Everywhere there was a shortage of food, of medical supplies and of medical help. Amputations had to be postponed because there were not enough surgeons.[89] In the widest variety of languages, men called for a bit of bread. Hundreds were

89   Author's Note: Eight Austrian physicians who had been captured refused to lend a helping hand. According to Prussian reports, they even refused to attend their own soldiers. The enemy, however, disputes this emphatically. The Austrian regimental surgeon, Dr. Kraus, declared in this respect, 'As one of those accused I must state as a matter of fact, that all of the Austrian and Saxon officers and about 900 men that were brought into the dressing station at the infantry barracks, the adjoining grammar school, the two churches and individual private houses, were cared for by us without any refusals so

happy if a kindly hand at least provided them with a drink of water. The shaken and the stoic were crowded together. A Saxon who had lost both eyes to a shot from the side, tapped his way around and passionately begged to be killed. Wounded Austrians and Prussians who wore the Schleswig Cross or the Düppel Medal, now renewed in common suffering their old wartime comradeship, and helped each other with advice and assistance.

The churches provided a particularly touching, and at the same time, graphic scene. Tattered and torn banners from the Thirty Years War hung on the walls between tall ornamental lanterns, baroquely carved and painted red. Hungarian Hussars sat on the steps of the altar, one wrapped in a blue and gold coat, the other in a white one. The bright light of midday fell on eagle feather and busby. Italians from Regiment Sigismund lay in the passages and niches, one with a rose between his pale lips. Bohemians from the 18th *Jägers* crouched in the pews and gazed imploringly at the portraits of the Virgin Mary, praying for help or for release. To the side, on the bare tiles and leaning against the pillared wall, was a Bohemian woman, beside her a wounded soldier of Regiment Chulai. The exhausted woman slept; the man did not stir. He had his arm around his nurse and her head on his chest.

Most of the officers were placed in private houses. Among the Austrians, forty or so in a room, were well known names, *Graf* Nicolaus Bethlen (a descendant of the *Siebenburg* Prince Bethlen Gabor), *Graf* Bulgarini of the General Staff (who later died of his wounds), *Graf* Pejacsevich, *Oberst* and Commander of the Liechtenstein Hussar Regiment, who two days later upon the arrival of the King, received permission to return via Dresden to Vienna while his wounds healed.

Some 2,000 wounded lay in Gitschin on the evening of the 30th, an equal number lay in the villages in the immediate vicinity of the battlefield. Their fortunes varied greatly. Those who had been brought to the Walditzer *Karthaus* [Charterhouse] (mostly Austrians) found loving care. Here (though there was no luxury) was adequate food, drink and care, and the warm hearted sisters who presided here, year in and year out, merely extended the scope of their daily duties.[90]

long as they were in Gitschin. *Generalärzte* Doctors Löffler and Bardeleben, the personal physician [*Leibarzt*] of His Majesty, Dr. Lauer, the *Oberstabsarzt* [medical major] Dr. Starke and a whole number of highly placed Prussian military can bear witness to my statement.' The contradiction might perhaps arise from the fact that after a certain point in time, the Austrian physicians did apply themselves for many weeks, but in the first days, disconsolate at their captivity and depressed by the strain, they declined to help.

90 Author's Note: The famous Wallenstein *Carthause* [Charterhouse, originally occupied by monks of the Carthusian Order] where the mortal remains of the Friedlander rested until they were transferred to Münchengrätz, has not been a monastery since the beginning of the 19th century, but has been for about twenty years, a prison. This happened in such a unique, and at the same time, so exemplary a manner, that we should say a word about it at this point. In charge of the facility, in which only serious criminals (none with sentences of less than ten years) are imprisoned, are twenty warm hearted sisters and their prioress. Aside from the prison's nuns, the inspector and a weak military garrison (which at the time of our occupation consisted of a few Austrian semi-invalids), there are no male personnel. The sisters take care of the entire administration and the immediate interaction with the prisoners, of which there are generally 700. A visitor wrote, 'It is amazing to see these twenty sisters, in their becoming habits, working and living with their accustomed calmness, amiability and gentleness, among these seven hundred murderers, thieves and arsonists. For the twelve years during which this female administration has existed, there has not been a single excess. For five years there has not been a single attempted escape. One has to see the respect that these criminals have for the sisters, especially for the prioress, and the way their faces light up with joy when [the prioress] walks through the work room or

Austrian prisoners and the wounded of both sides.

the cells and exchanges a few kind words with them ... The sisters administer the housekeeping and the work. Everywhere the prisoners, themselves, serve as their assistants. Only the most serious criminals are in chains, but all move freely in the great rooms, chambers and cloisters. Rarely is punishment necessary (most commonly removal from *communal* work). Everything is accomplished through love, kindness and gentleness. The roughest criminal becomes an obedient child. Religious services in this place are the most moving. The entire interior of the church, the altar, the chancel, the prayer stools, everything has been constructed by the prisoners themselves. The altar and the holy pictures have been made by them (mostly by artists who have been sentenced to 20 or 30 years for counterfeiting) and the wooden frames are elaborately carved. The merciful sisters sit in the choir stalls, next to the altar. The entire facility is perhaps unique both in its operation and in its successes.' (Since this was written there has been a major incident, and a new organization has already taken over the running of the prison, if we are not mistaken.

The numerous wounded that were brought to the little town of Lomnitz (near Eisenstadtl), received equally excellent care. Most of the Austrian wounded came from Regiment Constantin, most of ours from the *Leib* Regiment, which had to face the assault delivered by Brigade Piret at 8:00 in the evening. In Lomnitz,[91] granted, a unique case, the activities of the physician and the *Bürgermeister* were united in the same person, so that the administrative authority could directly assist the healing arts.

All the sadder was what happened in the villages, in which the hastily fleeing inhabitants had often left no more than emptied cottages and rubbish filled wells. In Unter Lochow wounded Pomeranians predominated, including *Lieutenant* von Weyher of Grenadier Regiment Nr. 12, King Friedrich Wilhelm IV, a young officer (only just arrived from the cadet corps) whose brain had been exposed when a shell fragment injured his skull. Others from the Pomeranian division had found wretched housing in Sobotka, Wohawetz and Wokschitz.

Most disturbing however, was the situation in Libun. The village itself had been shelled and half burned down. The church and parsonage had been turned into hospitals. In the bell tower were gathered all those who had died of their wounds or amputations. It was a long row. The parsonage was worst of all. Here lay the severely wounded, mostly on heaps of straw, Prussian, Austrian and Saxon officers, intermingled. Most of the Prussian officers belonged to the Fusilier battalions of the 8th, 12th and 48th Regiments which had captured Cidlina, Zames and Diletz from the Saxon Brigade Crown Prince. Here lay *Hauptmann* von Simon of the 12th Regiment, son in law of *General* Vogel von Falskenstein, shot through the chest and upper arm. Here, along a wall, lay *Lieutenants* von Borowsky, Tapper and von der Osten, all three from the 48th Regiment. Across from them were three Saxon officers, *Oberst* von Boxberg, his adjutant von Minckwitz and *Freiherr* von Seckendorf. In the same row with them was a young Austrian officer, Alois *Graf* Voss of the Savoy Dragoons. Nearly all died, including those for whom there was hope. The one who seemed most seriously wounded survived. This was *Lieutenant* Hellhof of the 12th Regiment. When the *Johanitterritter* von Werder (and he tells this himself) entered the young officer's room and asked him where he was wounded, [Hellhof] calmly said that he was seriously injured and pulled off the blanket, showing his questioner the stumps of both his amputated feet.

---

91   Author's Note: At the end of August there were still five Grenadiers of the *Leib* Regiment hospitalized in Lomnitz. Our path led us there. With us was an officer of that regiment, who had traveled from Prague to find out for himself what more could be done for the wounded. We entered. Who can describe the joy of the brave Grenadiers when they recognized their officer, under whom they had fought so courageously at the Cidlina. We soon found and greeted four of the five, now we sought the fifth. In the course of our search a fortunate circumstance brought us back to one of the first rooms. A fortunate circumstance, if nothing more! Already, during our first visit to this room of eight beds, we had noticed that for the entire time, two eyes had been fixed on us with a constant, painful expression, from a corner of the room. Now it became clear to us what this painful gaze had signified. The nearly motionless man lying there, with waxen face and that veiled expression that offers little hope of recovery, was also a Prussian, also a Brandenburger (of the 48th), a fellow countryman of those Grenadiers from the *Leib* Regiment, and merely because he belonged to another regiment, he had seen us pass him by like a stranger, without comfort or greeting. What bitter feelings must have passed through this man's heart as he lay there, abandoned and forgotten, while his fellow countrymen celebrated with old friends! Now however, the bitter cup was taken from him, and everybody redoubled their efforts to make things right with the involuntarily neglected sufferer. Granted, our only reward was the thankful smile of a dying man.

What a frightful sight! And it was *Lieutenant* Hellhof that recovered. By spring he was able to get around in a wheelchair and the winter months found him in Italy. (This is the same *Lieutenant* Hellhof who, during his travels in Italy, was insulted by a south German officer in the theater in Florence. This did, indeed, take place, but the cause of the incident has not been properly explained. For the sake of the officer's honour we prefer to believe that it was the result of a misunderstanding. When one has no feet, or has been severely wounded in the feet - we have ourselves, experienced such cases - one's movements are naturally clumsy, and one can thus be placed in a situation where one is unable to show the small considerations, the polite gestures, that would otherwise be expected. Unable to quickly [move one's legs], one sits as immobile as a toll gate in the theater, in the railway compartment or in a carriage, angry words are spoken before one can even explain. Thus, we excuse this painful scene. Any other explanation else would be too awful).

The church at Libun.

The Campaign in the Iser Region

The 29th had been a bloody day, but it was only the prelude! While hundreds awaited their first medical attention in the villages on the edges of the battlefield and under the arcades of Gitschin, the army pressed further south, to the decision.

The high command of the Austro - Saxon Iser Army has been severely criticized, and it must be granted, with justification. Two courses of action, or so it appears to us, were available. Either the Austro - Saxons should have resolved, from the very beginning, to hold the Iser line, stubbornly, firmly, and at all costs. Or they should have held nothing at all, but avoiding major engagements, fallen back to either Gitschin or Miletin, to link up with the main army for joint action.

However, the Austro - Saxons did neither the one nor the other. They gave up the Iser - line when it was still possible to hold it, and then they wanted to hold it after it was already lost. Whose fault was this? Primarily Benedek. Any subordinate, even a better one than Clam-Gallas, must come to grief on the contradictory orders of the Supreme Commander, if he who receives these orders, lacks the courage to break them. Sufficient proof may be found if we simply reproduce the orders that arrived from the Army High Command in the course of four days, at the Corps Headquarters or the Headquarters of the Crown Prince of Saxony.

Morning of the 26th: The Iser is not to be held, take post behind the Iser.
Noon of the 26th: The Iser is to be held at all costs.
Noon of the 27th: Prefer not to hold the Iser. Retreat to Gitschin.
Noon of the 29th: Hold Gitschin.
Evening of the 29th: Don't hold Gitschin.

Have there ever, in the course of a few days, been more changing, more contradictory or more confusing orders?

The position between Jung Bunzlau and Münchengrätz (actually a lost cause on a grand scale) was a mistake from the very beginning. Münchengrätz was marginal. The significant points were Turnau and Gitschin. The latter was such a favourable position, both strategically and tactically, that even on the evening of the 29th, all the prior mistakes could have been resolved, if instead of ordering, *Break off the fighting,'* the opposite order had arrived, *Hold the position by committing all forces and at all costs.* There however, Benedek failed. Up to that point, despite all the wavering and contradictions, he had at least held firmly (firm to the point of obstinacy) to *one point,* the first decisive blow was to be against Prince Friedrich Karl. He renounced this obstinacy at the very moment when just that obstinate perseverance would have had a certain chance of success. Obstinate and irresolute, each at the wrong time, the primary blame for the misfortunes of the Iser Army must fall to Benedek, and to a certain point (later we shall show to what degree) to *Graf* Clam-Gallas, who at his own request, was called before a military court martial.

A quarter of a year later, upon his acquittal, Clam-Gallas received the following letter from the Emperor:

My dear *General der Cavallerie, Graf* Clam-Gallas!
After the preliminary investigation confirmed the lack of any serious evidence against you, I was happy to grant your request for rehabilitation by a court martial, and I now express to you my entire pleasure that the verdict of the court martial recognizes your *total innocence* in every instance, and thereby, my army and the state affirm that the reputation and name of a courageous general, who has served myself and my house for long years with true devotion are free of any stain.

Schönbrunn, 13th October 1866.

So much for the letter of the Emperor, whose concluding words appear to us, to exceed the permissible measure of recognition. For however much we may assign the primary blame to the wavering of Benedek, Clam-Gallas is far from having led his army corps 'free from blame and stain.' Twice, if he had been more enterprising, he had opportunity to make a winning move, on the evening of the 26th and on the afternoon of the 29th. He would have (and he had the requisite means) achieved success. At Podol (on the 26th) he would have been victorious and would have recaptured Turnau (the means for so doing were at hand). The same held true, only on a larger scale, at Gitschin. When at 8:30 in the evening the order to break off the fighting reached him, victory was already within his grasp. The Austrian superiority was so great that if the right man had stood behind [the Austro - Saxon forces], our four brigades would have been smashed by the nine brigades and threefold superior artillery (to say nothing of the formidable position). That this did not take place cannot be blamed on Benedek (who would have been thankful for a victory under any circumstances, even one that he had not ordered). All of the blame for that falls on the inadequacy of the subordinate commanders.

So much for the conduct of our enemy's command on the Iser. Now a word regarding our own.

Accusations have been levelled against the High Command of the 1st Army, that its diversion towards Münchengrätz constituted a similar mistake to that which the Austrians committed by hanging on to the Iser position. However, our findings in this respect are, 'The fighting at Münchengrätz was brilliant in conception but superfluous ... it resembled ... besieging a fortress that one would have been better advised to entirely bypass. Instead of fighting at the Musky Berg on the 28th, on the evening of the 27th the 7th Division should have already advanced to Sobotka, and the 5th to Gitschin. Clam-Gallas would then have been outflanked and his communications with the main army severed.'

This criticism can perhaps be considered valid from a purely theoretical standpoint, but it overlooks the fact that at that time, our army had no [real] wartime experience, first it had to get to know itself. This particularly applies to *tactics* and not to *strategy*. It was indeed tempting to cut off 60,000 men, or even half that number, but accomplishing this (which perhaps was theoretically the only right solution), courted great danger if the tactical ability of the troops [did not match the strategic ability of the High Command]. *Above all, one wanted to take the safe course.*

It is from this viewpoint that the operations of the 1st Army from 26th to 29th July, especially the action at Münchengrätz, must be viewed. After Gitschin, when we started to appreciate our overall superiority, we began to operate more boldly. The Battle of Königgrätz was fought to a large degree in the confidence in this superior strength. We believed that in the worst case (if the Crown Prince failed to arrive), we could chance fighting against a two-fold superiority. After Königgrätz we may have gone too far in this boldness. It seemed as if it *must* work. However, what was more or less admissible after the 3rd of July was forbidden a week earlier.

The [original] army dispositions (of two army groups), which have been condemned by theory, and regarding which we too have some questions, cannot be decided by a traditional formula (which is always the easiest way). Time changes everything and each new [campaign] is never like the one before, each age demands its own solutions. This understanding, which does not preclude error, has led us to victory.

Book II

The 2nd Army to the Upper Elbe
From 1st to 3rd July

Contents

2nd Army to the Upper Elbe

The 2nd Army in Silesia

Two armies (if we consider the Elbe and 1st Army as a single formation) were now operating against the enemy.

The plan from the very beginning, was based on the union of the two armies on the upper Elbe, approximately in the vicinity of Gitschin.[1] In order to accomplish this, one army [1st and Elbe], moved out of Saxony on the 22nd and 23rd [June], the other [2nd Army], from Silesia on the 26th and 27th. We have followed the advance of one as far as Gitschin. Now we shall follow the advance of the other.

Immediately prior to the outbreak of hostilities, the 2nd (the so called Silesian Army) consisted of four army corps in the north of the *Grafschaft* (county) of Glatz, awaiting orders to march into Bohemia. The four corps were:

I (East Prussian) Army Corps, *Generallieutenant* von Bonin.
V (Posen) Army Corps, *General* von Steinmetz.
VI (Silesian) Army Corps, *General* von Mutius.
Guards Corps, Prince August von Würtemberg.

The Chief of the General Staff of the entire 2nd Army was *Generalmajor* von Blumenthal (who had already proven himself in the same position in the war against Denmark). The Commander in Chief was the Crown Prince [Friedrich Wilhelm]. We shall follow a brief biographical note with an account of the marches, concentrations and inspections that, in the first weeks of June, preceded the invasion of Bohemia by the 2nd Army.

Friedrich Wilhelm, Crown Prince of Prussia, was born on 18th October 1831 in the New Palace at Potsdam, and received his full name, Friedrich Wilhelm Nicolaus Karl, at his christening by Bishop Eylert on 13th November, the birthday of Queen Elizabeth. *Frau* Godet was in charge of his early upbringing.

When he turned eight, he started his schooling along with Rudolf von Zastrow and Adolf *Graf* von Königsmarck, who were the same age. The young Prince took to the [army] zealously, the Babelberg Park being the site of his first warlike games. Fortresses were built and stormed. One time it rained, and a servant brought him an umbrella. 'Have you ever seen a Prussian Prince under an umbrella?' So much for the umbrella.

---

1   Author's Note: This offensive, as we have indicated earlier, was a relatively late development. The defensive option was preferred until 14th June. We shall return to this later.

Frederick Wilhelm.

When he turned ten (18th October 1841), the Prince entered the *1st Garde Regiment zu Fuss* [1st Foot Guards Regiment], received the *Stern zum Schwarzen Adlerorden* [Star of the Order of the Black Eagle] and for his military studies, was placed under the tutelage of *Oberst* von Unruh, who had up to that point been Adjutant to the Prince of Prussia. *Professor* Curtius was in charge of his general education which started in 1844.

In 1847 and 1848 the Prince took part in shooting practice and exercises with mixed weapons, whereupon he was transferred on 3rd May 1848, to the 1st Guards Regiment for permanent service. Upon this occasion the Prince of Prussia delivered the following speech (at the swearing in ceremony at the Potsdamer *Lustgarten*):

My son now joins your ranks for permanent service. I hope that he will bring honour to his name and his lineage. The guarantee for that lies in the spirit God gave him, not in us, and you my son, my hope is that you, yourself, shall experience what your father discovered in the midst of his comrades. Gentlemen, it has been the greatest joy of my life to see how the loyalty and devotion of my subjects has never failed in the most difficult days both near and far! That I also wish for you. And so now, do your duty.

The Prince was not granted the opportunity to take part in the brief campaign in Baden shortly thereafter. In the following year (1850) he attended the University of Bonn and then undertook a greater journey. On 15th October he was appointed *Hauptmann* in the 1st Guards Regiment. In the following year he was entrusted with the independent command of the 6th Company. The 23rd of August 1853 (it was the fortieth anniversary of the victory of Grossbeeren[2]), provided the Prince with his first opportunity for a public speech. In the midst of a large circle of students, soldiers and veterans, all of whom turned up with flags and banners, the prince stated:

Forty years ago today on this field of battle, the victory was gained on which depended the salvation of the capital of this land. However, it had yet greater significance. At the same time it showed the world that Prussia could boldly enter the ring with any opponent.

On 15th October 1854, the Prince was placed in command of the 1st Battalion, 2nd *Garde Landwehr* Regiment, being promoted on 31st August of the following year to *Oberst*, and on 3rd July 1856, on the same day that ten years later would be so significant for him and that regiment, assumed command of the 1st Guards Regiment. He had just returned from Scotland, where his betrothal with the Princess Royal of England [Princess Victoria] had taken place at Balmoral. In the autumn of that same year, in response to the Prince's special request to also serve in the line, he was given command on 3rd October, of the 11th Infantry Regiment in Breslau, a position that he assumed on 1st November. The Prince took part in all the activities of the men, and was personally committed to their well-being. Not only did the Prince conscientiously perform his duties, he especially won the trust and affection of all his subordinates. On 25th January 1858, his marriage took place to the Princess Royal in London. On 8th February the people rejoiced as he brought his newlywed to the Prussian capital. On his wedding day the Prince was promoted to *General*.

On 1st July 1860, he was promoted *Generallieutenant*. On 18th October 1861, following the death of King Friedrich Wilhelm IV, he attended the ceremonial coronation [of his father] at Königsberg, in his capacity as Crown Prince of Prussia. The war against Denmark in 1864 took him to Schleswig - Holstein and Jutland. He assumed no command but observed operations at first hand. On 22nd February, before Düppel, he was under fire for the first time, and demonstrated, in addition to a rapid and perceptive insight into military matters, an objective and forgiving nature that rose above personalities and rivalries, assuring mutual cooperation [at Headquarters] and boding well for the future.

The opportunity soon arrived to justify this confidence, and under the most demanding of conditions. On 17th May he was named Commander in Chief of the 2nd Army, and on 2nd June,

2   Tr. Note: In the Battles of Grossbeeren, Blankenfelde and Sputendorf (23rd August 1813) an allied Prussian-Swedish army under Crown Prince Charles John (formerly Jean-Baptiste Bernadotte, Marshal of France) defeated the French under Marshal Oudinot, who were hoping to drive the Prussians out of the Sixth Coalition by capturing Berlin.

Fürstenstein Castle.

Military Governor of Silesia. On the 4th he proceeded to Breslau and thence to Fürstenstein, to set up his headquarters in the old castle, halfway between Breslau and the border.

Schloss Fürstenstein (described as the 'Pearl of Silesia,' in old travelogues) is the ancient seat of the *Grafen* von Hochberg. In 1847 the Hochbergs (in particular the Fürstenstein line), acquired the principality of Pless in Upper Silesia, in accordance with which the Grafen [Counts] assumed the title of Prince. The present Prince [*Fürst*] has improved the Schloss greatly, with renovations and additions. The library is one of the most extensive, especially with regard to the history of the Fatherland. The Schloss and its surroundings are filled with historical memories.

Near the Schloss are the lists where, in 1800, in the presence of King Friedrich Wilhelm III and Queen Louise, the Silesian nobility conducted a joust in knightly costume. The outer enclosure with the places where the knightly ladies sat, is still preserved. Among the historical items that are in the chambers of the ancient castle, are the writing desk on which Frederick the Great prepared the plan for the Battle of Hohenfriedberg[3] (the battlefield is a little less

---

3   Tr. Note: In the Battle of Hohenfriedberg (Striegau), Frederick the Great's Prussian army decisively defeated an Austrian army under Prince Charles Alexander of Lorraine, on 4th June 1745, during the War of the Austrian Succession.

than seven miles distant). In the 1820's King Friedrich Wilhelm IV, at that time still Crown Prince, enjoyed spending time there. Similarly, the present Crown Prince was a guest at Schloss Fürstenstein during his two extensive visits to Silesia in 1857 and 1859. Now, under different circumstances, he was again the guest of the Schloss. A letter from those days (the start of June) describes his presence as follows:

> The Crown Prince has been here for several days. He occupies the right-hand side of the main floor. The headquarters Guards is in the gatehouse of the Schloss, and the hundreds officers that go in and out, the cavalry orderlies that fly here and there, bear sufficient evidence that the peace of these valleys will soon give way to the pandemonium of war . . . The work demanded by the seriousness of the times, fills nearly the entire day. Only the time spent at table provides a few hours of relaxation, when the princely family, as well as the staff officers, gather around the Crown Prince on the terraces of the Schloss. Then a military band of one or other of the regiments appears on the garden terrace, and visitors from the town gather to enjoy the performance. Among the guests are some who are not there of their own free will. A few Windischgrätz Dragoons that had strayed on this side of the border were brought in yesterday. The Crown Prince presented them with gifts and sent them back to their regiment.

So much for the letter. It expresses the fear 'that the peace of these valleys will give way to the pandemonium of war,' and in fact, at the beginning of June, when the strict maintenance of a defensive [posture] was still a firm part of the political program, there could be little doubt that these Silesian valleys would become the theater of the war. The political situation excluded, as we know, any thought of attack. On 10th June the [intention to fight a defensive war] was still so firm that the Crown Prince concentrated his army, which had until then been positioned at the border of the Liegnitz and Breslau districts, nearer to Neisse in order to await an enemy attack with greater assurance behind this fortress and protected by the river of the same name. In accordance with this measure he also shifted his headquarters from Fürstenstein to Neisse. The defensive option was still prime until 14th June (the day of the Confederation Diet's motion). From that day on we looked upon ourselves as having been challenged, the political concerns no longer determined or limited our strategic movements. Now the first priority was no longer to maintain the peace, defensive thinking was abandoned, the offensive replaced it.

> On the 19th [of June] the order was issued for the army to be kept in readiness to advance toward the Bohemian border.
> On the 20th the Crown Prince issued his first army field order.
> On the 21st came the declaration of war.[4]
> On the 23rd the Crown Prince left Neisse, which had been his headquarters since the 10th.

---

4   Author's Note: This declaration of war, which was followed by the 'Manifesto' and the recall of ambassadors on both sides, took place by notification in writing, on the specified date (the 21st) of all enemy outpost commanders, by the Crown Prince, wherein was stated that, 'due to the Confederation Diet resolution instigated by Austria on the 14th, a state of war had in fact broken out, and the Prussian forces had received instructions to act accordingly.'

The banners and flags that had waved since the day of his arrival, from the tower of the town hall and from the Berlin gate, were taken down. Prior to this however, the commander summoned the officer corps and town officials one more time, and made the following speech:

> I am convinced that the fortress is in good hands. Trust the commanders, they deserve it. The orders that have been issued must be followed to the letter. I consider that I have been greatly honoured by the fact that my Royal Father has entrusted me with this army, which, if not perhaps chosen for immediate action, will offer good service to the Fatherland, namely to this province whose governor I have been named. You, gentlemen (turning to the officers), know your duty. I direct your attention to the history of Prussia, from which you know what tasks Prussia must fulfill. You are called upon to carry them out. You, gentlemen (turning to the officials) will have to endure great difficulties, but I believe that I can assure you, that this part of the province will not be the immediate theater of the war. If you have needs, turn to the King. In addition, I thank you for the quiet sympathy that you have shown to me regarding my recent loss.[5] The quieter this support was, the better has it been for me. I sincerely thank you all.

So spoke the Crown Prince on 23rd June. His words were so open, so heartfelt, yet they were carefully reserved with regard to the impending operations. There was no more deluding the enemy about the planned offensive however, since on this same day (23rd) the armies under *General* Herwarth and Prince Friedrich Karl, were already entering Bohemia. We could still leave the enemy in some doubt regarding the direction from which we would advance from Silesia however. Would we advance to the south or to the west, were we planning to operate in Moravia or in Bohemia ? We know now that the latter alternative (invasion of Bohemia) had been decided since the 19th. For that very reason it was desirable to conceal our intention to advance toward the west, and make it appear that our axis of advance would be toward the south. For this reason, on 22nd June, the two divisions of VI Corps were advanced toward Olmütz, and (on the 23rd and 24th) crossed the border at Kalkau, Friedeberg, Friedwald, Zuckmantel and at various other locations. Everywhere they spread the word that they were the advance Guards of the other army corps that were following them. Demonstrations at the southern point of Silesia toward Krakau took place with the same intention. Whether these feints actually deceived the enemy or not, we did succeed in entering enemy territory from Upper Silesia at the three specified points, without this march (behind the *Grafschaft* Glatz), being noticed or known to the enemy.

On the 25th the 2nd Army (less VI Corps which returned to its previous position at Neisse), was awaiting the invasion order at the three 'Gates of Bohemia.' The Crown Prince issued the following army field order:

> Soldiers of the 2nd Army! I have received the words of our King and Commander! His Majesty's attempts to maintain peace in the land have been in vain. With a heavy

---

5   Author's Note: His infant son, Prince Sigismund (born 15th September 1864), died on 18th June in the New Palace at Potsdam. Queen Augusta departed that same evening from Berlin to Neisse to console her son.

heart, but strong in his trust in the devotion and courage of his army, the King is resolved to fight for the honour and independence of Prussia, as also for the powerful new organization of Germany. Placed at your head by the grace and trust of my Royal Father, I am proud to commit my life and property [*Gut und Blut*] with you for the sacred good of our Fatherland. Soldiers! For the first time in over fifty years our army is facing a worthy foe. Trust in your strength, in our proven superior weapons, and realize that it is now a matter of conquering the same enemy that our greatest King once vanquished with a smaller army. And now, forward, with the old Prussian cry, 'With God for King and Fatherland!'

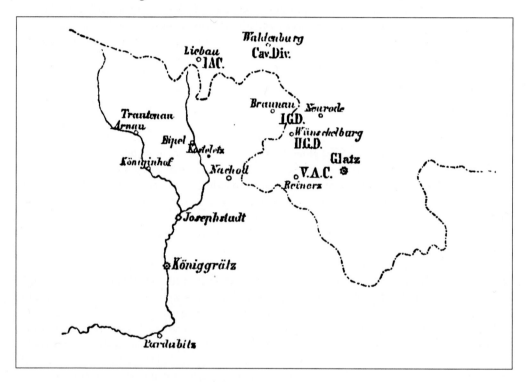

Initial deployment of the Prussian 2nd Army.

VI Corps in Upper Silesia

Detachments Knobelsdorf and Stolberg, the action at Oswiecim [Auschwitz]

As we closed our previous chapter (with the main body of the Crown Prince's army forming its columns at the border, ready for invasion), VI Army Corps was left behind on the river Neisse, in part to mask the concentration of the other corps, and in part to protect Upper Silesia for as long as possible. We shall initially turn our attention to VI Corps for reasons we shall later present.

The composition of VI Corps was:

11th Division (*Generallieutenant* von Zastrow).

21st Infantry Brigade, *Generalmajor* **von Hauenfeldt.**
 1st Silesian Grenadier Regiment Nr. 10, *Oberst Freiherr* von Falkenstein.
 3rd Lower Silesian Infantry Regiment Nr. 50, *Oberst* von Natzmer.
22nd Infantry Brigade, *Generalmajor* **von Hoffmann.**
 4th Lower Silesian Infantry Regiment Nr. 51, *Oberst* Paris.
 Silesian Fusilier Regiment Nr. 38, *Oberst* von Witzleben.
 2nd Silesian Dragoon Regiment Nr. 8, *Oberstlieutenant* von Wichmann;
 2nd Foot Battalion Silesian Field Artillery Regiment Nr. 6, *Major* Bröcker.
 Silesian Pioneer Battalion, *Oberstlieutenant* Dieterich.

12th Division (*Generallieutenant* von Prondzunski).

Combined Infantry Brigade: *Generalmajor* **von Cranach.**
 1st Upper Silesian Infantry Regiment Nr. 22, *Oberst* von Ruville.
 2nd Upper Silesian Infantry Regiment Nr. 23, *Oberst* Stein von Kaminski.
Combined Infantry Brigade, *Generalmajor* **von Knobelsdorff.**
 3rd Upper Silesian Infantry Regiment Nr. 62, *Oberst* von Malachowski.
 4th Upper Silesian Infantry Regiment Nr. 63, *Oberstlieutenant* von Eckartsberg.
2nd Silesian Hussar Regiment Nr.6, *Oberst* **von Trotha.**
 Silesian Cuirassier Regiment Nr. 1, *Oberst* von Barby.
 Silesian Uhlan Regiment Nr. 2, *Oberst* Baumgarth.
 Silesian *Jäger* Battalion Nr. 6, *Oberstlieutenant Graf* zu Dohna.
 1st Foot Battalion Silesian Field Artillery Regiment, *Major* Forst.
Reserve Cavalry;
 1st Silesian Hussar Regiment Nr. 4, *Oberstlieutenant* von Buddenbrock.
 Reserve Artillery;
 5 batteries under *Oberst* von Scherbening.

So much for the composition of VI Corps. We shall report elsewhere about its detachments which at times, reduced the corps to half its strength. The Commander was *General der Cavallerie* von Mutius.

Louis von Mutius was born on 20th March 1796, in Oels. His father (who died as a *General*), was at that time in the Würtemberg Hussar Regiment. His mother was a Lützow. Louis von Mutius entered the Silesian Cuirassier Regiment Nr. 1 (now *Leib* Cuirassier Regiment) at Juliusberg on 1st February 1813 at the age of 16. In May of that year he took part in the Battle of Gross Görchen, the rear Guards actions at Görlitz and Bunzlau, and the action at Haynau as *Portepée Fähnrich*, then (as of 20th May) as *Secondelieutenant,* receiving the Iron Cross 2nd Class for conspicuous bravery at Haynau. Of the other battles in the years 1813 and 1814, he took part with distinction in the Battle of Dresden, the actions at Graupen (Kulm), Libertwolkwitz and Gülden Gossa, the Battle of Leipzig and the actions at Montmirail and Etoges. Returning to the peacetime garrison of the regiment at Breslau on 6th July 1818, he was promoted to *Premierlieutenant* and there on 18th January 1819, married Marie, the youngest daughter of the future Commanding General of the V Army Corps, the Divisional Commander, von Röder. Although it would have been to his financial advantage to take over and manage the property belonging to the hereditary Seitenberg domain and his father's estate of Thomaswaldau, he chose to remain in the service and later, in order to avoid further substantial losses, sold it all, since his many transfers (a total of eleven) rendered it totally impossible to oversee the administration of this great landed inheritance by others.

In 1821 he was transferred to Posen as the duty Adjutant of the 10th Division and then in 1829, as *Rittmeister* of the 5th Cuirassier Regiment. In 1833 he was ordered to the corps headquarters of V Army Corps as Adjutant, then promoted with ante dated commission to *Rittmeister* and Squadron Leader in the 1st Cuirassier Regiment. That same year he was promoted to *Major* while retaining command of the squadron. On 20th March 1841, he became a permanent [*Étatsmässiger*] staff officer. The turbulent year of 1848 saw him transferred to Trier as commander of the 8th Uhlan Regiment.

He was fully engaged in military activity during the Baden Campaign of 1849. At the head of the mixed arms advance Guards of *General* von Webern's division, moving out of Saarbrücken, he fought in the action at Homburg in the Pfalz and at Rinnthal, the reconnaissance of Federbach at Muggensturm, the actions at Bischweier, Kuppenheim and Iffelsheim, thereby earning the reputation as an extraordinarily skillful, prudent and bold advance Guards commander. On 19th November 1849, he was promoted to *Oberstlieutenant*, and on 19th April 1851, to *Oberst*. These turbulent years brought several transfers. In November 1849, the 8th Uhlan Regiment came to Düsseldorf, then after the demobilization of 1851, to Bonn, and in the Autumn of 1852, to Elbing.   On 18th November 1852, von Mutius was named Commander of the 16th Cavalry Brigade and transferred from Elbing again to Trier. Here, on 13th July 1854, he was promoted to *Generalmajor*. In the winter of 1855, he took part as a member of the commission sitting in Berlin to revise the cavalry exercise regulations under the chairmanship of *General* (now *Feldmarschall*) *Graf* von Wrangel. In the spring of 1858, he was appointed Commander of the 13th Division, which involved his transfer to Münster, where he was also tasked with the provisional conduct of the business of the Corps Headquarters of the VII Armee Corps, and on the 22nd of that month, became *Generallieutenant*.

The following year, when the Austro - French war in Italy resulted in partial mobilization of the Prussian army, the King placed him in command of the 13th Division, and in November of that same year, transferred him to Neisse as Commander of the 12th Division. In 1860 he was named *Rechtsritter* of the *St. Johanniter Orden* [Order of St. John]. In 1861 he received the Order of the Red Eagle, 1st Class with Oak leaves and Swords, and performed honorary service to Grand Duke Nicolas of Russia at the coronation of King Wilhelm I in Königsberg. In August 1862 he was placed in charge of directing the exercises for the combined eight Guards Cavalry divisions and the three Horse Guards batteries at Berlin, and on 23rd October of the same year he was named Commander of the 11th Division. On 1st February 1863, he celebrated his fifty years of service in Breslau, his first garrison, with the heartfelt participation of his superiors, his subordinates and all who were close to him officially or socially. Two days earlier he had been named as Commanding General of VI Army Corps, and on the preceding day, he was awarded the *Kronenorder 1st Klasse* [Order of the Crown, First Class]. On the day of the celebration his former regimental comrade, the reigning Archduke of Sachsen Weimar, also decorated him with the *Grosskreuz des Falken Ordens* [Great Cross of the Order of the Falcon].

For months *General* von Mutius had conducted the business of the Silesian Corps Headquarters, of which he now assumed full command, in place of *General* von Lindheim, who had fallen sick and been granted leave. Under (*General* von Mutius) the relationship between the Corps Headquarters and all of the officials of the province were most friendly and cooperative. A Silesian by birth and still filled with a warm love for his homeland, nobody could have been better suited for the Silesian Corps Command. He enjoyed the entire trust of all Silesians, from the highest magnates to the simplest town dweller or peasant, he personally knew and took to heart their needs and wants that deserved attention. In September 1863 he was detached as umpire to the Field Maneuvers of III Army Corps. At the same time his energy was absorbed in watching the border of Silesia [to protect it] against the revolution in Poland. In June 1864, he was promoted to *General der Cavallerie*.

In May 1866 he was fully prepared for the mobilization of his corps. Always concerned for Silesia (which was in the front line), he had informed Berlin of the enemy's every move since the start of Austria's belligerent attitude toward Prussia. On 18th May he marched with the staff of VI Army Corps to join the Army, and toward the end of June, as we indicated at the beginning of this chapter, forming the rear and flank Guards of the 2nd Army, he and his corps, or more correctly, half of his corps (two infantry brigades and three cavalry regiments were detached) moved to the Habelschwerdt area. The subsequent chain of victories soon freed him and his corps from their duties as rear guard and made it possible for both to take part in the great action of 3rd July.

We must now give an account of that part of VI Corps, composed of *Landwehr*, that was entrusted with the protection of Upper Silesia against an enemy attack from Krakau or Olmütz. It consisted of a combined brigade formed from the 62nd and 63rd Regiments, the Silesian Uhlan Regiment Nr. 2 and the 6pdr battery von Balluseck. Active in the southwestern part of the province, in *Kreis* Ratibor, this 6,000 man Silesian force was named Detachment Knobelsdorff after its commander. Alongside Detachment Knobelsdorff, a second force, Detachment Stolberg, cooperated loosely with VI Corps.

It included no one from the regular army but consisted entirely of *Landwehr* and *Landsturm*. Its composition was:

Infantry for Home Defense.
    Battalion von Calliat, Battalion von Besse.
    Battalion von Kehler, Battalion von Kleist.
    Battalion von Osten – Sacken, Battalion von Schmidt.
Landwehr **Cavalry Brigade.**
    2nd *Landwehr* Uhlan Regiment.
    6th *Landwehr* Hussar Regiment.
    One volunteer *Jäger* company;
    One 6pdr *Ausfall* [sortie] battery (only arrived later).
A total of something over 5,000 men.

Detachment Stolberg was to take part in a brisk action. We take the following regarding its peculiarities from the notes of an officer who belonged to this corps:

The residents of Upper Silesia, so he writes, 'when they learned that the entire army was going into Bohemia and would leave them without protection, felt that they had been treated like step-children and were determined to attempt a general arming of the population, and to fight in the extensive forests of the province, rather than let the Austrian army into the land. Therefore, from the very beginning, there was much talk of forming a free corps and conducting partisan warfare. This had, after all, been the very theater of this sort of bitter fighting during the Seven Years War, and there were still old soldiers from the bold volunteer corps of 1806, 1807, 1813 and 1814. If there is anywhere in Germany that offers opportunities for irregular warfare, it is in Silesia. Broken terrain, forests, water courses, and on their banks, all kinds of willow. Whole areas are as if made for *Jägergefecht* [fighting by soldiers with a background as hunters and gamekeepers]. Along the Weichsel [Vistula] and its many smaller tributaries, are double, sometimes triple, often extremely high, embankments, their tops (as in all low lying areas) planted with willows. The riverbanks themselves are thick with trees and bushes, so that the *Jäger* can find fine cover everywhere. Thus, the terrain was suitable for guerrilla warfare. Above all there was a martial spirit that is always the most important factor. In order to avoid the evils that are inseparable from such a form of warfare, the government took matters into its own hands and formed an independent corps from the younger age classes of the *Landwehr*. That was a wise decision. The desires of the people and the interests of the regime coincided. Everything came together. Hardly were the notices posted when *Landwehr* volunteers came in from all sides, including older men who only belonged to the *Landsturm*. In no time the twenty one year old reservist and the forty year old *Landwehrmann* were together in the ranks. Among the *Jäger*, who were concentrated in a single company, there was a grandfather.'

'In like fashion,' so the notes say, 'were the officers of the detachments. Almost all belonged to the high Silesian aristocracy, and most would have been classified as over age. They came as volunteers, offering their service at their own expense and providing their own horses, and in such numbers that they could not all be employed with the troops. Thus, some forty or so were gathered by the staff, and thanks to their local knowledge of the border region and of the people, they formed a reconnaissance corps, mounted on good horses, such has seldom existed. Although many of these gentlemen held substantial estates in Austria and had large amounts of capital invested in Austrian industries, none of them hesitated for a moment to ally his fate with that of the Hohenzollern.'

Initiative, prudence and resolve could be guaranteed from such a force, and in the event, despite individual failures (because they were assigned missions beyond their capabilities), these local defense battalions, and yet more often their squadrons, repeatedly proved themselves in skirmishes and encounters, the most significant of which we shall now relate, the 'Action at Oswiecim.'

The action at Oswiecim

On June 21st and 22nd, Detachment Stolberg passed the declaration of war to the enemy at Oswiecim, destroyed the railway viaduct at Pruchna and the track from Krakau to Olmütz. On the afternoon of the 26th the High Command ordered [Detachment Stolberg] to make a strong reconnaissance across the Weichsel. This was entirely in accord with *Graf* Stolberg's intentions. The objective was twofold. First, to determine the strength of the enemy forces at Oswiecim, and secondly, to deceive the enemy regarding our plans, or at least to make him uncertain.

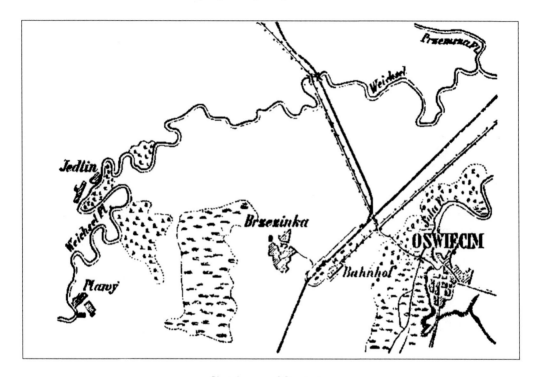

Sketch map of Oswiecim.

Reinforced by two Fusilier companies (10th and 11th) of the 62nd Regiment, the Detachment was mustered in the afternoon of the 26th at Nicolai, advancing to the border in the course of that day. The battalion (in part on wagons) took various roads to the Jedlin woods. Battalion von Calliat was ordered to demonstrate on the left flank from Myslowitz (to the Przemsza), where that battalion fought a small separate action. Early on the 27th, at 4:00, the Detachment moved out from the Jedlin woods with a strength of five battalions, the two Fusilier companies, the *Landwehr* Uhlan Regiment and two guns. It moved out on two roads:

The 11th Company of the 62nd Regiment, under *Hauptmann* von Massow, the *Landwehr* Battalion Osten - Sacken, the Uhlan Regiment and the two guns proceeded via Plawy.
The 10th Company of the 62nd, under *Hauptmann Graf* Königsdorff and the *Landwehr* Battalions von Bessel, von Kleist and von Schmidt proceeded toward Oswiecim via Brzczinka.

The remaining forces available to the detachment remained behind in a covering position at Plawy on the Weichsel. The second column, which proceeded via Brzczinka, was the first to go into action, initially at Brzczinka itself. The 10th Company of the 62nd Regiment, *Hauptmann Graf* Königsdorff, was in the lead, followed by Battalion von Bessel. After a stubborn resistance, the foremost houses of the village were captured. Finally, as the column that had crossed at Plawy, namely the 11th Company, under *Hauptmann* von Massow joined in the action, the village itself, was taken. The Austrians fell back on the Oswiecim railway station. Our forces followed along the railway embankment. When they reached the railway station, possession of which now became the exclusive focus of the action, the fighting entered its second phase. Our two guns opened fire and the now united infantry forces of our two columns, advanced against the railway station, which was probably defended by three battalions of Brigade Trentinaglia.[6] The large restaurant building (the most important point) was defended by the 4th Battalion of Regiment Mecklenburg. The assault seemed to be going well, all the sheds and adjoining buildings were taken by our advancing troops with great bravery. Only the restaurant building remained in enemy hands. Thus matters stood when our *Landwehr* Uhlans appeared, and through their outstanding action, added their weight to the scales, but unfortunately not enough to tip the balance.

Major von Busse, the Commander of the *Landwehr*, was seen advancing by two squadrons of *Grünne* [Green] Uhlans, who then suddenly disappeared from his sight. The *Major* immediately resolved to seek them out, and thereby to disengage our battalions that were fighting at the railway station by outflanking the enemy center. It was a long search, but when our 1st and 2nd Squadrons had reached the descending (far) slope of the railway embankment, the Green Uhlans (two weak squadrons) who had been waiting in the high grain, spotted them and immediately swung to the left, intending to break the Prussian line before it had deployed.

Major von Busse delivered a brief, pithy speech, had the trumpeter blow the *trot* and advanced with the two squadrons closed up. The enemy Uhlans seemed surprised by this calm behavior and hesitated, but then their dashing leader inspired them, rode forward, and at 50 paces, fired a volley. Two of our men fell and the attack continued. The Commander of the Green Uhlans initially clashed with *Major* von Busse who was charging ahead of his regiment, wounding him in the left shoulder, while the *Major* replied with two blows, one striking the rein [probably his left] fist of his opponent, the other hitting his head, so that his enemy sank from his horse. At almost the same moment, right beside the *Major*, *Vice Wachtmeister Graf* Lottum was wounded by two lance thrusts and one saber blow.

When they saw their commander in such fighting, the *Landwehr* Uhlans speared or cut down everyone that they came up against. The Austrians, for their part, realizing that this was a struggle for life or death, defended themselves fiercely. A bitter fight ensued and our squadrons

---

6   Author's Note: Together with Brigade Braisach, Brigade Trentinagli formed the 12,000 man strong garrison of Krakau. Both brigades consisted of only fourth battalions. Surprisingly (see also the action at Skalitz), these garrison battalions drawn from various fortresses, fought with outstanding bravery. Brigade Trentinaglia included the fourth battalions of Regiments Parma, Crown Prince of Prussia, Schmerling, Sachsen - Weimar, Rossbach and Mecklenburg. It is said that the last three of these were engaged at Oswiecim. Battalion Mecklenburg was definitely engaged.

took relatively few prisoners.[7] Only 15 enemy Uhlans succeeded in escaping, the rest were cut down. On our side only the 1st and 2nd Squadrons took part in the charge. The 4th arrived too late to join in the pursuit that continued to Oswiecim. The losses that accompanied this Uhlan encounter were substantial on both sides. We had 7 killed and 23 wounded, including (in addition to the two named officers, *Major* von Busse and *Graf* Lottum), *Lieutenant Graf* Ballestrem. The enemy lost 27 men according to his own account, more than twice that number according to our estimates. Killed were *Rittmeister Baron* Lehmann (posthumously awarded the *Ritterkreuz des Maria Teresien Ordens*) [Knight's Cross of the Order of Maria Theresa] and *Lieutenant* von Schönberg; wounded, *Rittmeister Baron* Bertoletti and *Lieutenant* Bartel. *Oberlieutenant Graf* zur Lippe was taken prisoner.

In the meantime, the affair was decided in the center, though not in our favour. Our two guns could not maintain their position against the enemy battery, and after firing 18 rounds (another report says only four rounds) they withdrew to the rear. Equally unfortunate was the assault on the restaurant building, which was repeated several times. The two Fusilier Companies of the 62nd, with *Landwehr* Battalions von Kleist and von Schmidt joining them in the first rank, pushed their attack to the extreme. *Hauptmann Graf* Königsdorf, commanding the 10th Company, was killed.

Oberstlieutenant von Schmidt and *Hauptmann* von Massow were wounded, but all their efforts foundered on the position, the valour, and perhaps also on the superior numbers of the enemy. Our *Landwehr* battalions were numerically weak and they finally fell back. The retreat began at 8:30 in the morning, covered by the Fusilier companies and the Uhlan regiment. Some individual units were badly mauled. The 62nd (only two companies strong), lost three officers and 29 men. Battalion von Kleist lost one officer and 49 men. Our entire losses totaled 172 men.

In Nicolai (where our forces returned towards evening), instead of friendly quarters our men found mostly locked houses and emptied rooms. When the first wounded and stragglers had arrived, the entire town was overwhelmed with panic and the residents had fled. They only started to return the following night when their concerns diminished to a reasonable level.

---

7   Author's Note: In this action and in the ensuing pursuit, the *Landwehr* Uhlan Joseph Schupka demonstrated exceptional bravery. He had six lance wounds to his head, a deep two inch saber slash on the left side of his neck, a saber cut on his right ear, another on his back and additional lance wounds to his left shoulder blade, right groin and thigh, a total of 12 wounds. Left lying for dead, he was captured. In the most chivalrous fashion (as was generally shown by the imperial cavalry officers on nearly every occasion), Schupka's bravery was later officially recognized as follows:

'In the fighting that took place on 27th June 1866, at Oswiecim, we witnessed the extraordinary bravery and courage with which the Royal Prussian Uhlan, Joseph Schupka, after the attack was completed, pursued our forces alone and attacked several of our men. He was finally surrounded, cut down from his horse and left for dead. During the course of the day this brave man was found still alive by locals and brought to Oswiecim where he was turned over to the local *Kaiserlich Königlich* [Imperial Royal] Military Command. We feel ourselves obliged to hereby honour and bear witness to this example of uncommon valour.

August Br. Bertoletti, *Rittmeister* I. Klasse. Johan Basté *Lieutenant*.
    königlich kaiserlichen 1st Uhlan Regiment
    Spital – Garrison at Krakau, on 30th July 1866.

Uhlans at Oswiecim.

All of the detachment had fought bravely but they had been assigned a mission that, good as they were in their own way, was beyond their capability. Battalions that had proven extremely usable in 'guerilla warfare' had been sent (with in part, deficient equipment), against a strong, well defended position, it was asking too much. Every home defense unit (we particularly think of the Guerillas and Tyroleans), even with the best spirit, is only of use within certain limits. Oswiecim provided a fresh demonstration of this truth. An attempt was made to conduct an offensive thrust with battalions that quite correctly bore the designation 'Home Defense' [*Landesvertheidigung*]. Unless we are mistaken, the six named battalions were taken back to Breslau for reorganization, they did not return [to active service] until 18th July. Until then the detachment was reduced to one *Jäger* company, the 2nd *Landwehr* Uhlans (which had excelled at Oswiecim), and the 6th *Landwehr* Hussar Regiment. This weak formation, outstandingly suited to guerilla warfare, was positioned for the [rest of the war] at Pless on the border. Its main mission was to watch the Weichsel crossings which it performed with great diligence. The cease fire that soon followed put an end to the border warfare.

On 15th July the *Jäger* Company had an interesting skirmish at Dzieditz. Because it is characteristic of the kind of irregular warfare conducted in this theatre, we shall briefly describe it:

The lull that followed the action at Oswiecim lasted until 15th July. On that day, because of reports that an all-arms detachment of Austrians was positioned behind Dzieditz, 50 *Jäger* advanced from Pless to the Weichsel (here the Weichsel is the border). The village of Hoczalkowitz is on our side, Dzieditz on the Austrian side. Essentially it was a matter of possession of the bridge. The *Jäger* officer heard cannon fire when he was a bit over half a mile distant. He ordered his men to march at the double quick and had the good fortune to reach the bridge before the Austrian infantry. In order to deny the enemy the protection of the high embankment on the Austrian side, the *Jäger* hastened over the stringers of the bridge and took position at the above mentioned embankment, which was about 150 paces from the exit of Dzieditz. A patrol was sent forward which was spotted by the enemy who sent a platoon of his infantry from Dzieditz toward the bridge. Their first impression was that there was only this patrol to deal with. Instead however, the Austrian platoon that was so carelessly advancing was met by the fire of 25 rifles at 150 paces. Only then did those who had not already been hit seek cover, which was not easy. The 50 [Prussian] *Jäger* had established a front of perhaps 150 paces, held by small groups at three firing positions. The embankment was constructed at this point with two bastion - like projections, between which lay the bridge. Willow bushes grew nearly everywhere along the top of the bank, so that the enemy *Tirailleurs* found themselves in a tight situation. They only caught an occasional glimpse of one of their opponent's heads, they never saw their enemy's body and had no idea of the numbers facing them.

Thus, the action continued until about 10:00. Every now and then an artillery shell whistled over the heads of both parties. Only now did the enemy think of what he had hitherto neglected, an advance on both flanks, but the decision came too late. The main body of our *Jäger* Company had by now arrived from Pless (on rack wagons that were always standing by), and had established themselves on the embankment that stood on the Prussian side of the Weichsel, to which the *Jäger* who had been engaged on the far side of the river, now fell back with great skill.

The Austrians, believing they had won the game, climbed the embankment on their side of the river with loud hurrahs. However the moment they appeared on the top, they were met with rapid fire from 90 rifles at extremely short range from the Prussian side, and were blown from the crest as if by lightning.

A firefight now developed that continued for several hours. Nobody could cross the bridge because it was under fire at a range of 60 paces. At about 1:00 the Austrians marched back to Kenty and we to Pless. The *Jäger* officer who had initiated this action was, in the tradition of Schill's followers (who created the 'Archduke of Dodendorf'), named the 'Archduke of Dzieditz'.

We now leave this digression (as the above descriptions of the 'guerilla war' in Upper Silesia must be viewed), to return to the main body of the Crown Prince's army, which we left in position at the Bohemian border on the 25th.

The Three Gates of Bohemia

On 25th June as we ended the chapter preceding the last, the concentration of the Crown Prince's Army was completed and each column (with the exception of VI Corps, which was to remain near Neisse), was ready to invade Bohemia. The three other corps were positioned in a narrowly drawn semicircle around the projection that juts into Bohemia from Silesia directly north of the *Grafschaft* [county] of Glatz.

> The I Army Corps had the right wing and held the line between Leibau and Schömberg.
> The V Army Corps had the left wing and stood between Glatz and Reinerz.

The Guards had the center and were between Neurod and Eckersdorf.

On the 26th the troops were brought forward to the border (The Guards were already across the border), the next day to pass through the 'Three Gates of Bohemia', namely;

> The Trautenau Pass (I Corps).
> The Braunau – Eypel Pass (Guards).
> The Nachod Pass (V Corps).

On the 27th this mission was accomplished, though incompletely at Trautenau.

The forcing of the 'Three Gates' was accompanied by much fighting. Before we go on to describe it, let us examine the eastern part of northeastern Bohemia, to which these frequently named three gates give entry. In so doing we shall have to repeat some of what has already been mentioned before.

The Elbe and its two tributaries, the Iser and the Adler, flowing here toward Saxony and Silesia, divide the entire northeastern quarter of Bohemia into three distinct parts.

> The first third (western part), is formed by the Elbe and Iser Rivers and the Lausitz Mountains.
> The second third (center part), is formed by the Elbe and Iser Rivers and the *Riesen Gebirge* [Giant Mountains].
> The remaining third (eastern part), is formed by the Elbe and Adler Rivers and the *Riesen Gebirge*.[8]

The Prussian advance proceeded through all three of these parts:

> The Elbe Army advanced through the first (western) part.
> The 1st Army advanced through the second (central) part.
> The 2nd Army advanced through the third (eastern) part.

---

8   Editor's Note: For some reason Fontane fails to mention of the Mettau. His original map has been redrawn to correct this omission.

We have already accompanied the Elbe Army and the 1st Army on their advance. Our present task is to follow the advance of the 2nd Army.

Because it was coming from the opposite side [of Bohemia], the advance went in the opposite direction. The Elbe Army and 1st Army, coming from the northwest, advanced to the south [east]. Because it came from the east, the 2nd Army, proceeded toward the [south] west. They would have to meet, either on the near or far side of the Elbe, [somewhere] between Arnau and Pardubitz.[9]

Because it had a shorter distance to go to the Upper Elbe, which essentially formed the rendezvous, the 2nd Army allowed the other armies several days head start. Five days later than the Elbe Army, four days later than the 1st army (Prince Friedrich Karl), the 2nd Army (Crown Prince) invaded Bohemia in three columns through the Three Gates, Nachod, Braunau - Eypel and Trautenau. The left wing column (V Corps) went through the Nachod gate.

V Corps – *General* von Steinmetz

The V Corps, (9th and 10th Divisions) consisted of battalions from Posen, West Prussia, Silesia, the Mark and Westphalia (thus differing from the other corps which usually represented a single province). The Posen Army Corps [V Corps] had only one actual Posen Regiment, the

---

9   Author's Note: The towns and small cities seated at short intervals on the Upper Elbe are, from north to south, Arnau, Königinhof, Jaromirz, Josephstadt, Königgrätz and Pardubitz [Fontane often refers to them as 'cities.' This is understandable since despite their small populations, they have an undisputable grandeur, however - we prefer towns]. Most of these had less than 5,000 residents, and had a mercantile, historical or military background. Arnau was known for its linen weaving industry, Königinhof (the old 'Queen's Court' of the Bohemian Queens) is known for the 'Königinhof Manuscript'. Pardubitz is noted for its Schloss, its horse stud, its Ring in old Bohemian architecture, and above all as the junction point of the railways that lead from Prague and Reichenberg, to Olmütz, Brünn and Vienna.
       Of particular importance are the fortresses of Josephstadt and Königgrätz. Königgrätz, apparently already of importance in 1055, is the older and more important of the two (population about 8,000). It is a Bishop's seat and has schools, seminaries (formerly also a Jesuit college) and four churches including a beautiful cathedral (whose spire is visible for miles).
       The protection provided by Königgrätz during the wars with Friedrich II was found to be inadequate. Therefore, it was decided to secure its flank with a second fortress, nearly 14 miles upstream on the Elbe. Accordingly, the fortress of Josephstadt was built in the years 1781 – 1787 where the village of Pless had previously stood. (At this same time the fortress of Theresienstadt was also built to the northwest, toward the Saxon border, again as protection against Prussia. Theresienstadt greatly resembles Josephstadt in its appearance and its layout).
       Josephstadt is located on the left bank of the Elbe. Its outer works, however, extend onto the right bank. Fields, gardens and meadows are contained within the works. The three main gates, provided with drawbridges, are the Königgrätz Gate, the Jaromirz Gate and the Neustadt Gate. In addition to these gates there are several other posterns (sortie doors), in case of need, for communication with the outside. The great houses (fifteen of which are dedicated to military purposes), the broad, straight, paved streets with (on the squares beside them near the gates) long heaps of stacked cannonballs, give Josephstadt a rather forbidding presence. On the great parade ground, surrounded by chains, rises the *Kirche de Maria Himmelfahrt* [Church of the Asumption of Mary] (built in 1808 – 1810), whose tower rises high above the fortress walls and provides a magnificent view of the Silesian mountains.
       Barely half an hour north of Josephstadt is Jaromirz, which until 1833, formed more or less a single town with Josephstadt since the civilians of Josephstadt were under the Magistrate of Jaromirz. Jaromirz consists of only a single road between two gates and has about 4,700 residents.

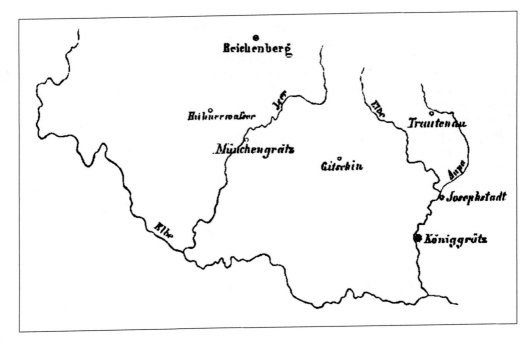

Principal rivers and cities of northern Bohemia.

58th. As for the three other regiments bearing the name of this province, the 18th was with III (Brandenburg) Corp, the 19th and 59th with the Army of the Main.

The order of battle of V Corps was:

9th Division (*Generalmajor* von Löwenfeld).

17th Brigade: *Generalmajor* **von Ollech.**
Westphalian Fusilier Regiment Nr. 37, *Oberst* von Below.
3rd Posen Infantry Regiment Nr. 58, *Oberst* von François.
18th Brigade: *Generalmajor* **von Horn.**
King's Grenadier Regiment (2nd West Prussian) Nr. 7, *Oberst* von Voigts – Rhetz.
Cavalry.
1st Silesian Dragoon Regiment Nr. 4, *Major* von Mayer.

10th Division (*Generalmajor* von Kirchbach).

19th Brigade: *Generalmajor* **von Tiedmann.**
1st West Prussian Grenadier Regiment Nr. 6, *Oberstlieutenant* von Scheffler.
3rd West Prussian Infantry Regiment Nr. 46, *Oberst* Walther von Monbary.
20th Brigade: *Generalmajor* **Wittich.**
4th West Prussian Infantry Regiment Nr. 47, *Oberst* von Massow.

6th Brandenburg Infantry Regiment Nr. 52, *Oberst* von Blumenthal.
Also, the 5th *Jäger* Battalion.
Cavalry:
West Prussian Uhlan Regiment Nr. 1, *Oberst* von Tresckow.

In addition, the 2nd Silesian Dragoon Regiment Nr. 8, *Oberstlieutenant* von Wichmann, and Brigade Hoffmann, both from VI Corps were also attached for the days of the invasion.

Karl Friedrich von Steinmetz was born at Eisenach, on 27th December 1796. His father was a Prussian officer, his mother was Baroness von Mosel. He was the youngest of three brothers. In 1806 he entered the cadet school at Culm. In 1808 (after Culm became Polish) he went to Stolpe. In Graudenz the cadets who had been transferred to Stolpe came under *Feldmarschall* L'homme de Courbière (the famous defender of Graudenz).

The military reputation and the good will of the *Feldmarschall*, made an impression on the young Steinmetz. In Stolpe he lived in a room that gave him a daily view of the Blücher Hussars when they rode out on exercise, thus giving him a great preference for the cavalry, especially for that particular regiment.

In 1811 Steinmetz came to Berlin. In February of 1813, with other cadets, he was assigned to the 1st Guards Regiment, which had at that time followed the King from Potsdam to Breslau. In Marcy, at 16¼ years old, he was commissioned and assigned to the York Corps. This appointment was painful to him because it made him an infantry officer. With a great lack of self-consciousness, he turned to the King (who held daily audiences at that time in Breslau) and expressed his wish to transfer to the Hussars. The King graciously refused his request, 'since there is a shortage of infantry officers', and so, after all sorts of incidents, he came to *General* York in Berlin. York greeted him in his usual manner, saying 'that he could not use him'. This arose in part from Steinmetz' small stature, in part from the fact that York generally wanted to fill all corps vacancies himself. The young Steinmetz took exception to this reception and replied, 'Then I shall return to His Majesty at Breslau.' York stared at him with wide eyes, ordered him to the parade ground and turned him over to the (then) 1st East Prussian Grenadier Regiment Nr. 1, Crown Prince of Prussia.

On 5th April he was already under fire. On the 29th of the same month, he took part in the famous action at Merseburg, in which the two Musketeer battalions of the 1st Regiment, under *Oberstlieutenant* von Lodenthal, fought alone against a superior enemy force six times greater than their own, where he was wounded in the arm by a ricochet. In the Battle of Gross - Görchen, on 2nd May, an enemy bullet penetrated his neckband but did not put him out of action. On the 19th May however, he was wounded at Königswartha, where a musket ball smashed his left middle finger. Despite this, two days later (21st May) he took part in the Battle of Bautzen, though on a horse of his uncle, the *Oberst* and Brigade Commander von Steinmetz. After the battle he went to Breslau to recover his health.

During the cease fire he returned to his regiment and took part in the action at Löweberg from 19th to 21st August, at Goldberg on the 23rd, in the Battle at the Katzbach on 26th August, the action at Wartenburg on 3rd October, the Battle of Möckern on 16th October and the action at Freyburg on 21st October. At Wartenburg on the Elbe, he led his rifle platoon with particular distinction. A cannon ball smashed both legs of the *Tirailleur* standing in front of him and threw [Steinmetz] flat on the ground. He sprang up and went onward. Only half an hour later did *Oberst* von Lodenthal draw to his attention the fact that the back of his overcoat and part of his trousers were missing. After the intense fighting at Möckern, von Steinmetz had the good fortune to be one of the five officers of the two Musketeer battalions of the 1st Regiment who was still unwounded. On that day the regiment lost 29 officers, 70 *Unteroffizier* [non-commissioned officers], five bandsmen and 829 ordinary soldiers.

In 1814 von Steinmetz took part in the fighting at La Chaussée on 3rd February, Chalons sur Marne on 4th February, Chateau Thierry on 12th February, as well as in the Battles of Laon on 9th March and Paris, on 30th March. He received the Iron Cross for the last two actions. After the last battle, von Steinmetz, unsurprisingly, visited Paris. However, he was so depressed by his lack of money that he only saw the Dome des Invalides before returning to his quarters. He hoped that one day, a lucky fortune would bring him back to Paris again.

Despite his youth and slight build, Steinmetz endured all of the strains of the war. He maintained his health by moderate living and by sleeping, whenever circumstances permitted. Above all, he showed little interest in carousing and far more interest in intellectual activities.

When war broke out again in 1815, the 1st Regiment was at Preussisch Minden. It moved forward but did not get into action. Towards the end of August, Steinmetz was again in the vicinity of the French capital and stayed in Meudon. He rode to the *Ludwigsfeste* [celebration of Louis XVIII's accession to the throne] in Paris with his landlord. When they arrived before the Tuilleries, they carelessly turned the horses over to a stranger, and in the most peculiar outfit (field cap and leather reinforced riding breeches), without badges of rank on his uniform, he mounted the stairs, where Louis XVIII had, in the meantime, opened the congratulatory reception. His landlord was turned away but Steinmetz was not stopped, neither by the Guards nor by the French officers in their dress uniforms. Rather they addressed him with true French courtesy and answered all his questions. In his travels through France he also became familiar with the northern provinces, which were then in part, still in a state of revolt. There were many incidents, namely in Rouen and Caen, however, he experienced neither attacks nor inconvenience, even though he moved freely among the people, often completely unarmed.

He marched with the 1st Regiment from France to Königsberg in Prussia, where he remained in garrison until 1818. On 26th May of that year, he was transferred to the 2nd Guards Regiment. Now came difficult days for the young Guards officer without means or additional funds. During the next year he was promoted to *Premier* [Lieutenant].

From the autumn of 1820 to the summer of 1823, Steinmetz attended the *Kreigsschule* [Staff Officer school], and in 1824 he was assigned to the topographical office where he was primarily concerned with the mapping of Posen and Silesia.

In 1815 he married his cousin, a daughter of *Generallieutenant* von Steinmetz, a resident of Frankenstein (in Silesia). *Generallieutenant* von Steinmetz (both uncle and father in law of our Steinmetz), asked the then Chief of the General Staff, *General* von Muffling, who was a friend of his, whether his son in law could join the general staff. Muffling declined the request pointing out that Steinmetz had no private income, he would have to make his career in the field.

And he made it 'in the field'. In 1829 he was promoted to *Hauptmann* and transferred again, this time to the Guards Reserve Regiment, then in 1835 to the *Kaiser Franz* Grenadier Regiment. He remained there for four years. In 1839, with simultaneous promotion to *Major*, he took command of the Guards *Landwehr* Battalion in Düsseldorf. In 1841 he was promoted to Battalion Commander in the Guards Reserve Regiment (Spandau).

He was in this post during the March Days [days of revolution]. In 1848 he and his battalion were brought to Berlin and there, during the street fighting, the Commander of the 2nd

Regiment, *Graf* von der Schulenburg, was wounded and the King gave Steinmetz command of this regiment.   Steinmetz joined the two Musketeer battalions (which had been chosen for the campaign in Schleswig-Holstein) in Havellande, while the Fusilier battalion remained in Stettin. The reserves were called up but there was no opportunity for exercises or firing practice, so it was that they marched to Schleswig. The battalions took part in the fighting in Schleswig and Düppel, and despite their incomplete training, performed outstandingly. After the campaign ended, while on parade, King Friedrich Wilhelm IV awarded *Major* von Steinmetz the *Orden pour le mérite* for his conduct in the war.

In October of that year, von Steinmetz was named as the Commanding Officer of the 32nd Infantry Regiment (at that time in Magdeburg). As everybody knows, shortly thereafter (November 1848) the [Prussian] *Nationalversammlung*[10] that was meeting in Berlin, was ordered to transfer its sessions to Brandenburg *a. H.* For the duration of its sessions, Steinmetz was named Commander of Brandenburg. Under his command was the Fusilier Battalion of the 31st Regiment, 6th Cuirassier Regiment, one battery of guns, and the Guards *Landwehr* Battalion from Magdeburg (the latter not very reliable because the current political situation in Magdeburg had more or less disorganized the battalion).

On 8th May 1849, von Steinmetz was promoted to *Oberstlieutenant.* In 1850 during the ominous developments with Austria, he and his regiment (the 32nd) proceeded to Kurhessen where he was named Commandant of Cassel. The officials and people proved cooperative. He wished to organize the returning Hessian soldiers and arm them from the arsenal that he had occupied, but this request was not approved.

As is well known, there was no war. Steinmetz led his regiment back, which was now garrisoned at Erfurt. A few weeks later (January 1851) von Steinmentz was promoted to *Oberst* and named Commander of the Cadet Corps, where he remained until 1854. On 13th July, shortly before he was named Commandant of Magdeburg, he was promoted to *Generalmajor.* During the first year of his time in Magdeburg he lost his only surviving daughter to typhus. He was deeply shaken.   Soon after the death of his daughter the *General* experienced visions, which gave rise to many fears, though [von Steinmetz] examined them quite dispassionately. Everything that he saw must have appeared all the more remarkable, as he perceived things that he had only thought possible for people in a condition of extreme excitation. Hitherto (as must be stressed) he had neither read of, nor given serious consideration to, visions of this nature. Later, as he became familiar with the literature relating to this question, he was amazed at the similarity with his own experiences.[11]

---

10   Tr. Note: After the March Revolution of 1848, the *Preußische Nationalversammlung* [Prussian National Assembly] was elected by equal and nearly universal male suffrage, to formulate a constitution for Prussia. It met in Berlin from May to November 1848. On 9th November 1848, the government expelled the *Preußischen Nationalversammlung* to Brandenburg an der Havel. On 5th December 1848, it was dissolved by Royal order.

11   Tr. Note: Long after Fontane wrote this, after von Steinmetz' death in 1900, Hans von Krosigk brought out, '*General - Feldmarschall von Steinmetz, aus den Familienpapieren dargestelt*', consisting primarily of letters and diary entries by von Steinmetz. This fascinating volume includes a lengthy (seventeen page) letter from Steinmetz to a close friend, describing in detail the visions of his deceased daughter Selma, and of other figures, including his two younger daughters. The letter is striking for its calmness, clarity and detail, and reveals a surprisingly sensitive side to *General* von Steinmetz.

In the spring of 1857, he was named Commander of the 3rd Guards Infantry Brigade, and in the autumn, Commander of the 1st Division, at which point he moved to Königsberg in East Prussia. In 1858 he was promoted to *Generallieutenant*. In 1863 he received command of the II Army Corps (Stettin), and in 1864, V Army Corps (Posen). That same year he was promoted to *General der Infanterie*.

As Commander of the 1st Division in the early sixties, he had led them for several days during the great I Corps vs the 2nd Division manouevres. This had been an extremely interesting and instructive exercise for him. The endurance of the troops, who at that time carried full packs and equipment throughout, gave rise in the *General* to great confidence in their capability to perform in the event of war. He did not have the opportunity to lead these troops (East Prussian) against the enemy. In Pomerania, where he commanded II Corps for a bit more than a year, he made the same discovery regarding the strength and endurance of the troops.

From May 1864, as mentioned above, he commanded V Corps (Posen). That corps was not surprised by the mobilization, neither the command nor the ranks. Everyone acted with commitment, zeal and self-sacrifice. Now the corps was ready for battle to protect the border. The corps trusted its commander, the commander trusted his corps, and all impatiently called for an attack. In the next section we shall see with what impetuosity, self-sacrifice and endurance it was carried out.

Marching through the pass.

Nachod – The Wysokow Pass – The Branka

As we said earlier, Nachod was the gate through which *General* von Steinmetz led V Corps into Bohemia (against an enemy who was advancing from the south).

Already, on the evening of the 26th, elements of our advance Guards had taken possession of the town and also the vital part of the Nachod pass.[12] The 'gate' required no further opening, merely to be held. Nevertheless, the business of moving a corps through a narrow defile would be difficult, the more so if the enemy, as could be expected, appeared in front of the pass. The following morning would bring proof of that.

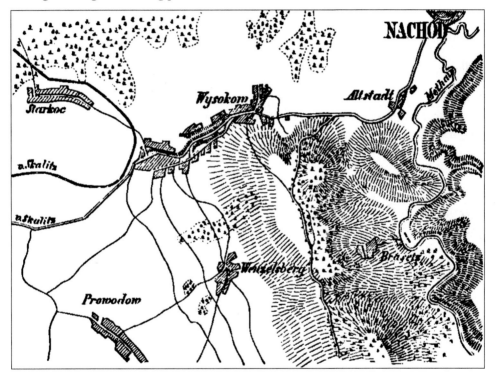

Nachod sketch map.

12 Author's Note: The occupation of Nachod on the evening of the 26th, was a minor action right on the border, which here is formed by the River Metau. As the point of our advance Guards reached the Metau bridge, it came under shellfire from the opposite bank. *Generalmajor* von Löwenfeld, who was with the advance Guards, immediately resolved to take the hills on the far side and to advance on Nachod (which had not initially been in the plan). A few rounds from two 4pdrs that had been ordered forward, soon drove off the enemy detachment (positioned at the Austrian toll house), which consisted of about one squadron of cuirassiers, two guns and a few infantry (probably of the 4th Battalion Khevenhüller, which was serving as the Josephstadt garrison). The bridge was then rebuilt. The 3rd Battalion of the 37th bivouacked between the Metau River and Nachod. One *Jäger* company occupied Nachod itself. At about 9:00 pm additional units from the advance Guards advanced as far as the Metau bridge. During the night of 26/27th June, the 2nd and 3rd Battalions of the 37th Regiment, two *Jäger* companies and one squadron of the 4th Dragoon Regiment were on enemy territory.

The town of Nachod, lying approximately in the middle of the pass, had little more than 3,000 residents. Its Schloss is famous as Wallenstein's birthplace. Until the time of the Hussites, it belonged to the Berka family, later the Smirziczkis, which was the family of Wallenstein's mother. After the Battle of the White Mountain (1620), *Graf* Terzky, Wallenstein's brother in law, became master of the castle. After the murderous night of Eger (25th January 1634),[13] Octavio Piccolomini was rewarded with the lordship of Nachod. An inscription at the inner Gate states that he was responsible for the present form of the castle. The Schloss stands on a crag that rises from the marketplace of the little town and is reached by stairs with 333 steps. The massive structure includes three courtyards that are surrounded by the dwelling and service buildings. The Piccolominis have long since died out, now one only finds their portraits, namely Octavio's, and a battlefield painting that is supposed to depict his victory over the French at Thionville. The Schloss now belongs to *Fürst* [Prince] Auersperg, in Prague.

So much for the town of Nachod, now we shall turn to the pass and describe the terrain. The first half, from the border as far as Nachod itself, was already in our hands. The second half, from Nachod to Wysokow, would follow. At that moment (the evening of the 26th) we had the possibility of debouching (the enemy was still about nine miles distant), however if he could get to second half (of the pass) before we could (as would actually prove true), he could attack the flank of this second half with superior forces, and thereby contest our possession, or as the case might be, the debouchment. In the event, the second half of the pass was the objective and the scene of the battle.

It was only the last phase of the battle that took place in the actual pass at Wysokow. The high points were primarily the battle for the possession of a plateau that lies south of the defile. We believe that we can best describe the main part of the battlefield and the terrain behind it as far as Nachod, with the sketchmap opposite and the accompanying profile line.

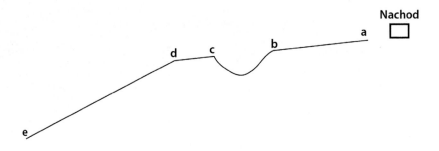

This is the line that our battalions hastening to the front had to follow. Debouching from Nachod, they first followed the major road leading over a high plateau from 'a' to 'b'. Then bearing off to the left, they descended into a major depression in the terrain, 'b to c'. Then at 'c' they had to clamber onto a second plateau, 'c to d'. Now at 'd', they faced the enemy who was attacking up the line 'e to d' and was barely being held in check by our advanced guards.

As the profile line indicates, the terrain was essentially favourable to us, and to a large degree made up for our inferior numbers. Our frontal position at 'd' gave us the advantage of an elevated

---

13   Tr. Note: Wallenstein was murdered in Eger on 25th February 1634.

position against the enemy who was attacking from the low ground, while the depression 'c to b' not only provided cover for the battalions of the main body, or as the case might be the reserve, but also provided the opportunity to concentrate, to form up and to spread out.

The main part of the fighting took place on the slope of the plateau, 'e to d', whose most suitable defensive positions extending from 'd', were held at the enemy's first appearance by the lead battalions of our advance - guard. The enemy, with greatly superior numbers, initially forced us back from our positions on the slope line 'e to d' back to the plateau line 'd to c'. This line we held, and recapturing the ground that had been lost, we finally pushed the enemy forces back down the slope line 'd to e'. With that, the action was decided in our favour. If we had failed to hold 'd to c' then we would have lost, not only the pass, but everything that was in the depression.

Therefore, as high points of the battle, we must deal with the depression 'b to c', the plateau 'c to d', and the slope 'd - e'. We shall deal separately with the concluding action at Wysokow.

First a few brief remarks regarding the three points named above. The depression is a part of the valley of the Metau that winds thence from the border. In it, halfway between Nachod and Wysokow, is the village of Altstadt, near which the Neustadt *Chaussée*[14] coming from the south, joins the Skalitz road (see sketchmap). The southern half of the plateau, which is divided by the Skalitz road, or to put it another way, by the pass at Wysokow, into a northern and southern half, is called the Branka.[15]

A wood, the *Brankawald*, extends for nearly two and a half miles north to south, on this southern part of the plateau. Parallel with it, immediately on its western front and still on the elevation of the plateau, runs the above mentioned Neustadt *Chaussée*, along which the Austrians were advancing [from the south].

On the slope of the plateau, which descends like a broad [glacis] to the plain below, are four sharply marked points, a farm field, a small wood, the village of Wenzelsberg[16] and again,

14   Tr. Note: *Chaussée* is an historic term used in German-speaking countries for paved rural roads, designed by engineers and originally planned for military movements.

15   Author's Note: 'Branka' means the opening, the portal, the pass. If the citizens of Nachod correctly informed me, in olden times, a thick, impenetrable wood covering the plateau north and south of Wysokow, formed the border between the mountains to the east, and the Aupa and Elbe valley to the west. In this dense forest there was a clearing where the *Chaussée* now runs and through which ran all the traffic between Silesia and northern Bohemia. This clearing was called the 'Branka'. It was an opening in the forest, a forest portal. In the course of time the word 'Branka' changed from the 'clearing in the forest' to the forest itself, and at the present moment, it refers to the entire forested ridge, before which the Neustadt Nachod *Chaussée* runs. On our maps only the northern-most portion, where the two *Chaussée* meet, bears this name. This (assuming the accuracy of my informants) is not correct.

16   Author's Note: On the slope of the Branka plateau, about half-way down, lies the Village of Wenzelsberg, extending in a straight line from east to west. Above the village, dating back to the earliest Christian time, is the Catholic Saint Wenzel's [Wenceslaus] Church, with an ancient wall around the churchyard, and an equally old separate standing clock tower [Ed. – both still there]. Below, at the Foot of the hill, stands the little evangelical church. The old Saint Wenzel's church, seen from a distance, is rather picturesque. Inside the church, which still shows signs of the fighting, are two oil paintings, representing the same occasion, 'King Wenzel holding a great gathering of the people on the Branka hill.' The larger somewhat older painting was struck by a bullet. The smaller painting, now above the altar, has the inscription in Bohemian, 'God will mercifully preserve us and our descendants'. The monument erected for the Austrian 6th Corps stands right by Wenzelsberg. A similar monument for 10th Corps stands at Trautenau.

another small wood. All four points were fought for. The cavalry action was fought on the farm field, (right by the plateau itself). At one time or another, elements of nearly all the regiments fought in the little northern woods [shown on map as *das Wäldchen*]. Wenzelsberg was where the men of the 37th won renown. The 58th held the little southern woods for hours.

We shall now turn to the description of the fighting, or of its individual moments.

Nachod.

The Encounter at Nachod

Early on the 27th, before daybreak, the Prussian V Corps (Steinmetz) was positioned with its main body at Reinerz, thus a little over nine miles east of Nachod. The Austrian 6th Corps (Ramming) was at Opoçno, thereby a little over nine miles south of Nachod.

Steinmetz's task was to pass through the 'Gate of Nachod' and then advance from east to west toward Gradlitz and the upper Elbe, along the line Nachod – Skalitz.

Ramming's task was to cover the (as yet incomplete) concentration of the Austrian main army at Josephstadt, by taking position between the upper Elbe and the Nachod Pass, for which purpose he was to advance from south to north toward the Nachod – Skalitz road.

If both parties were to fulfil their respective tasks, it would result in a meeting engagement of the two corps, one advancing toward the west, the other north toward Skalitz, presumably at right angles somewhere along the Nachod – Skalitz road. And so it came to pass but with the single difference that the Austrians, when they saw our column on the Wysokow plateau, swung to [their] right, thereby transforming an attack originally intended for our left flank, into a frontal assault.

The advanced guard action at Wenzelsberg until 12 noon

On the morning of the 27th, V Corps covered a bit over nine miles of highway, battalion behind battalion. The passage through the pass allowed no greater breadth.

The order of march was:

> The vanguard [*Vorhut*] of the Advance Guards [*Avantgarde*] (*Oberst* von Below).
> In Nachod:
>> 2 battalions of the 37th;
>> 2 companies *Jäger*;
>> 2 companies pioneers;
>> 1 4pdr battery (*Hauptmann* Schmidt).
> Main Body of the Advance Guards *(Generalmajor* von Ollech).
> In Schlaney (border village):
>> 1st Battalion 37th;
>> 3 battalions of the 58th;
>> 2 companies *Jäger*;
>> 3 squadrons Dragoons;
>> 1 4pdr battery (*Hauptmann* Michaelis).
> In Reinerz:
>> **Cavalry Brigade (*Generalmajor* von Wnuck).**
>>> West Prussian Uhlan Regiment Nr. 1
>>> 2nd Silesian Dragoon Regiment Nr. 8
>>> 1 battery horse artillery [12pdr smooth bore]
>> Main Body of the 10th Division (*Generallieutenant* von Kirchbach).
>>> 6th Regiment;
>>> 46th Regiment;
>>> 47th Regiment;
>>> 52nd Regiment;
>>> 4 batteries.
> In Rückerts:
>> Reserve (*Generalmajor* von Horn):
>> King's Grenadier Regiment (Nr. 7):
>> 2 batteries
>> Reserve Artillery (*Oberst* von Kameke):
>> 4 rifled and 2 horse – artillery [smooth bore] batteries.

Thus, Nachod itself was already occupied by the vanguard of our advance Guards. The occupation had taken place on the evening of the 26th and the pass, essentially, was in our hands. The section just beyond the pass (between Nachod and Wysokow) could be occupied since the enemy was not yet there with significant forces, or passed at that moment by our own forces. In the event that is what took place in the early morning of the 27th. Already by 7:00 or even earlier, the vanguard under *Oberst* von Below, passed Nachod and advanced on the road to Skalitz to the point where the road to Neustadt branches off [to the south]. Our vanguard, three battalions strong, was essentially in the depression (see profile). The hills ahead provided a panorama and von Löwenfeld [9th Division] halted here. The half battalion Kurowski (9th and 12th companies of the 37th Regiment) were ordered to head for Wysokow. There was no enemy there to interfere with this movement. The pass was in our hands, as was the immediately adjoining terrain.

Much was already won, nevertheless the numerical weakness of our vanguard (only 3 battalions) remained a great danger. Before the arrival of the main body of the advance Guards under *Generalmajor* von Ollech, and especially before the arrival of the main body proper, under *Generalmajor* von Kirchbach, these three battalions could be attacked by superior enemy forces and forced back into the defile, thereby rendering it impassable to our troops advancing from the border. *General* von Löwenfeld was aware of this danger, it was a matter of holding the plateau (or as the case might be, Wysokow) in the event of an attack, by committing all of his forces. The 37th (as we shall see, soon supported by elements of the 58th) fulfilled their mission in praiseworthy fashion.[17] [18]

17   Author's Note: Both regiments (as was the entire V Corps), were divided into half battalions, a form of organization which proved itself superbly, and which we present here:
Westphalian Fusilier Regiment Nr. 37 (*Oberst* von Below).
1st Battalion, *Major* von Lemmers.
     Half Battalion von Winterfeld (1st and 4th Companies).
     Half Battalion Vogelsang (2nd and 3rd Companies).
2nd Battalion, *Oberstlieutenant Freiherr* von Eberstein.
     Half Battalion von Schimonski (5th and 7th Companies).
     Half Battalion Braun (6th and 8th Companies).
3rd Battalion, *Major* von Ploetz.
     Half Battalion von Kurowski (9th and 12th Companies).
     Half Battalion von Bojan (10th and 11th Companies).
3rd Posen Infantry Regiment Nr. 58 (*Oberst* von Francois).
     1st Battalion, *Major* von Eberhardt.
     Half Battalion Schreiner (1st and 4th Companies).
     Half Battalion von Gfug (2nd and 3rd Companies).
2nd Battalion, *Major* von Haugwitz.
     Half Battalion Werneke (5th and 8th Companies).
     Half Battalion von der Horst (6th and 7th Companies).
Fusilier Battalion, *Major* du Plessis.
     Half Battalion von Gronefeld (9th and 12th Companies).
     Half Battalion von Suchodoletz (10th and 11th Companies).
18   Tr. Note: Kühne ('*Wanderungen ... Nachod*', pp.128ff, gives a detailed description and analysis of Steinmetz's use of half battalions and then criticizes their structure as failing to provide enough sufficiently trained officers to command the small companies. He also criticizes the disruption this organization made to the normal command structure that the entire Prussian army had been trained for. He sums up further discussion at length, saying, 'Our conclusion is that the Prussian 5th Army Corps did not achieve its victory as *a result of* the permanent formation of half battalions, but *in spite of it. General* von Lignitz ('*Aus Drei Kriegen* . . . , p. 3.) states that after the first three actions [Nachod,

At about 8:30 the vanguard of the Dragoon squadron that had been sent ahead on the Neustadt *Chausée* (thus to the south), reported the approach of the enemy. Strong columns were identified advancing toward the northwest, their march directed towards the villages that lay on the slope of the plateau, halfway between Nachod and Skalitz. Defense against this attack, whether it mounted the plateau from the south or from the west, was essential. *Generalmajor* von Löwenfeld made his dispositions thus:

One half *Jäger* company into the little woods between Wysokow and Wenzelsberg;
The 4th Dragoon Regiment and Battery Schmidt to its right to the unwooded portion of the plateau south of Wysokow;
Two half battalions, von Schimonski and Braun, to its left on that part of the plateau east of Wenzelsberg.

Half battalion Kurowski and 1½ companies of *Jäger* were ordered to the eastern end of Wysokow, to defend it against a sudden attack from Skalitz. The position was such that the Dragoons and artillery (including the companies detached to Wysokow), formed the right flank, the two half battalions positioned behind Wenzelsberg formed the left flank, and the small woods [*Das Wäldchen*] with its half company of *Jägers* was the center.

As these positions were taken the enemy arrived. It was Brigade Hertwek, which formed the head of the enemy corps. It consisted of IR 41 Kellner and IR 56 Regiment Corizutti [sometimes spelled Gorizutti] (both Polish regiments) [Ed: IR 56 was based in Wadowice and was certainly Polish. IR 41 was from Bukovina which had a mixed Jewish, German, Romanian, Ukrainian and Polish population; it is highly unlikely the 41st was entirely or even predominantly Polish], the 25th *Jäger* Battalion and one 4pdr battery. When he saw our position, *Brigadier Oberst* Hertwek immediately launched an attack. He deployed the column to [his] right, with front facing east, sent the *Jäger* and the brigade artillery forward, formed a first wave from IR 41 Kellner, and a second from IR 56 Corizutti. The battle began with a heavy bombardment from the Austrian artillery to which Battery Schmidt of the advance – Guards replied. This artillery battle, to which half battalions von Schimonski and Braun, contributed, ended by 9:30 to the Austrian's disadvantage. Their own report says, 'The enemy maintained heavy artillery and small arms fire, causing such significant losses in men and horses (due to the tactical advantage of his more elevated position), that our battery had to cease fire and fall back.'

The [Austrian] cannonade had been fruitless. Therefore, *Oberst* Hertwek decided to advance with his infantry (which up to this point had occupied a tolerably sheltered position) and storm the plateau. The 25th *Jäger* Battalion advanced on Wenzelsberg itself, IR 41 Kellner directed their attack to the left and right against the small woods that were immediately in front of [west of] Wenzelsberg]. One Battalion of IR 56 Corizzuti, was sent against the larger of the woods to the south in order (after their capture) to strike into the left flank of our position.

Our position however, had not remained the same. Reinforcements from the main body of the advance - guard, 1st Battalion 37th Regiment, von Lemmers, and the 1st Battalion 58th Regiment, von Eberhardt, had extended our position (to the south). Wenzelsberg was no

Skalitz and Schweinschädel] *General* von Steinmetz gave up the half battalions due to casualties resulting in a shortage of officers to command them.

longer our left flank, rather now it was the center. The northern woods [*das Wäldchen*] had now become the right flank, the southern woods [directly east of Wenzelsberg] had become the left flank. Half battalion Kurowski and the *Jägers* at the eastern end of Wysokow, had increasingly assumed the character of a right flank detachment and did not become involved in the fighting south of the *Chaussée*.

Our position had also gained in strength. The northern woods [*Das Wäldchen*], hitherto held by only half a company of *Jäger*, was now defended by the two half battalions von Winterfeld, and Schreiner. The southern woods (hitherto undefended), was now occupied by the two half battalions Vogelsang and Gfug. This strengthening of the flanks also strengthened the center (half battalions von Schimonski and Braun). One half *Jäger* company and six half battalions strong, we now awaited the attack of the enemy brigade.

This attacked with great bravery in four battalion columns, but all four columns were repulsed.[19] Our fire from the woods was too powerful, only the Austrian *Jäger* in the center reached the village of Wenzelsberg and occupied the cemetery. Advancing past the village, they seemed to be achieving some success, when they came under fire from the 2nd Battalion of our 37th Regiment (the frequently mentioned half battalions von Schimonski and Braun), which was concealed in a fruit orchard. Met by a destructive fire they had to fall back, but they retained a firm hold on Wenzelsberg.

Such was the situation at about 10:00. Our six half battalions had repulsed the attack of Brigade Hertwek. At 10:30 the fighting at Wenzelsberg entered its second phase.

The second brigade of Ramming's Corps, Brigade Jonak, had now arrived. It swung to [its] right and prepared to support Brigade Hertwek, which was preparing for a renewed attack. This support consisted initially of fixing our center and right flank, thereby providing Brigade Hertwek with the opportunity of delivering a powerful thrust against our left flank. The 1st and 2nd battalions of IR 56 Corizutti, which up to this point had come under little fire, were moved to the front and now advanced against the various woods south of Wenzelsberg.

However, here too the defense had been strengthened. The two half battalions Vogelsang and Gfug (from the 37th and 58th Regiments), which had repulsed the first attack at about 9:30, had in the meantime been reinforced with two additional half battalions Werneke and von

---

19   Tr. Note: Friedjung (v. 2, p. 53) describes the Prussian position and the Austrian attack thus: 'Hertwek disposed his forces in two waves. The first, two battalions strong, advanced with drums beating. Above were the Prussians, their skirmishers far in advance, concealed in the heavy crop of grain, behind them the unbroken firing line of the companies. The Austrians sent out a thin line of skirmishers fifty yards ahead [of their massed battalions]. Then the battalions stormed forwards. Each individual [battalion], in accordance with the regulations then in force, consisting of three close packed rectangles or *Divisionsmassenkolonnen* [division mass columns, a division being two companies together], which were only separated by narrow intervals, an ideal target for the incessant hail of lead.' He further describes the *Divisionsmassenkolonnen* on p. 254, '. . . Of the six companies of each battalion, each pair (a division) stood, one behind the other, so that three tightly packed rectangles faced the enemy fire. Between the divisions, regulations only allowed an interval of three paces [7½ feet] with the intention that the enemy would be crushed by the momentum of the *Massenkolonnen*. The Austrians hurled themselves into the battle in these rigid, inflexible formations. The officers could not exert any independent control, their purpose was restricted to marching ahead of the soldiers with sword in hand. The Prussians on the other hand, placed the highest emphasis on flexibility and maneuverability, their companies wherever possible, were directed against the enemy's flanks, pouring death and confusion into his tight packed ranks with their rapid fire.'

Gronefeld, both from the 58th. The second assault by Brigade Hertwek now went in against this reinforced, though still weak, force. Brigade Jonak was on its left, simply holding in check whatever other Prussian battalions were to the north and east on the plateau.

But this second attack also foundered. It was primarily directed (it was now 11:00) against a farmstead surrounded by orchards, that lay in front of the woods, part of the village of Schonow. This farmstead, shown on more detailed maps as *Sochor's Gehöft* [Sochor's farm], was held on our side by half battalions Werneke and Gfug, led by *Major* von Haugwitz. Near the farmstead *Generalmajor* von Ollech, Commander of the main body of the advance - guard, was on some high ground, along with *Oberst* von François and *Major* von Eberhardt, both from the 58th. In this second attack the enemy also advanced with great bravery. Their officers (who might have learned that their Polish battalions were facing a [Prussian] Polish regiment, the 58th), gave the commands loudly in Polish in an attempt to undermine the morale of our troops, but in vain. They fell back in the face of our fire. New columns of *Jäger* with infantry followed on, but *Major* von Haugwitz [of the Prussian 58th], now charged with hurrahs. [The two forces] meeting in the center of the projection formed by the southern wooded parcel. The battle continued, in part with the bayonet, as *Generalmajor* von Ollech rode toward the farmstead from the more elevated point where he had been. *Oberst* von François was at his side. The enemy immediately spotted the sparkle of the epaulettes. A *Jäger* officer (on horseback) rode into the firing line and speaking vigorously, pointed out the general and his companion. A moment later *General* von Ollech fell from his horse, seriously wounded by two bullets. Battalion drummer Braun immediately tore a needle gun from the hands of the nearest Musketeer and shot the *Jäger* officer from his saddle. The general had barely fallen when the men of the 58th (5th and 8th Companies) forced their way into the narrow strip of woods that lay to the north until, again coming into the open and halfway to Wenzelsberg, they reached a solitary house, the *Schonow Unterförsterei* [under forester's lodge].

Here prisoners were taken, all attempts by the enemy to recapture it failed. By now it was 11:30. The second attack by Brigade Hertwek, which as we have seen was a concentrated thrust against our left flank, was repulsed.

But a third attack was already in preparation. The enemy kept bringing up new forces. A third brigade, Brigade Rosenzweig, had just arrived to the left of Brigade Jonak, which at this point was inactive. Now Brigade Jonak launched its attack against our seriously depleted and already exhausted troops. The attack was supported on both flanks, to the left by Brigade Hertwek, to the right by Brigade Rosenzweig.

This time the attack succeeded. Our main body and reserve had not yet arrived and our men began to waver, first in the center (the village of Wenzelsberg), then also on the left flank (the southern woods, the farmstead and the forester's lodge). With a half right, front facing the enemy, the battalions of our advanced guard slowly fell back to the northeast as far as the place where the Nachod pass cuts through the Branka ridge. Only the northern wood [*Das Wäldchen*] and (according to the Austrian report) the church and the churchyard of the village of Wenzelsberg, were still in our hands, and Wysokow too, which had not yet been attacked.

The danger was clear and increased with each passing minute. It was evident that the enemy was attempting to make use of his advantage to force us back into the depression, thereby closing the pass and gaining the high ground. Brigade Rosenzweig, the 17th *Jäger* Battalion in the lead, advanced against the northern woods in dense columns. On the left and right the battalions of IR 55 Gondrecourt and IR 4 Hoch und Deutschmeister followed. Additionally, this was the moment that the [Austrian] Cuirassier Brigade Solms (which up to this point had remained at Kleny), stormed up the slope and onto the open plateau between Wysokow and the little northern wood [*Das Wäldchen*]. On our side all we had to meet this attack were single companies, the situation was critical.

The cavalry action on the Wysokow Plateau

As we said, the situation was critical, but only for the blink of an eye. The immediate danger, the cavalry attack, was quickly repelled. On our side Cavalry Brigade Wnuck emerged from the pass and threw itself, the 1st Uhlan Regiment in the lead, the 8th Dragoon Regiment following on the left flank, unhesitatingly upon the advancing enemy squadrons, the Ferdinand and Hessian cuirassiers.

A Prussian report (set down immediately after the action) outlined the encounter as follows:

> Our 1st Uhlans were in the lead. 500 paces to their rear, on the left flank of the Uhlans, the 8th Dragoons followed. Signal ... Deploy! ... Signal ... Gallop! ... Fanfare! Now our weary horses began to fly. With a thunderous hurrah we charged into the closed ranks of the advancing Cuirassiers. The Uhlans attacked their front, the Dragoons however, with their 4th Squadron leading, swung to the right and hurled themselves into the right flank and rear of the Emperor Ferdinand Cuirassiers. A furious fight ensued, a general mélée of lance, saber and pallasch [Austrian heavy cavalry sword], all intermingled. The long, broad pallasch of the Cuirassiers, struck like lightning in all directions, but our men had learned to parry and cut. The flank attack of the Dragoon squadron (*Rittmeister* von Walther) was decisive. *Lieutenant* von Raven, who was with this squadron, suddenly saw the enemy standard next to him. He, *Unteroffizier* Reudelsdorf, trumpeter Tuchale and several Dragoons threw themselves upon the powerful man that bore it and an unequal struggle developed. Von Raven made a grab, another saber stroke, and the enemy *Wachtmeister* sank from his horse. The standard was taken. The Cuirassiers were rolled up from the right flank and, driven into our Uhlans, where they lost a second standard.
>
> Our Dragoons that were pursuing the enemy, now came under heavy artillery fire. Incoming rounds killed men and the signal '*Appel*' [rally] called them back out of the fire. *Generalmajor* von Wnuck, the commander of the brigade, both regimental commanders, *Oberst* von Tresckow and *Oberstlieutenant* von Wichmann, bled from sword wounds to the forehead and neck. Ten more officers were wounded along with them in this short encounter.[20] The plateau was cleared, the attack of the enemy Cuirassiers thwarted.

---

20   Author's Note: Due to the great interest that this first cavalry encounter provoked on both sides, we list here the names of the officers who were wounded:
West Prussian Uhlan Regiment Nr. 1.
    Oberst von Tresckow in the right arm and left hand.
    Rittmeister von Glasenapp, loss of two fingertips.
    Premierlieutenant von der Marwitz, slash on right ear.

Such is the Prussian report. We shall now compare it with the Austrian account which states:

The Cuirassier Brigade Solms was only five squadrons strong and consisted of Cuirassier Regiment Emperor Ferdinand (four squadrons), and one squadron (the 2nd) of Cuirassier Regiment Prince Alexander of Hesse. The three other squadrons of this regiment were detached, two to Starkoç on the left flank, a third was attached to Brigade Jonak on the right. This last squadron (the 3rd) later took a decisive part [in the action]. The Ferdinand Cuirassiers, under *Oberst* von Berres, were in the lead. 700 paces behind them, on the left flank, the 2nd Squadron Hessian Cuirassiers, under *Oberst Graf* Thun followed. We mounted the slope at a trot then galloped away over the plateau. Prussian Uhlans now rode to meet our attack. *Oberst* von Berres, riding 50 paces ahead of the Cuirassiers, immediately fell upon the enemy, one of whom, presumably the commander of the Uhlans, was cut from his horse with a mighty stroke, right in front of his regiment. The Cuirassiers followed with raucous hurrahs. A mélée ensued, with cutting and thrusting, the [enemy] Uhlans performed well and many of our men were wounded by their lances. In this moment of total mélée, the Prussian 8th Dragoons threw themselves, several squadrons strong, into our right flank causing the Cuirassiers to waver. One standard bearer, already forced apart from his fellows and surrounded by a number of Dragoons, was wounded by saber and lance, and the standard torn from his grasp. The other standard bearer, in battle with the Uhlans, lost his horse and fell with more than twenty wounds. His standard, hacked and broken, was later found on the battlefield by the Prussians.

At this critical moment our Hessian Cuirassiers attacked. The 2nd Squadron (*Oberst Graf* Thun), followed by the Ferdinand Cuirassiers, plunged into the right flank of the Uhlans. The 3rd Squadron (*Oberstlieutenant* von Wagener), which as we know had been attached to Brigade Jonak, now attacked at the same time into the left flank of the Dragoons.

Oberstlieutenant von Wagener struck the enemy *Brigade General* von Wnuck [with his pallasch], *Rittmeister* Preiser cut the commander of the 8th Dragoons, *Oberstlieutenant* von Wichmann) from his horse. The enemy hesitated. The Dragoons (who outnumbered us decisively), fell into confusion. The dense tangle of combatants

Secondelieutenant and *Regiments Adjutant Graf* Reichenbach, slash on stomach (the horse had numerous wounds and had to be put down).
Secondelieutenant von Thun, slash on back.
Portepée - Fähnrich von Plessen, slash on head.
2nd Silesian Dragoon Regiment Nr. 8
Oberstlieutenant von Wichmann, slash on forehead.
Premierlieutenant von der Borne, slash on cheek and arm.
Premierlieutenant von Zawadzki, slash on right lower arm.
Secondelieutenant von Prittwitz, serious slash on head.
Also, the 2nd Squadron of the 1st Silesian Dragoon Regiment (Nr. 4), which took part in the fighting here, had three officers put out of action. These numerous wounds show how hotly this action, which only lasted about three minutes, was contested. *General* von Wnuck received his slash on the back of his head from an ordinary cavalryman, not from the Commander of the Hessian Brigade (Prince Solms, who led the enemy brigade, had earlier been a member of our Guards Cavalry and was then *Rittmeister* in the same West Prussian Uhlan Regiment against which he now fought).

moved eastward over the plateau. The Dragoons headed toward the rear toward Nachod.

Oberstlieutenant von Wagener, by choosing the right place and the right moment, had not only avoided defeat, but won a victory. We pursued the fleeing enemy but between Wysokow and the woods, we came under fire in the front and flank. Responding to the loudly shouted command, '*Kehrt euch*' [turn back], we returned to the edge of the plateau. Our victory was not achieved without losses. The Ferdinand Cuirassiers alone lost three dead and four seriously wounded officers, as well as 130 men and 142 horses. The Hessian Cuirassiers suffered fewer losses. The 3rd Squadron, which had struck the initial blow, had no significant losses with only one officer and a few men wounded. The suddenness of the attack, the surprise, the flanking of a flank attack that [the enemy] already believed to be victorious, that was what was decisive. Not the battle.

This description gives us the Austrian conception of the action.

The reports from the two sides agree on the following points:

1. That the West Prussian Uhlans and the Ferdinand Cuirassiers clashed frontally.
2. That the 8th Dragoons struck the enemy in the right flank.
3. That this flank attack disorganized the Ferdinand Cuirassiers and cost them two standards.
4. That immediately after this success the Prussian cavalry brigade retired.

So much is agreed, but why did Brigade Wnuck retire? This is where the reports begin to differ. The Prussian report says, 'Because the pursuing Dragoons came under shellfire.' The Austrian report says, 'Because *Oberstlieutenant* von Wagener struck the flanking Prussians in their own flank.' The Prussian report makes no mention of this flank attack. That it took place is beyond doubt. It is just as clear that it was an act of bravery and a spectacular tactical accomplishment, but how great was its effect? That is the question. We also wish to do justice to the enemy, the more so since in his account of this action, the recognition of what our cavalry accomplished is accompanied by the request, 'On our side, to honour the truth.' It is our honest endeavour to do this. However, we are afraid that our most generous concessions will not satisfy our enemy. He is inclined to impartiality in general, but so little inclined thereto in particulars. His undoubtedly excellent cavalry must be superior and victorious in every detail. That however, is more than we can concede. What was special in the cavalry action here in question, we will happily concede, as described in an Austrian special report (see Streffleurs *Zeittschrift*, March of 1867) which states that a number of Dragoons (large or small), was defeated by the 3rd Squadron Hessian Cuirassiers, and chased across the plateau. However spectacular and locally successful this attack may have been, it can have changed nothing in the overall outcome of the action. Everything happened too quickly, and the area fought over was too great. The attack cut off only a corner, it was merely an episode, not the turning point of the action. The enemy's own admission of our superior numbers, the limited number of [enemy] Cuirassiers carrying out the flank attack, and finally a glance at the enemy's losses in wounded, prisoners and trophies, all appears to leave us justified in our belief in a decisive victory. Perception stands against perception, report against report, but more than a thousand Prussian eyes watched Brigade Solms scatter to the west across the plateau, not Brigade Wnuck scatter to the east. It is hardly likely that a compromise will be reached after so many words have been exchanged.[21]

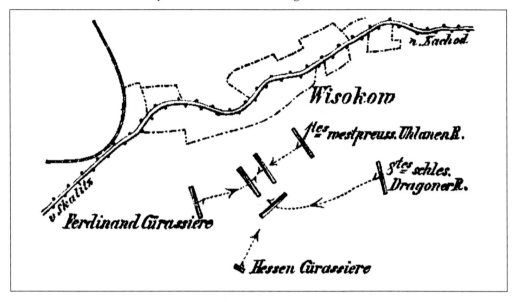

Sketch map of cavalry action by Wysokow.

21 Author's Note: Since we wrote the above, based on special reports of the regiments engaged, the General Staff works of both sides have appeared. These too leave the controversy just a sharp as ever.

The Austrian General staff observed:

The enemy Dragoons enveloped the right flank of our Ferdinand Cuirassiers. In this threatening moment the 3rd Squadron (under *Oberstlieutenant* Wagener) on the right flank and the 2nd Squadron (*Oberst Graf* Thun), on the left flank, cut their way into the enemy formations and pursued them across the plateau.'

The Prussian General Staff stated:

'Now that both sides had interpenetrated each other and were fully embroiled, a mighty hand to hand fracas developed that could not however, last for long. The envelopment of the enemy by the Dragoons soon proved so effective that [the enemy forces] fell back, at first slowly toward Wysokow, but then in total disorder along the edge of the village toward the west, Dragoons intermixed with Uhlans right on his heels.'

Who is right? Both sides stick to their colours, but an impartial third party, if he knows how to read between the lines, will be able to reach a decision. How difficult it is to discover the actual truth regarding even the simplest of events, can be illustrated by another, more personal episode from the engagement at Nachod. At the start of the action, the General Staff Officer of the 9th Division, *Oberstlieutenant* von Ziemietzki, rode (as a *parliamentaire*) to the enemy outposts to hand over a declaration of the Army High Command in which the commencement of hostilities was announced, and also a communication regarding medical personnel. In a statement of *Generallieutenant* von Kirchback we find the following: '*Herr* von Ziemietzki was held by the enemy until the action was ended. He had to experience the action with eyes blindfolded between two cavalrymen in the enemy ranks and was repeatedly in danger of being abused by Austrian troops.' The Austrian General Staff work, on the other hand, states, '*Obertlieutenant* von Ziemietzki had already handed over the documents at Kleny

Whatever the causes of the failure of the attack by Cuirassier Brigade Solms, it did fail, and that is sufficient for us. The brigade went back. The danger of a sudden cavalry assault on our battalions that had been forced back to the depression (that might at the very least have interfered with the debouchment of V Corps), was averted.

The 10th Division joins the action

The danger was averted but it reappeared in a new form almost immediately. In addition to the cavalry assault, Brigade Rosenzweig advanced against the northern woods and the Wenzelsberg church, and after a stubborn fight, took both from half battalions von Schimonski and Braun. Brigade Rosenzweig seemed to have accomplished what Cavalry Brigade Solms could not, forcing us back into the depression.

The Austrian account runs as follows:

> The enemy still held the large area of woods that extended north of Wenzelsberg over the plateau, and then onto the western slope as far as the depression.[22] The 17th *Jäger* Battalion was directed against these woods, followed by Regiment Gondrecourt. The assault succeeded. The enemy was forced back over the crest and the woods were successfully taken. Since the enemy seriously threatened the right flank of the brigade from the Wenzelsberg church however, it was advisable also to attack this part of the enemy position.
>
> Regiment Deutschmeister, led by *Oberst* Peinlich, was assigned the mission of assaulting the church and plateau from Wenzelsberg, which proved entirely successful. At the same time the church and the wall surrounding it were prepared for defense and held by a part of Regiment Deutschmeister, while the rest of the regiment took up position on the plateau and pursued the enemy with skirmishers.
>
> In this assault all the troops of the brigade suffered substantial losses to small arms fire. Nevertheless, order was maintained, and contact was established with the adjoining elements of Brigade Jonak (on the right).
>
> Since Brigades Jonak and Hertwek also carried out successful assaults on the hill at the same time, the enemy could be pursued further. While continuing to hold the woods and the church, Brigade Rosenzweig continued to advance to the east without meeting significant resistance.

So much for the Austrian report, which at least in its presentation of this part of the action, we must recognize as essentially correct. The assault of the three brigades had forced our advanced

and had returned to his troops, he was therefore no longer a *parliamentaire*. Since his release during the fighting was impossible, he was taken to Josephstadt.' (This says in effect, that if he truly was 'no longer a *parliamentaire*', then he was simply a prisoner, and in this case, there was no reason to let him return to his troops).

22   Tr. Note: This appears to refer to *Das Waldchen* on the map, which the author has, hitherto, described as the small woods to the north of the village of Wenzelsberg. Neither the author's map, the 1:25000 Prussian map, nor the map accompanying the Austrian General Staff Study show its extension into the hollow.

guard battalions back on the entire line. The woods north and south of Wenzelsberg, and finally the church located above the village, were all lost. We stood at the mouth of the pass, forced into the angle formed by the Skalitz and Neustadt roads, immediately south of the village of Wysokow. If we were forced back from here also, the day (perhaps more) would be lost. However, at this moment of pressing danger, help arrived.

The 10th Division, *Generallieutenant* von Kirchbach, eagerly awaited for so long, deployed from Nachod, crossed the depression and clambered up the Branka Hill to the hotly contested plateau. First to arrive was the 19th Brigade, *Generalmajor* von Tiedemann, Regiments No. 6 and 46, the 46th leading. Formed into six half battalions, the regiment attacked [*Das Wäldchen*] at the double, ejecting the 17th *Jägers* and IR 56 Gondrecourt, and then with a half left, went on to attack the Wenzelsberg Church (the '*Wenzelskapelle*'). This was held by a battalion of the elite IR 4 Hoch und Deutschmeister ('the children of Vienna'), who were defeated after a fierce fight.

The woods and the *Wenzelskapelle* were back in our hands.

The 6th Regiment followed the 46th (four half battalions strong, its Fusilier battalion had yet to arrive), which also advanced towards the [Wenzelsberg] woods, but then bore off to the right, passed over plateau on which the cavalry action had just taken place, and entered the village of Wysokow, which would now become the focal point of the battle. *Oberstlieutenant* von Scheffler, with three half battalions, occupied the southern half of the village, which traversed by a deep sunken road, formed the mouth of the pass. The northern half remained unoccupied. The ravine ran between the two halves.[23]

At almost the same moment in which the occupation of the village took place, the enemy attacked with his last brigade. The battle now entered its concluding phase but in order to describe this last moment of the action, we must go back half an hour.

The struggle for Wysokow

At about 12:00, *Feldmarschallieutenant* von Ramming, observing the advance of his first three brigades everywhere, resolved to break our last resistance with a strong blow to our right flank.

---

23   Author's Note: In order to understand the ensuing action in Wysokow it is necessary to be familiar with the layout of the village and with the order of battle of the 6th Regiment. The *Chaussee* (which is also the main street), runs as a sunken road of considerable width and depth and divides Wysokow into a northern and southern half. A second sunken road runs parallel to this, such that if the enemy is attacking the northern part of the village from the south, it provides him with a covered position from which he can fire on us without being hit himself. Further details of the extremely complicated layout would only confuse matters, the sketch will suffice. Only one further detail remains, that the western and eastern halves of the village are also sharply divided.

The order of battle of the 6th Regiment follows:

1st Battalion: *Major* von Wnuck.
    Half battalion von Thadden (1st and 3rd Companies).
    Half battalion von Bronkiowski (2nd and 4th Companies).
2nd Battalion: *Oberstlieutenant* von Gottberg.
    Half battalion von Heugel (5th and 7th Companies).
    Half battalion von Webern (6th and 8th Companies).
Fusilier Battalion: *Major* von Webern.
    Half battalion Fischer (9th and 12th Companies).
    Half battalion von Nitsche (10th and 11th Companies).

Brigade Waldstätten, which had not yet been committed, was directed to advance in three columns.

> The center column (2½ battalions) against Wysokow itself.
> The left column (1½ battalions) was ordered to bypass the village to the north.
> The right column (2 battalions) went south of the *Chaussée*, to [*das Wäldchen*].

When the *Feldmarschallieutenant* ordered this deployment, it could only be to secure the success that had already been achieved. The columns moved forward, however before they arrived, the deployment of the 10th Division and the rapid advance of 19th Brigade had completely changed the situation. The fighting continued. The Wenzelsberg woods [*das Wäldchen*] and the *Wenzelskapelle* were recaptured. Wysokow itself was occupied. It was no longer a matter of [the Austrians] securing success, the three columns of Brigade Waldstätten that were now advancing no longer had a success to secure, they had to recapture it. They accepted their new assignment and advanced to the attack.

Fighting in Wenzelburg village.

It appears that the right-hand column (2nd Battalion IR 9 Hartmann and 3rd Battalion IR 79 Frank), was the first to arrive. Its attack was directed against the protruding point of the Wenzelsberg wood, however it was met with rapid fire from its western margin, driving back first battalion Hartmann, then battalion Frank. The attack was repulsed.

The center column, a half battalion of the 6th *Jäger*, one battalion from IR 9 Hartmann and one battalion from IR 79 Frank, advanced against Wysokow and had more success. This center column came up against half battalion von Bronikowski, which *Oberstlieutenant* von Scheffler had moved forward into the western part of the village. After fierce fighting, half battalion Bronikowski had to fall back level with the two other half battalions von Webern and von Thadden but continued to hold the central and eastern portion of the village from the southern rim. The Regimental Commander was with them. Pursuing the advantage he had gained in the western part of the village, the enemy pushed on. His artillery gave him outstanding support and our losses mounted rapidly. *Oberstlieutenant* von Scheffler, *Major* von Wnuck, and many other officers and men were wounded in a few minutes. To make matters worse, the left hand column (a half battalion of the 6th *Jäger* and the 2nd Battalion IR 79 Frank) now appeared, some on the other side of the ravine, some enveloping our right flank.

All of our forces now congregated on our side of the ravine to secure the exposed flank with rapid fire. However the outcome was decided, not by the rapid fire, but by the additional commitment of the 20th Brigade (*Generalmajor* Wittich) which deployed its battalions to the right and left to support all the exposed points. First the Fusiliers of the 52nd and then the 47th passed through Wysokow and out the northern side, to counter those enemy forces attempting to envelop the village.[24] This engagement, supported by a nearly simultaneous Uhlan attack,

---

24   Author's Note: An officer of the Fusilier Battalion of the 47th gave the following striking description: 'We initially marched to the woods north of Wenzelsberg and took possession of them. Soon however, came the order to proceed to Wysokow. In order to accomplish this, we now bore to the right, over the gunfire swept plateau to the eastern end of the village. In order to get through this fire more quickly 'double time' was ordered, however it proved impossible to follow the order. In Wysokow our *Major* von Brandenstein wanted us to use the main street of the village to advance, but another battalion (of the 52nd) blocked the road so we had a moment of rest. The rifles were stacked and all made for the little stream that flows through the village. It was only muddy water but everyone drank and filled his canteen as much as time permitted. With renewed strength, with drums beating, we now moved on. *Major* von Brandenstein led us to an open space to the northwest, out of the village. We had hardly reached the hill when we were attacked by Austrian infantry columns and came under heavy fire from a battery positioned rather deep in the edge of the woods. While the first half battalion (von Vietinghoff) sent volleys after the [enemy] infantry columns that were retreating, the second half battalion (von Tschirschky) advanced against the battery, which kept them under heavy canister fire. Skirmishers were sent against the [enemy] detachment covering the battery (drawn from the 6th *Jäger* Battalion) and opened rapid fire against the gun crews and horses from a range of 300 - 400 paces, the effect was horrible. The battery attempted to withdraw but nearly all the men and horses were shot, three guns were left behind while the others fled behind the hill at whose edge they stood. In the meantime, our half battalion was now exposed since it had advanced a good deal farther than the first half battalion (which was now engaged with the 2nd Battalion of Regiment Frank). Now came reports that two squadrons [of cavalry], along with infantry, were approaching to take us in the right flank. In response to this threat, the second half battalion fell back on the first, taking advantage of a ravine, while the enemy cavalry was defeated by three squadrons of our 1st Uhlan Regiment. These were the 3rd and 4th Squadrons, *Premierlieutenant* von Berken and *Rittmeister* von Glasenapp. The [enemy] cuirassiers did not wait for the attack. Two guns were immediately captured by *Quartiermeister*

was decisive. The enemy fled and the other formations that were to the side, even the battalions of Brigades Rosenzweig, Jonak and Hertwek, that were now advancing on the entire line, now retreated.

The enemy himself described the final moments of the battle as follows:

At 12:30 (the moment when the [Prussian] 20th Brigade, Regiments 47 and 52, entered the action) the enemy launched a simultaneous and energetic attack against our three brigades on the right wing, *which were already seriously exhausted and had suffered considerable losses.* Nevertheless, they held their positions.

It was only when [Prussian] reinforcements (the King's Grenadier Regiment) entered the woods, and the enemy threw new forces into Wysokow (1:00), that our forces had to give up the ground they had gained. *Feldmarschallieutenant* Ramming ordered the retreat to Skalitz.

The retreat was now carried out, first on the right wing by Brigade Hertwek, then in the center by Brigades Jonak and Rosenzweig, under covering fire from the batteries, without the losing their tactical cohesion. Once they were on the open plain, Brigade Rosenzweig covered the retreat.

On our left wing, during the evacuation of Wysokow, the brigade battery lost its covering detachment as well as its horses and could only save three pieces (thus losing five). The Corps Artillery Reserve, whose position was exposed, also retired. The enemy pursued and after the crews of two guns were cut down, these too (two pieces) were lost.

The retreat to Skalitz was covered by the Corps Artillery Reserve and Cavalry Brigade Schindlöcker, which arrived at the close of the action. The enemy hardly harassed our retreat at all. The cannon fire fell silent at 4:30. The positions that we took up in Skalitz were as follows:

Brigade Waldstätten, left flank
Brigade Rosenzweig, center
Brigade Jonak, right flank
Brigade Hertwek was in reserve, behind Skalitz.'

So much for the Austrian report.

Flander and *Ulan* Buchwald, three others were left, stuck in the mud. This magnificent attack was no less outstanding than the earlier attack by six troops of the 8th Dragoons on some enemy infantry [*Jäger* and elements of IR 4 Hoch und Deutschmeister, and IR 20 Crown Prince of Prussia] in which a standard was captured. This gives the lie to the Austrian assertion that after the cavalry action on the Wysokow Plateau [12:00], Brigade Wnuck was no longer to be seen. It was these two cavalry regiments that caused substantial losses to the enemy, even after the cavalry action described above, capturing the enemy standard and guns. With that the enemy fell back and the three captured guns were carried off by our artillery horses. In the last moments of the fighting we suffered heavy losses, less from canister fired by the battery, than from the well-directed shooting of their covering detachment, the 6th *Jäger*, who concentrated their fire on our closed up half battalion, which lost two officers and thirty men in less than ten minutes.

The losses, the trophies

Nachod had been a bloody day, the more so for our opponent. They give their own losses (those of the cavalry division are not included) as 227 officers and 7145 non-commissioned officers and men (a third of whom were captured). Brigade Rosenzweig alone (Regiments Gondrecourt and Deutschmeister), lost about 1500 men. A soldier of the latter regiment, while still under the influence of the defeat, wrote in a letter sent later, 'Dear Parents. I greet and kiss all of you many times. I have already been so dejected by the many retreats and marches, day and night, that I truly believe that here and now is my final hour. On the 25th of June we came to the border. My God, that was awful, what I have seen in the first battle. It was at Skalitz (Nachod) on June 27th. Oh God, that was awful. We had to retreat because the Prussians always had a good position, in the woods and on the hills, and we were always out in the open. So many Deutschmeister have fallen there. The Deutschmeister Regiment has already been unlucky.'

On our side we lost 59 officers and 1061 men. The greatest losses were in the 2nd Battalion of the 37th, and the Fusilier Battalion of the 47th Regiments. The one lost four officers and 114 men, the other 93 men and two officers. Among the regiments, the 37th lost nine officers and 187 men, the 6th Regiment at most, eight officers and 134 men.

Dead, or dead as result of their wounds among the staff officers of V Corps were, *Major* von Natzmer of the 8th and *Major* von Rieben of the 4th Dragoons, Wounded were, *Generalmajor* von Wnuck, *Oberst* von Tresckow, *Oberstlieutenant* von Wichmann, *Oberst* Walther von Monbary, *Oberstlieutenant* von Scheffler, *Major* von Wnuck *et. al.* The serious wounds of *Generalmajor* von Ollech elicited much sympathy. Struck by two bullets almost simultaneously (one wounded his upper arm, the other smashed his thigh), his survival was due to the painstaking care he received, first in Frankenstein and then in Bethany Hospital. The wounds of the other staff officers were less severe.

The Crown Prince (who rode forward during the first half of the action and became so closely involved that his entourage felt called upon to draw their swords), was unharmed, as was *Admiral* Prince Adalbert, who was present on the left flank with the 58th regiment and the 4th Dragoons, observing the battle 'as an amateur.' He declined the request to expose himself less with the remark, 'Gentlemen, I don't see that well.'

The trophies of the day consisted of seven guns, one [infantry] standard and two [cavalry] standards. The two [cavalry] standards were taken from the Ferdinand Cuirassiers. One (currently in the Garrison Church in Potsdam) was conspicuous by its extreme age and had already gone through the battles of the Thirty Years War. It is on a staff over eight feet long on which are four times 30 gilded nails that originally secured the fabric, of which only a few traces of gold thread now remain. The gilded tip bears the double eagle.

Shortly after the cavalry action, the 3rd Squadron of the 8th Dragoons, *Major* von Natzmer, attacked some enemy infantry north of Wenzelsberg in an action that led to a long lasting controversy, too interesting and too unique to ignore. The first official report that the V Army Corps released after the battle states that in addition to the two [cavalry] standards, a regimental standard, indeed the regimental standard of the 3rd Battalion IR 4 Hoch und Deutschmeister, was captured. Thereupon the Commander of that ancient and honourable regiment responded in the November edition of the *Oestreichisch Militairischen Zeitschrift* as follows:

The Regiment Deutschmeister came away from the battle on 27th June at Nachod with its honour untarnished. As it formed into line of battle, the regimental flag remained furled. The furled flag was [then] struck by a musket round ... [and] broke apart in the center. The bearer of the regimental flag was thereby forced to take off the oilcloth cover, on which was written in large white letters the words 'Hoch und Deutschmeister Linien - Infanterie - Regiment Nr. 4, 3rd Feldbataillon,' to lay it aside, and to repair the broken staff sufficiently so that it could be carried. It remained in this state until after the battle of Königgrätz. The covering remained on the field at Wenzelsberg. The regimental flag itself however, was in the hands of its members.

In the battle at Skalitz on 28th June, the regimental flag was in no danger. It was in greater danger in the Battle of Königgrätz where the regiment had the difficult task of capturing the village of Rosberitz that had already been occupied by the Prussian Guards, and to take possession of the terrain between [Rosberitz] and Chlum, which had already been lost. The standard bearer fell. The regimental flag remained ours and we brought it, despite all the dangers of the retreat, to Königgrätz. Later in Vienna, the staff of the regimental flag was bound with a metal cylinder, and at the point of the break, a silver plate was attached on which is written, 'Shot through in the Battle at Nachod, in the assault on Waçlawice (Wenzelsberg) on 27th June 1866.

The identity of all the regimental flags of the regiment is confirmed by the fact that each of the nails (which were hammered in at the time of the flag's consecration), bears the name of the regiment. The Command of the Regiment further declares that neither the 1st, 2nd, 4th, nor any battalion of the regiment, lost a regimental standard. Herewith, hopefully, the entire matter is finally resolved in favour of the honour of our Fatherland's (Viennese) Regiment.'

On the appearance of this definitive declaration, whose credibility must be accepted as totally unimpeachable, even in the eyes of the enemy, came the following Prussian response :

In the Battle of Nachod, after the attack against Cavalry Brigade Solms, the 2nd Silesian Dragoon Regiment Nr. 8 also attacked infantry and *Jäger* close to the margin of the little woods north of Wenzelsberg with great success. Some of the 3rd Squadron broke up a cluster[25] in which was found a regimental flag. Six or seven infantrymen formed themselves closely around it and sought to defend it with admirable bravery. They fell however, under the sabers of the Dragoons, whereupon the regimental flag was thrown down. The arriving Squadron Commander, *Major* von Natzmer, ordered *Wachtmeister* Otto, who was with him, to dismount and pick up the regimental flag, and the trumpeter to blow *'Appel'* [rally]. The latter rode off. The *Major* and his *Wachtmeister* however, were shot before the regimental standard could be brought to safety. It was later found by *Major* von Webern and *Lieutenant* Thiel, as a half battalion of the 1st West Prussian Grenadier Regiment Nr. 6 passed the location where the fight had taken place. It was given to a trumpeter who brought it back to Nachod.

25   Tr. Note: *Knäuel* is usually translated as a knot or tight cluster. Infantry were trained to form *Knäuel* as well as squares when under attack from cavalry.

On the place where the attack had taken place, in addition to men of various *Jäger* battalions, were men of Regiment *Hoch und Deutschmeister Nr. 4* and Crown Prince of Prussia Nr. 20. Prisoners from the 3rd Battalion of Regiment *Hoch und Deutschmeister* stated with great assurance that they recognized the captured regimental standard as that of their battalion. That was the origin of the first report of the High Command of the 2nd Army regarding the capture in battle of the regimental standard of the 3rd Battalion of the above named regiment, an assertion which is proven wrong by the declaration of the regiment in question's Regimental Commander. Nevertheless, the fact remains that a regimental standard was taken in the Battle of Nachod which is now in the Garrison Church at Potsdam. To whom it formally belonged can only be determined by the Austrians.

The work of the Austrian General Staff, which has just been published, finally solved the controversy. The captured regimental standard belonged to IR 20 Crown Prince of Prussia. On our side many standards and flags were hit, none were lost. The standard of the 4th Dragoon Regiment was hit by two artillery shells, the second round tearing off the upper third and casting it to the ground. Two feet shorter than all the other standards as a result of emergency repairs, on 2nd August on the occasion of the parade on the field of Austerlitz, the regiment presented its regimental flag to King Wilhelm. News of the victory, the first significant one, gave rise to general jubilation in the land, especially in Silesia, which was the home of a number of the regiments that had fought there.[26]

The 'Eighth Dragoons' were the heroes of the day:

> *Hot was the day, hot was the war,*
> *The 8th Dragoons decided the victory.*
> *Major von Natzmer led his squadron,*
> *He grabbed the Deutschmeister regimental flag,*
> *His life was the price,*
> *Blessed with the knowledge of victory*

That has a serious ring to it but there were also happier verses in the Silesian dialect.

[Ed – Note. This dialect has subsequently fallen into disuse and thus it has not been possible to render a faithful interpretation. The verses are reproduced below in their original form].

> *Doas waar a Gewudel und a Gehudel,*
> *Ma soag vur Stoob nich wia an Knaul,*
> *Kenn Preußen kunnt ma vom Oesterreicher,*
> *Kenn Reiter underscheeden vom Gaul. . . .*

---

26 Tr. Note: Fortuitously the Prussian victory at Nachod, which caused jubilation throughout Prussia, came on the very day that King Wilhelm had previously proclaimed (on June 18th) to be a *Bettag*, or National Day of Prayer, '. . . a general Day of Prayer to be held with divine services in the churches as well as the closing of public businesses and cessation of labour, to the extent that the present situation allows.' (Pp. 159 - 160, Gentz und Vierow, *Geschichte des Infanterie - Regiments General - Feldmarschall Prinz Friedrich Karl von Preußen (8. Brandenburgischen) Nr. 64*, Ernst Siegfried Mittler und Sohn, Berlin, 1897).

> *Hie vergoaß sei Instrument der Trumpeter,*
> *U Beritt vergoaß der Undruffzier:*
> *Der 'Rudelsdurf' mit somst'm 'Tuchale',*
> *Die hieben ei uf a Cürassier.*

In the event it was the brilliant conduct of our cavalry that was celebrated, not only against the famed [Austrian] cavalry, but against all arms of the enemy.

The engagement at Nachod filled the hearts of our young troops with the joy of victory, but the day had more than moral significance. The difficult pass was opened, we were in Bohemia. The first step (often the most decisive) had been taken, it was the beginning of a series of victories.

As with all such events, its importance has on occasion been contested, unjustly in our opinion, considering how things went elsewhere on the 27th. We can assert that on this day, victory was only necessary at one location, and it did not matter whether it was the pass at Trautenau or Nachod that was opened. One of them however, had to be opened that day. Since the attempt at Trautenau had failed, and the Guards were still in the Eypel defile, it was of no small importance that at least one place had been cleared. We shall examine the significance of this and how the success on the 27th [at Nachod] differed from that on the 28th (Skalitz) in a later chapter.

The Encounter at Skalitz

The pass at Nachod was opened, V Corps had accomplished its invasion of Bohemia and a decisive location was captured. This was a great success, but only a first step, the Elbe must be reached and presumably crossed. In any case, no matter what, a union must be achieved with the other corps of the 2nd Army. Therefore, V Corps now proceeded toward Gradlitz. On the 28th *General* von Steinmetz decided to advance from the plateau of Wysokow toward Skalitz and to take this place (about halfway to Gradlitz), committing all of his forces (support of the 2nd Guards Division was anticipated). This task was by no means less difficult than that of the preceding day. If the enemy concentrated his forces there, as actually happened, it was hard to see how they could be defeated. Skalitz provided an outstanding defensive position.

We shall attempt a short description (compare this also with the sketch map of Nachod). The plain of Skalitz, which V Corps could look down on from its elevated position at Nachod [actually from the Wysokow plateau], was bounded to the north by a sharply defined range of hills, whose descending slopes can be deliniated by a line from Wysokow to Zlitsch, and which are pierced by three ravines, generally running from north to south. The villages of Nieder Wysokow, Starkocz and Zlitsch lie approximately at their mouths.

Between Studnitz and Starkocz, the ground west of the railway rises to the Schafberg (the highest hill), which commands everything as far as Skalitz. The railway itself crosses the plain past the Dubno pheasantry (which is well provided with good buildings and thick woods), on an embankment that, where the railway turns south in a great curve, attains a height of 15 feet and forms viaducts. The thickets of the pheasantry are 1500 paces from the town.

Parallel with this (from Zlitsch to the Aupa) is an insignificant ridge that at its southern end, forms the little (approximately 30 foot high) plateau, on which Skalitz itself is built. About halfway between Zlitsch and Skalitz, this generally insignificant ridge rises to achieve the proportions of a distinct hill, planted with fruit trees, which is called *Jägerhügel*. With its gentle slope toward Dubno, this low hill provides a generally favourable field of fire to the front, though it is commanded by the elevated ground north of the Zlitsch stream.

Skalitz itself, has a more favourable front. The margin of the plateau falls off steeply to its east and south. The railway is built into the slope and provides a good, tiered, firing position. The entrance to the town (especially around the *Chaussée* from Nachod), is covered by large houses and the railway station. The town itself is solidly constructed. On the far (western) bank of the Aupa, the hilly terrain extends to the bend in the river where the bridge is located, commanding the ground as far as the *Jägerhügel,* and beyond it, the richly cultivated plain as far as Wysokow. This is in general, a flat piece of fertile land, bounded by hills and the Metau and Aupa Rivers.

The Skalitz position was frontally strong (providing opportunities for two or three tiered positions), but it had two great weaknesses. The Aupa to its rear, and the narrow area of deployment available on the [Austrian] left, which was commanded by higher ground.[27]

The position would have been formidable, if its weaknesses could be avoided and its strengths maximised. In particular if the narrow, open, northern front of the town was closed off by field fortifications, if it was flanked by substantial quantities of artillery from the far side of the Aupa, and if the 6th Corps was positioned in Skalitz, and Archduke Leopold's 8th Corps was brought up via Spitta and Kleny, as soon as the Prussian attack developed. Then [the Austrians] would have been indisputably master of the situation, with the artillery of two corps and their great superiority in cavalry.

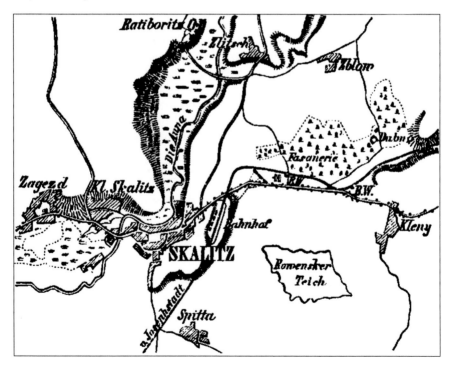

Sketch map of Skalitz.

27   Tr. Note: Kühne (pp. 14 – 18) provides an excellent description of the Skalitz position.

However, this did not take place. 6th Corps was positioned on the west bank of the Aupa, and 8th Corps, with three brigades[28] and two depot battalions (Crenneville and Degenfeld), took its place.

It was disposed thus:

> Battalion Crenneville: in the Dubno Woods (advanced position).[29]
> Brigade Fragnern: behind the Dubno Woods, in front of the Aupa heights (left wing).
> Brigade Kreyssern: to the right of the *Chaussée*, in front of the town (center).
> Brigade Schulz: to the right of Brigade Kreyssern, at the railway station (right wing).
> Battalion Degenfeld: in the marketplace and at the eastern entrance of the town.

All of these troops did not arrive in Skalitz before the early hours of the 28th. The first to arrive were Battalions Crenneville and Degenfeld, followed in rapid succession by the three brigades of 8th Corps. The brigade batteries were positioned alongside or to the rear of their respective infantry formations. The Corps Artillery Reserve went into position on the plateau before the eastern end of Skalitz, and took position on both sides of the *Chaussée*, two batteries to the south, three to the north. The enemy thus employed a total of eight batteries, or 64 guns.

The appearance and deployment of these forces was clearly observed by our side.

An eyewitness wrote:

> From 7:00 [am] or a bit later, the enemy was active. Clouds of dust swirled above Skalitz, and in the clear, clean air, we could clearly hear music playing in the town. Now and then a gust of wind would carry individual sounds, especially that of the big drum. We could observe the arrival of the troops for about 1½ to 2 hours, and we saw that the enemy must have brought up new brigades to fight against us.'
>
> In the event, our V Army Corps was facing an entire army, 70,000 men strong. In addition to the [Austrian] 8th Corps, 6th Corps had already gone into position as first reserve, 4th Corps was at Dolan, between Skalitz and Josephstadt, as second reserve. Nevertheless, *General* von Steinmetz resolved to attack. He disposed his forces as follows:
>
> The advanced guard (King's Grenadier Regiment Nr. 7 *et. al.*) was to advance from Wysokow to the railway embankment.
>
> The 17th and 22nd Brigades were to support the movement of the advanced guard to the right and left, or to precede it.
>
> The Main Body (10th Division) was to follow and envelop the enemy from right and left, storm the Aupa heights and enter Skalitz.

The action proceeded in accord with this plan. Before we describe the fighting, we shall point out the key points of the position with regard to our earlier description.

---

28   Author's Note: The 4th Brigade (Brigade Rothkirch) remained behind at Wildenschwerdt to protect the railway.
29   Tr. Note: Kühn, Friedjung and von Lettow- Vorbeck all agree that sending battalion Crenneville to the Dubno Woods was a tactical error which contributed significantly to the series of progressively ensuing disasters.

The Schafberg, the dominating height between Wysokow and Skalitz.
The Dubno Woods, pheasantry and *Unterförsterei* [under forester's lodge].
The railway curve between the pheasantry and the Skalitz railway station.
The Skalitz railway station and the Aupa heights.

The battle, itself, consisted of three main stages.

The capture of the Dubno Woods (shattering of Brigade Fragnern).
The clash at the railway embankment (shattering of Brigade Kreyssern).
Storming the Aupa heights, the capture of the railway station, entering the town.

Capture of the Dubno Woods

On the morning of the 28th, the positions of V Corps, including the 22nd Brigade, was as follows.

The 17th Brigade: Regiments 37 and 58, behind Nachod.
The King's Grenadier Regiment and the 10th Division north of Wysokow, in a valley.
The 22nd Brigade, Regiments 38 and 51, south of Wysokow, behind a burnt out farmstead.

The 17th Brigade moved out between 7:00 and 8:00 from its bivouac, which was far to the rear. It bypassed the town and Schloss of Nachod via roads to the north, reached the village of Studnitz, and then bore off to the left toward the Schafberg (between 9:00 and 10:00).

General von Steinmetz was already on the plateau of the Schafberg, which overlooked the wooded terrain as far as the Aupa heights. He had already ordered two batteries to go into position there. *Oberst* von Wittich (Chief of V Corps General Staff), observed from there by telescope, the advance of the Guards Cavalry Brigade (Prince Albrecht, son) toward Zernow. At the same time Austrian Cuirassier regiments appeared. *General* von Steinmetz ordered the batteries to open fire on the enemy cavalry. It was 10:00.

The 17th Infantry Brigade now reached the plateau of the Schafberg, swung its lead battalion to the right and formed into four waves (with full intervals) front facing Skalitz, the right flank of the first wave resting on the great sheep farm at Dubno. The deployment had barely finished when an extremely brisk shell-fire was opened on the brigade by the (30 to 40) guns of the batteries positioned north of Skalitz (10:15).

On our side, a third battery went into position north of the other two, but they all had to be pulled back [due to enemy fire]. The battery of smooth bore 12pdrs proved particularly useless at the great range of nearly 4,000 paces. In the meantime, the enemy batteries continued firing and put shell after shell into the position occupied by the 17th Brigade. Fortunately, nearly all their rounds bored deep into the ground and failed to explode, or merely threw up the sand without causing serious damage. The battalions unfurled their flags. The picturesque setting of the plateau and the bright sunlight heightened the beautiful martial appearance of the troops as they defied the hail of shells.

During this cannonade, *General* von Steinmetz received official word of the outcome of the Battle of Trautenau (on the 27th), as well as the resulting orders that had been issued to the

Guards Corps. Thus, he learned that he could not count on the previously promised support of the 2nd Guards Division, thereupon ordering that the attack proceed with his own forces. 'With the drums beating, forward!' The immediate objective of the attack was the woods at the foot of the Schafberg, between Dubno and the Aupa heights, the Dubno Woods. The 17th Brigade, Regiments Nr. 37 and 58, now advanced against [the Dubno Woods]. It was 11:00. However, at exactly the same time, the battalions of the advance – Guards (King's Grenadier Regiment Nr. 7, *Oberst* von Voigts – Rhetz), and the 22nd Brigade [*Generalmajor* von Hoffmann, from the VI Corps] that had advanced on the left flank, also entered the woods with hurrahs and joined the fight.

The leading half battalions crossed the eastern edge of the woods in four main columns, those from the 37th and 58th Regiments [17th Brigade] on the one side, those from the 7th [*Avantgarde*] and 38th [22nd Brigade, VI Corps][30] on the other. They took the southeastern corner, stormed the Dubno farmstead (the 38th in the lead) that was defended by the Crenneville Infantry and the 5th *Jäger* Battalion (which had arrived as reinforcements), and forced their way forward to the western border of the woods, their lines of attack crossing each other repeatedly and resulting in much confusion. There, where the road leading down from the village of Zlitsch reaches the *Unterförsterei* and then runs along the edge of the woods, the battalions reformed.

Up to this point the fighting had been relatively light. Nowhere, except at the Dubno [farm] buildings, had there been any determined resistance, and our losses had mainly resulted from the shell fire of the enemy batteries that had gone into position on the Aupa [heights]. However, although the wood itself had been taken without great loss, the terrain beyond it exacted far greater casualties. But first a few words regarding the ground that lay ahead.

As mentioned above, the road leading from Zlitsch to the railway and *Chausée* ran along the western edge of the woods. Rolling farmland planted with grain stretched for 1500 paces all the way to the Aupa, narrowing as it extended south between Skalitz and the railway embankment. A [small rectangular wood], densely planted with young pine trees, projected from the center of the [western edge] of the *fasanerie*, exactly at the location where, on the east side of the Zlitsch road stands the Dubno *Försterei* [the substantially built senior forester's lodge, sometimes referred to as a hunting lodge], flanked on both right and left by open fields and the hills rising above them.

The [Austrian] battalions retreating from the main part of the woods had established themselves here, in what the Austrian reports call the *'Gehege'* [the fenced in area – of young pine trees]. Now in closer contact with their reserves (that were between Skalitz and the Aupa heights), they were firmly resolved to halt [our] advance. The position was well chosen. In the *'Gehege,'* was a battalion of IR 15 Nassau with Battalion Crenneville to its left rear and the 5th *Jägers* to its right rear, the two last named units on elevated terrain. The position was thus in the form of a **T** [with the bar of the **T** parallel with the *Chausée* and the stem of the **T** extending into the *'Gehege'*].

This placed the enemy in a situation where they could meet any attack on their position [in the *'Gehege'*] with flanking fire. We wanted to eliminate this advantage before proceeding with the capture of the woods. At about 12:00 it was decided to take the elevated enemy positions

30   Tr. Note: *Generalmajor* von Hoffmann's 22nd Brigade, including Fusilier Regiment Nr. 38 and Infantry Regiment Nr. 51, belonged to VI Corps, and like all formations in the Prussian Army except *General* von Steinmetz's V Corps, was not organized in half battalions.

to the right and left [the bar of the **T**]. The 1st half battalion of the 58th advanced on the left against Battalion Crenneville, the 2nd half battalion of the 38th on the right against the 5th *Jägers*, and after not negligible casualties on our side, the flank positions were captured. Now was the moment to penetrate the *'Gehege'* itself. The Battalion of IR 15 Nassau, now stripped of its flank cover and already outflanked by the above named two half battalions, evacuated the untenable position and attempted to fall back to [the main Austrian army position on the Aupa heights], together with the two other formations that had already been defeated to its right and left. However, this retreat across an open field that provided no cover, was especially dangerous for the retreating battalions. The Nassau battalion lost a third of its complement, Battalion Crenneville (including the losses that had occurred in the Dubno Wood), lost half, the 5th *Jägers*, who diverted toward Zlitsch, had less substantial losses.[31]

The clash at the railway embankment

When the enemy saw us break out of the western margin of the Dubno Woods, and after a lengthy fight also capture the *'Gehege,'* he resolved to meet our advance with a counter attack. When he reached the Skalitz - Zlitsch road, he made a sudden right wheel through the cornfield as though he wanted to attack the *'Gehege'* and the Dubno Woods. Soon however, realizing that our attack was not only toward the west, but also towards the south (with the half battalions that had as yet not been heavily engaged), he changed the direction of his counter attack, swinging [south] toward the Nachod - Skaliltz *Chaussée*, to counter the danger there. Only a single battery, covered by *Jäger* and some infantry, kept to the more northerly direction and went into position on the road leading from Skalitz to Zlitsch in front of the *'Gehege,'* about 1,000 paces away. We present the events that preceded the capture of this battery before we go on to describe the fighting at the railway embankment.

Some of the 1st Battalion of the 38th Regiment, specifically the *Schützenzüge* [rifle platoons] of the 2nd, 3rd and 4th Companies, advanced from the *'Gehege'* across a bit of cornfield to a ditch that provided cover, as the enemy battery, hitherto covered by a hill, went into position in front of our 38th Regiment. *Oberstlieutenant* von Knobelsdorff, commander of the 1st Battalion of the 38th, then ordered the available rifle platoons to open rapid fire at 500 paces. About 14 horses immediately went down and the resulting confusion was evident. Only two guns opened fire, the covering infantry fired volley after volley, but the [Prussian] riflemen pressed forward with

31   Author's Note: In the above account, with regard to the battalions opposing us, we have in part based our description on the testimony of captured officers, and in part followed Austrian reports. However, the Austrian General Staff Work, which has appeared in the meantime, gives a different account. According to it, it appears that after the heavy losses suffered in the Dubno Woods, Battalion Crenneville retreated directly to Skalitz and that the *'Gehege,'* including its two flanking positions, was defended by the 5th *Jägers* and the entirety of IR 77 Salvator. Only after the position had already been lost did several parts of IR 15 Nassau appear to recapture it. These advanced across the ground between the *'Gehege'* and the railway, where they were met by such a murderous flanking and frontal fire (from the pheasantry), that they collapsed. *Generalmajor* von Fragnern was also killed in this attack. That is the official account of the enemy. We have declined to follow it unconditionally however. It is a natural and constantly recurring phenomenon, that the details in the firsthand accounts of the troops themselves, are generally closer to the truth than those given in the great military historical works that tend to focus more on the generalities than the specifics.

hurrahs and repeated their rapid fire at 200 paces, at which point everything fell apart to the degree that the remnants of the covering infantry and the gun crews sought salvation in flight. Five guns and two ammunition wagons fell into our hands. The battery commander, *Hauptmann* Prohaska, lay dead, *Oberlieutenant* Grosse, the *Oberfeuerwerker*, lay seriously wounded, between the guns the dead were thickly strewn. This success was not won without casualties on our side, *Hauptmann* von Kügelgen fell, 52 men were dead or wounded.

There was nothing decisive in these events. It was more a matter of a fine feat of arms, the more notable since it provided us with our only trophies of the day.

The main body of the enemy, as noted above, did not advance against the western margin of the woods however, but at the same time [as the attack on the 'Gehege'], advanced to the southwest corner in order to parry a threatened attack from there. In order to accomplish this, it had to march through the narrow ground between the *Chaussée* and the railway. When it entered that ground, we were already partially out of the woods.

The enemy columns belonged to Regiments IR 77 Salvator, IR 21 Reischach and IR 32 D'Este. On our side were half battalions from the 7th, 58th and 38th Regiments. Due to the importance of this fighting we detail it here.

The 3rd half battalion (von Natzmer) of King's Grenadier Regiment Nr. 7, moved out of the southwestern corner of the woods first, passed the [opening through the railway embankment], and immediately threw out skirmishers, advancing with its front facing Skalitz.

As soon as the half battalion passed the railway, it came under fire from enemy battalions that were already south of the *Chaussée*. At the same time, it took round after round of cannister from the guns that were positioned at the entrance to Skalitz. *Hauptmann* von Natzmer rode ahead of his battalion, loudly encouraging his men. His bravery contributed greatly to the half battalion making it through this murderous fire, continually advancing against the enemy. Finally however, they had to halt and seek cover in the *Chaussée* ditches since the rest of the regiment had not yet arrived. The two companies were too shaken by their losses (suffered in only a few minutes), to be able to advance against the battalions facing them with any prospect of success. A fire fight was conducted across the *Chaussée* which was overflowing with dead and wounded. *Hauptmann* von Natzmer was killed, *Portepée Fähnrich* Hoffmann likewise. In addition, six officers of this half battalion were also wounded, and this was only the prelude.

The actual assault by our side was carried out by three half battalions of the 58th, 38th and King's Grenadier Regiment, that broke out of the woods nearly simultaneously. The 6th and 7th Companies of the 58th, *Hauptmann* von der Horst, the 6th and 8th Companies of the 38th, *Hauptmann* Schrötter, and the 6th and 7th Companies of the King's Grenadier Regiment, *Hauptmann* von Kaisenberg. When half battalion von Natzmer was decimated, these were the half battalions that came against the enemy's advanced columns. We shall give the individual reports which, because the situation in general remained unchanged, have a certain relationship to each other. [In every case] our troops advanced, fell back, rallied, advanced again, repulsed the enemy, and captured the *Chaussée*.

Now we allow the individual half battalions to speak for themselves. As they do, examine our little map of Skalitz, on which, despite the limited space, the advance of these three half battalions (between the *Chaussée* and the railway), is quite clearly indicated.

First the men of the 58th:

' … the enemy … eager to avenge the humiliation of Nachod, advanced with a half right at the double to turn our left flank. *Oberst* von François, halting on a hillock, ordered our half battalion von der Horst to cross the railway and advance against the enemy. The drums beat, the trumpeters of their own accord, accompanied this with the signal to advance. As if on the parade ground, we advanced under shrapnel fire. *Major* von Haugwitz led our half battalion. It debouched from the railway cutting (at the southwest corner of the Dubno Woods) and marched on the far side [of the embankment] against the advancing enemy brigade, south of the railway. On its right was a half battalion of the King's Grenadier Regiment. Yet farther to the right was a half battalion of the 38th,[32] easily recognized on this day because they wore field caps [instead of helmets]. We advanced rapidly but soon the forward movement came to a halt. We had reached approximately the halfway point between the first and second railway underpasses, when we suddenly came under the effective fire of the [Austrian] battalions that had remained behind in Skalitz. We needed cover from this fire. *Major* von Haugwitz ordered us to cross over to the north side of the railway embankment. At that very moment this brave officer was hit by a bullet in the abdomen, just after he had his horse shot out from under him. He died of his wounds in the hospital at Reinerz on 24th July.

Losses mounted rapidly. *Lieutenant* von Manstein suddenly found himself in the midst of a group of Austrians that pressed in on him from three sides as, with individual riflemen, he crossed the railway (at kilometer stone 133). At that very moment, a shell that burst among the enemy also threw him to the ground and blinded him with the earth that it threw in his face. He considered himself lost. Then Musketeer Polein of his company (the 7th) grabbed him and dragged him into a small ditch under the whistling bullets. There he knelt down beside him and held off the approaching Austrians with his sure and steady fire. When finally the other men of the platoon came up, Polein bandaged *Lieutenant* von Manstein (who in the meantime had taken another round through his upper arm), with extreme care and carried him out of the fire to the dressing station. In so doing he was himself wounded by a shell in the thigh.

This report of the 58th was strikingly supplemented by a report of the 38th, whose half battalion Schrötter (6th and 8th Companies) had the right flank. From that we take the following:

With the King's Grenadiers on our left we reached the railway and crossed the embankment. We had hardly advanced 50 paces toward the station (between the station and the *Chaussée*) when we were inundated with a hail of shells and cannister and *Oberstlieutenant* von Wenckstern fell, killed by a shell. The half battalion suffered heavy losses of men and officers. The wounded *Hauptmann* Schrötter ordered us to fall back behind the railway embankment, since the half battalion of the 58th (*Major* von Haugwitz) had also fallen back to there through the railway underpass. A short rest, then *Hauptmann* von Rettberg assumed command, and after briefly rallying,

32   Tr. Note: It was only natural that the writer of this piece, himself a member of one of Steinmetz' (V Corps) half battalions, would speak of two companies as a '*half battalion*.' Infantry Regiment 38 belonged to von Mutius' VI Corps, which was not organized in half battalions.

the half battalion advanced anew, crossed the railway embankment and advanced toward the *Chausée*. Fresh losses, *Oberst* von Witzleben, our regimental Commander, who had advanced with the half battalion, was hit by a round from a rifle and sank from his horse. At that very moment new columns advancing in various directions, emerged from Skalitz. However, we were now ready for them. The 2nd Battalion Este [Austrian] advanced on the right and left to within 200 paces of the *Chaussée*. It was at full strength and despite our fire, continued to advance bravely. 100 paces from our half battalion, at the edge of a field, it crouched, halted and fired. We could see the officers leap forward with swords raised, encouraging the battalion to advance farther, but their efforts were in vain. The battalion held out for a few more volleys, then it turned, and closed up but at the run, retreated to the railway station. Our half battalion pursued, the drummers and trumpeters joining in. The remnants of Battalion Este retreated, some to the far side of the railway embankment, some to the buildings of the railway station which increasingly became the decisive point. Our men, too weak to force the ever strengthening railway station, took up a covered position alongside the *Chaussée*.'

With *Major* von Haugwitz (58th) on their right, *Oberstlieutenant* von Wenkstern (38th) on their left, half battalion von Kaisenberg (6th and 7th Companies) of the King's Grenadier Regiment, advanced in the center of our attacking line. The report says:

Half battalion von Kaisenberg emerged from the woods a little after half battalion von Natzmer, and after a stubborn fire fight, pursued the enemy infantry along the north side of the embankment. It now bore to the south, passed through the much mentioned railway cutting, and alongside the half battalions of other regiments, advanced toward the *Chausée* with skirmishers in the lead. *Hauptmann* von Kaisenberg was always 50 paces ahead of his men. This half battalion too, soon came under heavy artillery and small arms fire, and after beating off several small attacks, found itself facing a fresh, advancing Austrian brigade. It was Brigade Kreyssern, Regiment Reischach in the first wave. The brigade approached to within 100 paces of the half battalion under extremely heavy fire, still maintaining good order. It halted and the battalions of the first wave fired a volley, fortunately too high. Immediately after the volley, the brigade launched a bayonet attack but was brought to a standstill in the face of the half battalion, which remained in line and opened a rapid fire. The brigade could not get past this fire. It advanced to within 50 paces and then turned in flight. We too had suffered heavy losses. *Hauptmann* von Kaisenberg was seriously wounded in the head. Five other officers were also wounded.

This bloody fight with our three half battalions had shaken the enemy and halted his forward movement. The more so since, to the right and left of them, other half battalions from Regiments 7, 38 and 58, had also repulsed the enemy though with fewer losses.[33]

---

33 Author's Note: Leading the three regiments named above that were advancing on the right and left, was half battalion von Necker (2nd and 3rd Companies) of the King's Grenadier Regiment. Its involvement was significant. While half battalions von Natzmer and von Kaisenberg, following each other (with front facing Skaliltz), threw themselves against the advancing Brigade Kreyssern,

Under cover of their artillery, these two Brigades (Fragnern and Kreyssern), along with the still intact Brigade Schulz, began to retreat simultaneously, in part south to the Aupa, and in part through Skalitz. However, they still left sufficient battalions behind to mount a substantial defense against the concentric attack that we were now preparing against Skalitz.

We shall now turn to this final act of the battle.

Storming the Aupa heights, the railway station and the town

While a bitter fight raged on the narrow ground between the *Chaussée* and railway embankment, the decisive stroke was being prepared on the flank and in the rear. At 12.00, on the ground between the Dubno woods and the Aupa Heights, the main body of V Corps (the 10th Division) appeared, and as it had done the preceding day at Nachod, brought about the decision. In the first rank were the same regiments, the 6th and 47th.

The Divisional Commander, seeing how the battle had developed, divided his approaching division as it arrived, sending Brigade Tiedemann (in accordance with its original objective), to attack the Aupa Heights. He then redirected half of brigade Wittich (Regiment Nr. 47), from right flank to left, to finally tip the balance at the railway embankment and station, where [the Austrians] had mounted a last, desperate defense.

We shall first follow Brigade Tiedemann, on the right flank. A report stated:

> The 6th Regiment was in the lead. The thunder of the guns rolled loud above the chatter of the infantry fire as the 19th Brigade (Regiments 6 and 46), advanced along the right side of the ridge (which separated us from the Skalitz plain). Rapidly, soundlessly, the movement proceeded with muffled commands. Only individual officers stole a glance over the crest of the ridge, which was combed by shellfire. Directly in the path of our march, on the plateau north of Zlitsch, cavalry was visible that was advancing from Kosteletz southwards via Zernow. It was, in brightly shining cuirasses, the heavy Guards Cavalry Brigade under Prince Albrecht (son).
>
> As the 19th Brigade reached Dubno, the second wave of the 20th Brigade (Regiment Nr. 47) was ordered to launch a simultaneous attack, adjoining the left flank of the 19th Brigade, south of the *Chaussée*. In accordance with this order, and under heavy flanking fire, the six half battalions of the 47th Regiment crossed the fire swept embankment. (We shall return to this attack, which as already indicated, finally broke the enemy's resistance).
>
> We had almost reached Zlitch when the enemy batteries north of Skalitz began to pull out. Knapsacks were hastily discarded behind the last hillock by Zbow. Then, with

half battalion von Necker was on the railway embankment and could fire into the left flank of the attacking brigade. This contributed essentially to the overall success. It then advanced from the railway embankment to the *Chausée*, which was still held by individual groups of [Austrian] skirmishers [that had been thrown out by] the enemy brigade [during its advance]. *Hauptmann* von Necker advanced with his rifle platoons as far as the *Chaussée* ditches and became involved in a fire fight. After this had caused substantial losses without achieving any results, *Hauptmann* von Necker leaped up with his men and fell upon the (surprised) enemy. A short, bloody hand to hand fight ensued. The brave men who opposed us fell after a desperate defense.

a perfectly executed turn to the left, we charged the enemy troops on the *Jägerhügel*, who with the exception of the *Jäger* battalion, fell back into the town without waiting.

The brilliant charge of the 19th Brigade (praised by our comrades in the other regiments), was a magnificent sight. Captured Austrian officers later described how, ' ... they were totally surprised, not so much by the charge of twelve fresh battalions (half battalions) as by the speed and determination of the attack, emphasised by the short drumbeats, the advance at the double – officers leading, and the long, drawn out hurrah.' This charge was all the more decisive since the storming of the *Jägerhügel* (which was highly visible from everywhere), was like a signal that carried all of the other troops on the plain with it in the final assault. All of the battalions, from the extreme left flank to the extreme right flank, leaped forward and concentrically charged with jubilant hurrahs against the still mighty wreathe of fire at Skalitz.

Several groups of *Jäger* still attempted hold out. They defended their positions until they were only 50 paces from the bayonets of our battalions, but at 2:15, the Austrian left wing was swept from the heights down into the town as if by a storm wind.[34]

The 6th Regiment stormed through the northern entrance [to the town]. Between this and the *Chaussée*, where there was a second entrance, a half battalion of the 52nd Regiment advanced. The 38th advanced west of the railway, and on the *Chausée* itself, the 7th advanced (right through the barricades). Finally, leading elements of the 47th Regiment (which was engaged in heavy fighting against the railway station), entered the eastern and southern perimeter of the town. The left flank of the 47th made it to the marketplace. The town itself (in which, for example, the house of the royal Lippisch master builder Luppe, had to be stormed three times) was defended to the last by the 4th Battalions of Regiments Crenneville and Degenfeld.[35]

The capture of the railway station, as indicated in the above report, came just before the advance into the town. Now we turn to that event itself (the capture of the railway station) as described by an eyewitness. A member of the 47th wrote:

After we made the flank march via Studnitz and Zlitsch, the entire division was now on the right of our position, between Zlitsch and the Dubno *Försterei*. The Dubno woods were to our rear, the Aupa Heights before us. *General* von Steinmetz rode up to us. His orders were brief, to attack both wings of the enemy position. Regiments 6 and 46 were ordered to advance against the Aupa Heights (right wing), Regiments 47 and

---

34 Author's Note: Half battalion von Unruh (1st and 4th Companies of the King's Grenadier Regiment), appears to have fought at this location, only further north. Then, after a fight with the 24th *Jäger* Battalion in a gravel pit, where *Lieutenant* von St. Paul, adjutant to Prince Adalbert [Prince Adalbert of Prussia, founder the German Navy, who has already appeared in the front line at Nachod] was killed, helped storm the Aupa Heights.

35 Author's Note: The defense of Skalitz, including the railway station, was conducted by only six battalions, after the brigades had been ordered back by the Corps Command. Three of these (the 3rd Battalion Este and the 5th and 24th *Jägers*) were at the northern and northeastern entrances, two (the 4th Battalions Crenneville and Degenfeld) covered the eastern entrance of the town. The railway station was defended by the 31st *Jäger* Battalion of Brigade Schulz.

52 were to advance against the railway embankment and railway station (left wing). Only the leading regiments 6 and 47 actually got into action.

Thus, we had to take the railway station, the strongest point of the enemy position. We advanced in two waves, three half battalions in each. *Major* von Brandenstein commanded the first wave, *Major* von Heinemann the second. When the orders reached us, we were so far to the right that, in order to reach our objective (the railway station), we had to make a half left over the *Chaussée*, and then march nearly parallel with the enemy position for a good 1000 paces. It was no easy matter to maintain the proper front while taking constant fire in the right flank. As soon as we were level with the railway station it was 'By the right flank, march!' towards [the railway station]. Rifle platoons [*Schützenzüge*] of the 1st Battalion were thrown out in front, the regiment followed 70 to 80 paces behind, the waves at the regulation distance, the second flanking on the right, the half battalions in column to the center [*Colonne nach der Mitte*], left shoulder arms, drums beating in a calm march tempo. The degree to which we were able to maintain the regulation order in this advance (in part through tall standing grain) is best illustrated by the remark of an Austrian General that was reported by a prisoner, 'Look at that! The b - - - - are coming on as if they're on parade.' The two half battalions of the 1st Battalion climbed the railway embankment and stormed the railway station buildings. Only once was there a hesitation. We had nearly reached the embankment, and the enemy once more concentrated his fire on our center where the new battalion standard seemed to glow in the sunlight. The standard bearer fell as did the *Unteroffiziere* [non-commissioned officers] near him. For a moment the movement ceased but the commander of the half battalion, *Hauptmann* Bellay, the wave commander, *Major* von Bandenstein, and his Adjutant, *Premierlieutenant* von Desfeld, whose horses had been shot, immediately threw themselves into the gap. The latter grabbed the standard and we advanced. The Adjutant of the battalion, *Lieutenant* Hoffman, spurred his horse and with a few leaps, was first on the embankment. All followed, cheering. The infantry defending the embankment and the station buildings (mostly from the 31st *Jägers*), had either fled, surrendered, or found an honourable death in the last, futile resistance. Immediately after we advanced past the fortified farmsteads into the town. The battle was decided.

Skalitz was ours, the battle ended. There was no actual pursuit. Only artillery fire from the heights south of the town accompanied the enemy's retreat to Josephstadt (8th and 6th Corps).

At 4:00 our troops, exhausted by manouevring and fighting in the scorching heat of the sun, marched into bivouacs. Brigade Hoffmann (38th and 51st Regiments) provided outposts that were positioned on the far side of the Aupa, toward Josephstadt. In recognition of what it had achieved, the King's Grenadier Regiment was quartered in Skalitz. The 9th Division bivouacked north of the 10th Division south of the Nachod - Skalitz road.

The Austrian 8th Corps marched that same day to Salney. The 6th Corps, which positioned one brigade at Trebesow to receive the 8th Corps, followed toward Lançow.

Skalitz was a great success, though it was only gained with significant sacrifice. Our total losses amounted to 62 officers and 1,352 men. The King's Grenadier Regiment and Silesian Fusilier Regiment Nr. 38 lost the most, followed by Infantry Regiment Nr. 58. Among the wounded were the commanders of both of the latter regiments, *Oberst* von Witzleben and *Oberst* von François. We give the following numbers:

> King's Grenadier Regiment ....22 officers, 475 men.
> Fusilier Regiment Nr. 38 ....11 officers, 325 men.
> Infantry Regiment Nr. 58 ....11 officers, 146 men.

All of the *Hauptleute* [Captains, plural of *Hauptmann*] of the 2nd Battalion of the King's Grenadier Regiment (which had the heaviest losses - 14 officers and 292 men) were dead or wounded. *Hauptmann* von Natzmer was dead, *Hauptmann* von Lewinsky and *Hauptmann* von Bültzingslowen wounded. *Hauptmann* von Kaisenberg I, hit by two bullets, still led his half battalion onward against the enemy. The 2nd Battalion of the 38th Regiment had similar losses. The commander of the battalion, *Oberstlieutenant* von Wenckstern was killed, *Major* von Haugwitz of the 58th later died of his wounds.

The enemy losses were enormous. With essentially only two brigades (14,000) men actually under fire, he lost more than one third of his strength: 5,577 men, including 205 officers. Individual battalions lost up to half their complement, some even more.

Their losses:

> Battalion Crenneville (probably only 800 men strong) ....400 men.
> 24th *Jäger* Battalion...464 men.
> 5th *Jäger* Battalion...517 men.
> Regiment Salvator (three battalions) ....1,463 men.

Their losses in officers were: Regiment Salvator 42, Regiment Reischach 33, the 5th *Jägers* lost 19 officers, nearly its entire complement.

Skalitz was one of the bloodiest actions of the entire war, certainly for our enemy. Nowhere did he display greater courage. The attack of IR 21 Reischach, the conduct of Battalion Crenneville, but especially the conduct of the three *Jäger* Battalions (5th, 24th and 31st) was beyond all praise.[36] The great number of prisoners that fell into our hands (nearly 3,000 including 1,300 unwounded), does nothing to change that. It was only as the battalions realized that their heroic efforts were in vain that some elements panicked. Most of the prisoners were taken in Skalitz, itself, our entry from three sides cut off their retreat.

Generalmajor von Fragnern and *Oberst* Kreyssern fell at the head of their respective brigades.

The positions that were to have covered the concentration of the enemy armies at Josephstadt were now in our hands.

---

36   Author's Note: Numerous examples bear witness to the fierceness with which the enemy fought. *Lieutenant* Baron, adjutant of the 1st Battalion, 58th Regiment, was shot in the abdomen and fell from his horse. Lying on the ground he followed the victorious progress of the fighting with a joyful eye. Suddenly he found himself being attacked by a similarly wounded Austrian, who was crawling towards him with a rifle. Fortunately for him, he was still able to kill the enemy (who was aiming at him) with a shot from his revolver. (We append a sequel to this account. Two hours later, musketeers of the 58th were bearing *Lieutenant* Baron back to Skalitz on their rifles when the leader of a cuirassier patrol that was passing by, leaped from his horse, plucked a rose from a garden and laid it on the breast of the apparently mortally wounded man as a farewell. *Lieutenant* Baron did recover).

Fighting at Skalitz station.

The Fighting at Schweinschädel

The left wing of the Crown Prince's army was honoured with yet a third day of battle. On the 27th V Corps had advanced to Nachod and Wysokow, on the 28th to Skalitz, the 29th was to bring it to Gradlitz.

To prevent this advance, the [enemy's] second reserve, the Austrian 4th Corps under *Feldmarschallieutenant Graf* Festetics) had on the previous day, taken up position behind Skalitz on the great road leading to Josephstadt, at the village of Schweinschädel. Eight batteries had gone into position on the hills on both sides of the village. In and to the left of the village was Brigade Pöckh,[37] to the right (south of the village), Brigade Archduke [*Erzherzog*] Joseph, about

37   Author's Note: The detailed dispositions of Brigade Pöckh (which had to meet the main thrust), are as follows:

The 8th *Jäger* Battalion and the brigade battery, advanced to the northeast to the Trebesow brick kiln.
The 1st Battalion IR 37 Archduke Joseph was at the northern edge of Schweinschädel.
The 2nd and 3rd Battalions IR 37 Archduke Joseph were in the village itself, some in the [very large] dairy farm.
Regiment IR 51 Archduke Ferdinand was in front of Sebutsch, as a refused left flank.

Two battalions from IR 67 Schmerling of Brigade Archduke Joseph, which was positioned south of the *Chaussée*) [Confusingly there is a Regiment Archduke Joseph and a Brigade Archduke Joseph, both in the same corps], later participated in the defense of the sheep farm [*Schäferei*] and the brick yard [*Ziegelei*] between Schweinschädel and Sebutsch. One and a half battalions from Brigade Brandenstein

a mile behind Schweinschädel (also on the highway), Brigade Brandenstein. (The fourth Brigade of 4th Corps, Brigade Fleischhacker, was detached and was engaged at this very moment in the action at Königinhof.)

Reconnaissance on our side had informed *General* von Steinmetz of the enemy position. After the two bloody engagements on the 27th and 28th, [*General* von Steinmetz] was not inclined to engage in a third merely for the sake of it, and it seemed desirable to at least make an attempt to pass the enemy position (to the north via Chwalkowitz), in his advance to Gradlitz. During this flank march, only a left flank detachment (advancing on the great Josephstadt road), was to immobilize the enemy, whom it was expected, would fall back of his own accord when he finally became aware that he had been outflanked.

In accordance with this, *General* von Steinmetz issued his orders as follows:

> The 20th Brigade, Wittich, followed by Cavalry Brigade Wnuck, is to form a left flank detachment that is to advance (via Zajezd) on the great Josephstadt road, and then rejoin the main body of the corps at Miskoles.
>
> The 19th Brigade, *Generalmajor* von Tiedemann, is to proceed via Zlitsch and Ratiboritz to Weternik and Miskoles and reach the Chwalkowitz - Gradlitz road from there.
>
> The Main Body (9th Division, *Generalmajor* von Löwenfeld) is to follow the 19th Brigade.
>
> Brigade Hoffmann (Regiments 38 and 51) is to follow the Main Body.

The troops, needing rest and calm after their efforts of the previous days, did not move out of their bivouacs until 3:00 in the afternoon. First off was 20th Brigade (the left flank detachment under *Generalmajor* Wittich), which followed the great Josephstadt road as far as Trebesow [Trschebeschow] without meeting any resistance. Here its orders were to bear off to the right toward Miskoles, to unite with the 19th Brigade and the main body (9th Division), when it came under heavy fire from Schweinschädel, and became involved in fighting that rapidly took on a serious character.

Meantime, the 19th Brigade [*Avantgarde*] advanced on the Zlitsch Road in order to outflank the enemy position. After climbing onto the plateau from Chwalkowitz it had just reached the village of Miskoles, when the thunder of the guns coming from the [south], left no doubt that the left flank detachment [20th Brigade] was involved in a lively action with the enemy. It was impossible to simply leave the detachment (Regiments 52 and 47) on their own, and so the plan to bypass the enemy's left flank had to be given up. The 19th Brigade, von Tiedemann, was now ordered to disengage the 20th Brigade, *General* Wittich (which was already in action between Trebesow and Schweinschädel), with a powerful thrust to the south, into the enemy left flank.

In accordance with this order, the 19th Brigade swung to the left as it debouched from Miskoles, the 6th Regiment in the first wave, the 46th in the second, and coming from the north, attacked Brigade Pöckh which was positioned in the front, flank and rear of Schweinschädel.

(one from IR 12 Archduke Wilhelm, and a half battalion from IR 26 Grand Duke [*Großfürst*] Michael, took part in the very last moments of the fighting. In addition we mention in passing, that purely by chance, on this day, *Regiment* Archduke Joseph (belonging to Brigade Pöckh) and *Brigade* Archduke Joseph were under fire right beside each other.

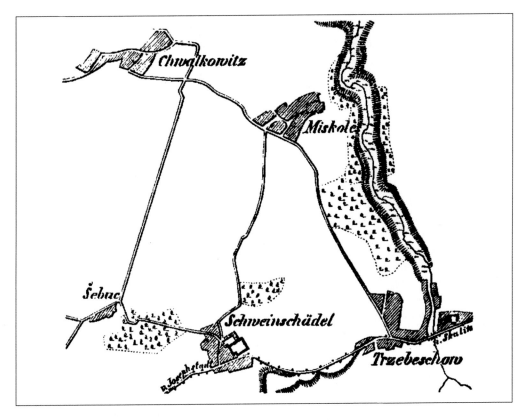

Sketch map of Schweinschädel.

The first assault hit the enemy 8th *Jäger* Battalion and swept it from the plateau into the villages below. A counter-attack from the 1st Battalion of Regiment Archduke Joseph was repulsed. In their irresistible advance, the half battalions of the 6th Regiment forced their way into the great dairy complex[38] that was defended by the 2nd Battalion, Archduke Joseph. Our men of the 46th (in the meantime included in the first wave) entered Sebutsch and the sheep farm that lay between it and Schweinschädel brickyard.[39] Two [Austrian] battalions of IR 67 Schmerling, the 1st and 3rd, that were positioned on the far side of the *Chaussée*, mounted a ferocious but ultimately unsuccessful counter-attack.

38   Tr. Note: The dairy farm was a large, enclosed, formidable complex of brick and stone. It had been loopholed and provided with firing platforms, thereby increasing its resemblance to that of a fortress. It formed the eastern and northern borders of [Schweinschädel] north of the *Chaussée* and east of the village street that led to Miskoles.

39   Tr. Note: The sheep farm was a long, whitewashed, solidly constructed, tile roofed, one story building, visible from afar and easily improved for defense. However, it was surrounded by orchards that obstructed its field of fire and provided attackers with a covered approach.

All of these movements were carried out simultaneously, but despite a courageous defense, the enemy was defeated in an extremely short time. His losses were already substantial, but they would worsen yet.

After taking the sheep farm and brickyard, the 46th occupied a position in the rear of the Austrian battalions still engaged in Schweinschädel, and now formed a sort of living wall, so that any [enemy] who tried to fall back from the front, had to undergo fierce flanking fire. The 1st Battalion IR 37 Archduke Joseph, which made this attempt, suffered enormous losses. Following that, the fighting died out. The line Schweinschädel - Sebutsch remained in our hands until three hours later when we voluntarily relinquished it.

On the enemy side, except for his numerous artillery, only Brigade Pöckh was really engaged. On our side Brigade Tiedemann (Regiments 6 and 46) was engaged. We take the following regarding the attack on the line Schweinschädel – Sebutsch, from the report of an officer of Grenadier Regiment Nr. 6. Much of it may serve as recapitulation of what has already been said:

> Thus, it became a matter of disengaging *Generalmajor* Wittich's 20th Brigade, which was on our left flank. As our leading elements debouched from Miskoles, they came under enemy shell fire. Now with a ' Left -March!' we mounted the plateau and advanced in a long line, front facing south, against the enemy position. It was 4:00. We now found ourselves on an elevated plain (whose southern slope, from Skalitz to Schweinschädel, followed the *Chaussée* to Josephstadt), dissected by broad, steep sided gullies, that ran south and cut the plateau into several high ridges. One of these ridges separated the villages of Schweinschädel and Sebutsch, Schweinschädel lying to the southeast, Sebutsch to the northwest. Both villages are so deep in their respective hollows that one cannot bring artillery to bear and can only see their roofs when within a few hundred paces. The ridge that separates them, also links them in a certain sense, in that there is a large sheep farm on the crest with a walled orchard extending south from it, and adjoining that on the side toward Schweinschädel, a large brickyard.
>
> The diagonal line across the ridge thus described, gives a general idea of the Austrian position. At its center, probably occupied by battalions of Brigade Pöckh, namely Regiment Archduke Joseph, was the sheep farm and the brickyard. In front of these two was the majority of their artillery. As for the villages themselves, Sebutsch, with its wretched huts was without tactical significance. Schweinschädel, with its massively built dairy, which took up nearly the entire eastern side of the village, provided ample means for defense. Sunken roads and fruit orchards surrounded by high walls lay before it. The doors of the northern front were blocked, the walls of the buildings provided with loopholes and firing platforms. Since none of these structures could be brought under artillery fire, we only became fully aware of these details when we stood right before them. The enemy might well have put up a more stubborn defense than we encountered, he did not fight badly, but neither did he fight well. As we advanced, the brigade came under shell fire and at the same time, rifle fire, from the sunken roads that were in front of it. Only then were the knapsacks left in a hollow in the ground where we rested twenty minutes.[40] During this time the 46th Regiment,

---

40 Author's Note: This rest was essential. Another letter states: 'Our advance against the village of

which had hitherto followed us as a second wave, came up on our right and into the first line. The attack now proceeded in four main columns. The left flank of Regiment Nr. 6 (half battalion von Webern, the 11th and 12th companies) took the eastern part of Schweinschädel, including the dairy. The 2nd Fusiliers from Trebesow, also joined the attack here.

The right flank of Regiment Nr. 6 (the 5th, 7th and 9th Companies) took the remainder of the village. The left flank of Regiment Nr. 46 took the enemy center, the sheep farm and the brickyard. The right flank of Regiment Nr. 46 took the village of Sebutsch.

Our two center columns, the right flank of Regiment Nr. 6 and the left flank of Regiment Nr. 46, were both involved in a joint attack on the sheep farm and brickyard. Our riflemen, officers in the lead, clambered over the orchard walls with the help of the climbing and vaulting that they had learned in the gym, broke open the barred doors, searched all the houses and outbuildings and gathered numerous prisoners from all sides. The actual fighting lasted barely ten minutes. It was a rapid and lasting success. It was only on the extreme right flank that half battalion von Gössnitz, the 9th and 12th Companies of Regiment Nr. 46, finally ran into trouble. Capturing Sebutsch in their first charge, the half battalion continued on and attacked a ridge between the village and *Chaussée* that was strongly held by the enemy. Met by volleys from several intact battalions of Brigade Brandenstein, our two companies were nearly shattered by the enemy fire. All of the officers of the half battalion were dead or wounded. The Adjutant, *Lieutenant* von Burghoff, assumed command of the remnant, led them back to Sebutsch and occupied the village. *Major* von Grolmann of the General Staff, was also wounded in this attack that failed with such heavy losses.

So much for the report. This check on our extreme right flank was insignificant in respect of the overall course of the action. The enemy, after suffering heavy losses at the three main points, the dairy, the sheep farm and the brickyard, found it advisable to calmly carry out his retreat to Josephstadt under cover of his batteries. *General* von Steinmetz, who for his part had only engaged in the action to [clear the road to Gradlitz], now issued strict orders to refrain from any pursuit of the enemy. All of the battalions that were engaged on the line Schweinschädel - Sebutsch, were pulled back onto the plateau.

An eyewitness wrote: 'One by one the sheep farm, the brickyard, and finally Schweinschädel, were evacuated by us. Our battalions slowly fell back to the hills, again under a heavy barrage of shells and rockets. As the last companies withdrew from Schweinschädel, the evening sun shone through the powder smoke and the thick clouds of dust, creating the illusion that the village really was going up in flames.'

The action at Schweinschädel cost the V Army Corps 15 officers and 379 men. The majority of the losses were suffered by the advance Guards, the 6th and 46th Regiments. The latter lost five officers (four killed) and 159 men. Both regiments had fought with great distinction. The

Schweinschädel was one of the most exhausting efforts of the war. In scorching midday heat we had to advance through fields of rape that stood chest high. You have no idea what an effort such an advance requires. Some people collapsed from exhaustion as if dead. Even the horses were exhausted and could barely get through.'

Fighting at Schweinschädel.

colours of the 1st and 2nd Battalions of the 6th Regiment were hit. The colour bearers, *Sergeant* Senftleben and *Sergeant* Franke, were wounded. Franke (2nd Battalion) was shot in the right arm. He took the colours in his left and stormed on forward with his battalion. (The sergeant's name was later engraved on the silver ring of the flag, which was hit four times at Skalitz and Schweinschädel).

A standard belonging to Regiment Archduke Joseph was captured by a *Gefreiter* [corporal] of the 2nd Battalion. *Oberst* Walther von Monbary (who, despite the head wound he had received at Nachod, remained with the regiment), had the battalion form a circle and promoted the *Gefreiter* on the spot to *Unteroffizier* and colour bearer. As already mentioned, the only other troops involved in the fighting were from the left flank detachment (especially Fusiliers of the 52nd), but their losses were less significant.

The Austrians lost 39 officers and 1,411 men, of which 1,026 were lost by Regiment Archduke Joseph. The rest came from the 8th *Jäger* Battalion and Regiment Schmerling.

It was 7:00 when the fighting came to an end. Under the protection of the Heavy Guards Cavalry Brigade (Prince Albrecht, son) all the wounded were brought to safety. The plateau was held by the rear guard (Brigade Tiedemann) of V Corps until 9:00. The main body had long since departed, passed Chwalkowitz, and at about 2.00, arrived in bivouac at Gradlitz.

With that, the Crown Prince's Army had for its part, reached the rendezvous.

The V Corps from Nachod to Gradlitz

The task assigned to V Corps had been accomplished. During the night of 28/29th *General* von Steinmetz dispatched the following telegram to the King:

> I report a second victory to Your Majesty that is greater and bloodier than that of the 27th (Nachod). Again, several trophies were captured. Numerous prisoners were taken. Skalitz is in my hands. Facing me was Archduke Leopold with 8th Corps.

That was early on the 29th, in the evening, after the action at Schweinschädel, he could add:

> 4th Corps has also been vanquished. The way to the Elbe is open.

Our V Corps made its way down from the Silesian mountains to the Upper Elbe in three stages, Nachod, Skalitz and Schweinschädel. Each stage was a victory. Three enemy corps were beaten, crippled, or forced back. This entire action was recognized by friend and foe as an outstanding accomplishment. Both the greatest dangers and the greatest honours were on the left wing, there is general agreement on this, but which of these three days bears the most distinction, which had the most significance. We too ask these questions.

The Austrians tend to underestimate the significance of Nachod. 'One who takes an impartial view of things (so says an enemy report) must admit that 6th Army Corps, *Feldmarschalllieutenant* Ramming, accomplished its mission on the 27th. For us the 27th was a strategic success in that, despite heavy fighting and substantial losses, we reached and occupied Skalitz.'[41] Those are smooth and skillfully chosen words. Not only do they touch upon the truth, they bring out some significant points, and yet we cannot agree with what they say. There is too much that they fail to say. If they were actually correct and entirely to the point, then Nachod would be reduced to a mere, 'hindrance to the [Austrian] march' that was fortunately and successfully removed. According to that, we wanted to prevent them from reaching a chosen objective. This, however, is unconditionally false. We did not position ourselves to block the advance of 6th Corps. Indeed, we were hardly in a position (with the few battalions that we had available at 10:00), to proceed offensively against them. It was more a matter of repulsing their attacks, attacks that he (the enemy) launched with all his forces, of his own accord. The enemy remains silent regarding these points. Skalitz was not reached [by the Austrians] thanks to the battle of Wysokow – Nachod, but in spite of it. A simple detour to the left would have brought the same result and avoided the defeat.

All of this seems to us to be incontrovertible. On the other hand, we can happily concede that Nachod was a greater victory for us than it was a misfortune for the Austrians. The enemy did indeed reach and occupy Skalitz, that is beyond question. However, this result (which we could not have prevented), could have been achieved at far less cost, thereby erecting a protective wall behind which Benedek could achieve the concentration of his army before leading it northwest against Prince Friedrich Karl. On a grand scale, regarding the big picture, the fighting on the

---

41 Tr. Note: This passage is at variance with the official Austrian General Staff Study.

27th did not [significantly] damage our enemy. His losses were simply expressed as a number, and that was 7,000 men.

Nachod was a defeat, that is indisputable, but it was a defeat that did not have far reaching effects, perhaps it was without strategic significance, not so Skalitz. The loss of Skalitz was of the highest strategic significance, not primarily because it was lost, but because of the special circumstances and conditions under which it was lost. Had these accompanying circumstances and conditions been different, then this new loss, just as that of the previous day, could be presented as relatively insignificant. If Benedek, while he carried on and completed his concentration undisturbed, had left 6th Corps behind to defend Skalitz, and if 6th Corps had then been beaten anew (or even half destroyed) while all of the other corps arrived at Jospehstadt, and then advanced (like the wind) toward the specified objective (Gitschin), then Skalitz would only have been a continuation of Nachod, a misfortune to be expressed in numbers, that could be more than cancelled out by a great, victorious blow against the [Prussian] 1st Army.

Therefore, the defeat at Skalitz was not such a great defeat in and of itself. It became so thanks to the particular circumstances under which it took place. First of all, instead of it being a second defeat of 6th Corps, it was the defeat of a new corps which had been diverted from its actual objective, the march toward Gitschin. This diversion from its original objective could only be justified by a resounding victory. A victory would have justified the temporary departure from the established plan, if it provided both the means and the way to regain the time that was lost. However, a new corps, which was originally tasked with a different mission, was engaged at Skalitz without adding victory to its standards. That made Skalitz, not merely a culpable inconsequence, not merely a defeat, but a *strategically* important defeat, disrupting plans and arrangements and preparing the way for further failures, or at the very least, allowing the chance of [an Austrian] victory to freely slip through their hands. Only now were Benedek's calculations rendered false, more through his actions than ours, more as the result of his errors than of our victory.[42]

Schweinschädel, by absorbing yet another fresh corps (the 4th), was simply a continuation of the previous errors, a continuation that put the seal on what had happened and made it irretrievable.

With reason, Benedek, whose initial plan cannot simply be condemned out of hand, has been harshly judged for his weakness and vacillation. Right up to the end, no definite plan was ever evident. Here he was more guilty than at Königgrätz. Half measures were the signature of the days from the 27th to the 30th. Steinmetz was the opposite, all clarity, iron will and energy.

Thus, things went as they did, and a spirit was born that allowed him to report in the telegram cited above, 'My troops are still full of courage and joy after two battles. They break out in loud

---

42 Author's Note: In this judgement we have constantly looked on Benedek (though also wavering and unsure) as holding to his original plan, i.e. to strike a blow against the 1st Army. If at a given moment, he had shown sufficient flexibility to entirely abandon his original plan, and instead to strike a blow against the 2nd Army, then all would not have been lost on the evening of the 28th. An energetic advance on the 29th with two intact corps (4th and 2nd Corps) in front, and the 6th and 8th Corps in reserve, could have made up for much, and provided him with breathing room and relative freedom of action. All that would only have been possible if he had the strength to decide instead of vacillating to the last.

jubilation.' If such was the mood of the troops on the 28th, by the 29th (Schweinschädel) the jubilation had become intoxication. The entire corps was filled with enthusiasm for Steinmetz.

An officer wrote from the camp at Gradlitz on the 30th:

> You know, he is like forged iron, and I am putting it mildly when I say that we have feared him more than loved him. All that, however, lies far in the past. Now we love him. He has conquered all, the Austrians and us. If early today, as the first shells landed in our camp, he led us to the Elbe and said to us, 'Now. Jump in,' I believe that we would have thrown ourselves into the river, packs and all, and would have waded and swum through it. He has caught our imagination, his name is the third word in every conversation. Steinmetz anecdotes go from mouth to mouth, both humorous and serious. Whether they are true or not is irrelevant. The mood from which they arise is genuine. At Nachod a *Hauptmann* called to him that he could no longer hold his battery. Steinmetz rode up and saw a picture of destruction. 'Yes, that won't work, but pulling back won't work, either. Go fetch help. I will stay here.' And so he did. As the incoming rounds burst, the cannoneers cheered and called out, 'Hurrah for Steinmetz!' Perhaps it was at that location where his old groom whispered to him, 'Excellency, the air is full of lead'. 'It's not hitting us', growled the old one to himself. This, 'It's not hitting us' went from mouth to mouth. It had a magic ring. At Skalitz I saw him when the report came that the Guards (engaged, at Burkersdorf) could bring us no help. He looked serious, more serious than usual, but his eyes, no matter how hard he blinked, still had something shining in them. The day before yesterday however, there was a cloud over him, as he rode past, our battalion had lain down to take cover. He shook his head. 'Fusiliers,' he called, 'today we are all going to die. But we want to go there. Let nobody lie on the ground until he is fallen.' At once everyone stood up ramrod straight. You know that he is supposed to have said when his wife died, 'Now I have only my God and the service.' We in 'the service' were not always pleased with that. Now we think otherwise.

Such was the mood of the corps. The King, however, expressed his thanks in the following letter:

> I learn from the reports of the Crown Prince, my son, as Commander of the 2nd Army, of the four day victory of such importance and decisiveness for the operations of the entire army, which you, *Herr General*, with your brave, excellent V Army Corps have fought. At the same time on the 27th and 28th, that you have been victorious in an independently conducted two day battle, so that I hereby express my royal recognition to the highest and fullest degree. It is thanks only to your energy and your effect on your brave troops that they, through their endurance and courage could face, and vanquish daily, fresh enemy corps. And you, *Herr General*, have the honour in so doing, of playing the largest part in contributing to the success of the difficult operations that I have assigned to the entire army, its concentration from Silesia and Saxony in Bohemia. In recognition of your great merit, as well as in recognition of the heroic achievements of your troops, I award you my *Orden des Schwarzen Adlers* [High Order of the Black Eagle] as well as the *Großkreuz des Rothen Adler Ordens* [Great Cross of the

Order of the Red Eagle] that goes with it, this however, *mit Schwerten* [with swords].
I am proud to award this highest decoration, for the first time since my late father
and King did so in the War for Independence, for great distinction before the enemy!
The Army and Nation will thereby read on your chest, what you have accomplished
through and for them, Your grateful, truly devoted King, Wilhelm.

And, as King and army, so was the entire land. Everyone felt Prussia has another York, and in
the *'Neuen Krieglsliedern'* [New Songs of the War], which followed our victories (as fast as the
victories themselves) it says, in dashing rhyme:

> *Steinmetz struck many a good blow,*
> *On a bloody day in June.*
> *That day became three,*
> *Each bloodier than the last.*
> *Steinmetz counted many fallen.*
> *None failed in their work for him,*
> *They struck hard, they struck true,*
> *And Austria was the hard stone.*

The image of *'Steinmetzen'* [the stone cutter] who finally mastered the hard stone, recurred in
all manner of shapes and sizes, and the Silesians and German Poles (as in the old style of *'Prinz
Eugen'* [Prince Eugene], sang in villages and inns;

> *Indeed the stone was hard and tough,*
> *But Steinmetz was not a fool.*
> *He kept hammering away on it,*
> *So that the sparks fell all around*
> *And the dust flew from it.*
> *Blood red was leaf and moss.*

Throughout the fatherland and beyond the borders of Prussia, all united in praising the 'brave
stone cutter' [*Steinmetzen*]. However, the one so honoured wrote, 'Fortune has made me more
humble than misfortune probably would have.'

The I Corps – *General* von Bonin

I Corps formed the right wing of the Crown Prince's army. Just as on the 27th when V Corps
had to advance into Bohemia through the Nachod gate, so I Corps had to push through the
Trautenau gate. Let us see how it performed its task.

I Corps, with the exception of Fusilier Regiment Nr. 33 (which was with the Elbe Army) was
complete and consisted exclusively of Prussian regiments. Its order of battle was:

1st Division (*Generallieutenant* **von Grossmann**):
    1st Brigade: *Generalmajor* **von Pape.**
        1st East Prussian Grenadier Regiment (Crown Prince) Nr. 1.

41st Infantry Regiment.
2nd Brigade: *Generalmajor Freiherr* **von Barnekow.**
3rd Infantry Regiment.
43rd Infantry Regiment.
Lithuanian Dragoon Regiment Nr. 1.

2nd Division (*Generallieutenant* **von Clausewitz).**
3rd Brigade: *Generalmajor* **von Malotki.**
4th Infantry Regiment.
44th Infantry Regiment.
4th Brigade: *Generalmajor* **von Buddenbrock.**
5th Infantry Regiment.
45th Infantry Regiment.
Leibhusaren - Regiment Nr. 1 and the East Prussian *Jäger* Battalion Nr. 1.
Reserve - Cavalry Brigade (*Oberst* **von Bredow):**
East Prussian Cuirassier Regiment Nr. 3.
East Prussian Uhlan Regiment Nr. 8.
Lithuanian Uhlan Regiment Nr. 12
In addition, a total of 16 batteries with 96 guns.

General der Infanterie von Bonin commanded the army corps. Adolf von Bonin was born on 11th November 1803. Enlisted in the Cadet Corps, he became a *Secondelieutenant* in the 2nd Guards Regiment when he was barely 18 years old. That same year (1821) he attended the *Kriegsschule* and was later assigned to headquarters duty with the Guards Corps. In 1833 he became personal Adjutant of Prince Adalbert, in 1838 *FlügelAdjutant* of His Majesty the King. He rapidly rose, becoming *Oberstlieutenant* in 1848, *Oberst* in 1851, *Generalmajor* and Commander of the 4th Regiment] in 1854, and in 1858, of the 1st Guards Infantry Brigade. That same year, after he had commanded the 5th Division in the autumn manoeuvers, he received the 1st Guards Division and was promoted to *Generallieutenant* when named as *GeneralAdjutant* to His Majesty the King. In 1864 he became *General der Infanterie.* In the previous year (1863) he was named Commanding General of I Army Corps.

I Army Corps was always considered one of the best in the army. The uniformity of its men, the vigour of the lineage from which it was recruited, the superiority of its horses, always gave it the caché of an elite force. The bravery and endurance with which the East Prussian regiments had fought during the Napoleonic wars, even during the unfortunate campaigns of 1806/7, lived on in its traditions. The people and the army expected much from this corps. Now we shall accompany it on its advance through 'the Trautenau Gate.'

Trautenau, about 4.6 miles from the Prussian border, was with Reichenberg, one of the most significant cloth towns of Bohemia. It is the center and main market for the flax spinning industry in all of Austria, and the prosperity of it individual firms, and the industriousness of its people, gave it an orderly and cheerful appearance. It has the character of a thriving English textile town. As in all Bohemian towns, the *Ringplatz* was its center, adjoined by two suburbs, the *Obervorstadt* (to the west) and the *Niedervorstadt* (to the east).

The population of Trautenau (approximately 5,000) is German. The Czech inhabitants form a foreign element that receives little consideration and contributes nothing to the character of the town. Its German population, its proximity to the border, and the weekly yarn and linen market, which is also usually much attended from Silesia, were the reasons that the commerce with the neighbouring Prussian province had always been of a friendly nature. The weeks and months immediately preceding the war had however, brought about a change. The decline in business and the needs of the workers had soured the mood.

So much for the town and its people. Now a word regarding its setting. Trautenau is on the right bank of the River Aupa, just over a mile west of the place where the river, coming from the west, makes a right angled bend to the south. The location of this bend in the river, where the village of Parcshnitz lies, is important. All of the roads that lead from Silesia over the mountains meet here and then continue, as a single road, to Trautenau. On 27th June, I Corps advanced on two of these roads.[43]

Until they reach the Aupa bend (at Parschnitz), these two roads run through narrow, at times canyon like defiles, which are difficult to pass through and could be closed by a few companies.

These difficulties disappear on the short stretch from Parschnitz to Trautenau (on the left bank of the Aupa where the broad highway has been upgraded to a *Chaussée)*, however they are replaced by new dangers. Ridges of significant steepness (with varying names) wall the valley on both sides, so that any attacker who wants to advance here is lost if his enemy is fortunate enough to have already taken up a position on these hills. Fortunately for us this had not happened. Had it been otherwise, the valley of the Aupa might well have become a 'Valley of Death' for us. We passed through the defile before the enemy arrived and before he took possession of Trautenau or the three hills encircling the town to the south, the Hopfenberg, Kapellenberg, and Galgenberg.

Now let us take a look at the enemy. 10th Corps was assigned the defense of the 'Trautenau Gate.' It arrived at the Upper Elbe on 25th June on its march from Olmütz and had bivouacked that day between Schurz and Jaromirz. The corps consisted of four brigades:

Brigade *Oberst* Mondl.[44]
   IR 24 Parma and IR 10 Mazzuchelli. 12th *Jäger* Battalion.
Brigade *Oberst* Grivicic.
   IR 2 Emperor Alexander and IR 23 Airoldi. 16th *Jäger* Battalion.
Brigade *Generalmajor* von Wimpffen.
   IR 13 Bamberg and IR 58 Archduke Stephan (the latter with four battalions, therefore no *Jäger* Battalion.)
Brigade *Generalmajor* von Knebel.
   IR 1 Emperor Franz Joseph and IR 3 Archduke Karl. 28th *Feldjäger* Battalion.

As usual, a 4 pdr battery and a squadron of cavalry were attached to each brigade. The reserve artillery consisted of five batteries (40 guns), so that the total artillery of 10th Corps consisted of

---

43   Author's Note: A third road, coming from the south where it follows the lower course of the Aupa, also forms a junction at Parschnitz. I Corps did not advance on this road, it was used by the 1st Guards Division, coming from Eypel. This [Guards Division] marched to Qualisch and turned when, at 3:00 in the afternoon, *General* von Bonin declined its support.

44   Tr. Note: The correct spelling is Mondel, however, the Prussian General Staff work consistently spells it Mondl, as does Fontane.

72 guns. The General commanding 10th Corps was *Feldmarschialllieutenant* von Gablenz, who arrived at the headquarters (which at that time were at Olmütz), on the 19th. The 10th Corps remained in camp on the 26th at Jaromirz. Only Brigade Mondl advanced to the northeast (to Prausnitz – Kaile), and thus toward Trautenan. The dispositions for the 27th were:

> Brigade Mondl was to move out early in the morning from Prausnitz – Kaile and attempt to be in Trautenau by 8:00 in the morning.
> The three other brigades of the corps were to move out of the camp at Schurz - Jaromirz at 8:00 in the morning and follow Brigade Mondl via Prausnitz – Kaile, to Trautenau.
> So much for the dispositions.

If the specified times had been strictly observed, Brigade Mondl would have arrived in Trautenau at the same time, or ahead of the [Prussian] *Avantgarde*. However, this did not take place, despite delays on our side, we arrived there first.

Now we shall follow the advance of our I Corps:

Austrian Dragoon.

Trautenau

As already mentioned in brief, I Army Corps advanced towards Trautenau on two roads:

> The 1st Division (on the left) followed by the Reserve Artillery, via Liebau and Golden Öls (a right flank detachment proceeded via Schatzlar and Ober - Altstadt).
> The 2nd Division (on the right) followed by the Reserve Cavalry, via Schömberg and Albendorf.

The rendezvous for the two division was the village of Parschnitz, where the roads joined at the bend in the Aupa.

The 1st Division, *Generallieutenant* von Grossmann provided the *Avantgarde*. This consisted of:

> 1st [East Prussian Grnds. Nr. 1 Crown Prince] and 41st Infantry Regiments.
> East Prussian *Jäger* Battalion Nr. 1.
> Lithuanian Dragoon Regiment Nr. 1.
> Three batteries.

The 2nd Division formed the Main Body, the 3rd [East Prussian Grenadier Regiment Nr. 3] and 43rd [6th East Prussian] regiments followed as Reserve.

The columns moved out at 4:00 in the morning. The distance to Parschnitz on each of the two roads was just under seven miles.[45] It was assumed that [both forces] would arrive at the rendezvous at about 8:00 and advance from there to Trautenau. The Main Body arrived at the appointed place at the designated time, not so the *Avantgarde*. This ran into considerable difficulties associated with the terrain (at Golden Öls the men had to march in single file) so that delay was unavoidable. It was 10:00 by the time that the *Avantgarde* reached Parschnitz.

At this point the Commanding General (von Bonin) ordered the following dispositions:

> The *Avantgarde* is to proceed up the Aupa Valley to Trautenau and is to occupy [the town] and the surrounding hills that command the town.
> The Main Body is to operate as the left wing, take the hills between Parschnitz and Trautenau, advance to the southwest and threaten the flank and rear of the enemy (his flank if he approaches from the south, his rear if he has already occupied Trautenau).
> The outcome of these operations will determine whether it will be possible for the army corps to advance farther westward to Arnau.

At this point it should be noted that one of the main reasons why we lost the battle, was because the main body (Left Wing) did not deploy its strength. The opening situation, even though giving cause for serious concern, was nevertheless favourable to us. The *Avantgarde* took the commanding heights (the Kapellenberg *etc.*) at noon (which could have been done by our forces

---

45   Tr. Note: The route assigned to the right wing Column was about one mile longer than that on the left, it was also more difficult to traverse.

without effort or sacrifice [three hours earlier] at 9:00). The oversight was thus made good, but at a bloody price, it was not a good omen. We now go to the two opening moments of the action, the occupation of Trautenau at 9:30, and the storming of the Kapellenberg at 12:00.

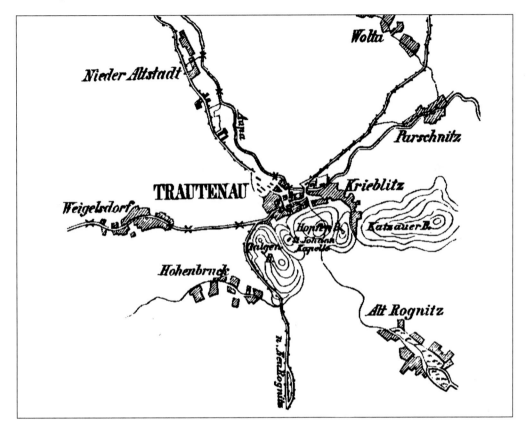

Sketch map of Trautenau.

An Austrian eyewitness[46] wrote:

> 'Early on 27th June' so says the enemy reporter, a resident of Trautenau, ' we were advised that food must be cooked by 9:00 in the morning for the four squadrons of the Windischgrätz Dragoons, who had formed the garrison of our town for several weeks. Shortly thereafter news arrived that an advanced detachment of our Windischgrätzers had already been engaged. Several had fallen. The appearance of our town soon assumed a curious aspect. A squadron of Dragoons held the marketplace. Riders and horse drawn vehicles hurried here and there and individual groups stood under the

---

46   Tr. Note: The 'eyewitness' was probably Dr. Hieronymus von Roth, the *Bürgermeister*.

arcades to exchange rumours and news. In all families there was great excitement and anxious expectation.

At 8:00 in the morning the squadron in the marketplace fell back toward Königinhof, and at brief intervals, other detachments of the Windischgrätzers arrived from Parschnitz and followed on the same road (toward Königinhof). The last detachment of Dragoons barricaded the so called *Spittelbrücke* [Spittel Bridge] in the Niedervorstadt [suburb east of the town] and then also withdrew. It was 9:00.

From the Trautenau church tower and from the Deanery, the Prussian troops, which halted at Parschnitz, could be clearly seen. Soon Prussian outposts could be identified on the northern hills right by Trautenau toward the Hummelhof [hill directly north of Trautenau, just west of Kommandeurhohe Spittlberg]. There were reports that the Austrian forces were moving towards Trautenau or Bausnitz. Their approach could not be observed from the town because the hills immediately south of Trautenau, the Galgenberg, the Johannesberg [variously referred to as the Kapellenberg – Church Hill, or the Johannesberg – Hill of St. John. The small chapel on the summit is dedicated to St. John] and the Hopfenberg, blocked the view to that side.

At 9:30 it was reported that the Prussians were advancing from Parschnitz in two infantry columns to the right and left of the road with the artillery on the road, itself. They had to halt in the *Niedervorstadt* at the barricaded bridge, and the Prussians immediately cleared the barricade without meeting any resistance. Approximately two or three squadrons of Prussian Dragoons crossed the Aupa above the *Mittelvorstadt* [Central suburb], and the infantry, following closely behind, entered the unoccupied town at 10:00 in the morning.

A Dragoon officer dismounted before the inn '*zum weißen Roß*' [The White Horse] and ordered a dinner for 18 [to be served] at 2:00 in the afternoon, along with quarters and stabling, and asked whether there were Austrian military forces in the town. Our answer was, 'Aside from the Dragoons with whom you skirmished and who withdrew an hour ago, there are no Austrian military forces in Trautenau.'[47]

Long columns of Prussians, one regiment after another, bands in front, now appeared in the square. Individual battalions stacked their rifles in the arcades and sought refreshments, which were offered to them from all sides. Other battalions only passed through the *Ringplatz* and continued onward toward the *Obervorstadt* [upper suburb, west of the town].

Their arrival may have lasted more than half an hour. The entire town was occupied by the Prussian forces and was entirely peaceful. Individual groups of people quietly watched the military performance. The inns were over-filled with soldiers. Then, suddenly, rifle shots could be heard to the west, from the *Obervorstadt*, which soon became continuous. Shortly after the Prussians had arrived, the vanguard (12th *Jäger* Battalion) of Brigade Mondl, which was approaching from Prausnitz - Kaile, took

---

47 Author's Note: This answer was entirely truthful. At that hour Brigade Mondl was not yet there. In any case, there could be no talk of 'being enticed into a mouse-trap.' The forces that we began to deploy were far too imposing, and Brigade Mondl too weak. These [enemy forces] were also defeated. All of the difficulties that we then had to overcome were not the result of enemy cunning, but of our own neglect.

up position on the hills south of the town, unnoticed by the residents of Trautenau. Individual *Jägers* occupied some of the houses of the *Obervorstadt* where a fire fight now developed. At the same time, the Windischgrätz [Dragoons] moved closer to the town, so close that they were directly on the right flank of the *Jäger* in the hills and on the slopes.

Fighting with Mondl, the Kapellenberg in the background.

The advance of the Windischgrätzer was also noticed by the Prussians, and three Prussian squadrons immediately advanced against ours. The enemy attack failed.[48]

48 Author's Note: It was the famous Lithuanian Dragoons that attacked. As is true of all of the cavalry actions of this war, controversy arose here too. Initially both sides bragged greatly, and while an Austrian report stated that 'The Lithuanian Dragoons were wiped out,' the Prussians said 'that the Yorkish Lithuanians defeat the Windischgrätz [Dragoons] daily.' That was too much on both sides. Nevertheless, the Austrian General Staff Work stated that (before infantry fire gave the action a different turn), 'the Prussian cavalry was defeated and pursued.' *Oberst* von Bernhardi, who led the 'Lithuanians' at Trautenau, has replied to this. His measured, carefully chosen words have the ring of

Within a few minutes 23 riderless Prussian horses came into Weigelsdorf. The battle was carried on by our *Jäger*, who with their accurate rifles, firing mostly from cover, exacted substantial losses from the Prussian Dragoons.

In the meantime the Austrian *Jäger* continued to move eastwards toward Parschnitz, some along the slope, some on the hill, while the main body of Brigade Mondl, hurried forward at the double, Regiments Parma and Mazzuchelli occupying the Galgenberg and Hopfenberg, but especially the Johannesberg (Kapellenberg) which lies between the two.

Now the action became livelier and more general. The Prussians positioned themselves firmly in the houses facing [the reverse slopes of these hills] and opened a murderous fire from the upper stories of the houses on the *Ringplatz*, and in the *Ober* and *Niedergasse* [upper and lower streets] against the Austrian brigade that was positioned in the hills. In the meantime, artillery fire could already be heard. We could see other Prussian battalions being sent to storm the heights. Soon the Kapellenberg was captured. It was a desperate struggle. The powder smoke obscured all clear vision. I myself, saw a Prussian officer enter one of the houses. 'Hold your fire', he called to the soldiers, 'Those are our men.' Brigade Mondl fought with great bravery. It attempted to hold the chapel, even after the Kapellenberg had been captured by the Prussians, but it had to fall back. Retreating step by step, they gave up their positions on the Galgenberg, Johannesberg and Hopfenberg,[49] and withdrew over the hills to the south, past the village of Hohenbruck where they established another position.'

truth. He said, 'The Lithuanian Dragoon Regiment acquired nothing but honour, attacking with 2¾ squadrons an enemy force of at least four squadrons at a full gallop, despite the unfavourable terrain, breaking through in places fighting hand to hand. However, while happily recognizing the brave and chivalrous action of the Imperial Dragoon Regiment, Prince Windischgrätz, we can neither concede victory to them nor confirm that they were left in possession of the battlefield, since as the result of heavy fire, both sides broke off the fighting *simultaneously* and fell back before a final settlement could be attained by the *arm blanche*.'

49 Author's Note: The capture of the three southern hills, the Galgenberg, Hopfenberg and Kapellenberg, was primarily achieved by the musketeer battalions of Regiment Nr. 41. The forces were distributed as follows:

The 1st Company held the houses on the eastern side of the marketplace;
The 2nd Company directed its attack against the Galgenberg;
The 6th Company against the Hopfenberg;
The 4th, 7th and 8th Companies against the Kapellenberg

In addition, the rifle platoons of the Fusilier Battalion, under *Hauptmann* von Buddenbrock, played a large part in the assault. The fighting that developed for the Hopfenberg and Kapellenberg was fierce, fiercest in the chapel itself. This chapel, a circular, rococo structure, filled with Madonnas and sacred pictures, with carved angels and haloes, was defended with extreme bravery by a detachment of IR 24 Parma. On our side it was the men of the 7th Company, under *Hauptmann* von Hanstein, and the fusiliers under *Hauptmann* von Buddenbrock, that carried the assault into the building. Our enemy (Polish) [East Galician, Polish/Ukrainian], squeezed and encircled by superior forces, finally fell back to the organ loft and refused to surrender. Now a fire fight developed inside the church, at such short range that the opponents could almost hold hands. The pews and floor began to show those well-known dark spots that cannot be washed away. An angel on the alter was shot through the shoulder.

So much for the enemy account. It generally agrees with the Prussian reports. The *Avantgarde*, as already indicated, had achieved with great effort at noon, what it could have attained with no effort at 9:00. A certain force was thereby expended that could have been employed at a later hour in the action, most probably to gain success.

Developments on the Left Wing

The capture of the Kapellenberg, which was achieved by 12:00 by individual *Jäger* companies and two battalions of Regiment Nr. 41, under *Oberstlieutenant* von Koblinski, was an *Avantgarde* success, not so with the retreat of the enemy to Hohenbruck and beyond. This withdrawal resulted primarily, if not exclusively, from the advance on the left wing. We now turn our discussion to this advance.

The Main Body of I Corps operated on the left wing and comprised Regiments Nr. 4 and 44, 5 and 45. The dispositions, as we know, essentially required [the Main Body] to advance against the enemy right flank, and thereby assist the *Avantgarde* in its task to occupy Trautenau, capture the hills to its south, and pursue the enemy to Hohenbruck.

Generallieutenant von Clausewitz (who commanded the left wing), brought Regiments 44 and 45 forward, formed an advance Guards of individual battalions and companies, crossed the Aupa about 500 paces west of Parschnitz, and then advanced against the southern hills. The defense was weak since Brigade Mondl, recognizing the importance of holding Trautenau, could only spare a few units (the 12th *Jägers* and a Battalion of IR 10 Mazzuchelli) to defend this position. The ground was extremely difficult, making a rapid advance nearly impossible. The enemy fell back slowly, initially past the Katzauer Hill to Kriblitz, then to Alt Rognitz and finally, past Alt Rognitz to Rudersdorf. It was a rifleman's fight, a sort of forest and hill hunt. The troops that were in the first line on our side were the Fusilier Battalion, and the 1st and 8th Companies of the 45th Regiment. Three companies of the 44th [Regiment] also joined them. The direction and style of combat was the same for all these units, which at various times supported each other.

The graphic account below is from an officer of the 45th, whose company (the 1st) was pretty much at the centre of things (thus the narrator could observe the course of the action to his left and right):

> *Oberst* von Boswell ordered our 1st Company to exert pressure on the enemy right flank. We took off our knapsacks and advanced onto the hills. It seemed to be *Jäger* facing us. Nevertheless they shot too high so we had few losses. The terrain was terrible but we pressed on, by noon the enemy seemed to be withdrawing everywhere . . . . The other companies of our battalion were no longer visible, so we simply directed our movement forward, and attempted to at least maintain contact with the rapidly withdrawing enemy. In so doing we took thirty to forty prisoners and probably discovered just as many dead and wounded. Soon, while constantly pursuing the enemy, we climbed a

---

The organ and organ loft were riddled with Prussian bullets. A *Major* and a *Hauptmann*, after repeated requests, finally surrendered. All of the [Austrian] men fell.

steep slope south of the village of Kriblitz and pushed on from there with a half left until we got to woods that were south (left) of Alt Rognitz.

At this moment the Divisional Commander, *Generallieutenant* von Clausewitz, who had reconnoitered the enemy's right flank, showed up and ordered our Company Commander (*Hauptmann* von Harder), to reconnoiter the enemy position again before he launched an attack on the woods that were in front of us. It turned out that not only the woods, but probably Alt Rognitz itself, was also occupied [by the enemy].

Three companies of the 44th Regiment had now arrived, with whom our 1st Company immediately launched a joint attack upon the woods. The enemy fell back with hardly any resistance on Alt Rognitz, which he now began to defend stubbornly with *Jäger* and other infantry. He held on particularly firmly near the church. For a moment our attack came to a halt until *Fähnrich* Milinofski broke off to the left and took the enemy in the flank, surprising him. At the same moment we charged (supported by the men of the 44th) with a hurrah, and took the village in the first assault ... The enemy fled, pursued by our fire. *Hauptmann* von Harder joined the skirmish line in order to personally lead the pursuit.

Fields of tall grain, which lay before Alt Rognitz and Rudersdorf, seriously hindered the pursuit. Nevertheless, it went forward quickly as far as the stream that cut the sunken road from Alt Rognitz to Saugwitz, and which flowed from west to east about 1000 paces before Alt Rognitz.

Here the ground between Saugwitz, Eypel, Unter and Ober Raatsch, Staudenz and Burkersdorf (the same terrain where, the following day, the Guards had fierce fighting) offered many opportunities for defense, and the enemy put up fierce resistance. Fighting continued here for a good hour. To our left, toward Saugwitz and Eypel, our 45th Fusiliers had taken a covered position. To the right, our 8th Company and two companies of the 44th shot it out with the enemy. We (the 1st Company of the 45th) and the 4th Company of the 44th formed the center. All in all, we were a little over two battalions strong. The enemy poured a hail of shells and cannister upon us without causing any losses. Everywhere the enemy fell back.'

Positions at 3:00

It was now 3:00. Our battalions on the left wing were in front of Alt Rognitz. The *Avantgarde*, on the right wing, had advanced as far as Hohenbruck.

At about this point *General* von Hiller [*Generallieutenant* Hiller von Gärtringen] reported to the Commanding General of I Corps and offered the assistance of the 1st Guards Division. *General* von Bonin declined his offer with thanks. He referred to the battlefield where the enemy was evidently retreating along the entire line.

It seemed that a complete victory had been achieved, but in actual fact it only appeared so. It was not Gablenz's corps that had been forced back, it was only his advance Guards (Brigade Mondl). The corps itself, at that very moment, was approaching with three brigades.

The overall situation (which was being celebrated prematurely), might be compared with the unhappy day in October 1806, when a General congratulated the Commanding Officer, Prince Hohenlohe, on his success. The momentary lull on the battlefield was considered to indicate the defeat of the enemy. However, it was only the [enemy] assembling his forces for the decisive blow. As Prince [Hohenlohe] accepted the congratulations the other side were speaking the historic words, *Ils se tromperont furieusement*. [They greatly delude themselves]. Here too, there was self-deception.

Brigades Grivicic and Wimpffen arrive 4:00 – 5:00

At nearly the same moment that *General* von Bonin declined help from the Guards, Brigades Grivicic and Wimpffen arrived. Only Brigade Knebel was still *en route*. *Feldmarschallieutenant* von Gablenz quickly deployed his forces. He had Brigade Grivicic advance on the right alongside Brigade Mondl, in a lateral, angled position, facing our left wing at Alt Rognitz, [while Brigade Wimpffen] attacked Trautenau and the three hills before it.

The appearance of these brigades had not gone unnoticed on our side, and as the enemy reports put it, caused visible confusion. *General* von Bonin (and this was good) did indeed issue orders to engage the enemy with all available forces. However, the *Avantgarde* that had been at Hohenbruck, did not fall back to the three hills [the Galgenberg, Johannesberg and Hopfenberg], but [all the way] to Trautenau, thereby removing itself from the fighting. In their place, the reserve brigade, *Generalmajor* von Barnekow, moved into the hill position and occupied the Kapellenberg, as well as the ground to its left. The serious fighting that now took place, was (so far as the right wing is concerned), exclusively conducted by this brigade. To it was reserved the privilege (at least *partially*) of making the day of Trautenau a glorious day for I Corps.

Up to this point, despite nearly nine hours of fighting, the battle had been characterized by a certain hesitancy, now it developed rapidly. While his three fresh brigades formed up for the attack, *Feldmarschiallieutnent* von Gablenz placed five batteries (a total of 40 guns) in a line to the south, between Hohenbruck and Kaltenhof, and had them open fire on the Kapellenberg, which was increasingly seen as the key to the position. The gunfire raged for an hour along the entire line. We now had two batteries (twelve guns) on the hill to reply.[50]

A third, Battery Böhnke, had already been forced to withdraw because it had been left with no support. Only when he believed that our position had been sufficiently softened up, did *Feldmarschallieutenant* von Gablenz order Brigade Wimpffen to storm the Johannesberg. Brigade Grivicic was ordered to support, or as the case might be, open the frontal attack with an energetic thrust against our left flank (our 44th and 45th were essentially positioned with front facing west).

We shall first follow Brigade Grivicic.

---

50 Author's Note: The author of the *Taktischen Rückblicke*, in his highly worthwhile pamphlet regarding the fighting at Trautenau (Berlin, F. Dümmler, 1869) remarks, with reason, regarding this miserly employment of artillery, 'An artillery officer who has a tactical eye for the terrain, will always find a place. At Trautenau there was no such person. Thus only a few batteries were brought into action, and these only for a few moments. The list of losses bears witness to their endurance in action. Of the 1,338 total men lost to the corps, the 16 batteries only lost seven wounded, and out of the overall loss of 78 horses, [the batteries] lost only two. Therefore, not even half a man per battery and one eighth of a horse. It was, quite certainly, not due to a lack of personal courage, but the ground seemed unfavourable and one did not want to expose the artillery to a possible setback. Therefore, most of the batteries were not even allowed onto the actual battlefield. There was no shortage of space or time to put all 96 guns in position. However, one would rather lose the battle than a single gun.'

An Austrian report stated:

> Our attack failed. It was an inspiring sight as our courageous *Oberst* Grivicic had the troops of his outstanding brigade first form up in two waves, and after a brief speech in Hungarian, accompanied by loud cheers, march forward to the strains of the Radetzky March to attack the wooded hills. However, it was in vain. The enemy held the position with stubborn determination. The needle gun was devastatingly effective.[51]

So much for Brigade Grivicic. Things went no better for Brigade Wimpffen, which launched its assault to the left [of Brigade Grivicic]. [Brigade Wimpffen] also formed in two lines of attack. Two Battalions IR 58 Archduke Stephan on the left of the *Chaussée*, two battalions IR 13 Bamberg to the right. The first wave attacked the Chapel of St. Johann, the second wave behind. An enemy report states;

> We watched with high expectations. The brigade climbed the rather steep slopes of the hill and crossed several sunken roads running parallel to the front, without losing its cohesion. To the music of the band, the battalions maintained their advance until extremely close to the chapel, at which point the attack came to a halt. Met with devastating small arms fire, the brigade was unable to go any further. Despite heroic endeavours, it had to fall back where it concentrated at Hohenbruck.

Thus, the assault of both brigades foundered. On the left wing (Alt Rognitz), the 44th and 45th, on the right wing (Chapel of St. Johann), the 43rd Regiment had repulsed the attack.

Once more there was success, but it almost seemed as if we had not recognized it as such. Instead of energetically concentrating the last of our battalions (which had indeed been stretched, but in no way worn out), instead of sending all the forces that were in Trautenau onto the endangered Hill of St. Johann, the only thought was to bring the forces that were already there, back to safety. The 44th and 45th, even though victorious, retreated to Parschnitz. The 43rd (only two battalions strong), was ordered to retreat through the position of Grenadier

---

51   Author's Note: A [Prussian] report (from a man of the 45th) states: 'Our *Oberstlieutenant* von Schmeling, fearing that our main position on the Kapellenberg could be compromised if the left wing fell back, resolved to commit his Fusilier Battalion and the 1st and 8th Companies of the regiment for the good of all. Calling on the companies by signal and word, he threw them against the first wave of the enemy, who was approaching in two compact columns. Two Battalions IR 23 Airoldi, one Battalion IR 2 Alexander, and the 16th *Jägers* Battalion, attacked on both sides. To the music of their bands, the four enemy battalions answered us with *Hochs* and *Hurrahs*, and so we clashed. The 8th, 10th and 11th Companies became involved in hand to hand fighting with two battalions that were assaulting without standards. After a brief fight the enemy fell back, although the officers did their best, trying all means, to get the men to renew the attack. A murderous rapid fire that decimated the two freshly assaulting [battalions], just as it had the battalions that had been [previously] repulsed, quickly made us the undisputed masters of the field. But we had heavy losses. *Hauptleute* von Gabain (10th Company), von König (8th Company) and *Lieutenant* Treuge, died a hero's death. *Oberstlieutenant* von Schmeling was wounded by a round in the right thigh, and with him, another hundred men were seriously or slightly wounded. The corpses of the fallen enemy lay in heaps. A sunken road on the left flank that led to our position, and through which the enemy hoped to withdraw, was filled with dead and wounded. Alt Rognitz and Rudersdorf were ablaze in several places.'

Regiment Nr. 3 (to Parschnitz). However, before this withdrawal could be carried out, the enemy launched his last, decisive attack, and came up against the same two battalions of the 43rd that had just repulsed Brigade Wimpffen. We now turn to a description of these final moments of fighting, essentially basing our account on the Austrian report.

The turning point, Brigade Knebel takes the Hill of St Johann 6:00

At 5:00, even before the attacks of Brigade Grivicic and Wimpffen had completely failed, Brigade Knebel appeared on the battlefield and was instructed to take a position astride the highway between Neu Rognitz and Hohenbruck. It had barely completed its deployment when Regiment Archduke Stephan fell back from the assault on the St. Johannes Chapel.

'*Generalmajor* Knebel now believed', so said the enemy report, 'that he could not stand by inactive, at a moment when the enemy could pursue the defeated Brigade Wimpffen and seriously threaten our own position at Hohenbruck. In addition, it seemed to the *Brigade General* that a final attack on the enemy position was worth the effort ... He resolved therefore, without waiting for orders, to join the action, and immediately instructed his entire brigade to advance and storm the Hill of St. Johann.'

The 28th *Jäger* Battalion, which had already advanced from Neu Rognitz to the hill on the right flank of the brigade, advanced along the woods that lined the quarry southeast of the chapel. In the center was IR 1 Emperor Franz Joseph, with its three battalions in closed up division masses [*geschlossenen Divisions Massenlinien*] in the first wave. IR 3 Archduke Karl followed in battalion masses [*Bataillons Massen*], in the second wave. The brigade battery went into position on the left flank and shelled the St. Johannes Chapel to cover the advance of the troops. These advanced in perfect order toward the Hill of St. Johann, where the two battalions of the 43rd[52] (Brigade von Barnekow), courageously attempted to hold the line, pouring forth a hail of bullets.

In this murderous attack, the 1st Battalion, IR 1 Emperor Franz Joseph, lost its Commanding officer, *Oberstlieutenant* von Habermann, as well as most of its officers, and initially had to fall back. A second attempt to take the hill (in which *Oberst* Du Rieux himself led the battalion [*Oberst* Du Rieux was the Regimental Commander]), also foundered since the men, already completely exhausted, were unable to climb the extremely steep final stretch. In the meantime, the 3rd Battalion, under *Major* Pilati, and the 2nd Battalion, under *Major* van der Sloot, managed to climb the western side of the hill, and regardless of the fire concentrated on their front and flank, dislodged the enemy from his position and captured the chapel. *Major* Pilati, the first of his battalion to make it onto the hill, was mortally wounded.

---

52   Author's Note: We consider this to be correct. [Prussian] accounts (with probable, intentional uncertainty), tend to suggest that the assault of Brigade Knebel hit Grenadier Regiment Nr. 3, more that the 43rd. That is extremely unlikely. The 1st Battalion of the 43rd alone, lost 238 men and almost half of its officers, whereas all three battalions of the Grenadier regiment only lost about 80 men. Aside from the men of the 43rd, only a weak contingent from the 41st held the most advanced row of hills. It was the 1st Company of the latter regiment, under *Hauptmann* von Gabain, that held out to the last on the Hopfenberg, and only started its retreat at the same time as the 43rd.

IR 3 Archduke Karl (which followed as the second wave) supported the attack of the Emperor Franz Joseph Regiment so closely, that a part of it stormed the hill at nearly the same time (6:15). It was led by its Commanding Officer, *Oberst* Pehm, who found a hero's death, as did *Oberstlieutenant* Wilhelm *Baron* Stenglin. The defeated enemy battalions now fell back through the battalions of the 3rd Grenadier Regiment to Parschnitz, followed thence by the latter regiment in echelons, after it too was forced to retreat by the Archduke Karl infantry. The 28th *Jäger* Battalion stormed the Kriblitz *Vorstadt* and forced the last of the enemy out [of Trautenau] into the Aupa valley. In the meantime, *Oberst* Grivicic and his brigade also made it onto the Katzauerberg [Katzau hill] east of Kriblitz. Brigade Wimpffen occupied the Hopfenberg. Thus, at about 7:00, three Austrian brigades were on the commanding hills while the last elements of the Prussian corps retreated in the valley. The cannon fire did not die out completely until about 9:30.

The storming of the Johannesberg by the Austrians was an act of unsurpassed bravery. During the entire campaign, perhaps only the action at Uettingen (in the western theater of the war), when the 36th Regiment took the Osnert,[53] is comparable. In the attack upon the Kapellenberg, both Austrian brigades displayed equal determination. That one was more fortunate than the other was due to the changed situation. Our power of resistance was crippled, weakening from one quarter hour to the next. Otherwise it is highly likely that Brigade Knebel would have shared the fate of Brigade Wimpffen. Even so, the outcome hung by a hair.

Fighting at the Kapellenberg.

---

53   Tr. Note: The last battle of the Main Campaign, in the Western Theater of the Austro - Prussian War took place on 26 July 1866 at Roßbrunn, Uettingen and Hettstadt. During this action the Magdeburg Fusilier Regiment Nr. 36 stormed the Osnert Hill [held by the Bavarians] suffering heavy casualties, including two battalion commanders.

We shall attempt to describe the locality (Hill and Chapel of St. Johann), whose possession was so hotly contested. Hohenbruck, lying horizontally in the low ground, provided a good place to form from [march] column to attack formation. Climbing from the low ground northwards, we reach a flattened ridge which, as we catch sight of the chapel (visible from afar), suddenly falls off steeply and forms a deep ravine. On the far side of this ravine a new hill rises, the Kapellenberg. At first sight it seems impossible to traverse the ravine and then climb [the Kapellenberg] under enemy fire, especially needle gun fire. The conformation of the ravine is such however, that it provides resting places for attacking troops in the smaller gullies that repeatedly cut through it. By taking advantage of these gullies, the enemy battalions were able to work their way relatively close to the Kapellenberg, so that only the final steep stretch (which was completely devoid of cover), had to be stormed. But however short this stretch was, it cost the blood of many hundreds of men. Here the front ranks of the Emperor Franz Joseph Infantry were mown down until the closely following battalions finally reached the hill, and attacking from two sides, forced our 43rd to retreat.

These (our men of the 43rd) provided their own description of the last, decisive moments of the battle. We take the following, referring to the 1st Battalion (which was the hardest pressed):

> The first enemy columns were repulsed by volleys followed by devastating rapid fire, before they were more than half-way up the hill. Now however, there was no wind to clear away the thick powder smoke that hung in the sultry air as suddenly, new enemy assault columns advanced through the broken ranks [of the first attack] with drums beating.
>
> After more rapid fire, in which the supports [*soutiens*] fired up to 25 rounds per man, the 1st and 2nd Companies were forced to evacuate the position at the chapel. Attacked in the front and right flank by several enemy columns, the supports had to fire in two directions at once. When the enemy columns were only 20 paces away, it became clear that further resistance would lead to capture, *no reserves or reinforcements were in sight*. *Hauptmann* von Normann therefore ordered the 1st Company to retreat, immediately followed by the 2nd Company. *Vice Feldwebel* Kirsch died a hero's death, *Lieutenant* Dewischeit (leader of the rifle platoon), was mortally wounded in the thigh. It was 6:30.
>
> In the meantime, the 3rd and 4th Companies under *Hauptmann Freiherr* von Braun, had also repulsed several enemy columns. When fresh enemy columns advanced and *Hauptmann* von Braun, was severely wounded by a shot through the chest, it became impossible for these companies to hold the position any longer. To the right, the chapel was also lost, and enemy bullets were already hitting the left flank. All of the companies now started to retreat to the north under intense enemy pressure. The 1st Company made its way through the northern end of Trautenau. The other three companies waded through the Aupa several hundred paces downstream. During the retreat over the Hopfenberg, the battalion's colours, which had been repeatedly hit, were in danger of being lost. The colour bearer, *Sergeant* von Gass - Jaworski, stumbled and fell down a slope and the pursuing enemy were just about to seize them, when the men of the 3rd Company immediately opened up a rapid fire. The swarm of enemy skirmishers fell back, and the retreat continued.

The retreat to Golden Öls

At 7:00 three Austrian Brigades stood on the three southern hills of Trautenau. Our forces down in the Aupa valley, initially retreated to Parschnitz. Everything now depended on whether the enemy mounted a pursuit. If he was still strong enough for an energetic push, our I Corps would be in extreme danger. Catastrophe was inevitable if the enemy threw our retreating columns into confusion with artillery fire from the hills, and at the same time closed off the Aupa Valley by pushing his right wing brigade (Grivicic) forward. We were spared this catastrophe. We were spared it, on the one hand, because the enemy forces were too exhausted, and on the other, because his forces like ours, did not have a clear overview of the situation. All unified command had long since ceased to exist. Weak, unplanned attempts to pursue and to endanger our retreat were repulsed by the Fusilier Battalion of the 4th Regiment and then by the East Prussian *Jäger* Battalion. We were fortunate in being able to conduct the withdrawal (through the mountains toward Liebau and Schömberg), with relatively few losses. The vital Golden Oels [choke] point, the actual pass and key point in the Aupa Valley, was held. It was after midnight (for some, 3:00 in the morning), when the troops, dead tired, reached their old bivouacs after nearly 24 hours of struggle.

As for the enemy, Brigade Grivicic remained in the hills south of Parschnitz (*Katzuer Berg*), while Brigade Wimpffen occupied Trautenau. *Generalmajor Baron* Koller assumed command of this half of 10th Corps. The other half (Brigades Mondl and Knebel) bivouacked in a position farther to the rear, by Neu Rognitz and Hohenbruck. The Commanding General of 10th Corps. *Feldmarschalllieutenant* von Gablenz was with them.

The losses, the 'Betrayal of Trautenau', retrospective

The action at Trautenau was fruitless and only resulted in losses. They were, as they had already been at Nachod and Skalitz, especially high on the enemy side, and were four times our own. The Austrians lost 191 officers (including 12 staff officers) and 4,596 men. Brigades Grivicic and Wimpffen, which had charged uphill in tightly packed assault columns under needle gun fire, suffered the heaviest losses. IR 13 Bamberg (Brigade Wimpffen) alone, lost over 500 men, including 369 severely wounded.

Prussian losses amounted to 56 officers and 1,282 men, including 86 missing. The four new regiments, the 41st, 43rd, 44th and 45th, had the heaviest losses, especially the 43rd (352 men).

Major von Hüllesheim, Commander of the 1st Battalion 43rd Regiment, died, not at the end of the fighting, as his battalion (with praiseworthy courage), repulsed the attack of a numerically superior enemy, but at an earlier hour (4:30), as the long enemy gun line prepared for the attack by Brigades Grivicic and Wimpffen. The very first shell that burst on the Kapellenberg killed the major along with *Premierlieutenant* von Keper who was next to him, also wounding the Battalion Adjutant, *Lieutenant* Sperling. *Major* von Nordenflycht, of Grenadier Regiment Nr. 4, fell on the left wing. Our side did not lose a single standard. Austrian standards were in danger more than once. Thus, in the report of Regiment Bamberg, we find:

> *Oberlieutenant* Otto Höffern von Salfeld played the greatest roll in saving the colours of the 2nd Battalion, which were in danger of being captured by the enemy, he held the battalion together with his courage.

This was in the fighting for the Kapellenberg, just after 5:00.

We still have to consider one further controversy; we mean the so called 'Betrayal of Trautenau.' This question has generated an entire literature of its own. While one side never tires of painting Trautenau as a 'fanaticized nest of Czechs' (it is a purely German town), the other is just as concerned to dispute that shots were fired and brands any mention of such as lying fiction. Now, with the days of excitement behind us, we can at least resolve the main points of the matter.

There can be no talk of a 'Betrayal of Trautenau.' It would have required the citizens or the governing body of Trautenau, to have lured our troops into the town with the express intention of ambushing them, in other words, a conspiracy. The investigation that was later conducted found not the slightest evidence for this, nor did the events in the town (even if we accept the worst interpretation) ever suggest it. We plead unconditionally not guilty regarding the overall conduct of the town and its governing body.

Our not guilty however, should not be taken to mean that there was not one single guilty person. So far as we know, there is not one single case of proven guilt, but we consider that given all the circumstances, it is more than likely some civilians did fire from windows and rooftops on Prussian soldiers. Dr. Roth (*Bürgermeister* of Trautenau) certainly disagrees.

However, he was not everywhere, he could not be, and he certainly goes too far in his eagerness to deny guilt when he claims the role as counsel for the defense for every single person (elsewhere he speaks of the bitterness of many hundreds of workers who had become breadless) and calls on 'truth loving Prussian men, who saw shooting from the houses of Trautenau,' to give their names. As far as the giving of names is concerned, he received his answer in the *Grenzboten*[54].

This answer stated:

> There are, in truth, many truth decent men who can and must bear witness that the Prussian troops were fired upon from the windows, and not by the Austrian military, for such were not present in the town. I could paint the house for *Herr* Dr. Roth, it is so clearly before my eyes, from which the first shot came. We were posted in the street closest to Parschnitz, between the Aupa bridge and the chapel. It was the corner house facing the chapel. In consequence that [house] was broken into, since the doors were barred, and searched. Subsequently I heard about five or six shots fired with short intervals between them. This was no self-deception such as *Herr* Dr. Roth would declare the case to be. Such a thing may well happen for an individual, but not for hundreds of men who are accustomed to look around themselves with sharp eyes.

One who recognizes the ring of the truth, will say that this has the ring of truth. Dr. Roth, of whose *bona fides* we have not the slightest doubt, also errs when he points out the folly of such an act of resistance by individuals against thousands. *Such scenes regularly repeat themselves.* Anyone who has ever been present in street fighting will bear witness. Uncritical, bereft of all clarity, with only a dark compulsion, victim of trembling excitement, the individual believes in

---

54 Tr. Note: *Die Grenzboten – Zeitschrift für Politik und Literatur* was a national liberal newspaper that appeared between 1841 and 1922. The Chief of Staff 2nd Army, was an anonymous contributor.

a mistaken perception of heroism and cunning, from the spirit of sacrifice and thirst for revenge, he dares the deed, and blind to the consequences, he throws the stone or fires his rusted rifle. It is not necessary that such actions take place every time, but when they do take place, they are perfectly natural. Thereby (in some circumstances) they may well be justified from a patriotic standpoint. We believe that such actions did take place in Trautenau. We do not judge their motives.

Finally, a retrospective look at the 'Action at Trautenau.' The conduct of the troops, with no special *elan* in the offensive (they were too tired), was impeccable in the defense, and at times (for example the 43rd), outstanding. A reporter says, with reason:

> Although the result of the day was unfortunate, the troops that were engaged in the fighting can look back on it with pride, for the ancient honour of the East Prussian regiments came through untarnished.

That is true, however regarding the leadership, it cannot be denied that it failed many times.

The means at hand were not employed, many battalions never even got into action, others arrived too late. There was no understanding of the bigger picture and there was a lack of energy. Where movement should have ruled, stagnation prevailed. Regiments were deployed where a company would have sufficed, individual companies were deployed where a regiment was needed. This was especially true of the left wing. Of the 12 battalions that operated there, less than half seriously engaged the enemy (and the enemy attacked with entire brigades).

Why it was that nothing took place in timely fashion will have to await the judgement of a later time. The original dispositions, the broad assignment of forces, was blameless. The inadequacies only began with the details. There is no question that this was felt very painfully by I Corps itself. The [Prussian] General Staff Work, generally measured and restrained in its statements, nevertheless makes the following judgement:

> I Army Corps was in a disadvantageous position throughout the entire day because Trautenau and the *commanding* heights were not occupied right at the beginning, thereby securing the debouching of the entire force. Its initial superiority (4 to 1) thus remained without influence. While the main body remained on the [left bank] of the Aupa, only *individual elements* fought on the [right bank], which were successively reinforced, but remained inferior to the constantly increasing enemy forces so that [the enemy] never had to face the entire [Prussian] force.
>
> The infantry fought nearly alone. They received little support from the cavalry and the greatest part of the artillery remained in positions from which they were unable to engage the actual battlefield. On the other hand, with full freedom of movement, the Austrians employed all arms and were able to establish complete superiority of their artillery (finally 40 pieces against 12).
>
> The presence of the 1st Guards Division up to 2:00 in the afternoon, which could have decided the action by a resolute advance into the enemy's right flank, was not employed. The *detached battalions and individual companies* from all [Prussian] brigades put up stubborn resistance.

These sentences, if at times veiled, contain all the complaints that could be made against the command of I Army Corps. The criticism expressed by a young officer, who apparently took part in the fighting, is more sharply expressed (also against the Austrian leadership):

> The entire 2nd Division (which arrived first) camped ineffectually on the valley floor east of Trautenau, in which any enemy battalions could cause them fearful losses from positions on the surrounding hills. It camped and awaited the arrival of the 1st Division, which was marching from Liebau.
>
> [The 1st Division] arrived at about 9:00, and about a half hour later, came the first Austrian artillery rounds. Indeed, at Trautenau the Austrian generals also initially committed grievous offences against the basic principles of war. The Austrians failed to occupy those hills from which they could have shot us to pieces without difficulty and thrown us back into the pass.[55] Instead they informed us of their presence by an ineffective, comical cannonade.
>
> The Commanding General [of 1st Corps] now decided to quit the mousetrap, and therefore dispatched a number of squadrons and several batteries from the unfortunate valley basin. We awaited the success of this 'first detachment.' Soon they returned and reported the terrain was unsuitable for cavalry, and that the artillery could not operate without covering forces.
>
> Now, finally, the infantry had to clamber up those steep slopes which the imperial [Austrian] generals had not yet occupied, for which we would happily award them a Life Saving Medal. For it was only thanks to this neglect that many of our men are still in possession of their lives, which otherwise, they would most certainly have lost. While several battalions clambered up that hill (on the left wing), several others marched forward to Trautenau, and from there, captured the less steep hills south of the town in stubborn fighting and with great bravery. This was the morning fight for the so called Kapellenberg.
>
> Eleven battalions and two (for a short time, three) batteries were then engaged in close quarter fighting with the enemy for 10½ hours. *Fourteen battalions and nearly all of the artillery of our corps did not fire a single shot.*[56] The captured Austrian officers however, expressed their amazement at the stubbornness with which our widely separated battalions fought.

55   Tr. Note: The young officer is referring to the Parschnitz Hill south of Parschnitz, which commanded the valley floor that 1st Army Corps was on. The Austrian Brigade Mondl had already established itself on the three hills commanding Trautenau, making full use of its limited forces, with strong positions on the Kapellenberg and Hopfenberg, and a weaker detachment securing its left flank on the Galgenberg.

56   Author's Note: This report is essentially correct. Whether 14 battalions (other reports speak only of five) fired no shot may remain an open question. However, there can be no doubt that at least half of all the battalions were not in any way energetically committed, or at the very least, did not make full use of their forces. That is clearly evident from the casualty list. The four old Regiments, the 1st, 3rd, 4th and 5th had a total loss of 300 men, including 60 killed, in an engagement that lasted about twelve hours. These numbers prove that the battalions in question were very lightly (some almost not at all), involved in the fighting. Compare this with the 5th Division at Gitschin or the 7th Division in the *Swiepwald* (at Königgrätz).

The homeopathic [sic; probably meaning 'in tiny quantities'] employment of our artillery remains an unsolved riddle. There was talk that the hills were too steep to climb, but this seems odd if one considers that Bohemian dung wagons made it up these hills, and Prussian artillery should certainly have been able to do at least as well with only moderate effort.

Come evening came the order to retreat. Everyone now believed that we would occupy the hills north of Trautenau, which provided a nearly impregnable defensive position, but the retreat continued until we were across the border. *A retreat was not necessary. To the contrary, the Commanding General should have ordered all [of his forces] to secure the success that had already been achieved: the advance through the pass into Bohemia.* Did it not occur to him that his retreat could endanger the entire Prussian strategic plan?

Those are sharp words, but probably not excessively so. We believe that these points must be raised. To remain silent regarding things that, to put it mildly, leave much to be desired, or indeed to cover up such events, is anything but our patriotic duty. A description that dwells on the toughness of the East Prussian regiments (because of their stubborn perseverance) and places Trautenau alongside Nachod and Skalitz, commits a grave injustice against the glorious Commander of V Corps. [*General* von Steinmetz] who with a sure eye and firm hand, fired every newly arriving battalion like an arrow, knew how to hit his target. To place everything on the same level confuses matters and deprives us of examples of true heroism.

The day of Trautenau was a loss for us, and the most deplorable fact is it need not have been lost. These remarks must suffice, now we move on to the description of that 'second day of Trautenau,' that made up for the first.

The Approach of the Guards

Between Nachod and Trautenau there is a third pass, the Eypel Pass, and through this 'third gate of Bohemia,' the Guards advanced. Already on the 26th (since here Bohemia protrudes nine miles into Silesia) an advanced guard had crossed the border. The route from the border to Eypel (which lies on the same vertical axis as Trautenau (to its north), and Nachod (to its south), extends for nearly nine miles from east to west.

The composition of the Guards Corps was:

1st Guards Division (*Generallieutenant* Hiller von Gärtringen).

    1st Guards Infantry Brigade: *Oberst* von Obernitz.
        1st Guards Regiment, *Oberst* von Kessel.
        3rd Guards Regiment, *Oberst* Knappe von Knappstädt.
    2nd Guards Infantry Brigade: *Generalmajor* von Alvensleben.
        2nd Guards Regiment, *Oberst* von Pape.
        Guards Fusilier Regiment, *Oberst* von Werder.
        Guards *Jäger* Battalion, *Oberstlieutenant* von Röder;
        Guards Hussar Regiment, *Oberst* von Krosigk;
        4 Guards batteries under *Major* Byschelberg;

2nd Guards Division (*Generallieutenant* von Plonski).
3rd Guards Infantry Brigade: *Generalmajor* von Budriski.
Emperor Alexander Guards Grenadier Regiment Nr. 1, *Oberst* Knappe von Knappstädt.
3rd Guards Grenadier Regiment Queen Elizabeth, *Oberst* von Pritzelwitz.
4th Guards Infantry Brigade: *Generalmajor Freiherr* von Loën.
Emperor Franz Guards Grenadier Regiment Nr. 2, *Oberst* von Fabeck.
4th Queen's Guards Grenadier Regiment, *Oberst* von Strubberg.
Guards *Schützen* Battalion, *Major* von Besser.
3rd Guards Uhlan Regiment, *Oberst* Mirus.
4 Guards batteries under *Major* von der Goltz.

The Heavy Guards Cavalry Brigade also was attached to the corps. Regiments *Gardes du Corps* and Guards Cuirassiers, under Prince Albrecht (son), also the Reserve Artillery, 5 batteries under *Oberst* Prince Kraft zu Hohenlohe Ingelfingen.

Prince August von Würtemberg commanded the corps. Friedrich August Eberhard, Prince von Würtemberg, was born on 24 January 1813 as the second son of Prince Paul von Würtemberg (from his marriage with a princess of Sachsen Altenburg). He entered the Würtemberg service in 1829, the Prussian in 1830, and joined the Regiment *Gardes du Corps* as *Rittmeister*. He became *Major* in 1832, *Oberstlieutenant* in 1836, *Oberst* in 1838. He commanded the Guards Cuirassier Regiment from 1840 to 1844. In 1854 (now *Generallieutenant*) he was given command of the 7th Division, in 1856 the Guards Cavalry, in 1857 III Corps, and in 1858, the Guards Corps. The following year he was given the rank of *General der Cavallerie*.

Only the new Guards Regiments (at that time combined as a division and commanded by *General* von der Mülbe), participated in the 1864 campaign. Now Prince August was given the opportunity to lead the entire corps into battle, and against a worthy foe. The orders for the 27th read, the Guards will advance toward the southwest to the middle Aupa (by Eypel) and establish contact with I Army Corps on the right, and V Army Corps on the left. It will follow them. The 1st Guards Division, after it had offered its assistance (fruitlessly) to *General* von Bonin whose forces were engaged in combat, proceeded to bivouac[57] that evening in and around

---

57 Author's Note: The advanced guard of the 2nd Guards Division (in fact its vanguard, comprised of several squadrons of the 3rd Guards Uhlan Regiment) engaged on the afternoon of the 27th in the cavalry action at Cerwenahora (Rothenberg). This action developed as follows. As the division arrived at its bivouac near Kosteletz, the thunder of guns could be heard from Nachod, and *Oberst* Mirus, Commander of the 3rd Guards Uhlan Regiment, was ordered to reconnoiter as far as Skalitz. He immediately moved out at the trot with the 1½ squadrons of his regiment that were immediately available to him. In the village of Cerwenahora, he learned that enemy cavalry had deployed on the far side of [the village] and he immediately attacked two enemy squadrons of Imperial Uhlans facing him at a distance of 900 paces. They were the Mexico Uhlans under *Oberst Graf* Wurmbrand. The shock of his charge was so great that he completely broke through the enemy line. Thereupon the Prussian Uhlans turned their horses back and the action developed into fierce individual combat in which, after twice surging back and forth, the Imperial Uhlans were thoroughly beaten and took flight. It is remarkable that before the Prussian attack reached the Imperial Uhlans, the latter fired a volley with their pistols, and also during the individual combat, repeated use was made of the pistols. Only a brief pursuit of the Imperial Uhlans was possible because a larger mass of enemy cavalry (according to a captured officer, eight squadrons) appeared at some distance. The enemy lost three officers, 65 men

Eypel. The 2nd Guards Division reached Kosteletz, about 4½ miles to the rear (southeast). The Reserve Artillery and the heavy cavalry were still further back. And so, to the 27th.

The orders for the 27th read - to the Aupa (Eypel), the mission for the 28th read - to the Elbe (Königinhof). This was only to be expected, however on the evening of the 27th, the question remained open as to whether it would be possible to carry out this advance or not. Both flanks were exposed. Reports from Nachod on the one side, from Trautenau[58] on the other, reported one success and one failure. These seemed to balance each other out. However, the failure at Trautenau was unmistakable, and for the moment, so far as I Corps was concerned, irreparable, while the success at Nachod could well be reversed at any moment by the three enemy army corps positioned at Skalitz. The situation was critical.

The ground was deeply incised by ravines and lacked any point from which [the commander] could obtain an overview (at least regarding approaching forces or forces already in position), it called for extreme caution. Nevertheless, action was required, the Prussian Guards could not start this war by turning back. Reconnaissance parties were sent out (early on the morning of the 28th), and if no insurmountable obstacles were revealed, Prince August von Würtemberg was resolved to attack. Outposts were positioned as far as Raatsch.

We shall now take a look at the enemy. The Austrian 10th Corps, as already mentioned, was positioned with two brigades (Wimpffen and Grivicic) in and near Trautenau, and two brigades (Knebel and Mondl) in and around Neu Rognitz. Thus, it adopted a hooked position. The two brigades that were concentrated by Trautenau stood in a horizontal line from west to east, the brigades bivouacked by Neu Rognitz stood in a vertical line from north to south. This position was only temporary, it was not be intended to be held. 10th Corps, in its advance from Königinhof to Trautenau on the 26th and 27th, resembled a large scale detachment. Its objective, to repulse our I Corps. Now having attained that objective, it was obvious that the detached corps should return to Königinhof, where Benedek was concentrating his army for the advance north.

This return [to Königinhof] was obvious, but the relevant order was hastened by a report that arrived at the [Austrian] Army Command during the night of the 27th/28th, stating that strong Prussian forces were positioned at Eypel and could cut the line of march of 10th Corps with an advance to the Trautenau – Königinhof road (approximately at Prausnitz Kaile). This would hit 10th Corps in the flank and at the very least, force it away from its immediate communication with Königinhof. In light of these circumstances, orders arrived at 10th Corps Headquarters early in the morning of the 28th for [the corps] to withdraw from the vicinity of the enemy forces at Eypel and proceed to Königinhof as soon as possible. Thus, both sides were possessed by the same concern, concern that the enemy might envelop their flank and cut them off, and

---

and 69 horses. The Prussian squadrons (during the individual combat and while [the force] rallied, two more squadrons of the 3rd Guards Uhlan Regiment came up) also suffered not insignificant losses. Three non commissioned officers and men were left dead on the field, three officers were wounded, *Oberst* Mirus with a minor lance thrust, *Premier Lieutenant Baron* von Dalwigk with two minor lance thrusts, and *Secondlieutenant Freiherr* von Ziegler, seriously wounded with a lance thrust in the mouth. 31 men were wounded.

58   Author's Note: *Major* von der Burg, of the Crown Prince's staff, and *Premierlieutenant* von Esebeck, of the staff of I Army Corps, brought news of the outcome of the action at Trautenau.

both had good reason. The fate that we were preparing for the enemy, could, if 10th Corps was promptly supported, also be in store for us.

After the relevant order arrived from [Army] Headquarters, Gablenz disposed his four brigades as follows:

> The brigades camped by Neu Rognitz (Knebel and Mondl), were to move southward, initially to Prausnitz – Kaile.
>
> The brigades camped by Trautenau (Wimpffen and Grivicic), the former (Wimpffen) to follow the direction taken by Brigades Knebel and Mondl, thus also proceeding via Neu Rognitz to Prausnitz Kaile.
>
> Brigade Grivicic was to advance, parallel to the above, to Alt Rognitz, cover the left flank of Brigade Wimpffen and threaten the enemy right flank if he advanced from Eypel.

So much for Gablenz's dispositions. While the enemy columns, in accordance with the above instructions, prepared to move out on the morning of the 28th, the Guards Command, based on the results of its reconnaissance, was resolved to attack these very enemy columns. Prince August von Würtemberg made the following dispositions:

> The 1st Guards Division was to debouch from the Eypel - Raatsch pass, advance westward, take Staudenz and Burkersdorf, and push on to the Trautenau Königinhof road.
>
> The 2nd Guards Division was to follow via Eypel and Raatsch, throw out two battalions to the right to cover the right flank of the 1st Guards Division toward Alt Rognitz.

This resulted in two victorious actions:

> 1. The action at Staudenz and Burkersdorf, by the 1st Guards Division.
> 2. The action at Alt Rognitz and the recapture of Trautenau by the 2nd Guards Division.

We now proceed to the separate descriptions of these two interesting actions.

The Fighting at New Rognitz and Burkerdorf (Soor)

The task for the 1st Guards Division concerned Staudenz and Burkersdorf. At 6:30 in the morning (28th) the battalions moved out. The Eypel pass is a little over two miles long and entirely contains the villages of Eypel and Ober Raatsch. There is a short stretch between the two villages that is pure ravine without houses. The *Avantgarde* (*Oberst* von Kessel) consisted of the Fusilier Battalions of the 1st, 2nd and 3rd Guards Regiments, the 3rd Battalion of the Guards Fusiliers, and individual companies of the Guards *Jäger* Battalion, as well as several squadrons of Guards Hussars. The 2nd Guards Infantry Brigade (*Generalmajor* von Alvensleben) followed as the Main Body, the 1st Guards Infantry Brigade (*Oberst* von Obernitz) as Reserve. By about 8:00 the *Avantgarde* was out of the defile and at Ober Raatsch. At 8:30 it received the order to attack.

The four battalions advanced together from Ober Raatsch to Staudenz. The Fusilier Battalion of the 3rd Guards Regiment formed the first wave, the other three battalions followed. The Hussars and Guards *Jäger* proceeded half left, the Hussars to Prausnitz – Kaile.

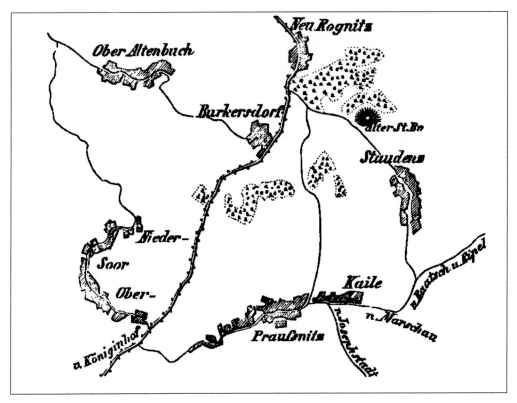

Sketch map of Burkersdorf.

Staudenz was reached and passed, there were still no losses. The first incoming rounds came as [the force] debouched from the village. Now the four *Avantgarde* battalions took up their attack formations as follows. The Fusilier Battalion of the 2nd Guards Regiment took the right flank, the 3rd Battalion of the Guards Fusilier Regiment the left flank.

The remaining two Fusilier Battalions divided themselves, and while two companies of the 1st Guards Regiment formed an extreme right flank (towards Neu Rognitz), two companies of the 3rd Guards Regiment formed an extreme left flank (toward Marchau), the remaining four companies took their position in the center. Thus, the attack proceeded as follows.

Between Staudenz and Burkersdorf, to the east of Burkersdorf, there is a wood next to the *Chaussée* leading to Prausnitz Kaile that consists of various smaller plantations (marked A on the map). These woods were taken in the first assault. There however, the attack came to a halt. In Burkersdorf, where Gablenz himself was in command, the enemy held firm and inundated our forces with such a hail of shells from his eight batteries (that had gone into position north of Burkersdorf, between it and Neu Rognitz), that no further progress could be made other than to hold the western margin of the woods by committing all our forces.[59] The disposition of our troops in the woods corresponded to the formation assumed for the attack. The Fusilier Battalion of the 2nd Guards Regiment, *Major* von Erckert, held the northwest corner, the 3rd Battalion of the Guards Fusiliers, *Oberstlieutenant Graf* Waldersee, the southwest corner. Between these two stood the half battalions of the 1st and 3rd Guards Regiment.

The action now proceeded to its second phase. The two Guards Batteries, Braun and Witte, went into action against the eight enemy batteries. At the same time the 1st and 2nd Battalions of the Guards Fusilier Regiment, advanced to support our advance - guard. The 1st Battalion headed for the southwest part of Wood A, the 2nd battalion *Oberstlieutenant* von der Knesebeck (following the 10th and 12th companies of the 1st Guards Regiment, which had advanced on the extreme right flank), initially proceeded past the quarry to the large woods southeast of the village of New Rognitz. This movement, rapidly executed, brought the fighting to a standstill, but no more could be achieved. It became increasingly obvious that the decision would be reached at Burkersdorf, which the enemy sought to hold onto with all his strength, along with the adjoining woods. The task now was to seize these from him, and it was accomplished.

Major von Erkert, with the Fusiliers of the Guards Regiment, had as we know taken a firm hold in the northwest corner of the Staudenz Burkersdorf woods, and carried on a brisk fire fight with enemy *Tirailleurs* who had sought cover behind fresh haystacks on a forward lying meadow. After about ten minutes, tired of the shooting, *Major* von Erkert led his Fusiliers in an attack against the corner of the village facing them. Other elements of the advance - guard, companies of the 1st Guards Regiment, joined them on the left. The Trautenau – Königinhof *Chaussée* was reached with a rush, and the northeast portion of Burkersdorf was taken after heavy fighting. Many prisoners were taken. A further advance however would be unsuccessful. Our forces were too fragmented. The enemy held the southern portion of the village with strong elements of IR 1 Franz Joseph. Unless our side received reinforcements, it would not be possible to transform the partial victory achieved by the capture of north Burkersdorf, into a complete one.

However, the moment was near when this would be done. Hardly had *Major* von Erkert's Fusiliers firmly established themselves beside the two companies of the 1st Guards Regiment (primarily the 9th) in North Burkersdorf, when shouts of hurrah, drumbeats and the trumpet call for a fast advance could be heard, one or two thousand paces to the left rear. It was the Main Body, the two Grenadier battalions of the 2nd Foot Guards Regiment, under *Oberst* von Pape,

59 Author's Note: Of the batteries that the enemy committed here, five belonged to the Corps Artillery Reserve and one each from Brigades Knebel, Mondl and Wimpffen. Five of these eight batteries were between Burkersdorf and the Neu Rognitz woods, some in front, some to the rear of the great road leading to Königinhof. As for infantry, at the start of the fighting the enemy only had Brigade Knebel in position, three of whose battalions (2nd and 3rd Battalions Archduke Karl and 3rd Battalion Emperor Franz Joseph) were on the left flank at New Rognitz, three other battalions (1st Battalion Archduke Karl and 1st and 2nd Battalions Emperor Franz Joseph) were on the right flank by Burkersdorf. Only when Brigade Knebel was defeated on both wings, the Neu Rognitz wing by the Guards Fusiliers, the Burkersdorf wing by the fusiliers of the 2nd Guards Regiment (thereby rendering 10th Corps' retreat down the Königinhof *Chaussée* impossible), did Brigade Mondl arrive at Neu Rognitz and join the action. Their involvement had only one objective, to free up the alternative route to the Elbe via Altenbuch and Pilnikau, which from Neu Rognitz, we also threatened to cut, and in part, had already done so. We shall return to this.

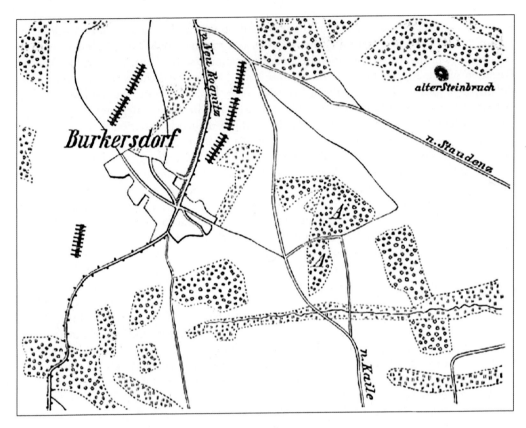

Sketch map of the Austrian artillery positions at Burkersdorf.

approaching at the double. These brought about the decision. Before we describe this however, let us go back a quarter of an hour and accompany these two battalions on their advance:

It was 9:15,' wrote an eyewitness, 'when our two Grenadier battalions debouched from Ober Raatsch. The battle was already raging in front of us, but there was nothing to be seen of our men who were engaged in this battle. We heard the chatter of small arms fire from the woods near Burkersdorf. Battery Braun had already gone into position east of Staudenz. Right beside it, in a thicket, was a company of *Jägers*. Not far from the battery, Prince August von Würtemberg and his staff were on a hillock. Seven or eight Austrian batteries were firing, two south, one west of Burkersdorf and four to the north, toward Neu Rognitz. Small arms fire could be heard from there, too. The enemy artillery fire was primarily directed against Battery Braun, which was under heavy bombardment. Their fire had already set Staudenz ablaze.

Such was the state of the fighting at 9:15. The description continued:

A quarter hour later (9:30), orders arrived from *General* von Hiller that the two Grenadier battalions were to advance in support of the four battalions that were already engaged in the Burkersdorf woods. The battalions immediately advanced to the woods. In the meantime the artillery fire had increased enormously, and showered the entire open area between Kaile, Staudenz and Burkersdorf with a hail of shells and shrapnel. Entire sections were covered with dust and dirt, but no one fell. Thus it was that wood A was reached, in which our *Avantgarde* had already established itself.

General von Hiller, who had been in A for the entire time, ordered the attack to continue. *Oberst* von Pape, to whom the order was directed, summoned the staff officers and *Hauptleute* to the front and gave out his dispositions. The companies were placed with platoon intervals between them [*auf Zugdistance*], the 7th and 8th Companies as *Soutien* [supporting] half battalions behind the left wing, skirmishers thrown out ahead. The company commanders were ordered to dismount from their horses. Then the companies approached from behind the edge of the woods that was held by the 1st and 3rd battalions of the Guards Fusilier Regiment, and on a given signal, everyone, company commanders in the lead, charged forward at the run with a thunderous hurrah. (This was the attack whose joyful hurrah had been heard by the Fusiliers of the 2nd Guards Regiment).

Some of the Guards Fusiliers joined the attack in small groups and ran forward, taking advantage of their advanced position. As they became aware of this, the Grenadiers called to each other, 'Get moving or the '*Maikäfer* [May bugs[60]] will beat us.' Amidst general laughter, they now charged as fast as they could to the woods. The startled enemy fired much too high, and the open, five hundred paces wide field of grain, was crossed with minimal losses.

The enemy fled, but nevertheless prisoners were taken from all three regiments that were engaged at Burkersdorf, Emperor Franz Joseph, Archduke Karl and the Parma Infantry.[61] One of our Grenadier regiments (1st) turning off to the right, forced its way into south Burkersdorf. The main attack however, proceeded without delay or hesitation in a straight line farther to the west, from wood to wood. At the margin of the woods, which adjoined the road leading from Burkersdorf to Prausnitz, *Hauptmann* von Kracht was seriously wounded, shot at close range through the chest. Thus it continued for a little over a mile, but when the pursuit reached the Trautenau – Königinhof *Chaussée*, our forces were barely adequate to take the withdrawing Austrian columns under fire. (12:00).

60 Tr. Note: The Grenadier's nickname for the Guards Fusiliers.
61 Author's Note: According to the Austrian General Staff Work, Brigade Mondl (Regiments Parma and Mazzuchelli) did not advance past Neu Rognitz, and accordingly could not have joined with Regiment Parma in the fighting at Burkersdorf, which was about a mile and a half farther south. Furthermore, the official Austrian report most specifically speaks only of Brigade Knebel, which held Burkersdorf and the woods north and south thereof, as far as Neu Rognitz. On the other hand, all of the Prussian reports agree that some of Regiment Parma were captured in and around Burkersdorf. Perhaps the contradiction can be resolved as follows: Gablenz had a personal *Stabswache* [Headquarters Guard], which he could select from any part of his corps. [Prussian] reports state that this consisted of a detachment from Regiment Gerstner. This however, is highly unlikely, since that regiment belonged to an entirely different corps (VIII Corps). Perhaps this *Stabswache* came from Regiment Parma.

So much for the report. We add that this decisive attack was supported along the entire line. On the left, the 1st Battalion of the 3rd Guards Regiment, which was also arriving, advanced toward Prausnitz Kaile. In the center, the *Avantgarde* battalion also took the southern part of Burkersdorf. On the right, the 2nd Battalion of the Guards Fusilier Regiment, under *Oberstlieutenant* von der Knesebeck, entered Neu Rognitz. Everywhere the enemy fell back. However, there could be no thought of further pursuit, our troops had all been in combat and were totally exhausted by the previous day's 27 mile march. Accordingly, the enemy retreat was undisturbed, neither from Neu Rognitz[62] nor from Burkersdorf, nor from the woods south of Burkersdorf. The retreat of the three Austrian Brigades proceeded, in an obligatory detour, via Ober Altenbuch and Pilnikau to the Elbe. They reached the river by 9:00 in the evening. Only small groups reached the great road south of Burkersdorf and marched directly to Königinhof and Josephstadt. The enemy's losses during this action cannot be determined precisely since most suffered elsewhere (at Alt Rognitz and Rudersdorf). There the fourth brigade of the corps, Brigade Grivicic, was nearly wiped out. We shall speak of that in the next chapter.

The 1st Guards Division lost 18 officers and 478 men at Burkersdorf and Neu Rognitz. Hardest hit was the 2nd Guards Regiment and the Guards Fusiliers, especially the latter. They lost five officers and 302 men, for the most part from the 2nd Battalion. Of the five officers, three *Lieutenants* von Byern, von Sydow and von der Mülbe II, fell at Neu Rognitz. They were buried in a thicket of young firs under heaped up blocks of rocks on the following day. Their epitaph read:

> *Death stretched out his hand to three young heroes.*
> *With God for King and Fatherland.*
> *The broad earth is everywhere the master.*
> *May their dust rest in peace, even far from the homeland*

62   Author's Note: An attempt was made from Neu Rognitz by our Guards Fusiliers to cut the enemy's line of retreat via Altenbuch, however battalion von der Knesebek which made the attempt, was soon forced onto the defensive. At about 12:00, they advanced from Rognitz and pushed Regiment Mazzuchelli (at the head of Brigade Mondl, just arriving from Trautenau), back with little trouble. This success however, did not last long. *Oberst* Mondl recognized the danger to his Brigade and Brigade Wimpffen (following behind), if the side road via Altenbuch and Pilnikau was blocked, since the main road via Burkersdorf and Prausnitz Kaile was already cut. Therefore, he immediately ordered that Neu Rognitz, the key point of the Altenbuch Road, be recaptured at any cost. Carrying out this order gave rise to a fierce fight. One and a half battalions of the Parma infantry, and half a *Jäger* battalion, advanced to the attack. The remainder of these regiments followed in the second wave. Our force fell back before this energetic assault with substantial losses. New Rognitz was lost and remained in the hands of Regiment Parma until the rest of the brigade, as well as Brigade Wimpffen and the Corps Train, had safely reached Ober Altenbuch, Regiment Parma then followed on. It is extremely likely that the fighting at Neu Rognitz began as the fighting at Burkersdorf was already decided in our favour, and it had no influence upon that. A greater influence, to the enemy's disadvantage, was failing to occupy Prausnitz Kaile which covered Gablenz' right flank and secured his line of retreat. *Feldmarschallieutenant* von Gablenz, had requested its occupation (his request was also endorsed by the Army High Command), however Brigade Fleischhacker (IV Corps), which (whose task it was) did not occupy Prausnitz Kaile, but Ober Prausnitz, situated nearly seven miles away. This deprived Gablenz from the very start of any freedom of action and forced him to think more of retreat than of victory.

Excerpts from letters written during those days, will shed light on individual episodes of the fighting. Thus, a Guards Fusilier who took part with his battalion (the 1st) in the assault from wood to wood, writes most strikingly:

We bivouacked at Eypel. The sun which awakened us, gave way to a bloody day. On the march, which we commenced at 6:00, we heard from the Guards Hussars that the enemy was on the other side of the next hills. We were extremely calm. The Austrians opened fire at such a range that we could see neither soldiers nor cannon. Our artillery replied but was immediately inundated with such a hail of shells that it quickly had to withdraw. We had 12 guns against their 64. We now advanced, took cover behind the houses of the village (Staudenz) and the air was immediately filled with the whistle of [shells].

Now we had to change position again. We proceeded through the village, which was already starting to burn, and hastened to a wood that was across from us and took cover behind the trees. The heavy [shells] tore through the twigs, but so far we had no losses. Now they began! We had passed through the first woods and had to cross a field of grain that was about 1000 paces wide in order to find cover in a second wood. That was what the Austrians were waiting for. Since they knew the exact distance from the edge of one wood to the other, they opened up with rapid shellfire as soon as they saw our leading [companies]. The first round immediately mowed down six men of the company. I saw them sink to their knees, hands pressed before their faces. Now it was, 'Forward, Get moving!'

So we came to the second wood. Our *Feldwebel*, a few non-commissioned officers and many men had fallen. We were again under artillery fire, but I pledge my solemn word, I did not lose my composure for a moment. My heart now throbbed with lust for battle as the *Oberstlieutenant* came to our *Hauptmann* with the order: The 4th Company has to take the edge of the next wood with the bayonet. With the command, 'Fix bayonets!', I thought once more of you, my beloved, and we threw ourselves upon the enemy with thunderous hurrahs. We entered the zone of mixed artillery and small arms fire. Things got pretty hot. The Austrians did not hold their ground.

Now there was a bigger wood to take, the third. We had to run another 1000 paces and drive off the enemy with the bayonet. Not a shot was fired. With *General* von Alvensleben at the point, all the officers in the lead, bayonets sparkling to the right and left, the entire battalion was dispersed, as far as the eye could see was only a field of soldiers, and so it went without a shot being fired. I myself, ran alongside our commander. 'Brave Fusiliers, I always thought of you like this! Hurrah!' And along with this, the beating of the drums, and see there, despite the flanking fire of the guns and small arms, the position was bravely taken. The Austrians fled and ran as fast as they could. We had now been under heavy fire for three hours. *General* Hiller von Gärtringen rode past us and expressed his joy through tears, that he had been able to see us like this and that he had experienced this glory. For our part, we were dead tired, exhausted. Many were missing.

An officer of the 2nd Guards Regiment wrote:

'A thousand greetings to all of you! Firstly, I am well and a glorious day lies behind us. I write these lines across from a great farmstead (at the southern edge of Burkersdorf). Six hours ago, it was still Gablenz's headquarters, now its *General* Hiller's. We nearly captured our friend and ally from Holstein there. Captured officers told us that he had considered it impossible for us to advance through the woods. Gablenz got away from us, but he left behind his war chest with 10,000 *Gulden*. *General* Hiller immediately allocated 2,000 *Thaler* for a hospital.

Let me now tell you how all this came about. Now we are victorious, but early today we were far from it. We were in a pocket not much better than a mousetrap. We had no idea how things were to our left, but this much we had learned, the Austrians had blocked things on our right (at Parschnitz). The situation was as bad as it could be, our morale not much better. For a moment the order was 'To the rear'. We were thunderstruck. So, the war that we had hoped for was to begin with a 'Retreat'. That seemed impossible to us. While we were still hanging our heads some Guards Hussars came back who had ridden to Staudenz and Burkersdorf early in the morning. 'Yes, we are encircled, but *the Austrians don't know it.*' 'Now, then, onwards' commanded Prince August von Würtemberg, and everyone let out their breath.

At this moment Divisional Chaplain Rogge from Potsdam, stepped before us, offered a short prayer and an inspiring speech. The first cannon shots mixed with the loudly spoken Amen! And now we advanced. At the moment we moved out we still hardly expected victory, but we wanted to sell our lives as dearly as possible. The first shells were something new, and to prove our politeness, were greeted with a threefold hurrah. Our men however, were immediately seized by a certain excitement, a lust for battle that irresistibly drove them forward. Granted, there is nothing more exciting and inspiring for solders than such a moment. The incessant thunder of the guns, the crack of the shells busting to left and right, and the merry whistle of bullets, all that excites the true soldier in a way that makes all though of danger completely disappear. Oh, our brave men! Who could not feel up to the most difficult mission with them? They call for decisive, indeed ruthless leadership. But when they are given it, they respond with complete and joyful devotion.

This day has taught me with so many examples of that, great and small, and the little examples are often the most heroic. Grenadier Dümling (a one year volunteer) hobbled as we advanced at the run, leaping after us with injured feet and could not be persuaded to stay back: 'On another day I would report myself sick, but *today I am well'*. And thus he made it to the end of the action, for hours. Heroism in little things always appears greatest to me.

And our *Sergeant* Gursch! Fritz will remember him, he fell beside him. Gursch lurched forward, and as he fell, planted his flag in the midst of the leading riflemen. He knew what he did. He knew his Fusiliers. There were terrible wounds. Some almost more remarkable than fearful. *Lieutenant* von Frankenberg's arm was bleeding as he rode up to us and brought a report. Now we heard what happened. A shell had torn off the head of a trumpeter (Krause) who was beside him, and the fragments of his skull had been driven into Frankenberg's arm like shell fragments.

It was a bloody advance from wood to wood, but the humorous ran alongside the horrible, and I shall close with a happier episode. During the fighting in the woods there arose a sudden clamour of laughter and joking. I saw many of our men who were standing around a prisoner, and exhibiting the most affectionate joy, shook his hand, hugged and kissed him. In response to my question as to what was going on, they said, 'It's Haschka's batman.' Now, you may ask, who is Haschka? Haschka was an Austrian *Oberlieutenant* of Regiment Parma who was in Berlin with the *Etappenkommando* [administrative headquarters] in Berlin during 1864 and 1865 and daily dealt with our regiment. He was extraordinarily popular. The joy of meeting his batman, who was immediately recognized by our people, was naturally great. The good fellow, however, now was upset because his master would now be without his services. We gave him brandy and cigars, everything that we had to hand and let him go, with many warm greetings to his master from his old friends.[63] And now, take good care of yourself. For us however, may we be granted many more days such as this *Day of Soor*.

'The Action at Soor.' This was the official name for the encounter of the 1st Guards Division on the 28th. And in fact, that fortified farmstead 2000 paces behind Burkersdorf, at which our pursuit ended, did indeed belong to the village of Nieder Soor, lying somewhat to the southwest. The opportunity was joyfully taken to couple [this action] with the victorious battle at Soor in the Second Silesian War, the more so since the situation today had so many features reminiscent of then. Thus, we find the following in Kurd von Schöning's description of the Seven Year War (Volume I, p. 47): 'The Prince was also present at the Battle of Soor, and during the retreat from Trautenau to Schatzlar, he came to the assistance of the hard pressed *General* von Bonin with troops at the decisive moment.' The 'Prince' referred to was Prince Heinrich. In other respects however, it is remarkable how the description fits, even with regard to the names!

The 1st Guards Division bivouacked in and around Burkersdorf, outposts were positioned as far as Nieder Soor on the *Chaussée* leading to Königinhof. The Austrian 10th Corps as noted above, reached the Elbe.

The Fighting at Alt Rognitz and Rudersdorf

About 4 ½ miles behind the 1st Guards Division, the 2nd Guards Division bivouacked in Kosteletz during the night of the 27th/28th. As the former moved out towards Burkersdorf on the morning of the 28th, the 2nd Guards Division initially headed from Kosteletz toward Eypel where it halted. Then came orders to advance from Eypel to the pass that extended past Raatsch, and to follow the 1st Guards Division. Already the thunder of the guns could be heard from the front.

It may have been 10:00 as the 2nd Guards Division received reports that about a mile and a half to the right, the enemy was in the village of Rudersdorf. This report was soon confirmed. It was decided to dispatch a detachment to the right flank. We shall return to this in greater detail.

First, however, we shall examine the enemy and his position.

---

63 Author's Note: Unfortunately, he was unable to deliver them, for as we learned later, *Oberlieutenant* Haschka was seriously wounded in this very action (at Burkersdorf) and died in a Prussian hospital.

Of the two enemy brigades (Wimpffen and Grivicic) that remained in and around Trautenau on the evening of the 27th, Grivicic received orders early on the 28th, to advance with front facing south, on the left flank of Brigades Knebel and Mondl (partly bivouacked, partly on the move), and by way of Alt Rognitz and Rudersdorf, to strike the right flank of the attacking enemy. This was a well-conceived manoeuvre which, had it succeeded (and it could have done if it had been executed between 9.00 and 10.00), would have driven a wedge between the two Guards divisions. This bold thrust, especially if supported by Brigade Wimpffen, could hardly fail to achieve a double success. Specifically:

> The 1st Guards Division, with its forward position already engaged, would be cut off;
> The 2nd Guards Division, stuck in the pass, would be unable to get out of it and, if it was lucky, would have to retreat to Eypel.

Each of these comprised a genuine danger. Two things averted it:

> Brigade Grivicic, and this was the most important thing, missed the right moment.
> Guards Grenadier Regiment Nr. 2 parried the thrust when it finally came.

Parrying this thrust was the action at Rudersdorf and Alt Rognitz which we shall now describe.

The 2nd Guards Division, *Generallieutenant* von Plonski, had formed an advanced guard consisting of the two Grenadier battalions of the Emperor Franz Regiment [Guards Grenadier Regiment Nr. 2]. The 2nd Battalion, *Oberstlieutenant* von Gaudy, took the lead, the 1st Battalion, *Major* von Böhn, followed. When the 2nd Battalion, still in the defile, reached the village of Raatsch, which was enclosed between high valley walls, *Oberstlieutenant* von Gaudy was ordered to climb the valley wall on the right with his battalion and to advance across the plateau toward the village of Rudersdorf, which was strongly held (the reports had been confirmed) by the enemy.

This was done. First the battalion climbed the steep side of the valley.

Once at the top, *Oberstlieutenant* von Gaudy called the company commanders together and made the following dispositions:

> The battalion was to advance on the direct route toward Rudersdorf, rifle platoons of the 5th and 8th Companies were to form the vanguard.
> The remaining platoons of the 5th Company were to form the main part of the advance – guard.
> The remaining platoons of the 8th Company were to cover our right flank.
> The 6th and 7th Companies were to follow the 5th company as a half battalion.

Now the battalion moved out. The sun blazed down, nowhere a shadow. The path led through fields of grain, dips and small woods. The first shots came after half an hour. The officers dismounted from their horses. Nothing could be seen of the enemy, no shako, no *Jäger* hat, only a cloud of smoke when a shot was fired, indicated the direction where (behind the tall grain) the enemy was to be sought. The first farmsteads of Rudersdorf that were not hidden in the valley, lay in bright sunshine. Most visible of all was a tall stone cross (crucifix) in front of the village, just to the left of the road. That was the main scene of the developing battle, and at the same time, would be a memorial for it.[64]

Oberstlieutenant von Gaudy rode at the head of the 5th Company. When the first shots rang out, he took his binoculars and focused on the closest farmstead, then said to *Adjutant* von Sydow, who was beside him, 'I see white coats. It is the enemy. Report that the village is occupied and that I will take it.' Those were the last words spoken by the brave officer who had already displayed outstanding courage and judgement in 1848 in Schleswig, and the following year, in the defense of the Prüm arsenal.

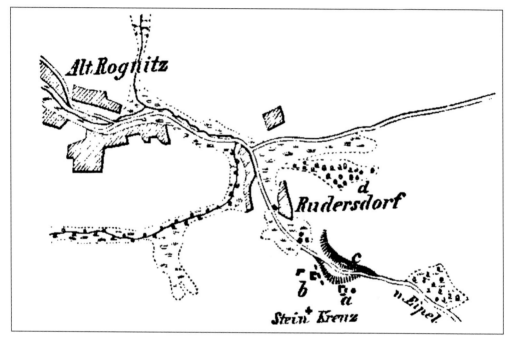

Sketch map of Alt Rognitz and Rudersdorf.

64 Author's Note: We add the following to the earlier description of the locality. Alt Rognitz and Rudersdorf lay, as was true for most of the villages in the area, in a long valley. The individual farmsteads were, in part, on the slopes, in part on the floor of the valley, with a small number on the plateau. The two villages were directly adjoining, Alt Rognitz was the main village, and at its highest point, was the picturesque Church of St. Johann and Paul. Rudersdorf was the smaller, southern half of the whole and is separated from Alt Rognitz by a cross. The inhabitants are German. [Ed Note: The road from Trautenau to Rudersdorf is mostly open, as it approaches Rudersdorf, a steep escarpment rises on the left, on which stands the Church of Saints John and Paul. In places the road passes through low rock cuttings. The escarpment is everywhere the most visible feature]. The actual fighting was limited to the southern point of Rudersdorf. As one approaches this from Raatsch, 200 paces before the beginning of the village, to its left, is the stone cross mentioned above, enclosed by a simple green iron fence, it is a work of remarkable artistic beauty. From the stone cross one has a view of the entire battlefield and of three or four farmsteads on the near side of the valley, then a stone quarry across from the farmsteads, on the right hand slope, and finally a little wood (towards Alt Rognitz) on the right hand plateau. These three points, the farmsteads, the stone quarry, and the little woods, were the focal points of the fighting. Finally, the stone cross, itself (the sketch map in the text emphasizes these points).

Events now took over and the platoons and companies advanced to the attack in their prescribed fashion.

The rifle platoons of the 5th and 8th Companies took the large, most fortified farmstead
(a). The 5th Company took the complex of buildings
(b)   immediately beside and behind it.
The 8th Company (advancing on the right flank) threw itself into a stone quarry
(c)   directly at the exit of the village, in the right wall of the valley.
The 6th and 7th Companies crossed the sunken village street running from left to right, climbed up the valley wall and advanced over the plateau on the far side into a small wood (d) right beside the village and valley.

All of these successes were achieved in little more than ten minutes. The troops had done their duty, but their bold advance had come at a high price. The two young officers, von Besser and Elert, who had led the rifle platoons of the 5th and 8th Companies against the large fortified farmstead were wounded, *Lieutenant* Elert seriously (shot through the abdomen). *Hauptmann* von Wittich was hit by a bullet in the nape of his neck as he advanced with his 5th Company against the adjoining, smaller farmstead. *Lieutenant* von Bärenfels, who assumed command, was hit by two bullets in the arm. Half battalion von Witzleben however, suffered the greatest losses.

We shall examine the advance of these two companies (6th and 7th) more intently, thereby recalling in detail what has been briefly described above.

Half battalion von Witzleben followed the 5th Company as the main body. When the half battalion reached the large fortified farmstead, it sent the rifle platoon of the 5th Company (the 5th Company was personally led by *Oberstlieutenant* von Gaudy) ahead. Von Gaudy immediately dismounted, placed himself at the front of the half battalion, and led both companies past the farmstead and down into the village. As he directed the half battalion to climb the facing wall of the valley, he was hit by two bullets, in the mouth and chest. He was dead on the spot. Men of the 5th Company carried him back to the farmstead.

When he saw his *Oberstlieutenant* fall, *Hauptmann* von Witzleben sprang to the front in that same moment and commanded, in a firm voice, 'Half right, march. By the right flank march; Halt!' Everyone obeyed, even the dispersed groups. Thus, he successfully led the half battalion to a corner of the valley that provided some cover, and at the same time, the opportunity to regroup.

This succeeded, but it was no place to stay. More desirable was a little wood to the right on the plateau, still at a significant distance and strongly held by the enemy. If it was taken, then [we would have cover] and be on the enemy's flank, commanding the valley.

Therefore, up and onto the plateau. So far so good, and now over the plateau to the woods. It might have been 300 paces. A tough piece of work. with skirmishers to the right and left they advanced. The half battalion was like a large, moving target.

Fire was heavy, especially from the left corner of the woods (where it adjoined the village) so that the half battalion involuntarily bore off to the right. *Hauptmann* von Witzleben, hit in the heart, collapsed. *Hauptmann* von Reitzenstein fell seriously wounded. *Lieutenant* von Weiher fell dead. All of the drums fell silent. The attack hesitated, but only for a moment. 'Forward!' , cried everyone, and despite fresh losses, the woods were taken. 70 prisoners were captured, the rest retreated, some to the left into the village, some to the rear through a gully to a facing hill that was also wooded.

The wood was ours, but it was not the time to celebrate. The troops were decimated, exhausted and disorganized. Bullets came from all sides. The battalion commander and *Hauptleute* dead or severely wounded. Moreover, suddenly came the question, where are the colours? The battalion colours were missing, the colour bearer too, *Portepée Fähnrich* von Schenk. They searched for him. There he lay at the margin of the woods, a youngster, shot through both legs. He had only been released from the cadet corps eight days before. He held in his hand the colours, with its tip half shot off (a bullet had hit the iron cross). *Lieutenant* von Sell, as the senior officer, assumed command. He stepped forward, took the tip together with the cross,[65] and kept it. He wrapped the oilcloth cover around his body like a sash, and returning to the woods, planted the flag in a clear spot where it would serve as a rallying point for the scattered men. Patrols were sent out. The remnants, 60 to 70 men, gathered round the flag. Some threw themselves on the ground in total exhaustion and immediately fell asleep.

The enemy seemed to be concentrating his battalions to recapture the woods. Columns were visible. The signal sounded the advance. Our men, still under heavy fire, especially from the left, were involuntarily forced further to the right, some into the open, some into another wood. It was now a matter of holding these woods by the village. *Lieutenant* von Sell quickly made up his mind. During this [involuntary] movement sideways, he suddenly shouted, 'Halt! March, March, Hurrah!' and leaping forward, he now led the men, inspired at that moment, joining in the Hurrah, as if to a new attack against the unoccupied woods that they had just abandoned. That cry had restored a certain *elan* to the demoralized troops, from that moment on, they were calm and held fast in the woods. The trunks of the trees provided some cover. Now there were only a few losses.

So much for the advance of half battalion von Witzleben. Let us now examine the overall situation as it was about 20 minutes after the start of the fighting:

> The remnants of the 5th Company, *Lieutenant* von Bärenfels, held the farmstead to the left of the village.
> The remnants of the 8th Company, *Hauptmann* von der Goltz, held the stone quarry on the right of the valley wall.
> The remnants of the 6th and 7th Companies held the little woods on the right hand side of the plateau.

Further advance was impossible. Thus, a fire fight developed from all three points which, thanks to the superiority of our needle guns and our covered positions, was carried on for a good hour

---

65   Author's Note: The tip had further adventures in the course of the day which led to remarkable scenes. *Lieutenant* von Sell, for all his efforts to preserve the tip of the flagstaff, nevertheless lost it in the confusion of the fighting. He instituted a search for it, but in vain. Others were to find it. When, about two hours later, 90 stragglers of the battalion led by a *Feldwebel*, proceeded across this little plateau, they saw the tip of the flagstaff lying in a field. They placed it on a young fir tree and carried this improvised flagstaff (sanctified by the old cross), before them as 'the remnant of the 2nd Battalion Emperor Franz,' into Trautenau. They personified the glory of the day. Thus, arose the rumour that 'the 2nd Battalion arrived in Trautenau 90 men strong.' However, as we have already indicated, these 90 men were stragglers. The battalion and it's colours still existed.

with varying success. This was where the famous 'Garibaldi' (a proper Berlin boy[66] who had followed the 2nd Battalion of the Franz Regiment from the day it moved out), excelled in his efforts to be of service. The troops, desperately thirsty, longed for a drop of water. Directly before them was a large well, but it was in the middle of the street and under fire from all sides which made it nearly impossible to approach. Garibaldi made his way to it, and while the bullets whistled around, he turned the crank and filled the bucket, and then the canteens from the bucket.

An hour passed and the hard pressed company held out but realized increasingly, that all the enemy needed was a single brief assault to throw our detachment (that had melted down to barely 200 men) out of our hard won position. The only question was why the enemy delayed so long. Finally, he gathered his forces, first attacking the farmstead to the left of the road and then the stone quarry, both of which he took.[67] The enemy pressed forward past the stone cross. *Hauptmann* von der Goltz, the only company commander still unwounded at this spot, led the remnants of his company back.

Only half battalion von Witzleben still held out in its advanced and exposed position. Probably it was not fully aware of its extreme danger. The enemy, after capturing the farmstead and the stone quarry, was already 1000 paces beyond our forlorn post. All that was needed was a swing to the left and all who were in the little woods would be cut off and captured. However, this was not to happen. At the very moment of extreme danger, the gunfire that became ever livelier on the flank and rear, gave rise to new hope that finally, help was arriving. And it had arrived, it was the 1st Battalion (von Böhn), so eagerly awaited for an hour. The action now entered its second phase.

Battalion von Böhn had initially followed Battalion von Gaudy, when the latter turned off to the right, [Battalion von Böhn] continued toward Prausnitz Kaile, but only for a short distance. When the battalion was about 200 paces past Raatsch, it was ordered to turn off to the right also to support the 2nd Battalion. Another Brigade would follow.

The corresponding movement was immediately executed, the plateau was climbed, and the two half battalions formed thus:

1st half battalion (1st and 4th Companies), *Hauptmann* von Witzmann.
2nd half battalion (2nd and 3rd Companies), *Hauptmann* von Bentivegni.

66   Author's Note: The actual name of this Berlin youth, who entered Trautenau the next day with an Austrian shako on his head, alongside the battalion's bullet torn colours, to the applause of all the troops in Trautenau, was Karl Lehmann. I saw him later in Prague. He wore a gray outfit, a military cap and shoulder straps of the Regiment Franz on his shoulders. He was highly regarded by the soldiers because of his courage, his modesty and his constant good humour. Thus, he was with them as they marched in. Since then, he was placed in a military orphanage for further training.

67   Author's Note: It appears that the stone quarry was voluntarily evacuated. From the moment the farmstead across from it was recaptured by the enemy, it became untenable. An eyewitness writes, 'Unfortunately the excavation was so shallow that, even lying down, one had no proper cover, so little that one of us was wounded in the nose, another in the heel. We were under cross fire from the front, from the houses of the village, from the strongly held little woods to the left of the village, and finally, even from woods to our rear. Many were wounded. The situation became ever more uncomfortable. We saw the enemy advancing on our left, the heat was unbearable. No one had a drop in their canteen. Finally, Bärenfels fell back. The Austrians forced their way into the farmstead and were now facing us. Now we also followed and fell back to the sunken road behind the stone cross.'

They now proceeded in essentially the same direction that Battalion Gaudy had taken an hour before. At about 1:00 both half battalions were within 500 paces of Rudersdorf. Here they came upon the retreating remnants (see above) of the 5th and 8th Companies, under *Hauptmann* von der Goltz. These now came under the command of the 1st Battalion.

Major von Böhn called a halt to allow the men (exhausted from the march and scorching sun), to rest, and above all, to [give him time] to review the situation. He saw that the enemy was following our retreating troops. [The enemy's] skirmishers were hidden on both sides in

Fighting at the stone cross.

cornfields and the woods. However, he had concentrated his main forces at the road itself. Here in the center, the farmsteads at the exit of the village were strongly held by Austrian *Jäger*. In front of this position however, almost at the foot of the stone cross, the enemy stood in dense columns, awaiting our attack. This was the 3rd Battalion IR 2 Alexander (Hungarian [Transylvanian]) *Major* von Böhn did not hesitate. He directed half battalion Bentivegni to the left, *Hauptmann* von der Goltz with the remnants of the 5th and 8th Companies to the right, against the woods that were filled with skirmishers. With the remaining half battalion von Witzmann, he charged the enemy center with hurrahs. A volley cut down the battalion that was standing at the stone cross in entire ranks, and rapidly pursuing the retreating enemy, our men established themselves at the entrance of the village. The farmsteads, which had been taken and held with such heavy losses were now captured for the second time. *Lieutenant* von Sydow, with some of the 8th Company, pushed forward to the Alt Rognitz church.[68]

The companies (6th and 7th) that remained in the little woods to the right on the plateau, attacked anew with flanking fire. Finally, fresh battalions arrived from the brigade that had been promised from the start. These were:

> The 1st Battalion of Regiment Elisabeth
> The Guards *Schützen* Battalion
> The Fusilier Battalion of the Franz Regiment

They drove the enemy off and were joined by fresh units from the 2nd Guards Division. The ever weakening opposition finally collapsed completely, surrounded on all sides and exhausted by two days of fighting. With no hope of relief and no possibility of breaking through, the greatest part of Brigade Grivicic now laid down their weapons. The Franz Grenadiers had done the real work, the battalions that followed on conducted a game drive, effortlessly harvesting the fruits of the victory with hardly any losses. Thousands of prisoners were taken.[69]

---

68   Author's Note: Among the grenadiers with whom *Lieutenant* von Sydow pushed forward to the church, two 'one year volunteers' shone, *Grenadier* Hasenpflug and *Gefreiter* Samuel. Only a few of the men of the 5th and 8th Companies still had the strength to follow. Most, after recapturing the farmsteads, collapsed, crying 'Water, Water.' It was brought to them, 'Garibaldi was again unwearying. As they pulled themselves together, to carry on the fire fight with the *Jäger*, they realized that a wounded Austrian lay by the previously mentioned well in the fierce heat of the sun, crying plaintively and begging someone to carry him out of the line of fire. *Lieutenant* von der Horst took pity and asked Grenadier Kucharsky to help him carry the man, since he alone was too weak to do so. Kucharsky immediately sprang forward saying, 'That is a good deed. The good Lord will help with that.' And so the two of them carried him out of the firing. The example of *Gefreiter* Samuel does not stand alone. Many times his fellow believers [Jews] excelled during the campaign. It was as if they had promised themselves that they would put an end to the old prejudices about their pacifism and incompetence. Three Jews were enlisted in the 1st Battalion of the *Leib* Regiment. One, overweight and no longer young, suffered horribly. His feet were sore, however he made it through the action at Gitschin in the scorching heat from beginning to end. He could not be persuaded to go to the hospital.

69   Author's Note: Large numbers of Brigade Grivicic that had spent the night hidden in the woods, were captured the following morning. Depressed by the fighting and their losses, they could not hope to break out. Some tried to slip through on their own, and some may have succeeded. Most however, came up against our outposts that were positioned in all of the villages and were taken after brief resistance. For example, 100 Austrians were captured by the village watch of the 3rd Guards Regiment, and about 120 more in Staudenz. The last prisoners of war showed how demoralized the Austrians already were. In Staudenz there were only four grenadiers from the 2nd Guards Regiment who had carried their seriously wounded *Hauptmann* (von Kracht) there the day before. At 4:00 in the morning came the sudden cry, 'The Austrians are coming.' The four grenadiers grabbed their weapons. Eleven litter bearers from the other regiment joined them. They hastily occupied the edge of the village and realized that a group of Austrians, about company strength, was advancing on the village. These 15 men, without an officer, opened a brisk fire. The enemy hesitated. Some of the 3rd Guards Regiment came to their assistance and two officers and 121 men surrendered. Some of the prisoners belonged to the 16th *Jäger* Battalion, some to IR 23 Airoldi (Polish) [the recruiting area for IR 23 was the Banat, it is unlikely that the predominant ethnicity was Polish], which had suffered extremely heavy casualties two days earlier in the fighting with I Corps. Along with *Brigadier Oberst* Grivicic, the Commander of Regiment Airoldi, *Oberst* Camerra, was also captured. Barely 2000 men from the entire Brigade reached their own lines.

Among them the courageous *Oberst* Grivicic (wounded) and his Adjutant. The victors, their prisoners in the middle, proceeded to Trautenau. This, on the evening of the 28th, had become a single great army camp, widely encircled by the battalions of the 2nd Guards Division.

Only one battalion was missing from the division, the 2nd Battalion Franz, it remained on the field that it had held so long, at the southern point of Rudersdorf, seeking out its wounded and burying its dead. We shall turn to this final act of the day.

Seven of the battalion's officers were wounded, three were dead. It was decided to bury these at the foot of the tall stone crucifix that had been shot up during the fighting [Ed. Note – still with bullets embedded in its stonework]. The three dead were sought and found. *Hauptmann* von Witzleben and *Lieutenant* von Weiher lay as they had fallen on the plateau. *Oberstlieutenant* von Gaudy, his valuables stolen, lay in one of the farmsteads that the pursuing enemy had occupied after the retreat of the 5th and 8th Companies. His revolver and his purse were taken from him. His watch chain (someone had been in a hurry) was torn off, but the watch itself was still in his breast pocket.

Burial party.

Evening had fallen. The moon rose as the remnants of the 2nd Battalion gathered around a grave at the north side of the stone cross which the one year volunteers of the battalion had requested (as a particular honour) to be allowed to dig. Then von Gaudy was brought up on a long plank (as in a burial at sea) and placed in the grave, von Witzleben beside him, von Weiher on top of them both. *Hauptmann* von der Goltz stood at the grave and spoke a few words that seemed appropriate to the moment, then a short prayer. All were deeply moved. The moon now shone bright in the heavens, 'Its light fell on the dead and on us, but it also illuminated the statue of Christ above us.'

As the grave was filled in, all who had stood around it returned to the nearby village. The officers sought lodging in the inns, but the situation there was terrible. Blood everywhere. Finally, they found a shed that bore none of the red traces of the fighting. They wrapped themselves in their coats and sought sleep, despite the horrors all around, it came.

We conclude with the fragmentary report of an eyewitness [in all probability an officer] who took part in the attack on the plateau and the woods. He presents a graphic picture, especially of the scenes that followed this fighting: '. . . and so we lay, hardly capable of action, in the woods that had been taken with so much blood, surrounded by the enemy in front, rear and left flank. But even more oppressive than the danger was the heat. The exhaustion and thirst reached the highest degree. The day before I had filled my canteen in Kosteletz with a passable local wine. There was a little bit left and I took a little swig. Immediately I was surrounded with men begging for some. It was impossible. All that was left in the canteen was one gulp. This must be saved for the wounded. I gave a few drops in the hollow of my hand to each, or at least to many, of the wounded, which they eagerly lapped.

After the fighting was over, as I went down into the village, I passed the place the we had suffered the heaviest losses. There lay Witzleben and Weiher, not far from each other. There were several wounded by Witzleben, who mourned him loudly. I was deeply moved when I saw his impressively beautiful corpse stretched out there. He was covered in blood. Two or three rounds through the chest had killed him . . . Below, in the first farmstead, lay Gaudy along with the other dead. We were not on good terms toward the end. Now I clasped the dead man's hand with the thought that there could be no hostility between us from now on . . . . There were many others, Wittich, Reitzenstein, Schenk, all severely wounded . . . .

We now attempted to write a few penciled lines to our families. In the meantime however, the loud cries of an old woman came from a little house across the way. She might well mourn. Her man lay dead, stretched out on the threshold of her house. A bullet had hit him in the forehead during the fighting in the village. . . . The combat reports were written. It was my lot to take them to Trautenau, where we presumed the divisional headquarters were. I rode off at about 8:30 on Wittich's white horse, armed with Horst's revolver. It was an extraordinary ride through sunken roads with the dead lying everywhere, some still from the previous day. I found the divisional headquarters in Trautenau and submitted the report. Then I looked for our *Oberst*. He was shaken as I told him of our efforts and our losses. I then rode out to the divisional bivouac where I found the two other battalions and stragglers from our own battalion. It was the 90 men with the improvised flagstaff, including men from my company. When they saw me they fell upon me and shook my hand. They believed that they were the only ones left from the battalion:

The next morning, I rode back to Rudersdorf through the valley that had been at the foot of our little woods and had separated us from the facing hill. In this valley there was tall grain. I could see many furrows in the grain and if I followed them, there was a dead Austrian lying at the end of each one. They had crept into the grain and there had been hit by our bullets . . . . I no longer found our battalion in Rudersdorf. I found it bivouacked in Raatsch. I was greeted on my return, and soon a generous meal was served, bouillon, chicken and buttermilk. The five captured officers of the 16th *Jäger* Battalion joined us. We chatted back and forth . . . In the evening we were in Trautenau.

There is hardly an event of the 1866 war that has received such varying judgement as this fight of the Franz Regiment, especially that of von Gaudy's 2nd Battalion at Rudersdorf and Alt Rognitz.

The enthusiasts have allowed themselves to be carried away, presenting the prompt, courageous execution of his orders by *Oberstlieutenant* von Gaudy, as an act of heroism that saved the entire Guards Corps. The critics on the other hand, have taken the position that the fighting at Alt Rognitz was irrelevant to the advance or security of the Guards Corps, and that first phase of this fighting was a mistake, indeed was an act of rashness.

Both viewpoints appear to us to have missed the real point. Events moved so rapidly in the forenoon of the 28th (the frontal action against Burkersdorf) and so strikingly, that even an assault into our right flank (which, after the previous negligence, could not have taken place before 12:00) could not have significantly altered the overall result of the day. In retrospect that is incontrovertible. As events turned out, an unchecked thrust of Brigade Grivicic would have been irrelevant, however, *had this thrust been executed two hours earlier and with two brigades*, our Guards Corps would have been in an extremely critical situation. The fact that, *by pure chance*, or as the result of failures by the enemy, things worked out more favourably for us, cannot retrospectively deprive the action of the recognition it would have gained under *other justified suppositions*.

So much for the significance or lack thereof, of the action itself. A word, too, regarding the conduct of the commander and his men. The manner in which *Oberstlieutenant* von Gaudy opened the action, and how the battalion (after having lost nearly all of its officers in the first ten minutes) carried on the fight, was neither an act of heroism, nor of rashness. Here too, there seems to be a middle ground. There was a definite order.[70] The attack was planned in careful obedience to this order and carried out courageously. What was attempted was not done on a whim, nor heroic fancy. What was done was only what was required, what was in accord with duty, what was, like the concept itself, simply correct. Those who praise and those who criticize the action must be willing to compromise. As always however, whatever the judgement of the informed regarding 'Rudersdorf and Alt Rognitz,' the feelings of the people have long since been made plain. Unconcerned with the military significance or insignificance of the action, they appreciated the bit of living poetry that deals with it. 'The Ballad of the Franz Grenadiers at Alt Rognitz,' with its folksong like refrain, 'How many are you, still? Say on, say on my son! 220 men of the 2nd Battalion,' has been a favourite on the streets and backcourts since the

---

70   Author's Note: The order read: 'The 2nd Battalion is to move up the valley. To the right there is a village. The enemy should be there (however these may be troops of our I Corps). *If it is the enemy, the battalion is to force its way through to Trautenau.'*

summer of 1866. The brave *Oberst* von Gaudy has also found honour in a song that speaks of him and his loyal men:

Still his stiff hand holds the sword,
His body soaked with blood.
He was our Oberstlieutenant,
Shot through heart and mouth.

Still, it was, a sweltering June night,
Drenched with tepid dew,
Shimmering white,

Lit by the light of the silent moon.
There at the crucifix of stone,
Drenched in the white glimmer,
His comrades in arms, volunteers,
Prepared his resting place.
At the foot of the cross and by moonlight,
Thus was the hero buried;
I know no better resting place,
No other could I have.

With God, for King and Fatherland,
So was the hero struck down.
We shall sing and speak
Of our Oberstlieutenant.

Sing and speak every hour,
Fritz Gaudy was his name.
He was shot through heart and mouth.
God help us all. Amen.

The Fighting at Königinhof

Significant success accompanied the action of the Guards Corps on the 28th. We briefly recapitulate as follows:

The passes of Eypel and Trautenau were opened.
Gablenz' corps was beaten in two actions (at Burkersdorf and Alt Rognitz). Brigade Grivicic was nearly wiped out.
The great roads to the Elbe lay open. The retreating enemy could only take up a position there under the protection of his fortresses (he did that).
Nothing stood in the way of the concentration of the entire 2nd Army on the plateau between Gradlitz and Königinhof.

In the event, the 28th had been the day of decision along the entire line between Nachod and Skalitz, Eypel and Trautenau, and had worked out in our favour. On the 29th, V Corps rapidly broke the enemy's resistance at Schweinschädel and advanced toward Gradlitz, while the Guards took Königinhof[71] by storm. Both corps, followed by I and VI Corps, thereby reached their rendezvous at the Elbe. We shall initially follow the Guards.

Following the action on the 28th, the 1st Guards Division held the line Neu Rognitz – Burkersdorf with its main body. The *Avantgarde*, with outposts toward Prausnitz, Soor and Ober Altenbuch, bivouacked in some woods either side of the Königinhof *Chaussée*. The night passed without incident. On the morning of the 29th (11:30) the *Avantgarde*, which had in the meantime been reinforced with a company of *Jägers,* two squadrons [of cavalry] and one battery, set out to occupy Königinhof.

Soon after 12:00 the *Avantgarde* (*Oberst* von Kessel) moved out. At its head marched:

> 3 troops of Guards Hussars.
> The 3rd Battalion of the Guards Fusilier Regiment.
> 2 companies Guard *Jäger.*

It was under the special command of *Oberstlieutenant Graf* von Waldersee of the Guards Fusilier Regiment.

The Main Body followed five hundred paces behind and comprised:

> The Fusilier Battalions of the 1st, 2nd and 3rd Guards Regiments.
> 2 Guards batteries.
> 2 companies of Guard Pioneers.

The distance from Burkersdorf to Königinhof is barely nine miles. The great heat and the sparse rations (the supply columns had not yet arrived and there was nothing to be had in the villages) made this march, for the most part through woods, one of the most difficult. We find the following descriptions:

> As we traversed this landscape of woods and rocks by Weiberkränke (that for about a half mile is called the *Königreich* Woods), and indeed as far as Rettendorf, we were presented with a sight that was as unexpected as it was disturbing to our soldiers' eyes. We saw the complete defeat of the enemy who had faced us yesterday. The entire *Chaussée* was strewn with discarded Austrian kit. There were knapsacks, coats (brand new), leather gear, shakoes, boots, cooking kettles, as well as weapons in numbers that

---

71 Author's Note: Königinhof, on the left bank of the Elbe between Arnau and Josephstadt, is one of the oldest Bohemian towns. It's centre is small but is completely surrounded by five suburbs, it has a Schloss and a deanery. In 1817 a Professor Hanka found an old Bohemian manuscript in the church tower (containing a considerable number of lyric and epic poems) now known as the '*Königinhofer Handschrift*' [The Königinhof Manuscript]. The controversy over the authenticity of this very interesting manuscript, we shall leave unsettled, only remarking that the revival of Czech literature dates from its discovery.

we could hardly count. Hundreds of rifles were thrown into the roadside ditches or scattered around, and just as many stacked in pyramids.

What had happened here? Each of us asked ourselves this question. Much larger numbers than we had seen must have passed through here and frightened by false alarms (perhaps in the night), had scattered in every direction. We had the impression of a total rout, and from this day on, we were convinced that the war would be soon and brilliantly ended. Even after a defeat, this should not happen to any army that could hope to stand against us on equal terms.

The march through the *Königreich* Woods may have lasted two hours. It was 3:00 when the *Avantgarde* emerged from the woods at Rettendorf, and now saw a broad landscape stretching before them, first meadows and fields of grain, then suburban farmsteads, then the town itself, with the shining ribbon of the Elbe, and on the far side of the river, a railway embankment and ridges.

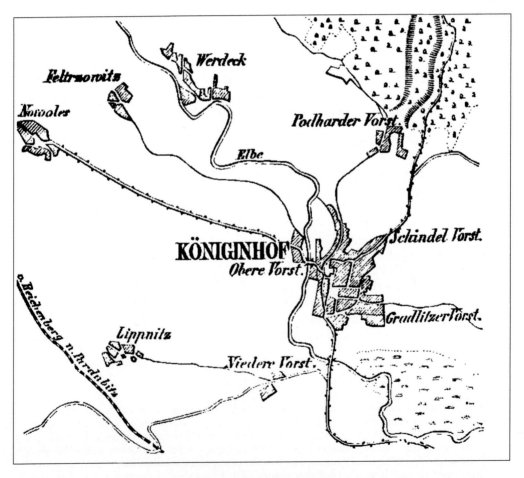

Sketch map of Königinhof.

On these ridges (thus to the rear of the town and river) could be seen withdrawing enemy columns, probably the remnants of 10th Corps. The [Austrian] army headquarters had taken two measures to prevent the line of retreat from being cut, or to make it more difficult. On the far side of the Elbe, batteries had taken up position on the ridges that could cover the ground as far as Rettendorf. On the near side of the Elbe, in Königinhof itself, was a rear guard consisting of IR 6 Coronini [4th Corps] under *Oberst* von Stocklin, with orders to stop the advancing enemy at that point.

This mission was as difficult as it was honourable. The position of the town, especially with regard to the two bridges over the Elbe, placed Regiment Coronini more or less, in a hopeless situation. In the event, things took such a course and a not insignificant part of Regiment Coronini was captured.

The fighting had three stages: a cannonade from Rettendorf, an infantry fight, and finally the capture of the town.

The cannonade

As the point of the *Avantgarde* (Guards *Jäger* and Guards Fusiliers) emerged from the *Königreich* Woods, retreating enemy columns were observed on the winding roads on the ridges on the far side of the Elbe.

Immediately (while the other troops of the *Avantgarde* continued their march on Königinhof), the two Guards Batteries of Braun and Eltester, were brought forward to a point south of Rettendorf and opened fire on the enemy columns on the far side of the Elbe, but the range was too great. Since the *Avantgarde* (calmly continuing its advance) had in the meantime reached a more advanced wood about 2000 to 3000 paces closer, and had taken position in it (front facing the town), one of the batteries was able to move to the southern edge of these little woods and fire directly on the town, shelling an old tower gate, which presumably offered us the nearest (northern) point of entry into the town.

The infantry fight

In the meantime, while the other battalions were still held back, the point of the *Avantgarde* had already emerged from the southern margin of the above mentioned small wood. Between this and the town itself was the Schindel *Vorstadt* [suburb], flanked on both sides by meadows and fields of corn. The enemy was hidden in these. *Oberstlieutenant Graf* Waldersee immediately took the offensive. To the left, east of the *Chaussée*, he had the 2nd *Jäger* Company and the 9th Company of the Guards Fusilier Regiment, advance with strong swarms of skirmishers against the meadow ground. The 12th Company followed, closed up with drums beating. On the right the 10th Company advanced. The 11th Company held the center, the *Chaussée*.

In the face of this offensive, the enemy evacuated his forward position and fell back to the edge of the actual town, but not without courageous resistance, repeatedly taking up intermediate positions while withdrawing. A report stated:

> The enemy riflemen lay hidden in the tall rye. They were at a disadvantage since they had to stand up to load their rifles, while we could remain under cover while reloading. The columns fell back, closed up, in good order. Their losses were significant as they

crossed the broad grainfields. The calm fire of the [Prussian] Fusiliers, and especially of the *Jägers*, was very effective. It was directed, always with special vigour, on the enemy when he was retreating. Very many dead and wounded lay in the grain, all shot through the head or chest. Thus, advancing on both sides of the *Chaussée*, we drew nearer to the town, which we now found to be held by enemy forces along its entire northern edge. We shot it out with them, after a quarter of an hour the enemy fire diminished.

The capture of the town

By now the Fusilier battalion of the 1st Guards Regiment, which had immediately followed the vanguard of the *Avantgarde,* had arrived. *Oberstlieutenant Graf* Waldersee, reinforced by four companies from this battalion, resolved to attack the town. He disposed accordingly:

> The 10th Company of the 1st Guards Regiment.
> The 11th Company of the Guards Fusilier Regiment.

The latter followed the former, both were to attack the town from the north. The other available companies were to advance on both flanks, and seek to capture the bridges, thereby cutting the enemy's line of retreat. The attack proceeded in accordance with this plan. Thus, we shall report;

> Regarding an encounter at the northern entrance to the town.
> Regarding street fighting on the part of the companies that entered the town.
> Regarding a skirmish at the bridges.
> And as the case may be, regarding a cannonade whose target was the bridges.

After the enemy fell back from his forward position, as we already know, he took post in the northern periphery of the town. All of the houses had been loopholed, roofs had been stripped of their coverings [tiles etc.] and a large farmstead at the beginning of the Trautenau road was fortified like a redoubt. The enemy held this farmstead. If he was driven from there, then the way into the town was open. The two above named companies attacked, 10th Company of the 1st Guards Regiment in the lead, and attacked with such energy that despite the, at times, courageous resistance, the farmstead was nearly taken in the first charge. A *Fähnrich* and 30 men were captured. The 11th Company of the Guards Fusiliers that followed found no more work and advanced to the marketplace.

During this brief encounter at the northern entrance to the town, the two 12th Companies of the two regiments most engaged in this action (1st Guards Regiment and Guards Fusiliers) entered from the right and left. The chance interaction of these two companies (which could not have been planned) led to some interesting street fighting. We shall attempt to describe it.

As the 12th Company of the 1st Guards Regiment (*Hauptmann Graf* Rantzau) approached the marketplace from the east, it was attacked by a column of approximately 250 men that was probably seeking a way out of the town by the southern Elbe bridge. A vigorous rapid fire contained the attack and forced the enemy column to turn off along a side street in the hope of now reaching the western Elbe bridge instead. They had made it about halfway between the market and the western bridge, when they ran into the rear of the 12th Company of the Guards Fusilier Regiment (which had entered the town from the northwest via the Podharder

Vorstadt), which was seeking the same objective as the enemy column, the western bridge over the Elbe. After a moment's hesitation, the Austrian column, under pressure from one enemy and here unexpectedly running into a new one, attacked. However, the rearmost half platoon of the Guards Fusilier Company reversed their facing and delivered such an effective fire that the enemy desisted from its attack. An officer who pressed forward shouting, 'Long live the *Kaiser*' was shot at a range of ten paces by a [Prussian] officer.

The resolution with which this half platoon of the Guards Fusiliers acted, while the rest of the company, unaffected by this incident, continued its march to the western Elbe bridge, caused the enemy column to turn back into the town. In so doing it had to come up against the same 12th Company of the 1st Guards Regiment before which it had, five minutes earlier, turned off toward the western bridge. The half platoon of the Guards Fusiliers followed, an encirclement became ever more likely. Only the confusion of side streets still offered an opportunity to escape.

The enemy column that we are following marched back into the town. From the suburb in which it found itself, it again reached the point (an old gate house of the actual inner town) at which the road began to go uphill until it reached the churchyard, when suddenly (in sight of our 12th Company of the 1st Guards Regiment that was positioned there), a wounded Austrian officer's horse scattered the tightly packed enemy column so that all pressed themselves against the houses, leaving a path through the middle. At the same moment an Austrian standard was raised in the center of this path.

The moment our leading riflemen saw the standard, they threw themselves with a hurrah into the path cleared by the wounded horse and fell upon the standard bearer. He held out bravely. Friend and foe pressed toward the flag. Fusilier Bochnia grabbed it, and although wounded four times, he managed to tear it from the enemy's grasp and bore it out of the struggling mass to the jubilant cheers of the Fusiliers who were pressing forward. Surprised by this incident and encircled, the entire enemy column laid down its weapons.[72]

The 12th Company of the 1st Guards Regiment, bringing its prisoners with it, reassembled on the marketplace. The 12th Company of the Guards Fusilier Regiment marched to the western Elbe bridge, and as it encountered no enemy there, continued along the edge of the town to the southern bridge over the Elb

The town was now ours. Regiment Coronini was either captured or expelled. Nevertheless, our situation remained critical. Not only did the enemy maintain a heavy fire from the hills on the far side of the Elbe, but there also appeared to be enemy columns (perhaps the remnants of 10th Corps and elements of 4th Corps), moving out of Josephstadt, that could suddenly change the direction of their march and attempt to recapture the position that had just been lost. [Austrian] *Jäger* had taken up positions in the houses and thickets on the far side of the river and were shooting it out with our forces.

The first objective must be to forestall any attempt to recapture the town. An attempt on our part by the Guards Hussars and Guards Fusiliers to advance across the bridge and to force

72 Author's Note: About 30 paces from the place where Fusilier Bocchnia captured the standard, a soldier of the Guards Fusilier Regiment had found a flag under the body of a dead Austrian, right by the wall of the churchyard. He lifted it up, but it was immediately torn from his grasp without his being able to see by whom. Probably several Austrians were hidden behind the churchyard wall, and from behind, tore the flag from the fusilier's hand. This unexplained event gave rise to an erroneous claim that *two* flags had been captured in Königinhof. This was not the case.

Fighting in Königinhof.

the enemy artillery to evacuate its position foundered. Therefore, there was nothing left but to destroy the bridge, or as the situation might demand, hold it until this measure could be executed. Guards Pioneers, *Hauptmann* von Adler, were brought up to destroy the bridge, and the 9th Company of the 2nd Guards Regiment was brought up to hold it. The enemy's fire now concentrated on these troops who were nearly bereft of cover. Hundreds of shells poured in. Two cut down 12 men. However, due to the importance of the position there was no alternative, the companies could not be spared.

The enemy finally gave up any attempt to recapture the town and completed his retreat (otherwise unhindered by us). In the meantime, the exhausted troops of our *Avantgarde*, and also the Fusiliers of the 2nd Guards Regiment, who were at the southern bridge over the Elbe, were relieved by four fresh battalions under *Generalmajor* von Alvensleben. Grenadier Battalion Petery, of the 2nd Guards Regiment[73] occupied the bridge. Other battalions searched the town

---

73   Author's Note: As Grenadier Battalion Petery arrived at the bridge to relieve the 9th Company of the same regiment, it too came under extremely heavy enemy fire. *Major* von Petery decided that it would be good to provide an example. He dismounted from his horse and had a footstool brought to him. The

and the suburbs and prepared the houses, especially on the southwest side, for defense. In so doing, it turned out that in one grand house, one of the Grenadiers found a piano and began to play. The cannonade continued. Suddenly came the cry, 'The Austrians are coming.' 'All the better, they can march to the music.' And the strains of *'Ich bin ein Preusse'* resounded over the marketplace [I am a Prussian, a popular Prussian marching tune of the time].

However, the Austrians did not come. Their total losses amounted to about 600 men, including nearly 100 dead, all from Regiment Coronini. Among those captured was *Oberst* von Stocklin (who had been wounded) as well as all of the staff officers. The lost standard belonged to the 3rd Battalion. On our side this success was attained with relatively few losses.

The 30th was a day of rest. The enemy limited his activity to a cannonade from the right bank of the Elbe. However, this cannonade (nearly ineffective) achieved nothing to alter the fact that the entire 2nd Army, as the result of three days of victorious combat, was now at the Elbe. All four corps had reached the rendezvous:

> V Corps (left wing) was at Gradlitz
> I Corps (right wing) was at Arnau
> The Guards Corps (center) was at Königinhof
> VI Corps was in support of V Corps

The 2nd Army had brilliantly accomplished its first mission, 'Debouch from the mountains in three columns to the Elbe.' On 1st July the Crown Prince issued the following Order of the Day:

> Only a few days have passed since we crossed the Bohemian frontier and already brilliant victories have accompanied our successful advance, as well as the attainment of our first objective, holding the Elbe crossings and union with the 1st Army. The brave V Army Corp, under the leadership of its heroic Commander, each day smashed a fresh enemy corps for three days in a row with amazing distinction. The Guards conducted two successful actions and forced the enemy back outstandingly. I Army Corps fought with extraordinary bravery under most difficult conditions. Five standards, two banners, 20 guns and 8.000 prisoners are in our hands and many thousands of dead and wounded show how great enemy losses must have been.
>
> Unfortunately, we have to mourn the loss of many brave comrades, who, either dead or wounded, are missing from our ranks. However, the thought of falling for our King and the Fatherland, united with the knowledge of having won the victory, will provide consolation to the dying and ameliorate their suffering. May God now continue to grant victory to our arms. I thank the generals and officers, as well as the soldiers of the 2nd Army for their bravery in battle and their endurance in overcoming the difficult conditions. I take pride in commanding such troops.
>
> Head Quarters, Prausnitz, 1 July 1866.
>
> > Friedrich Wilhelm,
> > Crown Prince

grenadiers wanted to place it in a safe place behind a house. 'Place it at the bridge. I can't see anything from there.' And so Petery sat down in the midst of the hail of shells and smoked his cigar. This did not fail to make a deep impression. Henceforth the men were as calm as their commander.

On the same day (1st July) that the Crown Prince issued this Order of the Day to the 2nd Army, the King arrived at the 1st Army (Prince Friedrich Karl) and set up his headquarters at Gitschin. On that day the 1st Army itself was well past Gitschin. Its extreme left wing (the 5th Division), was nearly in contact (only nine miles separated them) with the right wing of the 2nd Army. The union of the two armies took place two days later on the field of Königgratz.

Before we describe this decisive day, we shall look back on the enemy's actions from the 26th to the 30th.

In Retrospect

Benedek has been severely criticized by friend and foe alike, and perhaps most tellingly, also by those third parties that were not involved. Of his basic plan it is stated that:

> He violated certain fundamental principles. He was faced with two armies, one in front and one to the flank, one distant, the other close. Instead of turning against the nearby flanking enemy, and destroying him with superior forces, he stubbornly held to the plan, passing by the nearer enemy to throw himself on the more distant one. In marching past the flanking enemy, he exposed his right side and finally, deeply shaken by the flank attacks of the 2nd Army, had to recognize that he had neglected the fundamental principles of the conduct of war to the disadvantage of himself and his Emperor.'

Such is the judgement of him, briefly expressed in a pamphlet written by English Lieutenant Colonel Cooke. He wrote:

> The *Feldzeugmeister* misunderstood the strategic objectives of the campaign from the very beginning. Instead of merely halting the approach of Prince Friedrich Karl and attacking the Crown Prince with the main force, he did exactly the opposite and sought to hold the Crown Prince at the mountains while he marched with the main force toward Gitschin. This was an unfortunate measure. Its success depended on whether the four corps of the Crown Prince could be held in check by the two Austrian corps entrusted with this mission. The Crown Prince smashed the forces facing him. The three corps (2nd, 3rd and 4th) that had been ordered to reinforce the Austrians at Gitschin were recalled, and in this critical moment of the campaign, Benedek saw one part of his army overwhelmed by the Crown Prince, another part by Prince Friedrich Karl, while the three corps that could have provided him with superiority in one place, oscillated helplessly between both. Thus did he pay for his failure to respect the basic principles of the conduct of war.

We must agree with the criticism regarding the 'oscillation.' When he criticizes the basic plan however, then here again we must repeat that condemnation of Benedek in such form and generality, cannot be maintained as correct. Other factors that may also affect what is right, either as contributing factors or as decisive in themselves, are ignored. We suggest, as we write this - perhaps daring - statement, that it is quite likely the same with war as with art, that so called basic principles are only valid until they are overthrown by innovation or through an increasing number of exceptional cases.

So much for the generalities. In the case in question, it may well that an attack on the nearby 2nd Army might have been more natural and better than the stubborn persistence on first settling with the 1st Army at Gitschin. Nevertheless, as has been repeatedly stated, this persistence was not entirely reprehensible. The fact that it proved disastrous was due less to the unconditional defectiveness of the plan, than to the faulty and indecisive manner in which it was carried out. Benedek held stubbornly to his plan at a time when it would certainly have been better to give it up. Things had already gone so far that only a ruthless, determined push, could have saved the situation.

The question that must decide this controversy is simply this. Could Benedek, even after the fighting on the 27th (which as Benedek's plan required, should have been entirely avoided), still pass by the 2nd Army, and if he made it past, was it then probable that he could smash the 1st Army?

We shall attempt to find an answer to this. Benedek's situation on the 27th still gave him full freedom of action. 3rd Corps and 4th Corps were already on the right bank of the Elbe with Josephstadt to their rear. If the *Feldzeugmeister*, undeterred by the failure at Nachod, had directed 6th and 8th Corps over the Elbe during the night of the 27th/28th, and ordered 2nd Corps (still some way behind), at least as far as the Elbe, and then employed 10th Corps, which had been victorious on the day before (or if it was too shaken, a combined corps composed of various bodies of troops), to conduct a diversionary action against our 2nd Army which was, for the most part, still stuck in the passes, he would then have had ample time to be in Gitchin by noon on the 29th (certainly by early on the morning of the 30th), with five corps. If his arrival was certain, then it would have been an easy matter for the Austro Saxons to hold Gitchin from the 29th to the 30th. On the 30th it would be seven corps against four and a half.

We do not know what the outcome of this battle would have been, but who could deny that with such a numerical advantage, Benedek would have had a strong chance of victory. If victorious, the moral effect [of this victory] on any subsequent action with the army of the Crown Prince would be incalculable. Confidence in victory might well have more than made up for the numerical losses. We know very well that such armchair theorizing comes more easily than action, and that the course of events cannot be determined like a mathematical equation. We only wish to show that Benedek's plan was not unconditionally bad. The other plan (to deal with the enemy closer to hand), would have been better. [Benedek's original plan], only became disastrous when, in its execution, inconsistencies and contradictions arose that confounded and crippled it.

In the next section we shall see how, as his plan collapsed, Benedek himself finally collapsed, even before 3rd July brought about the actual catastrophe.

From 1st to 3rd July

Back and forth on 1st July, the Prussian position

The actions of our 1st and 2nd Armies, on the 27th, 28th and 29th, had resulted in a decisive convergence of the two great forces. Already on the evening of the 29th, contact had been established. On the 30th, the cavalry had established a direct, if still loose link. The 1st Guards

Dragoon Regiment, *Oberstlieutenant* von Barner, of the 1st Army, appeared in Arnau, which was held by the *Avantgarde* of the East Prussian I Corps. This was contact. An actual union of all our fighting forces was not yet intended.

Our position on 1st July was:

> The Elbe Army (right wing) between Zeretitz and Gitschinowes.
>   (*Avantgarde* as far as Hochwesely).
> 1st Army (center) on the line Aujezd, Horzitz, Miletin.
>   (*Avantgarde* as far as Gross Jeritz and Milowitz).
> 2nd Army (left wing) from Arnau via Königinhof to Gradlitz.
>   (*Avantgarde at* Ober Prausnitz).

This position covered an arc spanning 18 miles, but without depth. The choice was made to remain in this loose formation, which offered great advantages with few disadvantages. As the Prussian report stated;

> If the enemy was found in a position that could not be taken by a frontal assault, then one would have concentrated the entire force, only to then to separate it in order to make flanking attacks.

No genuine danger could actually arise from this loose formation since the individual armies stood only a short march apart.

The army remained in this position on 2nd July. Only the *Avantgarde* of the Elbe Army was advanced as far as Smidar. The days from 30th June to 3rd July, were essentially rest days, broken only by minor local actions, reconnaissance, skirmishes and ambushes. (The most interesting item of booty was the imperial field postal service). There was no significant action for two reasons. The army needed to rest, but no less important was the uncertainty of the enemy's location, where was the decisive blow to be struck. In other words, it was necessary to locate the enemy first in order to fix him.

Where was he? It was assumed that after Gitschin, he would have taken a position *behind* the Elbe, with the fortresses of Josephstadt and Königgrätz on either wing. However, he was on the near side of the river, as we shall now see.

The Austrian position, Benedek to the Emperor, Headquarters Königgrätz

In the meantime, the concentration of the Austrian army had been completed (on the 30th). All of the corps were at the appointed place on the Dubenetz plateau, right by the Elbe between Königinhof and Josephstadt. They were at the designated place, but in what condition!

The Austrian General Staff Work gives us the following insight into the situation on the 30th:

> Difficult hours dawned for the Army Command. It could no longer hide from the fact that its plans were thwarted and its strategy had totally miscarried. The army was now in the condition that had been planned for it since the start of operations [i.e. concentrated], but under highly unfavourable circumstances.

Gripped by the idea of leading the army into this apparently advantageous position, to fight the decisive battle, either against the entire enemy army, or farther west, against half the enemy army, missed the opportunity to attack and smash the nearer and isolated half army of the Crown Prince of Prussia on the 27th and 28th. However, several army corps were committed, *individually*, one after another, against each of the two half armies, with the purpose of covering the intended operation. Since the information given to [these corps] by the Army Command was neither clear nor timely, and in some cases non-existent, they were exhausted at all points in extraordinarily bloody fighting against superior enemy forces.

Each of the past three days had, with a single exception, brought only deplorable failures, while the enemy gained one easy triumph after another over the isolated Austrian corps, thereby accomplishing the difficult maneuver of uniting [his forces] before the Austrian army.

Such is the Austrian statement.[74]

In the event, only two corps, 2nd and 3rd, were still intact. All of the others had been in combat, and at least in part, suffered enormous losses, a total of 30,000 men or more. These were distributed (in round numbers) as follows; about 8,000 (Gitchin) from 1st Corps; 2,000 (Schweinschädel and Königinhof) from 4th Corps; 5,500 (Nachod) from 6th Corps; 5,000 (Skalitz) from 8th Corps, and 8,600 from 10th Corps (Trautenau, Soor and Rudersdorf). In addition to this, the Saxons (Gitschin) lost 600 men.

Thus, the equivalent of an entire army corps was already missing. Yet another factor was morale, the army had suffered a loss in trust and confidence. The magnificent army that had been so confident of victory at Olmütz, was now on the plateau of Dubenetz, but incapable of taking the initiative. Benedek resolved the pull the army back from Dubenetz, to a position farther to the rear. He telegraphed the Emperor, 'The debacle of 1st Corps and the Saxon Army Corps forces me to begin the retreat towards Königgrätz. Tomorrow my headquarters will be near there.'

At 3:00 in the afternoon of the 30th, the individual corps were informed of the intention to retreat. The decision itself, was justified in the following order:

74   Author's Note: The statement as presented here in the official Austrian work, namely a direct and nearly total condemnation of Benedek, is frequently criticized as unjust. 'Instead of admitting,' remarked a Prussian officer, 'that we were superior to our enemy in tactics, armament, organization, morale and intelligence, they would rather make *one* man responsible for the outcome of the war. Benedek was sacrificed as a scapegoat.' We do not share this opinion. Despite a keen regard for the brave and experienced man who faced us (a feeling that we have repeatedly expressed), and despite several attempts to justify his war plans, it is Benedek himself who bears the main responsibility for the failures, or at least the most egregious ones. In saying this we refer to what was stated earlier, *everything must finally founder in such a confusion of orders*. Benedek had the game in hand on the 28th, however he was unable to appreciate just how favourable the situation was, and he was definitely not capable of dealing with the enormity of his task (we shall return later to this). Whatever the deficiencies of the Austrian army might have been, the 6th, 10th and 8th Corps fought on the 27th and 28th with *consummate* bravery. The leadership was not bad and the balance of the scales, as we have seen, wavered. However, the lack of clarity at the highest level ruined everything.

The not inconsiderable losses that individual army corps have suffered in recent days, the necessity of giving the troops time to fully rest and reorganize, and after the army is finally concentrated, to prepare it for decisive blows, the need to re-establish regular supply after the recent rapid advances - all of this has caused me to decide to order the troops to a rearward position.

This measure must be conducted without any undue haste and in the strictest order, that requires the most determined and energetic conduct from all generals and troop commanders, whom I call upon here, in the name of the Emperor.

I require punctual completion of the dispositions, the maintenance of the strictest discipline and order on the part of the men, the avoidance of depressing statements and alarming rumours, and especially [that the supply trains stick strictly to their designated routes] so that the troops can move unhindered and with the greatest possible freedom, and if need be, fight without hindrance.

Everyone must realize the gravity of the situation and operate accordingly, otherwise, wherever I perceive or discover the slightest irregularity, I will treat the responsible commander with the uttermost severity.

I require of the entire army the most difficult test of its superb spirit, the curbing of its lust for action, perhaps the endurance of yet more hardships. I hope however, that the army will stand this test as it has done hitherto, wherever it has fought the enemy, with the most shining bravery beyond all praise.

Dubenetz, 30th June.

During the night of 30th June - 1st July, in accordance with these orders, the imperial army evacuated the position at Dubenetz, marched southwards (to the rear) to Königgrätz, and stood on the evening of 1st July, essentially as follows:

1st Army Corps at Kuklena.
2nd Army Corps at Trotina.
3rd Army Corps at Sadowa.
4th Army Corps at Nedelist.
6th Army Corps at Westar and Rosnitz.
8th Army Corps (alongside 4th) at Nedelist.
10th Army Corps at Lipa.

The Saxon Army Corps at Lubno, Nieder Prim, Nechanitz.

The 1st Light Cavalry Division at Stösser.
The 2nd Light Cavalry Division forward of Trotina.
The 1st Reserve Cavalry Division at Lochenitz.
The 2nd Reserve Cavalry Division at Westar.
The 3rd Reserve Cavalry Division at Sadowa.

The Army Artillery Reserve at Nedelist.

The Army Headquarters in Königgrätz.

This was the approximate position of the Imperial Army on the evening of 1st July. The retreat was carried out with essentially no disruption. Benedek had reconnoitered the terrain on the route from Josephstadt to Königgrätz. It was well selected for defense. The assault of the ever bolder enemy might founder against the defensive strength of this position, which at least offered significant *tactical* advantages.

The situation was still not hopeless, it only seemed so to the *Feldzeugmeister* as he rode over the field that was to be the burial place for his reputation. His strength had crumbled under the misfortunes and trials of the last four days. 'In the grip of a deep depression', says the Austrian General Staff Report, 'the *Feldzeugmeister* had already lost all confidence in himself, his staff, his army and the great cause for which it had gone to battle. At 9.45 (having arrived in Königgrätz), he received a telegram from His Majesty the Emperor, replying to his earlier communication in which he had informed the Emperor of the army's retreat.

The Emperor's telegram read:

> Although I have heard nothing ... since your reports of the 27th and 28th from Josephstadt, and then the telegraphic report of the 29th from Dubenetz, and despite the news of the retreat that became necessary to Königgrätz, I have great confidence that your energetic leadership will shortly achieve a favourable success, and that your strength will maintain order.

However, the report continues, these magnanimous words of the emperor could not restore the failing spirits of the unfortunate *Feldherr. Feldzeugmeister* von Benedek was not confident about the coming day, and at 11:30 in the morning, without the knowledge of anyone on his staff, sent the following telegram to the Emperor:

> I urgently beg your Majesty to make peace at any price; catastrophe is *inevitable* for the army. *Oberstlieutenant* Beck (the emperor's *GeneralAdjutant*, who had arrived at the headquarters during the previous night) is returning immediately.

The Emperor could not follow the advice of the Army Commander. No matter how unfavourable the latter might consider the condition of the army after all the misfortunes the individual corps had experienced, it could not justify entering upon negotiations with the enemy *before a battle had been fought*, and had itself decided the fate of the army and the state. Also, it would be unimaginable to anyone who had not directly experienced [recent] events, that the army was totally unfit for combat and that a catastrophe was inevitable. For that reason, negotiations with the enemy would be entirely premature and totally unjustifiable. His Majesty the Emperor thus replied telegraphically to the Army Commander at 2:10:

> It is impossible to make peace. I order, if it is unavoidable, that the retreat be initiated in the most orderly manner. Has a battle taken place?

The Army Commander (who had in the meantime regained a calmer, if not optimistic state of mind) replied telegraphically to the Emperor at 11:00 that night:

Your Majesty's telegram received, code understood. 6th, 8th and 10th Corps have suffered extremely heavy losses. 1st Corps, as I have personally ascertained today, and the Saxon Corps in part, are likewise extraordinarily battered and require several days to [recuperate]. 4th Corps has also suffered losses. Of eight corps, without having fought a [major] battle, merely from local actions, only two are entirely intact, but these two, [as well as the] cavalry and artillery reserve, are extremely fatigued. All require necessary rest, shoeing and other needs. 10th Corps in particular, also requires cooking gear.

The great losses experienced, are primarily due to needlegun fire, whose murderous effectiveness has uniformly impressed all who have been in combat.

After yesterday's experiences and the telegraphically reported debacle of the 1st and Saxon Corps, all of this has forced me to fall back to here. *En route* I found the massive train of the army, which could no longer be moved far enough to the rear, and if under such circumstances, an energetic enemy attack ensued, whether or not successful, before 1st Corps and the Saxons were reorganized and the army to some extent restored, catastrophe would have been unavoidable. Fortunately, up to this point, the enemy has not exerted pressure. Therefore I am allowing the army to rest this morning and moving the train to the rear. [The army] cannot remain longer here because, by tomorrow morning, a shortage of drinking water will develop in the camps. On the 3rd the retreat commences to Pardubitz.

If I am not outflanked, I can again count on the troops, and if the opportunity arises for an offensive thrust, I shall take it. Otherwise, I intend to bring the army back to Olmütz, so far as possible, and to carry out your Majesty's supreme orders, so far as lies in my power to do so, certainly with unconditional devotion.

So things stood in the evening of 1st July. The worst moment was already in the past. Dispatch of patrols was ordered in all directions and the following Army Order was issued:

In the morning (2nd July) the army will remain in the positions occupied today. The heavy baggage is to be sent to the rear during the course of the present night. (Detailed orders to follow). The train of the headquarters will remain in Raudnicka. The munitions train remains on the left bank of the Elbe at Königgrätz. The Army *Intendanz* [quartermaster branch] will be transferred on the 3rd of the month to Brünn. The Army Headquarters will be in the Prager suburb of Königgrätz in the Prague Inn [*Gasthofe zur Stadt Prag*].

To the outposts

A Prussian wrote:

'I hope the lines that I wrote you day before yesterday (29th) from Königinhof and that H. promised to forward, are already in your hands. The two days that have passed since then have not essentially altered the situation, only our brigade's situation has changed. We have now been moved forward as *Avantgarde*, and this afternoon, are on the right bank of the Elbe. Several battalions are in Daubrawitz, Liebthal and Sibojed.

My battalion is farthest forward, in the village of Dubenetz. The house in which I am writing these lines was still the Austrian headquarters last night. Only three days ago (in Burkersdorf) we were in Gablenz's headquarters. Now we are in Benedek's. Who knows what will come of all this.

Despite the fact that this is all Bohemian, we have been well received here. Königinhof seemed dead as we entered. Only a few old women remained. Here we found a dozen young girls, the first that we have seen since we marched into Bohemia. To all appearances they seem to be finding that they can live with us.

Several of our companies bivouacked outside the village. They are happy, laugh, sing, and the merry scenes such as you know from Düppel repeat themselves here. Since we can still count on two or three days of rest, if we generally count the days on outpost duty as days of rest, the men have built huts, some from leaves, others from straw, and with the help of street signs, have created a Carlstrasse and Grosse Friedrichsstrase.

One joy we experienced today was the arrival of the 1st Guards Dragoons, which as you might know, belong to the 1st Army. They came from the area of Gitschin and made a ride of just under 30 miles to Dubenetz (via Arnau). As we greeted them one could say that the chain was complete, contact established between the 1st and 2nd Armies. After a brief stay, they returned to the Army of Prince Friedrich Karl. That makes a total ride of almost 60 miles.

We have already made some good finds here, both in great and small. Thus we first found an officer's horse in the stall of a nearby farmstead, then the groom, and finally the luggage. We did not allow discretion to go so far as to fail to search the valise. It was amply outfitted, including (as always) maps of Brandenburg and of Berlin. They were all too confident. I already wrote you from Königinhof that all of the prisoners that we have taken so far wore thick coats, 'So that they would be able to enter Berlin in spruce white jackets.'[75] Officer's letters, which we took from an Austrian field post office, are all in agreement with that, and express the same spirit of overconfidence. They will 'give us a licking,' these and other similar expressions are repeated, even in letters that were written after Nachod and Skalitz, after Burkersdorf and Trautenau. Letters of the soldiers strike a very different note. They are moving in their fashion: 'Dear Peppi, I shall probably not see you again, for the Prussians kill everyone.' That certainly has a different ring. Today news of victory arrives here from all sides. We have become happily confident. We know full well that the main battle must still be fought, but we think that we shall conduct it well and successfully. Everyone hopes that this will all soon come to an end. We are now awaiting the King. Before a week has gone by much will have been decided.

Dubenetz, 1st July, evening.

75   Tr. Note: As recounted in the history of the 2nd Foot Guards (p. 74), when the captured Austrian soldiers were asked why they were wearing their heavy coats (in spite of the enervating heat) instead of their new white jackets, they stated that their officers had told them that the jackets must remain entirely clean for their entry into Berlin.

With the 1st Army, at least with the *Avantgarde*, the feeling was that the decision was near. One officer wrote:

Now let me tell you of my most recent experiences.Today at noon our Fusilier Battalion (27th Regiment) passed through Horsitz with the band playing, and marched to Gross Jeritz, a little over two miles in front of our division, which remained at Horsitz. We had barely reached Gross Jeritz when orders came to advance to Cerekwitz, a little over three miles further forward. A glance at the map left us in no doubt that we had been paced in an extremely exposed position, and what we have found in the last two hours, to be before and around us, has done nothing to make our position seem any less exposed. But I am getting ahead of myself:

It was already dusk when we halted before Gross Jeritz, and before we had left it behind us darkness fell. Fortunately we had found a German speaking man in the village whom we could use as a guide, obviously under constant watch. The tension mounted as after a quarter of an hour, our advanced cavalry patrols were fired upon. These hastened back and were no longer usable in the dark. Infantry patrols had to take their place. It was a most difficult situation. Our imaginations were overactive and we thought we saw rifle barrels shining behind every tree and bush, or a *Jäger's* feathered hat move.

Slowly we moved on, ever deeper in the night. We passed the village of Trzebobowitz, halfway there. The remaining half hour seemed to last forever. Finally we saw lights. A mighty building surrounded by a ring wall, emerged from the darkness, Schloss Cerekwitz. Behind [around] it was the village of the same name.

The Commander of our regiment (*Oberst* von Zychlinski), who was with the battalion in person, quickly made his dispositions. He led us through the gate of a tower, occupied the marketplace as well as the two main streets of the village, and put our 9th Company in the Schloss. It was all done quickly. They searched the extensive buildings, which were filled with [Austrian] stragglers who had fled here from Soor and Trautenau. They surrendered without resistance.

I now write to you from this Schloss. The mistress, a widow (Baroness von Kleeborn) is absent, but an estate manager, a housekeeper, a cook and a chambermaid remain. The latter (Räthe) is friendly with us. The cook too, will engage in conversation. She fixed us a warm beer, prepared supper and confidently placed the key of the pantry in our hands. We have found ample provisions in the house itself, and a stock of good beer in the adjoining brewery. Therefore, if you will, we sit here in the Bosom of Abraham, and if I add that I am writing these lines in a great chamber like room with two fireplaces, columns and a mahogany four poster bed, you may well have an attack of jealousy to know that I am housed like such a *grand Seigneur.*

But, do not envy me. We are sitting on a volcano and all of this could vanish at any moment. No more than two miles from here, on the slopes of a ridge, burn countless watch fires. From my room I can believe that, every now and then, I catch a glimpse of a man in their light. As we occupied the Schloss two hours ago and the numerous fires were visible, we still thought that it might be the bivouacs of the Elbe Army, or perhaps of our [1st Army] 8th Division. For the last hour, however, we have known that it is the enemy, at least an army corps strong. Our *Oberst* has sent reports to the Prince. If the enemy is as strong as the people here say (they speak of three corps and more) then we will have a battle within 36 hours. Perhaps the decision. God be with us.

Your . . .

Schloss Cerekwitz, 1st July (night).'

King Wilhelm in Gitchin

In the meantime, King Wilhelm had left his capital early on 30th June. The day before (29th) was a day of victories (Skalitz, Soor and Münchengrätz), there was jubilation and celebrations. That evening the King had spoken from the balcony to the people thronging around the palace, 'Great things have happened, but greater have yet to be done.' He now departed to fulfil this great mission. With him went his brother, *Generalfeldzeugmeister* Prince Carl and the Supreme Headquarters.

Headquarters consisted of the Chief of the General Staff, *General der Infanterie Freiherr* von Moltke, his Adjutant (*Major* Wright) and the officers of the General Staff. In addition were the Quartermaster General, *Generalmajor* von Podbielski, the Inspector General of Engineers, *Generallieutenant* von Wasserschleben, the Inspector General of Artillery, *Generallieutenant* von Hindersin, the Chief of the General Staff of the Artillery, *Oberst* von Bergmann, and a number of officers of the special arms of the service. In addition, from the Adjutant General's department, *Generallieutenant* von Alvensleben, from the suite of His Majesty, *Generalmajor* von Boyen, from the Military Cabinet, *Generalmajor* von Tresckow, from the Inspectorate of light Infantry [*Jäger und Schützen*] *Oberst Graf* zu Dohna, from the *Inspecteur der,* and of the *FlügelAdjutanten* of the King, *Obersten* von Steinacker and von Stiehle, *Oberstlieutenants Graf* Kanitz, *Freiherr* von Loë, *Graf* Finck von Finckenstein and *Major Graf* Lehndorff. Present in the headquarters (aside from *Generalfeldzeugmeister* Prince Carl of Prussia) were *General der Infanterie,* Minister for War, von Roon, the *Ministerpräsident Graf* von Bismarck, Prince Reuss, *Geheimer Legationsrath* Abeken, *Wirklicher Legationsrath Baron* von Keudell and a number of Prussian and foreign officers, including [Prussian] Prince Pückler - Muskau and the Duke von Ujest and [foreign] the Russian *Generalmajor Graf* Kutusoff, the Italian *Oberst Graf* Avet and the Mecklenburg - Schwerin *Major* von Brandenstein. The *Geheime Cabinetsrath* von Mühler, Chief of the Civil Cabinet, was also attached to the headquarters.

The *Stabswache* [Headquarters Guard], formed from contingents selected from all of the infantry and cavalry regiments of the army, under command of *Oberstlieutenant* von Krosigk, also belonged to the headquarters. The infantry was formed in a battalion, the cavalry in a squadron. It should be noted here that the latter rode in front of the royal carriage when the headquarters was on the move, rotating between Cuirassiers, Dragoons, Hussars or Uhlans. The infantry marched (often a day's march ahead) or followed when the headquarters departed. The King's journey, departing from the lower Silesian railway station, proceeded via Frankfurt, Görlitz and Zittau. When it passed through Prussian territory, it became a triumphal procession. Toward evening the King arrived in Reichenberg (Bohemia) and set up quarters in the Schloss of *Graf* Clam - Gallas, the same who had commanded the Austrian 1st Corps in the fighting at the Iser and at Gitschin. The King remained in Reichenberg until noon of 1st July, then moved his headquarters to Schloss Sichrow (the beautiful residence of Prince Rohan), and then on the 2nd, from Schloss Sichrow to Gitschin. The route there, past Libun[76] and Brada, passed through the midst of the battlefield. The war was now on all sides.

Prince Friedrich Karl (as always in the red uniform of the Zieten Hussars) came from his Horsitz Headquarters to the battlefield in an open hunting cart to meet his royal uncle, who immediately had him climb into his carriage and tell him about the fighting on the 29th and the condition of the 1st Army. Contact had been established with the 2nd Army (as we already know). Depending on how things went, the King would proceed either to Horsitz or Königinhof, either to the 1st or 2nd Army. The distance was not significantly different. At the moment when the King reached Gitschin, the decision had not yet been made, indeed could not be made, since it was not yet known where the great Austrian army was, whether it was on the near or the far side of the Elbe.

King Wilhelm in Gitschin.

76   Author's Note: In the village of Libun the King called a halt before a house that was identified as a hospital by the well-known red cross on a white banner. There he found seriously wounded officers of friend and foe. *Lieutenant* Hellhof, both of whose legs had been torn off by a shell, the Saxon *Oberst* von Boxberg, *Graf* Voss (Mecklenburg) of Dragoon Regiment Savoy *et. al.* The King immediately had note made of the name of *Lieutenant* Hellhof in the event that the wounded man might later need Royal grace.

An honour guard of Grenadier Regiment King Friedrich Wilhelm IV, whose 2nd Battalion had been in such fierce fighting and been decimated at Unter Lochow, stood on the Gitschin *Ring* (the King stayed at the inn). The appearance of the troops, helmet spikes shot off and worn out shoes, bore witness to how seriously they had been under fire. The King mustered the Guards. As he strode along the ranks, the men broke out in loud hurrahs that lasted as they presented arms until the end of the inspection. The magistrate and the council had also assembled at the marketplace to greet the king and request an audience. This was granted. The purpose was to assure the King that the citizens of Gitschin had *not* fired on the entering Prussians (on the evening of the 29th). The King answered;

> I wage no war with your nation, but only against the army that opposes me. If the citizens, however, take hostile action without any justification against my troops, I will be obliged to take reprisals. My troops are no wild horde and only require what is absolutely necessary to live. Your concern is to give them no reason for legitimate complaint. Tell the residents that I have not come to wage war against peaceful citizens, but only to defend the honour of Prussia from calumny.

The King then visited a hospital set up in the Jesuit church, in which were only Austrian wounded. The *Oberst* and Commander of the Liechtenstein Hussar Regiment, *Graf* Piacewitz, who had fallen into our hands seriously wounded (as already mentioned) received immediate permission, upon the recommendation of Prince Friedrich Karl, to travel to Vienna via Dresden. The King went further, ordering that all wounded Austrian officers could likewise be released to their homes if they gave their word of honour no longer to serve against Prussia in this war.[77]

It was from Gitschin that the King issued [his Order of the Day] informing the army that from now on *he would lead them personally*. The greeting read:

> 'Soldiers of my army! Today I come to you, my brave troops in the field, and offer you my royal salutations. In a few days, thanks to your courage and self - sacrifice, results have been gained in battle which are worthy to join the great deeds of our fathers. I look upon all the elements of my loyal army with pride, and I look forward to the upcoming events in the war with joyful confidence. Soldiers! Numerous enemies face us in battle. Let us rely upon the Lord God, the director of all battles, and upon our just cause. He will lead the banners of Prussia, so accustomed to victory, to new victories through your courage and endurance.
>
> Wilhelm.

After comprehensive discussions with the King, Prince Friedrich Karl returned to his headquarters in Horsitz. A General Staff officer reported during the afternoon, regarding the details of the positions, the nature of the ground, and the enemy's manner of fighting up to this point. The result of all these discussions was that a further period of rest (one or two days) was desirable for the troops who were seriously worn out, and that the military escort should be

---

77 This favour was later granted to unwounded imperial officers and happily taken up by them. After the war (and in our opinion, not entirely unjustly) it would have serious repercussions.

ready to escort the King to discussions with the Crown Prince at Königinhof at 9:00 the next morning. No one at the time this decision was made, had any inkling that 24 hours later, the great battle would already have been fought, and the outcome of the war would be decided.

We now turn to the 1st Army to show what changed the plans for the 3rd July and replaced them with the *decision for battle*.

The Day Before the Battle

The reconnaissance, *Major* von Unger's ride

On the morning of 2nd July, the 1st Army was positioned on the line Miletin – Horsitz – Wostromer. The III Corps (Brandenburg) had the left wing, II Corps (Pomerania) the right wing, IV Corps (Magdeburg – Thüringen) held the center. IV Corps also provided the *Avantgarde*. Farthest forward was the advance Guards of the 7th Division, Detachment Zychlinski, whose reports were decisive in the decision to give battle.

Detachment Zychlinski had been in the Schloss and village of Cerekwitz since the evening of 1st July. A letter that we shared earlier, shows us the route they took, the occupation of the Schloss, and finally the enemy campfires, which at a distance of a little more than two miles, burned on the opposite hills. The same letter also mentions the reports that later that same evening, were to be made in the Prince's headquarters, regarding the presumed strength of the enemy.

These reports were sent, but the importance of the situation required more certainty than could be provided by mere statements from staff at the Schloss and residents of the village. Personal observation had to determine the number of the enemy on the opposite hills, what troops were there, and the extent of their positions. The next morning was selected for that.

The night passed peacefully. By daybreak reinforcements arrived, the 2nd Battalion (*Major* von Busse) of the 27th Regiment. *Oberst* von Zychlinski, to secure himself against a sudden surprise attack, immediately reinforced both his wings, surrounded himself with a circle of outposts, and prepared the Schloss itself for defense with barricades and loopholes. He was resolved to hold out with his two battalions (the 2nd and Fusilier Battalions) to the last. A sentry with a telescope, who had to report on enemy movements, was posted in the tower of the Schloss' chapel. Patrols were sent out on all sides and numerous reports came back immediately stating that the enemy was foraging, that interminable columns of wagons were visible, and above all, that the enemy had positioned batteries of artillery in the direction of Lipa and especially in the clearings in the woods between Sadowa and Cistowes.

All of this was extremely important. There could no longer be any doubt that the enemy was in front of us. In order to avoid alarming the headquarters of the Prince with exaggerated statements, *Oberst* von Zychlinski decided on a direct reconnaissance, if possible, in the enemy's rear. He ordered *Premierlieutenant* von Heister (who led the squadron of Ascherslebner Hussars that was attached to the detachment), to take 15 horses and first locate the 8th Division (which was supposed to be on his right), then to reconnoiter the enemy on the road toward Lipa, then to return via Benatek. This was at 7:00 in the morning.

Premierlieutenant von Heister proceeded southwest, first checking Hnewcowes, where enemy *Jäger* had been during the previous night, then Sowetiz, then to Sadowa, near which he could get a view of the entire enemy camp. There he was to take prisoners. He had learned in the villages that an enemy *Jäger* company was in Ober Cernatek. Swinging to the right, he first rode along the *Chaussée*, then turned down a farm track, in order to make the sentries posted there believe that he was a Saxon cavalry detachment, unconcernedly riding along the way. Three hundred paces west of Ober Cernatek he came in sight of a picket (80 to 100 men strong) that seemed willing to be deceived. Our Hussars approached to 50 paces when a sentry opened fire. Our Hussars immediately charged and the enemy formed clumps and began to fire irregularly. Two of them did not have time to get away and were seized in front of the clump, despite the pursuing fire from the *Jäger*, they were safely carried off. Now it was a matter of getting back to Cerekwitz with them. They belonged to the 34th *Jäger* Battalion and stated that the Austrian 3rd Corps was on the Lipa hill. The watch fires that had shone the previous evening as far as Schloss Cerekwitz, had therefore belonged to this corps. It was impossible to learn from the prisoners whether other enemy formations were massed alongside or behind 3rd Corps, however the Czech populace, so far as they could be understood, suggested that there were. In fact, there was talk of the 'Saxons'.

The report was sent at about noon from Cerekwitz to Schloss Kamenitz [Headquarters of Prince Carl, 1st Army]. In the meantime, based on the earlier report from *Oberst* von Zychlinski, [Prince Carl] had already ordered a similar reconnaissance himself, and ordered a well mounted officer of his General Staff, *Major* von Unger, to proceed if possible, all the way to the Bistritz [stream].

Major von Unger (we will describe this reconnaissance in detail) initially proceeded to *General* von Fransecky at Horsitz, and from there to *General* von Horn at Gutwasser. What he learned at these two places essentially corresponded with the reports already received at Headquarters. It became increasingly evident that it was necessary to get behind the enemy outposts. *General* von Horn agreed to provide a squadron of the Thüringian Uhlan Regiment as an escort. However, since the horses had not yet been fed, *Major* von Unger decided to depart immediately with one *Gefreiter* and five Uhlans. The squadron was to follow on.

Major von Unger initially stayed on the main road, passed the most advanced Uhlan outpost of the 8th Division (adding the above mentioned Uhlan to his little force, thus bringing his number to 16), and bore off to the right on back roads, intending to get to the Bistritz or to the ridge directly in front of it (the Dub hill), which would give him a view of the Bistritz valley. The ride proceeded without interference from the enemy as far as a dip in the ground immediately before the above mentioned valley, also with a stream flowing through it. From the near side, *Major* von Unger immediately saw that the presumed Austrian camp on the far side of the ridge had placed outposts in this valley that ran parallel to the Bistritz. He saw this all the more clearly when the outposts were relieved. Now it became a matter of getting behind them. Therefore, it was necessary to ride down one slope and up the other, and in so doing, to avoid the villages in the valley that were in part, occupied by the enemy.

Major von Unger now proceeded toward the village of Klenitz (in the valley), but passing to the right of it. Before he was halfway down the slope, an Austrian Uhlan patrol came riding toward him from the opposite direction at a distance of 100 paces. The officers on both sides saluted each other. However, one of the Thüringian Uhlans, not noticing the salute, fired his pistol. By pure chance the bullet found its mark and the horse that had been hit (in the chest) went down, the rider with him, and the man behind him over the man in front. The entire enemy troop fell into disorder. The two Uhlans who had fallen off their horses were captured.

Closer to Klenitz our men ran into some villagers. The information that they provided agreed with the statements of the two captured Uhlans, the 3rd Corps was at Sadowa, and behind them towards Königgrätz, the 10th Corps and 1st Corps. The Saxons were at Problus. 3rd Corps had advanced one brigade (Brigade Prohaska), as far as Dub hill and beyond. If this was correct (and there could no longer be any doubt), the troops facing us belonged to 3rd Corps. In fact it was Brigade Prohaska.

In the meantime, our Uhlans had reached the valley floor. The little stream that flowed there was bordered on both sides by strips of boggy meadow that was difficult to cross. The horses sank in, it was difficult terrain. Finally, a sort of stone dam was found that made it possible to cross. *Major* von Unger, immediately recognizing its importance, left an Uhlan sentry, so that if pursued, he would be able to spot this only crossing point from afar. This foresight later saved him. He now proceeded up the hill, first passing isolated sentries, then passing close to the village of Dub. This, on the near side of the hill, was already full of Austrian *Jäger*. Not a shot was fired. It was obvious that our Uhlans (as had already happened with the villagers), were taken for Saxon cavalry. People even waved at them. Every greeting, obviously, was returned.

Major von Unger's reconnaisance.

Now our [patrol] had finally reached the crest of Dub hill, and before it lay the Bistritz valley. A single glance was enough to realise that we were facing a *large proportion of the entire enemy army*. One glimpse sufficed, but at the very moment in which our patrol reached the hill, a squadron of enemy Uhlans emerged from Sadowa (perhaps alarmed by the fleeing riders of the first patrol) and attacked. Combat was not the objective. Our patrol immediately turned, and now a fully-fledged chase commenced across broken terrain. The enemy Uhlans (on fresh horses), soon overtook ours despite the lead these had, and with great skill in handling their weapons (they were Poles) they tried to unsaddle our fleeing and ducking Uhlans, constantly circling with their lances.

The best rider, ten paces ahead of the others, pursued *Major* von Unger, thrusting his lance through the Major's jacket just above the hip, but he couldn't disengage, and was shot from his saddle by an *Unteroffizier* of our troop. Over hedges and ditches the flight continued. Now the Uhlan posted at the stream was visible, and a minute later the entire troop dashed safely across the stone dam. A fresh lead was gained when the [Prussian] Uhlan squadron that had been sent out from Gutwasser appeared on our side of the hill and stopped the pursuit.

This ride was carried out without losing a horse or a man. *Major* von Unger was back in Schloss Kamenitz between 6:00 and 7:00 in the evening. His report strengthened the decision to give battle, the more so as the various prisoners brought into the headquarters during the day all made identical statements to the effect that 3rd, 10th and 1st Corps were in the valley of the Bistritz.

The Prince was now determined (to forestall a possible enemy assault) to attack the enemy on the morning of the 3rd. At 9:00[pm] the corresponding orders went out to the commanders of both armies that were under his command (the 1st and Elbe Armies). At the same time he sent a letter to the Crown Prince in which he requested the cooperation of the 2nd Army the following day. It read:

> His Majesty the King has informed me of the task allotted to your Royal Highness for tomorrow (3rd July) to reconnoiter to the Aupa and the Metau. In the meantime, reconnaissance undertaken today on this side, and reports of outposts have indicated that extremely significant enemy forces have concentrated near Sadowa and Lipa on the road from Horsitz to Königgrätz. These have advanced their *Avantgarde* to Dub. Therefore I intend to attack the enemy tomorrow, 3rd July, and in accordance with the task assigned to me, push him back to the Elbe.
>
> Since strong bodies of enemy troops have also crossed from Josephstadt to the right bank of the Elbe ... [I am concerned that] in the event of an advance on my part towards Königgrätz, [they will threaten my] left flank. Such a diversion would force me to divide my force, in which case I would be unable to fully accomplish the desired objective, the destruction of the enemy corps.
>
> Therefore I request that your Royal Highness advance tomorrow, 3rd July, on the right bank of the Elbe with the Guards Corps or more [in the direction of] Königgrätz to secure my left wing toward Josephstadt. I particularly make this request since I cannot count on the prompt arrival of Bonin's corps due to the great distance, and since I presume Your Royal Highness will not come upon strong enemy forces in the reconnaissance you will undertake tomorrow. I add to the above that my left wing will be at Gross Jersitz and Cerekwitz.
>
> Signed Friedrich Karl,
> Price of Prussia.'

Lieutenant von Normann, of the Zieten Hussar Regiment was given the task of delivering this message. He reached Königinhof at 1:00 in the morning and was back in Schloss Kamenitz by 4:00.

Thus, the High Command of the 1st Army made all the preparations for a strong, perhaps decisive, blow for the next day. All of these arrangements required the approval of the King, who from the moment he arrived in Gitschin, had assumed supreme command of the entire army. Thus, *Generallieutenant* von Voigts - Rhetz, Chief of the General Staff of 1st Army, proceeded (by order of the Prince), from Schloss Kamenitz to Gitschin, to receive the [King's] approval, or his further orders.

General von Voigts - Rhetz arrived at 11:00 at night. The situation was critical. The troops of [Elbe and 1st Armies] were so weary from fighting since 26th June, and as the result of exhausting marches, that it had been considered necessary by all in the course of 2nd July, to grant the soldiers at least several days of rest. The distance of the 2nd Army from the presumed battlefield was substantial (for some corps 13½ miles). The King wavered. He first examined the possible enemy dispositions on the map (so far as they had been identified from reconnaissance). He then ordered that Generals von Moltke, von Roon, von Alvensleben and von Tresckow, be summoned for a council of war. This took place. It seemed that opinions differed little. The battle was agreed on. The King now issued his orders.

General von Voigts - Rhetz returned to Prince Friedrich Karl at Schloss Kamenitz with the permission to attack. *Oberstlieutenant Graf* Finckenstein, *FlügelAdjutant* of the King, was ordered to ride [from Gitschin] to Königinhof with written orders[78] to the Crown Prince for an immediate advance towards the probable battlefield. The departure of the King himself was set for 5:00 the next morning instead of 9:00 (as previously specified). The council of war was closed at 1:00 [on the morning of 3rd July]. It was 2:00 when the King retired for a short rest. During the night traffic was active on all the roads that led toward the Elbe from the west and the northwest. The Elbe Army was already on the march at 2:00. It marched (as ordered) from Hoch Wezzely to Smidar and from there to Nechanitz:

> The sky was sombre. One battalion after another came out of the wet bivouac. The columns marched past us in the gray dawn. Some of the officers asked in an undertone and seriously, 'So it's today?' It began to rain. The morning chill went right through us, we all had empty canteens. So long as we marched on the *Chaussée* (to Smidar) everything went fine. That would soon change. Not only did the rain continue, it steadily intensified. At Smidar we bore off to the left and now came onto muddy tracks.

---

78   Author's Note: The orders read: 'In accordance with information arriving at the 1st Army, the enemy has advanced over the Bistritz at Sadowa in strength, about three corps, which may be further reinforced, and therefore an engagement is to be expected with the 1st Army early tomorrow. According to orders, the 1st Army will be positioned early tomorrow at 2:00[am], on 3rd July, with two divisions at Horsitz, one at Milowitz, one at Cerekwitz, two at Psanek and Bristan, and the cavalry corps at Gutwasser. Your Royal Highness will immediately make the necessary arrangements to advance with all forces to support the 1st Army against the right flank of the presumed enemy concentration and attack as soon as possible. The instructions issued this afternoon under other circumstances are now no longer valid.

   Signed, von Moltke.'

   Graf Finkenstein rode via Miletin to Königinhof. Due to the importance of the document however, an identical second copy was sent via Kamenitz to Königinhof. Both copies reached the Crown Prince.

Then it was over ditches and meadows. It is a miracle to me how our artillery made it through at all.

Such was the report of an eyewitness.

At the vanguard of the 1st Army, which advanced on several roads, were divisions Fransecky and Horn. The Thüringian Division [8th Division *Generallieutenant* von Horn] kept to the main road and marched to Milowitz, The Magdeburg Division [7th Division *Generallieutenant* von Fransecky] advanced immediately to its left and proceeded from Horsitz via Gross Jeritz to Schloss Cerekwitz, which as we know, had already been occupied on the evening of 1st July:

> Although we had often marched in the dark, never had we moved out of the bivouac with empty stomachs and before daybreak. Everyone shivered. The deep darkness was intensified by an impenetrable fog that first settled around us and then began to dissolve in a fine, penetrating rain. The way was slippery so that the march, since we could not see where we stepped, became most uncertain and strenuous. Our packs had not been set aside and burdened us all the more, as with the difficult going, they shifted with the swaying of the body and threatened to pull us over.
>
> Under these conditions our mood was not especially elevated and the march took place, for the most part, in utter silence, only occasionally broken by the wisecrack of an irrepressible joker that cheered his comrades for a moment and then spread like wildfire.
>
> A halt was called when we were about half-way (to Cerekwitz). The day began to gray, but the sun did not come out. Instead, the rain now poured down on us. It might have been 5:00. Coffee was brewed from the iron rations we had with us. Some hastened to fetch wood and water. Others threw themselves down on the soft soil and fell asleep. The coffee refreshed us. Then forward again. For many this was their last meal.

Similar were the reports from all the divisions.

II Corps (Pommerania) advanced to the right alongside the Thüringian Division. III Corps (Brandenburg) followed as reserve. By 5:00 (earlier in some cases), the troops had arrived at their assigned positions. The valley of the Bistritz lay before them.

At 5:00 the King departed from Gitschin. With him was the entire headquarters staff, also *Graf* Bismarck. The King rode in an open carriage, dashing along the *Chaussée* through the puddles that were everywhere. The troops that the King passed broke into loud cheers as soon as they learned from the cavalrymen of the Headquarters Guards that their warlord was nearby. Each time such a jubilant cry reached his ear from afar, his serious expression changed to one of friendly warmth that he knew would always inspire his soldiers. The carriage stopped on the Dub hill where the King mounted one of the *Marstall* horses[79] that was waiting, a black stallion. He rode forward to the edge [of the valley]. There lay the Bistritz, Sadowa below, a wood behind, behind the wood, rising gradually was the Lipa hill and the village of that name. At that moment a flash could be seen through the fog, then the dull roll of gunfire, the first shot had been fired.

---

79   Tr. Note: *Marstall* at that time referred to the Royal Stable.

Book III

Königgrätz and After

Contents

---

1   Tr. Note: Throughout the text, the German *Swiepwald, Holawald* etc. has been used rather than the English *wood*.

Königgrätz

At the Bistritz, terrain, positions

Before we venture down from Dub Hill into the valley of the Bistritz, let us attempt to describe the broader picture. The Elbe, whose upper course almost forms a right angle, sweeps westward to enclose a rather extensive plateau, the Plateau of Gitschin. Let us cut a portion from this plateau whose eastern side is bounded by the course of the Elbe from Josephstadt to Königgrätz and whose western side is delineated by the line Horsitz – Neu Bidsow, giving us essentially a rectangle about nine miles long and nine miles wide, which we shall broadly designate as the battlefield of Königgrätz.

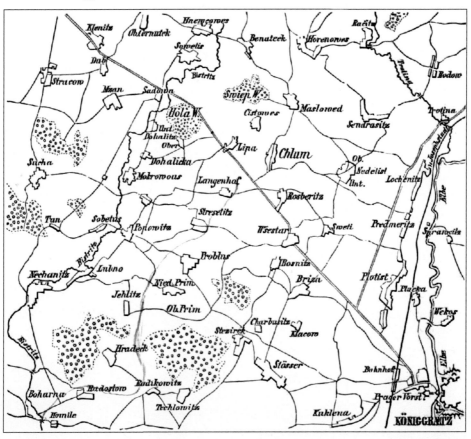

This rectangle, hilly and rolling (as is the entire plateau), is divided by the Bistritz stream into two nearly equal halves. On the western half, toward Horsitz and Gitschin, stand the Prussians. On the eastern half, toward Josephstadt and Königgrätz (the map only shows this half) stand the Austrians, between them lies the valley of the Bistritz.

Their respective positions were such that whoever launched an attack would first have to pass through the valley and then climb the hills on the far side. The Prussian position however, had the advantage of a good line of retreat over the Gitschin plateau, whereas the Austrian line of retreat led to the river Elbe which was almost immediately behind them. This was a great disadvantage that could hardly have escaped the eye of the *Feldzeugmeister*. Nevertheless, he chose this position because if the enemy pursued more rapidly than expected, it did at least provide an excellent defensive position.

To the front then. On the wings, only the [Austrian] right benefited from the natural strength of the position. Here there were several transverse ridges (at right angles to the frontal high ground), that extended across the barely 4½ miles between the Bistritz and the Elbe. These provided a natural obstacle consisting of three wall-like rows of hills that could neither be turned nor, if the defender did his duty, be stormed without heavy losses. The [Austrian] left wing position was weaker, the lower hills here providing the opportunity for an [enemy] outflanking manoeuvre that could provide access to their rear without a fight. The weakness of the position, a result of the [Austrian's] necessarily hasty deployment, could not however, (as we will later demonstrate) be utilized by our forces.

So much for the terrain on which our opponent had taken position, now we shall describe how their forces were deployed.

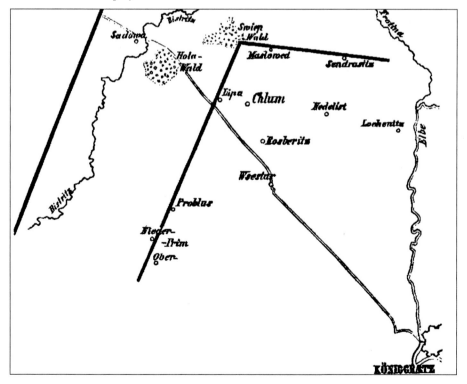

Relative axes of Austrian and Prussian front lines.

The Austrians stood massed in the centre on both sides of the Königgrätz – Lipa – Sadowa Chaussée . 3rd and 10th Corps were farthest forward with the 1st and 6th Corps behind them (as reserve). Alongside and behind them were the three Reserve Cavalry Divisions and the Army Artillery Reserve. 4th Corps, with 2nd Corps to its right, bent back in the shape of a hook, held the right wing. The Saxons and the Austrian 8th Corps were on the left wing, both covered by Edelsheim's 1st Light Cavalry Division (farther to the left).

To summarize then, the hilly nature of the battlefield was such that the Austrians on the far side of the Bistritz occupied a defensive position in the shape of a hook[2]. The long side facing west, the short side facing north, the highest points were where the two arms of the hook met. The much mentioned Maslowed Woods (*Swiepwald*) was an outlying bastion.

From the King's position on the Dub Hill [looking east] he could see the entire Austrian line of battle despite the fog and rain. Sadowa lay at his feet with its *Chaussée* and bridge over the Bistritz, the Sadowa woods [*Holawald*] beyond it, and beyond the woods themselves, the Lipa Hill. Benatek lay in the Bistritz valley to the left, Horenowes and Cistowes above it, the Swiepwald (almost within reach) lay between them. To the right, the Sadowa sugar factory, beyond that Dohalitz and Dohalitzka. Farther to the right, directly before Nechanitz, the Elbe Army was already under fire. Its advance was not visible from Dub, only the flashes of the cannon showed where the battle had commenced. Our forces were advancing to the Bistritz across the entire front (about 4.6 miles). The battle had begun.

We will now present an outline of the entire battle before we turn to the individual actions. Prince Friedrich Carl's plan was that the 1st Army (on either side of Sadowa) was to force a crossing of the Bistritz, storm (the Lipa Hill) behind it and thereby break through the enemy centre. The simultaneous advance of the Elbe Army via Nechanitz on the enemy's left wing, outflanking it as the case might be, was to support the main effort in the centre. At the moment the battle began, the Prussians did not yet know that they were facing the entire enemy army. They reckoned with three corps and the Saxons, that was the assumption on which the plan was based. The enemy however, was not facing us with half his army, but with his entire army. Fortunately, this possibility, while not believed to be the case, was included in our plans. For safety's sake, as we know, the Crown Prince had been requested to cooperate. If he came, and in the event his help was not urgently required, nothing would be lost. Whereas if his help was required, if we really were facing the entire enemy army, then victory depended on his intervention. We now know that the latter case was true.

Everything went well at the beginning. The Bistritz was crossed along the entire front. The advance guard of the Elbe Army took Nechanitz while three assault columns advanced in the centre: they were:

2   Author's Note: Our map is very generalized showing the hook shaped deployment and the general Austrian position. In particular, it would be impossible to exactly show the Austrian right wing since everything, from the very beginning, was in motion. One can only say that at the start of the action, the Austrian right wing was as our sketch shows, nearly at right angles to the actual front line. As the day progressed it swung increasingly from its hooked position toward an alignment with the front line. We shall return to this in greater detail later.

The 3rd Division (centre right), which occupied Dohalitzka and Mokrowous.

The 7th Division (centre left) which forced its way forward through Benatek to the Swiepwald.

The 8th and 4th Divisions (in the actual centre) which took Sadowa and occupied the Sadowa woods [hereafter referred to as the *Holawald*].

It was now 10:00. If we were able to take the Lipa Hill, the battle would be won before the Crown Prince [2nd Army] even arrived, however all attacks on this position failed. Fresh troops, Pomeranian, Thuringian, Magdeburg and, finally (from the reserves), Brandenburg regiments were led against the hill, but in vain. The advance came to a halt, individual battalions had to fall back, the centre was held but only with heavy losses.

Initially we looked to the right. If as expected, the Elbe Army advanced, if it outflanked the enemy and threatened his only line of retreat, the Königgrätz *Chaussée*, perhaps even cut it, then III Corps, which was being held in reserve, could be committed in the centre and achieve success. However, the desired rapid advance of the Elbe Army did not occur, no blame is attached to this, the situation on the right wing was similar to that in the centre, the hills, bristling with artillery, presented a defense that could not be broken on the first assault.

At this critical moment, when the anticipated outcome on the right wing had failed to materialize, it was clear that the decision could now only come from the left. And come it did. At about 3:00 in the afternoon the Crown Prince's army appeared from the north and struck into the flank and rear of the Austrian position. The two Guards Divisions, taking Chlum and Lipa in their first assault, drove like a wedge into the centre of the enemy flank. VI Corps advanced simultaneously to their left across the three ridges and took the enemy in his rear. To complete his misfortune, the Elbe Army simultaneously outflanked his position to the south. His only line of retreat, the Königgrätz *Chaussée*, might be cut at any moment from two sides.

In order to escape this impending doom, which entailed either capture or destruction of the army, [the enemy] ordered a hasty retreat. Cavalry and artillery sacrificed themselves, the latter especially, fighting to the end. The fact that they lost so many guns was not cause for blame but rather for fame, it is always easier to limber up and pull out.

The retreat proceeded across the Elbe and we shall deal elsewhere with the terror that accompanied it. What would the picture have been if the victor pursued! But there was no pursuit, our forces rested on the battlefield that had been so bitterly fought for.

Now we shall examine the battle in detail.

The Fighting at Problus and Prim

The Elbe Army was on the right wing. Facing it were the Saxons and behind them, the Austrian 8th Corps, initially only two brigades strong. On his right, the enemy maintained contact with his 10th and 1st Corps, his left flank was covered by the 1st Light Cavalry Division (Edelsheim).

The ground facing the Elbe Army as it arrived on the near side of the Bistritz, is best described as two valleys in succession with a central ridge between them. The initial Saxon plan was to hold this central ridge in force, in other words, to contest the enemy's passage at the first valley (through which the Bistritz flows). With this in mind on the evening of 2nd July, artillery positions were dug on this first ridge, the Hradek Hill. However, Benedek's dispositions did not allow for such a broad extension of his front, with the result that the actual Bistritz line was abandoned, and instead of holding the first valley, the second was chosen. The Saxons took up a position on the Problus – Nieder Prim Hill, with only individual battalions pushed forward to the Bistritz crossings. These advanced battalions were positioned as follows:

> In Tresowitz (right flank, only a little over a mile from Dohalitzka) the 5th Battalion.
> Between Tresowitz and Popowitz, the 6th Battalion.
> In Popowitz the 2nd Jäger Battalion.
> In Lubno the 9th Battalion.
> In Alt Nechanitz the 8th Battalion.
> In Nechanitz the 7th Battalion.
> In Kuncitz the 11th Battalion.

The task of the Elbe Army was now to force these Bistritz crossings (or at least the most important ones), to climb the Hradek Hill that lay behind them, and advancing from this hill through the second valley, to take the Problus – Nieder Prim position.

The front of the [Problus – Nieder Prim] position was quite strong. Its weakness was that it could be turned on the [Prussian] right and that it was overlooked by Hradek Hill.

The advanced guard forces the Bistritz and takes position on the Lubno – Hradek Line, 7:00-9:00

The advanced guard of the Elbe Army, *Generalmajor* von Schöler, moved out of Smidar at 3:30 [in the morning]. It advanced via Skriwan, Kralic and Kobilitz and was at the Bistritz by 7:00, seven battalions and two batteries strong. These seven battalions were:

> Fusilier Battalion of the 28th Regiment, *Major* Mettler.
> 2nd Battalion of the 33rd Regiment, *Oberstlieutenant* von Marschall.
> Fusilier Battalion of the 17th Regiment, *Oberstlieutenant* von Koblinski.
> Jäger Battalion Nr.8, *Major* Zierold.
> Fusilier Battalion of the 69th Regiment, *Major* Marschall von Gulicki.
> 1st Battalion of the 40th Regiment, *Oberstlieutenant* von Conrady.
> 2nd Battalion of the 56th Regiment, *Major* von Thielau.

The only substantial [but partially destroyed] bridge was at Nechanitz, otherwise, both upstream and downstream, there were only footbridges over the river so that if the army, especially the artillery, was to get to the other side of the Bistritz, Nechanitz must be taken. The Fusilier battalion of the 28th therefore attacked [Nechanitz] while the Fusilier battalion of the 17th and the 2nd Battalion of the 33rd, supported this movement on its left and right flanks, by advancing against Lubno and Kuncitz.

Kuncitz it appears was taken first, the 33rd pushed forward rapidly, the Saxon 11th Battalion that was fighting there fell back through the Hradek Zoological Gardens to Nieder Prim. The Saxon retreat and its immediate consequence, the appearance of our 33rd in the flank and rear of the enemy forces still fighting in Nechanitz, could not fail to influence the defense of this main crossing over the Bistritz.

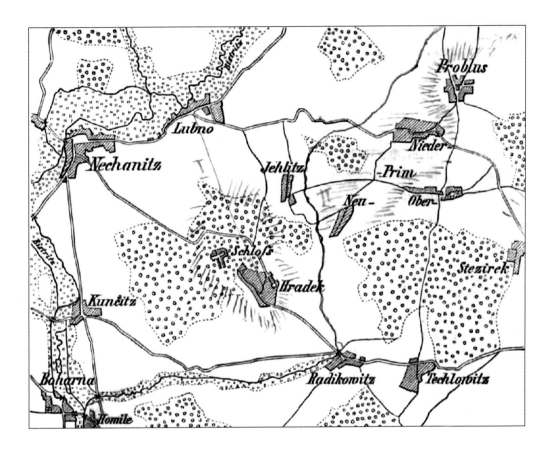

Alt Nechanitz (on the near side of the river) was taken effortlessly by our advancing 28th. Nechanitz itself was defended all the more stubbornly by the Saxon battalions fighting there, the 7th and 8th, and the Zenker Horse Artillery Battery that had gone into position in the churchyard. Only after the partially destroyed bridge over the Bistritz had been made passable using dismounted [barn] doors were our 28th able to advance and force the enemy out of Nechanitz. The 1st Company of the Saxon 8th Battalion, which had been in position right at the bridge, suffered not insignificant losses in this action. Battery Zenker also fell back.

The appearance of our 33rd in Kuncitz (as mentioned above) affected the defense of Nechanitz and played its part in causing the evacuation of this village. Similarly, this now began to influence the defense of Lubno, which had been conducted with great determination. The 9th Saxon Battalion, which up to this point had been supported by the *Granatkanonen* [shell guns[3]] of Battery von der Pforte, had defended the village perimeter, especially the houses at the

---

3   Tr. Note: *Granatkanonen* were short barreled, 12pdr, smoothbore shell guns designed to fire shell, shrapnel, cannister and round shot. Their range was shorter than the rifled pieces currently in use, but they had been retained due to their superior ability at firing cannister.

mill, with great determination and had exacted substantial losses from the advancing Fusilier battalion of the 17th (the battalion lost three officers and 80 men there).

Now with its left flank also exposed, [the Saxon 9th Battalion] fell back on Problus, the three battalions on the extreme [Saxon] right in Tresowitz and Popowitz (the 5th and 6th Battalions and the 2nd Jäger Battalion) also retreated even though they had not come under attack. Thus, the threat to the enemy left flank that had started at Kuncitz and progressed via Nechanitz and Lubno, now extended to the furthest extremity of the [Saxon] right wing.

All seven of the Saxon advanced guard battalions fell back to the Problus – Nieder Prim position. All seven of the Prussian advanced guard battalions followed them and took up a central position on the [first] ridge extending between Lubno and Hradek.[4]

Their positions from left to right, were:

Fusilier Battalion of the 17th Infantry Regiment.
Jäger Battalion Nr.8.
Fusilier Battalion of the 28th Infantry Regiment.
1st Battalion of Fusilier Regiment Nr.40.
Fusilier Battalion of the 69th Infantry Regiment.
2nd Battalion of Fusilier Regiment Nr.33.
2nd Battalion of the 56th Infantry Regiment.

The two advanced guard batteries, Wolff and Pilgrim, went into position in the centre of this position, also on the ridge. The second valley lay open and there, on the hills on the far side of the valley, lay the villages of Problus, Nieder and Ober Prim.

Artillery battle, the advanced guard captures Jehlitz, Neu Prim and the Pheasantry, 10.00 – 12.00

It might have been 10:00 when our advance guard batteries took up position and began to open fire. The enemy moved three rifled batteries to the hill between Problus and Nieder Prim and replied immediately. The cannonade gradually mounted in intensity as reinforcements arrived. Within the first hour the Saxons were reinforced by two Austrian batteries from 8th Corps (which was in reserve) ours were supported by two rifled batteries of the 15th Division (Canstein). By about 11:00, 34 [Austro Saxon] and 24 [Prussian] guns faced each other. Due in part to the long range (4000 paces) the cannonade was relatively ineffectual.

Generalmajor von Schöler, riding without concern between the lines, was unwilling to await the ever more uncertain outcome of the cannonade. He decided to go over to the offensive with his seven battalions and advance against the enemy position in three columns, left, right and centre. The many farmsteads and clumps of woodland in the centre of the valley favoured this advance in that they offered cover, and in the event, they were captured with minimal effort (including the woods between Popowitz and Problus). On the extreme right wing the

---

4   Tr. Note: As Strobl's maps show, Lubno is on the east bank of the Bistritz in the valley. The ridge under discussion rises just south and east of Lubno and extends south - southeast. Hradek is itself on the ridge, which then falls off to the southeast towards Radikowitz. Strobl's superb series of maps shows the position of each battalion or element thereof and its movements.

56th advanced to the Stezirek woods. In the centre, Jehlitz, Neu Prim and the most important position, the *Fasanerie* [the Pheasantry, a lightly wooded enclosure for rearing game birds] that lay between them, were taken by the 33rd and 40th. An attempt was made to advance beyond this to Nieder Prim but foundered on the strength of the enemy position. The pheasantry itself remained in our hands, at least for the time being.

Advance of the Saxon Leib Brigade, 12:00 – 1:00

We had gained ground and now stood on a line running approximately through the centre of the valley, nevertheless our advance had not deceived the Crown Prince of Saxony in respect of our numerical weakness. The 15th Division (Canstein), which was some way behind the advance-guard, had still not arrived, and therefore the enemy commander decided to go over to the offensive himself. The Saxon Leib Brigade, comprising Infantry Battalions 13, 14, 15 and 16, was shifted from the right wing of the enemy position (Problus), to the left wing (Nieder Prim), in order to advance from there and recapture Neu Prim and the pheasantry, the 12pdr smoothbore Battery Hering - Göppingen was ordered to support the attack.

Before we accompany the Saxon brigade in their advance, we shall first examine the Problus – Nieder Prim position and its defenders.

Problus and Nieder Prim, both on the crest of the ridge (the former with a prominent church), were put in the best possible state of defense by Saxon pioneers assisted by a detachment of Austrians. The Schloss [originally a Castle, but by 1866 most had evolved into elegant, walled country houses] and farm buildings of Nieder Prim were fortified by making loopholes, shuttering windows and creating breastworks as well as by digging infantry trenches and creating an abatis along the perimeter.

The 3rd Infantry Brigade was assigned the defense of the two villages. The 9th and 10th Infantry Battalions were in Problus along with the 3rd Jäger. The 11th and 12th Battalions and the 4th Jäger Battalion (this last from the Leib Brigade) were in Nieder Prim.

The remainder of the Saxon contingent were to be found as follows:

> The rest of the infantry (1st, 2nd and 4th [Lieb] Brigades) were in covered positions directly behind the crest of the hill between Problus and Nieder Prim, the 4th Brigade on the right, the 1st on the left and the 2nd northeast of both.
> The cavalry was on the right alongside the infantry to maintain contact with the Austrian 10th Corps.
> The Reserve Artillery was to the left rear.

The decisive engagement for this part of the battlefield would be at Problus itself. Immediately behind the Saxons, as mentioned earlier, was the [Austrian] 8th Corps. It held the woods of Bor[5] 1000 to 2000 paces east of the Problus – Nieder Prim line, Brigade Schulz on the right, Brigade Roth on the left, Brigade Wöber between them but further to the rear and nearly

---

5   Tr. Note: In 1866 Bor was a farmstead.

BERG SWITSCHIN   SCHNEEKOPPE

Problus.

reaching the eastern margin of the woods.[6] Still farther to the rear (outside the woods) was the Austrian Corps Artillery Reserve and the 3rd Uhlan Regiment, *Erzherzog* Karl.

The overall Austro-Saxon position therefore, was extremely concentrated and had an initial front (it was later extended) of barely 2000 paces and a depth of 4000 paces with the main strength on the right. This was the substantial force (40,000 men) that, in consideration of our weakness, now went over to the offensive. The Leib Brigade, as already mentioned briefly, advanced from behind the crest of the hill, band playing, from the right (Problus) to the left (Nieder Prim). It then wheeled and taking advantage of a depression in the ground (that extended between Neu Prim and Jehlitz) south of the village, vigorously attacked the woods of the pheasantry that were held by our 33rd and 40th. The 15th [Saxon] Battalion, preceded by a dense skirmish line, was in the lead. The 4th Jäger Battalion, breaking out of the western margin of the village (Nieder Prim), supported the offensive. The 12pdr shell gun Battery Hering – Göppingen, shelled our troops with shrapnel. The attack succeeded. Our 33rd and 40th had to fall back with not insignificant losses. All of the wooded areas as far as Jehlitz and Neu Prim were recaptured by the enemy who showed every intention of extending his success in the centre of our position.

At that moment however, the appearance of Prussian spiked helmets on his left flank halted the advance. This Prussian column was the 2nd Battalion of the 56th Regiment that had moved into the Stezirek woods (on our extreme right wing), then debouching from the northern margin of these woods with a half left, was now advancing against Ober Prim. The Saxons either overestimated these forces or the battalions of our 15th Division (Canstein) that were marching in a wide arc around Schloss Hradek, arrived sooner than expected (and sooner than we ourselves, expected). There is good reason to suspect the latter to be true. In any case, it was the surprise appearance of an indeterminate Prussian force from the southwest that brought the enemy offensive to a standstill. Covered by the 13th Battalion that wheeled toward the

---

6   Author's Note: All three brigades of 8th Corps moved out of their camp by Nedelist [NB Nedelist *not* Nechanitz] to these assigned positions, Brigade Schulz at 9:00, Brigade Roth (formerly Fragnern) at about the same time, Brigade Wöber (formerly Kreyssern) only between 1:00 and 2:00. This last brigade had provided two battalions for outpost duty the previous night. Since it could not wait for their return (a third battalion having been detached in the meantime), it arrived on the left wing with only about half its strength.

exposed flank, all of the remaining Saxon troops returned to the Nieder Prim position. Only the pheasantry remained held (by the 15th Battalion).

Advance of the 2nd Saxon Brigade, 1:00 – 2:00

The [Saxon] Leib Brigade's offensive, although it got off to a good start, only resulted in partial success. *Kronprinz* Albert [CIC of the Saxon forces] therefore decided to follow his initial thrust with a second in the same direction. The 2nd Brigade was chosen for this task. In order to prevent this advance being compromised again by exposing the left flank, the general commanding the Austrian 8th Corps was urgently requested to have one or more brigades advance toward Ober Prim. Ober Prim and its approaches were immediately occupied by Brigade Schulz (IR 8 Gerstner and IR 74 Nobili). This neutralized any immediate threat to the flank. The Austrians were so positioned that a simple left wheel would provide a solid wall of infantry behind whose protection the advance could commence. And it did indeed commence. The 2nd [Saxon] Brigade, brought from its reserve position at Problus to Nieder Prim, advanced in two waves just as the Leib Brigade had done previously, the 6th Battalion in the lead, over the rolling terrain between the pheasantry and Neu Prim toward the woods of Schloss Hradek that extended far to the east. Already our artillery position on the Hradek Hill was in danger when, again from the left flank (just as happened an hour earlier with the advance of the Leib Brigade) there arose a commotion that soon degenerated into chaos.

This time it was not distant Prussians that posed the threat but Austrians who, already broken and in some cases shattered, now threw themselves in wild flight into the flank of the advancing 2nd Brigade. After the misfortune that had befallen them, these [Austrians] that were supposed to form a covering wall, now produced more confusion than they had previously provided protection.

In order to understand these events, we must take our narrative back considerably in time and follow the Prussian 15th Division in its advance. This division, which had bivouacked behind Hochwesely nearly 14 miles from the Bistritz, despite its early start and rapid march, did not arrive at the bridge in Nechanitz until about 11:00. Here the division was ordered to keep to the right and advance via Hradek against the enemy left flank, especially against Ober Prim.

In accordance with these orders, at approximately 1.30, *General* von Canstein directed the 30th Brigade (von Glasenapp) against the Stezirek woods, and the 29th Brigade (von Stückradt) to the left against Neu Prim.

The Prussian brigades arrived at the locations specified for them (Neu Prim and the Stezirek woods) at the same time that the Saxon 2nd Brigade, its flank protected by the Austrian Brigade Schulz, began its advance from Nieder Prim. *General* von Canstein, who accompanied Brigade Glasenapp (Regiments Nr.68 and 28), ordered an immediate advance against the enemy flank, so that the Prussian advance from south to north collided directly with the Saxon advance from east to west. Between the two, on the line Neu Prim – Ober Prim, stood the Austrian Brigade Schulz, everything depended on the conduct of this brigade, but it failed. The Fusilier Battalion of the 68th Regiment in the lead, Brigade Glasenapp crashed out of the Stezirek woods with hurrahs and tore through the Austrian brigade, now positioned with front facing south, as if it was a sheet of paper, hurling one half to the right toward Ober Prim, and chasing the other half to the left, toward Neu Prim. Met there by fire from Brigade Stückradt, the flight took on a new direction (to the north) and flooded into the area between Nieder Prim and the pheasantry.

Rout of Brigade Schultz.

This was a disaster, for there, at that very moment, the 2nd Saxon Brigade was advancing to the attack. It was the worst possible timing! The very regiments (IR 8 Gerstner and IR 74 Nobili) that were supposed to provide protection for the offensive, now crashed in hopeless confusion into the left flank of the advancing Saxon battalions and swept the foremost (6th and 8th) along with them in flight. Caught in a hail of bullets from the crossfire of the two Prussian brigades, all of the opposing forces, including the two Saxon battalions, suffered heavy losses in dead and wounded. Only the outstanding conduct of the 2nd Saxon Jäger Battalion prevented a complete collapse. Brought forward from the second wave, band playing, it advanced in line toward the exposed flank. With skirmishers to the right and left, it allowed the swarm of fleeing men to pass through its lines which then closed up and commenced firing volleys at our pursuing battalions.

The Saxons returned to pass through the lines of their covering force behind Nieder Prim. The remnants of the Austrian brigade (which had lost close to 1000 men) concentrated in Ober Prim.

The 30th Brigade (von Glasenapp) captures Ober Prim, 2:00

This flank attack from the south, which as we have just described almost shattered the Austrian Brigade Schulz[7] and forced the 2nd Saxon Brigade to retreat, may not have achieved complete victory but it certainly got the process started. *General* von Canstein quickly decided to make the most of his success and ordered an attack on Nieder and Ober Prim. The latter, easily accessible as a flanking point, was taken first by the 30th Brigade.

The attack was made concentrically, the 68th Regiment, under *Oberst* von Gayl, approached the village from the south and southwest, the 28th, under *Oberst* von Gerstein from the south and southeast, the 68th first. In this action *Hauptmann* von Bolschwing of the 11th Company was killed. The village, which was bravely defended by the 3rd Battalion of IR 8 Gerstner, could only be taken, at least initially, one step at a time. However, as the 28th began to outflank the position and threatened to sever the line of retreat to the 'Bor Wood', the enemy evacuated the second half of the village, and pursued by our forces, fled in droves to the aforementioned wood (1000 paces to the rear). Halfway between Ober Prim and the edge of the woods the Austrian Brigade Commander, *Generalmajor* von Schulz, sank from his horse, mortally wounded in the chest by two bullets.[8] Whether as a result of the recent confusion [and probably the loss of many of their officers including the Brigade Commander] or because it [Ober Prim] did not seriously expose their own position (in the Bor woods), the Austrians failed to grasp the seriousness of the situation, the Saxons did not. They knew Ober Prim must be recaptured. If that failed, at the very least, the further advance of the Prussians from Ober Prim to Nieder Prim must be

7   Author's Note: The Austrian General Staff work, which has since come out, states that two brigades faced us at this location. Brigade Roth (so we learn) was ordered to support Brigade Schulz and to advance on the latter's left. Regiment Nr.77 Salvator took the lead, Regiment Nr.15 Nassau and the 5th Jäger Battalion followed. The brigade moved out from Ober Prim toward the Stezirek woods in good order, however as it entered the woods, the 5th Jäger Battalion, along with much of the Nassau Regiment, surged forward and became mixed up with Regiment Salvator resulting in confusion. It seems that at that very moment, our 68th thrust into the enemy's left flank and rolled it up. So much for Brigade Roth (Brigade Wöber arrived too late to be committed at this location). It might also be stated at this point that the Austrian 8th Corps had not had a good day on 3rd July. The Saxon report states this in no uncertain terms, and we have every reason to believe it. [The Austrian 8th Corps] displayed little of the extraordinary bravery with which the same corps (Brigades Fragnern and Kreyssern) [now Roth and Wöber] had fought at Skalitz. For our part, it is impossible to be precise in this, we probably had no more than three, certainly no more than six, battalions on hand and yet these sufficed to totally repulse twice their strength in enemy forces in less than half an hour. Only Ober Prim itself, as we shall show in the following pages, was well defended.

8   Author's Note: Men of the 28th Regiment, led by *Hauptmann* Perizonius and *Lieutenant* Tempel, attempted to carry the General (who lay in the midst of shell fire from his own batteries) off of the battlefield to Ober Prim. However, he died before they could get him to safety. His body was laid in the foremost barn and on the morning of 4th July, he was buried thirty paces from the village. His death aroused special sympathy among some of our troops. The 34th Regiment, which arrived soon after the action at Ober Prim, knew him from Rastatt [a Federal Fortress], where, shortly before the outbreak of the war, he had also been stationed and was a friend of the commander of the 34th Regiment, Oberst von Schmeling. At a later date, by order of the Emperor, the General was disinterred and re-buried in the cemetery at Königgrätz, where a monument had already been erected to him. (When the corpse was exhumed it showed two gunshot wounds in the left thigh, two in the left chest, one shot through the upper lip, the abdomen torn open by a shell fragment and the left arm and left leg broken.)

prevented. Accordingly, the Saxon 1st Infantry Brigade (that had suffered such heavy losses at Gitschin) now advanced from its reserve position at Problus to the Bor woods and took up a strong position, protected by an abatis, at the western margin of the wood, roughly level with Nieder Prim. The narrow patch of ground between Problus, Nieder Prim and the woods behind it (Bor), thus became a gap that would prove difficult and dangerous to cross since an advancing enemy would be exposed to a crossfire.

Simultaneously the Saxons commenced an escalating artillery barrage against Ober Prim. While the rifled batteries continued to fire from the hills at Nieder Prim on our artillery position at Hradek (with front facing west), all of the smooth bore shell gun batteries that were available to the Saxons, went into position at an angle to the five rifled batteries (with front facing south). Thirty guns now opened a formidable fire at extremely short range against Ober Prim, setting it ablaze and forcing our 68th and 28th Regiments to evacuate the village and seek cover outside of it in hollow ground and in the woods. This shellfire was so effective that our 30th Brigade was, at least for the time being, prevented from advancing from Ober Prim against Nieder Prim. In the meantime, the attack that would be decisive regarding Nieder Prim was launched from the other side, from the front.

The Reserve Artillery moves up, the 29th Brigade (von Stückradt) takes Nieder Prim

At about 2:00 *General* von Stückradt, whose brigade comprised the left wing of the 15th Division (Canstein), formed up to attack Nieder Prim. However, before he launched his assault, our artillery, which had hitherto fired from the Hradek Hill, moved forward to point blank range and now opened such a fire from 66 guns (the reserve artillery under Oberst von Bülow having arrived), that the enemy's 34 rifled guns could no longer maintain their position. As [the Saxon] fire began to slacken, the battalions of the 29th Brigade, the 65th and 40th Regiments, moved forward from the pheasantry and advanced in Sturmschritt [a fast run] against the village that was defended by half of the [Saxon] 3rd Brigade (the 11th and 12th Battalions) and by the 4th Jäger Battalion. The brewery, immediately adjacent to the Schloss, was already in flames. The 6th Company of the 65th Regiment forced its way into the village from the southwest and stormed the Schloss' courtyard. Other companies of the same regiment, along with those of the 40th and 33rd (the latter from the advance guard) followed on.

The 4th [Saxon] Jäger Battalion fought every step of the way as it evacuated the village which, along with the two infantry battalions mentioned above, it had stoutly defended despite five hours of ever increasing artillery fire. With no sign of disorder, it fell back past Problus to the northeast. Our forces were too exhausted for immediate pursuit.

The 14th Division (von Münster) storms Problus, 3:00

Problus fell at nearly the same time as Nieder Prim. This key position, key because it was the junction [between the Saxons and the Austrian army], would in any case have had to be evacuated after the loss of Ober and Nieder Prim. However, as the attack on Problus was being prepared, the two villages on its flank had not yet been taken and the overall situation was such that it was impossible to await the results of these actions. The urgent task at 2:00 was to disengage the centre, even if the Crown Prince did not come, or came later than expected. Such was the situation as *General* von Herwarth ordered the 14th Division to storm Problus.

After a march of nearly 14 miles on bottomless roads and across ploughed fields, the 14th Division (*Generallieutenant Graf* Münster-Meinhövel) reached Nechanitz at 1:00, Lubno at 1:30, and shortly after at 2:00, the woods between Popowitz and Problus that had already been occupied for three hours by the left wing battalion of the advance guard (17th Fusiliers). Here the two brigades of the division formed up for the attack, the 27th Brigade (*Generalmajor* von Schwarzkoppen), in the woods itself, the 28th Brigade (*Generalmajor* von Hiller) to its right rear at the southern point of the woods. The objective of the former was Problus itself (the church tower as *point d'appui*), the objective of the latter was the hill south of Problus.

The 27th Brigade advanced first, the Fusiliers and the 1st Battalion of the 56th Regiment in the lead. *General* von Herwarth, *Graf* Münster and *Generalmajor* von Schwarzkoppen took position at the front of the battalions and inspired the troops with stirring words. With colours unfurled and the regimental bands playing, the battalions now advanced from the woods, confident of victory. They had to traverse a stretch of nearly 1800 paces to the strongly held border of the village, under heavy artillery fire from front and flank (an enemy battery had gone into position at Stresetitz). The battalions kept up their advance, the Fusilier Battalion, with a half right, aimed for the southern half of the village while the 1st Battalion, heading straight ahead, went for the centre.

Hammered by incoming fire, the first of the dead and wounded began to fall. The Fusiliers suffered substantial losses, *Oberst* von Dorpowski was shot from his horse by a bullet in the thigh, *Oberstlieutenant* von Busse assumed command. Now the flanking companies of the Fusilier Battalion reached the edge of the village where the most difficult task awaited them. In the attempt to take the abatis and hedge that surrounded the village, *Hauptmann* von Montbart, *Hauptmann* von Bolschwing and *Permierlieutenant* von Consbruch were all killed by rifle fire, *Lieutenant* von Montowt was shot right through the heart. Seven other officers (all from the Fusilier Battalion) were more or less severely wounded within ten minutes. Two colour bearers fell, the colours were already in their third set of hands. Finally, they reached an earthen bank that ran close to the village and provided modest cover, here the Fusiliers threw themselves down and began to return fire.

The 1st Battalion whose job was to advance in the centre suffered fewer, but still significant losses. When it reached the line held by the Fusiliers, these now sprang up from behind the earthen wall and all together, from two sides (the 3rd Company under *Hauptmann* Michaelis having flanked the village to the north), advanced into Problus. A stubborn fire fight developed at the fences, hedges and buildings, especially in the cemetery. *Major* von Hymmen, commander of the 1st Battalion, disabled by a shot in the foot, was carried to the rear.

Major von Mutius assumed command. *Lieutenant* Madelung was struck dead, the last to fall. The far side of the village was taken and the enemy, who had fought with great valour (especially the 3rd Jäger Battalion), fell back in all directions. Two hundred prisoners, mostly wounded, fell in our hands. At nearly the same time, to the right of the 27th Brigade, the 28th (*Generalmajor* von Hiller) captured the hill between Problus and Nieder Prim. The preliminaries were nearly the same. As in the attack on the village of Problus, where two battalions of the 56th took the lead, two battalions of the 57th (and one battalion of the 17th) took the lead against the Problus Hill. Here the losses were fewer, in part because the terrain offered more cover. By about 3.00

The fighting around Problus church.

the village and hill of Problus were ours. The enemy, covered by his batteries, fell back to the northeast.[9]

Only the Bor Woods which lay, part on, part alongside his line of retreat, was still held at its northwest margin by the Saxon 1st Brigade and at its southwestern corner by battalions of the Austrian Brigade Wöber, especially by the 24th Jäger Battalion.

9   Author's Note: About one hour later, at the same time that the Austrian reserves (the 1st and 6th Corps) were brought up on the right, an attempt was also made by Brigade Piret, [1st Corps] against Problus on the left. With IR 18 Constantin and the 29th Jäger Battalion in the first wave and IR 45 Sigismund in the second, the brigade was ordered forward. Advancing under heavy fire from our skirmishers, [the Austrian brigade] forced the foremost *Tirailleurs* [skirmishers] who were posted in the hedges outside the village, back to the actual village itself, but then came under such heavy fire that it turned back after many officers and men, particularly from the 29th Jäger Battalion, fell to our bullets. *Oberst* von Ripper, Commander of Regiment Sigismund also fell. The enemy battery located by Stresetitz, continued its bombardment that had earlier set Problus on fire, until a later hour.

Totally exhausted, our forces did not pursue so that the enemy were able to commence their retreat without significant loss. The Saxons initially proceeded to Rosnitz and Briza. The brigades of 8th Corps followed in the same direction or took position by Charbusitz. The Elbe Army, less the 16th Division, which did not join in the action because it did not debouche from Nechanitz until 3:00, had accomplished its mission.

The enemy left wing was defeated, now it could be outflanked (by the 16th Division). The losses were great, 71 officers (22 of whom were dead) and 1557 men.

In the Centre – The Artillery Battle

In the centre (a left wing did not yet exist, it only developed later with the arrival of the Crown Prince), stood the 1st Army commanded by Prince Friedrich Karl, with the Elbe Army [whose actions have been discussed in the previous chapter] on the right. Here, as there, the task was essentially the same. It was a matter of driving in the enemy's forward positions, forcing a crossing of the Bistritz and depending on the circumstances, either storming the hills on the far side, or if these proved too strong, of holding the Bistritz line at all costs until the arrival of the Crown Prince.

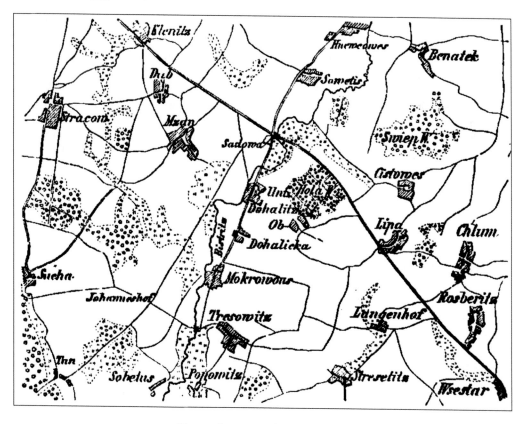

The northern part of the battlefield.

The forces available in the centre were six divisions strong: two Pomeranian, two Magdeburg/ Thüringian and two Brandenburg. The two Brandenburg divisions (the 5th and 6th) were held in reserve to the left of the Dub Hill, leaving four divisions for the attack. Three great attack columns were formed from these four divisions. The flanking columns to the right and left each consisted of one division. The centre column, however, was two divisions strong. All three columns attacked the enemy. In the centre we will deal with three distinct actions:

> One action on the centre right at Mokrowous and Dohalizka.
> One action in the actual centre at Sadowa, Dohalitz and the Holawald.
> One action on the centre left between Benatek, Maslowed, Cistowes and the Swiepwald.

The actions themselves, though with similar objectives, took different forms, also the losses they incurred differed widely. While the action on the centre right sustained the fewest casualties, that on the centre left was the bloodiest. Facing our three attack columns were the Austrian 10th and 3rd Corps positioned around Lipa, and the 4th and 2nd Corps on the Chlum – Maslowed line. Thus, four of our divisions fought against four of their corps. However, what was more to our disadvantage than the enemy's two to one numerical superiority, was his position on the hills on the opposite bank of the Bistritz, which was ideal for defense and especially favourable to artillery. All of the *Feldzeugmeister's* plans soon proved to be based on taking advantage of both of these factors, the outstanding position and his superior artillery. His orders directed that after lightly contesting the forward positions, [the Austrian forces were] to fall back to the main defensive line and there await the enemy without themselves going over to the attack. Only on [our] centre left, where the 7th Division conducted its famous battle in the Swiepwald, did our troops manage to engage in hand to hand fighting, all our other infantry assaults failed. We will return to the battle in the Swiepwald later but initially we will concern ourselves with the cannonade that now ensued, that continued for six hours, and can hardly find its equal in history.

In so doing we shall distinguish between two separate artillery battles based on the Austrian positions:

> The battle against Lipa.
> The battle against Maslowed [the Swiepwald].

The artillery battle against Lipa

Centered on Lipa, straddling both sides of the Königgrätz *Chaussée* stood [the Austrian] 10th and 3rd Corps, the left wing of 10th Corps extending as far as Stresetitz, the right wing of 3rd Corps as far as Chlum. Immediately in front of both corps, facing west and northwest, in entrenched positions, was a row of guns that stretched for more than a mile and became famous as 'the Lipa artillery position'. Initially comprising 17 batteries (seven around Lipa, ten to the west of Langenhof),[10] these 136 guns hurled their shells into the valley with a deafening

---

10   Author's Note: 3rd Corps originally had eight batteries, 10th corps nine. It seems however, that soon after the start of the battle, one horse battery from 3rd Corps was transferred from the northern side of the *Chaussée* to the southern side, resulting in the numbers seven and ten. The seven batteries near

thunder. The artillery fire was so heavy that three of 10th Corps' batteries had already exhausted their ammunition by 11:00. The general commanding that corps (*Feldmarschalllieutenant* von Gablenz), requested additional batteries from the 3rd Reserve Cavalry Division and also from Army Headquarters, in order to avoid even a momentary diminution in the intensity of the fire. Both requests were approved and two batteries from the Reserve Cavalry division and four batteries from the Army Artillery Reserve were released. At that point, shortly after 11:09, after the three depleted batteries of 10th Corps had been withdrawn, there were 20 batteries with a total of 160 guns near Lipa and Langenhof, and they now continued to fire uninterruptedly until the start of the retreat.

Let us now see what we had, with which to face the enemy artillery. Initially we had the twelve batteries of the 8th, 4th and 3rd Divisions, then at about 10:00 or a little later, these were augmented by four batteries of the Pomeranian Reserve Artillery under *Oberst* von Puttkamer. At about 12:00 these were joined by four additional batteries of the Brandenburg Artillery Regiment Nr.3 under *Major* Rüstow. Thus at 12:00 noon, our entire compliment of artillery facing the Lipa – Langenhof position consisted of:

Twelve batteries of the 8th, 4th and 3rd Division, 72 guns.
Four batteries of the Pomeranian Reserve Artillery, 24 guns.
Four batteries of the Brandenburg Artillery Regiment, 24 guns.

This gave a total of 120 guns, however at the given hour [12.00], little more than half were in action. The batteries of the 3th and 4rd Divisions, after achieving success at the start of the battle and having forced the enemy artillery that had advanced toward Sadowa, Dohalitz and Dohalitzka to retreat, could not maintain their position in the face of the fire from Lipa and were forced back piecemeal to the west bank of the Bistritz (with the sole exception of the 4pdr Battery Gallus, which held out to the last). The resultant loss was substantial, by noon we had only twelve batteries in action [72 guns] instead of twenty, to face an enemy 160 guns strong. Of these twelve batteries, three were to the north and nine to the south of the Königgrätz *Chaussée*. Those that were on our left went into position between the Holawald and the Swiepwald, those on our right between the Holawald and Dohalitzka. These twelve batteries that held out so heroically were.

On the left, between the Holawald and the Swiepwald (all three of the 8th Division):

6pdr Battery Anton.
4pdr Battery von Schlotheim.
4pdr Battery Kipping.

On the right, between the Holawald and Dohalitzka:

4pdr Battery Gallus of the 3rd Division.
4pdr Battery von der Dollen.

Lipa were positioned in tiers, three of them in the gun emplacements prepared the preceding day on the plateau between Chlum and Lipa, to the right and rear of the latter village.

4pdr Battery Bode.

6pdr Battery Möwes.

6pdr Battery Rautenberg, these last four of the Pomeranian Reserve Artillery.

6pdr Battery von der Goltz.

4pdr Battery Griess.

4pdr Battery Munk.

4pdr Battery Hirschberg, these last four from the Brandenburg Field Artillery Regiment.

72 guns in unprotected positions sought to hold their own against more than double their number of enemy pieces. From minute to minute it became ever more evident, as some batteries lost up to half their crews, that if no reinforcements came, we must be defeated in this uneven battle.[11]

But finally, they came. The Army Reserve Artillery under *General* Schwartz, had now arrived and advancing rapidly, went into position to the left and right of the Holawald, reinforcing [the position to the left of the woods] with four batteries, and that on the right with five. Our artillery strength thus increased from 12 to 24 batteries. Henceforth it maintained its

---

11   Author's Note: At this hour of unequal combat *Major* Rüstow also fell, seriously but not mortally wounded, he later died as the result of a double amputation. We quote the following report: '*Major* Rüstow was on the right wing with 4pdr Battery (Grieß) when he was informed that the ammunition was beginning to run out. He replied that it would be attended to immediately and rode back himself. He was on the *Chaussée* that runs from Unter Dohalitz to Dohalitzka, two to four paces from *Lieutenant* von der Bosch of the 5th Brandenburg Infantry Regiment Nr.48, when a shell burst in the roadside ditch and a fragment smashed *Major* Rüstow's right foot. *Lieutenant* von der Bosch turned in response to the cry for help from the trumpeter accompanying the *Major*, at the same moment that *Major* Rüstow sank from his horse. They picked him up and laid him in the roadside ditch. The wounded man repeatedly pressed *Lieutenant* von der Bosch's hand with the words, 'I shall now die. God grant us victory!' As he was being borne off on the litter, he waved his hand to the men nearby and said, 'Stay brave, men!' In Unter Dohalitz the duty surgeon, *Stabsarzt* Dr. Birawer, performed the amputation. [*Major* Rüstow] urgently requested [the doctor] to have him moved to the rear, since he feared falling into Austrian hands in his helpless condition. After the amputation, the amputated foot lay on the head end of his stretcher, he was carried into the village by *Lieutenant* von der Bosch, to whom he again stretched out his hand in farewell. In the hospital in Horsitz, to which he had been brought, he had to undergo a second amputation whose effects he did not survive. He died on 25th July 1866, after being deeply shaken by the news of the death in combat at Wiesenthal of his brother, a *Major* in the 2nd Westfalian Infantry Regiment Nr.15. 'In him the army has lost an excellent officer. Born in 1824 at Brandenburg, he entered the 2nd Artillery Brigade in 1842. In 1850 he resigned [from the Prussian army] and served in the Schleswig - Holstein Army as a battery commander at Idstedt and Missunde. In 1852 he returned to his old army and then, in 1864, took part in the storming of Düppel. At Gitschin he displayed his outstanding talent when he held out with four batteries of the 5th Division against the enemy's 90 guns. At that time one of his battery commanders described him as 'the ideal commander of an artillery division.' Impetuous in life, with an excitable temperament, he exhibited an unflappable calmness in battle. *Major* Rüstow was the younger brother of the well-known military historian W. Rüstow (Zurich). The latter wrote regarding his brother: 'It was immediately obvious that he was entirely at peace with the idea of a soldier's death. It is less well known that he remained true to the death to his gunner maxim, on 1st May 1866, he wrote to me, 'I am happy that in this campaign, I know exactly what I must do. Advance without having to maneuver much and then fire.''

strength at 100 guns, even after some batteries that had run out of ammunition or had suffered heavily, withdrew. It was not possible to further redress the inequality in numbers. 'Now (so says a report) an artillery battle developed that perhaps has never been equalled in history. It was not individual shots that one heard, but a continuous rolling thunder which, combined with the whistle and crash of shells flying and bursting, produced a deafening cacophony.' The gradually clearing day, by providing our [artillery] with a definite target, robbed the enemy of some of the advantages had he had hitherto enjoyed. Isolated infantry assaults that he attempted were repulsed and the approach of the 2nd Army began to make itself felt. The first signs of uncertainty became evident and at least made it possible for us to hold our own in the artillery battle that would rage on for another two hours. More was impossible. Victory would need to come from a different quarter.

The author of the *'Taktischen Rückblicken'* [Tactical Review] that we cited earlier in our description of the action at Trautenau said of this artillery battle, for which he had little admiration, 'The 1st Army waged what was essentially an artillery battle from 8:00 until 2:00, but did the artillery attain its goal? The objective could only be to create a breach in the enemy position (that the infantry could then assault) and thereby prepare for his destruction. But our guns could not even hold their own in the face of the imposing Austrian artillery. It became a matter of saving its own skin as best it could. If it had not been for the appearance of the Prussian infantry in the rear of the Austrian artillery, they would have had no reason to quit their position. Therefore, in this action the [Prussian] artillery had failed in its objective. If it had finally come to a frontal assault, would the artillery preparation have been sufficient?' We must first answer this question in the spirit of the author [of the Tactical Review] with a definite 'No!' There can be no doubt that our six hour cannonade had not shaken the enemy, nor had it prepared the way for an assault. But under the circumstances it appears doubtful to us whether any blame can be attached to this failure. Some things just cannot be forced. Will our artillery be blamed for the fact that, on 2nd February, it bombarded Missunde [in the Schleswig Holstein war] in vain? The question then, is not how much or how little our guns accomplished in the artillery battle against Lipa, rather, the question must be, did it accomplish what it could under the given, highly unfavourable circumstances? And, just as we answered the earlier question with a definite 'No,' we answer this one with an equally emphatic 'Yes.' Basically, there was nothing to be accomplished. 'Preparation for an assault,' in a situation such as that encountered at Lipa, was simply impossible as an artillery objective. At this point our guns had a fundamentally different [task], and that was to draw the enemy's fire upon itself so as to make the infantry's ordeal less fearsome. *And that it did!* Individual shortcomings can do nothing to change this fact.

The artillery battle against Maslowed

On the centre left, at Benatek, our artillery fought an even more unequal struggle. While the divisions fighting farther to the right at Sadowa, Dohalitz and Dohalitzka, the 8th, 4th and 3rd, mutually supported each other, our 7th Division fought virtually alone. The Swiepwald, whose interior would shortly become a bloody arena, lay between it and the great enemy artillery position at Lipa. This time the enemy's guns were positioned at Maslowed.

All that we had in action here were the four batteries of 7th Division. Very soon after the capture of Benatek and just before the start of the great fight in the Swiepwald, these batteries went into position south of and east of Benatek. They comprised the following:

12pdr Battery von Rotz.
6pdr Battery Kühne.
4pdr Battery von Nordeck.
4pdr Battery von Raussendorf.

Apart from minor realignments, these four batteries remained in virtually the same position for the next six hours. As the battle raged between Benatek and Maslowed, the opportunity to manoeuvre was extremely limited, all we could do was stick it out, the enemy's numerical superiority permitted nothing more. How great this superiority was we learn from the enemy reports that have since appeared. As at Lipa – Langenhof, here at Maslowed new batteries constantly joined the [Austrian] firing line, first four, then ten, then fourteen batteries. At about noon (and only for a short time) fifteen. They comprised the following and appeared in roughly this sequence:

The four brigade batteries of 4th Corps.
The six batteries of the 4th Corps Artillery Reserve.
Two batteries (from Brigades Würtemberg and Saffran) from 2nd Corps.
Three batteries from 2nd Corps Artillery Reserve.

A total of 15 batteries numbering 120 guns[12] were positioned in a broad semi-circle around Maslowed and directed their superior fire from this elevated position against our 24 guns.

The battle peaked at about noon, from then on (as the spearhead of the Crown Prince's [2nd] army began to arrive) the enemy had increasingly to protect his exposed right flank with ever diminishing forces. The brigades of 2nd Corps withdrew in echelon, taking up the hook shaped position facing north that was originally assigned to them, and of course, the brigade batteries followed the movements of their infantry. 4th Corps also withdrew. At 2:00 the enemy circle of artillery around Maslowed had disappeared and our four batteries now advanced to the hill from whence had come the fire they so long endured. From their new position they fired upon the enemy withdrawing to the southeast.

The 7th Division's artillery held onto the hotly contested ground just as heroically as did the rest of the division. It seems only right to remember them both.

Now we turn our attention to the infantry action in the centre, for which the artillery battle merely formed the greater framework.

12   Author's Note: The general commanding the entire Austrian artillery was Archduke Wilhelm.

The 3rd Division Takes Dohalitzka and Mokrowous

The 3rd Division (von Werder), bivouacked at Aujezd Sylvara and was at Psanek by daybreak. Orders arrived at 6:00 to advance to the line of the Bistritz. Three hours later (9:00) the division completed its change from column to battle formation south of Zawadilka, 2000 paces in front of Dohalitzka and Mokrowous. The 4th Division was on the left alongside 3rd Division and there was loose contact with the Elbe Army on the right.

Fog and rain made it impossible to make out the enemy's position on the Bistritz and the far side of the river. Only the flashes of the enemy guns made it evident that there was strong artillery facing us. The batteries of both 3rd and 4th Divisions went into position on the hill by Mzan, and opened fire with initial success, the foremost enemy batteries falling back to their main position at Lipa. This movement was interpreted by our side as an opportunity to push forward from Zawadilka against the villages on the far side of the Bistritz, Mokrowous and Dohalitzka.

The 6th Infantry Brigade, *Generalmajor* von Winterfeld, received orders to attack, and immediately advanced, Regiment Nr.54 in the first wave, Regiment Nr.14 in the second.

The Bistritz crossings (it was three to four feet deep here) were all destroyed but the troops waded through the stream without hesitation and after a short fight, *Hauptmann* von Pestel's Fusilier Battalion of the 54th Regiment, took Mokrowous. The 1st and 2nd Battalions, with the assistance of several companies of the 14th [Regiment] took Dohalitzka. There was only skirmishing with [the Austrian] Brigade Wimpffen. Facing us in Dohalitzka was the 2nd Battalion of IR 58 Archduke Stephan, in Mokrowous the 1st and 3rd Battalions of that Regiment, as well as the 2nd Battalion of IR 13 Bamberg.[13] Only the last attempted serious opposition, losing three officers and 70 men as prisoners from Regiments Bamberg and Archduke Stephan. The other losses were minimal. Meantime the pioneer sections restored the damaged crossings, allowing the 12pdr Battery Crüger and 4pdr Battery Gallus to follow the 6th Infantry Brigade. All the other [batteries] for the time being, remained on [the west] side of the Bistritz.

So far as the 3rd Division was concerned, the fighting with the Austrian outposts was over, now it faced the enemy's main position on Lipa Hill. It was at this time that the artillery battle which we described earlier commenced and continued for four hours. The infantry had no task other than to hold firm, to hang on. In Dohalitzka they fortified the church and schoolhouse, fortunate to find some sort of cover against the escalating shellfire. From time to time, along the entire line, a nearly irresistible pressure mounted to storm forward against the constantly firing Lipa Hill. However, the Commander of the Division (*General* von Werder), knew how to resist this pressure with the strictest orders. The fact that the losses here were less than in the centre at Sadowa, is largely attributable to the correctness of these orders and their prompt execution.

Now we shall turn our attention to this part of the battle.

---

13   Author's Note: These statements are based on credible enemy reports. According to the Austrian General Staff work (p. 263) it appears that, in addition to Brigade Wimpffen, two battalions of IR 3 Archduke Karl (Brigade Knebel) also took part in the lightly conducted defense of Mokrowous.

The 8th and 4th Divisions in the Holawald

The approach, the enemy positions

Two divisions, the 8th and 4th, advanced in the centre on Sadowa. The 8th Division, after a bivouac at Gutwasser, was at Milowitz by 4:00 in the morning, from here it received orders to advance. It proceeded via Klenitz and Dub, the advanced guard (Fusilier battalions from the 31st and 71st Infantry Regiments) occupied the Sadowa brickyard, the main body and reserve kept to the left and went into position behind the Roskos Berg [hill]. It was now 7:00.

After bivouacking at Wostromer, the 4th Division had reached Bristan by 5:00 in the morning. Here it was ordered to advance. It proceeded past Stracow to Mzan, which it occupied with its advanced guard (regiment Nr.49). The main body and reserve took up a covered position behind Mzan. It was now 8:00. The dispositions were such that the 8th Division was astride the Chaussée, the 4th, commanded by Generallieutenant Herwarth von Bittenfeld[14] a small distance to its right.

How stood the enemy? Lipa (or the Königgrätz *Chaussée*), was the boundary between 3rd and 10th Corps. *Feldmarschallleutnant* Gablenz commanded the 10th, Archduke Ernst of Austria the 3rd. Each of these two corps commenced the battle with two brigades on the hill, and two other brigades pushed forward to the Bistritz. Brigades Benedek and Kirchsberg of 3rd Corps were on the hill, as were Brigades Mondel[15] and Grivicic (the latter only four weak battalions strong) of 10th Corps. Brigade Benedek was between Chlum and Lipa, Brigade Kirchsberg in and around Lipa itself. Brigades Mondel and Grivicic in and around Langenhof.

That was the position on the hill. The four advanced brigades of the two corps, however, were positioned as follows:

> Brigade Appiano [10th Corps] in and around the Swiepwald.
> Brigade Prohaska [3rd Corps] in Sadowa, in the Holawald and Skalawald.
> Brigade Knebel [10th Corps] in the Sadowa sugar factory, in Unter and Ober Dohalitz.
> Brigade Wimpffen [10th Corps] in Dohalitzka and Mokrowous.

We have already described in a previous chapter the fighting that the last brigade had in both villages (what we have described as the centre right). In the actual centre, occupying a forward position were Brigade Knebel of 10th Corps and Brigade Prohaska[16] of 3rd Corps.

---

14   Tr. Note: to avoid confusion, note that there are two different Generals Herwarth von Bittenfeld, here *Generallieutenant* Herwarth von Bittenfeld, commanding the 4th Infantry Division of the II Army Corps of the Prussian 2nd Army. Earlier we met *General der Infanterie* Herwarth von Bittenfeld, Commanding General of the Elbe Army.

15   Tr. Note: The correct spelling is Mondel, however in the original text Fontane consistently misspells it Mondl.

16   Author's Note: Brigade Prohaska, to the left of Brigade Knebel, held Sadowa itself with the 34th Jäger Battalion and the 1st and 2nd *Roman - Banat* Battalions, the Holawald with the 3rd *Roman - Banat* Battalion, the Skalkawald with the 33rd Jäger Battalion and the terrain between the Holawald and the Skalkawald with the 4th Battalion* Gondrecourt and the 4th Battalion Corizutti. We give the detailed position of Brigade Knebel in another place.

The attack of our divisions that were advancing here, was now directed primarily against these.

The 8th Division takes the Holawald

At 8:00 the King appeared on the Dub Hill. The position of our divisions advancing in the centre was as follows:

> The advanced guard of the 8th Division at the Sadowa brickyard.
> The advanced guard of the 4th Division in front of Mzan.
> The main body and reserve of the 8th Division behind the Roskos Hill.
> The main body and reserve of the 4th Division behind Mzan.

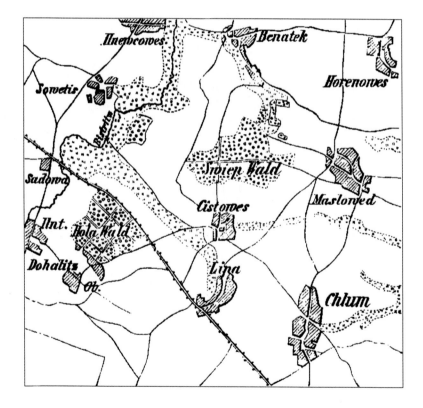

* Tr. Note: In peacetime all of the 80 infantry regiments of the Austrian army had three field battalions each. In the event of mobilization, each regiment activated a replacement battalion, the 4th Battalion. These 4th Battalions consisted of relatively untrained men and were therefore regularly used as fortress battalions or the like. Eight fourth battalions were assigned to the Northern Army, Infantry Regiments 7, 17, 22, 59 and 76. The fourth battalions of IR 55 Graf Gondrecourt and IR 56 Baron Corizutti were assigned to Brigade Procházka of 3rd Corps. (Heidrich, 'Der Kampf um den 'Svibwald' am 3. Juli 1866', p. 170).

Our batteries were already firing from the Roskos Hill and from Mzan.

The question was whether to force the Bistritz crossing at Sadowa, or to force the enemy to give up this important position (important because it controlled the *Chaussée*) by outflanking it to the right and left. The latter option was chosen. The advanced guard of the 8th Division was to keep up the skirmishing action that had already developed in front of Sadowa, while the main body of the 8th Division and the advanced guard of the 4th Division, were ordered to attack the Holawald (which lay behind Sadowa) from left and right. For the time being the main body of the 4th Division remained in reserve by Mzan. This double envelopment was conducted rapidly and with great precision. The 8th Division, outflanking the enemy in Sadowa on the left, was the first into the woods. Therefore, we shall initially follow it, but first a word about the Holawald.

Dohalitza Church.

The Holawald is a small wood about 1200 paces square. The Königgrätz *Chaussée* bounds its northeastern edge, Unter and Ober Dohalitz lie at either corner of the southern edge, Unter Dohalitz right on the Bistritz, Ober Dohalitz toward Lipa. Narrow tracks cut through the wood which rises slowly [in one direction] toward the [Lipa] Hill and [in the other direction] descends gently to the Bistritz.

Between [the river] and the woods is an open area 500 paces wide that later served for stationing reserves. At just this location (on its northwestern face) the enemy had prepared the woods for defense. Trees were felled and the chopped off crowns were employed to make a sort of interwoven abatis. The woods could offer only limited protection against artillery fire, the trees were too young, the trunks too thin. So much for the Holawald. Immediately after the fighting it was commonly called the Sadowa woods, however as the Swiepwald farther to [our] left was also given the same name, we have chosen to use the proper and original names of these two woods in our discussion, so as to avoid confusion.

'Attack the Holawald from the north,' read the orders for the 8th Division. The main body of the division, the two musketeer battalions of the 31st Regiment in the first wave, the two musketeer battalions of the 71st Regiment in the second wave, moved out immediately, wheeled round the Roskos Hill, constantly holding to the left, came under shell fire, reached Sowetitz, passed the Bistritz to the front and side of the Skalkawald that was held by the [Austrian] 33rd Jäger Battalion, and in a rapid advance, passed the retreating Battalions Corizutti and Gondrecourt, crossed the Königgrätz *Chaussée* and entered the northern face of the woods.

The fighting that initially developed at this location was insignificant. The main body of Brigade Prohaska (in Sadowa itself), realizing full well what our objective was, and at the same time knowing it would be cut off and captured if our enveloping columns reached the Holawald before it was out of the village, had evacuated Sadowa after token resistance and only held the woods themselves with a few troops, probably from the 34th Jäger Battalion and the Regiment *Roman - Banat*. These now fell back with light skirmishing to Lipa, those farther to the west, in the abatis and in the woods, were taken prisoner.

This initial success was attained with few casualties. Sadowa, the Bistritz crossing, the *Chaussée* and the Holawald were ours. The edge [of the woods] facing the enemy was held by individual *Schützenzüge* [skirmishing platoons[17]] pushed forward to the southern point of the woods and the village of Ober Dohalitz, which was already held by the advanced guard of the 4th Division, Regiment Nr.49.

The advanced guard of the 4th Division takes Unter and Ober Dohalitz

At the same time that the main body of the 8th Division received orders to bypass Sadowa on the left and attack the Holawald from the north, the advanced guard of the 4th Division, Regiment Nr.49, was ordered to take and hold the villages of Unter and Ober Dohalitz. The regiment had remained by Mzan since 8:00. *Oberst* von Wietersheim rode before his men, 'Soldiers,' he cried, 'In Berlin I promised His Majesty the King that we would knock the stuffing out of the enemy. Today we stand before the enemy, 49'ers, and we will knock the stuffing out of them, unfurl the colours, Regiment forward!' All three battalions moved out. The 2nd Battalion, *Major* von Tiedewitz, took the left flank, the Fusilier Battalion, *Major* von Rechenberg, the right flank, the 1st Battalion, *Major* von Salpius, followed on.

17   Tr. Note: In a company formed of two three-ranked platoons, the rear rank of each platoon included the best marksmen, who, when the company column formed for battle, detached from their original platoons to form a third two ranked *Schützenzug* which provided skirmishers, leaving the parent platoons with only two ranks. When skirmishers were deployed, only a portion, usually half or less, of the *Schützenzug* deployed as skirmishers, the balance of the platoon supporting them as *Soutien*, or supports.

The 2nd Battalion, with the 8th Company, *Premierlieutenant* von Mach leading, launched itself at the sugar factory halfway between Sadowa and Unter Dohalitz, crossed the ditch and fence, and with hurrahs, stormed into the factory buildings. The enemy fell back to the woods leaving a number of prisoners in our hands, probably from Brigade Knebel.

The Fusilier Battalion, passing through a field of hops between Mzan and the Bistritz, engaged in a short fire fight, then advanced on the right of the 2nd Battalion against Unter Dohalitz and after insignificant resistance, took the village. *Lieutenants* Gritzner (a shell later tore off his leg) and von Kehler, forced their way into a great barn and there captured two officers and 70 men from the 3rd Jäger Battalion and IR 49 Hess.[18] An eyewitness reports that,

The sugar factory.

18   Author's Note: These statements were most emphatically made by our 49'ers, therefore we have kept them in the text. It must be noted however, that the Austrian General Staff work only mentions two advanced brigades (Prohaska and Knebel) at this location and does not mention a third. However, there must have been such a third brigade here if our side's statements are correct, for the 3rd Jäger Battalion and Regiment Hess belonged to Brigade Kirchsberg, which according to the Austrian official report, was still intact at Lipa at this point and only made its assault from the hill three hours later. According to [the Austrian official report] the situation at that time was as follows: sugar factory: 28th Jäger Battalion and 3rd Battalion IR 1 Kaiser Franz Josef, Unter Dohalitz: 1st Battalion IR 1 Kaiser Franz Josef, between the sugar factory and Unter Dohalitz 2nd battalion IR 1 Kaiser Franz Josef.

'The officers presented their visiting cards and introduced themselves. We were not however, in the mood for the manners of the salon, and we simply sent them back to Mzan.

Thus, was the Bistritz crossed, Unter Dohalitz secured and the western corner of the Holawald nearly ours. All three battalions assembled and then, after a short rest, formed up in three columns, this time however, to advance *en ligne* toward Lipa. The 2nd Battalion was on the left, the Fusilier Battalion in the centre, the 1st Battalion on the right. As they advanced, the 1st Battalion, von Salpius, bore off to the right when it reached the point where the road forked toward Ober Dohalitz and Dohalitzka, and entered the northern outskirts of the latter village at the run, however the 54th was already there. Dohalitzka and Mokrowous had previously been taken by the 3rd Division.

The 2nd and Fusilier Battalions advanced to the southern edge of the Holawald, found some cover and then took Ober Dohalitz in similar fashion to Unter Dohalitz. The enemy fell back, skirmishing, to the hill. Our men sought to establish themselves in Ober Dohalitz, but before they had found any sort of protection at all, the infernal fire from Lipa began.

In the Holawald from 10:00 to 12:00

At 10:00 our position was:

> Four battalions of the 8th Division held the eastern edge of the Holawald, the 71st on the left, the 31st on the right, the first towards the *Chaussée*, the latter towards Ober Dohalitz.
>
> The 2nd and Fusilier Battalions of the 49th Regiment were in Ober Dohalitz and at the southern point of the woods (the 1st Battalion was in Dohalitzka).

Such was the position at the front of the woods. The reserves were immediately behind it and already in considerable strength. Everything that the 8th and 4th Divisions had available was here, concentrated in a narrow area thus:

Of the 8th Division:

Fusilier Battalion of the 71st	1 battalion
Fusilier Battalion of the 31st	1 battalion
2nd Battalion of the 72nd	1 battalion
Fusilier Battalion of the 72nd	1 battalion

Of the 4th Division:

Regiment Nr.61	3 battalions
Regiment Nr.21	3 battalions
Regiment Nr.9	2 battalions

Therefore 7 battalions in front of the woods, 12 battalions (as reserve) to the rear.

This was a significant force, strong enough to launch an assault, perhaps if pushed to the limit, even a victorious one. The order however, was not to go to the limit. 'The Holawald is to be held at all costs,' read all the orders, '[but] not to advance past the woods.' The stated mission was accomplished, but with extreme sacrifice, the losses were enormous. The position was held for three hours under shell fire from well over 100 guns, that all too often, switched from engaging our artillery, to the woods and village themselves. A soldier in the Holawald wrote:

> We sought cover, but where was cover to be found against such fire?! The shells broke though the clay walls like paper, finally setting the village ablaze. We fell back to the left into the woods, but it was no better there. Huge, jagged splinters from the trees flew everywhere. Finally, a kind of resignation settled over us. We took out our watches and counted. I stood beside the colours and in ten seconds four shells and one shrapnel round burst right in front of us. When the shrapnel burst in the air it came down like hail, and a beautiful ring of smoke rose in the air, ever widening until it vanished. I saw all that. Everyone felt as if he was in God's hands. Death was all around us, yet we were filled with calm.

At 11:00 the troops lining the edge of the Holawald, namely the men of the 71st, were so thinned out that the 8th Division committed its last battalions. They moved to the front, relieving battle weary formations where they could, but some, especially on the right wing where *General* von Bose commanded, would not leave, the 31st and 49th held there to the last.

From 12:00 to 2:00. The reserves are brought up

In the meantime, split into platoons and half platoons, it was evident that these heroic but exhausted soldiers were at a point where, in the event of an enemy offensive, their resistance would be broken. Therein lay the danger, and it was to prevent this, that the last reserves were committed.

Oberst von Michaelis was ordered to occupy the eastern edge of the woods with the 61st Regiment and to hold it. The *Oberst* sent the 1st Battalion, *Oberstlieutenant* von Beckedorff, along the second lane that ran parallel with the great road and occupied the entire eastern margin between the *Chaussée* and Ober Dohalitz with all four companies, but the previous scenes were repeated. The companies, seeking escape from the ever increasing fire, and decimated in an assault that was launched contrary to orders, shifted to the right into Ober Dohalitz, but found just as little cover there as in the adjoining woods. It appeared that all who were in the village pushed left into the woods, and all who were in the woods, pushed right into the village, but whether here or there, the danger and the casualties remained the same.

This shifting of the battalions toward Ober Dohalitz (only the 3rd Company remained in its assigned position) left the edge of the woods, except for a few isolated groups, nearly bereft of defense. *Oberst* von Michaelis, aware of the wide gaps, now moved the Fusilier Battalion, *Hauptmann* von Below, forward. The Fusilier Battalion advanced on the *Chaussée*, then moved to the right and into the empty spaces.

These reinforcements arrived in the nick of time. At 1.00 the enemy attempted to regain the ground they had lost in the morning, at Ober Dohalitz and the Holawald. Perhaps also, given that our positions had already been weakened, it might be more than merely a recapturing of positions lost, but a genuine offensive to break through our centre. In any case, the first enemy attempt had a tentative character. Two half battalions advanced, in closed formation [*geschlossen*].[19] Our 61st (and other troops to the left and right) allowed the enemy to approach to point blank range, then the *Soutiens* stepped into the intervals of the firing line and – *Feuer*! The Austrians dispersed and hastened back to their position south of Lipa.

Quick to take advantage of this success, our *Schützenzüge* now advanced, and making use of a cutting farther in front of the woods, attempted to shoot the horses and crews of the nearest enemy battery at a range of at least 800 paces. It appeared that this achieved some success, for suddenly a squadron of Mensdorff Uhlans that was covering this battery charged our *Schützenzüge* at the gallop.

Lieutenant L. shouted, 'Hold fast' and the Uhlans, virtually unharmed by our first volley, now surged over the skirmishers who were lying on the ground. In the next moment however, a hail of bullets from the woods scattered those [Uhlans] that were not already hit and scattered them in a wide arc as far as the *Chaussée*.

Mensdorf Uhlans.

A small troop returned the way they had come, the squadron leader at its head. Obviously, a brilliant horseman, he charged the officer commanding the *Schützenzug* and attacked him with his saber. Thus began a duel between the two battle lines, and in the midst of the gunfire. *Lieutenant* L. attempted to gain his opponent's left side in order to avoid the swiftly falling blows from his saber … but the bullet of a 61'er put an end to it.

19   Tr. Note: See earlier footnote on Austrian attack columns.

Advance of Brigade Kirschberg, 2:00

More and more troops were sucked into the frontline, the 2nd Battalion of the 61st Regiment and the 1st Battalion of the 21st.[20] *Generallieutenant* von Schmidt, constantly alert to the possibility of a breakthrough in the centre, believed that he had to counter this threat with all the forces at his disposal. Only two battalions of the 21st and two battalions of the 9th Regiment remained in reserve. Our position at the front of the woods at this hour was roughly as follows:

> On the left, toward the *Chaussée*, the 71st, 21st and 61st.
> On the right, toward Ober Dohalitz, the 49th and 31st.
> In Ober Dohalitz itself (thoroughly intermingled) the 49th, 61st and 31st.
> In Mokrowous, arrived from the right, the 1st Battalion of the 49th, *Major* von Salpius.

Thus, split apart, intermingled and decimated (Regiment Nr.61 had already lost 300 men) these units still represented a respectable force of at least eight battalions, a force that might well be damaged by enemy shell fire, perhaps might even be destroyed, but was still too strong to be overrun by an infantry assault on its own.

Unfortunately for the enemy he did make such an attempt, a more serious attempt, after his earlier attacks, as we have seen, had failed. Brigade Kirchsberg, comprising IR 44 Archduke Albrecht (Hungarian) and IR 49 Baron Hess (Lower Austrian), moved out of their covered position on the crest of the ridge and advanced down the hill, following the line of a shallow depression that extended towards Ober Dohalitz, IR 44 in the first wave. It was a magnificent sight, flags flying, regimental commanders in front. Our men, as if they had agreed in advance, allowed the battalion columns to approach to 350 paces and then opened up with a murderous fire. The columns continued to advance, halted and fired a proper volley but the battle was too unequal, they gave up the attempt, unbroken and in perfect order, they returned to their position on the hill, pursued by our fire. This effort was the last.

Among the fallen was *Oberst* von Binder, commander of the [Austrian] 49th Regiment, with a bullet through the heart. Half an hour later, only 300 paces farther on, the commander of *our* 49th Regiment, *Oberst* von Wietersheim, also fell, his thigh smashed by a shell. He had made

---

20   Author's Note: At about this same time or perhaps even earlier, from the Army Reserve (the 5th and 6th Divisions) the 2nd Battalion of the 12th, the 1st and Fusilier Battalions of the 18th, and finally, the 2nd and 3rd Battalions of the Brandenburg Fusilier Regiment Nr.35, were committed in the Holawald. With bands playing the two last named battalions, which had shone in the assault on Düppel [in the 1864 Schleswig - Holstein War] advanced, with a *Hoch* and hurrah for King Wilhelm. Prince Friedrich Karl called to them, '35'ers, today it is a matter of Habsburg or Brandenburg!' Thus, it was that they advanced into the woods in which so many of their comrades had already bled. A *Johanniter Ritter* [member of the Order of Saint John, or Hospitallers, devoted to providing medical attention to the wounded] who accompanied the advance described the moment as follows: 'I cannot remember a moment in my military career that ever brought me such satisfaction. The lane did not provide room for the column that was advancing on a broad front. As if they were going to a dance, the ranks separated, only to close up again a moment later. The incoming shells and falling branches were all ignored. The battalions wound their way through the thick woods at the run, separating and then reforming as if it was over a threshing floor. My heart beat harder. 'They are making it', I thought. But it was more than humanly possible. What was Düppel compared with the Lipa Hill! Holding fast was all that was possible.'

good his promise to the king, 'We will knock the stuffing out of the enemy', he succumbed to his wounds on 5th July, honouring his vow in death.

The 7th Division in the Swiepwald

The 7th Division advanced on the centre left [the extreme left wing of Prince Friedrich Karl's army]. It moved out of Horsitz at midnight and by 3:00 [am] was by Cerekwitz, which, as we already know, had been taken on the evening of the 1st July by *Oberst* von Zychlinski's two battalions of the advance - guard. *Generalmajor* von Gordon was in command of the entire advance - guard, four battalions strong.

Day broke, but in the falling rain it was still a gray dawning. The hours slipped by. The Divisional Commander, *Generallieutenant* von Fransecky, who would this day write his name in the annals of history, impatiently awaited the cannon fire from the southwest that was the signal to launch his own attack against Benatek, about 1½ miles south[east] of Cerekwitz. Finally, at 7:00 the thunder of the guns at Sadowa could be clearly heard, if muffled by the thick mist, it was time.

All four battalions of the advanced guard now formed up, the Fusilier Battalions of the 27th and 67th, under *Oberst* von Zychlinski, took the lead together with one squadron of the 10th Hussars. The two musketeer battalions of the 27th followed immediately behind. *Oberst* von Zychlinski, with Fusilier Battalion 27 to the right of the [Cerekwitz – Benatek] road, Fusilier Battalion 67 to the left, led those two battalions through high standing fields of grain toward Benatek. The enemy fired several ineffective volleys and evacuated the village, falling back to the south. Benatek was occupied. An immediate further advance proved impossible, for apparently, at the very moment that we wanted to debouche from the village, strong enemy forces appeared on the left flank, at Maslowed. *Generallieutenant* von Fransecky therefore issued orders to await the arrival of the main body of the division, Regiments Nr.26 and 66, before continuing the offensive.

The resulting pause in the fighting provided a good opportunity to carry out a visual reconnaissance of the battlefield from a vantage point directly in front of the village, and to a certain degree (granted, only very a very incomplete one) to examine the enemy positions.

The Swiepwald

A rifle shot's distance to the south is a wood that has subsequently become famous as the result of the 7th Division's battle. This wood, the Swiepwald, was barely indicated on the maps, at least there was no suggestion of its depth and extent. Now we know it and therefore we shall attempt a description.[21]

The Swiepwald is a forested hill rising to 917 feet at its highest point. It falls off steeply to the northeast, more gradually to the west and southwest. It takes the form of an irregular rhombus approximately 2000 paces long [east – west] and approximately 1200 paces wide [north – south].

---

21 Tr. Note: *Oberst* Ernst Heidrich's monograph (The Battle in the Swiepwald 3rd July 1866 – Sadowa Press 1905), provides the definitive description of the terrain and the battle, principally from an Austrian perspective.

Between the two opposite points, two substantial tracks run from east to west and from north to south, meeting at roughly highest point of the woods. The ground is full of knolls, saddles and gullies and the nature of the wood itself varies just as much as the terrain. Fir trees and oaks alternate, however one can say in general, that the western half has more tall timber, the eastern half more young oak plantations. On the day of the battle (which was significant for the infantry fighting) there were hundreds of cordwood [cut timber] stacks in the southeastern quarter of the woods [much of which had been cleared].[22]

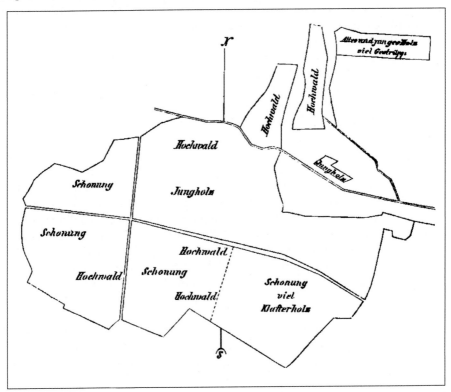

Sketch map of the Swiepwald.

22   Author's Note: We subsequently found the following description, in which the italicized lines are notable. 'This wood (so it says) the one usually known as the Swiepwald, was separated from Benatek by a meadow approximately 500 paces wide in which stood some tall, isolated trees. *Behind this meadow the wood, which has sharply defined edges, rises steeply uphill, forms a ridge, then a brushy ravine, climbs again and ends with its greatest breadth at the edge of the hill,* about five hundred paces from the village of Cistowes, which lies lower down in a hollow. The wood is composed in part of tall timber with and without undergrowth, in part young oak plantations in which at that time, cordwood was piled. Around Cistowes, with the exception of a few fruit orchards, is open farmland, but it then rises again, heavily wooded in parts, southward to the hills of Lips and Chlum.'

The enemy positions, which were certainly not visible from our side at that time, were as follows. Chlum was occupied, but by troops of the 3rd Corps (Brigade Appiano). Instead of being on the Chlum – Nedelist line, in other words, instead of holding the southernmost of the three [ridges] that we discussed earlier, the Austrian 4th Corps, *Feldmarschalllieutenant Graf* Festetics, had advanced to the central ridge (at Maslowed), indeed in part to the northern ridge too (Horenowes), and having wheeled half left, stood on the line Cistowes – Maslowed – Horenowes.

This advance, combined with a change of front in which the Austrian 2nd Corps was also partially involved, contributed greatly to that much discussed gap through which the army of the Crown Prince would later strike at the flank and rear of the Austrian position. While the army of the Crown Prince was provided with a great opportunity by 4th and 2nd Corps' left wheel and subsequent semi-circular envelopment of the Swiepwald, our 7th Division, which was advancing to fight *in* the Swiepwald, was presented with a nearly impossible task. Fortunately, it never knew it was facing odds of three to one.

This battle, the bloodiest and most confused of the war, we shall now attempt to describe. It will be a difficult task so in order to assist the reader's understanding, we beg forgiveness for our boldness in offering a comparison. For a moment let us forget about the woods and initially think of an abundantly subdivided oval structure with three courtyards and three gates. The three gates open to the south, the centre one being the main gate. The three courtyards behind it are connected by vaulted passages. High and low balconies, colonnades, jutting pillars, outdoor stairs, barred windows and cellar openings break the façade and enliven the picture. Rising above the courtyard to the right (viewed from the south) is a *Donjon*, a rectangular, massive tower whose battlements can only be reached by steep stairs that are difficult to access. This image may serve to lay the groundwork for an otherwise impossible discussion.

This oval structure with its three courtyards was hotly fought over. Three strong enemy columns advanced from the south against the three gates. The attacks to the left and right failed, the third and strongest column however, advanced through the great central gate. After bloody fighting that took advantage of the spaces between pillars and columns, and was conducted on stairs and balconies, [this third column] forced us out of the central courtyard and at the same time, thrust through the vaulted passages to the left and right into the two flanking courtyards. Thus, taken in the rear, we evacuated these, hanging on however, in the western courtyard behind an elevated row of columns, and in the eastern courtyard, by holding the commanding *Donjon*. Relief came just as even these were about to be seized from us by [the enemy] committing his last forces. The enemy withdrew. The three courtyards were recaptured.[23]

If we are able, with the help of this comparison, to present a picture of the battle in its broadest outline, it is clear that the battle in the Swiepwald was threefold in form, that it was fought on both wings and in the centre, that the two wings held until the breakthrough in the centre, and

---

23   Author's Note: This description is based on the belief that Brigade Poeckh, which advanced in the centre, provided the decisive factor that led to our defeat in the centre and also determined the fates of the two wings. The official Austrian description of this action, which has since appeared, provides a somewhat different picture. Once Brigade Poeckh, after its initial success, was finally repulsed with immense losses, what kept us defeated was the attack of an enemy double column that advanced on the flank, which entered the eastern courtyard through a side entrance. That is the modification required for our above picture, which otherwise remains the same. The further development is obvious.

that after that breakthrough, the entire wood was lost except for a few isolated pockets and the 'forest bastion' in the northeast. The few who held onto this high point would have the pleasure of being in the first rank in the final reconquest of the woods.[24]

Therefore, in accordance with this, we shall describe the battle in the following stages:

> The 14th Brigade (*Generalmajor* von Gordon) on the right wing.
> The 13th Brigade (*Generalmajor* von Schwarzhoff) in the centre.
> Battalions von Wiedner and Gilsa on the left wing.
> The defense of the Forest Bastion (the *'Donjon'*) on the northern edge.
> The reconquest of the woods.

This is the sequence that we shall follow in our account.

The 14th Brigade (*Generalmajor* von Gordon) on the Right Wing

Benatek was ours. Shots were exchanged from the southern edge of the village with enemy Jäger hiding in the Swiepwald. They were the 27th Jäger Battalion of Brigade Brandenstein (4th Corps). Behind and alongside them were IR 26 Grand Duke (*Grossfürst*) Michael and IR 14 Archduke (*Erzherzog*) Wilhelm, of the same brigade.

At 8:00 the advanced guard was ordered to take the woods. *Generalmajor* von Gordon, with the two Musketeer Battalions of the 27th Infantry Regiment took the right, *Oberst* von Zychlinski, with Fusilier Battalions 27 and 67 took the left. The outskirts of the woods were captured without significant loss and all four battalions pushed on, driving the enemy, particularly the 2nd Battalion Grand Duke Michael before them. The resistance was not uniform however, weaker toward the right, stronger toward the left (of centre). The 1st Battalion of the 27th Regiment, which formed the extreme right wing, passed the western point of the woods without casualties, suffering its first losses on the far side of the woods as it turned toward the village of Cistowes, located about 500 paces south of the [southern margin]. *Oberstlieutenant* von Sommerfeld, Commander of the 1st Battalion, fell in this advance. Two fortified farmsteads west of the village were occupied.

---

24 Author's Note: The Order of Battle of the 7th Division for 3rd July was:
    Advance - Guard. *Generalmajor* von Gordon.
        Infantry Regiment Nr.27 (*Oberst* von Zychlinski).
        Fusilier Battalion Nr.67 (*Oberstlieutenant* von Buttlar).
        Hussar - Regiment Nr.10 (*Oberst* von Besser).
    Main Body. *Generalmajor* von Schwarzhoff.
        Infantry Regiment Nr.26 (*Oberst* von Medem).
        Infantry Regiment Nr.66 (*Oberst* von Blanckensee).
    Reserve. *Oberst* von Bothmer.
        1st and 2nd Battalions [Infantry Regiment] Nr.67.
    During the battle the last named two reserve battalions were committed in the western half of the woods where the advance guard was fighting, so that the 14th Brigade was thus complete and to the degree possible in this action, represented a formation. On the other hand, two battalions, von Wiedner and von Gilsa, split off from the Main Body (13th Brigade), which is described as a formation in the Order of Battle, and formed a left wing. This will be examined more closely in the pages that follow.

Oberst von Zychlinski also went for this village, however his advance took him through the centre of the woods where he was embroiled in serious fighting from the very beginning, suffering infantry fire to his front, but more so, shell fire from Maslowed. Fusilier Battalion 67 was no longer in sight on his left. Instead, the 2nd Battalion 27th, which was marching on the left alongside the 1st, was placed at his disposal. Thus, it was not the two Fusilier battalions of the brigade, but the Fusilier and 2nd Battalions of his own regiment (Nr.27) that *Oberst* von Zychlinski led through the western half of the woods as far as its southern margin.

He reached that, and while the 1st Battalion had already established itself in the western farmsteads, he still had the northeastern corner of Cistowes before him, against which he now directed his attack. But the attack failed, Cistowes was strongly held. Advance units of Brigade Appiano (3rd Corps) had taken up position behind the houses and hedges, especially in the blockhouse like barns, and as the weakness of our columns could no longer remain hidden from the enemy, the 4th Jäger Battalion and one battalion of IR 62 Archduke Heinrich, advanced from Cistowes and chased our troops back into the woods.

Austrian storm columns attack the Swiepwald.

This assault was conducted with great boldness and skill, hitting our battalions on the edge of the woods in the flank and rear. The most advanced elements were cut off and captured, and our losses would have been much greater (Brigade Fleischhacker, advancing simultaneously on the left wing had just hit our 27th) except that at nearly the same time [9.30], two battalions of our 67th Regiment under *Oberst* von Bothmer now appeared in their rear and enveloped the enemy that was enveloping us.

An impending danger was thus averted by the appearance of these two battalions which constituted our only reserve, but not for long. The two battalions of the 27th were smashed, all of the *Hauptleute* were dead or wounded or missing. *Oberst* von Zychlinski, shot in the thigh and in great pain but still holding himself erect, led the remnants of his battalion toward the fortified western farmsteads of Cistowes where he found *Generalmajor* von Gordon and the 1st Battalion of Regiment Nr.27. The situation at this hotly contested location (between Cistowes and the edge of the woods) had only changed in as much as the two battalions of the 27th, had now been replaced by two battalions of the 67th, and in place of *Oberst* von Zychlinski, *Oberst* von Bothmer now assumed command.

He held on, as they had held on, however the enemy forces were constantly augmented and increasingly began to outnumber our own. A new brigade, Brigade Poeckh, initially attacked in the centre, and in the same way that the unexpectedly impetuous attack of Brigade Fleischhacker led to an envelopment of our 27th, so the equally impetuous advance of this new brigade (Poeckh) led to the envelopment of our 67th.

But this time too, help was not wanting. The 8th Division which at this very hour was marching past the Skalkawald toward Sadowa and the Holawald, was now approached for support. *Generallieutenant* von Horn acceded to this request and at the 67th's moment of greatest need, the Magdeburg Jäger Battalion and the 1st Battalion of the 72nd Regiment advanced from the northwest, and the enemy that was now in *our* rear (the 8th Feldjäger Battalion and IR 51 Archduke Karl Ferdinand of Brigade Poeckh), was now itself enveloped from the rear in the same way that the [Prussian] 67th had, through its appearance, enveloped the leading battalions of Brigade Fleischhacker (the 13th Jäger Battalion and IR 61 Grand Duke [*Grossfürst*] Thronfolger).

It was now 11:00 and this latest fighting had resulted in heavy casualties. Three companies of the 67th (the 1st, 6th and 7th) had lost 9 officers and 169 men in an extremely short time, including 6 officers and 57 men killed. The attempt to prevent the enemy from penetrating the wood had failed as his success in the centre, which was where he had directed his main assault, had enabled him to spread sideways [threatening] the rear of both [Prussian] flanks. It became quieter and quieter in the woods, even on the right, the enemy hesitated to deliver the final, decisive blow. Our men were too exhausted and too depleted to renew the battle from the scattered parts of the woods that they still held. Some of our isolated units had been forced off to the left, others had been beaten all the way back to the Skalkawald and the Holawald. The only cohesive formations were the 1st Battalion of the 27th, which held the western corner of Cistowes, and in the wood itself, on the extreme right, the help that had just arrived from 8th Division, the Magdeburg Jägers and the 1st Battalion of the 72nd. [The situation was grave] but General von Fransecky was determined to hold the forest with all the strength that he possessed.

So much for the broad outline of the battle on the left. The detailed descriptions that follow will complete the picture, and nobody has been able to provide a more lively or graphic account of the epic horror of these events than *Oberst* von Zychlinski himself, who stood for three hours (from 8:00 to 11:00) at the centre of this battle.[25]

We shall first listen to him:

<hr>

25 Tr. Note: *Oberst* Zychlinski tells his full story in '*Antheil des 2. Magdeburg. Infant. - Regim. No. 27 an dem Gefecht beim Münchengrätz am 28. Juni 1866 und an der Schlacht von Königgrätz am 3. Juli 1866.*' Another outstanding account of the 27th Regiment's part is told by Arnold Helmuth, who was a company commander in the 27th, in his '*Geschichte der letzvergangenen vier Jahre des 2. Magdeburgischen*

I stopped,' he says, 'waiting at the southern edge of Benatek. My musketeer battalion then came up alongside me on the right. I now ordered [my men] to move out and my Fusiliers took the margin of the woods that faced us without losses.

So far everything went well. We had hardly entered the woods however, when a frightful hail of bursting shells poured down on us, and the rifle bullets of the Jäger hidden in the woods, pelted us like driving rain. Everyone instinctively felt that the only way out was forward. Naturally, all command ceased, I had to seek to regain it at all costs. Then I found a footpath that led me to the western margin. I rode from east to west and back again, back and forth. The hail of shells continued with horrible intensity and before long, enveloped us from the left flank and rear. Again and again, riding here and there, I found myself in the middle of a chaotic mass whose centre was formed by my own battalion, surrounded by swarms of enemy skirmishers. Shells and cannister tore into us every moment from all directions. Rifle bullets flew around us, at the same time keeping us together since they came in equal measure from the front, both flanks and the rear, but we had to stay strong. *Ach!* My officers and men fell all around me, mowed down, dead and wounded. *Fähnrich* Hellmuth, our young hopeful, fixed me with an unforgettable look filled with pain as he took his farewell from me. *Lieutenant* von Zedwitz fell, seriously wounded in the shoulder. *Hauptmann* von Westernhagen was carried past me in the tangle of the woods. *Hauptmann* Joffroy had his severely injured hand bandaged and then immediately returned to lead his company.

My confused mass rolled onward toward the two isolated farmsteads of the village of Cistowes (at its west end). The 1st Battalion of the 27th had passed through the woods more rapidly and had already established itself there, however the enemy's ever stronger enveloping attacks, forced me to abandon the woods with the remnants of my battalion. We regrouped, and with drums beating, advanced against the main part of Cistowes, but in vain, we had to retreat.

We had already held on for two full hours when I again thought to encourage my men to attack Cistowes. I rode to the edge of the woods when a shell fragment fell right before my horse's feet, I had someone pick it up for me and stuck it in my pouch. Right after that another flew past my mare's nose so closely that it bruised her. She turned but I pulled her back again, then a rifle bullet passed through both her jawbones. She stood still as if she had taken root, I could not move her from the spot and had to dismount. A great stream of blood poured from the left side of her head. I remained by her for a good five minutes but could not bring myself to leave her.

Right after that I was shot through the thigh. It must have been at about this time that a shell fragment smashed my mare's lower back. Supported by *Oberstlieutenant* von Zedtwitz I went to the nearest of the two farmsteads by Cistowes. There I found my Brigade Commander (*Generalmajor* von Gordon) whose horse had been shot out from under him . . . we remained there to the last.

Infanterie Regiments Nr.27', 298 pages, entirely devoted to the 27th Regiment's actions in the 1866 War.

So much for *Oberst* von Zychlinski. As he said, he safely made his way to Cistowes without further incident at the same time that the 67th, under *Oberst* von Bothmer, arrived at the edge of the woods to relieve the 27th. An *Unteroffizier* of the 67th (*Freiherr* von Gablenz) describes his experiences as follows:

> ... We halted for an hour at Benatek, the village was already ablaze, then came orders to advance. We moved out and our hearts began to beat faster, for a short distance from us were some woods (the Swiepwald), in which our Fusilier battalion and the entire 27th Regiment, whom we were advancing to support, were already grappling with the enemy.
>
> We marched to the immediate vicinity of the woods in section columns. Then we formed up in platoons and the companies separated. Since we had to maintain frontal alignment with our other companies, as soon as we entered the woods our Battalion Commander, *Oberstlieutenant* von Hochstetter, ordered us to advance the left shoulder and reform platoons, after we had [earlier] broken up into half platoons. I must say at this point that the calmness with which this order was given, in the midst of the enemy fire, did not fail to have an effect on the men, who felt more secure, invincible, as they again closed up more firmly. Nevertheless, it was impossible to advance in the woods in close formation.
>
> ... It is difficult to describe the battle after we broke up again and fought in open order. It was nearly impossible for the officers to keep their platoons, or even smaller units, together. Every man fought pretty much on his own, but the hail of shells that fell on us, the branches and tree splinters that flew around us from all sides, forced us instinctively forward, in the simple hope that by further advances, we would get out of this critical situation. The ground before us rose steeply and I fell to the ground in the rush, crushed by the weight of my pack. As I got to my feet again my own unit was already far ahead of me and I had to join onto another. Thus, I came to the southern margin of the woods. I stepped out into the open to get a better look at the field of grain that lay before and beside us, from which enemy Jäger periodically emerged. Here I had the opportunity to see what an advantage our needle gun gave us. Seven Austrian Jäger emerged in leisurely fashion from the woods to my left, I sent a bullet among them to hurry them up. Five took off as fast as they could. Two others failed to heed my warning and turned toward me. Before they even had time to fire, my rifle was reloaded and one of my attackers wounded.
>
> Busy with these Jäger, I did not notice that the unit that I had joined onto had remained behind, meantime I saw a fresh Austrian battalion advancing in front of me, while the Jäger, whose retreat had been cut off, slipped out of the cornfields to the side. My situation was desperate, and it seemed to me that I had no choice other than to be shot or captured. In this situation I quickly resolved to follow the example of the woodsman who was followed by a bear. That is, I played dead, throwing myself face down in a ditch. As the Austrians advanced from both sides and came rather near me, I lay motionless, my limbs spread out, but I expected to feel the prick of a bayonet from someone who wanted to make sure whether I was really dead or not. I do not know how long I remained in this position, since the seconds seemed to stretch into eternity. I had to lie there until the battalion, which could not advance, retreated in defeat.

During the fighting we combatants lost all track of time. Our senior officers (there could be no thought of commanding) could only influence the men in their immediate vicinity by personal example, and this was not in vain. I cannot recall a single example where even one unwounded man surrendered. Nevertheless, no matter how we conducted ourselves, the possibility of complete annihilation drew ever nearer. Each time we believed that we had beaten the enemy, he advanced with fresh troops, and under fire from all sides, we had to fall back. At such moments our officers would say, 'Only another half hour!' and there was not one among us who failed to respond to this call with the resolve, 'Now if You, God, will grant me to live, then I will hold out for this half hour.

We shall now leave these detailed descriptions that portray the character of this fighting so graphically, so that we can return to the simultaneous advance in the centre of the Swiepwald.

The 13th Brigade (*Generalmajor* von Schwarzhoff) in the Centre

Generalmajor von Schwarzhoff's 13th Brigade entered the Swiepwald with *Generalmajor* von Gordon's 14th Brigade alongside and to the left. The Divisional Commander, *Generallieutenant* von Fransecky, was also present.

Marching at the head of the brigade was the Fusilier Battalion, *Oberstlieutenant* von Schmeling, and the 1st Battalion, *Major* Schweiger, of the 66th Regiment.[26] For the time being the rest of the brigade was held in reserve north of Benatek.

It must have been 8:30 as both battalions crossed into the woods. Directly in front of them, individual companies of the 27th and 67th Regiments were under extremely heavy fire. The appearance of the 66th disengaged them, and for the moment tipped the balance. The already shaken battalions of [the Austrian] Brigade Brandenstein, which up to this point had carried on the struggle alone (Brigade Appiano fought farther off to our right), quickly fell back as the 66th advanced in the centre as did the 27th Musketeers on the right, the entire Swiepwald was now in our possession. However, as we now know, this quick success would soon be contested, especially in the centre where the Austrians began their attempt to recapture [the woods] with increasing determination.

First was Brigade Fleischhacker. At 9:00 IR 31 Grand Duke Thronfolger, advanced in closed columns and forced our weakened formations back before the weight of its attack. *Generallieutenant* von Fransecky now ordered the four fresh battalions of the main body that were held in reserve behind Benatek, to enter the fray. Two (we shall meet them again later) bore off at 45 degrees to the left, the other two, the 1st and Fusilier Battalions of the 26th Regiment,[27] advanced against the centre and attacked the hitherto victorious battalions of Grand Duke Thronfolger. These, after an extremely courageous resistance, fell back.

---

26   Tr. Note: The 66th Regiment is well covered in Boeters, '*Geschichte des 3. Magdeburgischen Infanterie - Regiments Nr.66*', a remarkably clear and accurate account of the 66th Rgt. in the confused fighting in the *Swiepwald*, and Richard Gaertner, '*Die ersten 15 Jahre des Magdeburgische Infanterie Regiments Nr.66*'.

27   Tr. Note: For the actions of the 26th Regiment, see Fritsch, '*Der Antheil des 1. Magdeburgischen Infanterie - Regiments Nr.26 an der Kampagne von 1866 gegen Oesterreich*' and Stückrad, '*Geschichte des 1.*

For the second time our forces advanced to the southern edge of the woods, (finding good defensive positions amongst the stacks of cordwood), as the advance of the *third* Austrian Brigade (Brigade Poeckh, 4th Corps) again seriously jeopardized our success. This brigade advanced with great bravery, the 8th Jäger Battalion, with two Battalions from IR 21 Reischach and IR 32 D'Este to its left, [Ed: these battalions are from Brigade Wöber formerly, Kreyssern. The brigade was bivouacked in and around Nedelist on the 2nd July, the two battalions mentioned here were detailed for outpost duty and were seemingly left behind when the rest of the brigade moved south to take part in the fighting around Problus] and all of IR 51 Archduke Karl Ferdinand [Brigade Pöckh], attacked our exhausted, and by now disorganized battalions in front, flank, and soon in the rear.

Everything was chaos and confusion, bloody hand to hand fighting with rifle butts and bayonets, all the while under a hail of shell fire that was equally destructive to friend and foe alike. *Generallieutenant* von Fransecky, *Generalmajor* von Schwarzhoff, *Oberst* von Medem and *Major* Paucke lost their horses, *Major* von Schönholz was shot in the neck. *Premierlieutenant* Ewald, commanding the 11th Company and *Premierlieutenant* Wernecke of the *Landwehr* Battalion *Neu- Haldensleben* were fatally hit. *Lieutenants* von Platen and von Schierstädt fell, severely wounded. Three Westernhagens (two *Hauptleute* and one *Premierlieutenant*) were wounded. *Lieutenant* von Schulz suddenly found himself surrounded by several Hungarian infantrymen, heard a wild cry of *Eljen*[28] and collapsed, unconscious, run through with a bayonet. Like bees, in ever thicker swarms, the [Austrian] Jäger coursed through the woods. Our two battalions of the 26th Regiment that were fighting there had already lost 17 officers. Step by step they evacuated the woods and fell back to a covering position at Benatek.

This description of the battle in the centre is based on the Prussian version of events that formed soon after the war. The Austrian report however, as presented earlier, differs greatly. Perhaps the most remarkable thing is that *both sides* (something that hitherto may never have happened) willingly conceded defeat, both accounts closing with, 'After immense losses we fell back to a covering position.'

We shall first turn to, and then examine, the report of Brigade Poeckh:

> The assault began without preparation. By order of the Brigadier, *Oberst* Poeckh, only a few skirmishers were sent out in advance, thereupon the first wave of the Brigade charged downhill with irresistible impetuosity, over the bodies of our enemy and into the woods, 2nd Battalion Reischach and 1st Battalion D'Este on the left, all three Battalions Archduke Karl Ferdinand on the right, with the 8th Jäger Battalion in the centre. The enemy fled in great disorder. Then for a single moment hesitation overcame the heroic example of *Oberst* Poeckh, who was constantly at the head of his Brigade. The assault was rapidly renewed, but the men were exhausted, the constant up and down through woods and brush was more than their lungs could bear. They had to halt. Suddenly on a wooded hill to the right, a mass of Prussians appeared above us and commenced a murderous fire, here the brigade suffered its greatest losses, the

---

Magdeburgischen Infanterie - Regiments Nr.26, zweiter Theil, Die Letzten fünfundzwandsig Jahre 1863-1888., which is by far the best and clearest account of the part played by the 26th Inf. Rgt. In the *Swiepwald.*

28   Tr. Note: The Hungarian 'Hurrah.'

Brigadier and all but one of the staff officers fell . . . Cut off on all sides, there was nothing for it but to break out.[29] Sometimes fighting hand to hand with the enemy, only a small number succeeded in making their retreat. The remnants of the 8th Jäger Battalion escaped toward the left flank of the position with only four officers. The losses of 8th Jägers, like those of Regiment Archduke Karl Ferdinand and the two Battalions Reischach and D'Este, were immense. The first wave of Brigade Poeckh was nearly wiped out.[30]

The question remains, how to resolve the contradiction that *each* side [both Prussian and Austrian] considered itself to have been defeated! The answer is simply that [the formation] that finally defeated us, after we had, for our part, defeated the *first* wave of this brigade was, in fact, *an entirely different formation*, whose nearly simultaneous advance and success was entirely unknown to Brigade Poeckh. While the latter was going down to defeat in the front, two strong columns of [the Austrian] 2nd Corps (Brigades Würtemberg and Saffran) advanced from the flank through the eastern part of the woods, were victorious, and advancing rapidly, pushed into the centre and threw us out to the north (to Benatek). [The Austrian] 2nd Corps, which stood with two brigades at right angles to 4th Corps at the eastern margin of the woods and had our left wing as its first attack objective, thus delivered the decisive blow. We shall next describe its position and actions.

Battalions von Wiedner and von Gilsa on the Left Wing

The [Prussian] 2nd Battalion, *Major* von Gilsa, of the 26th, and the 2nd Battalion, *Major* von Wiedner, of the 66th Regiment had (as noted above) kept to the left as the four battalions of the 13th Brigade that were the last to be brought forward, reached the edge of the woods. This wheel to the left was the reason that, while all of the other parts of the 7th Division stood with front facing south, the two battalions named above went into action with front facing east. Here, to the extent that the confined area made such separation possible, they fought a separate action. Until 11:00 they continued this action without significant loss, the enemy battalions were mostly advancing in a diagonal line from southeast to northwest and merely brushed our left wing.

The [Austrian] 2nd Corps that had been facing it since about 9:00 with Brigades Würtemberg and Saffran (almost as if it did not want to diminish the honour of the 4th Corps by throwing the enemy out of the *Swiepwald* entirely on its own), satisfied itself for the time being by conducting a spirited fire fight across a broad stretch of meadow that extended between the eastern edge of

29 Author's Note: The 1st Battalion of Regiment Archduke Karl Ferdinand lost its direction in the process, and instead of keeping to the south, came out of the woods on its northwest side. Here *Rittmeister* von Humbert, who was with the 1st Squadron of the [Prussian] 10th Hussar in a hollow southwest of Benatek, immediately fell upon the surprised battalion, and without meeting any resistance, captured it, taking prisoner nearly 700 men (including 16 officers). This attack counts as one of the most outstanding actions of our cavalry in the 1866 campaign, due in part to its bravery, and in part to '*seizing the moment*.' It is easy, after the fact, to talk of mere 'luck'. One who grasps the opportunity properly, always has luck.
30 Author's Note: The 2nd wave of Brigade Poeckh, IR 37 Archduke Joseph, did not get into action at this time. Not until about 1:00, when the entire 4th Corps moved into the Chlum - Nedelist position did that regiment get into a belated and unnecessarily combat as it passed the *Swiepwald*.

the woods and Maslowed. This fire fight demonstrated the complete superiority of the needle gun, and perhaps even more, the superiority of our tactics. Battalions von Wiedner and Gilsa suffered few losses, while the opposing IR 57 Mecklenburg (all other formations were held in reserve, for the time being) suffered extremely heavy losses, and to no real purpose.

This is how things stood on the left wing until about 11:00, when suddenly the action began to take a different form. *Feldmarschialllieutenant* Mollinary, soon after taking command [of 4th Corps] from the severely wounded *Graf* Festetics [Festetics had a foot taken off by a shell fragment], convinced himself that assaults by individual brigades could accomplish nothing. He now resolved that instead of making uncoordinated attacks from the southeast, he would deliver a concentric attack from three sides. 2nd Corps, best positioned to deliver the attack from the east, was asked to cooperate and promised to do so, while from the south and east, the already defeated Brigades Brandenstein and Fleischhacker on the one side, and the fresh Brigade Poeckh on the other, moved out toward the Swiepwald.

We have already previously detailed the events surrounding the advance of these last named three brigades, especially the attack of Brigade Poeckh. Probably decisive to its success (a probability raised to a certainty in the Austrian account) however, was the attack that came half an hour later by 2nd Corps from the east. This attack, at least in its first stages, fell almost exclusively on the two Battalions Wiedner and Gilsa, especially the latter.

Before we follow this attack, we shall describe the positions of the enemy. In conformity with the movements of [the Austrian] 4th Corps, 2nd Corps, instead of holding the hooked Chlum Nedelist line, had also carried out a great wheel to the left and from 9:00 in the morning, stood as briefly noted above, with two brigades at Maslowed forming a right angle with 4th Corps. Brigade Würtemberg with IR 57 Mecklenburg thrown out to the right, held Maslowed. Brigade Saffran remained in reserve. These positions were held until 11:00, when with Brigade Poeckh having already entered the woods from the south, brigades Würtemberg and Saffran formed up for the attack. The 11th and 20th Jägers took the lead, directly behind in a long line were IR 64 Sachsen-Weimar (on the left), IR 47 Hartung (in the centre), and IR 80 Holstein (on the right). IR 57 Mecklenburg, which had up to that point conducted the fire fight on its own, was held back.

Now followed one of the bitterest actions of the day. The enemy battalions, preceded by skirmishers, advanced with great bravery. *Major* von Gilsa was wounded twice, first a minor wound to his arm which he ignored but the second, a bullet from an Austrian Jager, was more severe and he sank from his horse. Unwilling to relinquish command at such a critical moment, he rose to his feet and supported by his loyal bugler, Pieroh, moved back and forth in front of the battalion, praising the men and encouraging them to stand fast. Finally, as he felt his strength ebb away (he was mortally wounded) he turned over command to *Hauptmann* Fritsch: 'Now I shall die happy having seen how bravely my battalion has fought.'

Hauptmann Fritsch gathered what was left of the battalion and led them back to the edge of the woods for a fresh attack, but how the ranks were thinned! Of the officers, only himself and *Premierlieutenant* von Bismarck were still with the colours, half of the men were dead, wounded or missing and yet an attempt must be made, made at all costs. Forward! Forward! and again it was back into the woods. Colour Sergeant Täger sank to the ground, hit by two bullets at the outset, *Sergeant* Seibt grabbed the colours and sprang to the front. Not a shot was fired, and with a cry of *Gewehr zur Attack* [To the attack, rifle . . . right!], the assembled remnants of Battalion

Gilsa, and to their left, the 2nd Battalion of the 66th (*Major* von Wiedner), threw themselves at the advancing columns of Regiment Holstein, who now halted and fired a volley.

The ground was as flat as a threshing floor. Not a shot was fired. Our men fell to left and right, with drums beating the charge continued against an enemy who seemed to want to cross bayonets with us, but at the last moment he lost his nerve, and when we were within 40 paces he turned and fled. Now, instinctively and without waiting for the order, our ever dwindling band, which up to this point had not fired a single shot, halted and opened up with rapid fire [Schnellfeuer] on the retreating battalions. When *Hauptmann* Fritsch stopped the firing, the enemy columns were devastated. The dead and wounded lay in long rows, those who were still standing threw down their rifles and raised their hands in surrender.[31]

However, this success on the left wing was only temporary. Our two battalions (that had long since ceased to be battalions) were too weak to hold on for long against two brigades. Regiments Hartung and Sachsen - Weimar, despite the check experienced by Regiment Holstein, continued to advance. Regiment Mecklenburg formed up and attacked anew. In the face of superior forces, enveloped or exposed on both flanks, the remnants of our left wing had to fall back, some to Benatek. The enemy pushed on to the centre of the woods where they linked up with those parts of Brigade Poeckh that had advanced from the south and were already, in part, retreating. It was now 11:30.

'We die here!'

Most of the *Swiepwald* was now lost to us, of the surrounding area we still held Benatek, the Skalkawald and the northwest corner of Cistowes. As for the wood itself, aside from its western point, which the 72nd and Magdeburg Jägers still held, only the 'forest bastion' at the northeast edge remained in our hands. It was here that *Generallieutenant* von Fransecky assembled the scattered remnants of his division. At his side, spared as if by a miracle, were the remaining Brigade and Regimental Commanders, *Generalmajor* von Schwarzhoff, *Oberst* von Medem and *Oberst* von Blanckensee. The enemy, particularly his six Jäger Battalions, continued to stalk through the woods, when suddenly the hail of shells let up, soon the rifle fire too, but the ensuing hush offered little reassurance. Every man felt that it was the calm before the storm and that the enemy was preparing to seize the last parts [of the woods] still in our hands, especially the northeast bastion or '*Donjon*', as we christened it earlier. Any remaining doubt was put to

---

31 Author's Note: According to a description that *Hauptmann* Fritsch gave of this action, it was Regiment Mecklenburg Nr.57 that made this attack on the enemy right wing. He also names *Hauptmann* Matuschka, who was captured here. Nevertheless, we must accept the version published in the *Streffleurs Zeitschrift*, which appears to come from official sources, '*das II. Armee - Corps im Feldzuge von 1866*', that it was Regiment Holstein that advanced here in the assault. According to an accompanying sketch, the attack was as follows:

The 11th and 20th Jägers led the attack. The 64th, 47th and 80th are the Regiments Sachsen - Weimar, Hartung and Holstein (Italian). Regiment Mecklenburg (Polish), which had already taken a beating since 9:00, remained to the right rear behind Regiment Holstein and was only committed later. The report of 2nd Army Corps states, 'The troops (Jägers, Hartung and Sachsen - Weimar) entered the woods while Infantry Regiment Holstein Nr.80, despite its valour, could not attain success due to the open terrain over which it had to advance.'

rest when *Generallieutenant* von Fransecky, from his elevated position, observed the preparations for the enemy's final assault. The last brigade (Archduke Joseph) of 4th Corps advanced in front; from the east came all the available battalions of Brigade Thom, the 2nd Jäger Battalion, IR 40 Rossbach and IR 69 Jellacic, beside them were Brigades Würtemberg and Saffran, this was to be the decisive attack. It was obvious that our forces could not withstand such a renewed assault and yet this was what had to be done, the 'Bastion' would be held to the last man.

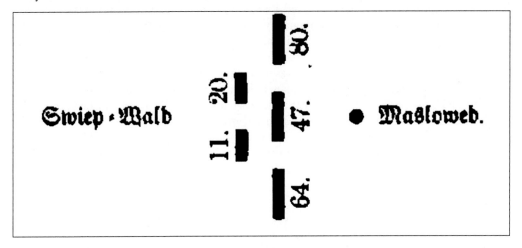

Proposed attack of Brigades Würtemberg and Saffran.

Generallieutenant von Fransecky put it simply, 'We die here!³²' We were ready to make the sacrifice, but God had other plans, *it was not required of us,* at the moment of greatest need, as always, help arrived. The attack did not take place. An eyewitness report:

> Initially we could not explain the reason, we had nearly given up all hope of assistance. Soon however, our spirits soared at the sight that now met our eyes, a division of Guards, advancing in perfect order like a [moving] wall. *The Crown Prince had arrived.*

32 Author's Note: That morning, at the very beginning of the action, the Divisional Commander had recognized the importance of this 'northern bastion' and ordered that it be held by two battalions. 'This corner is the pillar upon which the left wing rests and which cannot be lost.' And in the event, it was not lost. The Austrian General Staff Work ignores this fact and places the [Austrian] 2nd Jäger Battalion and Regiment Mecklenburg at this point at noon. That is an error. Perhaps [the error] is the result of the fact that parts of Brigades Würtemberg and Thom fought an extremely bitter action with our forces in the low oak brushwood which covered the northern slope of the open place that lay before the 'northern forest bastion', as well as in the bastion itself. In the course of this fighting the *eastern portion of this brushwood* changed hands repeatedly between attackers and defenders, the former then believing *that in gaining this territory they had also captured the only remaining portion of the woods.* However, to the side and rear of this brushwood, tall *Stammholz* [tall trees with trunks] which covered the eastern rim of the gully and extended to the Maslowed road, *was the actual position.* From there the defenders repulsed the attackers with rapid fire and also with aggressive counter attacks each time they attempted to approach. This is evident even today in the many graves which mark the boundary of the side of the 'bastion' that was attacked and cover the adjoining fields.

From time to time the helmets and bayonets glittered. We could not distinguish the individuals nor make out their features, but that calm, steady advance, at once gave us full confidence of victory, the victory that we had striven so hard for with the blood of so many comrades. Proud that success was now within reach, we could leave it to these advancing troops to claim the laurels.

Before we join them [2nd Army] in their advance, another word regarding the Swiepwald, for it was here more than anywhere else, that the outcome of the entire battle was decided. It consumed nearly two enemy corps, the two that were supposed to resist the thrust of 2nd Army as it approached from the north. When [this thrust] did take place, only a few remnants stood in the position that was to be held on the Chlum Nedelist line. The battle for the Swiepwald was a mistake for the Austrians, unless they could have won it and then broken through our centre with a flank attack against the Holawald. That much is now conceded, their own report states:

> In actual fact, the possession of the woods was not absolutely necessary ... So long as the northern front was adequately supplied with artillery from Lipa and Chlum, and the woods between well held by infantry to cover them [the guns], and finally if a number of batteries were positioned on the hills by Maslowed, then there need be no concern of an enemy advance from the woods against Lipa, Chlum and Maslowed. *The Swiepwald properly belonged to the domain of the Austrian artillery.* This alone would have sufficed. Individual enemy units might well hold out in the woods but would present no danger to the immediate surroundings. It would have been better if after the initial action of Brigade Brandenstein, no further attacks had been launched against the woods.

We will postpone the presentation of further statistics regarding this attack: numbers, hours and strengths. We shall merely recapitulate chronologically the four major attacks:

> Brigades Brandenstein and Appiano attack the east and west halves of the woods, 9:00.
> Brigade Fleischhacker attacks the western half of the woods and Cistowes, 9:30.
> Brigade Poeckh attacks the centre of the woods, 10:30.
> Brigades Saffran and Würtemberg attack the eastern margin of the woods, 11:00.

A fifth attack (as noted earlier) in which Brigade Thom was to have taken part, and which was intended to break our last resistance, did not take place.

The question regarding the strengths of the individual brigades has been much discussed. Initially it was considered that we had to deal with 56 enemy battalions in the Swiepwald. That appears to have been exaggerated. With the help of the Austrian General Staff work we can now exactly determine what we did have to face and what we did not, the situation was as follows:

Brigades Appiano and Brandenstein:	Battalions
4th Jäger Battalion	1
1st and 2nd Battalions Archduke Heinrich	2
1st Battalion Sachsen - Meiningen	1
27th Jäger Battalion	1

2nd and 3rd Battalions Grand Duke Michael 2
1st, 2nd and 3rd Battalions Archduke Wilhelm..3

Brigade Fleischhacker
13th Jäger Battalion 1
1st, 2nd and 3rd Battalions Coronini 3
1st, 2nd and 3rd Battalions Grand Duke Thronfolger.....................................3
1st Jäger Battalion (attached from Brigade Benedek) 1

Brigade Poeckh
8th Jäger Battalion 1
1st, 2nd and 3rd Battalions Archduke Karl Ferdinand....................................3
1st, 2nd and 3rd Battalions Archduke Joseph (fighting a subsequent action)...3

With Brigade von Roth from 8th Corps:
1st Battalion D'Este..1
2nd Battalion Reischach 1

Brigades Saffran and Würtemberg
11th Jäger Battalion 1
1st, 2nd and 3rd Battalions Sachsen - Weimar...3
1st, 2nd and 3rd Battalions Holstein 3
20th Jäger Battalion..1
1st, 2nd and 3rd Battalions Hartung...3
1st, 2nd and 3rd Battalions Mecklenburg...3
30th Jäger Battalion (from Brigade Archduke Joseph).....................................1
2nd Jäger Battalion (from Brigade Thom) 1

This gives (several of the units listed above barely came into action) a total of 43 battalions.

Therefore, we fought 14 against 43, a ratio of 1 to 3, in addition to which was the enemy's great superiority in artillery. Nevertheless, the enemy's losses were again out of all proportion. It is impossible to determine them exactly, since all of the brigades that were in action here were also the first to fight the Crown Prince's army, however they were probably not much less than 10,000.

The first wave of Brigade Poeckh, six battalions strong, was, according to Austrian reports, nearly wiped out. The 30th Jäger Battalion of Brigade Archduke Joseph (which only took part near the very end) alone lost 11 officers and 500 men. Other bodies of troops suffered similar losses. The higher ranking officers too suffered heavily. *Graf* Festetics, commanding 4th Corps had his right foot smashed by a shell right at the beginning of the action. *Generalmajor* von Brandenstein, *Brigadier Oberst* Poeckh, *Generalstabschef Oberst* Görz and many regimental commanders were dead or wounded. Well may an Austrian report say, 'Whoever witnessed the fearsome effects of the quick loading rifle and saw our troops heroically sacrifice themselves in repeated assaults, cannot fail to be amazed by them, and to agree that the Imperial Army was still capable of courageous deeds this day.'

The second half of the day bears further witness to that. Now we shall turn to it.

The Approach March of the Second Army

Oberstlieutenant Graf Finckenstein arrived in Königinhof at 4:00 in the morning, with him was a written order for the Crown Prince, commanding the entire 2nd army to advance.

At 3:00 in the morning the main body of the Crown Prince's Army was still on the left bank of the Elbe, in and behind Königinhof. Only I Corps (East Prussian) and the advanced guard of the 1st Guards Division were already over the Elbe, the former at Prausnitz Auhlejow, the advanced guard of the 1st Guards Division at Daubrawitz.

The 2nd Army Command issued the order to move at 5:00, detailing the advance only as far as the mid-course of the Trotina (in other words halfway between Königinhof and Sadowa), from there on, the formations must make their own decisions. The direction of [2nd Army's] march was from north to south and thus it would encounter the three great ridges that stretched between the Elbe and the Bistritz that we discussed in more detail in our earlier description of the ground.

The marching orders for the individual army corps were essentially:

> I Corps proceeds via Zabres and Gross-Bürglitz.
> Guards Corps proceeds from Königinhof to Jericek.
> VI Corps marches from Gradlitz to Welchow.
> V Corps follows VI Corps.

The position of the individual units was such that the advanced guard of I Corps, the 1st Guards Division, and the 11th and 12th Divisions should be the first to arrive on the battlefield, and so it was. The advanced guard of I Corps however, because it ran into particular difficulties *en route*, appeared nearly two hours later. Their arrival proved to be decisive.

Depending on distance [from 2nd Army Headquarters], the order to move had reached all of the corps and divisional commanders by 7:00 or 8:00. The alarm was sounded immediately and at 8:00 or as the case may be 9:00, 2nd Army moved out of its various bivouacs. The 1st Guards Division, the 11th and 12th Divisions advanced in three great columns between the Elbe and the Trotina, advance – guards first then the main bodies, with the Guards Division on the right, the 11th Division in the centre and the 12th Division on the left. They retained this configuration for the entire day, on the march as well as during the fighting.

In itself, the march was a superb accomplishment. The thunder of the guns, muffled, but always there, provided the impetus. The advanced guard of the 1st Guards Division covered nearly eight miles in two hours. At 11:00, while holding (more or less) to the prescribed line of march, not only did it reach the specified points of Jericek and Welchow, but the leading divisions had gone significantly further.[33]

33   Author's Note: The newly formed advance - guard of the 1st Guards Division, under Generalmajor von Alvensleben (hitherto the Fusilier Brigade von Kessel had the lead) consisted of the following, forming a left flank, and a right flank column:
Left Flank Column, *Oberst* von Pape:
    1st Battalion of 2nd Guards Regiment, *Major* von Petery.
    2nd Battalion of 2nd Guards Regiment, *Major* von Reuss.
    1st Squadron Guards Hussar, *Rittmeister* von Stralendorff.
    3rd and 4th Guards Jäger Companies (von Arnim, von Lettow).
    1st 6pdr Battery, *Hauptmann* Braun.
Right Flank Column, *Oberst* von Werder.
    1st Battalion of the Guards Fusilier Regiment.
    2nd Battalion of the Guards Fusilier Regiment.
    3rd Squadron Guards Hussar, *Rittmeister* von Rundstedt.
    5th 4pdr Guards Battery, *Hauptmann* von Eltester.

The advance guard of the 1st Guards Division was in Zizelowes.
The advance guard of the 11th Division was directly north of Racitz.
The advance guard of the 12th Division was to its left, (though separated from it by the Trotina[34]) at the Horicka Hill.

The main bodies of the divisions followed close behind.

Our position at 11:00 was on the line Zelkowitz – Racitz – Horicka Hill, we had reached the northern border of the battlefield and the first enemy artillery shells began to arrive. In front of us lay a depression with the village of Horenowes in the hollow and a ridge on the far side. This ridge was the first ridge across the approach, the famed 'Hill with the two Lindens' [*Zwei Linden Höhe*], the Horenowes Hill.

The Artillery Battle Against the Horenowes Hill

Capture of Horenowes, Racitz, Trotina

At 11:00 as we said, the three advance – guards of the leading units, 1st Guards, 11th and 12th Divisions, were facing the Horenowes ridge, and beyond the junction of the Trotina and Trotinka, the Horicka Hill. The points held by our advance guard were, from right to left: Zelkowitz, Wrchownitz, Frantower Mill and Habrina:

The 1st and 2nd Battalions of the Guards Fusilier Regiment in Zelkowitz.
The 1st Battalion of the 2nd Guards Regiment and the 4th Guards Jäger Company in Wrchownitz and the Frantower Mill.
The 1st and 2nd Battalions of the 50th Regiment at Racitz.
The three battalions of Regiment Nr.23, with two battalions of the 22nd further back in Habrina, at the (northeastern) foot of the Horicka Hill.

When they had arrived in these positions, the advanced guard halted to await the arrival of their respective divisions, in particular the artillery. The ridge that they were facing did not show any sign of a strong infantry presence, but there was every reason to anticipate such a presence on the far side. In any case, whatever the situation might be with regard to the enemy infantry, [the advances guards] were too weak to capture such a strong artillery position as the Horenowes Hill appeared to be.

---

34 Author's Note: The course of the Trotina made a significant separation between the 11th and 12th Divisions, even though they marched only an extremely short distance from each other. Thus, it was that the first half of the fighting was more of a joint operation involving the 1st Guards and 11th Divisions rather than the 11th and 12th Divisions. Only after the 12th Division crossed the Trotina at its confluence with the Elbe at about 12:00 or 1:00 (on a level with Sendrasitz) did this change, and the two Silesian divisions then attacked jointly. In addition, it is necessary to clearly distinguish between the *Trotina* and the *Trotinka* [see map]. The two streams join by Racitz, the *Trotinka* coming from the east, the *Trotina* from the north, the name of the conjoined streams now being the Trotina. Just before the Trotina enters the Elbe is the village of Trotina, with the Trotina Mill just a bit to its north.

In the hollow at its foot, there was no water course, but in all other respects the leading elements of 2nd Army at 11.00, stood in a position very similar to that which 1st Army had faced at Lipa since 8:00. Just as the [enemy] artillery position at Lipa faced west, so the [enemy] artillery position at Horenowes faced north.

The ground where our forces stood provided a good overview. As the heads of our columns became visible, the enemy batteries, at least for the most part, were firing toward the west, on Benatek and the Swiepwald. It was only gradually, as they became aware of the impending threat from our direction, that they shifted their guns to the right and their fire towards the north. Three artillery positions were evident: a strong one in the centre and two weaker ones on either wing. The main gun line was on the ridge between Horenowes and Racitz, partly in front of, and partly to the right and left of the historic 'Zwei Linden Höhe'. Five batteries fired from here, one from Brigade Thom and four from 2nd Corps Artillery Reserve. On the enemy left wing, west of Horenowes, two batteries (one each from Brigades Würtemberg and Saffran) were already in action. On the enemy right wing, near the village of Trotina, were the eight guns [one battery] of Brigade Henriquez. Thus, we were facing a total of 64 guns.

Our reserve artillery was still well to the rear; fortunately however, the Divisional Artillery had already moved forward during the march so that at 11:45:

Two Guard's Batteries, Braun and Eltester were on the right wing.
Four batteries of the 11th Division, under *Major* Bröcker were in the centre.

About 45 minutes later two batteries of the 12th Division, under *Major* Forst, were able to open fire against the entire enemy gun line. As the main battle developed in the centre, *Major* Bröcker provided a brief description:

Our four rifled batteries (in the centre) were combined to make a single large battery, whose front line (800 paces long) extended from Wrchownitz and the Frantower Mill, and whose left wing was still about 1000 paces from Racitz. In this position we were able to outflank the enemy's right wing. The range was 2500 paces. Two Guard batteries fired on the right alongside us. The first rounds fired by our side came from the 4pdr Battery von Garezynski. Soon the artillery duel was fully ablaze on both sides, our 24 guns faced 40, which fired with extraordinary accuracy, which was not surprising, since firing from a defensive position, one generally is firing at known ranges. This was obviously the case here, for round after round was right on target, and his 8pdr shells would have caused us many losses if we had not had the foresight to place our guns at 30 pace intervals (since there was no shortage of room), and if all his shells had burst. The fact is that his fuses failed to function in three quarters of his shells. Ours worked better. Individual guns pulled out, two ammunition wagons blew up.'

So much for the report. The fire constantly intensified and in the space of one and a half hours, our four batteries had fired some 600 rounds and received rather more in return without achieving a result. Then finally, at 1:15, the enemy suddenly broke off the action and his entire line began to retreat. The seven batteries that had faced our centre and right wing proceeded in haste, back over the second ridge to the third, the Chlum – Nedelist ridge, meanwhile the

[Austrian] batteries on the [Prussian] left, having initially advanced to the level of the Trotina mill, fell back to Lochenitz. We pushed forward along the entire line.

Zwei Linden Hohe.

There were two basic reasons for the sudden breaking off the action by our enemy. First, at about 1:00, our artillery position in the centre and on the right had been significantly strengthened by the arrival of the Reserve Artillery under *Oberst* von Miesitschyeck, as well as several divisional batteries, so that we could now reply to the fire of 64 guns with 90 of our own. Secondly, our infantry had advanced under the cover of this superior fire and had, in part, captured the villages of Horenowes, Racitz and Trotina which lay immediately in front of the enemy artillery position. The enemy was now in part exposed to being outflanked. We shall next describe the actions that led to the capture of these three villages.

The capture of Horenowes

Wrchownitz, as mentioned earlier, was held by the 1st Battalion, 2nd Guards Regiment,[35] *Major* von Petery. *General* von Alvensleben, observing the increase in our artillery fire since about

35   Author's Note: The 2nd Battalion, *Major* von Reuss, 2nd Guards Regiment, which arrived in Zizelowes at the same time as the 1st, had received orders from *General* von Hiller to immediately advance to Benatek to support the 7th Division that was so hard pressed in the Swiepwald. *Oberst* von Pape, Commander of the 2nd Guards Regiment, accompanied that battalion on its march. At 12:15 it arrived in Benatek. The village was ablaze and showed signs of heavy fighting with piles of dead and wounded in the ruins. *Oberst* von Pape initially rode forward toward the Swiepwald in order to apprise himself of the situation. 'There (so writes the *Oberst*), I was met by a terrible picture. The brave regiments of the Magdeburg division must have had a fearsome fight and still the incessant thump of the shells, the crashing of splintered of trees and the constant rattle of small arms fire, made it hard to conceive how it had been possible for them to hold their position for such a long time against the colossal superiority

12:30, and at the same time, the advance of the main body of the 1st Guards Division, now ordered the capture of Horenowes, which was about 1000 paces to our front. *Major* von Petery, who had already been waiting impatiently in Wrchownitz, attacked immediately, dispersing his leading companies into skirmish order with instructions to reform again close to the village. He did this to give his battalion the best possible protection from the enemy shrapnel.

Horenowes itself was held by two battalions of IR 40 Rossbach, the pheasantry south of the village was held by the 2nd Jäger Battalion, which had already fought in the Swiepwald. The perimeter of the village had been barricaded, as had the streets and houses, and it seemed as if there would be a stubborn defense. This however, hardly materialized. The 4th Guards Jäger Company, *Hauptmann* von Lettow, which was in the first line of the attack, together with the 1st, 2nd and 4th Companies of Battalion Petery alongside them, broke into the village in their initial rush. The enemy fired smartly from the houses and cellars but soon surrendered when hard pressed, 300 prisoners were taken.

The companies fought on through the village and continued their assault, wheeling half left against the 'Hill of the Two Linden Trees, from which the last enemy batteries pulled out, seeing that the village was in our hands and that they had lost their infantry cover. The pheasantry was captured at nearly the same time. Attacked by the 3rd Company of the 2nd Guards Regiment, *Hauptmann* von Herwarth III, the [Austrian] 2nd Jäger Battalion fell back after a brief fight.

The Schützenzug under Lieutenant Chorus pursued the retreating enemy, while the rest of the 3rd Company also proceeded to the 'Hill of the Two Linden Trees.'[36]

The capture of Racitz

At about the same time (probably 15 minutes earlier) that *General* von Alvensleben ordered the 1st Battalion of the 2nd Guards Regiment forward against Horenowes, *General* von Zastrow ordered the 1st Battalion of the 50th Regiment against Racitz, which was held by two battalions of IR 69 Jellacic. Directly behind it, in wooded hills on the right bank of the Trotina, was the 9th Jäger Battalion (Steiermärkers) belonging to Brigade Henriquez. Racitz itself was taken

---

of the enemy. Their stubbornness could only give rise to the highest admiration and amazement. It was natural that the officers and men greeted our arrival in this most serious situation with great joy.' Even as *Oberst* von Pape wanted to lead Battalion von Reuss against the Swiepwald, the battalion was ordered back to the division and given 'The trees on the top of the Horenowes Hill' *as point de vue*, as were so many other formations that day.

36   Author's Note: *Lieutenant* Chorus, in relentless pursuit of the enemy, became completely separated from his battalion and only rejoined it two hours later at the Lipa woods. In this time, he was fortunate enough to proceed through the centre of the enemy main body and to accomplish a brilliant *coup de main*. Halfway between Chlum and Nedelist he came upon an enemy battery with 12 guns. At 600 paces he opened fire, however when this proved insufficient, he advanced to 300 paces, and even though under heavy cannister fire, fired so effectively at [the battery's] covering infantry, that they fled. Thereupon he concentrated his platoon's fire on the battery, so disturbing its crews that *Lieutenant* Chorus felt the moment had come to capture the battery. With loud hurrahs he and his platoon charged forward, receiving another salvo of cannister when 20 paces from the muzzle of the guns. However, since the battery was too far above them, the cannister swept harmlessly above their heads. The next moment he and his platoon were in the battery, whose four right flank guns they captured, while a passing company of the 3rd Guards Regiment took the remaining eight. *Lieutenant* Chorus, congratulated by the Crown Prince for this magnificent feat of arms, received the *Pour le Mérite*.

in the first rush. The attack proceeded with the 1st and 4th Companies advancing in front, while the 3rd covered the left flank and the 2nd followed in reserve. The commander of the 1st Company, *Hauptmann* von Schlutterbach, celebrated the anniversary of his action at Lundby[37] with the capture of Racitz, 250 prisoners and one standard were taken.

Up to this point the 50th had suffered hardly any losses, these now began to mount as it passed through Racitz to the south, and then advanced against the wooded hills on the right bank of the *Trotina*, where, as mentioned above, the 9th Jäger Battalion was positioned. This received our two leading companies, the 1st and 4th, with well aimed fire from the edge of the woods which had been fortified with abatis. After a brief fire fight our men charged, whereupon a Jäger Officer stepped forward and waved a white handkerchief stuck on the point of his sword.

'Our *Hauptmann* (so writes a man of the 50th) immediately ordered us to cease fire, which happened instantly. We now unsuspectingly climbed the hill to take the enemy's rifles but suddenly, when we were at a range of about 150 paces, they opened fire. Fortunately, one of them fired before the others, in effect announcing the treachery that they had in mind. We threw ourselves on the ground in a flash so that the volley passed harmlessly over us. Now however, enraged, we charged and took no prisoners, we put them all to the sword, the enemy officer who had dared commit this dastardly deed had six gunshot wounds.'

So much for the report. The leading unit of the 11th Division (1st Battalion of the 50th Regiment) thus drove not only two Battalions of Regiment Jellacic out of Racitz, they also drove out the enemy Jäger that were holding the woods behind it and forced them back over the plateau, all the way to Sendrasitz. The rout of this Jäger battalion was the work of the 50th alone. The 12th Division now took a larger part as it advanced on the left bank of the Trotina, and at that very moment, waded across the stream to the right bank and took the enemy in both flanks with several half battalions of Regiment Nr.23. We now shift our attention to this advance on the extreme [Prussian] left wing.

The capture of the Horicka Hill, Trotina Mill, and the village of Trotina

Shortly after 11:00, the head of the 12th Division stood, as we know, at the foot of the Horicka Hill. Facing it at a considerable distance (by the village of Trotina), was Brigade Henriquez with IR 27 König der Belgien in the first rank, IR 14 Hessen in the second. Between our position and that of the enemy, on the right bank of the Trotina as far as the southern point of Racitz, was the afore mentioned 9th Jäger Battalion. The next point that we had to secure was the Horicka Hill. It was in our hands by about 12:00 or a little later, and just as at Horenowes and Racitz, our victorious battalions pushed on to take the ridge behind. The 12th Division also advanced further south to maintain its alignment with the advancing divisions on its right.

Generallieutenant von Prondzynski split Regiment Nr.23 into six half battalions and put them in the lead. When at about 12:45, the advancing half battalions were level with our 50th Regiment which was engaged with the [Austrian] 9th Jägers on the far bank of the Trotina,

---

37   Tr. Note: In the Battle of Lundby (3 July 1864, Second Schleswig - Holstein War), a Danish company attempted a bayonet charge across open ground but was stopped by rapid fire from the Prussian needle guns, 20 meters in front of an embankment behind which the Prussians were lying. This battle was the last in the 1864 Schleswig - Holstein War and provided the first real demonstration of the deadly effectiveness of the Prussian needle gun against massed formations.

Generallieutenant von Prondzynski held back half battalion Fehrentheil (6th and 8th Companies) and had the remaining five half battalions wheel to the right and attack the enemy in both flanks. The 23rd waded the stream, at times with the water up to their armpits, and took the Jäger Battalion from right and left, thus bringing about an immediate result. As we have seen, the Jäger retreated to Sendrasitz, with our forces following. At this very moment, probably in order to disengage the Jägers, Brigade Henriquez advanced from the village of Trotina. In the lead was the famous IR 27 König der Belgien, the same regiment that had stormed the Danish position at Oversee with outstanding courage and driven the Danes from their position under its then *Oberst*, Duke Wilhelm of Würtemberg. The brigade's artillery battery advanced to the hill of the Trotina Mill at the same time.

However, this brief offensive movement, though it may have provided a breathing space for the retreating Jäger, did not effectively counter the advance of our 23rd, which was joined in its advance by the Silesian Jäger Battalion Nr.6. The half battalions advanced on both sides of the Trotina, on the right to Sendrasitz, on the left to the Trotina Mill and the village of Trotina itself. Especially decisive was this last movement because it enveloped the Regiment Belgien on its right flank. A platoon from the second company of Jäger Battalion Nr.6, under *Lieutenant* von Oldenshaufen, took possession of the mill. Half battalion Fehrentheil passed Rodow (near which a bursting shell put several men out of action), entered the village of Trotina on the run and there took many prisoners. In its haste, it neglected to thoroughly search the houses in which hundreds of the enemy were hidden, who then found opportunity during the night to slip away over the Elbe or to Josephstadt.

After our capture of Trotina, Brigade Henriquez fell back to Lochenitz on the Elbe. We shall meet it again here at a later hour.

On the Maslowed Hill

Our position at 2:00

By about 2:00 the village of Trotina was in the hands of 12th Division. Thus, our extreme left wing had already progressed halfway across the rear of the still unshaken enemy forces at Lipa and Chlum.

Generallieutenant von Prondzynski, who had pushed his division to the limit in his determination to avoid falling behind, was probably now slightly ahead of the two divisions fighting alongside him. The 11th Division in the centre and the 1st Guards Division on the right were constantly advancing and had moved on from the capture of the first ridge to take the second. The leading formations of all three divisions were again, essentially in line. The main bodies of the divisions were immediately behind [the advance – guards] or had already advanced into the interval between them. The artillery went into position. After the capture of the above villages, our forces were on the ridge between Maslowed[38] and Sendrasitz, with the *third* ridge

---

38   Author's Note: Maslowed was captured after a brief struggle by the 4th Guards Jäger Company under
      Hauptmann von Lettow, possibly with the cooperation of some of the 2nd Guards Regiment (Battalion
      Petery). The 3rd Battalion [of the Austrian] Sachsen-Weimar Regiment was responsible for the village's
      defense. The Austrian General Staff Work, to the extent that it mentions this battalion (Sachsen-
      Weimar), fails to mention this brief action in Maslowed, but speaks of a defense of the village by the

now before them. Our advance to this position, with the exception of the village fighting for Maslowed, met no opposition at all.

While we were still on the Horenowes Hill, we saw retreating enemy columns which, so far as we could make out, were attempting to reach the third ridge between Chlum and Nedelist, without showing any sign of attempting to hold the intervening ground at all [i.e. the second ridge]. Their intention was so obvious that our side resolved to do everything possible to prevent the withdrawal. Since (given the significant lead that the enemy had) this was impossible to accomplish with infantry, *Generalmajor Graf* Bismarck ordered an attack on the withdrawing battalions with his Combined Cavalry Brigade (3rd Uhlans and 2nd Dragoons) that were on the Horenowes Hill.

The attacking force split into two, the 2nd Dragoons together with the 1st and 5th Uhlan squadrons under *Major* von Steinbrück on the left, the 2nd, 3rd and 4th Uhlan squadrons under their commander *Oberstlieutenant* Heinichen on the right. Both attacks had similar outcomes. The squadrons rode down or took prisoner the smaller clusters of infantry they encountered *en route but* had to turn back with losses when they attempted to break up the battalions that had formed square.

The attack on the 3rd Battalion of Regiment Sachsen - Weimar that formed the rearguard was particularly bloody. As we know [the 3rd Battalion] held Maslowed to the end, and then preceded by a battery of artillery, fell back in close order over the second ridge to Nedelist. *Oberlieutenant* Heinichen led his squadrons against this battalion. The approach was brilliant. The deeply sunken roads were crossed at the gallop, the swarms of skirmishers that the battalion had thrown out were ridden down, and despite the first volley that the squadrons received at 40 paces, the square was broken with the first shock. The enemy was already starting to lay down his weapons when the squadrons came under artillery and rifle fire from a range of 12 paces. *Oberstlieutenant* Heinichen, who had ridden against the front of the square with his usual energy and coolness, took four bullets, one of which entered his neck through his left jawbone and killed him on the spot. He sank soundlessly onto the neck of his horse and then to the ground, right before the square. His horse too was hit by four bullets[39], and the Battalion Sachsen - Weimar resumed its withdrawal, unhindered.

This cavalry attack probably took place at around 1:30 or 1:45. While it was taking place (as noted above) leading elements of the 1st Guards and 11th Divisions advanced under heavy shell

---

2nd Battalion IR 68 Steininger. This can be explained by the fact that Maslowed was variously occupied during the long ebb and flow of the battle by friend and foe alike. The 2nd Battalion Steininger, when it entered the village, found it long since evacuated by our Guards Jäger and held it, uncontested, until the 2nd Guards Division that was advancing in this direction toward Lipa, captured it in a second fight.

39   Author's Note: Immediately after the attack was over, his body was taken by men of the 1st Squadron of the regiment to the crypt of the Horenowes cemetery where he was buried the next day. He remained there until January 1868, at which time a friend of the deceased, Amtsrath Dietze, exhumed the body and had it transferred to Barby, where it was interred on the 25th January. The deceased was spared the painful news of the death of a brother and two other close relatives, who were killed as Hannoverian officers in the battle of Langensalza. King Wilhelm honoured the memory of this outstanding officer with the following inscription which was inscribed on a silver sleeve and attached to the standard of the 1st Brandenburg Dragoon Regiment Nr.2. 'During the Battle of Königgrätz, on 3rd July 1866, the Commander of the Regiment, *Oberstlieutenant* Heinichen, fell at the head of the regiment near this standard.'

fire, but otherwise unimpeded, from the first ridge to the second, and a quarter of an hour later stood on the ridge between Maslowed and Sendrasitz. The enemy right wing (4th and 2nd Corps), had in the meantime re-established the (original) hooked position that he had left during the fighting in the Swiepwald. Now he faced two of our divisions advancing between Chlum and Nedelist, particularly the 1st Guards. The ensuing hours were to see fierce fighting, but first it is necessary to describe the enemy position, as least in broad outline.

The enemy position at 2:00

The hooked position that 4th and 2nd Corps now adopted, ran essentially between Chlum and Nedelist and incorporated four earthworks [schanze]. Schanze IV was directly in front of Chlum, Schanze I in front of Nedelist [Schanze IV was at the northern end of Chlum facing north, Schanze I was approximately midway between Nedelist and Sendrasitz, also facing north]. These field fortifications (constructed during the previous night) were left unoccupied and thus were of no significance during the course of the action. We only mention them because they provide excellent markers in relation to the enemy position and make orientation easier.[40] In, by and behind Chlum, was Brigade Appiano of 3rd Corps. To its left (in the Lipa woods) was Brigade Benedek [also 3rd Corps]. In front of Chlum were three batteries in the approximate area of Schanze IV, with a fourth behind the village.

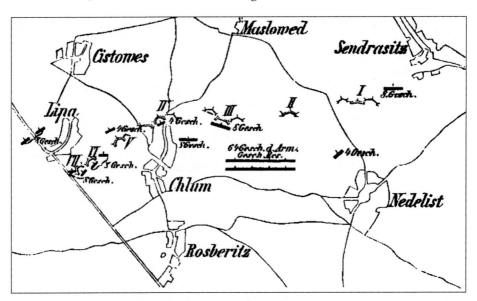

Austrian gun emplacements between Lipa and Nedelist.

40   Author's Note: Three more positions, already described in relation to the great artillery battle against Lipa (Fortifications V, VI and VII) were to the left of Chlum in and around the Lipa woods. However, for the part of the battle described here they had no significance, even as markers. Our map was prepared from an Austrian sketch. It does not fully agree with our statements in the text, these are more accurate. The difference is in the batteries to front and rear of Chlum. There were more batteries there than are shown on our sketch map.

To the right, beside Chlum, on the ground between Schanze IV and Schanze II was 4th Corps, formed up in two lines:

> The intact Brigade Archduke Joseph, together with three Jäger Battalions Nrs. 8, 30, 27 and two batteries, comprised the first line.
> The remnants of Brigades Brandenstein and Poeckh, along with one battery comprised the second line (The 4th Brigade of the Corps, Brigade Fleischhacker, was still in Cistowes, we shall meet it later).
> In the interval between Brigades Poeckh and Brandenstein in the second line, eight batteries of the Army Artillery Reserve under *Oberstlieutenant* von Hofbauer had gone into position.

To the right, alongside 4th Corps and the Army Artillery Reserve, on the ground between Schanze I and II, and soon to the rear of Nedelist, were [2nd Corps] Brigades Thom, Würtemberg and Saffran. Further to the right of these was the 2nd Light Cavalry Division and to the right of that, almost on the Elbe, Brigade Henriquez.

Thus, our advancing divisions came up against 120 guns and six brigades between Chlum and Nedelist. Nevertheless, it appears that the three brigades of 2nd Corps mentioned above (Brigade Henriquez was not involved at this point), did not attempt any serious opposition but concerned themselves with making good their escape to the Elbe. This premature concern for its own safety that characterized the entire conduct of 2nd Corps on the afternoon of the 3rd, has been justly criticized. 4th Corps, though it may have been insubordinate, even mistaken, in wheeling to the left and committing itself too deeply in the battle for the Swiepwald, at least did its best to make amends through stubborn persistence and self-sacrifice.

Of our two divisions that were advancing against the Chlum – Nedelist line, the 11th took Nedelist and pushed on from there. We shall meet it again, and also the 12th. But the bloodiest fighting that developed principally involved the 1st Guards Division, which, driving all before it, took nearly the entire position in the first rush.

We shall now examine the details of the Guard's action.

Grenadier Brigade von Obernitz Captures Chlum

We last saw the advanced guard of Brigade von Alvensleben at 2:00. At this time:

> The 1st and 2nd Battalions of the Guards Fusilier Regiment, and the 2nd Battalion of the 2nd Guards Regiment, were about 1000 paces east of Maslowed.
> The 1st Battalion of the 2nd Guards Regiment was about 1200 paces south of Maslowed, in a shallow depression that extended between Cistowes and Nedelist. This Battalion, Battalion von Petery (the same one that had captured Horenowes), was closest to the enemy in Chlum (approximately within rifle range).

All four battalions were advancing when they were ordered to halt by *Generallieutenant* von Hiller. Upon receipt of this order, for the time being, they went into reserve and the two other brigades of the 1st Guards Division, Grenadier Brigade von Obernitz and Fusilier Brigade von

Kessel, now marched past them toward Chlum, initially taking the line between Shanze IV and Schanze II. When Brigade Obernitz passed Battalion Petery it was 2:15.

At about the same time, the Guard Artillery (eight batteries strong), which had closely followed the infantry, took up a diagonal position between Maslowed and Nedelist, and opened fire. It consisted of the four divisional batteries, Braun, Eltester, Witte and von Schmeling, in the front line, together with the four batteries of the Reserve Artillery, under *Oberstlieutenant* von Miestitscheck, behind them in the second line. The Guard Artillery, 48 guns strong, now engaged the enemy's 120 guns.[41] The fire now increased to an incredible intensity, at the same time the artillery battle between Lipa and the Bistritz also reached its height. It was no longer possible to distinguish individual shots, only a continuous rolling fire that shook the air and ground. Over 500 guns were engaged along the whole front, it is questionable whether comparable numbers fired at any one time at Borodino, Leipzig or Waterloo.

During this deafening barrage, the advanced guard brigades, Brigades von Obernitz and von Kessel, moved against the Chlum – Nedelist line. We shall initially follow the first assault on Chlum.

Chlum, a village with a church, is situated on the hill of the same name (Chlum Hill). It is elongated and runs from north to south, such that the southernmost part with the pretty church (visible from afar) is on the highest point, while the rest of the village falls off increasingly to the north. It is irregularly built and consists of the poor wooden huts typical of the area, only a few houses are substantially constructed, and all are surrounded by gardens. Communication is by two roads, one running the length of the village [north-south], the other crossing it [east-west], and meeting in the centre at right angles. The cross road [east-west] is short, slightly sunken and cuts the village noticeably into a northern and a southern half. The western part [of the cross road] forks on leaving the village, one branch goes to Cistowes, one to Lipa, the eastern part [of the cross road] goes to Nedelist. The longitudinal road runs north to Maslowed and south to Rosberitz. Generally, all of the roads and lanes are more or less sunken.

The most important aspect of the configuration of the ground, is that there is no point in the village, or even in its immediate surroundings, that provide a clear view of the foot of the hill. That can only be achieved when one is right at the top of the slope. We shall see how significant this will be to the events that will soon unfold.

Chlum, as we know, was held by Brigade Appiano. Some parts of the brigade had taken part in the battle for the Swiepwald, but by 11:00 almost everything had been pulled back to the hill. The position at 11.00 as follows:

41   Author's Note: It is improbable that the battle was actually conducted with such unequal forces, certainly not for long. We can assume that only the 64 guns of the [enemy's] Army Artillery Reserve really caused us problems. The guns of 4th Corp, which were mostly to the [enemy's] left, did not play a major role. These batteries, which had already been firing since 8:00 in the morning, had in part expended their ammunition, and in part suffered heavily. Our infantry advanced so rapidly that the batteries on the enemy left wing were either captured or forced to pull out. This created a more or less numerical equality on both sides. The artillery of the 11th Division under *Major* Bröcker that was advancing on the left beside our Guard Artillery, seems to have played no significant part at this stage of the battle. Only after the capture of Rosberitz did it again become spectacularly involved, as the closing act of the great drama began to unfold.

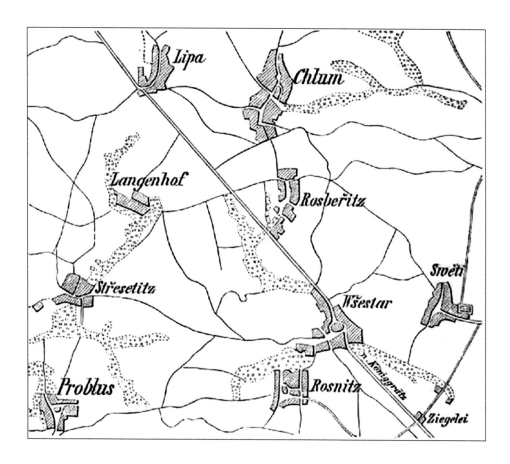

The 2nd and 3rd Battalions IR 46 Sachsen-Meiningen were in Chlum.
The 1st Battalion Sachsen-Meiningen, the 4th Jäger Battalion and the greater part of IR 62 Archduke Heinrich, were behind Chlum on the hill (the smaller part of Regiment Heinrich remained in Cistowes).

These positions however, very much to the enemy's disadvantage, were not held. As our cannon fire from the Horenowes Hill steadily increased after 1:00, and the 2nd Battalion Sachsen - Meiningen began to suffer losses, *Generalmajor* von Appiano, who was present in Chlum, ordered that the troops on the hill withdraw to behind the crest. Accordingly, the battalions concerned moved off [eastwards] and formed up at the foot of the hill. The cover that this new position temporarily provided would come at a high price. The [Austrian] officers had a premonition, saying to themselves that the hill which was now being voluntarily relinquished, would need to be retaken before long, but the [Brigade Commander's] order left no choice.

At about 2:00 the new position was occupied and the 1st Battalion Sachsen - Meiningen, the 4th Jäger Battalion and Regiment Archduke Heinrich, now stood at the *foot* of Chlum Hill, west of Rosberitz, toward the *Chaussée*. Only the troops that were actually holding Chlum remained in their former position. The 2nd Battalion Sachsen - Meiningen, *Oberstlieutenant Baron* Schimmelpening, continued to hold the northern half of the village. The 3rd Battalion, *Major* Jaczkowsi, occupied the eastward half of the cross road, in a dip in the ground that led toward Nedelist. The positions were such that the battalions had neither a clear view of the enemy nor contact with each other.

Defense of the village was entrusted to the Commander of the Sachsen - Meiningen regiment, *Oberst* Slaveczki. It appears that this was not a particularly fortunate choice. He was near sighted and seemed to have no more than the vaguest idea of the existence of a second Prussian Army, or of the possibility of its appearance. To the last, he responded to reports that were brought to him [of enemy sightings] with the same phrase, repeated over and again, 'You are a doom-monger.' He had taken up position with the 3rd Battalion.

At 2:30 (we are basing the following on an Austrian account) fresh reports came, one after the other, that, ' Prussian columns are trying to break through between Chlum and Nedelist.' *Oberst* Slaveczki shook his head, took a look for himself and calmly announced, 'Those are Saxons.'[42] For a moment his assertion)that there was no enemy nearby) was in fact correct. In the broken ground our columns would suddenly vanish only to reappear in the next instant. Now, as if springing from the earth,[43] they threw themselves on the [enemy's] 3rd Battalion, positioned at the eastern arm of the cross road. The assault first hit the [enemy battalion's] right flank (*Oberst* Slaveczki was on the left). The regimental adjutant dashed over to report to him . . . . the *Oberst* cut him off with, 'You are a doom-monger,' those were his last words. Our forces broke through in three or four places, enveloped the leaderless fragments and dispersed, killed or captured the entire battalion within five minutes. Some fugitives from the left flank made their way to the foot of the hill and formed up alongside the 1st Battalion, *Major* Noak.

The Prussian assault continued along its original axis and cut right through the centre of the village, thus forming a human barrier. When it was unable to break through this barrier, the entire 2nd Battalion surrendered at once.

As we know, the 2nd Battalion held the northern half of the village. During the intense fire fight, *Oberstlieutenant Baron* Schimmelpenning had gone to the eastern end of the village [to ascertain what was going on]. Quickly realizing that he was in danger of being cut off with his entire battalion, he dashed back and issued orders to move back across the fateful cross road into the more elevated southern half of the village. The [enemy] companies set out in a hurry, but ours were quicker, the door was shut, the barrier complete. A weak attempt to break through collapsed in the face of the Prussian riflemen, who, already established in houses and hedges, commenced a rapid fire. *Baron* Schimmelpenning fell, and before another five minutes had passed, 100 men of the 2nd Battalion were dead or wounded, 600 captured. In no more time

---

42   Tr. Note: Thus also demonstrating a total misunderstanding of where the Saxon forces were on the battlefield.

43   Author's Note: To someone who knows Chlum, the [Austrian's] total surprise will be less hard to understand than to someone who has never seen it with their own eyes. With justification an Austrian report says: 'It was a cloudy day and visibility was limited. In addition, the grain in the fields stood as tall as a man and the columns entering it vanished immediately from sight. Finally, several depressions extending from Maslowed to Chlum and Nedelist made it possible for the advancing columns to approach unseen, only here and there the flash of a rifle that disappeared just as quickly. Thus, the enemy was only clearly seen when he was felt.'

than it has taken us to describe these events, Chlum was ours and the key to the enemy position was in our hands.

It was the 1st Battalion, *Major* von Kleist, of the 1st Foot Guards Regiment, that had achieved this brilliant success with a flanking assault from the east (assisted by the 1st Guards Jäger Company, who had distracted and confused the enemy from the north). Only when Chlum was ours did the enemy seem to realize the full significance of the loss. The moment that the [Austrian] officers had foreseen had arrived. The hill must now be recaptured from the bottom. The 1st Battalion Sachsen - Meiningen, *Major* Noak, advanced with great bravery and despite serious losses, constantly closing ranks, had already made it halfway up the slope when an Austrian Uhlan regiment (we shall later return to this) charging up from the *Chaussée*, suddenly turned aside to escape our rapid fire, and in so doing collided with the 1st Battalion Sachsen – Meiningen, that was also advancing up the hill. In an instant the entire body of troops was ridden down, shattered, wiped out. *Major* Noak lost his horse. Fighting on, on foot, and endeavouring to make good the disaster, he was severely wounded and captured. The battalion colours were lost beside him after an honourable fight (two colour bearers fell).

Vincenz Cristofek, *Hauptmann* in Regiment Sachsen - Meiningen, whose account of the battle at Chlum provided most of the material we have presented, closed his description with the following statement:

> The Uhlans came and went like a whirlwind, their passage was marked by their and our dead. That was the help that they brought to us. At this hour of the day only the Regiment Sachsen - Meiningen fought in Chlum. The fact that it did not flee the scene *en masse*, as some have dared to claim, is evidenced by its losses, 620 dead and wounded. Although beaten, the regiment can take pride in the fact that, in the campaign of 1866, just as in 1859 in Italy, the regiment fought against the Guards and did so with some degree of honour. The Regiment Sachsen - Meiningen, however, has not received just recognition.

We have happily quoted these words. The heavy losses of the regiment should at least lead the Austrians to a less negative judgement. Indeed, it does appear that individual elements (namely the 1st Battalion, which had six officers killed and nine wounded) fought with admirable bravery. On the whole however, neither the position nor the leadership, not the conduct of the regiment deserves special praise. Our guardsmen destroyed it with no significant effort. It was a *battue* [a game drive]. Hundreds surrendered without making any attempt to resist. Already softened up, having awaited the enemy for seven hours and finally encountering him where he was not expected, it seems that faced with the 'giants of the 1st Guards Regiment' (that too had its effect), panic swept over entire sections of the regiment, namely the 2nd Battalion. Thus, was Chlum taken and held against a first attempt to recapture it. The key to the enemy position was in our hands and remained so. Surprise had temporarily crippled the enemy's strength.

Among those who were totally surprised by the capture of Chlum was Benedek himself. He was on the high plateau between Chlum and Lipa, 300 paces from the village. He had no hint of what was taking place so near on his right flank. According to the Austrian account, General Staff Colonel, *Oberst* Neuber, brought the first report at 2:55: 'Have you seen the enemy in Chlum?' asked the *Feldzeugmeister*. '*Ja*, I was met with rifle shots.'

For a moment the *Feldzeugmeister* seemed indecisive about what to do (so says the report), then he dashed off at the head of his numerous suite to see for himself. A [Prussian] Guards company that had already established itself outside the village of Chlum welcomed the staff with a murderous fire that laid out a host of men and horses. *Major* and *Flügeladjutant Graf* Grünne was killed, *Feldmarschalllieutenant* Henikstein and *Major Fürst* Esterhazy, had their horses shot out from under them. The suite scattered in all directions, most seeking to escape from the deadly fire by dashing downhill to a factory building. However, the enemy was already there too, receiving the staff with new fire. Archduke Wilhelm was wounded. As if this was not enough, at that very moment two of our own [Austrian] batteries shelled the houses in which the enemy was located with such a hail of shrapnel, that the Army Commander and all of his staff, for several minutes, were faced with the alternative of being killed by enemy rifle bullets, or by their own shrapnel. Finally, they were fortunate enough to get out of the cross fire.'

Benedek himself, rode to Lipa. The General Staff officers scattered westward in order to prepare the attack of the two reserve corps. We shall deal with these various attempts to recapture [Chlum] in the subsequent chapters.

Benedek and his staff come under fire from Chlum.

Fusilier Brigade von Kessel Takes Rosberitz

Fusilier Brigade von Kessel (which consisted of only three battalions), immediately followed Grenadier Brigade von Obernitz, pushing forward into the intervals [between the Grenadier battalions] and then also wheeling right as it crossed the line between Schanzes IV and II, sending several volleys after the withdrawing enemy.

However, the right wheel of the Fusilier Battalions did not take place simultaneously, the points from which the wheeling movements commenced varied, as did the points at which they ended. Only the move to the right was shared by all three [battalions]. The Fusilier Battalion of the 1st Guards Regiment, *Oberstlieutenant* von Helldorf, struck the elevated southern point of Chlum at nearly the same time as the 1st Battalion of the 1st Guards Regiment cut through the centre [of Chlum], and captured the 2nd Battalion Sachsen -Meiningen. The appearance of the Fusilier Battalion contributed substantially to this rapid success, especially through the capture of a battery of Horse Artillery that was positioned on the west side of Chlum and which had poured cannister into the 1st Battalion (the 3rd Company in the first rank), as it pushed [westward] along the cross road toward Lipa. Seven guns were captured, one escaped.[44] Battalion von Helldorf remained at the south end of the village where, with others, it repulsed repeated attempts to recapture Chlum and later took part in the bloody battle for Rosberitz. We shall meet it again as we describe that action.

The 3rd Battalion of the Guards Fusilier Regiment, *Graf* Waldersee, made its right wheel from a point several hundred paces farther south. Instead of hitting the southern point of Chlum, it hit the sunken road linking Chlum and Rosberitz down which it began to advance. It then received orders to cross the sunken road and halt the approach of an enemy battalion that was advancing uphill from the *Chaussée* toward Chlum.

Graf Waldersee's men, already formed up in two half battalions, immediately faced west and advanced against the rapidly approaching enemy. At that very moment, a significant body of enemy cavalry that seemed to have the same objective, and to be advancing in the same direction as the attacking Austrian battalion, caused [Battalion *Graf* Waldersee] to halt and form line (to better meet the charge).

As this was taking place the enemy cavalry reached the hill. It was the Austrian Brigade Schindlöcker, with the Kaiser Uhlans and Cuirassier Regiment Franz Joseph in the first wave, Cuirassier Regiment *Graf* Stadion in the second. The leading regiments were formed in squadron column, close beside each other. The cuirassiers approached in splendid order with long, even strides, the Uhlans beside them were in a somewhat looser formation. Both regiments rode directly against our line of Fusiliers. The first volley came at 250 paces, which seemed too high as the cuirassiers continued their charge, however, when our officers shouted, 'Aim lower!' horses and riders began to go down. At 120 paces the leading squadron of cuirassiers turned to the right, the 2nd Squadron rode to the same range and suffered the same fate, the 3rd [Squadron] disintegrated under fire and the remnants of the entire regiment now charged into

---

44 Author's Note: The battery, nearly captured by surprise, was Horse Artillery Battery Nr.7 of 3rd Corps under *Hauptmann* van der Gröben [the 'van' is correct]. When [*Hauptmann* van der Gröben] heard that Chlum had been captured, he advanced his battery to within two hundred paces of the edge of the village and shelled our debouching column. 'The enemy rapid fire, however,' says the Austrian report, 'caused such devastation among the gun crews and horses that, in a moment, *Hauptmann* van der Gröben, one officer, 52 men and 68 horses fell.' A Prussian artillery officer described this advance of the battery, with no cover, to a range of 200 paces in brief, 'In human terms, an act of heroism, in artillery terms, sheer nonsense.'

the Uhlans,[45] all then fleeing in confusion toward Rosberitz.[46] Cuirassier Regiment Stadion of the second wave did not attempt an attack, merely riding forward to the hill and then following the two retreating [routing] regiments.

The enemy losses resulting from this disastrous and incomprehensible assault were enormous. 250 men lay on the ground including the Commanding Officer of the cuirassier regiment, *Oberst* von Koziebrodski. The 3rd Squadron (comprising eight officers and 160 men) sacrificed all of its officers and 134 men dead or wounded. Of more importance was the fact that in their wild flight, the cuirassiers and Uhlans had severely disrupted the 1st Battalion Sachsen - Meiningen as we saw in the previous chapter, partially contributing to the defeat of this outstanding regiment.

It must also be noted at this point that, immediately after the defeat of the cavalry attack and after the capture of the 1st Battalion Sachsen - Meiningen, Battalion Waldersee and Company von Görne advanced to the northwest corner of Rosberitz, from which position they also repelled further attacks from the *Chaussée* to recapture the Chlum - Rosberitz position. These attacks were perhaps conducted with inadequate forces, but certainly however, with inadequate determination. The *determined* attempts made by the reserve corps to recapture the position in question (and we shall return to these in detail) took place nearly an hour later.

The Fusilier Battalion of the 2nd Guards Regiment, *Major* von Erckert (only three companies strong after the 9th Company, *Hauptmann* von Görne, became separated) advanced farthest to the south to a point where it's right wheel not only missed Chlum but even the ground between Chlum and Rosberitz, and instead struck Rosberitz itself. This, which was only weakly defended by the retreating Austrians, was quickly taken.

The advance of Battalion von Erckert to the point from which it carried out its right wheel can best be described as a chain of small engagements, a series of fortunate attacks on the one side, of repelled assaults on the other. The 10th and 11th Companies formed the right flank [of the battalion], their line of advance leading them past the east side of Rosberitz. When they had

---

45   Tr. Note: It may sound a bit overdone to say that the Austrian cuirassiers 'charged' into the Austrian Uhlans in their mad dash to escape, but that is exactly the impression, and to a large degree, the effect, produced on the unfortunate recipients. Repeatedly during the day, cavalry in flight rode down their own infantry and artillery and their victims described it just as if they had been ridden down by hostile forces. In a similar incident during the great cavalry battle near Stresetitz, fleeing *Hessen* Cuirassiers, in mad confusion, crashed through the columns of the retreating Saxon infantry, trampling anyone and anything that stood in their way. The diary of a Saxon officer says, 'A column of Austrian cavalry threw itself upon us in a manner that was in no way different than if they had the enemy before them. Wherever there was any gap, the riders broke through the infantry (in column of platoons), spreading confusion everywhere, and where there was no gap, they sought to break their way through by force.' (From footnote, pp. 246 - 7, *Der Antheil des Königlich Sächsischen Armeecorps am Feldzuge 1866 in Oesterreich.*)

46   Author's Note: On the left wing of Battalion Waldersee, which repulsed this cavalry assault, was the 9th Company (*Hauptmann* von Görne) of the 2nd Guards Regiment. Following the right wheel of the two Battalions von Helldorf and *Graf* Waldersee, it became separated from its parent body, finding itself initially in the path of the battalion marching farther to the south. Company von Görne subsequently attached itself to the Guards Fusiliers (Battalion Waldersee) in all subsequent actions. During the engagement with Brigade Schindlöcker it formed part of the first line, participating in the destruction of Cuirassier Regiment Emperor Franz Joseph (some of the 2nd Battalion of the 1st Guards Regiment also took part in this episode of the fighting).

almost reached the northeast corner of the village, they were suddenly attacked by two enemy battalions, probably from Regiment Archduke Heinrich, which fell upon them with the cry 'Es lebe der Kaiser' [Long Live the Emperor]. The 10th Company responded in quick time, rifles on the right, to the beating of the drums. Both sides now charged to the attack, the next moment would show who had the stronger hearts. The first enemy battalion came to within 80 paces, halted, wavered, and then turned back, followed by a rapid fire which reduced them to utter confusion, the other battalion suffered a similar fate from the fire of the 11th Company.

Brigade Appiano in flight.

The 12th Company, *Hauptmann* von Kropff, advanced in line on the left of the 10th and 11th, beating off an enemy battalion, firing on an enemy battery causing substantial losses and then advancing to the *Chaussée* (initially keeping close to the east side of Rosberitz before bearing off again to the south). There it stood, a few hundred paces past the two other companies, when a large confused mass of enemy troops (several battalions of infantry mixed with cavalry), suddenly appeared from the southern corner of the village, apparently retreating toward Wsestar and Sweti [Presumably the remnants of Brigade Appiano, perhaps also Brigade Brandenstein].

Hauptmann von Kropff immediately formed his [company] for action and opened fire. The shooting continued for five minutes but due to its length and depth, the enemy column couldn't return fire and passed, mute and inactive, like a towed target. The results were horrible, it was nothing short of murder and *Hauptmann* von Kropff, refusing to continue [the slaughter], had his men cease fire and withdrew to Rosberitz where he assembled the company at the southern point of the village, in a plum orchard behind a massive barn. The 10th and 11th Companies had already taken position to the left and right of this barn. It was now 3:00.

The Advanced Guard of 1st Guards Division Takes the Lipa

The rapid success of Brigades Obernitz and Kessel was significantly helped by advances on both sides:

> On the left flank, Nedelist was captured by advanced elements of the 11th Division. On the right flank, the Lipa woods were taken by the advanced guard battalion of the 1st Guards Division which was again in action.

We describe elsewhere the occupation of Nedelist. Here we shall initially deal with the capture of the Lipa woods. A confrontation had already developed on the approach to these woods, we shall recount this first.

The clash with Brigade Fleischhacker

The advance - guard, Brigade von Alvensleben, four battalions strong, positioned itself near Maslowed. Battalion Petery was in front of the village, the three other battalions were on the (eastern) side. All the battalions had encountered the enemy, and now, unusually [for an advance guard], found themselves to the rear of our other two brigades, which had already advanced much farther. In order to explain this, it is necessary first to turn to the enemy.

While the other brigades of [the Austrian] 4th Corps marched off to the Chlum - Nedelist line as we have already mentioned, Brigade Fleischhacker remained in and around Cistowes. Several hours had elapsed when the brigade commander began to feel (and for good reason) that if he didn't pull back and rejoin the other brigades of his corps, he would be lost. In order to carry out this manoeuvre, *Oberst* Fleischhacker chose to withdraw along a narrow, half mile long meadow, that formed a shallow valley between Cistowes and Nedelist [This valley, which rises to a saddle approximately a quarter of the way between Cistowes and Nedelist before falling away to the east, is roughly 2½ miles long. Fontane's 'half mile' reference probably refers to the meadow itself]. Battalion Petery was already in this meadow just in front of Maslowed, a meeting engagement therefore, was inevitable.

It was probably around 2:30 as the enemy brigade moved out of Cistowes in a long column. The [Austrian] Hussar Regiment Nr.7 Prince Friedrich Carl of Prussia, to the fore, followed by the Brigade Battery, then the 13th Jäger Battalion and finally IR 6 Coronini and IR 61 Thronfolger. As it passed the northern outskirts of Chlum, the leading Hussars almost level with Schanze III, they ran into Battalion Petery which had simultaneously arrived at the same location. Immediately coming under fire, the leading squadron was destroyed, the others scattered, and a 'stag hunt' now ensued for a quarter of an hour across a considerable stretch of the battlefield. The swirling, dispersed Hussars sought to escape in all directions, but wherever they tried to turn, left toward Maslowed, right toward Chlum, or in a wider arc toward Horenowes or Racitz, they were met by enemy fire or, where they blindly leaped into our batteries, were felled by the gunners with handspikes and sponge staffs. Several groups dashed from Maslowed to Sendrasitz where they encountered the Crown Prince and his staff (who had just appeared at that location) and were captured by our own Guard Hussars, who were riding at the head of the

2nd Guards Division.[47] The battery of Brigade Fleischhacker suffered a similar fate and coming under fire at various locations, lost nearly all of its guns. The infantry battalions of Brigade Fleischhacker had in the meantime proceeded unscathed toward Nedelist. Here however, the head of the column came up against Battalion Petery and the first wave of our advance – guard, the 1st and 2nd Battalions of the Guards Fusilier Regiment. As soon as he became aware of the approaching enemy column, *Generalmajor* von Alvensleben threw the right flank battalion, the 2nd Battalion of the Guards Fusilier Regiment, *Oberstlieutenant* von der Knesebeck, into the flank of this column, which, enveloped by our skirmishers, in part surrendered, in part scattered or fled back to Cistowes, pursued by Battalion Knesebeck. Here the two remaining guns of the brigade battery fell into our hands.

The capture of the Lipa Woods

While *Generalmajor* von Alvensleben sent Battalion Knesebeck against the withdrawing enemy column, the other three battalions of the advanced guard continued their advance thus:

> The 1st Battalion of the 2nd Guards Regiment, *Major* von Petery, which was about 1000 Paces ahead, passed through the northern point of Chlum and took up a position at the Western boundary of the village.
> The 1st Battalion of the Guards Fusilier Regiment, *Major* von Tietzen, formed up into company columns and advanced in various directions.
> The 2nd Battalion of the 2nd Guards Regiment, *Major* von Reuss, including the 3rd Guards Jäger Company, *Hauptmann* von Arnim, advanced as a compact body against the Lipa woods.

The Lipa wood, a [small] irregularly shaped plantation of young trees between Chlum and Lipa, provided with abatis, infantry trenches and gun emplacements, was held by Brigade Benedek (1st Jäger Battalion, IR 78 Sokcevic and IR 52 Archduke Franz Karl). The latter regiment (Franz Karl) was in a forward position west of Chlum, Regiment Sokcevic was to the rear, east of Lipa, the brigade battery was also in the woods, the 1st Jäger Battalion was in Lipa itself. The entire brigade, which had originally been facing west towards the Bistritz, now reversed its facing and turned east, towards Chlum.

As it started to climb the rather steep hill, Battalion Reuss came under fire from the woods and immediately launched a frontal attack, pinning the enemy in position, while the 3rd Jäger Company advanced on the right (from the north), and two companies of Battalion Petery, which as we know was directly beside Chlum, advanced on the left (from the south). Battalion Reuss, which was in the lead, advanced from east to west in company columns with two platoons of the Guards Fusilier Regiment under *Lieutenant* von Obernitz in the front rank.

Now the enemy artillery opened up and raked the ground, while Austrian troops moved to the edge of the woods and commenced firing volleys. At this moment *Major* von Reuss was

---

47   Author's Note: Among those captured was a young imperial officer who complained vociferously as if the whole matter was an insult and an example Prussian arrogance. He was allowed to go on like this for a while. Finally, a Guards Hussar lost his patience, saying, '*Herr* Comrade, calm down. If it is so displeasing to you to be our prisoner, you shouldn't have allowed yourself to be captured.'

knocked from his horse by a shell as he galloped from the right flank towards *Oberstlieutenant* von Neumann, who was on the left. Everyone who saw him fall knew that he had been killed but it was impossible to halt or delay. *Oberstlieutenant* von Neumann immediately assumed command and taking advantage of the lull following the Austrian volley [they were reloading] (which was too high), led the companies, skirmishers to the fore, against the edge of the woods with the cry 'Marsch, Marsch.' At nearly the same moment the Guards Jäger Company von Arnim, forced its way into the Lipa woods from the north and part of Battalion von Petery entered from the south.

Although some of the enemy fought back desperately, they generally only put up only weak resistance, the vigour with which the assault was conducted seems to have disconcerted them. More than 1500 men surrendered in entire groups, mostly from Regiment Archduke Franz Karl, numerous stragglers from other regiments were also captured and sent to the rear under strong escort.

Our own losses were limited though the death of *Major* von Reuss, an excellent officer, was greatly mourned. A search for his body could not be made until the following morning. He was found at the spot where he fell, in a field of oats between Chlum and Cistowes, about 500 paces from the northern exit of the village. A 4pdr shell had torn off the left side of his chest and shoulder, the shell, which had failed to burst, lay beside the body.

The attempted recapture

The Lipa woods were captured. All of the companies that had been involved passed through it in different directions, but essentially from northeast to southwest, and took up positions at the opposite border [of the woods] parallel with the *Chaussée*. Battalion Petery took the left flank with a half company of the 1st Guards Regiment and the 3rd Company of the Guard Fusiliers.

Hardly had this position been taken when it became evident that the enemy, who had just been ejected from the woods, was going to attempt to recapture them. Thus, what had been attempted little more than a quarter of an hour earlier, only two or three hundred paces away at Chlum, would be repeated here. As the reserves of Brigade Appiano had earlier attempted to retake Chlum Hill, so the reserves of Brigade Benedek would attempt to retake the position that they had just lost [the Lipa woods].

The direction of the attack was such that it must strike the foremost companies (1st and 4th) of Battalion Petery which had taken cover in an irregular hollow (half sunken road, half gravel pit), to await the impending attack. The Grenadiers required only brief encouragement to stand firm and fire calmly, they answered as if with a single voice, 'Don't worry. Let them come!'

And they came, nearer and nearer. Under a hail of shells that opened the attack, the Austrians advanced from the Chaussée up the hill in typical formation, apparently in six division columns,[48] two abreast and three deep, with the skirmishers only about ten paces in front. Our

---

48   Author's Note: At this time there has long been uncertainty regarding which units made this attempt to recapture the Lipa woods. According to the Austrian General Staff Report it can only have been the 2nd and 3rd Battalions of the Croatian Regiment Sokcevic that advanced [side by side] in six division columns (one Austrian 'division' comprised two companies, thus each battalion was six companies - or three 'divisions' strong). In less than ten minutes the two battalions lost eleven officers, three *Hauptleute*, four *Oberlieutenants* and four *Unterlieutenants* killed. According to the Austrian General Staff work

two companies awaited their approach, rifles ready. When the enemy were about 100 paces away the volleys of the 1st tore into them, then those of the 4th Company, then again the 1st and then the 4th. Despite all this the columns continued their advance. The Grenadiers now opened up with a heavy rapid fire and the Austrian battalions wavered, turned back and then fled down the hill. In the meantime, *Hauptmann* von Herwarth III also had the 3rd Company of Battalion Petery, which had been farther to the rear, advance to the edge of the woods and fire into the flank of the retreating battalions. Those parts of the 1st Guards and Guard Fusilier Regiments that were nearby were also active in repulsing this attack.

The enemy losses were enormous, his dead and wounded lying so thick that it was impossible an hour later to pass through the area on horseback. Hardly a man was hit on our side, the Austrian skirmishers fired much too high. The report of an eyewitness (from the 2nd Guards Regiment) said,

> The attack was delivered with great elan. The commander of the regiment, who was riding a white horse, showed immense courage and was always in the lead. He and his horse went down together under our hail of bullets. If the Austrian column had advanced another 60 paces, they would have trodden our two companies into the ground. But their strength failed at the last moment.

Thus, this attack too was repulsed, just as the one against Chlum Hill had foundered. *Brigadier Oberst* Benedek, seriously wounded, led the remnants of his brigade back toward Langenhof.

The Advanced Guard of the 2nd Guards Division Takes Lipa

Apparently Lipa itself was taken at the same time as the Lipa woods. Just as the woods were captured by the advanced guard of the 1st Guards Division, *Generalmajor* von Alvensleben, so Lipa was captured by the advanced guard of the 2nd Guards Division, *Generalmajor* von Budritzki. The battalions of this brigade followed Brigades Obernitz and Kessel and had, in crossing the meadow ground between Maslowed and Chlum, wheeled half right against the northern edge of the village of Lipa.

The village of Lipa, with its southwest margin right by the great *Chaussée*, had the same significance for the enemy as Sadowa had for us. Accordingly, every effort was made to provide it with the greatest possible defensive strength. Innumerable batteries, positioned in tiers, surrounded it on all sides. In addition, it was protected by abatis at its northern and western margins. Attempts had been made since 8:00 in the morning to advance in the centre against Lipa but without success, no further attempts had been made since 11:00. Nevertheless, what had failed frontally was now to succeed from the flanks and rear. After taking the woods, the

---

some of IR 13 Roman Banat [a Grenz regiment from the military frontier], under the personal leadership of *Oberst* Baron Catty, Chief of Staff 3rd Corps, also attacked the Lipa woods, in which attack *Oberst* Catty was seriously wounded. This attack cannot be the one referred to at this point. It probably came a quarter, perhaps even half an hour later and since it was merely a demonstration (to cover the withdrawal of Brigades Kirchsberg and Prohaska), was conducted with a relatively small force, probably one or two divisions.

capture of Lipa itself was only a matter of time, and it came about initially as the result of an attack by the Guards *Schützen* Battalion, led by *Major* von Besser.

About 300 paces north of Lipa was a shallow valley given over to meadow, the side of the valley closest to the village was held by Austrian Jäger. Concealed in a field of tall grain that that extended as far as the meadow itself, they exacted the first losses from our skirmishers.

Realizing that our advance would not be stopped by these losses, the enemy Jäger fell back to the northern half of the village which was strongly held by troops of the 3rd Army Corps. Our Guard Schützen immediately pursued, such that:

> The 3rd Company, *Premierlieutenant* von Bassewitz, advanced in the centre against the north side of the village.
>
> The 4th Company, *Hauptmann* von Gelieu, advanced on the left against the northeast corner of the village.
>
> The 2nd Company, *Hauptmann* von Laue, advanced on the right against the northwest cornerof the village.

(The 1st Company, *Premierlieutenant* von Massow, which had participated in the rout of the Friedrich Karl Hussars at Maslowed, was still some way to the rear).

The leading platoons of the three companies were in open order with the *Soutiens* [support companies] positioned wherever possible under cover, waiting to reinforce the skirmish line if required. This happened almost immediately and as we approached the woods, the Commanding Officer ordered that everyone adopt skirmish formation. With loud hurrahs the three companies threw themselves into the stubbornly defended village, keeping to the direction given above, the *Hauptleute* leading, the Commanding Officer (*Major* von Besser), galloping ahead of the *Tirailleurs* of the 3rd Company. The 4th Company, von Gelieu, ran into opposition first and had to take an abatis that lined the (northeastern edge of) the Lipa woods before it could enter the village itself. The two other companies, at least initially, ran into less difficulty and stormed into the village from the north and northwest.

The enemy, especially Jäger from the 1st, 3rd 5th and 17th Battalions,[49] put up a desperate defense. Each house had to be taken individually and artillery, firing from higher up, swept the village streets with cannister and shell, causing us significant losses. In order to escape this fire and at the same time to neutralize it, the skirmishers stormed one position after another with redoubled energy until they reached the western and southwestern margins of the village, captured the high ground and forced the brigade batteries in the immediate vicinity to withdraw.

The losses suffered by our Guard Schützen Battalion in enveloping and capturing the village were not insignificant. *Hauptmann* von Laue, who had already pushed as far as the eastern *Chaussée* ditches of the great Königgrätz highway, was shot through the right knee from the brickyard (which the enemy held to the very last). *Secondelieutenant* Bethusy - Huc was hit in

---

49   Author's Note: According to consistent [Prussian] statements, prisoners were not just from the above named four Jäger battalions (1st, 3rd, 5th, and 17th) but also from the 9th. This is entirely possible. The 1st and 3rd Jäger Battalions had been in and around Lipa since early in the morning with the 17th by Rosberitz, thus only 2000 paces further back. As for the 5th and 9th (these battalions fought by Problus and Trotina), the prisoners in question were probably fragments of the two combined Jäger battalions (Nr.33 and 34) that belonged to Brigade Prohaska and which had also taken up position close to Lipa.

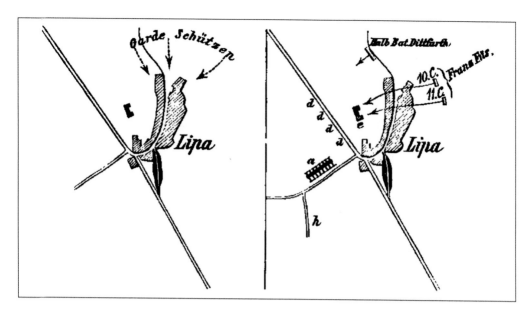

The fall of Lipa.

the forehead and fell dead on the spot, as he led his platoon into a newly built farmstead right at the entrance to the village. *Gardeschütz* Wende of the 2nd Company was hit by a shell that separated his torso from his legs, leaving it 20 paces away.

The two other battalions of the advanced guard of the 2nd Guards Division, the Fusiliers of Regiments Franz and Alexander, also played a significant part in the fight for Lipa. Two Fusilier companies (the 10th and 11th) of Regiment Franz, entered Lipa almost exactly in the same place (the northeastern corner) as the Guards Schützen Company von Gelieu. However, while the Guards Schützen fought their way down the length of the village street, [the Fusiliers of the 10th and 11th Companies Regiment Franz] fought their way across the village and captured the brickyard (e) in the open ground between the village and the *Chaussée* that was especially stubbornly defended. In so doing *Premierlieutenant* von Rechenberg was killed. A few minutes later *Premierlieutenant* von Notz also fell as he led his 10th Company against the *Chaussée* ditch that was strongly held by enemy Jäger (dd).

The enemy force, which was composed of fragments of various battalions, was driven off or captured and the *Chaussée* occupied. On its far side however, in front of Langenhof, three batteries (24 guns) of the great artillery line that had prevented our 8th and 4th Divisions from breaking out of the Hola woods since 9:00 still held on. After Lipa had fallen, and realizing the enemy was in their rear, half of these attempted to limber up and pull out, but their attempt collapsed under the fire of our Alexander Fusiliers, who were right beside them. The other twelve guns (a) which had remained in position and continued firing against the Bistritz line, were captured by various units advancing across the *Chaussée,* by Guard Schützen under *Hauptmann* von Gelieu, by Franz Fusiliers under *Lieutenant* von Delitz, and by Guard Fusiliers (who had advanced to this point from the Lipa woods) under *Lieutenant* von Mirbach. The gunners held out to the last with true heroism. When our forces were already within 50 paces, one of these guns, with only three of its crew remaining, fired its last round against Dohalitz.

The enemy centre was broken through, *Lipa was ours*. Our most advanced formations, surrounded by numerous captured guns, had reached Langenhof. In the very last moments of this fighting, the Commander of the Franz Fusiliers, *Major* von Delitz, was wounded in a manner that was as unusual as it was painful. A shell tore off the neck of a Fusilier, and the buckle of his stock hit the major standing behind him in the mouth like a shot (at approximately this time, or a little later, *Oberstlieutenant* von Pannewitz, Commander 2nd Battalion of the Elizabeth Grenadiers, fell. His *Adjutant, Lieutenant* von Wurmb, fell with him. An artillery round killed them both

The 11th and 12th Divisions Take Nedelist and Lochenitz

Here we break off our description of the Guards action and turn back to the left wing of the Crown Prince's army, to the VI Army Corps, which was advancing with equal speed. At 2:00 or perhaps even a little earlier, the 11th Division reached and captured Sendrasitz, and the 12th Division, the village of Trotina. After a brief rest, both divisions resumed their advance southwards, the 11th Division towards Nedelist, the 12th to Lochenitz. We shall follow them both.

The Capture of Nedelist

After repeated attacks by three squadrons of [Austrian] s Regiment Nr.12, Haller, who had vainly attempted to stop the advance, Nedelist was taken without serious fighting. After their earlier battle [in the Swiepwald], Brigades Saffran and Würtemberg that were holding the village, were in no condition to put up any serious resistance. Only the four batteries of the Army Artillery Reserve that were positioned and in action directly west of the village, held out and caused us substantial losses.

An officer of the 50th Regiment writes regarding this advance;

> Our 2nd Battalion, *Major* von Berken, took the lead.[50] When it reached the hill west of Nedelist, the main body of the battalion came under such horrendous shell fire that it had to enter the village. Only the long line of skirmishers, which was already about 300 paces ahead, continued to advance and sought shelter in a shallow depression, the previously mentioned meadow that extended from Cistowes and Chlum, toward Nedelist. The Schützenzug of the 8th Company, *Lieutenant* von Both (which kept to the left and had become separated from the other skirmishers), quickly climbed the next hill. An enemy officer who showed himself was shot down. Concealed by the grain, the skirmishers advanced up the hill until they suddenly saw artillery in action. With a loud hurrah the platoon threw itself upon the guns. Five managed to fire without suffering much damage. A sixth, whose crew were shot down or fled, was fired

50   Authors Note: The three battalions of Regiment Nr.50 separated en route from the Frantow Mill to Nedelist. The 1st Battalion, *Major* von Sperling, was first into Racitz. The Fusilier Battalion, *Major* von Galisch, was first into Sendrasitz, while the 2nd Battalion, *Major* von Berken, took the lead against Nedelist. Thus, a sort of rotation took place in the advance from village to village.

by an officer [when our men were] 15 paces distant. It blew away several of our men, but those who followed them took the gun and immediately felled the officer. Two guns that succeeded in pulling out were brought to a halt by rifle bullets before they made more than 200 paces and were captured. The worst moment came when another battery unlimbered on our flank at a range of 300 paces and fired on our platoon of skirmishers with cannister. The brave skirmishers threw themselves down among the captured guns, finding cover behind them, and now shot up the enemy battery so effectively that it ceased firing and pulled out. Nine guns were captured.[51] In the meantime, the main body of the battalion, which had swung out to the left, had firmly established itself in the weakly defended village of Nedelist (2:30). This was now in the midst of the battle, and fighting raged left and right. The Divisional Commander, *General* von Zastrow, resolved to wait until his regiments had concentrated at this location before continuing the advance. At about 3:15 this concentration was accomplished. We shall now see how the 11th Division continued the action.

The Capture of Lochenitz

The capture of Lochenitz by the 12th Division took place half an hour later than the occupation of Nedelist. We left [the 12th Division][52] at 2:00 at the Trotina. After the fighting south of Racitz (on the banks of the Trotina), the main body of the division had continued southwest with five half battalions of Regiment Nr.23, and Jäger Battalion Minkwitz, sharing to a greater or lesser degree in the fighting of the 11th Division, first at Sendrasitz and then at Nedelist. The smaller part of the division on the extreme left flank had taken the village of Trotina after a short fight, and now advanced toward Lochenitz. The Commander of the Division, *General* von Prondzynski, was also there and assembled what he still had available:

Jäger half battalion Müller.
The Fusilier Battalion, *Major* von Lyncker, of the 22nd Regiment.
The 6th and 8th Companies of the 23rd Regiment.
The 6th Hussar Regiment.
Two rifled batteries under *Major* Forst.

51   Author's Note: Various units cooperated in the capture of these guns west of Nedelist (their number cannot be precisely determined). Schützenzüge of the 50th Regiment, as mentioned a above, a Schützenzug of the 2nd Guards Regiment under *Lieutenant* Chorus and two companies, von Arnim and von Lobenthal, of the 3rd Guards Regiment. The guns that the enemy lost here belonged to the Army Artillery Reserve, from which the 3rd and 4th Divisions (a total of eight batteries) went into action by Langenhof, the 1st and 2nd Divisions west of Nedelist. The 7th Battery of the 2nd Division suffered the greatest losses. The *Hauptmann*, 27 men and 41 horses had already been put out of action as they continued firing with cannister at the [Prussian] *tirailleurs*, who had advanced to within close range. *All of the guns were lost.* Two ammunition wagons had already been blown up in the original position (by Horenowes). The other batteries suffered fewer losses, at least here. It must be remembered that they had taken up repeated positions as they fell back, sacrificing themselves in an attempt to cover the retreat of the army, first from positions by Wsestar and Sweti, finally in a flanking position by Plotist.
52   Author's Note: After leaving the 1st Battalion of Regiment Nr.22 in Habrina, the 12th Division consisted of only five battalions: Regiment Nr.23 with three battalions, Silesian Jäger Battalion Nr. 6 and Fusilier Battalion Nr.22.

This was all that was available for the capture of Lochenitz.

Lochenitz, a village that ran parallel to the Elbe, lying between the *Chaussée* and the railway embankment, was occupied by IR 27 Konig der Belgien. They had orders to hold this position until the remainder of Brigade Henriquez had completed its withdrawal. It appears that the regiment essentially carried out its mission.

General von Prondzynski initially made it his business to form a reserve from the Jäger half battalion Müller, the 8th Company of the 23rd Regiment, *Hauptmann Graf* Henneberg, and the 11th Company of the 22nd Regiment. He positioned these at the crossroads formed by the Lochenitz to Sendrasitz road and the *Chaussée*. He then pushed Fusilier Battalion Nr.22 along the narrow strip between the railroad and the *Chaussée*. The enemy believed that he had to oppose this advance with a counter attack of his own, but he was thrown back into the village by the Fusiliers after a short fight. Individual platoons of the 22nd followed close on their heels, soon coming under intense cannister and rifle fire (the colour bearer, *Sergeant* Metzner was twice wounded and twice sank to the ground but was only persuaded to relinquish the colours with difficulty). The outskirts of the village were captured at the same time the 6th Company of the 23rd Regiment, pushed into the northwestern corner that led to Maslowed.

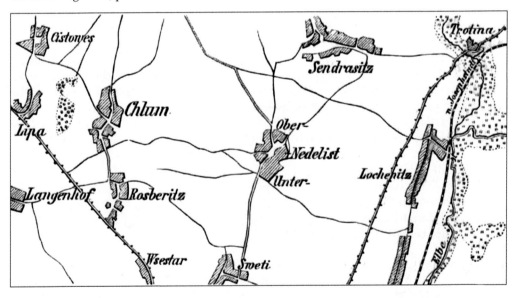

The *Soutiens* attempted to take Lochenitz in the flank farther to the south, but at that very moment, bugle calls rang out from all parts of the village, making it clear that the enemy intended to complete his withdrawal across the Elbe as quickly as possible. In order to do as much damage as could be done with the forces available, *Major* von Lyncker sent the 9th and 10th Companies against the east side of the village. If this succeeded, if our forces got to the bridges before the Austrians, then all who were still in the village would be taken prisoner. That was the intention of our Upper Silesian Fusiliers, as they crossed the railroad embankment (under heavy enemy fire) and waded across the Trotina near its confluence [with the Elbe], up to their chests in muddy water. When they reached this point, they saw the enemy crossing the Elbe 400 paces farther south. In order to intercept them they would now have to [swim] the Elbe. *Hauptmann* von Gottberg, in the heat of the moment, leaped into the river with his company and could only be restrained by repeated orders to return to the bank from *Major* von Lyncker (who had one horse shot from under him in the fighting for Lochenitz, and another mortally wounded), otherwise the Elbe, which had risen that day, would probably have swallowed up the entire company.[53]

The attempt at envelopment, despite all the haste and courage with which it was carried out, had failed. Accordingly, *Major* von Lyncker decided to pull the companies back, again wading through the little river (from left to right) and instead of attempting an envelopment, to simply pursue [the enemy] through the village to the bridge. By the time that this had been decided, the last enemy units had already crossed. It became evident that the Austrians had started to construct a pontoon bridge over the Elbe alongside the existing bridge. Thus, from the very beginning, they had planned to use Lochenitz as a crossing point for the retreat of their right wing. The enemy pontoon bridge, 12 *Hackets* and all that goes with them [a *Hacket* was a wagon with everything required to make a single section of bridge], were in part in the water, in part still on land, with a large number of dead pioneers and draft horses among them. An upturned enemy gun stood undamaged in the village street, an ammunition wagon close by. Numerous wounded and unwounded enemy soldiers were captured near the bridge and in the gardens and houses, yet more who had hidden themselves got away during the night.

At 3:00 the third ridge and its extension to the Elbe were in our hands. Our three leading divisions now stood on the line Chlum – Nedelist - Lochenitz. At 3:00 our three leading divisions held the Chlum - Nedelist - Lochenitz line, thus we closed our previous chapter. The 1st Guards Division extended its arms far in advance (Rosberitz was taken) while its body was in Chlum and the Lipa woods. The advanced guard of the 2nd Guards Division, the Guard *Schützen* and the Alexander and Franz Fusiliers, held Lipa and Langenhof.

Our forces had a magnificent view from the high plateau between Chlum and Lipa. Nearly at the foot of the hill, barely 2000 paces away, one could see the imposing masses of the Austrian Reserve Corps (1st and 6th), directly around Rosberitz and stretching to Wsestar, Sweti and Rosnitz. Behind them were numerous cavalry regiments, probably 15 to 20 and an equal number of batteries, all in all, a good 40,000 to 50,000 men. Farther on toward Problus, in the clearing weather, the rising smoke of intense artillery fire could be seen, thus giving an idea of the extent of the battle.

It was a splendid sight, but at the same time, one that could arouse concern. The forces that we had assembled at Chlum and Lipa amounted at most to 12,000 men who, if attacked by the enemy's reserves, would have to hold their own against a numerical superiority of four to one.[54]

---

53   Author's Note: The Upper Silesian Regiment proved itself here and elsewhere that day as true '*Wasserpolacken*' [water Poles!]. Individual companies waded once through the Trokinka, twice through the Trotina and finally, they even attempted the Elbe.

54   Author's Note: There were, including the advance - guard of the 2nd Guards Division, 12,000 men at the most, aside from casualties and men who had been detached. The 2nd Battalion of the 3rd Guards Regiment was far ahead toward Sweti, the 2nd Battalion of the Guard Fusilier Regiment was well to the rear in Cistowes. Thus, the defense of the Chlum - Lipa position [would be left to] the advance - guard. Little help could be expected from the 11th Division, which was concentrating by Nedelist.

Advance of the Austrian Reserves.

The force ratio was so heavily against us, the enemy artillery still outnumbered ours so greatly, that their renewed attempt to recapture the Chlum position might seem justified. Nevertheless, it was certainly a mistake. We now know how dubious our position really was and its numerous weaknesses, but Benedek could not know this and he had no right to simply assume what he did not know. For him the simple fact had to be, that with the appearance of our 2nd Army on the battlefield, our forces could be expected to double, thus he should not hope to accomplish against our entire force, what he had hitherto failed to achieve against the half.

Yet again the proper moment for the offensive had been allowed to pass. At 11:00 the *Feldzeugmeister* could have advanced with his reserves, or at 12:00, the 4th and 2nd Corps (supporting each other where possible) could have advanced against the *Swiepwald*, Benatek and Sadowa woods. This advance might still have had a chance of success, but 12:00 was the last time. Now, a full two hours later, it must have been apparent that the moment had passed and that he should use his reserves to cover a retreat, rather than to attempt to retrieve what had already been lost. That he chose the latter course was his most egregious error and made defeat inevitable.

Nevertheless, mistake or not, recapture was decided upon and the columns set themselves in motion. We have two main attacks[55] to differentiate, a fragmented attack by 6th Corps and a

---

55   Author's Note: We have already, in the previous chapter, described the attempts to recapture Chlum that were made before 3:00, mostly with extremely inadequate forces. There were five:

The attack of the 1st Battalion Sachsen - Meiningen (Brigade Appiano).
The attack of the 1st and 3rd Battalions Archduke Franz Karl (Brigade Benedek).

coordinated attack by 1st Corps. Both attacks failed. The assault of 6th Corps captured Rosberitz, but Rosberitz was only an outwork and not the actual objective itself. The real objective was Chlum, and this, despite every effort, was not taken. The outcome of the battle depended on possession of this elevated position that commanded Rosberitz (which was beneath it). With Chlum, we held the key to victory.

We shall now detail the battle that developed around Chlum and Rosberitz.

Commitment of the Austrian Reserves (6th and 1st Corps)

As we said in the previous chapter, the recapture of Chlum had been decided upon, and 6th Corps, *Feldmarschialllieutenant* Ramming, was given the order to attack. This order, much anticipated by his officers, was greeted with enthusiasm. The recent events [at Chlum and Lipa] had caused some disquiet among the troops which could only get worse with continued inactivity. *Feldmarschialllieutenant* Ramming had his corps prepare for action, two batteries commenced (an inadequate) preparatory fire, then Brigade Rosenzweig advanced towards Chlum with the 17th Jäger Battalion and IR 4 Hoch und Deutschmeister in the first wave, IR 55 Gondrecourt in the second. Their task was to bypass Rosberitz and directly attack the main position itself, the 'fortress'[at Chlum - Lipa]. However, coming under heavy fire from Rosberitz, both waves gave up their primary objective, and instead of attacking Chlum, directed their attack against the 'outwork' at the foot [of the hill], the village of Rosberitz. The Jäger battalion and the Deutschmeister Regiment [IR 4 Hoch und Deutschmeister, the 'house regiment' of Vienna, and one of the best in the KK army] forced their way into the southwest corner and centre of the village. Regiment Gondrecourt,[56] which formed the second wave, turned into the northern third of the village, from which position it probably turned again toward Chlum Hill. After a short fight, which was carried on with great ferocity over the garden fences of the southwest

The attack by individual battalions of Grand Duke Michael and Archduke Wilhelm (Brigade Brandenstein).
The attack by two Battalions Archduke Heinrich (Brigade Appiano).
The attack by two Battalions Sokcevic (Brigade Benedek).

The last was the most serious. The third and fourth foundered before they could deploy their forces. Most of these attacks were launched from Rosberitz, two (the second and fifth) from the Lipa woods and the village of Lipa.

56 Author's Note: The Austrian General Staff Work does not explicitly name Regiment Gondrecourt in the attack on Rosberitz. Rather the relevant passage states, '*Generalmajor* Rosenzweig ordered the 17th Jäger Battalion and Regiment Deutschmeister to occupy Rosberitz, which was in flames, while he personally carried on the attack against Chlum with Regiment Gondrecourt (second wave).' This seems to mean that the fight against Rosberitz was only conducted by the Jager battalion and the 'Deutschmeister'. That, however, can hardly be the case. All [Prussian] reports speak of six clearly evident columns that approached the northern third of Rosberitz from the west, and even if we look upon these six columns as only division columns (one division equals two companies), then, if they belonged exclusively to Regiment Deutschmeister, there would have been nothing significant left over for the capture and occupation of the southern half of the village, at least nothing adequate. We therefore believe that it was highly probable that Regiment Gondrecourt, which advanced here in tightly closed masses, *kept its eye on Chlum* while shoving our five weak companies aside simply brushing through the northern corner of Rosberitz.

corner (where the 3rd Battalion Deutschmeister was attacking), our forces had to fall back to the gully and sunken road that ran between Rosberitz and Chlum, this hillside would now be the main theater for the next half hour. Repeated attacks were attempted but all failed. We shall come back to this. First, we shall describe the various phases of the battle for Rosberitz.

The battle for Rosberitz

The village of Rosberitz was principally held by Fusilier Brigade von Kessel. The brigade comprised three battalions echeloned from south to north, operating virtually independently of each other and barely maintaining contact (Battalion von Helldorf had become a combined battalion in the confused, ebb and flow of fighting). We said that our forces stood echeloned in three parts. Now the enemy too approached in three main columns, each column composed of several division columns, swinging both of his wings to the right and left while directing the centre column against the south end of the village. He clearly intended to take Rosberitz, which he viewed simply as a temporary distraction, by simultaneous attacks in front, flank and rear. It succeeded. We shall now follow this fight minute by minute.

The battle for the south end of the village

At the south end of the village (and here we go back a half an hour) was the Fusilier Battalion of the 2nd Foot Guards Regiment, *Major* von Erckert. All three companies (the 9th was at the north end of the village) remained in the positions they had taken after the capture of Rosberitz. The 10th Company held the furthest point of the *Chaussée*, the 11th and 12th Companies behind it, to the right and left. The 10th Company maintained a lively fire fight at little more than 20 paces with a battalion of Jägers which was in good cover behind trees and the *Chaussée* ditches. The Jägers then launched a snap attack but it was repulsed, those that had advanced the farthest falling back and returning to their positions on the far side of the *Chaussée*. It was inadvisable however [for the Prussians], to take advantage of this momentarily favourable situation with a bayonet attack since, aside from a few companies in the centre of the village, there was no immediate support to the rear, they simply had to hold on.

This would prove to be an increasingly difficult task. The fighting up to this point had only been the overture, now the enemy poured an unbelievable volume of artillery fire into Rosberitz, preparatory to his main attack.

The southern part of the village burst into flames. The entire area was literally saturated with shells, shrapnel and cannister. Fragments of trees, stones and splinters flew around and wounded many. The shells (also Prussian) smashed through the buildings, toppling walls that buried wounded and unwounded alike. Great clouds of dust caused by the smashing of bricks and mortar rose into the air, it was like the end of the world, however the Fusiliers held on, worthy of the old breed, the Schill Fusiliers. Whole ranks fell without wavering a foot. Their brave commander, *Major* von Erckert, remained on his horse in their midst, facing the Austrian Jägers whose number seemed to increase rather than diminish. A bullet hit his horse in the neck. As he bent forward to examine the wound, he himself was shot in the upper arm and side, and at almost the same moment, in the neck, knocking him back in the saddle. He sank from his horse and was carried out of the village (to the east) where he was laid down at the edge of a field of grain.[57]

Hauptmann von Kropff assumed command of the three companies. The situation was critical. After nearly an hour of incessant, heavy fire, cartridges began to run short. They were carefully removed from the dead and wounded but this could not continue for long, especially since a new assault was being prepared. As the Austrians felt our fire begin to slacken (due in part to the shortage of cartridges), and because they considered our position to be adequately weakened by the raging artillery fire, they now formed the three strong attack columns (which we mentioned at the start of our chapter), of which the centre column exclusively, the eastern column at least partially, hit the southern end of Rosberitz.

Our exhausted, weakened companies, virtually incapable of resistance due to the shortage of ammunition and completely disorganised, could no longer withstand the pressure. Bereft of any support, they fell back. Now the Austrians advanced to within ten paces of the confused mass, but having entered Rosberitz from different directions, they were now so densely packed that they got in each other's way. *Premierlieutenant Graf* Rantzau, slipped and fell to the ground. In his state of utter exhaustion, he was unable to get back up immediately, and in order to hold off the advancing Austrians and to sell his life as dearly as possible, drew his revolver and fired into the approaching multitude. This stopped them short and *Lieutenant* von Horn, taking advantage of the moment, rushed towards the Austrians, gathered up the fallen man and brought him to safety.

In the 11th Company there was a group of around 20 men who were still with the colours and who did not want to retreat because of *Fähnrich Sergeant* Gursch. This brave *Unteroffizier* advanced against the Austrians with flag held high and sought to carry the rest with him. The tip of the flagstaff was hit by a cannister ball and rang with a clear-sounding note, without however showing any sign of damage. Since the Austrians were also pushing in from the east side, the colours were in extreme danger. The enemy forced their way through the farmstead and leaped over the fence intent on making it their own. The little [Prussian Colour guard] was however, inspired to a heroic defense and was unwilling to let the standard be torn from their grasp while they still lived. *Lieutenant* von Bersen (who was shot in the hip while defending it) and *Portepée Fähnrich* von Bülow, threw themselves into the struggle and only their most extreme efforts managed to save the colours. No Austrian hand defiled the sacred object. All three companies then fell back to the previously mentioned sunken road between Rosberitz and Chlum. We shall meet them again there.

The battle for the centre of the village

In the centre of the village, *Oberstlieutenant* von Helldorf held on with a weak battalion composed of three combined companies. These three companies belonged to different parent formations. They were:

---

57   Author's Note: Enemy battalions later passed over him at this location, taking him for dead. In fact, he did not lose consciousness for a moment and observed it all. An Austrian general remained near him for a long time and watched the defeat of his troops with icy calm. It was later said (whether correctly or not remains to be seen) that it was *Graf* Gondrecourt.

The 4th Company (*Premierlieutenant* von der Knesebeck) of the 1st Guards Regiment.
The 2nd Company (*Premierlieutenant* von Löwenfeld) of the 3rd Guards Regiment.
The 9th Company (*Hauptmann* von Oppell) of the Fusilier Battalion of the 1st Guards Regiment.

Prince Anton von Hohenzollern was in the last named company.

Events in the centre of the village were essentially the same as those at the southern end. Our three companies were able to hold out against the first weak attacks but the same envelopment that wrested the southern end of Rosberitz from our grasp, did the same in the centre. It is difficult to say exactly which column hit this part of the village. The enemy came from both directions, but it may have been the eastern column that hit Battalion Helldorf in the same way that Battalion Erckert was hit by the centre column. Even more than the enemy's numerical superiority was his appearance from every direction, there could no longer be any talk of tactics, it was a brawl, every man for himself. *Oberstlieutenant* von Helldorf, in the midst of fearsome artillery fire, was attempting to consolidate his three companies in the centre of the village. He was riding towards the road that led from Rosberitz to Nedelist, intending to halt and reposition his men toward the east, when a shell fragment hit the left side of his head. He fell from his horse without making a sound, arms outstretched. He died as the adjutant of the Fusilier Battalion, *Lieutenant* von Müller, reached his side.

Any real leadership was now impossible. The men fought in individual groups, attempting to hang on to each house and each hedge, but the enemy grew stronger, surging forward in tightly packed masses. It was then that Prince Anton von Hohenzollern fell, severely wounded. The sheer weight of the attack forced our broken troops to the northern end of the village and then up the hill toward Chlum. *Herr* von Woyrsch, who went through this fearsome half hour beside the prince, gave the following account, at the same time describing the battle, itself.

I kept close to the Prince von Hohenzollern, around whom there was now a group of no more than 40 men. We 40, together with a company of the 3rd Guards Regiment that had held on in the village, determined to fight it out until reinforcements arrived, and they couldn't come soon enough.

Fortunately, we no longer had as much trouble with shellfire since the nearest enemy was now within 50 paces, and thus too close for their own artillery. However, one man after another fell to rifle bullets and soon there were only six of us, then the Prince was hit in the knee. Three of us rushed over to bring him to safety but we had barely gone ten paces when the Prince was hit by two more rounds. Then one of us was shot, a second was hit on his belt buckle, I too was hit twice but with no damage done. The first [spent] bullet hit me on the stomach, the second pierced my pocket handkerchief in a most extraordinary manner. We had just brought the Prince to a house and started to cut off his boots and bandage him, when we heard the Austrian signal to advance. I reached for my rifle, preferring to die rather than be captured when a friendly word from the Prince, who endured his extreme suffering with calm and patience, brought me to my senses. Realizing that resistance at this point, without the slightest hope of success, would only endanger the life of the Prince, I surrendered.

Constantly fighting, the companies fell back in small groups from the centre of the village to the sunken road between Rosberitz and Chlum. The 4th Company of the 1st Guards Regiment lost all but one of its officers killed or wounded and the most junior Lieutenant (*Lieutenant* von Werder), assumed command. The 2nd Company of the 3rd Guards Regiment held out to the last and covered the retreat.

The battle for the north end of the village

Oberstlieutenant Graf Waldersee held on in the northern end of the village with the 3rd Battalion of the Guards Fusilier Regiment to which, as we have previously mentioned, the 9th Company of the 2nd Guards Regiment, *Hauptmann* von Görne, had attached itself. Due to its greater numbers and better position, it held out somewhat longer than *Major* von Erckert and *Oberstlieutenant* von Helldorf, but eventually it too had to fall back.

The [Austrian] western column, which had not touched the southern end of Rosberitz and merely brushed the centre with its right flank companies, now hit the northern end of the village with its full weight. Presumably it was the entire second wave of Brigade Rosenzweig, Regiment Gondrecourt. Our five companies were too weak to resist this mass onslaught. Fighting, they evacuated the northern end of the village and fell back up the hill along the road from Rosberitz toward Chlum, its sunken nature affording some protection. *Hauptmann* von Görne climbed out of the sunken road for a better look and immediately fell with a rifle bullet through the abdomen. Yet more losses were to be mourned. The company remained in this position for a quarter of an hour.

The Assault on Chlum

In the meantime, the Austrians had established themselves in Rosberitz. Those [Prussians] remaining, wounded or unwounded (about 70 men), were taken prisoner. To the extent that it had been committed, the [Austrian] 6th Corps had done its duty. Once more victory seemed to smile on the *Feldzeugmeister*, but it was the last smile, and a fleeting one at that.

The capture of Rosberitz was undoubtedly a success, however even though this success was not to be underrated, it accounted for little. Morally, as with any success, it was significant, tactically, as has been stated repeatedly, it was of no consequence. Whoever controlled Chlum, controlled the battle. If the *Feldzeugmeister* had succeeded in capturing this point [Chlum] from Rosberitz, then indeed much would have been won and much lost. Just as the enemy had committed the last available battalions of 3rd and 4th Corps to recapture Chlum between 3:00 and 4:00, now, an hour later, he committed the fresh forces of 6th and 1st Corps to the same objective. It might even have succeeded. Eight of the nine brigades of the two reserve corps were still intact, only Brigade Rosenzweig had been in action as we know, and with some success. As they became available, brigades and battalions were now set in motion.

A [Prussian] report stated:

> After a short rest the Austrian battalions advanced toward the slope, some directly to our front, some outflanking us to the west. To escape being outflanked, our ravaged companies [in Rosberitz] fell back from the sunken road that ran up the hill, to another sunken road that ran across the slope and provided a better line of defense and a better

field of fire. This retreat, although conducted over such a short distance, exacted a heavy toll, especially for Company von Görne. *Lieutenant* von Pape, already wounded in the arm and side, was cut down by a shell fragment that went through his abdomen from side to side and when on the ground, took another rifle bullet in the right hip. He died the next day at Chlum. *Portepée - Fähnrich Graf* Schwerin was shot in the thigh, a wound which later proved mortal. *Portepée - Fähnrich* von Fallois, who had only come to the regiment from the Cadet Corps on 18th June, received one shot through the lower abdomen and five shell fragments in the back. All the officers of the company were killed or wounded, everyone else who fought here also suffered heavy losses.

[The retreating forces] finally made it to the sunken road that ran across the slope and here *Oberstlieutenant Graf* Waldersee brought the entire movement to a halt. He planted the flag of his battalion in the ground and exhorted the assorted survivors to rally round it and to hold their ground, just as in the *Swiepwald* it was a case of not one step back. A dense skirmish line took up its position in the sunken road and awaited the enemy.

[The enemy] seemed to be hindered in his movements by his own massed formation. Soon however the mass began to flow, and pouring out of Rosberitz, individual columns set out directly up the hill. Others debouched to the left and right from the edges of the village and sought to support the frontal attack by enveloping the flanks. The Jäger horns sounded the advance and the notes of the hymn, '*Gott erhalte Franz den Kaiser*' [God Save Franz the Emperor] could be clearly heard from the advancing columns that drew ever closer.

Battalion Waldersee and those who had attached themselves to it, lay with rifles ready when an artillery salvo suddenly crashed out from the left. A guards' battery (the 4pdr Battery Eltester) had gone into action 150 paces away and spewed death and destruction into the tightly packed enemy ranks. The range was so short that they fell by the hundreds but nevertheless, the columns continued to advance. A Jäger battalion marching in front that hitherto had been heading for the sunken road, now swung to the left and charged the battery, but it was suicide. The battalion collapsed under fire from the battery in front, and from the Guard Fusiliers on its left. The attack was repulsed, and the enemy fell back to the northern edge of Rosberitz, where they held on grimly.

Such was the attack as recounted by one of our men.[58] However, what appeared to be one great action as seen from the Chlum Hill, was actually a conglomeration of attempted assaults that followed one after the other, but with the exception of the last one (we shall return to that), without coordination. 6th Corps itself launched four attacks:

Generalmajor Rosenzweig, as already noted initially led IR 55 Gondrecourt.
Feldmarschialllieutenant von Ramming led Regiment IR 60 Prince of Wasa.

---

58   Author's Note: Another report said, 'The enemy advanced everywhere, from the village, from the right and the left of the village, over the field towards us, up the hillside, everywhere closed up battalions (more than twenty) reached a certain point, swirled in confusion and retreated. Even in the advance his lines got crossed, the retreat was complete chaos. All in all, a colourful but confused picture of a battle.'

Oberst Jonak IR 20 Crown Prince of Prussia.
Generalmajor Hertwek his entire brigade.

All these attempts however, lacked coordinated support and barely made it halfway up the slope. The sole exception was Regiment Gondrecourt, which achieved temporary success and reached the church in front of the village, but there the attack collapsed, and they were forced to retreat to Rosberitz with enormous losses.

However chaotic the situation appeared, the *Feldzeugmeister's* sharp eye could hardly fail to see that the efforts of 6th Corps had failed, above all, because of their fragmentary nature. That at least could be corrected, and thus ensued the last great attack, the massed attack of 1st Corps. There is an enemy report on that attack, we shall let it speak.

> During the battle for Rosberitz the Austrian 1st Corps deployed to the right, and as it saw 6th Corps fail to gain possession of Chlum, set out to recapture this key position itself with a planned and energetic assault. Under the fire of its battery located on the slope southeast of Rosberitz, Brigade Poschacher moved out from [Rosberitz] while, to its left, Brigade Ringelsheim also advanced against Chlum.

We shall follow each of the two columns.

IR 34 King of Prussia led Brigade Poschacher up the slope using the sunken roads, driving off the weak Prussian units that had reoccupied Rosberitz,[59] but when it came within range of the sunken road that ran *across* the slope, it suffered such enormous losses (a total of 1600 men) that IR 30 Martini had to be brought forward to relieve it. Part of Chlum Hill was captured, but the attack failed to reach the village itself.[60]

---

59   Tr. Note: According to Strobl (p. 124), after the retreat of 6th Corps, Rosberitz was hastily reoccupied by Guards Battalion II/3 and other dispersed elements of the Prussian Guards.

60   Author's Note: We take the following from a special report of our Guards Artillery, against whose reserve batteries, the attack of the 'Iron Brigade' (Poschacher) was primarily directed, and which bears witness to the confusion of this battle and to the extraordinary bravery of the enemy, but especially to the grave danger that momentarily threatened our position in Chlum.

'At 4:30 Brigade Poschacher advanced and climbed the hill southeast of Chlum with Regiment King of Prussia, and to its right, the 18th Jäger Battalion. Batteries von Heineccius, von Mutius, von Werder and von Eltester stood fast. The Commander of the Reserve Artillery, *Oberst* Prince Hohenlohe, saw the columns advancing up the hill on our left and thinking that they were our own retreating infantry, rode toward them intending to ask them to cover our flank. Looking over towards the batteries to see what was happening, he turned back and found to his surprise that he was among the Austrian 18th Jägers, some of whose officers he personally recognized and whom he had hosted two years earlier in the barracks at the Kupfergraben in Berlin. The Austrian Jäger disregarded the two lone riders, and as he and his orderly extricated themselves from their ranks, he ordered the three Batteries Heineccius, Mutius and von Werder to fall back, Battery Eltester remained. The attack of the Austrian brigade was primarily directed at the space between the 4pdr Battery von Werder and the 4pdr Battery von Eltester, which latter was positioned nearly 1000 paces to the left of Battery von Werder. An infantry attack, probably by Regiment King of Prussia, but which according to the Austrian report was Regiment Martini (which had been brought up to the front as support), advanced to within 100 paces of Battery Eltester but was then briefly stopped by cannister fire and by the volleys of the 10th Company of the Guard Fusilier Regiment. Taking advantage of the momentary hesitation, Battery

IR 42 King of Hannover with the 26th Jäger Battalion to its right, comprised the first wave of Brigade Ringelsheim, IR 73 Duke of Würtemberg the second. Thus, the entire brigade advanced toward Chlum with the right wing by the farmstead at the *Chaussée* bridge. Brigade Leiningen followed as reserve with Brigade Knebel of 10th Corps, which joined the attack of its own accord, to its left

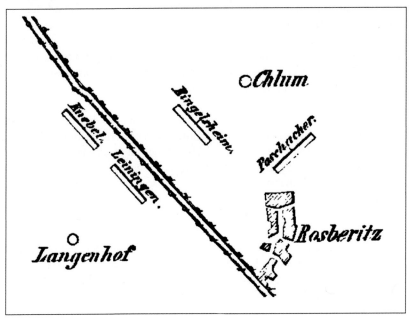

Sketch depicting 1st Corps counter-attack on Chlum.

Due to its strength, this attack promised success. Brigade Ringelsheim however, had barely passed the *Chaussée,* when it was deluged from the hills on both sides and from the village of Chlum, by small arms and artillery fire from the [Prussian] batteries that had gone into action at the southern end of Chlum. Nevertheless, the brigade pushed on.

In order to protect it from a [Prussian] flank attack, *Generalmajor Graf* Gondrecourt had Brigade Leiningen's battery go into position and open fire, Brigade Leiningen itself would swing out to the left and advance. IR 38 Haugwitz and the 3rd Battalion IR 33 Gyulai made it to the crest of the ridge northeast of Langenhof but were halted by heavy infantry fire and then by the sudden appearance of [Prussian] cavalry. Brigades Leiningen and Knebel formed square, briefly fired on each other and then began to retreat once they realised that the attack had foundered. Brigade Poschacher, whose brave leader had been killed in the first assault, followed them down from Chlum Hill, and after them, Brigade Ringelsheim [Ed: *Generalmajor* Ferdinand Poschacher von Poschach is now interred in the graveyard of the Church of the

Eltester limbered up and pulled out. (It was probably the cannister fire of Battery von Eltester that exacted the greatest losses from the assaulting enemy).'

Transfiguration in Chlum, not far from where he fell. A contemporary bust of the *Generalmajor* (by the British sculptor Alexander Stoddart) was placed in the church in 2015].

In this battle (which lasted about 20 minutes) and in the retreat to Rosberitz and Wsestar, 1st Corps lost 279 officers, 10,000 men and 23 guns, more than half of its entire complement. All this sacrifice was in vain. Chlum was not recaptured. The outcome of the day was decided.

The Recapture of Rosberitz

The 1st and 11th Divisions decide the outcome

The enemy retreated to Rosberitz, but it was clear from our position in the sunken road that he had not given up the game. Troops assembled and reformed, was a third and last great attack planned, and if it was, were we in a position to resist it? The enemy still had three intact brigades available, Hertwek,[61] Waldstätten and Abele. Was it likely that the battered battalions of the 1st Guards Division would be able to withstand the assault of 20 new battalions? Who could answer this question in the affirmative ?

Then the situation suddenly changed. A lone rider with a blackened helmet galloped up to our thin line from somewhere in the rear, 'Gentlemen, is there still anything left to do here?' It was the battery commander of I Corps, who found it hard to believe that the dense, immobile columns at the north end of Rosberitz were enemy. Soon however he learned the truth and battery after battery galloped into position alongside each other, Lithuanian Dragoons appeared to cover them, the Heavy Cavalry Brigade, *Gardes du Corps* and Guards Cuirassiers (a splendid sight!) came up between Nedelist and Sweti. The 4th Guards Infantry Brigade, Regiments Franz and Augusta moved up. The Crown Prince had by now arrived on Chlum Hill, and the advanced guard of I Army Corps with Regiments Crown Prince and Nr. 41, along with the East Prussian Jäger Battalion, *Major* von Sommerfeld at the head, marched past him through Chlum. *Generallieutenant* von Hiller was at the southwest exit of the village, right at the spot where the battalion must pass. He had been there for an hour directing the action, it was an exposed position but one that offered the best view of the field. *Major* von Sommerfeld galloped over to him to report.

> Thank God that you are here! What do you bring with you?
> My battalion, followed by the advanced guard of I Corps.
> Now everything will be good!

At this very moment *Generallieutenant* von Hiller clutched his chest, '*Herr Kamerad*, help me. I am wounded,' those were his last words. A shell fragment had pierced his chest from the side, he sank from the saddle without another sound. Thus, died *General* von Hiller at the moment of victory, a victory for which he and his division had committed their last strength.

A simultaneous flank attack by the 11th Division (von Zastrow) had in large part contributed to this splendid success. We left [the 11th Division] at 3:00 after the capture of Nedelist by the

---

61 Author's Note: Brigade Hertwek had already been sent forward but had made it no further than halfway up the hill, nor had it suffered any significant losses.

2nd Battalion of the 50th Regiment, pausing for more than half an hour to allow the division to concentrate at the northern end of the village. Then by order of the Corps Commander, *General von Mutius*, Brigade Hoffmann (Regiments 51 and 38), headed toward Rosberitz while Brigade Hanenfeld (Regiments 10 and 50), proceeded toward Sweti and Wsestar.

Both brigades advanced so rashly and impetuously, that an officer of Brigade Hanenfeld later answered the incredulous question of why it suffered so few losses by saying, 'We didn't have time to fall.' Sweti was taken by the 10th Regiment. The 51st pushed on from the east into Rosberitz at nearly the same moment that the advanced guard of I Corps reached the village from the north. The entirely coincidental concurrence of these attacks (they were not pre-planned), completely threw the enemy off balance and dealt him the final blow.

Both brigades, which had pressed forward so relentlessly (first to the *Chaussée* and then across it), did more than any other formation to accelerate the enemy's withdrawal by threatening his line of retreat. We shall meet these brigades again at the capture of Briza and Klacow (6:00).

Forward! King Wilhelm on the Lipa Hill

Even as the battle raged around Rosberitz, perhaps at the very same moment when the leading elements of I Corps debouched from Chlum, the King, who had followed the course of the battle for eight hours from the Roskos Hill, ordered an advance along the entire line. The 1st Army, which had only been held back at the Bistritz with great effort, welcomed their commander's order with joy. The divisional batteries that had been in action there, dashed off on the *Chaussée* toward Lipa, to their left the 9th and 21st regiments advanced (the 'Colberg Regiment' in the first wave), directly to the right of the *Chaussée* the brave defenders of the Holawald, the much depleted battalions of the 31st, 71st, 49th and 61st Regiments broke out of the little woods with a hurrah, and yet farther to the right, the regiments of the 5th and 6th Divisions, which had up to this point been held in reserve, now advanced via Dohalitzka and Mokrowous. The advance proceeded toward Lipa, Langenhof and Stresetitz, on a front four and a half miles long. An awesome spectacle now stretched beyond the Lipa Hill which provided an overview of the entire battlefield, even the advance of both wings.

An eyewitness wrote:

> The fog that had hitherto hung densely over the bloody field of honour tore apart, and suddenly one could see the entire Prussian army advancing in a wide arc toward the southeast, brigade by brigade, battalion by battalion. All pressed forward with the bands playing. My eyes filled with tears that I was granted this experience, many indeed, were granted this. We shook each other's hands again and again in inner gratitude to the Almighty Provider of all that is good, that He had allowed us to take part in such a great deed, that He had made us participants in this spectacle. The Prussian armies pressed implacably ever forward toward Wsestar and Briza, toward Stresetitz and Problus, the Guards, I and VI Corps on the left, Herwarth on the right with the Rheinland and Westphalia. I remained where I was and savoured the most moving spectacle of my entire life in silent, indescribable joy.

In front of the infantry or passing them on the wings, the cavalry now broke into the enemy with *the King at their head*. Another report said:

King Wilhelm himself, followed by his suite, rode at the forefront of this great advance, sitting astride his noble beast that ever since has born the proud name of Sadowa. It was a moment filled with symbolic meaning. As he reached the Lipa Hill, the point around which the bloody battle had turned for seven hours, the late afternoon sun burst through the dark rainclouds, casting a golden glow over the field, the field that was now his. The Guards troops that were here recognized him and we were presented with a spectacle that surpassed anything we had ever seen or known. Men of all the battalions, Guards, Schützen, Franz, Alexander, Elizabeth Fusiliers, all thronged around their victorious Warlord, surrounding him and kissing his hands.

He, himself, wrote, 'I had to allow it.'

The King galloped across the plateau, past Langenhof to the cavalry action that broke the enemy's resistance. Nearly surrounded by fleeing Austrian cavalry and in danger of being swept away with them, *Graf* Bismarck rode up to the king, 'As a *Major* I have no advice to give your Majesty on the field of battle, but as *Ministerpräsident*, I must request that your Majesty not expose yourself to danger in this manner.' The King acceded to this request.

We shall describe the cavalry action itself in the next chapter.

The Cavalry Engagement at Stresetitz

It was 3:30 when the King himself, already at the forefront, gave the widely heard order, 'Cavalry forward!' Near him, between the Roskos Hill and Sadowa were the two light brigades, von der Gröben and Wilhelm von Mecklenburg, these formed part of Cavalry Division Hann.[62] Both brigades immediately moved off, advancing on the left of the *Chaussée* and up the slope toward the Lipa Hill,[63] but before we follow the action, let us examine the battlefield as it was at that moment.

The enemy's entire front line was now in retreat and for the most part had already passed Sweti and Rosnitz. The attack of his 6th Corps had failed and only the five brigades of 1st Corps still held the ground between Rosberitz and Wsestar. Three of these brigades (to which as we know, Brigade Knebel of 10th Corps had voluntarily attached itself) had assaulted Chlum. The

---

62 Author's Note: Cavalry Division Hann consisted of the Heavy Brigade von der Goltz and the two Light Brigades von der Gröben and *Herzog* Wilhelm von Mecklenburg. The two latter consisted as follows:
Brigade Wilhelm von Mecklenburg.
    Brandenburg Hussar Regiment (Zieten) Nr.3.
    2nd Brandenburg Uhlan Regiment Nr.11.
    2nd Guards Dragoon Regiment.
Brigade von der Gröben.
    Thüringen Hussar Regiment Nr.12.
    Neumark Dragoon Regiment Nr.3.
Of the maps in the text, the Chlum area essentially includes the area of the cavalry action.

63 Tr. Note: The definitive study of the great cavalry action near Stresetitz is '*Der grosse Kavalleriekampf bei Stresetitz in der Schlacht von Königgrätz am 3. Juli 1866*' by Barthold von Quistorp. Unfortunately, the original edition with maps is extremely rare. Strobl's 'Königgrätz' has the best and most complete maps of the entire battle of Königgrätz.

formidable gun line on both sides of Lipa no longer existed and those batteries that had not pulled back to cover the retreat from new positions, had been captured.

Of the five [Austrian] cavalry divisions,[64] the two light divisions (Taxis and Edelsheim) covered the right [northern] and left [southern] flanks of the retreating army. The two Heavy Cavalry Divisions still in the immediate vicinity of the battlefield were the 1st Division (Prince Holstein) behind Wsestar, and the 3rd Division (*Graf* Coudenhove) behind Stresetitz, however they were also in retreat. In the centre and to the [Prussian] right [the south], stretched an open, semicircular plain, bordered by the villages of Langenhof, Problus and Rosnitz. Only beyond it and to the [Prussian] left [the north], where the enemy stood on the broken ground between Rosberitz and Chlum, was the battle still raging.

Thus, stood matters when at about 4:00, the two light cavalry brigades of Division Hann reached the plateau. Directly in front of them were the companies and half battalions of the 9th, 31st and 35th Infantry Regiments that had advanced from the Holawald, Dohalitzka and Mokrowous. Langenhof was held by troops of the Guard. The Batteries Gallus and Munk had engaged the enemy, while the other batteries of II and III Corps, with the 12th, 21st and 49th Regiments between them, followed on in a broad line.

The cavalry action (against Division Holstein) between Rosberitz, Langenhof and Stresetitz

Brigade von der Gröben was the first to reach Lipa. Both regiments, the Thüringen Hussars on the left, the Neumark Dragoons on the right, were already advancing towards Langenhof when they were ordered to bear left toward Rosberitz, from whose southern point, an enemy infantry battalion had emerged onto the *Chaussée*. However, this command only reached the Thüringen Hussars which swung left as ordered, followed by the two left flank squadrons (the 4th and 5th) of the Neumark Dragoons, the three other squadrons of the Dragoon regiment continued riding toward Langenhof.

As he advanced, *Oberst* von Barnekow, who led the Thüringen Hussars, realized that in addition to the original Austrian battalion designated for attack, two others, accompanied by artillery, had also emerged from the edge of the village (the Austrian report says it was the retreating Brigade Leiningen but is no more precise than that). To reduce his exposure to artillery fire and to avoid giving the [enemy] battalions time to form up, the *Oberst* ordered his Hussars to charge. The first enemy battalion was completely ridden down and scattered but immediately thereafter, the left wing of the Hussar regiment received a volley from the next battalion, and at almost the same time, a blast of cannister from the artillery. The right wing came under equally heavy fire and there was a momentary pause before the 3rd Squadron charged into the clustered infantry [Austrian infantry, if they had time, would form square when attacked by cavalry, if dispersed or if surprised, the infantry was trained to form 'clusters' with whatever numbers were available], while the 2nd and 4th charged the battery. The commander of the guns was cut from his horse and at this point it looked as if the Hussars would carry the day, however

---

64   Tr. Note: Now that we are dealing with cavalry and not infantry, the term division usually refers to a larger formation comprising a number of brigades (see previous footnotes for the composition of Prussian Division Hann and Austrian Division Holstein). It should be noted as a general point however, that occasionally two squadrons of Austrian cavalry were referred to as a 'division'.

at this moment of general confusion, a large body of enemy cavalry appeared on the narrow strip of ground between Wsestar and Rosnitz. It was the 1st Reserve Cavalry Division (Prince Holstein), with Brigade Schindlocker on the right and Brigade Solms on the left and somewhat to the rear (Brigade Solms had been engaged with our 1st Uhlans and 8th Dragoons on the plateau between Wysokow and Wenzelsberg [Battle of Nachod 27th June]).[65]

The 4th and 5th Squadrons of the Neumark Dragoons, who were to the right of the Hussars and had not taken part in the action against the clustered infantry, were the first to see the approach of Brigade Schindlöcker. The 5th Squadron, swinging off to the right behind the 4th, attacked the flank of the Stadion Cuirassiers and broke through the leading squadron, but then became entangled with the squadron behind, and was drawn into the enemy's forward momentum, finally becoming a part of it.

The Thüringen Hussar Regiment, to which the 4th Squadron of the Neumark Dragoons had attached itself, had in the meantime continued with its attack [on Brigade Leiningen] when it too saw the mass of enemy cuirassiers. Since it was still involved with the enemy infantry, and it was impossible for it to turn against the cuirassiers, *Oberst* von Barnekow had 'Assembly' [*Appel*] blown and tried to withdraw his Thüringians in good order. However, the Stadion and Emperor Franz Joseph Cuirassiers, together with the Nicolaus Hussars of 1st Corps, pursued him and thus a colourful, intermingled mass of Austrian and Prussian Hussars, Dragoons and cuirassiers, surged on toward Langenhof in a wild melee.

At this critical moment for our Hussars and Dragoons, the Pomeranian 4th Uhlan Regiment (part of II Army Corp's divisional cavalry), appeared on the Lipa Hill. *Oberst* von Kleist, Commander of the regiment, immediately had the signal blown to form up for action and threw his force, with the 1st and 2nd Squadrons in echelon, upon the enemy cuirassiers. After eight to ten minutes of stubborn fighting in which *Oberst* von Kleist was cut from the saddle, they were able to repulse the cuirassier brigade and pursue it over the plain (the 3rd Uhlan squadron also joined in this action). Then our thoroughly disorganized Hussars, Dragoons and Uhlans turned and rode back to (the east of) Langenhof, to rally under the protection of the 4th Uhlan Squadron which had remained in reserve.

However, before the rally could take place, a third stage of the action ensued. While the remnants of Brigade Schindlöcker withdrew toward the south, to Langenhof, the second brigade of Cavalry Division Holstein, Brigade Solms, now advanced. At this point we had no

65   Author's Note: The Order of Battle of Division Holstein was:
       Brigade Solms;
              Ferdinand Cuirassiers;
              Hessen Cuirassiers;
              Emperor Max Uhlans [Tr. Note: Named after the Emperor Franz Joseph's younger brother
              Maximillian, briefly Emperor of Mexico during Napoleon III's ill-fated expedition of 1861].
       Brigade Schindlöcker;
              Stadion Cuirassiers;
              Emperor Franz Joseph Cuirassiers;
              Emperor Franz Joseph Uhlans.
       The two regiments of Uhlans did not take part in the action that now developed. The Emperor Franz
       Joseph Uhlans had been badly mauled by our fire south of Chlum and their remnants stayed near
       Sweti, where the Emperor Max Uhlans were also positioned covering the artillery (south of Chlum our
       volley fire had, as we know, also wiped out the 3rd Squadron of the Emperor Franz Joseph Cuirassiers,
       so that Brigade Schindlocker now only consisted of seven squadrons, Brigade Solms having only eight).

forces available to hand, the squadrons that were assembling by Langenhof were not sufficiently recovered to attack the approaching cuirassiers, nor even to successfully parry them. The enemy horsemen, two squadrons of Ferdinand Cuirassiers who were slowly approaching, closed up, but rather than attack our rallying cavalry, turned instead toward the sheep farm and rode past it on both sides.

The sheep farm itself had been occupied by Schützen of the Colberg Regiment, between it and the village of Langenhof, a company of the same regiment had formed up in close order with its left flank exposed to the approaching Ferdinand Cuirassiers. These however showed no signs of attacking them (the Colberg company, the Austrian reports speak of a feigned attack), rather galloping past its front at a range of about 50 paces and thereby coming under such a murderous rapid fire, that nearly all [of the cuirassiers] who had approached the sheep farm were cut down.

At this very moment fresh cavalry forces also approached on our side, though only weak at first. One and a half squadrons of the Zieten Hussars (Brigade Mecklenburg) jumped the watercourse just east of Langenhof and attacked the right flank of the already shaken cuirassiers, rolling them up and pursuing them south toward Rosnitz. Enemy artillery fire put a stop to the pursuit and the Zieten Hussars, under *Rittmeister* von Thiele, returned to a covering position south of Langenhof.

This however did not conclude the action against Cavalry Division Holstein. Of the four Cuirassier regiments of the division, the Hessen Cuirassier Regiment (reportedly only two squadrons strong) was still intact and apparently had no intention of quitting the field without crossing swords. They trotted directly towards Langenhof but at this point we only had one and a half squadrons of the 4th Uhlan Regiment and two and a half squadrons of Zieten Hussars, that under the command of *Oberstlieutenant* von Kalkreuth, had just cleared the above-mentioned water course, and had taken position in a small sunken meadow with their left wing against Langenhof. To the south (northeast of the sheep farm) were yet another one and a half weak squadrons of the 4th Uhlans. The Commander of the 2nd Cavalry Division, *Generalmajor* von Hann, was with the Zieten Hussars. He himself provides the following description of the encounter that now developed.

> I had ordered the one and a half squadrons of the 4th Uhlan Regiment to attack the right flank of the advancing cuirassiers, while the Zieten Hussars were to attack their front. The two squadrons of Hessen Cuirassiers calmly approached in perfect order and I drew my adjutant's attention to their outstanding comportment. The officers had taken their place in front and one could hear them calling to their men, Close up! Close up! but then they suddenly turned to the left and tore off to the northeast, initially toward Rosnitz, closely pursued by the Hussars and Uhlans. Not much more was to be heard from the cuirassiers, for they rode in a tightly packed mass so that one could not get in among them. Nevertheless, their losses must have substantial while our own were quite insignificant. The pursuit was continued until we came under fire from the Austrian artillery near Rosnitz. Only then was the 'Assembly' blown.

Thus, ended the complicated cavalry action on the plain between Rosberitz and Langenhof. It was really a series of individual related actions in which, on our side, the Commander of the Cavalry Corps, Prince Albrecht [Father] took part. [There were two Prinz Albrechts in the Prussian army, father and son. General der Kavallerie Prinz Albrecht von Preußen K. H. (father) was Commanding General of the Cavalry Corps of Prinz Friedrich Karl's 1st Army. *Generalmajor* Prinz Albrecht von Preußen K. H. (son) commanded the 1st Heavy Cavalry Brigade that was attached to the Guards Corps in the Kronprinz 's 2nd Army]. All of the enemy's cuirassier divisions, first as brigades, then as regiments, had come into action and everywhere they had to give way. We shall return, later, to see the extent to which our infantry and artillery had shared in bringing this about.

The cavalry action (against Division Coudenhove) between Stresetitz and Problus

As we have seen, *Generalmajor* von der Gröben's order to attack the enemy infantry emerging from Rosberitz, only reached the Thüringen Hussars and the two left flank squadrons of the Neumark Dragoons. The remaining three squadrons (1st, 2nd and 3rd) of the latter regiment, under *Oberstlieutenant* von Willisen, continued in the direction they were headed and went past Langenhof to Stresetitz, where they took position in a small depression in the ground. They had barely found cover when they spotted an enemy cuirassier brigade approaching from the direction of Rosnitz, it was half of Cavalry Division Coudenhove,[66] Brigade *Fürst* Windischgrätz.

The enemy brigade slowly approached *Oberstlieutenant* von Willisen, who immediately fell back, partly to draw the enemy cavalry into range of the [Prussian] infantry that was forming up further to the rear, and partly to enlist the support of other Prussian cavalry if he went over to the attack. The enemy brigade continued its advance at a steady trot. The Dragoon regiment now had to come to a decision, and after falling back a bit further, it wheeled to face the cuirassier brigade, which had in the meantime, also deployed thus:

> Regiment Prince Karl of Prussia in the front.
> Regiment *Graf* Wrangel following on the wings in divisions [in this case a division is two squadrons].

The two opponents were now so close that *Oberstlieutenant* von Willisen, his right flank nearly in contact with the enemy, threw himself upon them with '*Marsch - Marsch!*' The impact was tremendous with both sides breaking through the opposing lines. The 3rd Squadron hacked its way into the cuirassiers' rear and a general hand to hand combat ensued until the cuirassiers, unable to withstand the pressure of our three squadrons, slowly fell back fighting.

---

66   Author's Note: The Order of Battle of Division Coudenhove was:
         Brigade *Fürst* Windischgrätz:
                  Prince Karl of Prussia Cuirassiers.
                  Wrangel Cuirassiers.
                  Uhlan Regiment Archduke Karl Ludwig.
         Brigade *Generalmajor* Mengen:
                  King of Bavaria Cuirassiers.
                  Graf Neipperg Cuirassiers.
                  Alexander Uhlans.
    Uhlan Regiment Archduke Karl Ludwig was probably detached, at least it was not mentioned in the after-action report nor in the casualty list.

At this moment the 2nd Brandenburg Uhlan Regiment Nr.11, *Oberstlieutenant* Prince zu Hohenlohe (Brigade Mecklenburg), drew near the battlefield east of Stresetitz, leaped over a sunken road and in squadron column, charged the enemy's left wing. Shaken by this massive blow, the main body of the enemy fell back and fled southward with their standard, while roughly one and a half squadrons, also belonging to the left wing and taken in the rear by the Uhlans, was driven northward toward the broad sunken road running east from Stresetitz. Those that did not go down in the sunken road, were felled by lances or by the bullets of the 35th Regiment which had arrived there. The right wing of the enemy cuirassier brigade, which was least disordered by the shock of the Uhlan regiment, continued their attack towards the north. The infantry of the 35th and 49th Regiments who stood in their path were courageously attacked, but in both cases the attack was beaten off. Nevertheless, the enemy brigade continued their charge against a great gun line consisting of five batteries that had been drawn up between Langenhof and Stresetitz. It was here that the heroic bravery of Brigade Windischgrätz was brought to an end. Received with cannister, the enemy horsemen, especially the Prince Karl Cuirassiers (which here, were fighting against their Prussian *Chef*[67]), were crushed.

Those who were not killed were for the most part wounded and captured. According to Austrian sources, the losses of the two regiments, Prince Karl of Prussia and *Graf* Wrangel, amounted to 378 men and 470 horses. *Generalmajor Fürst* Windischgrätz, always at the forefront of his brigade, was among the severely wounded. Even *Feldzeugmeister* Prince Karl was affected by this charge.

The second half of Division Coudenhove, Brigade Mengen, initially followed Brigade Windischgrätz. When *Generalmajor* Mengen saw more Prussian cavalry advancing from west to east, he wheeled to face them and charged, Alexander Uhlans on the left, King of Bavaria Cuirassiers on the right with the Cuirassier Regiment *Graf* Neipperg following behind.

The cavalry *Generalmajor* Mengen had spotted advancing from Problus was the 1st Guards Dragoon Regiment, the leading formation of Cavalry Division Alvensleben (which was itself advancing via Nechanitz).[68] [69] The distance between the two forces shrank as if they were flying and once the battle lines had been drawn, the Dragoons (in squadron column) attacked the

---

67   Tr. Note: The reader is here reminded of the practice, standard at the time on both sides, of regiments honouring a famous figure, domestic or foreign, as their *Chef*.

68   Tr. Note: Remember that as the result of an error, Division Alvensleben had been detached from Prince Karl's 1st Army Cavalry Reserve at the start of the day and sent to *General* Herwarth von Bittenfeld's Elbe Army (to Prince Karl's great annoyance), where it languished on the west bank of the Bistritz for most of the day.

69   Tr. Note: Cavalry Division von Alvensleben, after the detachment of Cavalry Brigade Prince Albrecht (Son) consisted of Heavy Brigade von Pfuel and Light Brigade von Rheinbaben. At 3:00 the entire division was ordered to move out from Johanneshof, Light Brigade Rheinbaben crossing the bridge at Nechanitz shortly after 4:00. This brigade, which was the only one to get into action (and essentially, only with its leading regiment) consisted of:

1st Guards Dragoon Regiment, *Oberstlieutenant* von Barne.;
1st Guards Uhlan Regiment.
2nd Guards Uhlan Regiment.

The Guard Dragoons suffered losses (from shellfire) even before they reached the actual battlefield. *Rittmeister* von Bodelschwingh was struck down not far from Lubno.

Alexander Uhlans. The two regiments rode through each other, then the Dragoons turned and after a fierce combat, drove some of the Uhlans north to Stresetitz, some south towards Problus, surrounding and capturing the remainder.

As mentioned above, the [King of Bavaria Cuirassiers] had advanced immediately to the right of the Alexander Uhlans but before they were able to wheel left and give a fresh twist to the fighting by attacking *our* left flank, the [Prussian] Blücher Hussars of Pomeranian Division Werder, appeared on the plateau and immediately attacked *them*. The enemy was pinned down before he could even form his line, the boldness of the action defeated him, and he fled to the rear [70] with the Blücher Hussars in pursuit. During this pursuit however, [the Blücher Hussars] ran into the [Prussian] 1st Guards Dragoons and the two regiments, mistaking the other for the enemy, began to exchange blows.

Following the actions above, the first wave of Brigade Mengen was dispersed, with Uhlans and cuirassiers dashing all over on the plain, but the bloodiest part of the fighting was yet to come.

Those Alexander Uhlans who had fallen back to the south, had by this time reached the southeastern corner of Problus, where *Hauptmann* Caspari of the *Rheinisch* Field Artillery Regiment, had positioned his battery. The Uhlans, met with a salvo of cannister, wheeled in a wide arc to the north of Problus and sought to rejoin the main body of their regiment that was in full flight toward Stresetitz. However, they only arrived in time to share in its fate, and those that escaped being driven onto the lances of the 1st Guard Uhlans who had just appeared, went down to the infantry fire coming from the village. Eighty to one hundred horsemen who initially escaped the general slaughter, now headed for the place where King Wilhelm (who had in the meantime appeared on this part of the battlefield) was watching events. It was a critical moment. *Flügeladjutant, Oberstlieutenant Graf* Finkenstein, galloped over with the two troops of the [mounted] Staff Guard that were on hand, intending to charge the Uhlans, but the left flank companies of the Brandenburg Fusilier Regiment Nr.35 that were present, eliminated the danger with their fire and drove the Uhlans, who were vainly seeking an escape, back toward Problus. Only a few of the horsemen that made it to Problus were able to escape toward the south.

Cuirassier Regiment *Graf* Neipperg, despite its not insignificant losses, did not get into action. The entire Division Coudenhove retreated, in part behind Briza, in part behind the 2nd

---

70 Author's Note: According to the Austrian General Staff Work it was not the Bavarian Cuirassiers that were engaged here, but the Neipperg Cuirassiers. *ALL* other accounts however (including Austrian ones), agree with our text. The casualty lists provide additional confirmation, although these too, are not that useful due to misprints, omissions and contradictions. The Austrians have a tendency to tidy everything up, doing so when it presents a good appearance. A stranger with an eye for figures will find this irritating. First, he struggles to solve the riddle until he finally realizes that he has fallen into a bottomless morass where, the harder he tries to find firm ground, the deeper he sinks. This kind of statistical game is typical [of official Austrian publications] and will only be improved when an internal reform is instituted. The Bavarian Cuirassiers lost six officers, the Neipperg Cuirassiers lost one. These numbers only make sense if the two regiments had been mistaken for each other in the General Staff Work (which we do not underrate in other respects), so that it should be revised to read, 'A thrust of the Neipperg Cuirassiers broke up the hand to hand action. The Bavarian Cuirassier Regiment wheeled to the right, no longer coming into action' (according to Austrian reports it lost, in addition to six officers, 56 men and 122 horses).

Reserve Cavalry Division [von Egbell] that was northeast of Klacow. The Austrian General Staff Work speaks highly of the cavalry when at the end of the relevant passage it says, 'The two Cavalry Divisions Holstein and Coudenhove had not sacrificed themselves in vain. The retreating army was able to complete its movement to and over the Elbe free of harassment by the enemy cavalry.'

So ended, if we consider the separate actions as a whole, the greatest cavalry battle of modern times. Not even at Waterloo, where Napoleon sacrificed his cuirassiers to the English artillery, had such numbers faced each other with the *Arme Blanche* [cold steel]. In total both sides fielded more than 30 squadrons, so that the fields surrounding Stresetitz, Langenhof and Problus, shook with the hooves of nearly 10,000 horses.[71] The losses of the two enemy cavalry divisions were heavy. According to their own figures, they lost 1256 men dead or wounded and nearly 2000 horses. Our losses too were high, particularly the Neumark Dragoons, which had the hardest fighting and fought with great bravery. They lost 12 officers and 189 men, a loss matched by only one of the enemy regiments (Cuirassier Regiment Prince Karl of Prussia).

As is true of all the cavalry actions of this war, especially 'The Great Cavalry Battle near Stresetitz', both sides took a contradictory view and both sides claimed victory, in particular the Austrians. Their General Staff Work states that, 'Brigade Solms assembled [after the action] in the depression east of Langenhof and remained there for more than a quarter of an hour despite incoming fire from all sides. However, just as at Stresetitz (Brigade Mengen), *the Prussian cavalry did not reappear here either.*' This is refuted simply by the fact that while the confused fighting between Stresetitz and Problus had not yet reached its conclusion, we already had two regiments (the 1st and 2nd Guards Uhlans) nearby. Neither regiment came into action however, as by the time they arrived on the field, there was nothing left for them to do.

We are confident that we have entered upon this discussion without prejudice, indeed with a certain predisposition towards our opponent. The courage of these excellent regiments and the misfortune that attended them, together with a desire to see the best in our enemy, inclines us to favour the Austrians in this as in many other things. A most detailed study of events however, has led us to the conviction that in this great cavalry battle, with all its confused and contradictory moments, the Austrian cavalry was defeated, not by bad luck, nor the fire of our artillery and infantry, but by our own cavalry themselves. In the end, after we had overcome our initial setbacks, we beat them, man to man and saber to saber.

It cannot be asserted however that we inflicted sufficient losses on the enemy to make him quit the field. On the contrary, our sabers (the lance was somewhat more effective) accomplished little against the thick, white coats [cloaks] of the cuirassiers. But despite our incapacity with the *arme blanche* to directly inflict death or injury, the shock of our attacks, forcing the enemy horsemen to give way before us, here one way, there another, drove him onto our firing lines in the rear and were thus the cause of the enormous losses that he subsequently suffered. Where the forces were evenly balanced (as in the two attacks of the Neumark Dragoons) we defeated him in proper cavalry fashion with *Choc* [shock], through the weight and force of the attack.

---

71   Author's Note: In contrast with other accounts, most of which have chosen to divide the overall action into three parts, we have divided it into two. Not only was there a battle on both sides of Stresetitz, there was also a battle against two separately appearing enemy divisions, thus two actions in total. If however, one is not content with this simple two fold division, there is nothing left but to come up with four, or perhaps more correctly, six individual actions.

With the exception of one case only (the Ferdinand Cuirassiers), the enemy had not been shaken by infantry fire prior to our attack taking place.

All of this is only said in [our own] defense, we would be the last to criticize the Austrian cavalry whose heroism is already a part of history. Those who witnessed it have been unstinting in their praise. 'These outstanding regiments', so one of our own writes, 'have the right to take pride in their place, as equal to the best cavalry in Europe. We had to fight them, but we can only record their defeat with soldierly sympathy. It was distressing to see the 'white coats' melt away like snow in the sun.'

Austrian Uhlans and Cuirassiers in a wild melee.

The Retreat

While the cavalry battle exacted an ever increasing toll of men and horses, it gained some time for the retreating [Austrian] infantry, who rolled on towards Königgrätz and the Elbe crossings, sometimes in good order, sometimes close to dissolution. The brigades of 1st Corps, [some] reduced to half their complement, fled through Wsestar and Rosnitz, while Brigade Abele (still intact) covered their retreat. There was no actual pursuit over the Charbusitz – Klacow – Briza line other than the fire of our artillery[72] which followed the enemy and speeded his retreat.

---

72 Author's Note: Our artillery (which has come in for increased criticism of late) maintained an extraordinary level of activity to the very end. Batteries of *all* the army corps competed strenuously to follow the advancing infantry (namely the 11th Division), and at times even overtook them. From one half hour to the next and often more frequently, positions were changed so that in the end, five, ten and finally more than thirty batteries occupied the lines Langenhof - Rosberitz, then Wsestar - Sweti,

There can be no doubt that had our cavalry pursued him directly, or indeed cut off his line of retreat (which was a distinct possibility), it would have resulted in the capture of even larger numbers of prisoners and the complete destruction of his army. Our artillery fire did indeed achieve extraordinary results however, and by the time darkness fell, the entire Austrian army was overcome with panic.

There were a number of probable causes for this. Not only was the fortress [of Königgrätz] closed [and declared 'off limits' by Benedek himself] to the fleeing army, the local area had been [deliberately] flooded thus completing its isolation. Traffic on the approach roads was jammed, and from that moment on, the situation became catastrophic. As was repeatedly stated in the later hospital reports, those at the back clambered over the top of the infantry that was wading and swimming in front, using them merely as ballast, as bridges to reach the far bank. We must leave it to others to decide how much of this was exaggeration, but it was in these final hours that the majority of the losses took place.

Letters written at the time paint a graphic picture. An Austrian military surgeon reported:

It was between 4:00 and 5:00 [in the afternoon], the retreat had already started, and we surgeons were fully occupied with bandaging the wounded, many hundreds of whom were still awaiting transport. Suddenly our own cavalry (cuirassiers and Uhlans along with artillery and supply wagons), crashed into us and surged off toward Königgrätz. Many cavalrymen fell and were trampled by the horses behind, wagons toppled over and crushed those on foot, we were never so close to death as during this retreat. The dressing station disappeared, and men shouted, 'Save yourselves!' Eight thousand leaderless horsemen [Ed: something of an exaggeration] dissolved in flight carrying along many of the wounded with them. In the midst of the screams we could hear the thunder of cannon, and shell fragments fell among us. Thus, we were swept along by the crowd without knowing where or how it would end up. I had given up any thought of survival and could only hope for salvation by some extraordinary chance. Suddenly there was water in front of us, a railway embankment to the right and a sunken road to the left which was completely blocked with our ponderous supply wagons and wagons full of wounded, behind us was an immense body of cavalry. We were ordered to cut the horses' harnesses and abandon the wagons, those of us on foot were near to desperation. Repeatedly, we waded through water that rose above our knees, fearing every moment that we would drown or be trampled underfoot. Finally, we made it to the railway station that was 2000 paces in front of Königgrätz (which was completely barricaded). Many broke through the barricades, others leaped over them, I ran behind it along with thousands of infantry. Finally, we reached the Elbe, waded through it, clambered over palisades, went on up to our necks through a second arm of the river,

and finally Charbusitz - Klacow - Briza. There another heavy cannonade was directed against the final enemy artillery positions at Stösser, Freihöfen, Ziegelschlag and Plotist. Here the battle and pursuit stopped with the 11th Division having advanced essentially to the same line:

   Brigade Hanenfeldt (from Sweti) via Briza;
   Brigade Hoffmann (from Rosberitz - Wsestar) via Rosnitz and Klacow.

It was at Klacow where, in front of the 1st Army, the advanced formations of the 2nd and Elbe Armies linked up.

climbed a rise, leaped over felled trees and arrived, exhausted, in a little wood at 1:00 in the morning, where we collapsed from fever and exhaustion. Several of my fellow sufferers built a fire and thus we lay, warming ourselves at the fire to avoid freezing to death. At 3:00 we set off again, still dripping wet, the villages we passed were empty, no villagers, no livestock, no food, not even drinking water, everyone had fled, scattering the livestock and consuming the food.

Another report stated:

We now held the *Freihöfen* [a sort of peasant commune] south of the *Chaussée*. Masses of retreating troops passed us on all sides and headed for Königgrätz where, because of the twisting roads that led to the gates, a dreadful confusion had developed. The floodgates had been opened [deliberately as part of the Königgrätz defenses], and soldiers that had been crossing what were at first, dry meadows, suddenly found themselves in a deepening expanse of water. Hundreds drowned and everyone crowded onto the narrow roads, horse drawn artillery overturned, fleeing soldiers of the Italian regiments fired their rifles. In short, it was like the crossing of the Beresina.

However, in the midst of all this panic, individual regiments would provide shining examples of discipline, bravery and self-sacrifice. Above all it was the artillery, continually moving to new firing positions, that held on to the last, sacrificing itself with rare devotion and determination.

But they did not stand alone. The 1st Saxon Jäger Battalion with the Crown Prince of Saxony in the centre, made their way (in close order) through the midst of this chaos, and with the city [Königgrätz] to their left, marched down the railroad to Pardubitz.

Several Austrian regiments did likewise. The Chulai Regiment [IR 33] found itself surrounded on three sides, but all had given their word before the start of the battle that they would rather die than surrender, and they kept their word. The jewel of the regiment, its colours, was not taken by the enemy, but was instead passed from hand to hand until it reached the top of a hill from whence it could be brought to safety. Inspired by the same love of honour, the Hungarian Regiment Wasa [IR 60], proud of its ancient reputation, held fast in the midst of the retreat and fired volley after volley. Finally, as its losses grew too great, the *Oberst* commanded, *'Gewehr über'* [shoulder arms], however the regiment did not want to retire and one of the soldiers knocked the *Oberst* down. When the nearest officer sprang forward to cut down the soldier, he himself was shot in the side. Discipline was broken but courage remained. Other regiments did likewise, though not many. Two bands left a moving impression on this terrifying scene. Standing apart from the general confusion, in a meadow in front of the railway embankment, they played the national anthem and the Radetzky March to encourage the fleeing troops and recall them to honour

The Evening of 3rd July

The view from Chlum Hill was wonderful, as the rays of the setting sun shone brightly on the fortress of Königgrätz. The battlefield, like a broad panorama, was framed by the mountains, above which dark clouds chased and collided with each other as if continuing the battle. The sun at first threw a dark red glow that paled in the clouds, light lingered in the heavens, and below, on the far side of Problus, now and then a few shells flashed as they burst.

The enemy, by now broken into many parts, dispersed and made good his retreat to Pardubitz. The 2nd and 4th Corps (we have already dealt with 2nd Corps) had already crossed the Elbe at Lochenitz, Predmetitz and Placka, soon after 3.00. As for the other corps, only a small proportion had made it to the far bank of the Elbe, some through Königgrätz, some using the bridges to its south. The greatest part of the army still remained on the near side [of the Elbe] and moved southwards on and beside the railway embankment.

For the most part it did so unmolested. At about 7:00, orders were issued that 1st Army was to place outposts toward Königgrätz, 2nd Army toward Josephstadt, and the Elbe Army was, 'to the greatest extent possible, pursue the retreating enemy toward Pardubitz', but this possibility was extremely limited. The 16th Division, *Generallieutenant* von Etzel, was too weak and the other troops too exhausted by their exertions and the battle.

The various divisions bivouacked, essentially as follows:

> The 14th, 15th and 16th Divisions (Elbe Army) near Problus, Prim and Stezirek.
> The 3rd Division at the Bor woods, the 4th at Holawald, the 5th by Wsestar, the 6th at the Roskos Hill, the 7th and 8th between Lipa, Langenhof and Stresetitz (First Army).
> The 1st Guards Division by Wsestar, the 2nd Guards Division south of Langenhof (Second Army).
> The 11th Division by Briza; the 12th by Sweti (Second Army).
> I Corps west of Rosnitz (Second Army).
> V Corps, which arrived on the battlefield at 8:00, south of Rosnitz (Second Army).

The Crown Prince had arrived on Chlum Hill with Prince Friedrich Karl before the battle had even ended. The two congratulated and embraced each other in pride and joy at the victory. From there the Crown Prince turned farther south to seek out his royal father on the plateau.

> It was a long time,' so says a letter, 'before we found him (the King). Wherever we went, he had already been, leaving behind rejoicing troops. Our ride too was like a triumphal procession, 2nd Army thanking its general who, at the right moment, had led them to victory. Finally, we could see the King in the distance and the Crown Prince joyfully headed toward him with us behind, spurring our weary horses to a last effort. The King stretched out his hand to his victorious son, unable to speak for joy. The Crown Prince grasped it and covered it with kisses until the King took him in his arms, pressed him to his breast and tenderly kissed him. No words were spoken, all present looked on with moist eyes. Finally, the King found words, just what I do not know, but certainly words of the most lustrous recognition, for he then awarded the Crown Prince the *pour le mérite*.

The troops camped so densely, and the most varied divisions were crowded so close together, that the most extraordinary scenes of meeting and greeting took place. Friends who had not seen each other for 30 years, many not since the days when they were cadets or young lieutenants, found each other again on this hotly contested field of victory.

The campfires burned at 9:00 and the bandsmen played 'Now thank we all our God' [Nun danket alle Gott, the famous Leuthen Chorale], a thousand throats and a hundred thousand hearts joined in. In the sunken roads that led down from Chlum to Rosberitz lay the dead, the wounded, and the exhausted of both armies. They could no longer be at strife. It was reminiscent of the famous scene from the Battle of Torgau[73] where friend and foe alike, exhausted and freezing, huddled round the watch fires and agreed that whoever had been defeated in the course of the day would be the other's prisoner.

While the weary fell asleep, the King drove back to the inn at Horsitz where he found nothing more to sustain him than a cup of tea and a sofa. The initial report that was telegraphed to Berlin read, 'Today we fought and gained total victory over the Austrian army, near Königgrätz, between the Elbe and the Bistritz, in an eight hour battle. Enemy losses and trophies are not yet counted but are significant. At least 20 cannon. All eight corps fought, but with great and painful losses. I praise God for his mercy. We are all well. The Governor should fire victory salutes.'

The next morning the King wrote to the Queen, summarizing the events of the previous day:[74]

On the 2nd Fritz Karl left me at about 3:00 in the afternoon after a council of war in which it was decided the give the men, who have been exhausted by marching and fighting, one or two days rest. However, at about 10:30 in the evening *General Voigts Rhetz* was back with me again with reconnaissance reports, which indicated that significant bodies of enemy troops had moved from Josephstadt to Königgrätz between 8:00 and 3:00, on this side of the Elbe. Prisoners stated that the army had concentrated between the Elbe, the Bistritz and Königgrätz. It was therefore proposed we take advantage of this favourable situation and offer battle. I positioned the 1st Army with II, III and IV Corps in the centre, Sadowa before it. *General* Herwarth with his 1½ corps to advance on the [enemy's] left flank via Nechanitz, Fritz with the 2nd Army (Guards, I, V and VI Corps) to advance from Königinhof with his left wing on the Elbe, against the enemy's right flank.

It was already midnight by the time I had settled everything with *General* Moltke, setting my departure for 5:00 in the morning since the army had to move out at 2:00. I had nearly 18 miles to drive and still did not entirely believe that the enemy could be positioned on this side of the Elbe. However, that would soon prove to be correct. As I mounted my horse in the little village of Dub, it rained and continued to do so with lengthy interruptions throughout the day. As I drove past the troops I was constantly greeted with hurrahs.

The fighting began at 8:00 with fire by the II Corps artillery, as I arrived in Sadowa and took my position on a hill. This corps was to my right. The 8th Division (Horn) crossed the Bistritz at Sadowa and attacked the wooded hill in front of it but

---

73   Tr. Note: The Battle of Torgau, 3rd November 1760, was one of the bloodiest battles in the Seven Years War in which Frederick the Great's Prussian army gained a costly victory over a larger Austrian army.

74   Author's Note: We present this letter, in part because it has become a historical document, and also because it recapitulates the events of the day most graphically and with extreme brevity.

gained little ground due to the fierceness of the defense. The 7th Division, *General* Fransecky, deployed further to the left with similarly fluctuating success. Herwarth entered the fighting from Nechanitz after 1½ hours, which from now on, was mainly an artillery battle for nearly five hours, mixed with infantry fighting in the forested hills. We eagerly awaited the arrival of the 2nd Army, for in this long artillery battle, the artillery had already repeatedly exhausted its reserve ammunition. The infantry action surged back and forth. Finally, we discerned the first signs of the approach of the Guards Corp, but we could not see the fighting since it was taking place on the far side of a hill and we could only perceive it due to the enemy flanking position.

Despite this envelopment and despite Herwarth's generally slow advance, the enemy held fast in the centre. Now the 9th Brigade (Schimmelmann), the *Leib* and 48th Regiments, were advanced to support the attack in the centre. I rode forward through the regiment, which greeted me with loud jubilation, while Piefke[75] had the band play '*Heil Dir im Siegerkranz*' a moving moment! Suddenly the artillery fire in the centre slackened and cavalry was called for, a sure sign that the enemy was beginning to weaken.

I now left my hill because the issue was being decided by the flank attack of the 2nd Army, and I rode forward with the cavalry. Here I first met the 2nd Guards Division and some of the Guards Fusilier Regiment, advancing with drums beating and twelve captured cannon in their midst. The jubilation that broke out when these troops saw me is indescribable. The officers kissed my hands which I had to allow this time, and thus I continued ever forward, though under constant cannon fire, from one troop to another, and everywhere with the never ending cries of hurrah! Those are moments that can only be imagined, only understood by experiencing them! I also met the troops of the I, VI and V Corps and also my [own] infantry regiment. [I met] only the 8th Jäger Battalion of VIII Corps and only the 17th Regiment of VII Corps. The others had already advanced too far in pursuit of the enemy.

Now our cavalry regiments broke forward. A murderous cavalry action developed before my eyes, Wilhelm at the forefront of his brigade, 1st Guards Dragoons, the Zieten Hussars and the 11th Uhlans against Austrian cuirassiers and Uhlans that were totally defeated, and the field of battle, which I trod immediately afterward, was horribly strewn with cut up Austrians, dead and alive! The infantry again advanced as far as the edge of the Elbe valley, where there was still heavy artillery fire from the far side of this river, into which I also came and from which Bismarck earnestly removed me. I then continued to ride all around in order to greet troops that I had not yet seen where I also met Mutius, Würtemberg and Bonin. All of these encounters were indescribable. I was unable to find Steinmetz and Herwarth.

What a sight the battlefield was! We counted 35 cannon. It looked as if more than 50 had been captured, and several standards. Rifles, knapsacks and cartridge pouches were everywhere. At this point we estimate 12,000 prisoners, including 50 captured

---

75   Tr. Note: Johann Gottfried Piefke, 9th September 1817 – 25th January 1884, a German conductor, *Kapellmeister* and composer of military music. He was Bandmaster of the 8th Infantry Regiment in Berlin and was famous for the many marches he composed including the *Königgrätzer Marsch* (composed after the Battle of Königgrätz).

officers. But now the other side of the coin! Our losses have not yet been determined, but they will be high. You already know that *General* Hiller of the Guards was killed, a great loss! Anton Hohenzollern has four wounds in the leg, I do not know how he is doing today, he must have been enormously brave. Erckert is seriously wounded, as is *Oberst* Obernitz with a head wound. The 1st Guards Regiment has such heavy losses that it has been reformed as two battalions. You can imagine how moved I was, and in such mixed fashion, joy and sadness.

Finally, late on at 8:00, I met Fritz and his staff. What a moment, after all that we had experienced, and at the end of this day! I myself awarded him the *Pour le Mérite*. He burst into tears, for he had not received my telegram announcing the award,[76] therefore it came as a complete surprise! I returned here at 11:00 without anything, so that I had to camp out on a sofa.

Trophies and Losses

Five standards, 160 guns, many thousands of rifles, and 20,000 prisoners were in our hands, but more significant than all that, was the realization that this victory had decided the war. The dualism had met its end, the *Bundestag* was dead and a new Germany had been born.

A great result, but at a high cost. On that day we lost 359 officers and 8794 men, including 99 officers and 1830 men killed. The 7th Division suffered the heaviest losses in the *Swiepwald*, followed by the 1st Guards Division at Chlum and Rosberitz. Here are the losses of the regiments that were in the most intense action.

In the *Swiepwald*:

26th Infantry Regiment	26 officers	709 men
66th Infantry Regiment	13 '	476 '
27th Infantry Regiment	25 '	444 '
67th Infantry Regiment	17 '	400 '

Chlum and Rosberitz:

1st Guards Regiment	13 '	380 '
2nd Guards Regimen	10 '	251 '
3rd Guards Regiment	4 '	246 '

---

76 Author's Note: The Crown Prince wrote (in his diary) of this meeting: 'Finally, after much searching and questioning we found the King. I reported the presence of my army on the battlefield to him and kissed his hand, whereupon he embraced me. Neither of us could say a word for a long time, then he found words again and told me that he was happy that I had achieved such great success and demonstrated capability of leadership. He had, as I knew from his telegram, awarded me the *Pour le Mérite* for the previous victories. I had never received that telegram and so my father and King awarded me our highest military service order on the battlefield where I had decided the victory. I was deeply moved by it and those around us also seemed moved.'

In the Hola woods:

49th Regiment	5 '	327 '
61st Regiment	10 '	370 '
31st Regiment	10 '	207 '
71st Regiment	9 '	291 '

Problus and Prim:

56th Regiment	14 '	341 '
28th Regiment	12 '	213 '

Of the generals, *Generallieutenant Freiherr* von Hiller was dead, *Generalmajor Graf* Groeben wounded. Our other losses in staff officers totaled 32.

Of those, killed or died of their wounds:

Oberst von Wietersheim, Commander of the 49th Regiment.
Oberstlieutenant von Helldorf of the 1st Guards Regiment.
Oberstlieutenant von Pannewitz of Regiment Elizabeth.
Oberstlieutenant von Sommerfeld of the 27th Regiment.
Oberstlieutenant Heinichen, Commander of the Brandenburg Dragoon Regiment Nr.2.
Major von Reuss of the 2nd Guards Regiment.
Major von Gilsa of the 26th Regiment.
Major Rüstow of the 3rd Field Artillery Regiment.

Especially grievous was the death of *General* von Hiller, who fell at the decisive moment of victory (as his father did at La Belle Alliance). Here follows a brief summary of his life.

Wilhelm, *Freiherr* Hiller von Gärtringen (an old noble family originally from Graubündten), was born on 28th August 1809 in Pasewalk, Pomerania. In 1826 he entered the 1st Guards Regiment[77] attending the *Kriegschule* [war college] from 1834 until 1837. He went on extended leave in 1842, spending his time observing the fighting in the Caucasus until 1844, when he returned and was promoted *Oberst* in 1856, and *Brigadier* in 1859. In January 1866 he received command of the 1st Guards Division, the same division in which he had commanded both a brigade and a regiment and in which he had started his military career. He entered Bohemia at the head of this division, fighting with it in the victorious actions at Burkersdorf and Königinhof. Instinctively recognizing that Chlum would be decisive, he advanced with [the 1st Guards Division] against it. Chlum, and immediately thereafter, Rosberitz, were both taken. We have already described these actions in detail.

---

77   Author's Note: He wrote in later years, 'I was fortunate to be the youngest member of this outstanding regiment, which deserved this designation and had constantly earned it. Who better to judge it than one who had received his first military education in it … The spirit of the old Prussian service that was founded by Friedrich Wilhelm I, the outlook and values that formed the basis of the Prussian officer corps had survived most vividly from generation to generation, in the old nursery of the Prussian army in Potsdam.'

During this fighting and the subsequent events' (so writes a surviving companion in arms) *General* von Hiller remained on the hill at the southwest exit of Chlum, at the location which provided the freest and broadest view and as such, was also extremely exposed, but was the most suitable place for the divisional commander. His troops, widely dispersed due to the terrain and by the rapidity of his advance, fought all around him at all the points we have mentioned. His adjutants were constantly in motion to maintain contact within the division. One of them, the young, ebullient and optimistic The Losen, was killed at the northern exit from Chlum. The general, at the southern end of the village, was often entirely alone. Only a few members of the 1st Foot Guards were near him during that unprecedented artillery barrage, remaining calmly in the saddle for more than an hour and a quarter.

That was probably an hour and a quarter of deep inner excitement! It is true that the attacks of the Austrian infantry up the slope were repeatedly repulsed, but the isolated position of the division resulting from its bold advance to the fateful Chlum Hill became increasingly critical from one moment to the next. *Rosberitz was lost.* Then four batteries of the Guards Reserve Artillery showed up just in time and opened up with a well aimed, heavy fire on the columns of the Austrian reserves. Imagine his feelings as the general viewed the battlefield! How it must have reminded him of his father's glorious day at La Belle Alliance! As his father had done, he too had plucked the bloody laurels with his heroic, bold advance. He could hardly doubt that it would lead to victory. Already the enemy was beginning to retreat, and only one concern could still trouble the general, whether the other corps of the 2nd Army would arrive soon enough at Chlum, to throw their full weight into the scales against the enemy's flank attacks. We now know how the division hastened toward the decisive point and how at the very moment of consummation of this uniquely significant mission, which it seems, had been passed from father to son, a shell struck him dead from the saddle.'

Wilhelm von Hiller was dignified, upstanding and strict, with dark eyes and hair, serious and reserved in conduct and movement. With those whom he knew and whom he trusted, he was open and spoke freely. With those whom he did not know or did not care for, he could display a chilly reserve that was perhaps, more foreboding than he intended. The chivalrous basis of his thoroughly noble nature characterized his entire being and secured for him the admiration of the best. He was greatly mourned. The King, in his letter to the Queen, named him first among the fallen. '*General* Hiller of the Guards was killed, as you already know, *a great loss.*' Songs named him 'the son of the Lion of Plancenoit:

A warrior was he, pure as steel,

> *Who knew how to win victories.*
> *He led the King's Guards to battle,*
> *Herr Hiller von Gärtringen.*
> *The fresh laurels of Trautenau*
> *Wound around his heroic brow*
> *Death for King and Fatherland*
> *He found at Chlum.*

Along with the death of *General* Hiller, the fate of the young Prince Anton von Hohenzollern stirred special sympathy. The King's letter also was most flattering in its statement, 'Prince Anton von Hohenzollern was enormously brave.' The occasion of his mortal wound has been extensively described already, we shall add only a little thereto.

Before the start of the war the Prince was travelling in the Orient. He hastened back to his regiment (1st Guards Regiment), arriving just before it moved out. He cheerfully bore all the hardships of the march with his comrades and subordinates. In the successful actions at Staudenz, Burkersdorf and Königinhof, he was a shining example of self-sacrifice and courage to all around him. On the 3rd he led a platoon of the 9th Company. At the front of his platoon he took Rosberitz and played an outstanding part in the defense of this village until he was seriously wounded by four bullets in the thigh. Captured and then freed, the youthful hero was brought to Königinhof. He died there after thirty three days of intense suffering. His last words were, 'I am greatly relieved to know that I am the one among the Hohenzollerns, whose death bears new witness to the courage of our brave army.'

> Our losses were great and painful, but they shrink beside those of the Austrians. Because the Imperial State [Austria] had never before fielded such a large army, or if it had, never committed it to a single decisive battle, the losses in men and material were greater than ever before. And just as the overall losses were immense, individual regiments lost up to half their compliment. Well might a soldier of the *Deutschmeister* Regiment write:

> Dearest Parents, the 3rd of July was the Battle of Königgrätz. It has only been fifteen minutes since I returned from it. I shall remember the 3rd of July until the day that I die. On the 3rd of July in only another quarter of an hour we would have had the Prussians. That day will remember, the 3rd of July. That is when it happened. That day we had to retreat. Oh God, that was bad. I threw away all that I had. Everyone wanted to be the first to get away. Oh God, I shall always remember the 3rd of July.

We have already listed the trophies we captured from Austria. It lost over 44,000 officers and men, including 26,000 missing. Of these 26,000 only 20,000 were captured, so that we must attribute the difference (6000), for the most part, as dead and mortally wounded. We shall probably never have exact and absolutely reliable figures for the Austrian losses. Once the great storm is over, then either interest diminishes (the dead are dead) or the numbers are altered in accordance with the differing viewpoints. Therefore, the figures given in the first weeks, despite individual errors, often remain the best. That '*convenu*' [politely agreed upon] that plays such a part in military history has not yet had time to find expression. The only lists that are unquestionably reliable, are those listing the fallen officers by name.[78]

---

78   Author's Note: The above words were written before the appearance of the Austrian General Staff Work but we believe, with good reason, that even after the appearance of that work what we said remains valid. On the other hand, we must affirm that with few exceptions, there can be no talk of an *official* whitewash of the facts or even of a reduction of the actual losses. On the contrary, here and there one gets the impression that the Austrian General Staff has occasionally added or subtracted five hundred, more or less, merely to make the enemy of that time happy.

The various Austrian military journals may vary considerably in their statement of losses. In round numbers however, give or take a few hundred, 1st Corps lost about 10,000, 4th Corps 9,000, 3rd Corps 6,500 and 2nd Corps 6,000 men. Thus, 4th and 1st Corps each, lost more than our entire army. The Saxons suffered least (despite heavy losses in dead and wounded) but their excellent discipline held them together, and their captured and missing numbered only in the hundreds.

Remarkable, as in nearly all of the Austrian wars, is the large number of senior officer casualties:

Generalmajor von Schulz of 8th Corps.
Generalmajor von Poschacher of 1st Corps.
Oberst Prinz Hohenlohe - Langenburg of 1st Corps.
Brigadier Oberst Poeckh of 4th Corps.
Generalstabsoberst von Görtz of 4th Corps.
Oberstlieutenant im Generalstabe von Gareiss of 4th Corps.

Also eight regimental commanders:

Oberst Binder of Regiment Hess Nr.49.
Oberst Slawecki of Regiment Meiningen, Nr.46.
Oberst von Ripper of Regiment Sigismund Nr.45.
Oberst Graf Bissingen of Regiment Steininger Nr.68.
Oberst von Reitzenstein of the 8th Jäger Battalion.
Oberst Bergou of Regiment Martini Nr.30.
Oberst Zerebs of Regiment Chulai Nr 33.
Oberst von Lebzeltern of Regiment Corizutti Nr.56.

All of the above were killed or died of their wounds. The total number of officers killed ran to well over 500. The number of wounded was three to four times as many. These numbers bear shining witness to the bravery and self-sacrifice of the Austrian Officer Corps. In 1849 at Novara, the officers marched in a long line before their men and almost personally won the victory. We repeat that this casts a bright light on the officer corps, but conversely, almost a shadow over the army.

Rüstow is right when, in relation to Prussian and Austrian losses, he concludes, 'The perception is that the Prussian officer corps suffered only relatively slightly greater losses than the men, this perception speaks favourably for Prussia. There can be no higher praise of the general spirit of the troops than this. For this essentially means that the officers do not have to expose themselves to an extraordinary extent in order to move their men forward or keep them on the spot. This is especially well illustrated by the 7th Division in the *Swiepwald*. The significantly greater losses of officers on the Austrian side only shows how much better is the general material of the Prussian [army].' This statement appears correct to us but we must confess in this regard, how disinclined we are to under rate or offend the defeated enemy.

Regarding Austria's losses on that day we must remember that it also lost its *Feldherr*, or that it lost its *faith* in him, it amounts to the same thing. After 3rd July, Benedek was to all intents and purposes, a dead man. Even before the defeat in all its horror became clear, he knew what defeat signified for the Emperor, the country, and for himself. Well might he feel a desire to escape it all. When he saw (so it is said) the likely outcome of the battle, he sought death, plunging into the midst of the storm. Well might he have repeated that historic line, 'Will no damned bullet hit me?' [attributed to Frederick the Great at the battle of Kunersdorf]. Officers who realized what was going on inside him did not shrink from him, but sought to cover him to the end (one was wounded). They succeeded, perhaps more than he to whom they were rendering that act of love desired. Otherwise he remained externally calm and showed no sign of weakness. 'I have lost everything but life itself,' he is supposed to have said. Soon after midnight he was in Hohenmauth. At 3:00 in the morning he dispatched the following telegram to the Emperor:

> After more than five hours of brilliant fighting by the entire army and the Saxons, in locally fortified positions before Königgrätz, with the centre in Lipa, the enemy managed to gain a foothold, unobserved, in Chlum. The rainy weather held the powder smoke close to the ground so that it prevented clear vision. Thereby the enemy succeeded in penetrating our position at Chlum. Suddenly and unexpectedly coming under heavy fire in the flank and rear, the nearby troops wavered and despite all efforts, it was impossible to halt the retreat. At first [the retreat] moved slowly, increasing its speed as the enemy exerted pressure until all were over the military bridges on the Elbe as well as at Pardubitz. Losses cannot yet be determined, but are certainly extremely serious.

The effect of this telegram, which was then wired to all capital cities, was like a thunderbolt.

The Emperor in the Hofburg collapsed. In the Tuileries one stood, crushed, before a finely spun, now shredded, web [a reference to Napoleon III]. Cardinal Antonelli is said to have cried out, 'The world is collapsing' [Casca il mondo].

As with the rulers, so with the people. In France it felt like another Waterloo, yet the people who seemed most calm were those where the blow must be felt most directly, in Vienna. The population bore up well, perhaps because they were more outraged and bitter than broken and miserable. 'Away with the old state of affairs', this call was louder than, 'Down with the Prussians'. The *Neue Freie Presse* [The New Free Press], one of the best and most esteemed newspapers, wrote:

> We have lost a great battle and will have to bear the consequences of a decisive defeat, whether the war will now be carried on with a commitment to the most extreme means, or whether there will be an armistice as the first step in the conclusion of peace. Venice will be turned over to the Emperor Napoleon so that Italy will be satisfied. The South Army under Archduke Albrecht [will be] brought [north] and the rallied remnants of the North Army, united with the army that just gained victory at Custozza, will face the Prussians.
>
> That all sounds fine and well, however what is generally said is also true, that since the fateful battle of Königgrätz, the North Army no longer exists as a tactical body. It is true that one of the most beautiful armies that Austria has ever put in the field was not only beaten by the Prussians, but dispersed, captured and destroyed. It is true that the Prussians have gained a victory such as no one had dreamed possible. Thus, we fear that the South Army too, can no more appear in time and place to stop

the enemy, to successfully defend the Imperial Capital and repulse the victoriously advancing Prussian army.

There is only one solution. Our present regime - or another, must decide to set the political machinery in motion and do what is needed. Above all that means an appeal to the feeling of what is right and honourable, to the inspiration of the people of Austria and the solution of the Hungarian question by means of an Imperial initiative in the grand style. Today it is no longer a matter of party programs, of centralization, of federalism or dualism. Today the very existence of the empire is at stake, its position, its power, its worth, its right, its honour. Who can fail to recognize these truths?

The voices 'from the camp' sound bitter. Our army has been sacrificed for what has been elevated to an *Idée fixe* since the battle of Oeversee,[79] that assaults with the bayonet and musket butt are the proper tactics. Our infantry advanced until they fell, but the leaders should have learned from the losses of the first battles, that it was not the way to success, that one does not achieve victory with dead battalions. Nevertheless, they remain loyal to this erroneous doctrine. We believe that this disregard for human life can be cited as a product of the system, but we will leave it to the reader's acuity to discern the cause. In Russia, where the same ideas prevail, the same results can be seen. One can bring men to the point where they know how to die, but do not understand how to win.

And another letter stated:

We have been ruined by two things, a blind underestimation of the enemy and a presumptuous overestimation of our own forces and means. The most recent days have finally given rise to the conviction that the art of war has become a profound branch of knowledge, and that battle is no longer a mere slugging match from which he who 'goes at it' blindly with the heaviest fists, emerges as the victor. Despite all of the millions that we have spent for military purposes ... we have lost the campaign, not because our soldiers were less courageous ... but because our military doctrine is obsolete, our strategy debased, our tactics antiquated. With all our millions ... we have failed to accommodate ourselves to the new system of conducting war and therefore the old has collapsed under the weight of a new.

The 'system' has been condemned (and rightly so), the system in state, school and army. Just as the 'twenty-four pounder' won the Danish war, so has the 'system' lost this war. Not Benedek, at least not in the eyes of the people. They support him, their old favorite, with rare loyalty, and provide a beautiful example of forbearance and enduring love, an example rarely matched in history. His mistakes are granted, but the poet's lines seem to live in all hearts:

Even the bloodiest son of misfortune,

---

79   Tr. Note: The Battle of Oeversee, or Sankelmark, took place on 6 February 1864, between the Austrian forces under *General* Ludvig von Gablenz and Danish forces retreating from the Dannevirke.

Even the most heroic warrior,
Who has been vanquished by unhappy fate,
Lives on in the esteem of men.

Since in the pages that follow (even though he successfully leads his shattered army to Moravia) we only catch a fleeting glimpse of the Imperial Supreme Commander, we shall now add a brief account of how his career ended. He continued to bear the high command until his arrival in Olmütz, thence he proceeded to Vienna where a court marital was instituted to 'pass judgement' on him. Peace had long since arrived and our troops had evacuated Austria when the Court Martial finally rendered its verdict. But there was no actual verdict, rather an evaluation, a legal opinion, an historic assessment of character:

> Difficult as it is, we must repeat the harsh words, that *Feldzeugmeister* von Benedek was unfortunately not up to so great a task, and that there are mistakes in his plans and dispositions that cannot in any way be justified by the rules of the military art . . . . However, Benedek's errors in the conduct of the war were not due to negligence, nor lack of energy, nor indifference, nor carelessness. No one could have striven with better will and greater zeal, for the victory of our army and the honour of Austria's arms.
>
> However, political and military relationships, as they became evident before and during this unfortunate war, required for their mastery one of those brilliant military leaders that are so rare in history, and among whom *Feldzeugmeister* Benedek, for all his outstanding soldierly virtues, can no longer be reckoned. That this is so, after what has happened, we can only mourn ... but *there is no book of law that declares the lack of the highest intellectual gifts a punishable offense,* and nothing else can be rendered in such cases than the essential atonement, which consists of the immediate and lasting removal of the subject from the level of employment for which he was not suited, a punishment that weighs all the more heavily, the higher and more distinguished that level of employment was.'

These words were essentially correct. History will judge him more gently.

The Day After the Battle

It was late in the day when things came to life in the bivouacs, the men had slept the sleep of the dead, but now began the searching and the burials. There were terrible sights, but the men got through it, some due to the elation of victory, some through fatigue and exhaustion, yet others were desensitized by the intensity of their experiences. One fact is certain, the men dealt with it, they kept their calm. Those who could, wrote, and many tears fell on the paper, but they also laughed again, a soldier's heart does not stay sad for long.

Where time and place permitted, under fruit trees, in the shadows of a barn, men sat together and talked about their experiences of the previous day. The favorite themes, of course, were the acts of heroism. Here one talked of a 15 year old *Fähnrich* who had just come from the cadet corps, who captured as many cannon as he had years, there of a drummer who, after the loss of his drumsticks, beat out the assault with his bloody fingers, yet again of an entire band that, surprised and surrounded in the woods, made its way to freedom with tuba and trumpet. There were additional special examples.

At Dohalitz a wagon was behind a gun that had lost its team. The driver watched curiously as the battery commander galloped over:

'Harness your horses to the gun, quickly!'
'As ordered, *Herr Hauptmann*.'
'Were you a soldier?'
'4th Artillery Brigade Sir.'
'Then you can replace the wheel driver who has been shot.'
And he did. At another place the talk was less heroic than comical.
'What are you going to do with that goose?'
'She is wounded, *Herr Lieutenant*, I have merely rescued her.'

In the 7th Division they talked about the hunt, where for a good ten minutes entire units had taken part, as between Cistowes and Chlum, a startled hare appeared. Pomeranian Grenadiers had captured a [Austrian] General's wagon that was fiercely defended (more energetically than many positions) by a Leverrier [?] bitch who was lying on the wagon seat with four pups. There was the stirring story of a Saxon *Hauptmann's* hound that howled and pulled [at people] until they followed him into a field of grain where, unable to move with wounded feet, they found his master under the stalks of grain.

There was no shortage of such stories. An officer bent down to pluck a four leafed clover for his bride at the very moment a shell whizzed right over him. As he hastened to the nearest ditch to fill a canteen with water for a wounded Prussian lying beside him, an Austrian Jäger was felled by a Prussian bullet in the middle of his Samaritan deed. These stories and many more passed from mouth to mouth. At the edge of the Sadowa woods two wounded men of the 71st Regiment had dragged themselves to the foremost ditch, as on the far side of the *Chaussée*, a Guards battalion advanced across the field to Lipa, flag flying, band playing. The two wounded got up, looked at each other and joined in, but the one did not make it to the end. Death had silenced him. Thus, the men talked in the bivouacs.

We however, shall make another trip over the battlefield, to scenes as they were on the next day. Our path takes us again from the right to the left wing.

Graves were being dug in the Problus cemetery, and mostly one did not have to carry the dead far, for they lay thickest in the cemetery itself. The cemetery, as in all modern battles, was a favourite location. The dead fall to the dead. A shell had torn a great hole in the church tower, the rectory was riddled, eleven bullets were stuck in the priest's bedroom. A sentry was posted by the great well to save the remaining water for the wounded. At the western edge of the village, behind a hedge, lay long rows of Saxon Jäger. Farther to the west, in the direction from which our attack had come, lay our men of the 56th. A funeral procession emerged from the cemetery, it was Fusiliers of the 9th Company who had borne their brave leader, *Hauptmann* von Monbart, to his grave. They had, in haste, built a simple coffin for him and decorated his last resting place with flowers. These brave men did honour to themselves in honouring their leader, as they lowered him into his grave, right by the church, they scratched his name on the wall of the house of God. Before the sun set there were many other names beneath his.

From Problus to Mokrowous is a half hour's walk. Here the meadow ground looked as if it had been plowed. Men of the 54th had spent the night in a dairy, in the morning they carried a litter on which lay two bodies, a Galician Catholic and a Pomeranian Protestant. The local priest followed in rich vestments, beside him a Protestant clergyman in field coat with brassard and pass. The one prayed his *de Profundis* and *Pater noster,* the other closed with 'Our Father.' The Catholic clergyman took the shovel and threw earth in the grave, then he passed it to the Protestant clergyman who now did the same. An eyewitness wrote, 'I got the general feeling of, I believe in one holy, universal, Christian church.'

Dohalitzka is next to Mokrowous. In the centre of the village, on an open square, stands a great crucifix surrounded by five magnificent linden trees. A shell had struck one of them and had splintered a branch the size of a man. The splinters lay all around, but the crucified Christ was intact. Before him, all powers must bow. In the beautiful church, visible from afar, were over a hundred wounded. Some hobbled in the aisles of the high vaulted church, most lay around the altar and looked upon the statue of the crucified Christ. The organ and pulpit had been removed and the windows shot out, yet it was still the house of God, those within bearing powerful witness to the homily, 'Oh come unto me, all ye that labour and are heavy laden, and I will give you rest' [Mathew 11:28]. And they *were* weary and heavy laden. One lay with his skull split so that his brain was visible, another's shoulder was torn off, he died. They lowered him into the grave on a common linen sheet (he was otherwise untransportable). There he lay in his nakedness, his wide-open eyes that no one had closed, stared from the depths of the grave toward heaven. Everything was in short supply, no straw, no water. A chaplain offered an Austrian *Rittmeister* a fragment of ship's biscuit and a drop of wine. Tears flowed from the eyes of the revived man and he blessed the hand that had done so much for him with so little.

A pretty path leads uphill from Dohalitzka toward Sadowa, a mere twenty minute walk. Here in Sadowa, the severely wounded lay in the sugar refinery between the kettles and the hydraulic presses of the sugar house. The inn where the wounded officers had been brought was already empty. *Oberstlieutenant* von Pannewitz, of the Elizabeth Regiment and *Freiherr* von Putlitz of the 49th had breathed their last here. They had already found their graves right by the statue of [Saint John] Nepomuk that stands beside the inn, right by the road 'under the apple trees of Sadowa.' Faithful hands had erected a simple cross. The Catholic grave digger kneeled and prayed while the last words were spoken.[80] Dying Austrians must also have lain at the inn. A group of soldiers, Pomeranians from the Colberg Regiment, found a little amulet in the cracks between the boards and tried to decipher the inscription. They only succeeded when an officer joined them. The inscription was in French, 'Mary, conceived without sin, pray for us.' It might have been left here by the Hungarian *Oberst* Serinny, Commander of the Würtemberg Regiment who spent the night hours in this room before he was transported to Horsitz. *Oberst* Serinny, as the *Johaniteritter* von Werder gave him a piece of *Commisbrod* [army bread] and a bit of Madeira, had taken it with the thankful words, 'And I cannot even hope to perform the same loving service for you.'

---

80   Author's Note: 'He always did that, and moved me with his devotion,' said Pastor Kessler of Brandenburg. 'In parting he asked me for a token of remembrance, and I gave him a little book so suitable for a grave digger, *'Tode der Frommen und Gottlosen'* [Deaths of the Pious and Godless]. His joy was beyond words and, with many tears he kissed my hand.

Benatek village 4th July.

In Upper Dohalitz, which consisted of only ten to twelve cottages, things looked grim. All of the wounded who could still move, mostly Austrians, had dragged themselves [out of the buildings] into the courtyards and gardens, the others were burned to death. For twenty four hours they had had nothing to drink but the night time dew. When at last help came, one heard nothing but the cry, '*Woda, Woda*', and when water was brought to them from a nearby pond, '*Dzieki, Dzieki*' [Polish for 'thanks, thanks'] came from their trembling lips.

The situation in the *Swiepwald* and in the villages that surrounded it, in Cistowes and Benatek, in Maslowed and further back, in Cerekwitz, was similar to that in the Hola woods, at whose southern point is Upper Dohalitz. Many men of the 27th and Guards Fusiliers lay in Cistowes, and what scenes in the village lanes! A Jäger, leaning against the wall supported by his rifle, stone dead. In a well, whose enclosure was smashed, a dead Uhlan who had fallen in with his horse. One of the barns was filled with Austrian wounded, one man from the Banat, from Regiment Coronini, was shot through the chest. With pitiful coughing he attempted, spasmodically, to remove the coat from his blood covered chest, he was unsuccessful, nobody understood him. Finally, someone noticed that there were still 30 cartridges in the pocket of his coat, their weight was preventing him breathing.

Cerekwitz, which had been outside the area of actual fighting, showed few signs of destruction, but in its Schloss, which had been converted to a large hospital (Dr. Wilms, who was a member of the *Geheimer Rath*,[81] ran the hospital in a manner later recognized by friend and enemy alike, as outstanding), were seemingly endless rows of beds. On one of them lay *Hauptmann* von

---

81   Tr. Note: Since the 17th century, the *Geheimer Rath* was the highest governing body in each of the individual German states.

Westernhagen of the 27th, shot through the chest. He shared the hope of all with injured lungs, 'I think that I shall get better.' The doctor consoled him, 'If that is the case with me, God's will be done.' Not far from him lay another officer of the 7th Division, he knew that he was going to die. When the clergyman got to his bed he softly said, 'I feel that my wound is mortal, my sins, of which I have committed many, trouble me deeply and I wish that I could start a new life. *Ach*, when one is young that is how one lives.' He was still for a bit then he said, 'I will probably die, but I would like to live.' A Fusilier of the 66th was carried into the hall of the Schloss, he had only just been found in a field of grain. He had been shot through the mouth and a thick bloody froth was on his lips, when one of the nursing sisters came to him and offered him a drink of wine he replied, '*Ach ja*, how I would like that, but I would soil the bottle.' All who heard him had tears in their eyes at this evidence of self-denial.[82]

There was also a hospital in the Horenowes Schloss. Here lay *Oberst* von Zychlinski. His servant had found for him a big jug of cream that had been hidden, and as the cream refreshed the *Oberst*, Pastor Besser from Waldenburg treated the jug of cream like an inheritance. It was shared with friend and foe alike and an Austrian *Hauptmann* of Regiment Mecklenburg, who had as he put it, received two bullets in the arm from the 'Prussian pea shooters,' declared that in

---

82   Author's Note: Fusilier Nuglisch of the 26th Infantry Regiment was also here in Cerekwitz. He was seriously wounded in the lower leg and later died. A paper was found in his writing case addressed to his wife. Among the many thousands of letters that were written at the time, there can be none better than his to show the best that we have, and what actually gave us victory. There is nothing simpler and more moving than the letter of this simple man, therefore we present it to you.

'I was wounded on 3 July 1866 in my left lower leg, by a shell fragment in the fighting at Maslowed (*Swiepwald*). It was an immense bloodbath. The people lay as if they had been mowed down . . . . We Fusiliers of the 26th Regiment stormed a hill with oak woods which the enemy defended strongly. Suddenly we realized that we had been completely cut off. The Austrians fired from three sides. In this crossfire I was severely wounded in the left lower leg by a shell fragment. As I was lying there in my pain I saw that the Austrians had again gained the upper hand and forced our people back . . . . I also saw with horror how they shot my wounded comrades who were lying there or struck them with musket butts. As they approached I played dead, but the monsters couldn't restrain themselves and struck me with their musket butts on the left hip bone. However our people drove the Austrians back again and I thanked my Father in heaven when I saw Prussians again . . . . The fortunes of war swung back and forth. Finally the Crown Prince came . . . . My dear reader, seeing a battlefield like this is amazing and makes a deep impression on the soul . . . . I was carried from the battlefield on the morning of 4th July to a nearby village and was left lying in a barn with several comrades. That afternoon my left boot and trouser leg was cut off and I then received the first bandages. I have been grazed by rifle bullets which are not serious, one on the left hand, one on the right cheekbone just below my eye and one on the left loin . . . . My dear almighty God and Saviour, Jesus Christ, has this day taken me under his paternal care . . . . I have the most intense yearning to see my beloved wife and children again, they who lie so close to my heart, and my good old mother. To know that I was near them would be balm for my deep wound. Even if I must die in the hospital in Magdeburg, I would sleep more peacefully in the military cemetery [there] than here in foreign soil. My loved ones could visit me then, decorate my grave with flowers and direct a prayer to God. My dear children would then know where their father was, even though he was in the grave. I shall however, pray to our dear Lord that he restores my health, that he gives me the strength to endure my pains. But I speak like my Lord and Saviour ' Not my will, but Thine be done' . . . I write this on my bed of pain . . . . If I die here, then I want this satchel and all that is in it to be sent to my wife. She lives in Magdeburg, Schmiedhofstrasse Nr.13. I am Fusilier Wilhelm Nuglich of the 1st Magdeburg Infantry Regiment Nr.26, 12th Company. If however I die in Bohemia, then as God wills, so God does, and that is well done.'

the 'whole damned campaign' nothing had tasted so good to him as this jug of cream. However, such cheerful pictures were rare. *Major* Noak de Huniad of Regiment Sachsen - Meiningen, a Serb by birth, was only lightly wounded. He hurried through all the passages of the Schloss and called for a priest, an *Unteroffizier* of his regiment was dying. Finally, he found what he was looking for, a Lutheran clergyman came to the ward of the Greek Orthodox Szegediners and gave him the consecrated host. At that very moment eleven [civilian] prisoners were brought into the courtyard of the Schloss. They had fired on one of our patrols from the edge of the *Swiepwald* and were surrounded and taken. Several of them had cartridges in their coat pockets, one old greybeard had several dozen needle gun cartridges in his sleeve. One was captured with the still warm rifle in his hands, the others had thrown theirs away. Probably these eleven rascals (four of them were later hanged) were members of a gang that had plundered the dead during the night of 3/4 July on the entire battlefield, particularly in the Holawald and Swiepwald, and it must be said, wretchedly murdered many of the wounded so as to then be able to rob them as dead. It is only too credible that awful deeds of all sorts took place, among which the stories of fingers that had been cut off so as to more easily remove rings are the most innocuous. We will leave a veil over the most horrible ones. Only the following finds a place here. An officer wrote.

> I was on duty on 4th July and had to pass over the battlefield. Whole rows of dead lay beside their rifles, mown down by cannister as they charged. Alongside them were the trophies of our victory, weapons, rifles, powder wagons, cannon. On one of them was written in chalk, 'I captured this cannon - Gottlieb Janke.' Under this another wrote, 'That is not true, I took it K. Hencke.' But I will tell you of other things. We came into a wood that lies between the three villages of Cistowes, Benatek and Maslowed (the *Swiepwald*). There the fighting had raged fiercely. A group of dead Austrians lay one on top of the another. At a little distance we saw some rascals who seemed to be busily engaged in plundering the bodies. In order to frighten them off, like vultures, we fired our revolvers and indeed they disappeared or seemed to. At that very moment, to our horror, at least twenty of those we had thought dead stretched out their arms and begged for water with weak voices. The small amount that we had with us was soon gone. I promised an Austrian *Oberst* who lay in front of the copse that we would return as soon as possible with water and a doctor and rode to the next village. However what help to be found there? Finally, I succeeded but two hours must have passed. When we returned to the woods we hardly recognized the spot. The Austrians had all been plundered, they lay there without uniforms, none of them stirred anymore. I stepped over and called, 'Here is water, water!', but all in vain, *they lay there, still*. I could no longer distinguish the Austrian *Oberst* among the dead. Horrified, we left the woods.[83]

83 Author's Note: There were other examples of Christian charity, unfortunately only scattered. We give such an example. Between Upper Dohalitz and Dohalitzka lay a man of the 49th, forgotten, suffering unspeakable agonies, no living being nearby. 'Already I thought myself close to death (so he later said) when a young girl appeared, a big wine jug in her hands, and gave me a drink. Then she brought water and washed and bound my wounds. I felt that God sent his angel.' The name of the heroic girl who helped many others in similar fashion, was Josepha Kalina, a Czech. Otherwise it must be said that it is extremely questionable whether the battlefield vultures were just Bohemian scoundrels. Many reports speak of '*Marodeurs*' [marauders], and there are many indications that such strange figures followed our own army.

Leaving the *Swiepwald* we then turn toward Chlum, to end our wanderings there. It was said that *General* Herwarth von Bittenfeld rode from Problus to Chlum early on the 4th. His son was in the Guards and his father's heart wanted to know how things had gone. As he rode out of Rosberitz toward Chlum he stopped, looked into the sunken road and shook his head, saying, 'This is worse than Problus,' and it was worse than Problus. A chaplain wrote;

> What a sight awaited us when we finally reached Chlum. Right at the exit of the village, in a sunken road, we came upon the hoofprints of the 'Red Horse' of which the Apocalypse speaks.[84] Step by step the signs of the Grim Reaper increased. Our ponies shied, a dead horse lay in the road, then another, beside it the body of the rider, an Austrian Uhlan, his saber still in his stiffened fist. On both sides of the road, whose loamy soil was coloured red (another report says, 'It was like a red stream ran down the sunken road'), between shattered wagons and carts, lay heaps of dead. The battlefield here was covered with the bodies of handsome tall men of the 1st and 3rd Guards Regiment, Guards Fusiliers from Battalion Waldersee, Braunsberg Jäger and Fusiliers of the 2nd Guards Regiment. And so we came to the churchyard. What sharp discord did the name 'cemetery' give today; every grave was decked with a fresh corpse.

In the Chlum church, whose tower and roof had been hit by several shells, the wounded lay so tightly packed that it was only with extreme care than one could move among them so as to hurt none. Resting on the altar, wrapped in his field coat, lay *General* von Hiller. Death had not wiped that friendliness from his face that he was noted for in life, rather it had transfigured it. Beside him lay *Major* von Reuss. Many of the wounded looked upon the dead and breathed to themselves, 'If only I was one of them.'

Prayers were spoken, German, Polish, Bohemian and Hungarian, loud and soft. In the sacristan's house beside the church, in a narrow room, lay two Prussian officers, *Lieutenant* von Pape of the 2nd Guards Regiment and *Hauptmann* von Braun of the 43rd Regiment, both near to death. *Lieutenant* von Pape, shot through the liver, suffered intensely and no medication could relieve his pain. 'Ach, this is not good', he said in a weak voice. *Hauptmann* von Braun, shot through the lungs, longed for a drink of soda water but there was hardly any water in Chlum. Some of the wells were dry, some intentionally stopped up and polluted (an unbelievably shortsighted act on our enemy's part). Water had to be brought with great effort from the pond at the lower end of the village. Then, when a fresh drink arrived, everyone stretched out their hands, 'Pastor, sir, I beg you, me too, I beg you, me too.'

On the evening of the 4th, the burial on Chlum Hill took place, the same spot on which the previous day's fighting had been decided. It provided a good view of most of the battlefield. Alongside the grave that had been dug for *General* von Hiller were nine further graves which were to take the bodies of the other fallen officers of the 1st Guards Division. As the result of a misunderstood order however, most of these had already been buried at another location.

Only *Oberstlieutenant* von Helldorf found his last resting place beside von Hiller. Not far from the graves, a great number of the captured guns had been collected. The King had come from his

---

84 Tr. Note: Revelation 6:4, 'And there went out another horse that was red: and power was given to him that sat thereon to take peace from the earth, and that they should kill one another: and there was given unto him a great sword.'

The church at Chlum 4th July.

distant headquarters (a two hour journey) to honour his fallen general, even in death. The Royal Princes also attended the ceremony, all of the officers of the division were there too. Divisional Chaplain Rogge stepped up to the graves and spoke on the text, 'The noblest in Israel are slain on this hill. How are the heroes fallen!' Visibly moved after the ceremony ended, the King threw his handful of earth into the two graves, then it was *'Legt hoch an!'* [Present arms, aim high] and the bullets whistled above the dead.

The next day *Oberst* von Pape buried his only son. His last resting place had been prepared by his comrades on the north side of the Chlum church. The grave was laid with green twigs and leaves, and the departed was lowered into it, wrapped in four military coats. The regimental band played the hymn, 'What God does, that is well done' and concluded with 'How peacefully you rest.' The chaplain who conducted the service wrote, 'There I saw what strength the Christian faith provides. The father's heart may well have bled from many wounds, as he had to leave his son here in foreign soil, but he remained steadfast and firm, and as the ceremony ended and the grave was closed, he turned to the officers of his regiment that were gathered around him with the words, 'Gentlemen, that lies behind us, we however go forward with God, for King and Fatherland.'

There were burials everywhere on the broad field, mostly quiet, in mass graves without song or music. The love of the comrades had barely found enough time to erect a simple, nameless cross. But our hearts also beat gratefully for those, the nameless.

> *Sleep still and true,*
> *Until the last day,*
> *When a new morning,*
> *May quicken you again!*
> *Golden memories bloom,*
> *As you rest.*
> *In victory was it granted to you,*
> *To die for the Fatherland.*

Early on 5th July the Army moved out, marching south. The work was done, the wounded in their wards (hard enough), the dead in their graves, but not all, there were just too many of them. Even by the 8th the field had not been fully cleared.[85] An officer of VI Corps, who rode over the battlefield that day from Nedelist where he had a command, has given us the following description:

This past Sunday (8th July) I had my horse saddled, the 'Bella' whom you know, to ride alone one last time over the battlefield. I had nothing with my but my servant and a great black hunting hound, the gift of a dying Austrian officer. Sitting in my bedroom I did not know what I would find. The setting sun already cast its last rays on the field as I rode out of Nedelist, and the cool evening breeze carried the stink of the corpses and blood toward me. Anyone who was not accustomed to this stench would faint on the spot. I knew it well enough and rode on in order to get to Chlum and Sadowa, where the main battle had been fought.

Dead silence reigned all around, only broken at times by the uneasiness of my horse and hound. As soon as we came to the place where a wounded man had lain, Bella snorted, flared his nostrils and stamped his hooves on the ground, the hound ran in circles round the designated spot and howled horribly. Only after encouragement with the spurs did the horse move forward, finally a lark flew up, climbing singing into the sky, but with a song such as I have never heard elsewhere. It climbed more than it sang.

I rode further without having any specific purpose in mind. *Ach*, what a sad scene was presented here! Around twenty dead were lying around the statue with open, broken eyes, directed toward the statue of Mary. Others held rosaries and crucifixes in their hands, they had probably prayed until their last breath. The bodies exhibited all sorts of wounds, only a few seemed to have died at this spot. Most had crawled there to end their lives in sight of the statue of the Mother of God. I sprang from my horse and kneeled down to pray for the dead.

---

85   Author's Note: The Bohemian villagers refused, in part, to help digging graves, and growled to themselves in Czech, 'Let the Prussians bury those that they killed.' More than once they only went to work when a section stepped forward and the command was given 'Prepare to fire!' That seemed to help every time and then even the most nationalistic understood German. (Such isolated incidents in no way altered the fact that the better class of Czechs were generally more favourably disposed toward us than the German Bohemians.)

I rode back via Wsestar and Sweti. Close to Sweti, on an elevated position where a battery must have been located, was a sponge staff. An Austrian artilleryman was leaning on the sponge staff as if he was asleep. He had been shot under both arms and stood like a shadow against the ever darkening heavens. It moved me deeply, I still see that picture in mydreams.

From Königgrätz to Before Vienna

On 4th July

Prague itself was among the trophies of 3rd July although it wasn't occupied until the 7th. Before we turn to this however, let us spend a few moments on the 'Day of the Battle', not with scenes resembling those with which we closed the previous chapter, but with events of a more general, if less significant nature. The first opened with a Hussar's stroke.

On the morning of the 4th, *Lieutenant* von Wrangel of the Guard Hussars was ordered to advance with 30 men towards the fortification of Königgrätz and to reconnoiter the enemy's outposts (our own outposts were about a mile before the city, beyond the range of the fortress guns).

Von Wrangel moved out and about 2,000 paces from the fortress, encountered a long column of baggage, ammunition, medical and supply wagons, easily 300 of them, surrounded by a mass of Austrian and Saxon wounded, thus preventing the fortress guns from firing on the road. This protected, to a certain degree, the movement of our troops. *Lieutenant* von Wrangel rode on with two Hussars to post a *vedette* near the fortress. Here he suddenly encountered an Austrian double sentry post which was positioned on a bridge across an arm of the Elbe, only 80 paces from the Hussars. Both sides were surprised but the situation demanded rapid action, with a few steps von Wrangel had galloped over the bridge and demanded the surrender of the sentries with drawn revolver. They surrendered, and then an amazing scene ensued. In contact with this outpost were other posts at intervals of 100 paces, surrounding the fortress in a semicircle. In order to bring these in, *Lieutenant* von Wrangel blew on his signal whistle, waved with his hand and called to them. Within a half hour the chain of outposts had vanished, and we had taken 35 men prisoner (according to another version, only 12).

Convinced by these events of the complete demoralization of the enemy, *Lieutenant* von Wrangel believed that he could go further. It did not seem impossible to him that the fortress would capitulate. Therefore, while the main body escorted the prisoners, von Wrangel, with a single Hussar, galloped to the gate of the fortress, waving his pocket handkerchief to make it clear that he was a *parliamentaire*. He was received at the door and taken, blindfold, to the Commandant, *Generalmajor* von Weigl. The Commandant received him in the presence of his staff and accepted the improvised declaration, 'His Royal Majesty the Crown Prince stands before Königgrätz with a victorious force of 150,000 men. The entire Austrian army is in flight. The fortress, cut off from any contact with its army, cannot withstand an attack. Therefore, in order to forestall unnecessary bloodshed, the Crown Prince offers the Commandant the opportunity for an honourable surrender.'[86] Such was the self-confidence with which the proposal

---

86   Author's Note: The garrison of the fortress consisted only of three 4th battalions of Regiments

was presented that *General* von Weigl requested 24 hours to consider it so that the details of the surrender could be determined. *Lieutenant* von Wrangel then brought this message to the Crown Prince, who then had the negotiations, as fortunate as they were unexpected, continued by a General Staff officer. However, they collapsed, it was later asserted that the Austrians never had any serious intention of surrendering. We can leave it at that.

The appearance of the Guard Hussars at Königgrätz and the subsequent negotiations, took place on the morning of the 4th. In the afternoon *Feldmarschiallieutenant* Gablenz [commander of the Austrian 10th Corps], appeared at the Royal Headquarters in Horsitz and proposed the cessation of hostilities, since after the great action of the previous day, the campaign was decided. He was given the response that [Prussia] was indeed prepared to negotiate a definitive peace on political grounds, but that an operational standstill of the Prussian army was out of the question. *Baron* Gablenz, who was not empowered to negotiate, had to be satisfied with this and left the Supreme Headquarters under escort. (He returned again on the 8th to propose, under certain conditions, a ceasefire of no less than 8 and no more than 12 weeks. Since the objective of this proposal was clearly to gain time for the South Army to be brought up from Italy, this did not result in any negotiations either. *Baron* Gablenz spoke to the Crown Price, the King did not see him). On 4th July King Wilhelm also issued the Army Order in which he spoke to his soldiers of the victory attained:

Soldiers of my armies assembled in Bohemia! A series of bloody and glorious actions has made possible the junction of our assembled forces in Bohemia. I see from the reports presented to me, that these results have been achieved by the unfailing leadership of my generals and the devotion and courage of all of the troops. For those very reasons, despite all of the exertions and deprivations of recent days, the army has, under my leadership, energetically attacked the enemy in a strong position near Königgrätz, captured the well defended position after intense fighting and gained a glorious victory. Many trophies, over a hundred captured cannon and thousands of prisoners, bear new witness to the courage and devotion in which all arms of the service have competed with one another. The day of Königgrätz has exacted great sacrifice, but it is a great day for the entire army upon which the Fatherland looks with pride and awe. I know that you will continue to meet my expectations, for Prussian troops always know how to unite their heroic spirit with that discipline, without which great success cannot be attained.

                                                                                    Wilhelm.

The Garde Landwehr in Prague

Before we follow our three great armies on their further progress to the Danube, let us in a bloodless interlude, follow the advance and imminent detachment of a fourth army, that

---

Mazzuchelli, Airoldi and Grand Duke Constantin. They belonged to the brigade of *Generalmajor* Tomas, who was in Josephstadt with the 4th Battalions of Regiments Khevenhüller, Degenfeld, Haugwitz, Ramming and Crenneville.

likewise on 3rd July, arrived on our right wing (admittedly after the battle was over) in and around Nechanitz. It was the Guards *Landwehr* Division Rosenberg.[87]

A letter that we have provides information regarding the efforts that were made to reach the battlefield in time:

We moved out of Kopidlno (which we had reached the evening before) early in the morning. The distance to Königgrätz was about 22½ [English] miles. The roads had turned to mud, it was miserable. Nevertheless, we forced march and whoever or whatever fell by the wayside was left lying. At 11:00 we were in Bitschow, still nine miles from the battlefield. I was given nine houses for the company, in which I assigned them quarters for an hour and a half. The horses had to be housed in the front room of an abandoned house but soon settled down in these unfamiliar quarters when their oats were poured into the emptied drawers of a chest. Two retired Austrian captains, twin brothers, who had turned over their sofa to me, gave me a cup of coffee, a pipe and tobacco, filled my saddlebag with hard boiled eggs, and one after the other, assured me that 'The Prussians march like the devil.' Then they had an *Amsel* [a species of Thrush] whistle the *Mantellied*[88] while I tried to catch a bit of sleep. Then the 'Alarm' was blown and 15 minutes later we marched out of the town. In the woods, half an hour farther east, we could already hear the thunder of the battle and proceeded to a hill where we could see the movement of columns, the fire of artillery and the surge of battle. We continued on to Nechanitz, the big houses were full of wounded, the churches full of prisoners. Forward by a forced march to the battlefield, an inspiring thought that dispelled our weariness but it was terrible. There were many dead, Austrian cavalry either cut down or shot down, eight places were on fire . . . . We bivouacked on the sodden ground, wet and hungry. Only the next morning did we learn that the decisive battle had been fought.

87   Author's Note: The Guards *Landwehr* Division, under the command of *Generalmajor* von Rosenberg - Gruszcynski, formed the first echelon of the Reserve Army Corps. The second echelon was the *Landwehr* Division Bentheim. Just as the Guards *Landwehr* Division Rosenberg followed the Elbe Army (it had, for example, relieved [the Elbe Army] in Dresden), so *Landwehr* Division Bentheim followed Division Rosenberg. *Generallieutenant* von der Mülbe commanded the two divisions. Their compositions was as follows:
    Guards *Landwehr* Division von Rosenberg - Gruszcynski.
        1st Guards *Landwehr* Regiment, *Oberstlieutenant* Ranisch.
        2nd Guards *Landwehr* Regiment, *Oberst* Fronhöfer.
        1st Guards Grenadier *Landwehr* Regiment, *Oberstlieutenant* von Roehl.
        2nd Guards Grenadier *Landwehr* Regiment, *Oberst Freiherr* von Putlitz.
    Combined *Landwehr* Infantry Division von Bentheirm.
        2nd Pommeranian *Landwehr* Regiment Nr.9, *Oberst* Orlovius.
        4th Pommeranian *Landwehr* Regiment Nr.21, *Oberst* von Suchten.
        1st Westphalian *Landwehr* Regiment Nr.13, *Oberstlieutenant* von Rekowsky.
        2nd Westphalian *Landwehr* Regiment Nr.15, *Oberstlieutenant* von Rentz.
    The Army Corps also contained a combined *Landwehr* Cavalry Division and a Reserve Field Artillery Regiment.
88   Tr. Note: A song occurring in the musical comedy (*Liederspiel*) Lenore (1829) by K. von Holtei (Oxfordindex).

The division was not granted a lengthy rest, it had to achieve its march objective. Already at 4:00 [in the morning], it was ordered to follow the enemy toward Prelautsch. At 5:00 it was shifted west (roughly toward Prague) in order to cover the right flank of the march of the three great army columns. Reinforced with two rifled batteries of the 7th Artillery Regiment, the division initially marched to Podiebrad, where it crossed the Elbe, and then proceeded in two days via Sadska and Ober Pocernitz, to the immediate vicinity of Prague. Prague was not held by the enemy. At noon on the 7th the leading elements of the division, the 1st Guards *Landwehr* Regiment, under *Oberstlieutenant* Ranisch was in the village of Chwala, an hour from the capital and a card, with the following message, was sent on to the *Bürgermeister*, Dr. Belsky:

> Ranisch, *Oberstlieutenant* and Commander of the 1st Guards *Landwehr* Regiment, designated Commandant of Prague, desires that the higher civilian officials come out to the village of Shwala so that they can discuss the occupation of the city in its own interests.

As a result of this card, at 4:30 in the afternoon, the *Bürgermeister* and the Cardinal Archbishop *Fürst* Schwarzenberg, drove out to Chwala in the Archbishop's carriage. When the carriage arrived before the village, the members of the deputation held white flags out of the window openings and the entire group were halted by our sentries. The gentlemen then exited their carriage and were escorted to the quarters of *Oberstlieutenant* Ranisch. The Cardinal delivered a speech in which he implored the victors to take to heart the wellbeing of the city. Dr. Belsky spoke in the same vein. *Oberstlieutenant* Ranisch informed them that Prague would receive a garrison of 8,000 men and in general, gave the most reassuring promises. The deputation returned to the city and entry took place on the morning of the 8th, in the meantime the main body of the division had arrived. *Generalmajor* von Rosenberg took his position at the front, and in the midst of a great throng (only the Imperial officials had fled) proceeded with drums and fifes through Carolinenthal and the Spittelthor into Prague, along the Spittelstrasse to the Josephsplatz.

The 1st Guards *Landwehr* Regiment immediately proceeded to the Hradschin where the Prussian flag was hoisted. The regiments that followed occupied the Joseph and Ferdinand Barracks. The *Bürgercorps*, where they were on watch in the *Altstadt* [Old City], at the gates and on the *Kleinseite*, were relieved. Only the posts on the Wischerad, in front of the *Provinzialstrafhaus* [the provincial jail] and the *Invalidenhause* remained in their hands. Twelve guns went into position directly before the Hofburg and off duty infantry carried their needle guns (at least at the start). Nevertheless, the caution of the one side and the avoidance of the other did not last long. Contact between the men of the *Landwehr* and the local citizens became friendlier each day. The people were soon convinced that the 'terrible Prussians' were not all that terrible. As a sign of growing trust, Austria's favorite dish was set before them, but here the friendly innkeepers made a mistake. As a Prague newspaper wrote at the time, 'We really had the best intentions toward the Prussians when we served them the favorite meal of our own soldiers, dumplings [*Knödel*]. Our guests however, seemed not to particularly care for this delicacy, and thus the dumplings, ordinarily the occasion of soldierly contentment, were distributed by the Prussian *Landwehr* men among our poor folk.'

Days in Prague were days of recovery, for even though they had not come up against the enemy, the Guards *Landwehr* Division had not lacked strenuous exertions. Now the men enjoyed the benefits of a great city, and in addition, a comfortable billet. In the afternoon hours all the streets were filled with curious *Landwehr* men who admired the historic buildings, the splendid monuments, the Teinkirche, the Nepomuk bridge and the Kettenbrücke [Chain Bridge]. In the morning one could even see individuals swimming in the river through the arches of the bridges. The beautiful sites were also visited, the officers especially visited the Schwerin Memorial, erected in gratitude to the '*Feldmarschall* who had fallen with the flag at Prague.'

The evenings presented a particular picture of contentment. The entire off duty garrison assembled on the two Moldau islands where Prague's fashionable set was accustomed to gather, in merry mood and elegant dress for the concerts.

The occupation of Prague was significant for more than one reason. It put an end to the authority of the Imperial officials (who could incite an uprising in our rear). It covered the flank of our army towards Bavaria, and provided, admittedly with a substantial detour, a rail link between Turnau and Pardubitz. In other words, our army regained unbroken rail communication with the north, in spite of [the Austrian held fortresses of] Josephstadt and Königgrätz. Throughout the entire course of the campaign, Prague remained occupied by our forces, though the garrison was changed. The Guards *Landwehr* Division moved on to Brünn and were replaced by *Landwehr* Division Bentheim.

The Austrian Army as Far as Olmütz

The Retreat to Vienna

Prague was ours. Holding it had never been part of the *Feldzeugmeister's* plan and after the catastrophe of the 3rd, it was totally out of the question. Keeping the army together and not splitting it into detachments as it retreated south, was his main objective. Benedek correctly resolved to assemble the remnants of his army under the protection of the fortress at Olmütz, allowing it to rest and recuperate, and imbuing it with fresh spirit.

Here the *Feldzugmeister* displayed all his talents, especially in the clear and resolute manner in which it was carried out. It was a matter of preventing the dissolution of an army that was *en déroute* [in flight] and concentrating it at a given location. It happened quickly and without confusion, the troops one might say, exceeding expectation. Three army corps (1st, 3rd and 6th) and the Army Artillery Reserve proceeded via Hohenmauth, four corps (2nd, 4th, 8th and the Saxons), along with the [2nd] Light Cavalry Division, *Taxis*, via Wildenschwerdt. Only these two roads were available and by the 11th the army was in the great fortified camp around Olmütz. The 10th Corps, the [1st] Light Cavalry Division Edelsheim and the three heavy cavalry divisions were ordered back to Vienna, 10th Corps was to be transported by rail.

Benedek's plan (to prevent our advance on Vienna by taking a flanking position at Olmütz) was not carried out. Probably even before King Wilhelm's decision to, 'leave only the 2nd Army before Olmütz and advance with the two other armies via Brünn and Znaym to the Danube,' the Emperor himself issued the order to give up the position at Olmütz, and hasten with all of the corps to the endangered capital. This order had to be obeyed and the *Feldzeugmeister* immediately issued the appropriate instructions. 3rd Corps and a portion of the Saxons were sent south in forty trains, all of the other corps however, according to a march plan issued on 13th July, were to march on foot via Kremsier, Göding, and Stampfen, down the valley of the March River and thence to Vienna. On the 14th, the 4th and 2nd Corps moved out, on the 15th, the 8th and 1st Corps successfully passed the line to which our 2nd Army (already past Olmütz and directly on their right flank), had advanced. The serious action in which the retreating 8th Corps became involved, left no doubt that an unhindered retreat[89] down the valley of the March to Vienna or Pressburg, would be impossible. Therefore, the *Feldzeugmeister* decided to alter the direction of the main body of his army. Orders were issued to abandon the [river] March line and to swing out left (thereby crossing the Little Carpathian Mountains), following the valley of the Waag River, reaching Pressburg circuitously, and then on to Vienna.

We shall return to this. The Austrian corps (still the 4th, 2nd, 8th, 1st and 6th) again proved themselves in performing an outstanding march.

It was impossible to follow them directly as it would have caused our 2nd Army (which formed our left wing), to move increasingly to the left and thereby lose contact with the other two armies. So, we did not interfere with the enemy's march, and while his five corps followed the route described above, we proceeded in a straight line toward the capital city, or more correctly, toward the land that lay between Vienna and Pressburg, the Marchfeld. Since we (namely our 1st and Elbe Armies), were at least level with the enemy as he began his circuitous march, our forces were presented with the opportunity of arriving on the Danube before him. If that succeeded, while we could not absolutely deny him the possibility of reaching Vienna, we would at least force him to swing farther out, and by further detours, come to the aid of the endangered capital from the south instead of from the east.

Such a result seemed highly desirable since it would delay the junction of the enemy armies. Therefore, all efforts were made to insert our forces between the enemy army proceeding from Olmütz, and the enemy army that was already at Vienna. Our 7th and 8th Divisions celebrated yet another day of great achievement, however just as the fruit of these exertions were being plucked and the 'Battle of Blumenau' was about to open the gates of Pressburg, the armistice took effect. This was on the 22nd July. The fighting in the eastern theatre concluded with the action at Blumenau. It was preceded by a number of encounters, some big, some small, and we shall return to these in due course but first, leaving aside all warlike matters and limiting ourselves to the peoples and landscapes of this march, we shall accompany our three great columns on their progress through Bohemia and Moravia. We shall let eyewitnesses speak and go back and forth between the two armies.

Through Bohemia and Moravia

'Pardubitz, 6 July,
The Advance Guard of our 2nd Army[90] arrived here yesterday. We have the headquarters of the Crown Prince here. The King and the Supreme Headquarters are expected

---

89   Author's Note: An unhindered retreat became all the less probable when on that same day (the 15th) serious fighting took place at Tobitschau and Prerau with the advance guard of the 1st Army. A flank attack (from Brünn against the vital rail point at Göding) was conducted and thus the withdrawing enemy could be certain at somewhere along the [river] March, our armies would seriously endanger his right flank.

90   Author's Note: Our three armies, marching in three great columns, had met on the battlefield of Königgrätz, and (on the 5th) they departed from it in three columns to follow the retreating enemy via Pardubitz to Olmütz. They maintained their relative positions, the 2nd Army (Crown Prince) took the left wing, the 1st Army (Prince Friedrich Karl) the centre, and Elbe Army the right wing. In other

tomorrow or the day after. Of all the Bohemian cities that I have yet seen, Pardubitz is the *most* Bohemian, with great, picturesque charm. It lies at the confluence of the little Chrudimka river and the Elbe. Two suburbs adjoin the city and actually exceed it in numbers of houses and inhabitants. Of the two city gates, the green and the white, only the first is provided with a tall, slender tower. Handsome houses with Italian gables surround the spacious *Ringplatz*. The *Rathaus* [city hall] catches the eye on the west side, on which can be seen the coat of arms of the former Lord of Pardubitz, which are at the same time, the Coat of Arms of the city, the front half of a white horse on a red field. There is an interesting story behind this coat of arms. One night, when King Wladislaus II of Bohemia was with the army of Friedrich Barbarossa before Milan in the year 1158, Bohemian warriors scaled the walls of the Lombard capital and entered the city. Heavy fighting broke out and the Bohemians, confronted by superior forces, had to fall back through the gate through which they had already admitted some of their own troops waiting outside. A knight, *Ritter* Jezek von Pardubitz, only made it back to the gate as the Milanese dropped the portcullis, falling on his horse and splitting it in two. The Bohemian knight lifted the front half of the horse onto his shoulders and bore it before his king, who was so pleased with this heroic deed that he awarded the brave knight the half horse as his coat of arms.

Beside the *Rathaus* is the Schloss, the most important building in the city, built by Wilhelm von Pernstein in the 16th century. In his time, it was an important citadel, but now it serves only peaceful purposes, its spacious rooms are used for residences,

words, the three armies set out in towards Vienna via Olmütz (left), Brünn (centre), and Znaym (right). The following table best presents the lines of march that they followed.

July	2nd Army	1st Army	Elbe Army	Headquarters
5	Opatowitz	Prelautsch	Chlumetz	Horsitz
6	Pardubitz	'	'	'
7	'	Hermanmestetz	Neuhof	Pardubitz
8	Hohenmauth	Chrast	Goltsch Jenikau	'
9	Leutomischel	Richenburg	Deutsch Brod	Hohenmauth
10	Mährisch - Trubau	Neustadt	Iglau	Zwittau
11	'	Pernstein	'	'
12	'	Brünn	Trebitsch	Czernahora
13	Opatowitz	'	'	Brünn (In Moravia
14	Konitz	'	'	'
15	'	'	Znaym	'
16	March to the right by the Guards and VI Corps from Olmütz to Brünn	Pawlowitz	March to the left from The Znaym - Vienna Road to the Brünn-Vienna road.	'
17		Lundenburg	Mittelbach - Wülfersdorf	'
18		Feldsberg	'	Nicolsburg to the 29th
19		Duernkruth	'	'
20		Ebenthal	Wolkersdorf -Gaunersdorf	'

The 2nd Army (Crown Prince), as of the 16th, ceased to exist as one body and operated in three parts: I Corps (East Prussia) was left behind to observe the fortress of Olmütz. VI Corps (Mutius) and the Guards shifted to the right, toward Brünn, behind the 1st Army, only V Corps (Steinmetz) advanced in the originally planned direction, southward down the March. On the 19th it reached Napagedl, on the 20th Ungarisch Hradisch.

offices and an archive, some are empty. The bastions are now gardens with pavilions, the battlements are now alleys and paths, the moat has been transformed into a little garden, the slopes below the walls are planted with fruit trees and vineyards. The exterior of the castle, to which one has access through a side street from the square, is imposing. One must pass through three gates and an arched bridge to get to the actual stronghold.

The present importance of the city comes from its ever growing rail traffic, its splendid, nearly mile long double railway station, and above all, its *horse races*. At the start of October, when the races take place, high born cavaliers stream in from Bohemia, Vienna, Hungary, Prussia *etc.,* so that at this time, Pardubitz houses more of the upper nobility than many medium or large sized German cities. It swarms with jockeys, liveried servants, grooms, stablemen and racegoers from Prague. Immediately after the racing, hunting with hounds begins and extends well into November. The broad plain offers the most favourable going and at the same time, the numerous ponds and meandering streams add to the variety and excitement of the sport.

Pardubice.

The number of inns is in proportion to the liveliness of the city and after the exertions of recent days, we made the greatest possible use of their presence. The martial and ever changing picture that the market place presents is enthralling, and one friendly reunion follows another. May we too be so blessed. We live in hopes that the great work is already accomplished and that the war is coming to an end.

Hermanmestetz, 7 July

Archduke Wilhelm von Mecklenburg has arrived here with the newly formed advance guard of the 1st Army, consisting of the entire 60th Regiment with the Fusilier battalions of Regiments 18 and 48, the 4th Jäger Battalion and some artillery and cavalry. Everything here is very different from the villages and cities we have previously passed through. The panic which the defeat at Königgrätz occasioned among the country folk has not extended south of the Elbe, and no one has abandoned the houses or farmsteads. Everyone is working, peasants work the fields, the villages throng with women and children and the shops offer their wares for sale.

Our marches are seldom on the main roads, most are on narrow country roads or over meadows and past low lying water mills, which give the landscape great charm. From the crests of the hillocks that we reach now and then, we look across a broad, fruitful plain, and on the horizon, at a distance of about twenty five to thirty miles, a blue mountain range that separates Bohemia from Moravia. Everywhere the grain is magnificently golden and perfects the rural scene.

The town of Hermanmestetz is thoroughly and entirely Bohemian [Czech]. Only a few of the residents, even of the better classes, speak German, and the signs on the shops and inns are all in Bohemian. As soon as the troops marched in and were released to their quarters, they pounced on the shops and called for tobacco and cigars, the same for coffee which was soon entirely sold out. Every taproom is filled with a hungry crowd that greedily calls for food, beer and wine. Knapsacks are heaped on the benches, rifles piled in the corners, and the men crowd around the tavern tables as each try to win the innkeeper's attention. Even though hungry and thirsty, the soldier's mood is always good.

When darkness falls the noise stops and the throng in the streets vanishes as the men seek their night's lodging. Some sleep in the houses on straw, others in barns, many in the gardens for there is not enough space in the houses, and aside from this, many prefer the mild summer air to a stuffy room. And thus, deep silence now reigns in the previously noisy town, and the only sounds that one hears are the steps of a sentry and the whinny of a horse.'

Chrast, 8th July.

Our 1st Army under Prince Friedrich Karl, is now here and distributed around Chrast. The 8th Division is in the town itself, the main body is on the road between Mährisch and Trübau, while the Elbe Army is advancing toward Iglau on our right. There is much talk of peace, but the army continues its advance while taking all precautions. The fields were searched in sequence by skirmishers who kept the same pace as the marching troops, searching through the grain with the same care and caution as if they were hunters who wanted to find the fox in his den. The infantry march cheerfully and content, with trouser bottoms rolled up, not seeming to feel the weight of their heavy knapsacks and cooking kettles. The helmets have suffered more than any other part of the equipment in this campaign, many are missing their spike which has usually been torn away by a bullet or shell fragment. Some helmets look as if in the heat of the fighting, they were tossed down and trampled under the feet of the ranks marching behind. The bandoliers are no longer all that white and the boots have lost all traces of polish. The half-starved artillery horses, whose ribs project as the result of the heavy exertion and sparse fodder, still trot briskly, almost without stretching their harness. The straight, steel cannon roll easily on the country roads behind the teams and seem easy work for six horses. When the ground is softened by cloudbursts as at Königgrätz however, then it is another matter.

The army is still marching in several columns, and from every height one sees long blue lines, snaking through the countryside like serpents. Disappearing in sunken roads, winding through villages, appearing and disappearing again in copses and thickets, they extend for miles from front to rear. Always looking directly ahead, the troops seem to be marching toward the fortress of Olmütz, under whose walls the Austrians have a fortified camp in which they are said to have more than 100,000 combat ready troops and 400 guns. Here it is said, the Austrian army thinks to block the Prussian route to Vienna.

Today we have again passed through a generally productive land whose inhabitants have not fled before us. Again, we marched on country roads, at times shaded by fruit trees, then again over lush, blooming meadows that extend over limestone, covered only with only a thin layer of soil. In many places the rock is exposed, rising twenty to thirty feet high, forming wondrously shaped grottoes and caverns around which cluster silver fir and white pine, and at whose feet bloom wild roses, hawthorn, foxglove and nightshade.

All of the farmsteads and cottages are built of brick and even the smallest village glories in a church with a tower, on whose highest point is usually a great, often gilded, onion-shaped dome, a feature that seems unique to the Slavic lands. Here one sees none of the little wooden huts, for the residents of this region are more prosperous than the people north of the Elbe, and when we crossed this river, we left behind the cottages built of pine wood, so many of which fell victim to the artillery fire of friend and foe alike. All of the houses we enter here are extremely clean, the furniture without colour and polish, but washed and scrubbed to a whiteness that one does not meet in northern Bohemia. All of the brasswork, all the iron and steel objects sparkle and shine, often to the equal sorrow of guest and host when [troops] are billeted there with their dusty coats and dirty boots that seem out of place in this world of cleanliness. Here too the inhabitants sigh about the war, for their crops have been damaged. Soldiers of both armies have been quartered with the people (the Austrians retreated through this area a few days earlier), and many among them have sons and brothers in the Austrian military service. But there is no animosity between them and the Prussian soldiers. In fact, the latter are so cheerful that even the most hostile person would find it hard to take offence at their behaviour.

Tonight, the headquarters have been established in a local monastery, the priests are still here but have turned over the greater part of the house to Prince Friedrich Karl and his staff, military wagons and horses have been brought within the enclosure.

Officer's servants go whistling through the corridors and cells, and the building would soon seem just like a barracks if the priests did not walk round offering food and drink to the officers and soldiers in a friendly fashion. For even though we are considered as enemies of their land, and perhaps also of their church, they still know that the army has made a long and difficult march, and they practice that charity which should be the unifying bond between all Christians.

Radiating from the church and cloister, the little town, whose white houses shine in the sun, extends in four streets built almost at right angles to each other. Between and behind the houses one sees quaint little gardens, and beyond lie the fields whose heavily laden ears of grain are ripening for the harvest. The bells of the church sound slowly for vespers, for it is Sunday. Several women, shawls drawn over their heads in Bohemian fashion, walk at this very moment under the portal of the church, and one sees them crossing themselves at the entrance with holy water. All of this presents a picture of the deepest peace, but the numerous bayonets before every door, the constant thronging of the soldiers walking the streets, the wandering shopkeepers who have placed their stalls before the door of the church and argue with the soldiers about the price of black cigars and schnaps, make it all too clear that this friendly little town is at present the headquarters of an army that has just come from the field of battle, and is again advancing to force their enemy into yet another battle, for it is obviously in the interest of the Prussians to press hard on the heels of the retreating Austrians and force them to fight, before they have the opportunity to reorganize.

Brünn, 14 July.

Four days ago, we left Bohemia behind us and are now in the midst of Moravia, the day before yesterday, the 12th, the advance guard of our 1st Army entered Brünn, the capital of Moravia. The first half of our march to Vienna is completed, and the second half at least does not seem contested. The enemy continues to retreat, he is in a fortified camp at Olmütz, but we shall leave him there and march on past him.

Brünn has 50,000 residents and is charmingly situated. Here, for the first time since we entered Bohemia, we feel surrounded by culture. We can buy, if for a high price, anything our hearts desire, and it is interesting for the silent observer to see how thousands of weary, exhausted, souls, find new strength here. I belong to both, meaning to those that are recovering and to those who observe. Even the theater has suffered no interruption unlike other places. Yesterday evening I heard 'Martha' and relaxed in my seat in the stalls. The opera was well performed, the chorus and orchestra were excellent and the solo performances would have satisfied any reasonable critic. In front of me was a *Lieutenant* of the [Austrian] Hessen Cassel Hussars who had been captured in the fighting at Saar. I met him again later in the '*Schwarzen Bären*' hotel and heard from Prussian comrades that his horse had fallen and thus he was captured. He was a handsome, fit looking young man who did not look as if he would have willingly fallen into our hands.

This morning I visited the famous Spielberg that rises directly from the west side of the city. The Schloss, which has served for the past seven years as a state prison, is now used as a barracks and after the hasty departure of the Austrian garrison, it still looked grim enough. The vaulted chambers that had served for the confinement of prisoners, were for the most part, subterranean, without light and icy cold. All their traces of brutal tyranny produced a terrible impression on the visitor, hail to the great, humane Emperor Joseph [II] who kept them here! Among others, I was shown the cell in which the notorious *Pandur, Oberst* von Trenk[91] was imprisoned. His remains are interred in the crypt of the Capuchin monastery.

In Brünn we find ourselves on historical ground, less than five miles to the east is the battlefield of Austerlitz, before us the Marchfeld that had already seen Romans fighting Hungarians. Perhaps we shall meet the enemy there. The day that awaits us will be hot, Perhaps thousands will be consumed by its scorching heat:

> All of the lips that for us pray,
> All of the hearts that we crush,
> Comfort and protect them, eternal God!

The hearts and senses of the poor, hard hit people of this land, are sorely oppressed, the hopes of peace that emerged yesterday were, for many, like a breath of fresh air.'

Brünn, 16 July.

What wonderful contrasts! Emperor Sigismund ruled the Mark Brandenburg from here, and so badly, that finally the House of Hohenzollern had to put an end to the ghastly mess. At that time the Mark was given to the *Markgraf* Jobst von Mähren who sucked the unfortunate Brandenburg lands dry in order to build castles and the like. Now, nearly 500 years later, the *Fürst* [Prince] of the Mark Brandenburg has established his headquarters in Brünn, and the children of the Mark enliven the streets, for all of the true regiments of the Mark, (the 8th, 12th, 24th, 35th, 48th, 60th and the 64th), have been in Brünn for three days with *General* von Manstein. At that time the nobles and burgers of the Mark took their orders from Brünn. Now men of Brandenburg administer the Brünn police, the mail and all the city departments whose administrators have fled.

Yesterday (Sunday) the King ordered field services for the regiments of the 5th Division, it had arrived in the afternoon behind the 6th and 7th Divisions, and moved out early toward Lundenburg.

An altar was set up on the highest spot of the so called Josephstädter Glacis, between the *Statthalterei* [Governor's palace] and the quarters of *Generalfeldzeugmeister*

---

91   Tr. Note: Franz *Freiherr* von der Trenck, born January 1st 1711, died in the Spielberg Prison in Brno, October 4th 1749. Born in Italy, he was a Prussian with Austrian citizenship and large estates in Croatia. He had a checkered and highly colourful career, replete with numerous instances of brutality and alleged corruption. He earned most of his fame during the War of the Austrian Succession, as the leader and commander of a unit of *Pandurs* (Pandours), light troops in the Austrian army (one could almost describe them as tribesmen) which specialized in 'irregular warfare.' Later in his career he was convicted by military court martial of a variety of misdeeds and was sentenced to imprisonment in the Spielberg, where he died in 1749.

Prince Karl von Preussen. Its beautiful flowers and the particularly pleasing setting provided a contrast with the thoroughly martial surroundings. On three sides of [the altar] stood the Leib Grenadier Regiment, the 12th Grenadier Regiment, Prince Karl von Preussen, and the 48th (the younger brother of the Leib Grenadiers), each with three battalions, their flags beside the altar to right and left. On their right was the Military Choir, and behind it, artillerymen of the *Feldzeugmeister* Brigade. To the left were the regimental bands, and behind these, the Brandenburg Pioneer Battalion, all of them sons of the Mark Brandenburg. The King appeared at 9:30, accompanied by the Grand Duke of Mecklenburg Schwerin (who will shortly depart for Leipzig to assume command of the 2nd Reserve Corps that is being formed there), and the Princes Karl, and Friedrich Karl, of Prussia, followed by the general adjutants, *Generalen à la suite*, *Flügeladjutanten* and all the military personnel of His Majesty's Headquarters, the *Ministerpräsident Graf* von Bismarck, as well as the generals present in and around Brünn. The Field Service was held in accordance with the norms prescribed in the 'Kirchenbuch für den Armee' by the Divisional Chaplain of the 5th Infantry Division, who preached a lively sermon based on the sentence, 'Not us! Not us! No, to Him alone the honour.' The effect was all the greater as the entire setting, the place where it was held and the still fresh memory of what they had just experienced, perhaps even more, the thought of what was impending, set a serious and receptive mood. The service closed with two verses of 'Now thank we all our God, 'the general prayer and the blessing, with thousands of local residents standing around in perfect silence.

Early today the cavalry of the *Stabswache* [headquarters guard] rode off toward Lundenburg. Yesterday, at the railway about fourteen miles from here, there seems to have been a fight with the enemy for we could hear the rumble of cannon fire that became more distant to the east. The news is we have captured another 18 cannon (at Tobitschau and Rokeinitz) and that the Austrians no longer want to hold their position.

Brünn, 17 July.

The railway has been cut at Göding. Lundenburg (a vital junction) is occupied. Benedek can no longer employ the railway to transfer the army corps concentrated at Olmütz, to Vienna. They must now go via Pressburg, and on foot.

Only the future can tell whether these corps still have the will to fight, I doubt it. That is what the coachman from Lundenburg told me. He is really an Austrian soldier but surreptitiously deserted his regiment, preferring to work for his cousin as a stableman than be shot dead, thanklessly and to no purpose, for the Emperor of Austria. Many of his comrades have already done the same as him and more would like to do it as soon as they find an opportunity. The deplorable lack of patriotism and the absence of a national spirit is widespread, especially among many of the Austrian soldiers. The individual officers, for the most part, are brave and loyal, indeed many officers would rather seek death than survive defeat. However, the majority of the common soldiers seem unaffected by the outcome of the battles, and are completely indifferent to the distant fate of the Empire of Austria, of which many have no conception at all. The extraordinary number of prisoners taken by the French in Italy in 1859, and again by us here in Bohemia and Moravia, is directly due to the spiritual apathy of the men of the *Kaiserlich königlich* Army [92]

92   Author's Note: The great number of prisoners that Austria has lost in its last two wars, and also in its battles against the 'First Empire,' cannot find any explanation other than the above. Many have only a vague loyalty to the Habsburg Monarchy and would rather see it destroyed than continue. Nevertheless, it would be a mistake to view all that has happened from this perspective, and to presume on any general anti-Austrian sentiment, or even a general indifference. Not only in its German core provinces, but also in the west and south Slavic lands, in the Polish and even in the Italian provinces, the Emperor has loyal subjects and all they need to become a real threat to us, is organisation. The country folk have already risen, especially in the country between the upper Elbe and the Silesian border, and already, on 14th July, the Commander of the 12th Division, *General* von Prondzynzki (who remained behind to maintain the encirclement of the fortresses of Josephstadt and Königgrätz), has had to issue the following proclamation:

'Ten peasants and farmhands in the Königgrätz area, have dared to treacherously fire on Royal Prussian troops, whereby they have been captured and been condemned before the court martial in Pardubitz. I take this opportunity to warn the populace against such conduct. I have hitherto been moderate, but I hereby make it known that any civilian who is captured with weapons in hand, will suffer the death penalty, and that for every Royal Prussian who is wounded or killed, a nearby farmstead will be burned to the ground. If Royal Prussian military personnel are fired on from a locality and the perpetrators are not surrendered, then all of the inhabitants of the municipality will be arrested for the deed and the locality will, depending on the circumstances, be burned down.'

(If the reports we have received are reliable) The ten peasants and farm labourers mentioned in the proclamation were shot. A similar execution took place in Skalitz, but all of these measures remain ineffective, for in the vicinity of Königinhof, there have been instances where civilians have fired on individual solders and small detatchments.* On our side it was believed, at least initially, that we were dealing with '*Räubergesindel* [bandits], but we are now convinced that this is not a matter of 'bandits' but of *Landsturm* [local defense units] and that in all these cases, we are dealing with patriotic men who have taken up weapons for their Emperor, their church and their homes. This is to qualify the opinions that are expressed above in the text, in the letters from Brünn.

*The most interesting such ambush may well be the following: 'On 16 July (so states an *Unteroffizier* of the light field hospital of the Guard Corps), we arrived at Müglitz (Bohemian Mohelnice, a town of 3400 inhabitants, Kreis Olmütz, on the March) and remained there overnight. On the 17th we rode to the village of Grossbeutel, only five minutes from the town, to requisition a wagon. I was in the process of driving the wagon away when my *Gefreiter* galloped up and reported that outside of the village, an armed mob of civilians had Prussian infantry in their midst and were bringing them toward the town. This seemed suspicious to both of us and we hastened toward them along in a covered alley. When they suddenly became aware of us, they fired on us and drove the three infantrymen that they had in their midst before them with blows from rifle butts. In a flash I had the revolver that I had captured at Königinhof in my hand, and the *Gefreiter* his pistol. With a loud hurrah, we fell upon the mob, which consisted of twelve armed peasants. Yet again they greeted us with a volley. I shot down two of them. One knocked the *Gefreiter* to the ground. The three infantrymen that they had captured, one from the 4th, one from the 5th and one from the 45th Regiment of the Crown Prince's army, were suddenly freed by our attack and bravely helped us, even though they had no rifles. Two peasants begged for quarter but were cut down without mercy. Our three freed prisoners were entirely covered with shotgun wounds and we had to get them to safety, for a whole mass of people came out of the village with scythes, muskets, hatchets and sticks. *Even women and children took part*. We could not deal with such superior numbers and wanted to get away from their bullets. I was fortunate during the attack, but during the retreat one of the peasants put a bullet through my shoulder and another grazed my neck. The *Gefreiter* had already received an axe blow to his foot. I endured the pain, and as quickly as our wounds allowed, we attempted to escape. After five hours of arduous marching we finally came

Brünn, 20 July.

The divisions of our 1st Army had long since moved south, first to the Thaya, then to the Danube. I still kept my command here, in the morning I finally followed. I took advantage of this final day once more to visit the Spielberg, which has such an infamous reputation in the history of Austria. It is a moderately high hill, and from its top one has a good view of Brünn, built in a semi-circle around it, with its many towers, old palaces and cloisters - and in direct contrast - giant factory buildings with their tall smokestacks and broad drying areas. In between them are green meadows, shaded gardens, wide avenues and broad fields of vegetables, for which this area is famous. Steeply sloping hills with deeply incised valleys extend right up to the suburbs, while the distant horizon is bounded on two sides by the foothills of the southern Carpathian Mountains. It is a veritable panorama that one enjoys from the Spielberg, and if it is not especially beautiful (for to this eye, water is totally absent, and although the hills are indeed fertile, most of them are bare and lack the adornment of woods), it is interesting because one has a wide view over an extensive part of Moravia. The favourable position of this isolated hill occasioned the construction, from the earliest times, of a strong castle, continually strengthened and extended, and was for a long time one of the strongest citadels of the monarchy. That is no longer the case, as a fortress the Spielberg is worthless against modern artillery. Most of the walls and bastions have been torn down, and in their place are beautifully arranged walks, shaded, circular flower beds, even a skittle alley, so that the Spielberg is now one of the most popular promenades, and one of the most patronized places of amusement for the residents of Brünn. Only two great barrack blocks and several other buildings, which form a closed quadrangle on the top (now occupied by the Prussians and set up as hospitals because of the healthy air) remind one of its recent past.

Here in these buildings are the ghastly, subterranean prison cells, arranged with truly refined cruelty, in which for too long, Austria let its political prisoners languish. Here too is the low, narrow, sparsely illuminated cell in which Silvio Pellico was kept from 1822 to 1830 under the harshest possible conditions, because he wanted to free his Italian Fatherland from Austrian rule, and elevate it to a great, united, free kingdom. Political prisoners will always remain a sad necessity, and any state which hopes to maintain a stable form of government has not only the right, but the duty, to punish and render harmless individuals who rise against the majority, and would disturb the peace of its citizens by their unruly pride. However, such deprivation of freedom does not have to be carried out with cruelty, the necessary imprisonment should not become an instrument of revenge.

About nine miles from Brünn is the famous battlefield of Austerlitz, which played such a decisive part in history. I examined it closely several years ago, but the terrain has been so transformed by changes in agriculture that it is nearly unrecognizable. The famous pond, which was so fateful for the retreating Russians, where Napoleon

upon Prussian troops. I reported the events and immediately a squadron of Guard Cuirassiers and a company of the Emperor Franz Regiment proceeded to the village to capture the guilty.'

had the ice smashed with his cannon balls so that many drowned, has now been completely drained and transformed into fruitful fields. The peace that followed took a significant amount of territory from Austria. Will the peace that is soon to be made do the same? Probably not, Prussia cannot make use Austrian territory and therefore will not have it.'

Wolkersdorf (near Vienna), 21 July.

You have followed the advance of our three armies, the 2nd Army initially proceeded toward Olmütz, the 1st to Brünn and the Elbe Army to Znaym. We (the Elbe Army) again had the right wing. Our path led us down the great imperial highway. This was not the road on which the Austrian army had retreated, it went past Olmütz farther to the east. The enemy cavalry (Edelsheim) that was before us, which was to delay our advance, accomplished little. They only showed themselves in the distance and rapidly fell back before our advance so that our advance guard only rarely managed to engage the enemy with its cavalry.

We dashed through Moravia just as quickly as through Bohemia. Nowhere did the enemy attempt any serious resistance. From Znaym the Elbe Army entered the Arch Duchy of Austria and thereby into a land of the German language, which is only sporadically encountered in Bohemia and Moravia. We departed from Znaym on the 16th, and since the 20th, have been in the immediate vicinity of Vienna. The advance guard, on the hills by Wolkersdorf, can see the proud imperial city, with Stephen's Tower lying at its feet. Our soldiers were jubilant and greeted this view as just reward for their strenuous march since Königgrätz. It was a magnificent evening that the spectacle made even finer. Vienna and its sea of houses was clear in the distance, the main buildings and the Schönbrunn were easily recognizable. Behind, the dark mass of the Vienna woods, in the foreground, the plain of the Marchfeld, to the east, the heights of the Carpathians. In the Marchfeld, with its rich fields and friendly villages, one could recognize Wagram, Aspern and Esslingen. To the right, on the left bank of the Danube, the Bisam Berg, which is also supposed to be fortified by the enemy, and then the Upper Austrian highlands. It was a glorious panorama, hitherto never seen by a Prussian army. Our soldiers also feel this and will risk everything to reach the next great objective, Vienna.

These excerpts that we have shared above, have led the reader in stages from the battlefield of Königgrätz, to the spires of Vienna. As stated in the introduction, they have served to provide portraits of the landscape, villages, [towns] and cities, land and people, as well as typical and representative moments from the march itself, as they appeared at the time. In what follows, we shall accompany our three great armies for a second time, but now with the intention of providing a description of the various actions in which they became involved with the enemy rearguards in their rapid pursuit.

The Fighting at Saar and Tischnowitz – 1st Army, 10th-11th July

Day after day the pursuit continued, and despite the lead that the Austrians had gained from the evening of the 3rd to early on the 5th, we stayed hard on their heels all the way to the Danube. This resulted in all three of our columns being involved in numerous encounters with the enemy, some light, some substantial. The 1st Army, whose progress we shall now describe, marched in the centre via Brünn and fought actions at Saar and Tichnowitz.

The fighting near Saar on 10th July. Pomeranian Uhlans against Radetzky and Hessen-Cassel Hussars

Cavalry Division Hann was in the vanguard of 1st army and by noon of the 9th, having ridden via Prelautsch and Chotebor, reached the hamlet of Wojnomestetz, near the Moravian border. The 2nd Pomeranian Uhlan Regiment Nr.9, *Oberst Freiherr* von Diepenbroick – Grüter, was in the lead. It was learned that enemy Hussars had left the place a few hours earlier and had fallen back to Saar, but their lead was too great and it would not be possible to catch them. Next morning the march was resumed toward Saar.

> The 9th Uhlan Regiment was again the leading the division
> The 1st Squadron, *Rittmeister* von Schickfus, was the leading squadron.
> The 4th Troop, *Lieutenant* von Seckendorff, was the leading Troop.

The terrain was hilly and in part overgrow with fir trees so that it was extremely difficult to obtain an overview. Fresh traces of bivouac alongside the highway showed that the enemy had spent the night there. The Uhlans continued south for nearly five miles when, this side of the village of Strizanow, *Lieutenant* von Sekendorff ran into a troop of Hussars which he attacked and chased before him. Suddenly an officer with about forty horsemen charged out of a farmstead by the highway and threw themselves upon our Uhlans. Both sides rode into each other, however after a few moments the Hussars turned and fled. Two enemy sutlers, who had attempted to make it up the steep sides of the highway with their wagons, to get to the open fields, nearly blocked the road in their attempt. The Hussars behind them, who attempted to ride through this involuntarily erected barricade, were unsaddled by lance thrusts or captured. Only the officer and 10 to 15 men got away. On our side, *Lieutenant* von Bülow II, who had acted as reconnaissance officer and had voluntarily joined in the attack, was wounded in the forehead by a sword cut. A halt was made before Saar.

Lieutenant von Seckendorff was ordered to search Saar and regain contact with the enemy, which he did, being received with carbine fire on exiting the far side of the town. There he saw two squadrons of Hussars formed up for action by the sunken road that led toward Wattin, but a hill blocked any further view. He halted, and when one of the enemy squadrons advanced, fell back [through Saar], followed by the enemy who went into position on our side of the town, and opened up a rather vigorous carbine fire. For our part we awaited the arrival of the other squadrons (the 2nd had been detached). Shortly afterwards the regiment had assembled before Saar. The next objective was to regain possession of the town and there was a special reason to avoid any delay. The regiment's adjutant, *Lieutenant* von Naso, had ridden into the town with *Lieutenant* von Seckendorff's troop to obtain more accurate information regarding the enemy, but since the hill that rose on the far side interfered with his reconnaissance, he returned without success. On his way through the town however, he noticed the church tower, which promised an extensive view. He climbed the tower, leaving his horse in the care of an *Unteroffizier* below. Hardly had he reached the top when he saw, to his dismay, that the advance guard had been forced back and that the *Unteroffizier* who was holding his horse was swept up in the retreat. The cries of the townsfolk and their constant pointing to the tower made it clear that he had not gone unnoticed. He found himself in a difficult situation, the next moment threatened him with death or captivity. With cocked revolver in hand, he took his place at the upper exit of the narrow tower stairs, ready to sell his live as dearly as possible, however he was spared this extreme.

At nearly the same moment in which the three squadrons of the regiment assembled before Saar, the *Unteroffizier* (who had fled) reported the desperate situation of *Lieutenant* von Naso, and *Oberst* von Grüter immediately ordered an advance to free him. The First Troop of the 1st Squadron under *Lieutenant* von Bülow I, was in the lead, followed by the rest of the 1st, 3rd and 4th Squadrons. The lead formation ran into the enemy at the entrance to the town. The [Austrian] Hussars advanced in the square and fired their carbines. They repeated this maneuver several times. At the market place *Lieutenant* von Bülow ordered an attack. With loud hurrahs his Uhlans charged the Hussars, who turned and fled.[93] Thus the chase continued to the exit from the town where a half squadron had blocked the sunken road. Although the Uhlans had become dispersed in the pursuit, they threw themselves resolutely on the enemy and forced him to fall back to the support squadron standing behind. In this action, *Lieutenant* von Bülow had his horse shot out from under him.

In the meantime, the rest of the 1st Squadron, *Rittmeister* von Schickfus, passed through the town and since there was no room to form up, attacked in formation of threes [presumably road column]. After a vigorous hand to hand fight the enemy was repulsed. Our 3rd Squadron, *Rittmeister* von Maercken, pursued them. The enemy, now two squadrons strong, fell back

93   Author's Note: We take the following graphic description of the action from the letter of an eyewitness. 'A lively fight began right before the market place. The famous Austrian cavalry were attacked by the somewhat worn out Prussian horsemen and the lance came into open battle with the saber. The Uhlans formed a line across the road and walked forward a short stretch, then broke into a trot, lances high with the black and white pennants fluttering in the wind, but where the road broadened into the market place, a short sharp word of command, a clear bugle call, and the points of the lances lowered and the horses broke into a gallop, the riders, with their rein hand bent low on the horse, the shaft of the lance gripped firm in the other, the point with fluttering pennants to the fore. Even as the Prussians broke into a gallop, the Austrians were also in movement. With a more open formation and moving faster, they charged, flinging the blue, yellow embroidered coat from their shoulders to leave the sword arm free. Sabers held high, the small, wiry horses strictly in hand, they drew nearer, nimble and light, and threw themselves upon the Prussians as if they wanted to leap over the points of the lances. The Uhlans fell back heavily before the assault, but they held their own and pushed forward at the walk. The enemy parried the lances with their sabers but could not reach the riders. Soon however, the ground was covered with horses and riders that had been ridden down and who attempted to get up again. Unsaddled Hussars chased riderless horses with trailing reins. They rode against the firm Prussian line like a wave that surges against a cliff, and like the wave, broke. The Prussians, bigger, stronger men on heavier horses, forced the smaller Hussar and their light horses to retreat or unsaddled them due to their sheer weight and bodily strength. Indeed, often the shock was so great that steed and man, recoiling, rolled thrashing on the ground.'

quickly along the road to Gross Bitesch. *Rittmeister* von Maercken broke into a gallop, the distance separating him from the Hussars shrank, the rearmost enemy squadron then formed front but in vain. In a trice it was broken through and the chase continued, friend and foe intermingled, for about three and a half miles on the miserable, slippery, stony roads to the village of Wattin. The Hussars defended themselves bravely, but they had to give way. Finally, the total exhaustion of the horses forced *Rittmeister* von Maercken to break off the pursuit.

Our losses consisted of one man killed, one officer and seventeen men wounded, including the *Sergeant* and regimental clerk Dieskau, bleeding from eleven wounds. (Dieskau, at the beginning of the campaign, had requested as a special favour to be able to exchange the pen for the saber. He was granted his wish and after the loss of an eye, was restored to his former position as regimental clerk.)

The enemy, one squadron each of Radetzky and Hesse-Cassel Hussars, lost three officers and 32 men captured. Among the officers captured was *Rittmeister Graf* Lichtenberg.

The fighting at Tischnowitz 11th July – 2nd Guards Dragoons against the Wallmoden Uhlans

To the left of Division Hann, which formed the right flank of the 1st Army, the Light Cavalry Brigade of Duke Wilhelm von Mecklenburg advanced along the river Schwarzawa[94] toward Brünn.[95] On the 10th his brigade reached Rozinka. Early on the 11th it moved out to the southeast with the 2nd Guards Dragoon Regiment, *Oberst* von Redern, in the lead, the 1st Squadron, *Rittmeister* von Korff, the leading squadron and a troop under *Lieutenant* von Dieskau, the leading troop. The advance was slow since to the right and left, wooded ravines and steep hills made reconnaissance difficult. Near Olschy, a little over two miles from Tischnowitz, they ran into the first enemy cavalry (the Wallmoden Uhlans, as it later turned out), who showed themselves in front and on both flanks. *Oberst* von Redern immediately directed a squadron to right and left in order to drive off the enemy's flank detachments, while the advance guard under *Lieutenant* von Dieskau (accompanied by *Major* von Schack) continued toward Tischnowitz.

Tischnowitz lies on the left (the far bank), of the Schwarzawa, its suburb, Vorkloster, lies on the right (the near bank), town and suburb are linked by a bridge. In Vorkloster our advance guard came up against one troop of enemy Uhlans, fell upon them, and chased them over the bridge into Tischnowitz. Here however the attack halted. Two Austrian squadrons were in the market place and with the cry, 'The Prussians are here,' saddled up (they had just fed the horses) and fell *en débandade* [in disorder] upon the approaching troop of Dragoons, driving them out of the town. But not for long. By now the 1st Squadron, under *Rittmeister* von Korff, was there and the second attack on Tischnowitz was launched. The clash took place on the Schwarzawa bridge, between the town and its suburb. The Uhlans appeared to want to form an impenetrable line but our Dragoons, sabers drawn and horses firmly in hand, approached them

---

94   Tr. Note: The Schwarzawa is a tributary of the Thaya River. Brünn is located at the confluence of the Schwarzawa and the Zwittawa.

95   Author's Note: We remember that Duke Wilhelm not only led his own brigade (2nd Guards Dragoons, Zieten Hussar, 11th Uhlans), that belonged to Cavalry Division Hann, but also led the advance guard of the 1st Army. This included, in addition to his brigade, Infantry Regiment Nr.60, Fusilier Battalions 18 and 48, the 4th Jäger Battalion and three batteries.

smartly and only let their horses go at the last moment, hurling themselves forward between the Uhlans. *Major* von Schack was wounded by a lance thrust in the left shoulder, however his men pressed so close to the enemy that their lances were useless. The hand to hand fighting lasted only a moment. *Rittmeister* von der Knesebeck, the commander of the enemy squadron, was cut from his horse and the Uhlans then turned and fell back to the town pursued by the Dragoons who, under the influence of their officers, retained their good order. When they had reached the street that led to the market place, the Uhlans again attempted to form a front, but our Dragoons immediately attacked anew and the mere weight of their horses together with the force of their sword strokes, forced the enemy back.

Fighting at the Tischnowitz market.

The combat was intense and drawn out, the horsemen packed together so tightly that they could hardly use their weapons. They wrestled with each other and tried to pull each other from their horses. The horses, frightened and wild, stamped, reared up and kicked, however the weight of the Prussians was overwhelming. They forced their enemy back to the marketplace where the statue of the Madonna looked down on the fighting from atop her column. Here an Austrian officer was hurled from his saddle by a tall Prussian Dragoon of almost unbelievable strength.

Another Austrian was forced down in his saddle by the grip of a Prussian Dragoon so strongly that his backbone broke. In general, the lighter Austrian riders could not withstand the greater force. They turned and hurried out of the town where they passed through the Sachsen Cuirassier Regiment, two other Uhlan squadrons and a battery. There was no pursuit due to the inequality of the forces. It was Cavalry Brigade Soltyk that faced us here. The enemy lost two officers and 53 men, some dead and wounded, some captured. We lost two dead and ten wounded.

The Fighting at Kralitz and Biskupitz – 2nd Army on 14th July

The 2nd Army, as we know, was marching towards Olmütz (to the left of the 1st Army which was proceeding toward Brünn). It too had encounters with the retreating enemy, the first on the 7th and 8th of July. On the 7th a mixed command under *Oberstlieutenant* von Barnekow (the 1st and 5th Cuirassier Regiments, Uhlan Regiment Nr.10, which had contributed 200 of its strongest horses together with 100 similar from the 2nd *Leib* Hussar Regiment), captured one company of the 4th Battalion of Regiment Deutschmeister with a strength of three officers and 140 men. The wagon column, with which this company marched as escort, escaped. The next day (the 8th) was less fortunate when the 2nd *Leib* Hussar Regiment, intending to attack the Haller Hussars, was heavily shelled and lost 16 men and 19 horses (only 11 according to another report). After these encounters on the 7th and 8th, Cavalry Division von Hartmann, which provided the lead formation of the 2nd Army, went for nearly a week without further contact with the enemy. Then (on the 13th) the division reached Konitz, level with Olmütz. The 2nd Hussar Regiment had advanced east of the road to Olmütz, Uhlan Regiment Nr.10, south of the road to Prossnitz. They were now so close to the enemy (who had concentrated around Olmütz) that an encounter could be expected at any minute, and in the event, that is what happened.

The 1st Leib Hussar Regiment at Kralitz

The *Leib* Hussar Regiment (not the 2nd *Leib* Regiment – garrison at Posen Lissa - which had been pushed forward the previous day from Konitz to Olmütz), but the 1st *Leib* Hussar Regiment (garrison Danzig, scouting ahead of the 2nd East Prussian Division, *Generallieutenant* von Clausewitz), had the first encounter on the afternoon of the 14th. After a nine hour march, the regiment arrived at 5:00 in the afternoon at Prossnitz. As it was about to bivouac, several squadrons of enemy cavalry were seen withdrawing near the village of Wrahowitz. The 2nd Squadron under *Rittmeister* von Winterfeld, was ordered follow and to observe them.

The retreat continued as far as Kralitz. The enemy (comprising two squadrons of the Saxon 3rd Reiter Regiment, although they claimed it was only two troops), who had assembled again near the side of Kralitz, was starting to fall back into the village itself, when *Rittmeister* von Winterfeld, seizing the moment, gave the signal to attack. A hand to hand fight developed between the wall of the cemetery and a farmstead, since the enemy, jammed into the narrow space, could not fall back quickly. *Lieutenants* von Keudell and von Holzendorff along with 16 Hussars were wounded there, two men were killed. The enemy fell back to Biskupitz, his losses were one officer and 16 men.

The Silesian Cuirassier Regiment at Biskupitz

Barely two hours later, the Silesian Cuirassier Regiment had to survive a fight that, despite all of the bravery with which it was conducted, had a less favourable outcome.

The regiment had received orders to advance via Prossnitz and Tobitschau to Prerau (there to destroy the railroad), reaching the village of Biskupitz at about 8:45 in the evening. About 300 paces west of the village, they came up against a half battalion of Austrian infantry from Regiment Sachsen Weimar, which immediately formed square. Our cuirassiers, *Oberst* von Barby riding in front, advanced by squadrons to the attack. The 1st Squadron advanced and received a volley, the 2nd followed it, then the 4th, and finally on the left flank, the 3rd. They rode through the fire and encircled the square. One report says, 'The volleys looked strange by night but could not stop our squadrons. All of the officers who came at the square cleared the bayonets that were advanced against them with elegant jumps of the sort you would see in peacetime on a racetrack. The squadrons followed and the enemy lay on the ground.' So far so good. However, while our cuirassiers called upon them to lay down their weapons, a second infantry formation (probably from Regiment Holstein) approached from Biskupitz under cover of the fading light and opened fire. The horses, shying in the darkness, could not be brought to advance towards the muzzle flashes and were forced to retreat, bivouacking this side of Biskupitz, toward Prossnitz.

Our losses were substantial. *Lieutenant Graf* Lüttichau lay dead on the field from a thrust through the abdomen. *Lieutenant* von Elssner died the next day from a shot through the chest. 'Tell my father that the thought of his grief is the only thing that makes it hard for me to die.' While he was inside the square, *Lieutenant* von Tschammer - Osten had his right index finger shot off. *Lieutenant* von Seherr - Thoss, *Lieutenant* von Matzdorff and *Portepée - Fähnrich* von Wostrowsky received bayonet wounds in neck, shoulder and chest. *Lieutenant* von Russer, who fell down inside the square was taken prisoner. Our total losses amounted to 20 dead and wounded.

There is also an Austrian report of this action which is essentially in agreement with ours, only it does not mention the approach of a second infantry formation that decided the action. It states, 'The Silesian Cuirassier Regiment advanced against the square that was formed by the 15th and 16th companies of Regiment Sachsen - Weimar, commanded by *Hauptmann* Kneufel - Herdlitzka and attacked it with the greatest energy. Despite the volleys it fired, the enemy riders broke into the square and forced it apart. However, the courageous men of the Sachsen – Weimar Regiment defended themselves with the bayonet, capturing one of the enemy officers who penetrated the square, finally forcing the enemy cavalry back with loud hurrahs. We lost four men. With the help of this magnificent feat of arms the position of the advanced guard Brigade at Biskupitz, as well as that of 2nd Corps (*Feldmarschialllieutenant Graf* Thun) by Tobitschau, was secured for the night.

The Fighting at Tobitschau and Prerau – 2nd Army on 15th July

More important than the encounters above, in which only our cavalry were involved, was the action at Tobitschau on 15th July. In order to understand this combat, it is necessary first to examine the overall situation of friend and foe. The details that follow are a recapitulation of what has already been said.

On the 10th and 11th the main body of the enemy was concentrated around Olmütz when orders arrived from Vienna to bring the army to the Danube, indeed to the gates of Vienna itself. This order had to be obeyed and by the 12th, the transport of troops by rail had begun. On the 13th a march plan was drawn up for all of the five corps that were still camped around Olmütz, and on the 14th they began to move down the valley of the March via Kremsier, Göding, Stampfen and Pressburg, or as the case might be, Vienna. 4th Corps and 2nd Corps formed the first echelon.

Our 2nd Army whose advanced guard was already past Olmütz, attempted to disrupt this first echelon with an attack on its flank (from Prossnitz). That resulted in the previously described actions near Kralitz and Biskupitz which accomplished little more than disturbing the enemy, who continued his march. Our losses (namely at Biskupitz) were more significant than his. That was on the 14th. All in all, it amounted to a failed attempt against the right flank of the first echelon (4th and 2nd Corps). The 15th brought a repetition of the events of the previous day but achieved a more significant outcome and resulted in the enemy having to modify his route of march.

Again, two enemy corps, the 1st and 8th, moved out. The 1st on the far [eastern] bank of the March via Prerau, the 8th on the near [western] bank of the March via Tobitschau. Just as on the previous day, we were determined to disrupt the march of these two corps (the second echelon). However, what had been attempted with extremely inadequate forces on the 14th, was to be attempted on the 15th with more substantial ones, namely the entire Division Hartmann and an infantry brigade. This produced an entirely different result as we shall see.

The fight at Tobichau – Brigade Malotki and Cuirassier Brigade von Schön against Brigade Rothkirch

We said that early on the 15th, the enemy moved out of Olmütz on two roads, 8th Corps via Tobitschau, 1st Corps via Prerau. Both roads ran from north to south. Our forces were on the [Austrian] flank by Prossnitz, a small city (south of Olmütz) on a level with Tobitschau and Prerau. A thrust from west to east that was to strike the latter location (Prerau) and destroy the railroad there, must first hit Tobitschau. And so it came to pass, that the action at Tobitschau took place several hours before the attack on Prerau. The formations that were to carry out this flank attack were:

> Brigade Malotki (Regiments 4 and 44) of I East Prussian Army Corps.
> 4 pdr Battery Magnus.
> Cavalry Division von Hartmann.

The latter consisted of:

> Cuirassier Brigade von Schön (1st and 5th Cuirassier Regiment).
> Light Brigade von Witzleben (2nd *Leib* Hussar and 10th Uhlan Regiment).
> *Landwehr* Brigade von Frankenberg (1st *Landwehr* Uhlan and 2nd *Landwehr* Hussar Regiment and two horse artillery batteries.

All of these elements, with the exception of Light Brigade von Witzleben, got into action.

The terrain is flat and crossed with individual ridges but above all, with many watercourses, all of which essentially run from north to south. The main river is the March, which runs down the middle of the broad stretch of ground between Prossnitz and Prerau and is joined to right and left by the other courses. On the stretch that is relevant to our description of the combat, these tributaries of the March run nearly parallel to and alongside the main river, so that in going from Prossnitz to Prerau, one has to cross:

First (right before Tobitschau) the Blatta.
Then (just past Tobitschau) the March.
Finally (first by Traubeck and then [again] by Prerau) the Beczwa.

Yet more water courses run parallel to these and thus the approach can only be made over a series of bridges[described as a 'bridge defile']. The two points that must first be secured in order to prevent a thrust towards Prerau becoming too foolhardy, were Tobitschau and Traubeck.

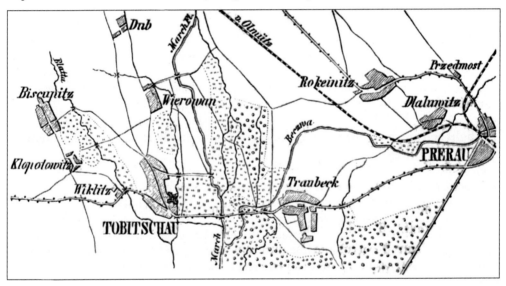

Sketch map Tobitschau to Prerau.

Initially, the Blatta River, before Tobitschau, had to be crossed. In order to accomplish this, three villages and their bridges on the near side of the [Blatta] river had to be taken. These three villages were Wiklitzer Hof, Klopotowitz and Biskupitz. For any further information, look at the accompanying sketchmap. We now go to a description of the action itself.

The Infantry Action. Brigade Malotki occupies Tobitschau and Traubeck

In order to cover his withdrawal, the enemy had occupied Tobitschau and the adjoining ground (to the south) with Brigade Rothkirch of 8th Corps. This was the only Austrian brigade that had not yet been in action. It consisted of Regiments IR 23 Mamula and IR 71 Leopold (of Tuscany), an Uhlan squadron and a 4pdr battery. This was the force that opposed Brigade Malotki.

General von Malotki moved out of Prossnitz shortly after daybreak. He immediately formed his brigade for action with front facing east on the plateau between the Wallowa stream and the Blatta river, with Battery Magnus on the left wing. The position extended from the Wiklitzer Hof to Klopotowitz, Cavalry Division Hartmann took position on the extreme left wing, and with it the two horse artillery batteries. As this position was being taken, large enemy columns, especially artillery, could be seen immediately beyond the Blatta River, withdrawing southward on the road leading from Olmütz, towards Tobitschau.

As we saw the enemy, so he saw us. Recognizing the threat facing him from such a close flanking position, he had three batteries (24 guns) from the Corps Artillery Reserve, deploy and open fire, intending to limit our advance and take our battalions in the left flank. Our three batteries, Battery Magnus and the two horse artillery batteries, immediately went into action themselves and a brisk cannonade soon developed. We will shortly see how this part of the battle went. In the meantime, even before the artillery had fired a shot, the Fusilier Battalion of the 44th Infantry Regiment, which was in the first wave, advanced against the Wiklitzer Hof, the 2nd Battalion against Klopotowitz, with the 1st Battalion advancing between them. Since the villages were not held by the enemy, the battalions marched down the eastern side of the plateau into the valley of the Blatta River, initially only under fire from the enemy artillery. The river was sufficiently broad and deep that it could only be crossed by the two available bridges at the Wiklitzer Hof. If the enemy had known this, the crossing would have been extremely difficult for the brigade and without support, perhaps impossible.

Fusilier Battalion 44, which was the first to cross the bridge, ran into two enemy companies on the far side, probably the enemy's right flank cover. These had not seen our approach, and promptly made for a small wood northwest of Tobitschau, where a skirmish developed. Meantime, the 1st Battalion deployed to the left of the Fusiliers while the 2nd Battalion inserted itself between the other two battalions. Grenadier Regiment Nr.4 followed this movement and also crossed the bridge with the Fusilier Battalion at its head. Two companies of the latter were ordered to take Tobitschau, thus enveloping the enemy left flank and gaining the crossing over the March and its subsidiary branch. For the time being the rest of the Grenadier Regiment followed on.

The first wave now advanced against the western edge of the wood, receiving extraordinarily heavy shell fire from the left, and equally heavy rifle fire from the front, nevertheless it resolutely advanced, preceded by strong swarms of skirmishers. First the edge, and then the wood itself was taken with hurrahs, the advance then halting at the far side (of the wood) to reassemble the companies. The enemy battalions that had held the wood fell back eastward to the *Chaussée* and occupied the rather deep roadside ditches. Momentarily the fight came to a standstill, on our side *Oberstlieutenant* von Behr, Commander of the 44th Regiment's Fusilier Battalion, was killed in this attack.

Finally, but far too late, the enemy realized that his main objective should be to keep the road clear and force us back over the Blatta River, so he attempted to advance with his battalions and attack the eastern margin of the woods. He was received at short range with such a murderous rapid fire however, that he immediately fell back across the *Chaussée* and again occupied its roadside ditches. In the meantime, our troops had sufficiently reformed so that they could debouche from the little woods, and in a second rapid advance, defeat the enemy battalions which initially fell back to a meadow east of the *Chaussée*, but then turned north toward Olmütz and Wierowan, and the adjoining Rakodau. Here too our 44th (2nd Battalion) pursued the enemy and occupied both villages. Brigade Rothkirch, together with the brigades that followed, fell back again to Olmütz.

Just as the 44th on the left had taken Wierowan and Rakodau, in front of the Wiklitzer Hof, the Grenadiers of the 4th Regiment reached and occupied Tobitschau and later, Traubeck. Our forces ran into substantial resistance in both places. The crossings of the three rivers (Blatta, March and Beczwa) were now in our hands and Prerau, the actual objective, was within reach of our cavalry. However, before we describe the cavalry thrust that was directed against Prerau, we must describe an episode of the fighting at Tobitschau. This was the famed attack of the 5th Cuirassier Regiment that played such an important role in the course of the fighting.

The Advance of the Cuirassier Brigade – The West Prussian Cuirassier Regiment Nr. 5 Captures 18 Cannon

On the left wing as we said, the 44th (2nd Battalion) forced its way forward to Wierowan and Rakodau. However, before this advance was possible, the enemy artillery that had gone into position in front of these villages at the start of the action, had to be silenced or captured. This was accomplished by the 5th Cuirassier Regiment. *General* von Hartmann, not content with the support given by his two horse artillery batteries (along with Battery Magnus) provided for the advance of Brigade Malotki, ordered Cuirassier Brigade von Schön to find another crossing farther up the Blatta River, so that depending on circumstances, it might enter the action on the far side of the river. The brigade descended into the broad meadow of the Blatta between Klopotowitz and Biskupitz and had just found a rather poor bridge, when the adjutant of the division, *Premierlieutenant* von Rosenberg, reported that the enemy's massed battery that was fully engaged in firing, was without any cover.

Immediately *Oberstlieutenant* von Bredow advanced across that bridge with three squadrons of the West Prussian Cuirassier Regiment and formed up for the attack. The enemy may well have seen our cuirassiers but was initially in doubt as to whether they were Prussian or his own. He then however, shelled the Silesian Cuirassier Regiment, which remained in the meadow, while the West Prussians, making skillful use of a depression in the terrain, vanished from his view. At a range of 900 paces, *Oberstlieutenant* von Bredow, with his adjutants, *Rittmeister* Schach von Wittenau and *Premierlieutenant* von Rosenberg right beside him, charged the gun line with the 2nd Squadron. The 4th Squadron followed behind on the left as the second echelon, the 1st Squadron was moved to the right to cover against any cavalry that might advance from Wierowan. Thus, the cuirassiers charged into the enemy battery despite shell and cannister fire, and with loud hurrahs, rode down all before them so that 18 guns, seven ammunition carts and all of the teams (168 horses) were taken along with two officers, four *Unteroffiziere* and 164 soldiers. Only two enemy guns and several ammunition carts managed to escape in time. The *Hoch* to the King that arose from the jubilant group would not end and as the captured guns were taken back over the Blatta by our own drivers, and they filed past the Silesian Cuirassiers, even the prisoners joined in the general hurrahs.

It has been asserted with good reason that this action was one of the finest in the history of the Prussian cavalry. With a difficult defile in their rear [a metaphorical 'defile 'comprised of the series of bridges], a battery of 18 guns was attacked and nearly all were taken. The entire crew

The West Prussian Cuirassiers seize 18 cannon.

manning the battery were up to that point unwounded, our infantry with their fire support not yet come up. Only the splendid courage of the brave horsemen and their leader, as well as the extremely skillful use of the terrain [the dead ground], brought about the incomparable success of the attack. The regiment had only ten wounded [Von Bredow would repeat this coup de main in 1870 at the battle of *Mars La Tour* in his famous 'Death Ride'].

The fighting at Prerau (Rokeinitz)[96]

Tobitschau along with Traubeck were taken, the bridges and highway opened, the line of retreat (to Prossnitz) secured. Cavalry Division von Hartmann was now in a position to accomplish its actual mission, to seize Prerau and destroy the railway and telegraph there. Before it [Division Hartmann], the road from Tobitschau to Prerau ran through an open plain for two miles but then entered some woods, and on its far side, drew near to the high running Beczwa River until it reached Prerau. It was evident that there was no room here to deploy an entire cavalry division, the more so because south of the road to Prerau, the ground was badly broken and the long Tobitschau defile lay to the rear. Nor could there be any talk of surprising the enemy infantry in Prerau after some of his infantry, which had fought at Tobitschau and Traubek, had

---

96   Tr. Note: More generally spelled Roketnitz.

retreated there. Furthermore, fresh enemy forces had been reported north of Tobitschau, on the road from Olmütz, by Dub. It was decided therefore, to make the attack with only a part of the division and keep a reserve so that if required, *Generalmajor* Malotki could resist a possible enemy attack. These were the considerations that persuaded von Hartmann to commit only a part of his division to the planned operation, it was as follows:

> The 4th Squadron of the Posen Uhlan Regiment Nr.10 (accompanied by *Oberstlieutenant* von Barnekow, the Commander of the regiment).
> The 2nd, 3rd and 4th Squadrons of the 2nd *Leib* Hussar Regiment under *Oberstlieutenant* von Schauroth.
> The 2nd *Landwehr* Hussar Regiment under *Oberst* von Glasenapp.
> The horse artillery battery of VI Army Corps under *Hauptmann* le Bauld de Nans.

The above troops were brought forward of Traubeck, the horses were fed and allowed to drink there. It was quite unusually hot, and both man and beast suffered under the scorching rays of the sun. The troops had been pushed to the limit in recent days by arduous marches (one squadron of the *Leib* Hussar Regiment had not unsaddled in 65 hours).

Reconnaissance revealed that it would not be possible to advance to Prerau in a straight line, and that it would be preferable to cross the Beczwa north of the road, and then join the road from Olmütz to Prerau on the far side of the railway. An extremely good ford was found and soon the river and railway had been crossed. On the far side [of the railway] the force formed up for action with the Uhlan squadron and the *Landwehr* Hussar Regiment in the first rank, the 2nd *Leib* Hussar Regiment in the second.

Directly before the right flank of the first rank, a hill stretched off to the right on which was the village of Dluhonitz (in other reports, as also on our sketch map, Dlaluwitz). To the left, in low ground, level with the second rank, was Rokeinitz. On the far side of this village the terrain rapidly rose to a substantial height. The road from Rokeinitz to Prerau remained in the low ground between the hill of Dluhonitz and that on the far side of Rokeinitz. A formation of enemy infantry could be seen opposite the right wing of the first rank (the Uhlans), their skirmishers approaching in the tall grain. Opposite the centre of the first rank (*Landwehr* Hussars), on the hill, was a larger formation, apparently a battalion. The bayonets glinted in the bright sunlight. To the left, the tail end of a considerable column of wagons stirred up clouds of dust on the road from Rokeinitz to Prerau.

General von Hartmann had brought the horse artillery batteries forward at the same time as the cavalry (as far as a thickly tree lined avenue that led from Dluhowitz to Rokeinitz) and ordered them to open fire against the enemy infantry. The battery fired its first rounds at 1200 paces and the square was observed to be restless. This was the signal for the advance of the first wave. The squadron leaders were told that each should pick his own special objective and pursue it ruthlessly. *Oberst* von Glasenapp, with the 1st and 2nd Squadrons of his *Landwehr* Hussars, chose the battalion on the hill (centre). It was still shaken and in full retreat when it was ridden through, encircled, cut down or captured. To their right the Uhlans rode against the infantry seen there. These made a better stand and the squadron was received with irregular fire.

Oberstlieutenant von Barnekow and *Lieutenant* von Richtofen had their horses shot out from under them. *Fähnrich* von Bornstedt was shot through his lower leg. Several Uhlans and eight horses were hit, but the square was ridden down and broken, in part captured, in part pursued into Dluhonitz. Only the fire from the edge of the village halted the Uhlans. The 3rd Squadron of the *Landwehr* Hussars turned (left) against the wagon train on the *Chaussée*, which was now gripped by indescribable panic. The drivers had cut the traces and fled, some of the wagons had been driven into each other, others lay sideways in the *Chaussée* ditches. Still farther to the left, *Rittmeister* von Seydlitz with the 4th Squadron, had discovered some infantry hastily clumped together.[97] He rode against them and took 50 men prisoner.

All of these successes now enabled the 2nd and 3rd Squadrons of the *Leib* Hussar Regiment (second rank), to seek their share of the day's laurels. Spotting some enemy at the exit from Rokeinitz, they resolved to attack them, but a sunken road provided the enemy with protection. *Lieutenant* von Stosch (following *Premierlieutenant* von Blumenthal as leader of the 3rd Squadron after Blumenthal was seriously wounded in the first attack), gathered his men again, but the sunken road caused the second attack to fail too. The 2nd Squadron was initially more successful, but it too had to fall back before heavy flanking fire that exacted significant casualties.

Despite these local failures, the attack had been an overall success, however it merits serious examination. The enemy (under the personal command of *General Graf* Gondrecourt, if prisoner statements are reliable), had in the meantime, gained time to bring up substantial forces to oppose the [Prussian] assault. On the hills north of Rokeinitz, two batteries of artillery went into action, their rifled guns pouring shells into the field. At the same time four, according to other statements, five squadrons of Haller Hussars appeared from Prerau. It was time to assemble the brigade and think of retreat, however before this could be accomplished, another serious encounter developed, rich in honour but also in casualties. *Oberst* von Glasenapp, when he saw the Haller Hussars approaching his flank and rear, turned against them. He later wrote the following description of this closing part of the action:

> Even as I was in the process of organizing the troops and squadrons of my *Landwehr* Hussars came the cry, 'Hungarian Hussars are cutting off our retreat,' and I saw a column of enemy Hussars in my rear. Nevertheless, their appearance did not cause me any particular concern, the more so since their slow, measured approach, did not suggest very serious intentions. I therefore continued to organize [my force] but had '*Apell*' blown for those who had been detached. I now swung my squadrons around to go against them. At that very moment I received reports that another column of enemy Hussars was advancing out of the gully to the right of Przedmost, also to our rear, but they too were only advancing slowly.

---

97   Tr. Note: The German term for a small group of infantry, hastily assembled to repel cavalry, is *Knäul*. The standard tactic for infantry under attack from cavalry was to form either a *Carrée* (a square) or a *Knäul* (a clump). The *Carrée* (as described in the *Infanterie Exerzir Reglement Chapter 14*) took time to form and required the entire battalion. Smaller bodies of infantry, if caught in the open by cavalry, formed a *Knäul*. It lacked the regularity of the *Carrée*, but presented the attacking cavalry with a tightly packed mass of infantry with bayonets extended in every direction. In the 1866 war the Prussians regularly dispensed with both the *Carrée* and the *Knäuel*, finding that the rapid fire of their needle guns was fully effective in repulsing cavalry attacks from the same kind of firing line they would employ against infantry. The disadvantage of the *Carrée* and the *Knäuel* was that, the moment the attacking cavalry had cleared the field of fire, they also presented massed targets that invited immediate slaughter when exposed to artillery fire or to the rapid, concentrated fire of Prussian needle guns.

It did not seem advisable to me to make the intended attack on the enemy advancing from Dlaluwitz, since my rear was too exposed. On the other hand, I considered it just as inadvisable to seek an over hasty exit from this trap, because that would have encouraged the enemy, but discouraged my Hussars. I therefore had troops detach from the right wing and then, proceeding half right, walk towards the enemy in order to see how they would react, upon which I then intended to base my further actions. This proceeding at a walk had the result that the enemy, who was approaching at a slow trot, halted, and also began to walk. The column from Dlaluwitz then turned on the spot, following my movement in order to maintain its front against me, while the column in my rear followed me. I employed the time thus gained to give instructions to the squadron leaders. The leader of the 1st Squadron, *Premierlieutenant* von Zastrow, was ordered that as soon as I gave the command 'Front,' to immediately turn his troops that were marching behind, and attack the enemy column that was following in our rear, while the rest of the 2nd and 3rd Squadrons were ordered that, on my command 'Front', each was to individually turn left and charge the enemy column that was now on our left flank. In the meantime, the regiment had gained enough time to shift far enough along the front of the enemy column, so that the direct line of retreat to *General* von Hartmann was open, and [the regiment] was now only exposed in the flank. In considering this improved situation I felt that it was now time, true to the old Prussian cavalry tradition, to make good this opportunity which might never again be offered to myself and my brave Hussars, to measure ourselves against an enemy of the same arm [Hussars], even if he was three to four times our number. Our line of retreat was open, having that, a plucky rider can deal with many disadvantages, even if he does not succeed. The ratio was such that we, with a total strength of 160 men (all of the others had been detached), were facing two columns, the greater on the left, with three squadrons, the smaller in our rear, with two squadrons. The commander of the Haller Hussars later told me this.

I therefore gave the commands, 'Front! ' and 'March, March!'. My brave Hussars carried them out precisely, courageously throwing themselves onto the enemy in the prescribed manner, as rapidly as their totally exhausted horses permitted. Surprised by this attack, the enemy halted, and tightly packed, defended themselves where they stood. Born toward the enemy by my brave horse so that I was far ahead of my Hussars, I exchanged a few slashes with the enemy commander and his adjutant by way of preparation and then forced my way into the lead squadron, where I was so tightly encircled and covered with blows that, before I could cut my way out or my Hussars could cut me free, I fell from my horse, bleeding from nine cuts (six to the head and neck, three to the arms).

With our limited forces, it was impossible to break through and scatter the massed enemy. Nevertheless, the Hussars sought to cut their way through undaunted, and the fighting continued for about a quarter of an hour until, called back by the signal, *'Apell!'* blown repeatedly by order of *General* von Hartman, they broke off the fight and fell back toward the railway embankment, (where the rest of the detachment, the Posen Uhlans and *Leib* Hussars had already assembled), not pursued by the enemy. And just in the nick of time, since once the enemy recovered from his initial shock, and realized the limited strength of [our] detachment, he advanced from all sides to cut us off from the ford, but he did not succeed.

So much for *Oberst* von Glasenapp's report. The regiment (remember that its strength was only 160 men) suffered heavy losses. In addition to three men dead, five officers and 52 men were wounded, thus more than a third. *Lieutenant Graf* Rothkirch - Trach had seven wounds, and only his faithful horse saved him from capture. *Oberst* von Glasenapp fell into enemy hands. Shortly after his capture he was brought to Prerau, where he was bandaged. *Feldzugmeister* Benedek visited him afterwards, hugged and kissed him, and in the presence of his entire staff, praised him highly for his own bravery and that of his Hussars. That very evening *Oberst* von Marburg of the Haller Hussars, with his entire officer corps, appeared to express his highest respect for him and his regiment. Thus, the enemy honoured the brave officer and his troops in most a chivalrous fashion. *General* von Hartmann went back to Tobitschau as evening approached and there united his division.

The result of the day was that the advance of the second enemy echelon (8th and 1st Corps) was disrupted at Tobitschau by Brigade Malotki, and at Prerau by a detachment of Cavalry Division Hartmann. We have already indicated that this thrust of the 2nd Army from west to east, and a similarly directed thrust by the 1st Army against Göding and Lundenburg, made the enemy movement along the March River impossible, and forced him to bear off to the east and the valley of the Waag. We shall return to that.

Raid Against Humpoles and Pilgram (Elbe Army on 8th, 9th, 16th and 22nd July

The Elbe Army, which as we know marched on the right wing, on the great imperial highway, also had its skirmishes and encounters, but they were lighter, less bloody, and in most cases, amounted to no more than a brief contact with the enemy. Nothing outstanding happened, but much that was audacious, spirited and amusing, ambushes and adventures succeeded each other. The King's Hussar Regiment (from Bonn) marched in the vanguard of the Elbe Army, and ever alert, ever in the saddle, always close on the enemy's heels, experienced a series of humorous scenes and vigorous pursuits, a colourful mixture of fortune and misfortune, of success and failure, that individual participants have narrated in lively and charming fashion. We select individual accounts from these, first regarding the raid of the 2nd Squadron (*Rittmeister* von Massonneau) against Humpoles and Pilgram.

Against Humpoles and Pilgram (8th and 9th July)

'After a long march from Czaslau to Habern,' so he says in his description, 'the 2nd Squadron of the King's Hussar Regiment was quartered near the latter at Schloss Barocz of *Baron* von Mrowicz. Our joy regarding the first cantonment that we had enjoyed since 15th June was great, especially since it seemed as though the hospitality and amiability of our host and his daughter, made up for much that we had endured during the last three weeks. After a good dinner that stood in great contrast to the simple noonday meals in bivouac, a small ball was arranged. The ladies took part most willingly and we thus forgot for a moment the war with its misery and horrors.

The little company was waltzing over the parquet in a colourful mix, when an orderly arrived bringing an order to the *Rittmeister* that resulted in the immediate sounding of the alarm. Everyone dashed down the steps in extreme haste, ran to his horse, and within a few minutes, the squadron was lined up in the courtyard of the Schloss.

We headed out on the road toward Humpoles and soon discovered that is was a matter of a provisions column of several thousand wagons that had passed Swetlau, which we were near three days earlier. So it was that we rode a good five hours in the mountainous terrain, nearly always at the trot. Darkness had long fallen and there was but little to see of the enemy. We came unexpectedly upon a sunken road that was difficult to negotiate because it was so narrow, and now several supply wagons that we had come upon *en route* and had brought with us, got stuck.

Suddenly there was gunfire ahead of us. *Lieutenant* von Böselager (who led the advance – guard) reported that he was in front of Humpoles and under infantry attack. Our situation was critical. We were wedged between the rock walls of the sunken road and the wagons behind, and thus we could not retreat, nor did we so desire. In any case, we wanted first to learn how strongly the town was held by the enemy, and then attempt to throw them out. *Fähnrich* von der Schulenburg was therefore sent to support the *Rittmeister*, and thus we resumed our advance. As we later learned, we were facing Austrian police (which are also combatants among the Austrians) and Saxon infantry, and we shot it out with them for a good half hour. Since it was dark there could be no talk of aiming, there were few wounded. Thus for example, a detachment of police in the side street fired a volley at one of our patrols at ten paces, hitting nobody and to cap it all, after they had thrown away their rifles, they were captured by the patrol.

In the meantime the squadron itself had also pressed forward, mopped up the main street and positioned itself in the market place. The enemy fell back from the town (firing constantly, since he probably thought we were far stronger than we were), and soon reached the woods and swamp that extended right up to the town. Further pursuit was impossible for cavalry. Things were also lively in Humpoles. The *Bürgermeister* was hauled from his bed and soon appeared in a black swallow tailed coat before the *Rittmeister*, greeting with much bowing, his uninvited guests, who loudly demanded food. Therefore, there was slaughtering and cooking and never did food taste so good as here in the night, at the fire in the market place in Humpoles. For all that, our situation was not entirely without danger. We were nearly 23 miles from any other body of troops and in the immediate vicinity of the enemy, who could return in strength at any moment. In addition, we could expect nothing good from the citizens. The *Rittmeister* however, found a very effective means to deal with the latter. He had wood, straw and tar brought into the square and declared that in event of any hostility or disobedience, he would set the entire place ablaze. This insured us against the citizens, whom we suspected would make contact with the enemy and betray us. We secured ourselves as best we could with sentries and *vedettes*. We spent the night in the marketplace troubled only by the pouring rain, each man by his horse, serving as his own picket stake.

We moved out early in the morning in order to give the convoy, which we were catching up with, no opportunity to get ahead. After several hours march we came to the old abbey of Seelau, and could clearly see a long row of wagons in the mountains. They had turned off the main road at Trelowitz, and now seemed to be heading towards Patzau. Scarcely had they spotted us when the wagons took off at a gallop. A troop under *Graf* Pourtales was sent in pursuit, and after half an hour's chase, we overhauled them. A few shots were exchanged, but finally the police, our acquaintances from the previous evening, threw themselves sideways into the bushes. Finally, after a horse of the first wagon had been shot and the traces had been cut on many others, we forced the wagons to stop and drove them toward Trelowitz, back to the squadron. Aside from a few policemen, there were only postal and telegraph officials on the wagons. An individual who had been dragged along by the enemy as a 'Prussian spy' was also freed. The wagons were loaded with oats, flour and other victuals. Upon a closer search we also found a considerable amount of money, which, although it was claimed to be 'funds for the poor' and 'private property', was taken to Iglau along with all the rest under command of the *Vice Wachtmeister Graf* Dönhoff und Rieck, with a strong escort, where it arrived safely that same night.

After a short rest, the squadron moved from Trelowitz toward Pilgram, where according to local reports, the main body of the column had gone. We sacrificed our horses last strength, but they were too far ahead of us. We were within three hours of them when we arrived in Pilgram, but we had to give up our pursuit just before we reached our objective since the column was now behind the Austrian outposts, and we had to give our horses some rest after such a strenuous march (in the two preceding days we had ridden nearly 77 miles).

The next morning, since we could go no further forward, we proceeded sideways toward Iglau, back to the advanced guard of the Elbe Army. Granted, we had not completely achieved our objective, taking only 52 wagons. We had to be satisfied with entering Iglau with our captives, 16 in number, where we were greeted warmly by our comrades of the advanced guard with loud hurrahs.

The encounter near Hollabrunn (16th) – The raid to Stockerau (19th and 20th)

The week following the raid against Humpoles and Pilgram went more smoothly. Until the 14th, the King's Hussars remained at in the van of the advance – guard, and advanced over the Thaya. The 15th was a rest day. On the 16th two squadrons (the 2nd and 4th) continued their march on the imperial highway. This march (led by *Major* Prince Heinrich von Hessen und bei Rhein) was a simple maneuver to cover the left flank of the Elbe Army as it advanced to Laa, and leave the enemy believing that our entire right wing army was following on this road. The two squadrons named were given neither infantry nor artillery, sacrificing strength for mobility. Nevertheless, it was only a demonstration, a ruse. The audacious ride went to Stockerau. We take the following from the notes of an eyewitness:

Early on the 16th we moved out of the bivouac (near Znaim). We came right up to a village before the little town of Hollabrunn and saw three enemy cavalry regiments, 20 guns, and one Jäger battalion, on a hill on the far side. This mighty force did not impress our two squadrons. We rode boldly into the town, requisitioned forage and victuals for 10,000 men and food for about 100 officers. The residents did not refuse, but brought what was required into our bivouac on wagons, we did not unsaddle since we had to be ready for a serious fight at any moment. A patrol was dispatched and returned almost immediately with two prisoners from the Savoy Dragoon Regiment.

We remained there on the 17th, posted piquets and *vedettes* and sent large patrols into the countryside where again, two Hungarian Hussars from Regiment Liechtenstein were captured. We soon received news that the enemy had retreated and so we followed him on the 18th to Ober Hollabrunn, but nothing came of it.

On the 19th we advanced toward Stockerau, nearly 14 miles south on the Danube [Stockerau is not on the Danube, but separated from it by the 'Forest of Au'], it was a splendid ride, however we would not reach it this day. Initially we passed the wondrously beautiful Schloss of *Graf* Schönbrunn, and learned that Brigade Appel had been there two days before, and that we now had Brigade Wallis before us. We had fine old Hungarian wine and bread and butter brought to us on the *Chaussée*, and after we had breakfasted well, it was on to Sierndorf, a Schloss of *Fürst* Colloredo. Here we occupied the courtyard of the Schloss with both squadrons, posted piquets and barricaded the place. The Schloss is gorgeous with a large park, we had enough fodder and oats for our horses, we ourselves dined in the ancestral hall, where those of the prince's servants who had remained behind, served us. Stockerau remained our objective. We had learned that an Austrian detachment was there, which we hoped to intercept. Therefore, at 5:00 in the morning, the 2nd Squadron went left flanking until it was in position behind the town, the 4th went directly in. Unfortunately, the enemy had already flown the coop, we merely made a good requisition, even getting a roe buck. Then we heard reports that the enemy was approaching in great strength and had cut us off on three sides. We retreated, taking our provisions with us, and safely reached Schloss Sierndorf. We posted piquets toward Stockerau and were soon in action with Hungarian Hussars. We fought it out with them, but they gave way and moved off to the side. That same evening we returned to Göllendorf (just after we left Sierndorf, a battalion of Austrian Jäger tried to ambush us) and bivouacked by a great monastery. On the 21st we reached Hollabrunn, from whence we had begun our raid. We remained there until the next day (the 22nd), and then marched through sunken roads, narrow defiles, and over steep hills, to the left of the road to Nieder Hollabrunn. There we were jubilantly greeted, we had already been given up for lost. That same day the cease fire started.

In the closing hours of the war, just before the cease fire began, there was an interesting but indecisive action involving substantial forces. We shall present this in the next chapter

The Action Near Blumenau on 22nd July

The final action, the 'Action near Blumenau' as we call it, the 'Action near Pressburg' to the Austrians, was more significant than all of the actions on the long road from the Elbe to the Danube. Our objective was to prevent the union of the Austrian army that was already on the Danube, with those parts of the North Army that were still *en route*. If this succeeded, if after a victorious fight before the gates of Pressburg we were able to take Pressburg itself, then we would stand between the two Austrian armies. This would force the North Army arriving on the Danube, to make a wide detour to the left, cross at Komorn, and arrive in Vienna from the south. Such a circuitous march could hardly be accomplished in less than five or six days, which would allow the 120,000 strong 1st and Elbe Armies, concentrated in the Marchfeld and on the Russbach, to deliver a decisive blow against Vienna.

Before we deal with that action, let us first describe the situation and the locality. The situation on the evening of the 21st was as follows. In Vienna and in camp toward Florisdorf were [the Austrian]:

> The 5th and 9th Army Corps [Part of the South Army, returning from Italy].
> The 10th and 3rd Army Corps [Part of the North Army, retreating from Königgrätz].

In other words, aside from the [Vienna] garrison, the force comprised two corps of the South Army and two corps of the North Army. The last two corps (10th and 3rd), had either gone directly to Vienna after the 3rd July, or had set out from Olmütz when our army appeared on its flank. [This Prussian Army] had by its thrusts against Tobitschau, Prerau, Göding and Lundenburg, forced the Austrian forces to divert to the east. These [Austrian] forces, 4th, 2nd, 8th, 1st and finally 6th corps, and the Saxon Division Stieglitz, were attempting, by forced marches and despite a substantial detour, to arrive in Pressburg before us (on the right wing of the South Army that was already on the Danube). For our part however (as we indicated above), we were making similar efforts to thwart this, and by occupying Pressburg, to block the union of the Army that was already at the Danube, with those parts of North Army which were still *en route*. One could say there was a race between friend and foe to see who would reach, or as the case might be, capture, Pressburg first. And now a word about the locality.

Between Vienna and Pressburg lies the Marchfeld, bounded to the south by the semi-circle of the Danube, to the north by the semicircular curve of the railroad. The river March forms its eastern border (entering the Danube at right angles, four and a half miles [west] of Pressburg). To the west the Marchfeld extends to Vienna, to the east (to Pressburg and beyond), were the *kleine Karpathen* [small Carpathian Mountains]. Therefore, whoever desired to get to Pressburg on the east bank of the March River (and this was our objective), would have to pass through the foothills of the Carpathian Mountains. The only road running northwest to southeast (the road from Marchegg to Pressburg), could best be defended at the villages of Kaltenbrunn and Blumenau, where it ran through a valley with slopes rising on either side to the right and left[98] about four and a half miles [north] of Pressburg.

And here it was defended. Therefore, if we were to reach Pressburg by the shortest route, we either had to take the pass at Blumenau, or skirt it using virtually impassable mountain trails. We shall see that to assure success, both were attempted, and essentially both were attained. When the cease fire was announced, as both parties agree, our side was poised to achieve a great success. The question remains, and we shall go into this later in more detail, whether we would have been in a position to keep this success, or whether our gains would have vanished. Now we

---

98   Tr. Note: A saddle extended west from Blumenau across the valley to Kaltenbrunn, providing an excellent position for the Austrian artillery.

move on to describe the fighting itself. In so doing we shall inevitably have to deal with some of these points again.

On our side, the IV Army Corps was selected for the march on Pressburg. It was the same divisions (7th and 8th) that had shone in the fighting in the Swiepwald and the Holawald on 3rd July, and through their renowned endurance, had contributed so much to the victory. *Generallieutenant* von Fransecky, Commander of the 7th Division, was entrusted with command of the army corps for the operation against Pressburg. The Commander of the 15th Brigade, *Generalmajor* von Bose, assumed command of the 8th Division. The latter division had already marched since the 17th on the left [east] bank [of the March]. On the 21st, the 7th Division crossed from the right to the left bank at Anger, and advanced to Stampfen. Early on the 22nd our troops detailed for the operation against Pressburg were positioned as follows:

The 8th Division (farthest forward) was south of Bisternitz.
The 7th Division (a little over two miles behind) was by Masst [Maaszt] and Stampfen.
The reserve artillery of IV Army Corps (five batteries under *Oberst* Scherbening) farther north by Zohor.
Cavalry Division Hann west by Marchegg.

A total of 19 battalions, 24 Squadrons and 78 guns. We note that three battalions were missing from the original 22 battalion strong army corps. The 4th Jäger Battalion was detached to the advanced guard of 1st Army, the 2nd Battalion of the 27th Regiment was rear area garrison in Horsitz, the 2nd Battalion of the 26th Regiment performed a similar duty in Brünn.

Facing our forces on the Austrian side were Brigade Mondel of 10th Army Corps and the entire 2nd Army Corps. However, it must be pointed out, that at the start of the action, only two brigades of this approximately 30,000 man strong enemy force, Brigades Mondel and Henriques, were in place and that even at noon, when the cease fire took effect, a not insubstantial part of 2nd Army Corps, *Feldmarschialllieutenant Graf* Thun, was still on the far side (east side) of Pressburg.

At about 5:00 in the morning the advance began. *Generallieutenant* von Fransecky had his forces disposed so that he would hold the enemy frontally with the 7th Division and Regiment Nr.72 (attached for the day), while 15th Brigade under *Generalmajor* von Bose, marched around the enemy's right flank, and positioning itself between Blumenau and Pressburg, gained the enemy's rear. The plan however, did not work out as intended. The available time was short, seven hours at most, but it might have been enough if circumstances had been different. *General* von Fransecky waited for information regarding the advance of the flanking column, but it had a difficult march, and finally when the report arrived, it was too late. The moment had passed.

We shall initially accompany the 7th Division in its advance. Early in the morning it proceeded from Stampfen to Bisternitz, a little less than two and a half miles in front [north] of the villages of Kaltenbrunn and Blumenau. A cavalry encounter between the 3rd Squadron (*Major* von Hymmen) of the 10th Hussars, and two weak squadrons of the Austrian Emperor Franz Joseph Uhlans opened the action. The Uhlans were defeated, *Major* von Hymmen wounded. This took place at 7:00 in the morning. While we opened fire from south of Bisternitz with 36 guns, our infantry advanced on the hills to left and right and attempted to take Kaltenbrunn with the right column (2nd Battalion of the 72nd and Fusilier Battalion of the 66th Regiment) while the left column (1st and Fusilier Battalions of the 72nd, Fusilier Battalion of the 27th and all three battalions of the 67th Regiments) attempted to capture or to advance close to Blumenau. Five more battalions, the 1st and 3rd of the 26th, the 1st and 2nd of the 66th and the 1st of the 27th Regiment followed. At 8:30 the batteries of the Reserve Artillery also joined in from south of Bisternitz. At 9:30, since their fire was unsuccessful, *Oberst* Scherbening pushed [them] forward on the right. All in all, we did not gain the upper hand in this artillery battle. Given that the enemy artillery positions had been superbly selected, it would have been difficult at best, to take the pass before we knew that the flank march had been successful, and that report did not arrive, resulting in the failure of the operation. This was all the more regrettable since the flanking column had achieved its objective in brilliant fashion. We now follow it.

At 6:00 in the morning the 15th Brigade moved out. *Generalmajor* von Bose formed a left and a right wing column. On the left the 31st Regiment, on the right the 71st. Foresters and peasants were assigned to each column as guides. So began the march over the mountains to the Gemsenberg, directly north of Pressburg and in the [right] rear of the Blumenau position, this was where the columns were to unite. This movement was carried out with great exactitude and essentially without interference from the enemy. *Oberst* Avemann, who led the right wing column (Regiment 71) was the first to arrive at the foot of the Gemsenberg. There he came up against the 2nd Battalion IR 27 King of the Belgians (Brigade Henriquez), placed his Fusilier battalion at the front, attacked and threw the 'Belgians' off the Gemsenberg with heavy losses. The defeated battalion fell back westward to Pressburg (the railway station). The left wing column (Regiment 31) also arrived at the Gemsenberg immediately after this action.

Generalmajor von Bose, quickly realizing that it was more important to get into the rear of the Blumenau position than to occupy Pressburg, immediately deployed his forces with Fusilier Battalion 71, which was to remain in its position at the Gemsenberg, with front facing south to cover his rear, while he himself led the rest of the brigade, with a right wheel past Eisenbrunnel (where, after a short fight, the 9th Jäger Battalion was defeated) into the Mühlthal and on to the railroad. Here he stood, exactly halfway between Blumenau and Pressburg, with his five battalions between the echeloned enemy brigades. After taking this position he reported to *Generallieutenant* Fransecky that he was between Kunstmühle and Prohaskamuhle in the rear of the Blumenau defile. This report did arrive,[99] but before it did, the cease - fire went into effect along the entire line in front of Blumenau, and the action was broken off before it entered its decisive phase.

As we have already mentioned, a rather heated literary battle is being waged over what the outcome of the action would have been. Both sides, apart from a few isolated voices, are convinced that they would have been victorious. We too, shall not withhold our opinion.

---

99   Tr. Note: As Stresetitz makes clear, in *Die Letzte Operation* . . . , (p. 439), and Friedjung, Ditfurth and von Lettow-Vorbeck in their works, Bose's report did not make it back in time. By that point Column Württemberg had already broken the chain of Uhlan relay riders that Bose had left behind him and contact was entirely cut off between Bose's force and *General* Fransecky's. The first word from Bose (p. 456) arrived after he left the negotiations for an armistice demarcation line, which had begun at about 11:45, leaving *General* von Stülpnagel negotiating with the Austrian *Hauptmann* von Wiser. As *General* von Fransecky rode a few hundred paces toward Blumenau he met an adjutant of the 8th Division who reported that 'After a victorious fight, Brigade von Bose has reached the *Kunstmühle* before Pressburg, thereby cutting off the enemy's retreat to the city.' This did not simplify negotiations, as the question now was, just who was cut off by whom. Had von Bose's force cut off Mondel's brigade at Blumenau, or had Württemberg's column cut off von Bose.

We consider that in accordance with a clearly conceived plan and despite great difficulties, the two brigades had outflanked a strong enemy frontal position with great precision, and to employ once more that well known word, with 'elegance'. We consider that the enemy's spirit had been broken since the day of Königgrätz, and that we were superior to [the enemy] not just in leadership and armament, but also in morale. Thus, it appears probable to us, that if the action had been continued for even a single hour longer, the two [Austrian] brigades near Blumenau would have been encircled and captured, before the three brigades in and around Pressburg would have been in a position to hasten there and turn the tide in favour of Austria.

This supposition is entirely based on the assumption of our superiority, a superiority that we do not assume out of vanity, but which we had proven in a series of bloody battles. If this superiority is not conceded however (and the enemy certainly does not concede it), if the enemy believes that the battalions facing ours were of equal worth, and on that basis, looks upon the action as a chess game whose probable outcome depends entirely on the positions[100] of the pieces, then we must admit to significant doubts as to whether we could claim the victory out of hand. We were in the position where the one who would attack from the rear is, himself, attacked from the rear, and while we would dig a pit for two enemy brigades into which they must then fall, three other brigades are digging a pit for us into which (if the pit diggers are fast enough) we ourselves must fall. We do not believe that this would have taken place. The disparity in morale was too great, but it must be said the visible position of the pieces does not speak unequivocally in our favour. This situation at the start of the cease fire was essentially as follows:

We repeat that only a picture of the situation, a general overview, is presented by the above lines and numbers. The separated Fusilier Battalion of the 71st, as well as the detached enemy

100 Author's Note: Immediately prior to the cease fire the enemy position was:
In front, facing the 7th Division (Fransecky) were:
     7 battalions of Brigade Mondl.
     1 4pdr (Brigade) battery.
     9 squadrons Uhlans.
     1st and 2nd Battalions IR 14 Hessen.
     2 8pdr batteries of the Army Artillery Reserve.
     2 Horse Artillery batteries.
In the centre, cut in half by our enveloping column toward Blumenau:
     9th Jäger Battalion.
     IR 27 Belgien.
     IR 40 Rossbach.
Toward Pressurg:
     IR 69 Jellacic.
     IR 64 Sachsen Weimar.
     1 8pdr battery of the Corps Artillery Reserve.
In Reserve (near Pressburg) were:
     48 guns (6 batteries).
     3rd Battalion IR 14Hessen.
     IR 80 Holstein.
While the entire Brigade Würtemberg was taking us from the east in the flank. So much for the enemy positions at noon. Our sketch avoids these details, and for the sake of clarity, shows the elements fighting in the centre as more definitely separated to the north and south than was in fact the case. In reality the battalions were closer behind and alongside each other without any such significant intervening space as our sketch shows in the centre.

Jäger detachments are not shown to avoid confusing the picture. Unshaken in our confidence in victory, we have also been fair to the enemy and presented all that would tilt the scale in his favour.

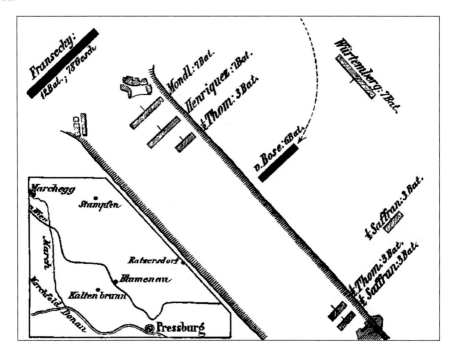

Blumenau.

Along with the ongoing controversy, there is yet another question to be raised, whether, when the cease fire was practically a certainty, the action at Blumenau might have been avoided. Entirely aside from the fact that war is not the place for such considerations, the possession of Pressburg was a valuable enough prize to be worth a certain amount of risk. The capture of this city would not only have provided new evidence of the energy and ability of our army command but would also have provided considerable relief to our seriously exhausted troops. This result was not achieved, and thus one can mourn the sacrifice, but it was only in order to win the prize that the commitment was undertaken.

Our total losses included 8 officers and 199 men. Two officers (*Lieutenants* von Rohrscheidt and von Petersdorff of the Fusilier Battalion of the 71st) died. The latter battalion suffered the heaviest losses. The Austrians lost 470 men, more than a third of their overall losses came from IR 27 Belgien.

By agreement [terms of the armistice], our troops that had been in action fell back to the demarcation line Marchegg – Bisternitz – Stampfen.

Translator's Bibliography

(Books I, II , III plus a list of useful maps)

(Anon – Hoffmann) I was unable to locate a copy for my own use, but I include this reference for the sake of a more fortunate reader, Hoffmann's discussion of the battlefield of Königgrätz in Vol. 4 of the 1867 *Streffleur's militärische Zeitschrift I.*

Das Gefechtsfeld und das Treffen bei Trautenau im Kriege 1866' in '*Streffleurs Österreichische Militärische Zeitschrift, XI. Jahrgang, Zweiter Band* and *Dritte Band*, Vienna 1870.

Das Gefechtsfeld von Soor (Neu-Rognitz und Rudersdorf), in '*Streffleurs Österreichische Militärische Zeitschrift, XI. Jahrgang, Vierter Band*, Vienna 1870.

(Anon – *Oberst* von Pape) *Das Zweite Garde - Regiment zu Fuß in dem Feldzuge des Jahres 1866*, Julius Sittenfeld, 1868, Berlin. An excellent, highly detailed, very readable, 176 page account. A basic source.

(Anon) *Der Antheil des Königlich Sächsischen Armeecorps am Feldzug 1866 in Oesterreich. Bearbeitet nach den Feldacten des Generalstabes.* Sächs. Generalstab (Hrsg.), Dresden, Carl Höckner, 1869. This Saxon official history is outstanding for detail, accuracy and honesty and includes an excellent map of the southern, left wing of the battle of Königgrätz.

(Anon) *Exerzir-Reglement für die Infanterie der Königlich Preußischen Armee vom 25 Februar 1847, Neuabdruck unter Berücksichtigung der bis zum 3. August 1870 ergangenen Abänderungen'*, Verlag der Königlichen Geheimen Ober - Hofbuchdruckerei, Berlin, 1870.

Clear, concise, the basic 'first source' regarding Prussian infantry formations and small unit tactics.

(Anon, though according to Friedjung, *Vorherrschaft . . . Bd. II*, p. 98) the author was *Feldzeugmeister* R. V. Samonigg, who was, in 1866, General Staff Officer of Brigade Fragnern).

Das Gefecht von Skalitz am 28. Juni 1866, Wilhelm Braumüller, Wien und Liepzig, 1914. Samonigg's maps of the action at Skalitz are indispensable.

(Anon) *Der Nebel von Chlum, militärischer Beitrag als Schlaglicht auf die officielle öster. Sowie preussische Darstellung des Feldzuges 1866 von Einem der Nord-Armee*, Steinhaufer, Prague, 1867. Surprisingly productive! The first part suffers from factual inaccuracies and an almost polemic style and intent. Once the author gets to discussing the battlefield, the morale of the Austrian troops and the battle itself, he provides interesting and productive insights. Highly critical of Benedek.

(Anon – H. Jacobi) *'Im Felde': Erinnerungen eines einjährigen Freiwilligen vom Füsilier - Bataillon des Kaiser-Franz Garde-Grenadier Regiments aus dem Feldzuge in Böhmen und Mähren*, Stille & van Munden, Berlin, 1867. Highly readable, fascinating 116 page account.

(Anon– Kuehne) *Skizzen aus dem Feldzuge von 1866*, Eduard Döring, Potsdam, 1868. The description of 7th Infantry Division's battle in the *Swiepwald* is brief (17 pages) but unsurpassed for its vivid clarity.

Barry, Quintin *The Road to Königgrätz: Helmuth von Moltke and the Austro- Prussian War, 1866*, Helion, Solilhull, 2010.

Bassett-Powell, Bruce *Armies of Bismarck's Wars, Prussia, 1860-67*, Casemate, Philadelphia & Oxford, 2013.

Besser, L. von *Die Preußische Kavallerie in der Campagne 1866*, Verlag von Alexander Duncker, Berlin, 1868.

Birago, Karl *Ritter* von *Untersuchungen über die europäischen Militärbrücken und Versuch einer verbesserten, allen Forderungen entsprechended Militärbrücheneinrichtung*, Anton Strauss's se. Witwe, Vienna, 1839.

Blazek, Matthias *Die Schlacht bei Trautenau, der einzige Sieg Österreichs im Deutschen Krieg 1866*, Ibidem Verlag, Stuttgart, 2012.

Bleibtreu, Cart *Königgrätz*, Carl Krabbe, Stuttgart, 1903.

Boguslawski, A. V *Die Entwickelung der Taktik von 1793 bis zur Gegenwart*, 2nd edition, Ernst Siegfried Mittler und Sohn, Berlin, 1873.

Boeters *Geschichte des 3. Magdeburgischen Infanterie-Regiments Nr. 66*, Ernst Siegfried Mittler und Sohn, Berlin, 1897. A remarkably clear and understandable account of the 66th Rgt. in the confused fighting in the *Swiepwald*.

Broecker, Rudolf *Erinnerungen an die Thätigkeit der 11. Infanterie Division und iherer Artillerie während des Feldzuges 1866,*. Königliche Hofbuchhandlung, Berlin, 1867.

Carr, William *The Origins of the Wars of German Unification*, Longman, London & New York, 1991.

　　Schleswig-Holstein 1815-1848, A Study in National Conflict, Manchester University Press, Manchester, 1963.

Chevalier, Hauptmann *Die Elb-Armee im Feldzuge von 1866*, Verlag von Max Mälzer, Breslau, 1869. Excellent 78 page account, gives the Prussian viewpoint to go along with the official Saxon account.

Craig, Gordon A *The Battle of Königgrätz, Prussia's Victory over Austria, 1866*, Greenwood Press, Westport Connecticut, 1975 reprint of 1964 J. B. Lippincott edition.

Dicey, Edward *The Battlefields of 1866*, London, Tinsley Brothers, 1866.

Ditfurth, Moritz von *Benedek und die Taten und Schicksale der k. k. Nordarmee 1866*, L. Seidel & Sohn, Vienna, 1911. Volume 1, Events prior to Königgrätz, volume 2, Königgrätz, volume 3, post Königgrätz.

Ditfurth is absolutely essential reading for a full understanding of the campaign in Bohemia. His descriptions of both Austrian and Prussian movements and actions are extremely clear. He is the only source I have found that clearly presents the Austrian actions and the reasoning behind them. Much that all other sources leave as incomprehensible and illogical, if not downright reprehensible,   become entirely understandable, even reasonable, given the context in which they occurred. Ditfurth describes and analyzes the events from the Austrian viewpoint without being partisan or distorting the facts. He is also the only source that gives details on the actions of the Austrian artillery and is excellent on cavalry actions. Ditfurth , himself, took part in the great cavalry battle near Stresetitz as an *Oberlieutenant* in the 10th Cuirassier Regiment, Brigade Mengen of Cavalry Division Coudenhove.

Dolleczek, Anton *Geschichte der Österreichichischen Artillerie, von den frühesten Zeiten bis zur Gegenwart,* reprint of 1887 self-published work in Vienna, by Akademische Druck – u. Verlagsanstalt, Graz – Austria, 1973.

    Monographie der k. u. k. österr.-ung. Blanken und Handfeuer - Waffen', reprint of 1896 Kreisel & Gröger, Wien edition by Akademische Druck – I. Verlagsanstalt, Graz, Austria, 1970.

Eckardt, Walter & *Die Handwaffen des brandenburgisch-preußisch-deutschen* Otto Morawietz *Heeres 1640 -1945,* Helmut Gerhard Schulz Verlag, Hamburg, 1973.

Fiedler, Siegfried *Kriegswesen und Kriegführung im Zeitalter der Einigungskriege,* Bernard & Graefe Verlag, Coblenz,

Fontane, Theodor *Der deutsche Krieg von 1866,* Verlag der königlichen Geheimen Ober - Hofbuchdruckerei ®. V. Decker), Berlin, 1870. Excellent reprint available, Eugen Diederich's Verlag with excellent reproduction of the many fine illustrations and sketch maps. Also available in English translation,

Friedjung, Heinrich *Der Kampf um die Vorherrschaft in Deutschland, 1859 bis 1866,* 2 vols), J. G. Cotta'sche Buchhandlung Nachfolger, Stuttgart und Berlin, 1916. This and von Lettow - Vorbeck are the mutually complementary indispensable studies of the 1866 Austro-Prussian war and of the Battle of Königgrätz. The original has maps that are not included in the print on demand reprints. The author continued to revise his work so the final 10th edition is the one for study. Friedjung also includes maps of actions in Italy.

Fritsch *Der Antheil des 1. Magdeburgischen Infanterie Regiments Nr.26 an der Kampagne von 1866 gegen Oesterreich,* Verlag von Emil Baeusch, Magdeburg, 1867.

Gablenz, Heinrich von *Meine Erlebnisse im Feldzuge 1866 als Landwehr - Untroffizier im 4. Magdeburgischen Infanterie-Regiment Nr.67,* Verlag von Stilke & van Muyden, Berlin, 1867. (100 pp.)

Gaertner, Richard *Die ersten 15 Jahre des Magdeburgische Infanterie Regiments Nr.66,* Ernst Siegfried Mittler und Sohn, Berlin, 1876.

Groote, Wolfgang von & *Entscheidung 1866, der Krieg zwischen Österreich und Preußen* Ursula von Gersdorff *Herausgegeben vom Militärgeschichtlichen Forschungsamt durch Deutsche,* Verlags-Anstalt, Stuttgart, 1966.

Hoenig, Fritz *Untersuchungen über die Taktik der Zukunft entwickelt aus der neueren Kriegsgeschichte,* 4th edition, Militär-Verlag R. Felix, Berlin, 1894. Includes excellent 30-page account of 28th Infantry Brigade of the Elbe Army at the Bor farmstead and adjoining Briza Woods at Königgrätz.

Helmuth, Arnold *Geschichte der letzvergangenen vier Jahre des 2. Magdeburgischen Infanterie Regiments Nr.27,* Ernst Siegfried Mittler und Sohn, Berlin, 1870. Two hundred and ninety-eight pages almost entirely devoted to the 27th Regiment's actions in the 1866 War, An outstanding, detailed, source level account of one of the key regiments at both Münchengrätz and in the *Swiepwald* at Königgrätz. At the time of the fighting in the *Swiepwald*, Helmuth was a *Premierlieutenant* in the badly battered 11th Company, which had already lost its *Hauptmann, Graf* Finckenstein, on the extreme left wing.

Hozier, H.M. *The Seven Weeks War: Its Antecedents and its Incidents,* J. B. Lippincott & Co., Philadelphia, 1867, (two volumes), original edition worth finding for its excellent maps. Hozier was the London Times correspondent with the army of Prince Friedrich Charles. His descriptions of the terrain for 2nd Army's actions are particularly valuable. His accounts of actions of the Crown Prince's army are very inaccurate. Cost moderate, readily available.

Huber, Ernst Rudolf *Dokumente zur Deutschen Verfassungsgeschichte, Band 1.*
    Deutsche Verfassungsdokumente 1803-1850, München, Kolhammer, 1961.
    Dokumente zur Deutschen Verfassungsgeschichte, Band 2:
    Deutsche Verfassungsdokumente 1851-1918, München, Kolhammer, 1964.

Jähns, Max *Die Schlacht von Königgrätz,* Leipzig, 1876. Approximately 500 pages devoted entirely to Königgrätz, make this the most detailed and extensive account of the battle. Includes a great deal of material from regimental histories and personal memoirs.

JN (*Major* Nosinich) *Rückblick auf den Krieg 1866, I. Band,* Wien, 1868. Austrian interpretation of the war, immediately after its conclusion. Strongly partisan but valuable reading, especially for initial positions of Austrian 3rd Corps prior to receipt of Benedek's dispositions for battle. Ditfurth provides a far more extensive, non-partisan but Austrian view written forty years later. Indeed, I consider Ditfurth one of the finest accounts written by anyone on either side, right up there with Jähns, Friedjung and von Lettow - Vorbeck.

Kaiserlich-Königliches Militär-Geographisches Institut, Wien:
    Iglau-Land: Böhmen/Ober-Österreich/Nieder-Österreich/Mähren (= General-Karte von Mittel-Europa 1:200 000. 96. 33° 49').
    Olmütz-Land: Mähren/Preußen/Schlesien/Böhmen (= General-Karte von Mittel-Europa 1:200 000. 74. 35° 50').
    Wien-Land: Niederösterreich/ Ungarn (= General-Karte von Mittel-Europa 1:200 000. 121. 34° 48').
    Brünn-Land: Niederösterreich/Mähren (= General-Karte von Mittel-Europa 1:200 000. 97. 34° 49')
    Lundenburg (= General - Karte von Mittel - Europa 1:200,000.   Maßstab 1:200.000. 33° 49').
    Pressburg-Land: Niederösterreich/ Ungarn (= General-Karte von Mittel-Europa 1:200 000. 122. 35° 48').

k.k. Generalstabs-Bureau für Kriegsgeschichte (referred to in translator's notes as 'Austrian General Staff Study')
    Österreichs Kämpfe im Jahre 1866 (4 vols), Verlag des k. k. Generalstabs, Vienna 1868. The maps accompanying the original edition are not included in print on demand reprints. The Austrian history's maps are more detailed, even than von Lettow - Vorbeck's and are

invaluable, though difficult to come by. Nearly the entire set of maps are included in the three volumes of Ditfurth's work, in pockets at the back.

Kahnte, Helmut & Bernd *Lexikon Alte Maße, Münzen und Gewichte*, Bibliographisches Institut Annheim/Wien, Zürich, Meyers Lexikonverlag, 1987.

Kessel, Gustav von *Die Ausbildung des Preussischen Infanterie-bataillons im praktischen Dienst*, Verlag E. S Mittler und Sohn, Berlin, 1863.

Kirchbach, Hans Ferdinand *Die Theilnahme des 5. Armee Korps an den Kriegerischen Ereignissen gegen Oesterreich in den Tagen von 27 Juni bis 3. Juli 1866, spezieller der 10. Infanterie Division, Extra-Abdruck aus dem 'Beiheft zum Militair-Wochenblatt' 1868, Heft I., III., V. und VI.* Ernst Siegfried Mittler und Sohn, Berlin, 1868. A basic source for actions of 5th Army Corps. 156 pages.

Koch, H. W *A History of Prussia*, Dorset, New York, 1978.

Krosigk, Hans von *General-Feldmarschall von Steinmetz, aus den Familienpapieren dargestellt*, Berlin, 1900, Ernst Mittler und Sohn.

Kühne, *Major Kritische und unkritische Wanderungen über die Gefechtsfelder der Preußischen Armee in Böhmen 1866*, 4 vols: *Das Gefecht bei Nachod; Das Gefecht bei Skalitz, Das Gefecht bei Soor; Das Gefecht bei Trautenau* and discussion, Berlin, 1875, Ernst Siegfried Mittler und Sohn. Kühne's analysis of the terrain and action is indispensable for an understanding of these actions. Kühne's maps of these actions are the best maps available for Skalitz, second only to Strobl's for Trautenau and Wysokow (Nachod), showing different stages of the battles for Nachod, Skalitz and Trautenau.

Kunth *Unter der Fahne des 2. Bat. Franz*, Berlin, 1867. Here I include a book that I have not yet been able to obtain for my own reading. I have seen so many fascinating quotations from this in Max Jähns and Richard Schmitt that I include it for the reader's benefit as an excellent source.

Liebeneiner, Hugo *Theilnahme des 4ten Magdeburgischen Infanterie Regiments Nr. 67 in dem Feldzuge gegen Österreich im Jahre 1866*, Verlag G. Basse, Quedlinburg, 1869. 134 pp.; extremely clear and informative.

Lignitz, Viktor, von *Aus Drei Kriegen, 1866-1870-71 – 1877-78*, Ernst Mittler und Sohn, Berlin, 1904.

Lettow -Vorbeck, Oscar von *Geschichte des Krieges von 1866'*, Berlin, 1892-1899 (3 vols). This, with Friedjung, is indispensable for study of the 1866 Austro-Prussian War and for Königgrätz. The original edition is worth the cost and difficulty of locating copies for the excellent annotated maps, many topographic, of all significant actions of the war. All of the base maps of the individual actions, without annotations showing unit dispositions, are available in *Moltkes Militärische Werke IV.3 Die Schlacht, Karten, Karten zu Moltkes Kriegslehren, Die Schlacht*, which is far easier and less costly to find.

Moltke, Helmuth von, *Moltkes Militärische Werke II, Die Thätigkeit als Chef des Generalstabes der Armee im Frieden, Moltkes Taktisch- Strategisch Aufsätze aus den Jahren 1857 bis 1871: Memoire an Seine Majestät den König vom 25 Juli 1868 über die bei der Bearbeitung des Feldzuges 1866 hervorgetretenen Erfahrungen* and *Betrachtungen vom Frühjahre 1867 über Konzentrationen im Kriege von 1866* and *'Anlagen Nr. 9 bis 18* providing orders of battle of Prussian Armies in the 1966 campaigns. Ernst Siegfried Mittler und Sohn, Berlin, 1900.

Moltkes Militärische Werke, III, Kriegsgeschichtliche Arbeiten, zweiter Theil. Kritische Aufsätze zur Geschichte der Feldzüge von 1809, 1859, 1864, 1866 & 1870-71, Betrachtungen über das Gefecht von Trautenau am 27. Juni, 1866 und über die Kämpfe des V. Armeekorps bei Nachod, Skalitz und Schweinschädel vom 27 bis 29 Juni 1866, Ernst Siegfried Mittler und Sohn, Berlin, 1899. *Moltke's Militärische Werke IV., Kriegsleheren, Dritter Teil, Die Schlacht, Schlachtenverlauf und Schlachtenkarakteristik, 1. 1866, Relation über die Schlacht von Königgrätz* Ernst Siegfried Mittler und Sohn, Berlin, 1912. See note above regarding the map volume.

Malet, Alexander *The Overthrow of the Germanic Confederation by Prussia in 1866*, London, Longmans-Green & Co., 1870.

Müller, Hermann von *Die Entwicklung der Feld-Artillerie in Bezug auf Material, Organisation und Taktik, von 1815 bis 1870: Mit Besonderer Berüucksichtigung der Preussischen Artillerie auf Grund Officiellen Materials*, Verlag von Robert Oppenheim, Berlin, 1873.

Nipperdey, Thomas *Germany from Napoleon to Bismarck, 1800-1866*, Princeton University Press, Princeton N.J., 1996 (English translation of' *Deutsche Geschichte, 1800-1866* (1983).

Ortenburg, Georg *Waffe und Waffengebrauch im Zeitalter der Einigungskriege, Heerwesen der Neuzeit, Abteilung IV, Das Zeitalter der Einigungskreige, Band 1*, Bernard & Graefe Verlag, Koblenz, 1990. An outstandingly valuable and useful volume in a superb series of the weapons, organization and tactics of the armies of the time. A basis starting point for anyone trying to gain an understanding.

Waffe und Waffenbegrauch im Zeitalter der Revolutionskrieg, Heerwesen der Neuzeit, Abteilung III, Das Zeitalter der Revolutionskrieg, Band 1, Bernard & Graefe Verlag, Koblenz, 1988.

Pauer, Dr. Bernhard *Trautenau, 1866, Erinnerungen, Erlebnisse und Schriftstücke aus dem Kriegsjahr in und bei Trautenau*, Selbstverlag des Verfassers, Trautenau, 1891.

Petrossi, Ferdinand *Das Heeerwesen des Österreichischen Kaiserstaates, ein Handbuch für Officiere Aller Waffen*, 2 vols, Wilhelm Braumüller, Vienna, 1865. The two volumes total over 800 pages, abundantly illustrated, of detailed information about organization, equipment and tactics of the Austrian army on the eve of Königgrätz. Petrossi provides, for the Austrian army, the same as, or even better than the detail that Witzleben provides for the Prussian.

Pflanz, Otto *Bismarck and the Development of Germany: The Period of Unification, 1815-1871* (vol. 1 of 3 vols), Princeton University Press, Princeton , N.J., 1990.

Preussen Armee: Grosser Generalstab: Kriegsgeschichtliche Abteilung: *Der Deutsch-Danische Krieg, 1864*, Ernst Siegfried Mittler und Sohn, Berlin, 1886. A reprint of the maps accompanying these volumes is available, *Landkarten Pläne und Skizzen, Deutsch- Dänischer Krieg 1864*, Verlag Rockstuhl.

Preussen; Armee: Grosser Generalstab: Kriegsgeschichtliche Abteilung (cont.): *Der Feldzug von 1866 in Deutschland* (2 vols, the first is text, the second annexes. The annexes include only two maps, one of the action at Blumenau and the other of the action at Dermbach. The remainder of the annexes are primarily orders of battle for each action), Berlin, 1867.

Quistorp, Barthold von *Der Grosse Kavallerie - Kampf bei Stresetitz in der Schlacht von Königgrätz am 3. Juli 1866,* Verlag Joseph Graveur, Neisse, 1870. Accurate, detailed, strictly factual. Original necessary for its five detailed, 1:1250 maps. Strobl's detailed maps of this action in his study of Königgrätz are fully sufficient to study this action if Quistorp's are unavailable.

Regensberg, Fr *1866, Band 1: von Dresden bis Münchengrätz – Gitschin – Custoza,* Franckh'sche Verlagshandlung, Stuttgart, 1903-1905.
   1866, Band II: Nachod, Trautenau, von Skalitz bis Königgrätz, Franckh'sche Verlagshandlung, Stuttgart, 1905–1906.
   1866, Königgrätz, Ein Schlachtbild, Franckh'sche Verlangshandlung, Stuttgart, 1903.
   1866, Letzte Kämpfe und Friedensschluß, Franckh'sche Verlagshandlung, Stuttgart, no date given.

Although Regensberg is seldom referred to in scholarly publications, I find his accounts extremely readable and detailed. I generally reread Regensberg before I explore particular action in detail for a remarkably clear account which, occasionally, includes a detail missing elsewhere.

Roth, Hieronymus von *Achtzig Tage in preussischer Gefangenschaft und die Schlacht bei Trauetenau am 27. Juni 1866,* Carl Bellmann's Verlag, Prag, 1867.
Rothenberg, Gunther Erich *The Army of Francis Joseph,* Purdue University Press, West Lafayette, Indiana, 1976.
   The Austrian Military Border in Croatia, 1522 -1747, University of Illinois Press, Urbana, 1860.

Schirmer, Fritz *Das Treffen von Blumenau – Pressburg am 22. Juli 1866: Eine kriegsgeschichtlilch-Taktisch Studie,* L. W. Seidel & Sohn, Vienna, 1904. The original edition of this excellent study includes 9 detailed maps and 4 landscape drawings.
Schlieffen, Alfred von *Canna,* Ernst Mittler und Sohn, Berlin, 1925.
Schmidt – Brentano *Die Armee in Österreich, Militär, Staat und Gesellschaft 1848-1867,* Harald Boldt Verlag, Boppard am Rhein, 1975.
Schmitt, Richard *Die Gefechte bei Trautenau am 27. Und 28. Juni, 1866, Nebst einem Anhang über Moderne Sagenbildung,* Friedrich Andreas Perthes, Gotha, 1892. Excellent study of Trautenau. Extends Kühne's outstanding study. Has no maps of its own, so virtually requires Kühne for his maps, 111 pages on the first day of Trautenau, 96 on the second day, Burkersdorf, Alt - and Neu - Rognitz, Soor.
Schwarz, Herbert *Gefechtsformen der Infanterie in Europa durch 800 Jahre,* Dr. Herbert Schwarz, Munich, 1977.
Seebach, von *Geschichte des 4. Thüringischen Infanterie Regiments Nr.72, 1860-1910, unter zugrundbelegung der von Oberstlieutnant Fabricius im Jahre 1879 geschriebenen Geschichte neu Bararbeitet,* Uhland'sche Buchdruckerei, Stuttgart, 1910. Fabricius 1879 edition did not include the 1866 War.
Showalter, Dennis *The Wars of German Unification,* Arnold, London, 2004.
   Railroads and Rifles: Soldiers, Technology, and the Unification of Germany, Archon Books, Hamden, Connecticut, 1975.
Sperling, Eduard *Geschichte des 6. Ostpr. Infanterie Regiments Nr.43.,* Königsberg in Pr., 1874.

Steefel, Lawrence D *The Schleswig-Holstein Question*, Cambridge, Mass., Harvard University Press, 1932.

Steinitz, *Major* Eduard *Ritter* von Steinitz, published as 'einem Generalstabsoffizier': *Von Königgrätz bis an die Donau* (5 vols).

    Der Rückzug der Nordarmee vom Schlachtfeld des 3. Juli

    Die kritischen Tage von Olmütz im Juli 1866. From the arrival of the North Army Headquarters at Olmütz on the 9th to the evening of 15th July.

    Das österreichische Kavalleriekorps Holstein und das Vordringen der preußischen Hauptkraft gegen Wien.

    Die letzte Operation der Nordarmee 1866, [from the 15th of July to the armistice, continuation of *'Die kritische Tage von Olmütz'*.

    Die Donauverteidigung.

Contrary to standard practice, I have included the listing of all five volumes, due to their importance, so that the reader will be able to search for them, even though, to date, I have only been able to locate and study *Das österreichische Kavalleriekorps Holstein . . .* and *Die letzte Operationen der Nordarmee 1866.* These volumes by von Steinitz are the definitive sources for the actions following Königgrätz, presenting them from the Austrian viewpoint but without prejudice.

Strobl, Adolf *Königgrätz, Kurze Darstellung der Schlacht am 3. Juli, 1866*, L. W. Seidel & Sohn Verlag, Vienna, 1903. Clear, concise (176 pages), a totally factual summary with all relevant orders and reports. Six orders of battle and 38 sketch maps. These are by far the most detailed of all maps of the action at Königgrätz, showing the positions and movements of each formation at various times and at major focal points of the action. His account of the details of commitment, formations and movements of forces and elements thereof is rivaled only by Ditfurth for the Austrian side.

    Trautenau. Kurze Darstellung gleichnamigen Treffens am 27. Juni 1866. . . mit 2 Ordres de bataille und 10 Skizzen, L. W. Seidel & Sohn, Vienna, 1901.

    Wysokow (Nachod). Kurze Darstellung gleichnamigen Treffens am 27 Juni 1866 . . . mit 2 Ordres de bataille und 11 Skizzen, L. W. Seidel & Sohn, Vienna, 190. In this case I have made an exception to the basic rule of only including references in my bibliography that I have personally used for this project. I have not yet been able to locate a copy of this item.

However, Strobl's works on Königgrätz and Trautenau have proven so valuable, with their many superbly detailed maps that I am including his work on Wysokow (Nachod) for the benefit of the reader who might not otherwise learn that Strobl also did this study of Wysokow (Nachod).

Stückrad *Geschichte des 1. Magdeburgischen Infanterie Regiments Nr.26, zweiter Theil, Die Letzten fünfundzwandsig Jahre. 1863 – 1888*, Ernst Siegfried Mittler und Sohn, Berlin, 1888. By far the best and clearest account of the part played by the 26th Inf. Rgt. In the *Swiepwald*.

Sybel, Heinrich v *The Founding of the German Empire by William I*, tr. by Marshall Livingston Perrin, PhD. (*Gött.*), Greenwood Press, New York, 1968 reprint of Thomas Y. Crowell & Co., 1891. (Original, *'Die Begründung des Deutschen Reiches durch Wilhelm I'*, München, Leipzig und Berlin, 1889).

Vatke, Theodor *Mein Sommer unter den Waffen. Aufzeichnungen und Erinnerungen aus dem Böhmischen Feldzuge im Jahre 1866,* former *Gefreiter* in Kaiser Franz Garde-Grenadier Regiment Nr. 2, Stille & van Munden, Berliln, 1867. Excellent and highly readable account, 135 pp.

Verdy du Vernois J *Im Hauptquartier der Zweiten Armee 1866,* Berlin, 1900.

Walker, Col. B *The Battle of Königgrätz,* Helion and Company, Solihull, 2006.

Wandruszka, Adam *Die Habsburgmonarchie 1848-1918, Band V, Die Bewaffnete and Peter Urbanitsch, Macht,* Verlag der Österreichischen Akademie der Wissenschaften, Wien, 1987.

Wawro, Geoffrey *The Austro-Prussian War: Austria's War with Prussia and Italy in 1866,* Cambridge University Press, Cambridge, 1996.

Weberstedt *Geschichte des 4. Magdeburgischen Infanterie Regiments Nr 67. Ergänzte und bis 1899 fortgeführte Aufgabe Die ersten 25 Jahre des 4. Magdeburgischen Infanterie Regiments Nr.67 dargestellt von Heinrich,* Ernst, Siegfried Mittler und Shon, Berlin, 1899. This includes another truly excellent extremely detailed account of the fighting of the 67th Rgt. in the *Swiepwald.*

Wirtgen, Rolf *Das Zündnadelgewehr, Eine militärtechnische Revolution im 19. Jahrhundert'* E. S. Mittler & Sohn, Herford und Bonn, 1991.

White, Jonathan R *The Prussian Army, 1640-1871,* University Press of America, 1996.

Winter, Frank H *The First Golden Age of Rocketry: Congreve and Hale Rockets of the Nineteenth Century,* Smithsonian Institution Press, Washington & London, 1990.

Witzleben, August von *Heerwesen und Infanteriedienst der Königlich Preußischen Armee,* 10th edition, Verlag von A. Bath, Berlin, 1868. The 'ultimate source' on structure, organization, tactics and much more on the Prussian infantry. I worked from the 1868 edition but would very much like to obtain the 1864 edition for the situation 'on the eve of the 1866 war.' Witzleben provides, for the Prussian infantry the same level of detail that Petrossi does for the Austrian.

Von Zychlinski, Franz *Antheil des 2. Magdeburg. Infant.-Regim. No. 27 an dem Gefecht beim Münchengrätz am 28. Juni 1866 und an der Schlacht von Königgrätz am 3. Juli 1866 aus dem Briefe an einem Freund,* Verlag von Julius Fricke, Halle, 1866. An outstandingly readable account of the actions of the 27th at Münchengratz and in the *Swiepwald.*

Note on Maps

Military history without maps is incomprehensible. I have found that, without a doubt, Kühne's maps are the most detailed and invaluable for the actions of the 2nd (Crown Prince's) Army. Kühne describes and analyzes the terrain and actions in detail and has detailed topographic maps showing positions and movements of the elements involved, in some cases with as many as four or five maps for a single action. Samonigg's maps of Skalitz go even beyond Kühne's, just as his analysis extends Kühne's from an Austrian viewpoint. For those actions that Kühne does not cover (those of the Elbe and 1st Army [Prince Friedrich Carl's] and Königgratz, itself, von Lettow - Vorbeck's excellent detailed maps, mostly contour maps at a scale of 1:25,000, are my favorites. The superb maps accompanying the Austrian General Staff study sometimes provide greater detail, however the Austrian maps are shaded to show relief, sometimes so darkly that it is hard to make out detail. Ditfurth's three volumes include the maps from the Austrian General Staff study in pockets at the back, which offers another way to get copies of the superb but hard to find maps from the Austrian General Staff Work. I find that I regularly work back and forth between von Lettow-Vorbeck, Kühne, and the Austrian Staff Study maps. The best maps for following larger movements and gaining a general perspective are the superb sheets put out by the *Kaiserlich-Königliches Militär-Geographisches Institut, Wien* @ 1:200,000 that are listed in bibliography.

Summation

I consider Heinrich Friedjung, Oscar von Lettow - Vorbeck, Moritz *Freiherr* von Ditfurth, Max Jähns (for Königgrätz itself), Adolf Strobl (for Wysokow / Nachod, Trautenau and Königgrätz) and Kühne (for all of the actions of the Prussian 2nd Army), along with Theodor Fontane, himself, as the absolutely essential sources for any serious study of the Campaign in Bohemia. Eduard *Freiherr von* Schweinitz' series of five volumes on the Austrian actions after Königgrätz is definitive for that period.

Edward P Steinhardt